AF830825

China–Europe Tax Treaties

Lorenzo Riccardi · Giorgio Riccardi

China–Europe Tax Treaties

Selected Tax Treaties and International Taxation

Springer

Lorenzo Riccardi
Shanghai University
Shanghai, China

Giorgio Riccardi
RsA Asia
Shanghai, China

ISBN 978-981-19-3562-6 ISBN 978-981-19-3563-3 (eBook)
https://doi.org/10.1007/978-981-19-3563-3

© The Editor(s) (if applicable) and The Author(s), under exclusive license to Springer Nature Singapore Pte Ltd. 2022
This work is subject to copyright. All rights are solely and exclusively licensed by the Publisher, whether the whole or part of the material is concerned, specifically the rights of translation, reprinting, reuse of illustrations, recitation, broadcasting, reproduction on microfilms or in any other physical way, and transmission or information storage and retrieval, electronic adaptation, computer software, or by similar or dissimilar methodology now known or hereafter developed.
The use of general descriptive names, registered names, trademarks, service marks, etc. in this publication does not imply, even in the absence of a specific statement, that such names are exempt from the relevant protective laws and regulations and therefore free for general use.
The publisher, the authors, and the editors are safe to assume that the advice and information in this book are believed to be true and accurate at the date of publication. Neither the publisher nor the authors or the editors give a warranty, expressed or implied, with respect to the material contained herein or for any errors or omissions that may have been made. The publisher remains neutral with regard to jurisdictional claims in published maps and institutional affiliations.

This Springer imprint is published by the registered company Springer Nature Singapore Pte Ltd.
The registered company address is: 152 Beach Road, #21-01/04 Gateway East, Singapore 189721, Singapore

Dedicated to our Eurasian friends, partners and colleagues, with a special thank you to Edward Sheehan, Luigi Wang, Nicola Alessandro Cieri, Diyang He, Marco Rumhein, Simone Restaino, Mauro Dong, Mauro Dellisanti, Luca Zheng, Pasquale Frieri and Yu Zhang.

Contents

Historical Background to International Treaties

International tax treaties are the foundation and thus a crucial component of the tax rules and treatment of international payments and incomes. Of the international tax treaties, the vast majority follow either the United Nations Model Double Taxation Convention between Developed and Developing Countries (UN Model) or the Organisation for Economic Co-operation and Development Model Tax Convention on Income and on Capital (OECD Model).

However, the history of international tax agreements dates to prior to the foundation of the UN at the end of World War II. These initial agreements were primarily based within Europe and between contiguous states where the treaties were predicated upon the similarity of both nations tax systems, therefore these early tax treaties were limited in their international nature. Nevertheless, these early treaties did establish the foundations which underpin the modern international taxation system, particularly with respect to concepts such as reciprocity and the minimising of the burden of double taxation. This principle of reciprocity is at the heart of the OECD Model upon which most modern tax agreements are based.

Reciprocity in early international relations was seen as the granting by one nation of certain commercial privileges to another, whereby the citizens of both are placed upon an equal basis in certain branches of commerce. It may be understood that reciprocity is theoretically attributed to every legal norm of international law, it should not be automatically assumed that reciprocity is the basis of all international treaties, as most international treaties now follow multilateral most-favoured-nation treatment in their relations.

In 1823, the United Kingdom introduced a law based upon reciprocity which enabled any country to export goods to the United Kingdom as long as the open access to that country's markets was freely available to British ships.

This early preference for reciprocal trade continued until the signatory of the 1860 Cobden–Chevalier Treaty trade agreement between the United Kingdom and France, which brought about the status of most-favoured-nation. This agreement introduced the interpretation of the most-favoured-nation clause, which resulted in the harmonisation of trade concessions in all participating states. This shift to however

© The Author(s), under exclusive license to Springer Nature Singapore Pte Ltd. 2022

L. Riccardi and G. Riccardi, *China–Europe Tax Treaties*,
https://doi.org/10.1007/978-981-19-3563-3_1

was not seen in international tax treaties, the importance of reciprocity remained, the most notable example being in the Austria-Hungary and Prussia for the Prevention of Double Taxation signed on 21st of June 1899, which introduced regulations for the avoidance of double taxation on the basis of reciprocity. The treaty gave to the Minister of Finance the authority to introduce regulations on such occasion where the treaty differed from national law to prevent the issue of double taxation arising.

In the twentieth century a number of other methods for providing relief from double taxation have been identified. Double taxation can be relieved by one jurisdiction unilaterally not imposing tax on income earned in another jurisdiction, by one jurisdiction reducing the amount of tax payable in that jurisdiction for any tax paid in another jurisdiction on the same income or by allocating taxing rights for different types of income between jurisdictions. Interestingly, the early tax treaties chose the allocation method of relief that continues to prevail in modern tax treaties. Further, the early tax treaties adopted the fundamental principles of allocating taxing rights based on the source of income or the residence of the taxpayer. Modern tax treaties continue to allocate taxing rights based on these same principles.

The early tax treaties also established central concepts such as 'permanent establishment', which determines where a business pays tax. These mutual agreement procedures for dispute resolution back to the 1899 treaty, which provided for a non-binding, negotiation-based process between the parties on specific issues.

The introduction of the 1899 treated was initiated due to an introduction of personal income tax, and an acquisition tax in the Austro-Hungarian empire in 1898, whereas Prussia already had similar taxes in force, thus for citizens living in the border regions, double taxation became a frequent issue due to the porous nature of borders at the time. The 1899 treaty introduced taxation rights to the country of domicile and to the country of source in relation to acquisition taxes. Article 1 provided that taxpayers would only be liable for direct state taxes in the country where they had their domicile or in the country of residence if there was no domicile. Utilizing a concept now commonplace in all tax treaties, Article 2 of the treaty allocated the right to tax business profits to the country where the permanent establishment was located.

The next recorded double tax treaty was signed between the Austro-Hungarian Empire and Liechtenstein and followed on from the precedent set by the 1899 stipulating the right to tax business profits to the country where the land, buildings or business establishments were situated and the right to tax the income of individuals to the country of domicile.

The next decade prior to the first world war saw a multitude of double tax treaties signed between the Germanic states, which shows the common still evident to this day, of the signing of treaties between nations with significant cultural ties or economic ties.

Legal nature of tax treaties

Treaties are contracts between sovereign nations, this is clarified in Article 2 of the Vienna Convention on the Law of Treaties, which applies to all treaties, provides:

"A treaty is an international agreement (in one or more instruments, whatever called) concluded between States and governed by international law."

As Article 2 of the Vienna Convention states, the name used is not critical to the functioning of the agreement, and that the subjects of the treaties are the nations rather than third parties such as citizens or taxpayers. Therefore, treaties impose obligations upon the nations rather than the citizens, who should only receive benefits from the treaty. For some nations treaties are self-executing, whether as for other nations national law must be implemented before the treaty may take effect.

As stipulated by Article 26 of the Vienna Convention, treaties are binding States and must be performed in good faith, this is a principle known as *pacta sunt servanda.* In other words, if a nation develops a reputation for the breach of contract, other nations will be reticent to contract with them.

As discussed in the historical background to tax treaties, reciprocity is one of the fundamental underlying principles. This can be seen for example in most bilateral tax treaties in the treatment of tax rates, if for example articles referred to dividends in a treaty provides for a maximum withholding tax on dividends paid by a resident company to shareholders resident in the other contracting State, that maximum rate will apply equally in both contracting states. This reciprocal obligation applies to both States regardless of the volume of taxes being paid. If for example a double tax treaty between a developed nation and a developing nation is signed, the vast quantity of dividends is likely to be paid to shareholders in the developed nation, however the withholding rate is equal in both nations, leading to a larger benefit for the residents in the developed nation. Likewise, the exchange of information and the assistance in collecting of taxes will apply in both directions.

The Process of Negotiating Tax Treaties

Double tax treaties typically develop from periods of enhanced relations between both contracting nations.

When initiating a discussion or proposal for a double tax treaty, nations will prioritise those which have significant levels of trade and investment between both parties, however some nations have taken the approach of using a double tax treaty, or a revised double tax treaty as a diplomatic incentive for other diplomatic ventures, a recent example is whereby the People's Republic of China has ratified new double tax treaties to countries which have joined its belt and road project, a prime example being Italy, which signed a second double tax treaty with the PRC in 2019.

The process of negotiating a double tax treaty occurs over two rounds, of which both countries host one. Both nations shall exchange their model treaties and their objectives for the treaty. The first round of negotiations is to primarily decide upon the text to be used as the treaty basis. The second round of negotiations focuses on article-by-article discussion.

After an agreement is concluded, it is typically signed by a ambassador or senior office from the ministry of finance, at this point the treaty is considered signed, however it is not ratified and not effective. Different nations have their own internal ratification procedures, however there is a typical lag period of approximately two years from signature to ratification.

Once a treaty is ratified and effective there is the possibility for the party nations to mutually amend the treaty. This is typically done through the entrance into a Protocol between both nations which is considered an annex to the double tax treaty. Just like the treaty, the protocol must also be ratified, rather than just signed, as according to international law's jurisprudence a protocol is an international treaty.

© The Author(s), under exclusive license to Springer Nature Singapore Pte Ltd. 2022

L. Riccardi and G. Riccardi, *China–Europe Tax Treaties*,
https://doi.org/10.1007/978-981-19-3563-3_2

The United Nations Model and OECD Model Tax Conventions

There are two prominent model tax treaties—the United Nations Model and OECD Model Conventions, however many nations have adapted their own preferred model treaty which may be an amalgamation of both the UN and OECD standards.

As discussed previously the first recognisable treaties emerged in the decades prior to World War One in the twentieth century. Following WW1, with the creation of the League of Nations, the league attempted to create model conventions in 1943 and 1946, however the dissolution of the league prevented widespread adoption of the treaties. The work of creating new model treaties was taken up by the OECD in the 1960s, when the first Model Convention was published. This model convention is accompanied by a commentary on each article. These OECD Commentaries are crucial to the interpretation of the tax treaties, and have been used as reference points even between nations which are not OECD members. The OECD Commentaries contain comments and observations by the member countries on specific articles and how they aim to interpret the articles in their own treaties.

The United Nations established the United Nations Economic and Social Council (ECOSOC) of the United Nations Ad Hoc Group of Experts on Tax Treaties between Developed and Developing Countries in resolution 1273 (XLIII). This group developed the United Nations Model Taxation Convention between Developed and Developing Countries in 1980, which has been subsequently revised in 2001 and 2011.

The UN Model follows the template established by the OECD Model and most of its provisions are identical to those in the OECD. The core difference between the two conventions is that the UN Model has less restrictions on the taxing rights of the source country.

As an example, Article 12 (Royalties) of the OECD Model and Article 12 of the UN Model differ as the OECD Model does not prevent the source country from imposing a tax on royalties paid by a resident of the source country to a resident of the other country. Another difference is with the treatment of furnishing services in a country for 183 days or more which constitutes a permanent establishment under

© The Author(s), under exclusive license to Springer Nature Singapore Pte Ltd. 2022

L. Riccardi and G. Riccardi, *China–Europe Tax Treaties*,
https://doi.org/10.1007/978-981-19-3563-3_3

the UN Model, whereas under the OECD Model the furnishing services becomes a permanent establishment only if the services are provided through a fixed place of business that must exist for more than 6 months.

Objectives of Tax Treaties

Tax treaties at a general level are instruments to facilitate international trade and investment between the signatories, through the process of removing the impediment of double taxation. This general purpose is followed by more specific and situational reasons for a double tax treaty.

The first purpose, the elimination of double taxation is founded upon the rational that if income trade and investment is taxed by two countries without relief, the double taxation would naturally deter trade and investment. As an example, the UN model in Article 4 (2) (Resident) established a rule to allow a taxpayer that is a resident in both countries to be a resident in only one of the countries for purposes of the treaty. Most issues of double taxation have been successfully resolved over the last five decades of model treaties, however one common remaining issue is that of countries approach the interpretation of an arm's length when establishing transfer prices in transactions between related parties.

Aside from the reduction of double taxation the historical emphasis on the elimination of double taxation should not obscure the fact that most tax treaties have another equally important operational objective—the prevention of tax evasion and avoidance or double non-taxation. In other words, the fundamental principle is that treaties should apply to ensure that income is taxed once, and only once. These objective counterbalances the elimination of double taxation. Just as double taxation imposes an inappropriate barrier to international commerce, the tolerance of fiscal evasion and avoidance offers an inappropriate incentive to such commerce. Although the elimination of tax evasion and avoidance is an objective of most tax treaties recognized by both the United Nations and the OECD, there are few provisions in typical tax treaties that are designed to achieve it.

In addition to the two principal operational objectives of tax treaties, there are several ancillary objectives. One ancillary objective is the elimination of discrimination against foreign nationals and non-residents. Any country entering into a treaty wants to ensure that its residents who carry on business in the other contracting State are treated the same as the residents of that other State who carry on similar activities. A second ancillary objective is to facilitate administrative cooperation between

© The Author(s), under exclusive license to Springer Nature Singapore Pte Ltd. 2022
L. Riccardi and G. Riccardi, *China–Europe Tax Treaties*,
https://doi.org/10.1007/978-981-19-3563-3_4

the contracting States. This administrative cooperation has three main dimensions: exchange of information, assistance in the collection of taxes and dispute resolution.

The exchange of information in the typical tax treaty can be an important tool in combating tax evasion and avoidance and to ensure that taxpayers receive treaty benefits. The United Nations and OECD Model Conventions both provide that each contracting State will lend assistance in the collection of tax assessed by the other State as if the tax were its own. Finally, most treaties provide a mechanism in their treaties—the mutual agreement procedure—for resolving disputes concerning the application of the treaty. This procedure is often used to resolve transfer pricing disputes.

One of the most important effects of tax treaties is to provide certainty for taxpayers. Certainty concerning the tax consequences of cross-border investment is an important factor in facilitating such investment. Tax treaties have an average life of approximately 15 years. As a result, non-resident investors know that, despite changes in the tax laws of the source country, the basic limitations in the treaty on the source country's right to tax will continue to prevail. For example, if company A, a resident of country A, licenses residents of country B to use intangible property developed by company A, company A will know (for example) that the rate of withholding tax on royalties provided in the treaty between it and country B will continue to apply even if country B increases that rate under its domestic law.

Although it may not be an objective of a tax treaty, the allocation of tax revenues from cross-border activity between the two contracting States is certainly an effect of the treaty. As a result, the treaty negotiators should be acutely aware that the provisions of the treaties they are entering into will determine how much tax revenue will be subject to domestic tax. For example, if a country agrees to a 5% rate of tax on interest under Article 11 (Interest), its tax on interest paid by residents of the country to lenders resident in the other country will be limited to 5% of the total interest paid and the other country's tax revenues will be whatever its tax rate on its residents is less the 5% tax paid to the source country.

Contents of a Typical Tax Treaty

As previously discussed, the structure of the UN and OECD models are broadly similar, and any derived double tax treaty between nations will likely follow the precedent established by the models. This section will briefly discuss the chapters and articles of the typical double tax treaty.

Chapter 1 is composed of Articles 1 and 2, of which Article 1 identifies the persons that are affected by the treaty, and Article 2, which lists the taxes covered by the treaty.

Chapter 2 provides Articles 3, 4, and 5, which provide for the general definitions, the definition of resident, and the definition of permeant establishment respectively.

Chapter 3 provides the substantive rules of the treaty on how to manage the various types of income, typically over Article 6 through to Article 21.

The Articles and the types of income are as follows:

Article 6—Income from immovable property.
Article 7—Business profits;
Article 8—Income from the operation of ships or aircraft in international traffic and boats in inland waterways transport;
Article 9—Profits of associated enterprises and transfer pricing;
Article 10—Dividends;
Article 11—Interest;
Article 12—Royalties;
Article 13—Capital gains;
Article 14—Income derived from professional and independent services;
Article 15—Income from employment;
Article 16—Directors' fees and remuneration of top-level managerial officials;
Article 17—Income derived by artistes (entertainers) and athletes;
Article 18—Pensions and social security payments;
Article 19—Income derived by government employees;
Article 20—Income derived by students, business trainees and apprentices;
Article 21—Other income; in other words, income not dealt with in Articles 6–20.

© The Author(s), under exclusive license to Springer Nature Singapore Pte Ltd. 2022

L. Riccardi and G. Riccardi, *China–Europe Tax Treaties*,
https://doi.org/10.1007/978-981-19-3563-3_5

Chapter 4 contains Article 22, which depending on the treaty will either deal with the taxation of other incomes or the taxation of capital.

In this Chapter which is composed of Article 23 predominantly provides for two methods of mitigating double taxation, either through the exemption method or the credit method. Should the contracting State where income arises be entitled to tax the income as established in Chapter 3, the contracting State in which the taxpayer is resident is obligated to provide relief from double taxation. Under the exemption method, the residence country excludes or exempts the income from residence country tax. Under the credit method, the residence country taxes the income but provides a deduction from that tax for the tax paid to the source country on the income.

Chapter 6 covers the so-called Special Provisions, from Article 24 through to Article 28. Article 24 prevents discriminatory taxation by the source and residence countries. Articles 25, 26 and 27 provide for administrative cooperation between the contracting States. Article 28 reinforces the fiscal privileges enjoyed by diplomats and consular officials.

Chapter 7 issues the method to bring the treaty into effect and the means to terminate the treaty.

Relationship between tax treaties and domestic law

International treaties are not always directly effective in the signatory countries, jurisprudence suggests that if there is a conflict between domestic law and a treaty, that the treaty will prevail.

Tax treaties do not impose upon the persons in identified in Article 1, rather tax is imposed by domestic law. Therefore, we can state that tax treaties have a relief effect, but they do not replace the domestic law. For example, should a person resident in Country A according to its domestic tax laws, is also considered to be a resident of Country B according to its domestic tax laws, the tie breaker rule shall only apply to the taxes that are directly referenced by the treaty.

Introduction to Chinese Taxation

Legislative Background and Tax Reform

The Chinese tax system has recently developed closely to the economic growth of the country. The entry of China into the World Trade Organization (WTO) and the economic boom that has characterized past and recent years have made clear the necessity of overhauling a regulatory system in order to provide stability in the administration of the country, even in the tax field. The desire of becoming a leader in the Asian area, keeping up with the major world powers, has led China to make numerous amendments to improve and adapt the tax system to the rapid expansion of the economy and at the same time, to attract an increasing number of foreign companies.

As a result, a significant tax system overhaul was achieved on March 16, 2007 with the enactment of the Enterprise Income Tax Law, which then came into force on January 1, 2008. The new scheme joined together two systems of corporate income tax previously separated, the Domestic Invested Enterprises and the Foreign Invested Enterprises. The main purpose of the reform was to standardize tax treatments for foreign and local companies, removing privileges for foreign companies and formulating new tax legislation in harmony with Western laws.

Sources of Chinese Tax Law

Competent authorities with the power to legislate within the tax field are the following:

- National People's Congress;
- State Council;
- State Administration of Taxation; and
- Ministry of Finance;

© The Author(s), under exclusive license to Springer Nature Singapore Pte Ltd. 2022

L. Riccardi and G. Riccardi, *China–Europe Tax Treaties*,
https://doi.org/10.1007/978-981-19-3563-3_6

The National People's Congress (NPC), with its Standing Committee, is the supreme legislative authority in China, while the State Council, which is headed by the Premier, is the main executive organ of government.

The State Administration of Taxation and the Ministry of Finance are the organs empowered to interpret tax laws and regulations and to issue circulars, notices, and rulings about fiscal issues. The State Administration of Taxation is also responsible for tax policy and the administration and collection of taxes.

Tax Classification

There are different types of taxes levied on individuals and entities, which can be classified into the following categories:

- Direct taxes

  i. Individual Income Tax
  ii. Company Income Tax

- Indirect taxes

  iii. Value Added Tax
  iv. Consumption Tax

- Other taxes

  v. Stamp duty
  vi. Deed tax
  vii. Land VAT
  viii. Resource Tax
  ix. Vehicles and Vessels Tax
  x. Environmental Protection Tax
  xi. Tax surcharges

- Customs duties

  xii. Import duties
  xiii. Export duties

Individual Income Tax

The individual income tax is the income tax levied on Chinese citizens and foreigners residing in China or having a source of income in the country that is subject to taxation.

The tax liability depends on the status of residence in China and on the source of the income.

Company Income Tax

The company income tax is levied on China resident enterprises and China non-resident enterprises with and without a permanent establishment in China.

The standard tax rate is 25%; lower and preferential rates are available for companies engaged in specific sectors and industries.

Taxpayers of the Chinese Company Income Tax are resident enterprises (including companies incorporated in China and companies not incorporated in China but effectively managed and controlled in the country) and non-resident enterprises with permanent establishment in China (which are taxed on their China-sourced income and non-China sourced income effectively connected with the establishment) and without permanent establishment (which are taxed on their income generated in China).

The Company Income Tax is paid on the income generated from the sale of goods, provision of services and transfer of ownership as well as income from dividends, interests, and royalties.

Value Added Tax

The Value Added Tax (VAT) is one of the indirect taxes applied on the purchases and sales of goods, services, intangible and immovable properties.

For small-scale taxpayers, including new established enterprises and companies with an annual sales amount lower than 5 million CNY, the VAT is levied at a rate of 3%, but they are not allowed to offset input VAT with output VAT nor entitled to apply for VAT refund in case of exports.

For general VAT taxpayers, the VAT rates have been amended several times during the past years. Currently, general VAT taxpayers are subject to VAT at rates ranging from 6 to 13%; VAT is considered a neutral tax since general VAT taxpayers are allowed to credit input VAT paid on the purchases of goods and services against the output VAT collected from the sales of goods and services.

A specific announcement jointly issued by Ministry of Finance, State Administration of Taxation and General Administration of Customs have lowered the VAT rates from 16 to 13% and from 10 to 9%, after a previous adjustment introduced in May 2018. The revised VAT rates have been implemented from April 1, 2019.

Taxable item	VAT rate (%) until 31.03.2019	VAT rate (%) from 01.04.2019
Sales of goods	16	13
Leasing of movable property	16	13
Processing and repair services	16	13

(continued)

(continued)

Taxable item	VAT rate (%) until 31.03.2019	VAT rate (%) from 01.04.2019
Transport, postal, basic communication, construction services	10	9
Transfer of land use rights	10	9
Sale of real estate	10	9
Agricultural products, food and edible oil	10	9
Tap water, heating, air conditioning, hot water, gas	10	9
Books, newspapers, magazines, audio and video products, electronic publications	10%	9%
Feed, fertilizers and pesticides	10%	9%
Dimethyl ether	10%	9%
Other goods stipulated by authorities	10%	9%
Services not included above	6%	6%
Export	0%	0%

Consumption Tax

The Consumption Tax is an indirect tax levied on producers and importers of certain goods classified as "luxury" or "non-essential", such as tobacco, alcohol, fireworks, jewelry, cosmetics, motor-vehicles, etc. There are specific sub-categories with different tax rates and mechanisms for calculating the tax base.

Other Taxes

The other categories of taxes include:

- **Stamp duty tax**, levied on contracts (including sales, purchase and loan contracts), corporate documents and books with rates varying between 0.005 and 0.1%;
- **Deed tax**, calculated and levied on the transfer of ownership rights for land and real properties. The tax is levied on the transferee and the rates vary from 3 to 5%;
- **Land VAT**, calculated on the income resulting from the allocation or transfer of land use rights and buildings;
- **Property tax**, levied on the owner or lender of property and based on the value of the land/buildings and the leases;
- **Resource tax**, imposed on entities engaged in mining, the extraction of natural resources and production of salt within PRC;

- **Vehicle and vessel tax**, levied on the owners of certain categories of vehicles and vessels;
- **Environmental protection tax**, imposed on the entities responsible for emitting pollutants, solid wastes, and noise pollution.
- **Urban construction and maintenance surtax**, a surtax calculated on the amount of indirect taxes payable by the taxpayer. Depending on the location, the surtax rate is 7% (for urban areas), 5% (for county areas) and 1% (for other areas);
- **Education surtax**, a surtax imposed on the amount of indirect taxes payable by the taxpayer at a rate of 3%;
- **Local education surtax**, which is imposed on the amount of indirect taxes payable by the taxpayer at a rate of 2%;

Customs Duties

Customs duties are applied on the goods imported into China and on specific goods exported to other countries. The amount of customs duties on import/export of goods is calculated on the value of the goods multiplied by the corresponding rate; the value of the goods results from the customs declaration. This usually follows a regular check by competent authorities; the single rate is defined from its HS-code (code similar to the INTRASTAT European classification) that identifies the specific product category (Taxable Entities Covered).

Individual Income Tax

The National People's Congress enacted the Individual Income Tax Law for the first time on September 10, 1980, entering into force on the same day. In the following decades, there have been numerous amendments made to the original text with the last dated August 31, 2018, when the National People's Congress announced the promulgation of a revised text of Individual Income Tax Law of the People's Republic of China to be implemented from January 1, 2019.

The organ carrying out the control and administration of Individual Income Tax (IIT) is the State Administration of Taxation, which is also responsible for the collection and distribution of tax revenue together with local tax offices in provinces and metropolitan cities locally in charge of tax administration. Tax revenue is then divided between central and local governments.

Tax Residence

The revised Individual Income Tax Law divides taxpayers into two categories: resident taxpayers and non-resident taxpayers.

The definition of the resident taxpayer includes individuals who are domiciled in China (for family relationships, economic interests or possession of a home registered under their own name) and individuals who are not domiciled in China but have resided in China for 183 days or more during a tax year.

From the other side, non-resident taxpayers include individuals who are not domiciled in China and that have resided in China for less than 183 days during the tax year.

A tax year begins from January 1 and ends at December 31.

The IIT liability of each individual depends on his/her tax residence status.

Tax Liability

Individual taxpayers who are domiciled in China are subject to IIT on their worldwide income, including income sourced in China and income sourced outside China.

Individual taxpayers who are not domiciled in China but have resided in China for 183 days or more for more than 6 consecutive years, are subject to IIT on their worldwide income starting from the seventh year of tax residence.

Individual taxpayers who are not domiciled in China but have resided in China for 183 days or more during the tax year and are tax resident in China for no more than 6 consecutive years, are subject to IIT on their income sourced in China and their income sourced outside China but paid by a Chinese entity. The portion of income sourced outside China and paid by an overseas entity is exempt from China IIT.

Individual taxpayers who are not domiciled in China and have stayed in China for less than 183 days during the tax year are subject to IIT on their income sourced in China.

Individual taxpayers who are not domiciled in China and have stayed in China for less than 90 days during the tax year are subject to IIT on their income sourced in China and paid by a Chinese entity.

Only the days in which the individual has stayed in China for 24 h are included in the counting, while those days in which the individuals stayed less than 24 h are excluded.

Individuals who have dual employment and work both in China and abroad can determine their income sourced in China and the related tax liability based on the actual working period in days in China. In this case, the days in which the individuals stayed less than 24 h in China are counted as half day.

Worldwide Taxation and Six-Year Rule

According to the revised IIT Law, individuals who are considered tax resident in China shall be subject to China IIT on their worldwide income. However, individuals who are not domiciled in China and that have not been tax resident in China for more than six consecutive years can be exempted from China IIT on their income sourced outside China that is paid by an overseas entity. Individuals who are not domiciled in China will be therefore subject to China IIT on their worldwide income starting from the seventh year of tax residence.

The six-year period shall be counted starting from January 1, 2019 and shall be counted again if the individual leaves China for more than 30 days on a single trip in any year during which he resided in China for 183 days or more.

Income Classification

The Individual Income Tax Law lists different categories of income subject to the individual income tax:

1. Income from wages and salaries;
2. Income from remuneration for personal services;
3. Income from author's remuneration;
4. Income from royalties;
5. Income from business operation;
6. Income from interest, dividends, and bonuses;
7. Income from lease of property;
8. Income from transfer of property; and
9. Contingent income.

The incomes listed in items 1–4 are aggregated in the comprehensive income and subject to the individual income tax on a consolidated basis.

The incomes listed in items 5–9 are computed separately from the comprehensive income.

Calculation of Taxable Income

For comprehensive income received by a resident individual, the taxable income is calculated as the gross income less the standard deduction (60,000 CNY/yearly), the social contributions, the special additional deductions and any other deduction provided by the law.

For a non-resident individual, the income from wage and salary is taxed after deducting the standard deduction (5000 CNY/monthly).

For income derived from labor services and royalties income, the taxable income shall be the gross amount less the deduction of 20%.

For income from author's remuneration, the taxable income is determined by deducting 20%, with an additional deduction of 30% from the resulting amount.

For business income, the taxable amount is determined as the remainder after deducting costs, expenses, and losses from the gross income generated in the tax year.

For income derived from leasing of property, the taxable income is the remainder after deducting 800 CNY (or 20% of the amount received) from the total amount received.

For income derived from the transfer of property, the taxable income is the capital gain calculated as the difference between the total proceeds and the original cost of the property and reasonable expenses incurred in the transfer.

For interest, dividends and other occasional income, the taxable income is determined based on the amount received each time.

Individual Income Tax Rates

For comprehensive income, progressive rates ranging from 3 to 45% are applied on the taxable income calculated after subtracting all the allowed deductions:

Income tax rate on comprehensive income (yearly basis/CNY)

From	To	Tax rate (%)	Quick deduction
Not exceeding 36,000		3	0
36,000	144,000	10	2520
144,000	300,000	20	16,920
300,000	420,000	25	31,920
420,000	660,000	30	52,920
660,000	960,000	35	85,920
Exceeding 960,000		45	181,920

On a monthly basis, the tax rates are:

Income tax rate on comprehensive income (monthly basis / CNY)

From	To	Tax rate (%)	Quick deduction
Not exceeding 3000		3	0
3000	12,000	10	210
12,000	25,000	20	1410
25,000	35,000	25	2660
35,000	55,000	30	4410

(continued)

(continued)

Income tax rate on comprehensive income (monthly basis / CNY)			
From	To	Tax rate (%)	Quick deduction
55,000	80,000	35	7160
Exceeding 80,000		45	15,160

For business operation income, progressive rates ranging from 5 to 35% are applied on the taxable income calculated after deducting costs, expenses, and losses:

Income tax rate on business operation income (yearly basis CNY)			
From	To	Tax rate (%)	Quick deduction
Not exceeding 30,000		5	0
30,000	90,000	10	1500
90,000	300,000	20	10,500
300,000	500,000	30	40,500
Exceeding 500,000		35	65,500

For interest, dividends, income from leasing and transfer of property and occasional income, a rate of 20% shall apply.

Social Contributions

Chinese employees are required to make contributions for social insurance, including pension, medical, unemployment, maternity, and work-related injury insurances and the housing provident funds. Foreign citizens are also required to participate in social security schemes, even if at the moment the implementation varies from city to city.

Both employee and employer shall contribute to social security schemes and the amount of these social contributions is calculated based on the employee's average salary calculated in the previous year and the rates determined by local Authorities.

The rates currently applied in Shanghai and Beijing are as below:

Item	Shanghai		Beijing	
	Employer (%)	Employee (%)	Employer (%)	Employee (%)
Pension	16	8	16	8
Medical	9.5	2	10	2
Work-related injury	0.26	–	0.4	–
Maternity	1	–	0.8	–
Unemployment	0.5	0.5	0.8	0.2
Housing fund	7	7	12	12

Special Additional Deductions

Besides the standard deduction of CNY 5000 monthly (equal to CNY 60,000 yearly), the Individual Income Tax Law and its Implementing Regulations provide additional deductions from taxable income for children's education, continuing education, treatment of serious disease, the caring for the elderly, house loan interest and rents.

Item	Qualifying conditions	Annual deduction
Children's education	Pre-school Compulsory education Intermediate education Higher education	12,000 CNY/child
Continuing education	Formal education Professional education	4800 CNY 3600 CNY
Medical fee for serious disease	Self-paid medical expenses over 15,000 CNY	Actual expense not exceeding 80,000 CNY
House loan interest	Mortgage on first house	12,000 CNY
Housing rental fee	Not owning a property in the city of work	9600–18,000 CNY
Elderly dependent care expenses	Parents and grandparents aged 60 years or elder	12,000–24,000

Tax Allowances for Expats

Foreign employees can be exempted from individual income tax on certain benefits received during their employment in the territory of China. Such deductible allowances include:

- housing, meal and laundry allowances received in a non-cash for or on a reimbursement basis;
- reimbursement of reasonable relocation expenses upon commencement or cessation of China assignment;
- travel expenses for a couple of return flight tickets to home country;
- language training and children education expenses.

All the expenses shall be supported by relevant documentation.

Foreign employees will be allowed to enjoy such allowances until the end of 2021; from January 2022 foreigners can benefit only of the special additional deductions introduced for Chinese employees in 2019.

Withholding and Final Settlement

Employers are required to withhold the individual income tax at the payment of the remuneration: for wages and salaries, the tax shall be withheld on a monthly basis, while for author's remuneration, royalties and remuneration for personal services, the tax shall be withheld at each payment.

The revised IIT Law introduced a new withholding system, according to which the resident taxpayers earning a salary are subject to individual income tax withholding based on the cumulative taxable income.

A final IIT settlement shall be handled by the taxpayers between March 1 and June 30 following the tax year if the withholding tax on their comprehensive income has not been correctly applied at source, if they have earned overseas income, if they have to apply for a refund or if they earned taxable income in two or more working places.

Company Income Tax

The current Company Income Tax Law and its implementing rules have entered into force on January 1, 2008, responding to the demand of an action able to adapt the wholly foreign owned enterprises taxation with local firms' taxation.

Company Income Tax Rate

The standard rate of the company income tax is 25%; reduced and preferential rates are granted to those enterprises operating in certain industries and geographic areas. For example:

- high-tech enterprises are eligible for a reduced rate of 15%;
- enterprises operating in encouraged industries and established in the Western regions are eligible for a reduced rate of 15%
- from 2019 to 2021, small low-profit companies with a taxable income up to 3 million CNY, a number of employees not exceeding 300 and total assets not exceeding 50 million CNY are eligible for reduced rate of 20%, to be applied on 25% of the income up to 1 million CNY and on 50% of the income exceeding 1 million CNY and up to 3 million CNY.

Taxable Entities

The company income tax is levied on resident and non-resident enterprises. For the purpose of the taxation, are considered as resident those enterprises that are incorporated in China or incorporated outside China but effectively managed and controlled in China. Resident enterprises are taxed on their worldwide income.

Non-resident enterprises are those not included in the definition of resident enterprises and can be further divided into two categories: non-resident enterprises with a permanent establishment in China. For these entities, the income sourced outside China may be exempt from taxation.

Type of company	Taxable income
Resident company (incorporated in China or effectively managed and controlled in China)	Worldwide income (income sourced in and outside China)
Non-resident company with a permanent establishment in China	Income sourced in China and the income sourced outside China that is connected to the permanent establishment
Non-resident company without a permanent establishment in China	Income sourced in China only

Categories of Taxable Income

The Company Income Tax Law provides a list of revenue considered taxable:

1. Revenue from the sales of goods and provision of services;
2. Proceeds from the transfer of tangible and intangible properties;
3. Dividends received from private and listed companies;
4. Interest, rental, royalties, and revenue from donations; and
5. Other income.

The Source of the Income

A relevant issue is to identify the source or the origin of the profits of a company: non-resident enterprises are subject to tax only on the portion of the income generated within China or effectively connected with the permanent establishment.

The source of the income shall be determined according to the art. 7 of Implementing Rules of Company Income Tax:

1. For revenue from sales of goods and provision of services, the source is determined in accordance with the place in which the activities occur;
2. For income from transfer of immovable properties, the source is determined according to the place where the property is located;
3. For income from transfer of movable properties, the source is determined according to the place of the transferring enterprise;

4. For income from transfer of equity, the source is determined according to the place where the invested enterprise is located;
5. For dividends, the source is the place of the enterprise which makes the distribution;
6. For income from royalties, rental and interest, the source is determined according to the place of the enterprise paying the income;
7. For other income, the source is determined according to the State Council.

Tax Liability and Computation

The taxable income for Company Income Tax is determined by starting from the total income (including all the taxable revenue from sale of goods, provision of services, transfer of goods and related rights, dividends, interest, rental and royalties, along with donations and other non-operating income and deducting the non-taxable or exempt items).

The total income is then deducted by items as not-taxable income and expenditure incurred during the course of business, including costs, expenses, losses on disposal of assets, depreciation and carry-forward losses.

Withholding Tax

Non-Resident companies without a permanent establishment in China are subject to Company Income Tax which is withheld at source on income earned within PRC's territory. The taxable income may consist of earnings from dividends, royalties, interest, rental, and capital gains. To determine the origin of a source of income it is recommended to consult the art.7 of EITIR, where the Chinese Legislator has laid down principles to verify the provenance of sources and their possible liability to corporate income tax.

The withholding tax on income from Non-Resident companies without a permanent establishment in China is equal to 10% unless otherwise stated.

Withholding Agent

In China, withholding tax is levied on Non-Resident companies providing services to China-based business. The income tax payable on such income derived by Non-Resident enterprises shall be withheld at source, and the client, becoming a withholding agent, has the responsibility to transfer this amount to the State Treasury in name and behalf of the tax bureau. The process ends with a tax return delivered within seven days after the payment.

Tax Computation and Deadlines

The Company Income Tax is calculated multiplying a tax base by its applicable rate and then subtracting tax credits previously accrued thanks to preferential treatments and taxes already paid abroad. The annual CIT declaration must be filed within 5 months after the closing of the fiscal year which always coincides with the calendar year as stated in the Company Income Tax Law. Advance payments are finally required, based on quarterly interim financial statements released every three months and followed by a net balance adjustment sum paid by the Authority after the submission of the annual CIT declaration.

Anti-avoidance Rules

The Company Income Tax Law provides a series of anti-avoidance rules aimed at designing a general framework in line with the principles adopted in the legal systems of Western countries:

- standard on transfer prices between related parties
- standard on Controlled Foreign Companies
- standard on Advance Pricing Agreement between a Firm and Financial Administration about transaction prices between related parties
- standard on Cost Sharing Agreement that involves the deductibility of common costs charged to intra-group companies
- legal obligation to document ongoing transactions between the entity and its affiliated companies ("Related Party Transaction Annual Report")

The tax authority has also introduced a general anti-avoidance clause that enables local officials to make adjustments in a wide range of cases:

"If an enterprise engages in a business arrangement without bona fide commercial purposes that results in reducing its taxable revenue or taxable income, the tax authorities in charge have the right to make adjustments based on reasonable methods."

Transfer Pricing

General Framework

The Circular no. 42 issued in 2016 by the SAT introduces a three-tiered documentation framework providing a new landscape for transfer pricing practice in China, in line with the main guidelines provided by OECD.

The transfer pricing documentation includes a master file, a local file, and a special issue file.

Enterprises having only domestic related-party transactions are not required to prepare the above files.

Related-Party Definition

An enterprise is a related party to another enterprise, organization or individual if one of the following conditions is met:

- one party directly or indirectly owns at least 25% of the equity of another party or a third party directly or indirectly owns at least 25% of both parties;
- one party takes a loan from another party (other than an independent financial institution) in an amount equal to or more than 50% of the borrower's actual paid-in capital, or 10% or more of the total debts are guaranteed by another party (other than an independent financial institution);
- more than half of the senior management or at least one senior member of the board of directors who may control the board of one party is appointed by another party, or at least half of the senior management or at least one senior member of the board of directors who may control the board of both parties is appointed by the same third party;
- more than half of the senior management of one party are also senior management of another party, or at least one senior member of the board of directors who may control the board of one party is also a senior member of the board of directors of another party;
- the normal operation of production or business of one party is dependent on the industrial property or proprietary technology licensed by another party.

Master File

The requirement of the master file applies to enterprises that during the year have carried out overseas related-party transactions for an aggregate value exceeding 1 billion CNY or to enterprises that have carried out transactions with overseas related parties and which financial statements are consolidated by an ultimate holding company that has prepared a master file. In the second case, the master file is prepared by the ultimate holding company and shall be provided to the Chinese subsidiary.

Local File

The enterprises required to prepare the local file are those with:

- An annual sum of related-party transactions related to tangible assets exceeding 200 million CNY;
- An annual sum of related-party transactions related to intangible or financial assets exceeding 100 million CNY; or
- An annual sum of other related-party transactions exceeding 40 million CNY.

The related-party transactions covered by an advanced pricing agreement shall not be included in the local file.

Special Issue File

A special issue file is required if the enterprise has entered or has implemented a cost-sharing agreement or falls under the thin capitalization requirement, with a debt-to-equity ratio exceeding 2:1 (for non-financial enterprises) and 5:1 (for financial enterprises).

Country-By-Country Reporting

The Chinese resident enterprises that are the ultimate holding company of a multinational group with consolidated revenue over 5.5 billion CNY or that have been nominated as the CbC reporting entity by their group are required to prepare a CbC report.

China at a Glance

Official name	People's Republic of China	Capital city	Beijing
Currency	Yuan Renminbi (CNY/RMB)	Official language	Chinese
Time zone	UTC + 8 (China Standard Time)	Population (2018)	1395 million
Area	9.6 million km^2		

Gross Domestic Product 2020, by regions[a]					
Region	GDP 2020 (CNY bn)	GDP Growth 2020 (%)	Region	GDP 2020 (CNY bn)	GDP Growth 2020 (%)
Anhui	3868	3.9	Jiangxi	2569	3.8
Beijing	3610	1.2	Jilin	1231	2.4
Chongqing	2500	3.9	Liaoning	2512	0.6
Fujian	4390	3.3	Ningxia	392	3.9
Gansu	902	3.9	Qinghai	301	1.5
Guangdong	11076	2.3	Shaanxi	2618	2.2
Guangxi	2216	3.7	Shandong	7313	3.6
Guizhou	1783	4.5	Shanghai	3870	1.7
Hainan	553	3.5	Shanxi	1765	3.6
Hebei	3621	3.9	Sichuan	4860	3.8
Heilongjiang	1370	1.0	Tianjin	1408	1.5
Henan	5500	1.3	Tibet	190	7.8
Hubei	4344	−5.0	Xinjiang	1380	3.4
Hunan	4178	3.8	Yunnan	2450	4.0
Inner Mongolia	1736	0.2	Zhejiang	6461	3.6
Jiangsu	10,270	3.7	**National**	**101,599**	**2.3**

[a] *Source* National Bureau of Statistics of China

International trade 2020[a]	Export	Import	Trade balance
Merchandise (CNY billion)	17,932.6	14,233.1	3309.6
Service (CNY billion)	1935.7	2628.6	−692.9

[a] *Source* National Bureau of Statistics of China

Foreign direct investment 2020[a]	Inflows	Outflows
FDI (CNY billion)	1000.0	759.8

[a] *Source* National Bureau of Statistics of China

Company income tax rate (%)	25	Withholding tax on royalties (%)	10
Withholding tax on dividends (%)	10	Losses carry forward (years)	5
Withholding tax on interest (%)	10	Individual income tax rate (%)	3–45
Standard VAT rate (%)	13	No tax area for individuals (CNY)	60,000

Appendix: Tax Revenue

Main Items of China General Public Budget Revenue

in CNY billion[a]	2017	2018	2019	2020
Budget revenue	**17,259**	**18,335**	**19,038**	**18,289**
Tax revenue	***14,437***	***15,640***	***15,799***	***15,431***
Domestic value-added tax	5638	6152	6234	5679
Domestic consumption tax	1023	1632	1256	1202
VAT and consumption tax from imports	1597	16873	1581	1453
VAT and Consumption tax rebate for exports	(1387)	(1591)	(1650)	(1362)
Corporate income tax	3212	3532	3730	3642
Individual income tax	1197	1387	1038	1156
Resource tax	135	163	182	175
Urban maintenance and construction tax	436	483	482	460
House property tax	260	288	298	284
Stamp tax	221	219	246	308
Urban Land use tax	236	238	219	205
Land appreciation tax	491	564	646	646
Vehicles, Tonnage, Tobacco leaf tax	94	99	112	115
Vehicles purchase tax	328	345	349	353
Tariffs	300	284	290	256
Farm land occupation tax	165	131	139	125
Deed tax	491	573	621	706
Other tax revenue	0	0	1	0
Non-tax revenue	***2822***	***2695***	***3239***	***2858***

[a] *Source* National Bureau of Statistics of China

Tax Revenue Breakdown

Item	2000	2005	2010	2015	2020
Domestic VAT	455	1079	2109	3111	5679
Business tax	187	423	1116	1931	0
Company income tax	100	534	1284	2713	3642
Individual income tax	66	209	484	862	1156

(continued)

(continued)

Item	2000	2005	2010	2015	2020
Other taxes	450	632	2,328	3875	4926
Total tax revenue	1258	2878	7321	12492	15431

In CNY billion

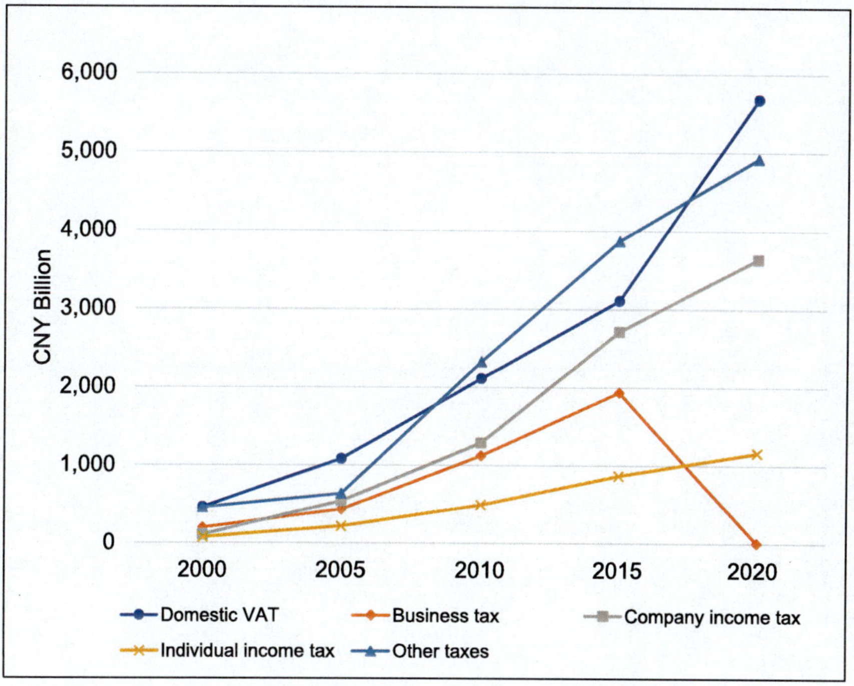

An Overview of China Europe Trade and Economies

European Economies

Geographical Europe, as defined by the United Nation, is composed by 45 economies, made of approximately 745 million people, with a combined GDP, in 2019, of 21 trillion US dollars (2019 has been chosen as benchmark in order to avoid the effect of the pandemic on data). The largest economy is Germany, with a GDP of 3863.3 billion, followed by the United Kingdom, France, and Italy. The smallest economy is San Marino, with a GDP of 1.6 billion USD, followed by Montenegro, Kosovo, and Moldova. Luxembourg, Switzerland, and Norway are at the top regarding GDP per capita, while Moldova, Ukraine, and Kosovo are the European economies with the lowest GDP per capita.

Economy	Region	Population, (mln persons)	GDP current prices (billion USD)	GDP per capita (USD)
Albania	Southern Europe	2.9	15.4	5373
Austria	Western Europe	9.0	447.7	50,023
Belarus	Eastern Europe	9.5	62.6	6604
Belgium	Western Europe	11.5	517.6	45,176
Bosnia and Herzegovina	Southern Europe	3.5	20.1	5742
Bulgaria	Eastern Europe	7.0	66.3	9518
Croatia	Southern Europe	4.1	60.7	14,950
Cyprus	Southern Europe	0.9	24.3	27,720
Czech Republic	Eastern Europe	10.6	247.0	23,214
Denmark	Northern Europe	5.8	347.2	59,795
Estonia	Northern Europe	1.3	31.0	23,524
Finland	Northern Europe	5.5	269.7	48,869

(continued)

© The Author(s), under exclusive license to Springer Nature Singapore Pte Ltd. 2022

L. Riccardi and G. Riccardi, *China–Europe Tax Treaties*,
https://doi.org/10.1007/978-981-19-3563-3_7

(continued)

Economy	Region	Population, (mln persons)	GDP current prices (billion USD)	GDP per capita (USD)
France	Western Europe	64.8	2707.1	41,761
Germany	Western Europe	83.0	3863.3	46,564
Greece	Southern Europe	10.7	214.0	19,974
Hungary	Eastern Europe	9.8	170.4	17,463
Iceland	Northern Europe	0.4	23.9	67,037
Ireland	Northern Europe	5.0	384.9	77,771
Italy	Southern Europe	60.4	1988.6	32,947
Kosovo	Southern Europe	1.8	8.0	4442
Latvia	Northern Europe	1.9	35.0	18,172
Lithuania	Northern Europe	2.8	53.6	19,267
Luxembourg	Western Europe	0.6	69.5	113,196
Malta	Southern Europe	0.5	14.9	30,650
Moldova	Eastern Europe	3.5	11.7	3300
Montenegro	Southern Europe	0.6	5.4	8704
Netherlands	Western Europe	17.2	902.4	52,368
North Macedonia	Southern Europe	2.1	12.7	6096
Norway	Northern Europe	5.4	417.6	77,975
Poland	Eastern Europe	38.0	565.9	14,902
Portugal	Southern Europe	10.3	236.4	23,031
Romania	Eastern Europe	19.5	243.7	12,483
Russia	Eastern Europe	146.7	1637.9	11,163
San Marino	Southern Europe	0.0	1.6	47,280
Serbia	Southern Europe	7.0	51.5	7398
Slovak Republic	Eastern Europe	5.5	106.6	19,548
Slovenia	Southern Europe	2.1	54.2	26,170
Spain	Southern Europe	46.7	1397.9	29,961
Sweden	Northern Europe	10.3	528.9	51,242
Switzerland	Western Europe	8.5	715.4	83,717
Ukraine	Eastern Europe	41.9	150.4	3592
United Kingdom	Northern Europe	66.9	2743.6	41,030

Source International Monetary Fund, year 2019
Note Data for Andorra, Liechtenstein, and Monaco are not included as they are not available at the time of writing

European Economies: Openness to Business

Regarding openness to business, the values for Corporate Income Tax span from 35% in Malta and 9% in Hungary and Montenegro. The top scores in the Doing Business ranking are awarded to Denmark, the United Kingdom, and Norway, while the lowest scores are given to San Marino, Liechtenstein, and Bosnia and Herzegovina. In this ranking Germany is 10th, France 16th, and Italy 34th. The top three countries for FDI instock in 2019 have been the United Kingdom, the Netherlands, and Switzerland, while the top three countries for FDI inflow in 2019 have been the Netherlands, Ireland, and the United Kingdom. All countries but Andorra, Kosovo, Liechtenstein, Monaco, and San Marino have a Double Tax Agreement with China, while 27 out of 45 are part of the Belt and Road Initiative, with Italy, Russia, and Poland being the main economies being part of it.

Economy	DTA with China	Belt road	Company income tax 2021 (%)	Doing business score 2020	FDI instock (million USD)	FDI inflow (million USD)
Albania	YES	·	15	67.7	8811	1281
Andorra	NO		10	–	–	–
Austria	YES	·	25	78.7	205,634	4643
Belarus	YES	·	18	74.3	14,513	1293
Belgium	YES		25	75.0	566,116	9707
Bosnia and Herzegovina	YES	·	10	65.4	8755	528
Bulgaria	YES	·	10	72.0	51,856	1223
Croatia	YES	·	18	73.6	29,866	1365
Cyprus	YES	·	12.5	73.4	445,091	24,248
Czech Republic	YES	·	19	76.3	170,682	7577
Denmark	YES		22	85.3	105,748	930
Estonia	YES	·	20	80.6	27,476	3044
Finland	YES		20	80.2	78,353	8170
France	YES		25 (from 2022)	76.8	868,691	33,965
Germany	YES		30	79.7	953,306	36,359
Greece	YES	·	22	68.4	40,513	4631
Hungary	YES	·	9	73.4	97,841	5205
Iceland	YES		20	79.0	8705	−241
Ireland	YES		12.5	79.6	1,120,301	78,234
Italy	YES	·	24	72.9	445,741	26,569
Kosovo	NO		10	73.2	4501	304
Latvia	YES	·	20	80.3	17,948	789

(continued)

(continued)

Economy	DTA with China	Belt road	Company income tax 2021 (%)	Doing business score 2020	FDI instock (million USD)	FDI inflow (million USD)
Liechtenstein	NO		12.5	64.8	–	–
Lithuania	YES	·	15	81.6	20,411	975
Luxembourg	YES	·	25	69.6	128,422	−11,421
Malta	YES	·	35	66.1	205,758	3573
Moldova	YES	·	12	74.4	4792	589
Monaco	NO		26.5	–	–	–
Montenegro	YES	·	9	73.8	5652	453
Netherlands	YES		25	76.1	1,749,779	84,216
North Macedonia	YES	·	10	80.7	6350	365
Norway	YES		22	82.6	167,475	4298
Poland	YES	·	19	76.4	236,506	13,220
Portugal	YES	·	21	76.5	161,640	8234
Romania	YES	·	16	73.3	97,095	5971
Russia	YES	·	20	78.2	463,860	31,735
San Marino	NO		–	64.2	–	–
Serbia	YES	·	15	75.7	43,964	4281
Slovak Republic	YES	·	21	75.6	59,750	2449
Slovenia	YES	·	19	76.5	18,135	910
Spain	YES		25	77.9	751,510	12,406
Sweden	YES		20.6	82.0	339,543	20,568
Switzerland	YES		11.9–21.6	76.6	1,350,682	−21,740
Ukraine	YES	·	18	70.2	48,906	3070
United Kingdom	YES		19	83.5	2,075,271	59,137

Source UNCTAD and RsA Asia report, year 2019 unless otherwise indicated

European Economies: Trade

The top exporters are Germany, the Netherlands, France, and Italy, while the main importers are Germany, the United Kingdom, France, and the Netherlands. Germany, Russia, the Netherlands record the highest trade surplus, while the United Kingdom, France, and Spain mark the highest trade deficit. Germany, the Netherlands, France, the United Kingdom, and Italy are the economies that engage the most in international trade, while Andorra, Montenegro, Albania, and Moldova engage the least in absolute terms. It should be noted that the figures for the Netherlands might be inflated by the Rotterdam effect.

Economy	Imports (million USD)	Exports (million USD)	Total international trade (million USD)	Trade balance (million USD)
Albania	5897	2716	8612	−3181
Andorra	1752	142	1894	−1610
Austria	184,964	179,021	363,986	−5943
Belarus	39,342	32,930	72,272	−6412
Belgium	426,198	444,563	870,762	18,365
Bosnia and Herzegovina	11,159	6578	17,737	−4581
Bulgaria	37,176	33,303	70,479	−3873
Croatia	28,026	17,381	45,407	−10,645
Cyprus	9167	3460	12,627	−5707
Czech Republic	178,248	198,511	376,759	20,262
Denmark	97,533	110,699	208,232	13,166
Estonia	18,015	16,124	34,139	−1891
Finland	73,500	73,333	146,833	−167
France	651,179	569,732	1,220,910	−81,447
Germany	1,234,222	1,489,158	2,723,381	254,936
Greece	62,218	37,874	100,093	−24,344
Hungary	119,814	123,616	243,430	3802
Iceland	6542	5224	11,766	−1318
Ireland	98,483	169,779	268,262	71,297
Italy	473,512	532,663	1,006,175	59,151
Latvia	18,717	15,489	34,206	−3228
Lithuania	35,612	33,124	68,736	−2488
Luxembourg	23,991	16,508	40,500	−7483
Malta	7072	3007	10,079	−4065
Moldova	5842	2779	8621	−3063
Montenegro	2909	465	3374	−2444
Netherlands	635,967	709,229	1,345,197	73,262
North Macedonia	9471	7189	16,660	−2282
Norway	85,013	102,685	187,697	17,672
Poland	261,998	264,013	526,011	2015
Portugal	89,924	67,060	156,983	−22,864
Romania	96,530	76,873	173,403	−19,658

(continued)

(continued)

Economy	Imports (million USD)	Exports (million USD)	Total international trade (million USD)	Trade balance (million USD)
Russia	254,052	418,796	672,848	164,744
Serbia	26,730	19,630	46,360	−7101
Slovak Republic	90,049	89,682	179,731	−366
Slovenia	43,962	44,866	88,829	904
Spain	371,929	333,622	705,551	−38,306
Sweden	158,690	160,543	319,233	1852
Switzerland	277,001	313,866	590,867	36,865
Ukraine	60,607	50,066	110,673	−10,541
United Kingdom	691,801	468,817	1,160,618	−222,983

Source UNCTAD, year 2019
Note Data for Kosovo, Liechtenstein, Monaco, and San Marino are not included as they are not available at the time of writing

European Economies and China: Import, Export, and Trade Balance

Dealing with European economies trade with China, Germany is the top importer from China and the top exporter towards China, with a trade surplus of 18 billion USD in 2020. The Netherlands and the United Kingdom record the highest trade deficit with China, with 66 and 52 billion USD respectively. The Netherlands and the United Kingdom are the second and the third top importers from China, with 79 and 72 billion USD respectively, while Russia and France are the second and the third top exporters towards China, with 57 and 29 billion USD respectively.

Economy	Import from China (billion USD)	Export to China (billion USD)	Trade balance, (billion USD)
Albania	0.571	0.079	−0.49
Andorra	0.003	0.0004	0.00
Austria	3.41	6.64	3.23
Belarus	2.11	0.889	−1.22
Belgium	20.76	7.84	−12.92
Bosnia and Herzegovina	0.12	0.072	−0.05

(continued)

(continued)

Economy	Import from China (billion USD)	Export to China (billion USD)	Trade balance, (billion USD)
Bulgaria	1.55	1.37	−0.18
Croatia	1.57	0.138	−1.43
Cyprus	0.893	0.025	−0.87
Czech Republic	13.74	5.13	−8.61
Denmark	7.47	6.01	−1.46
Estonia	0.864	0.281	−0.58
Finland	2.95	4.19	1.24
France	37.34	29.71	−7.63
Germany	86.82	105.26	18.44
Greece	7.04	0.773	−6.27
Hungary	7.4	4.28	−3.12
Iceland	0.1	0.104	0.00
Ireland	4	14.04	10.04
Italy	32.94	22.25	−10.69
Latvia	1.05	0.2	−0.85
Lithuania	1.81	0.487	−1.32
Luxembourg	0.949	0.276	−0.67
Malta	1.36	0.388	−0.97
Moldova	0.145	0.06	−0.09
Montenegro	0.113	0.057	−0.06
Netherlands	79.01	12.79	−66.22
North Macedonia	0.156	0.227	0.07
Norway	3.53	7.27	3.74
Poland	26.74	4.32	−22.42
Portugal	4.19	2.77	−1.42
Romania	5.13	2.64	−2.49
Russia	50.58	57.18	6.60
San Marino	0.007	2.86	2.85
Serbia	1.62	0.497	−1.12
Slovak Republic	3.03	6.43	3.40
Slovenia	3.45	0.508	−2.94
Spain	27.54	10.35	−17.19
Sweden	8.37	9.47	1.10
Switzerland	5.09	17.49	12.40
Ukraine	6.88	7.79	0.91
United Kingdom	72.61	19.76	−52.85

Source United Nations COMTRADE, year 2020

European Economies and China: Two Main Import Categories from China

Looking specifically at the goods categories imported from China by European countries, it is noticeable that Germany, the top importer from China in Europe, demands "electrical, electronic equipment" as first import category in 2020, followed by "machinery, nuclear reactors, boilers", with a value of 20.65 and 18.94 billion USD respectively. The same categories are repeated also for the Netherlands and the United Kingdom, the second and the third top importers from China.

Economy	First category	Value (billion USD)	Second category	Value (billion USD)
Albania	Machinery, nuclear reactors, boilers	0.085	Electrical, electronic equipment	0.072
Andorra	Pharmaceutical products	0.0009	Rubbers	0.0009
Austria	Electrical, electronic equipment	0.946	Machinery, nuclear reactors, boilers	0.860
Belarus	Electrical, electronic equipment	0.381	Machinery, nuclear reactors, boilers	0.346
Belgium	Machinery, nuclear reactors, boilers	2.90	Electrical, electronic equipment	2.76
Bosnia and Herzegovina	Machinery, nuclear reactors, boilers	0.021	Electrical, electronic equipment	0.020
Bulgaria	Electrical, electronic equipment	0.319	Machinery, nuclear reactors, boilers	0.304
Croatia	Electrical, electronic equipment	0.334	Machinery, nuclear reactors, boilers	0.242
Cyprus	Ships, boats, and other floating structures	0.322	Machinery, nuclear reactors, boilers	0.125
Czech Republic	Electrical, electronic equipment	7.22	Machinery, nuclear reactors, boilers	3.72
Denmark	Electrical, electronic equipment	1.13	Machinery, nuclear reactors, boilers	0.986

(continued)

(continued)

Economy	First category	Value (billion USD)	Second category	Value (billion USD)
Estonia	Electrical, electronic equipment	0.327	Machinery, nuclear reactors, boilers	0.139
Finland	Electrical, electronic equipment	0.698	Machinery, nuclear reactors, boilers	0.562
France	Electrical, electronic equipment	6.56	Machinery, nuclear reactors, boilers	6.11
Germany	Electrical, electronic equipment	20.65	Machinery, nuclear reactors, boilers	18.94
Greece	Machinery, nuclear reactors, boilers	1.29	Electrical, electronic equipment	1.02
Hungary	Electrical, electronic equipment	2.81	Machinery, nuclear reactors, boilers	1.35
Iceland	Electrical, electronic equipment	0.017	Machinery, nuclear reactors, boilers	0.016
Ireland	Machinery, nuclear reactors, boilers	1.01	Electrical, electronic equipment	0.49
Italy	Electrical, electronic equipment	6.96	Machinery, nuclear reactors, boilers	5.58
Latvia	Electrical, electronic equipment	0.253	Machinery, nuclear reactors, boilers	0.171
Lithuania	Electrical, electronic equipment	0.328	Machinery, nuclear reactors, boilers	0.260
Luxembourg	Machinery, nuclear reactors, boilers	0.608	Mineral fuels, oils, distillation products	0.095
Malta	Machinery, nuclear reactors, boilers	0.315	Mineral fuels, oils, distillation products	0.255
Moldova	Machinery, nuclear reactors, boilers	0.036	Electrical, electronic equipment	0.030

(continued)

(continued)

Economy	First category	Value (billion USD)	Second category	Value (billion USD)
Montenegro	Plastics	0.018	Electrical, electronic equipment	0.014
Netherlands	Electrical, electronic equipment	26.83	Machinery, nuclear reactors, boilers	20.63
North Macedonia	Electrical, electronic equipment	0.043	Machinery, nuclear reactors, boilers	0.039
Norway	Electrical, electronic equipment	0.461	Vehicles other than railway, tramway	0.455
Poland	Electrical, electronic equipment	7.50	Machinery, nuclear reactors, boilers	4.61
Portugal	Electrical, electronic equipment	0.997	Machinery, nuclear reactors, boilers	0.673
Romania	Electrical, electronic equipment	1.05	Machinery, nuclear reactors, boilers	1.03
Russia	Electrical, electronic equipment	10.75	Machinery, nuclear reactors, boilers	10.19
San Marino	Toys, games, sports requisites	0.001	Machinery, nuclear reactors, boilers	0.001
Serbia	Machinery, nuclear reactors, boilers	0.470	Electrical, electronic equipment	0.338
Slovak Republic	Electrical, electronic equipment	1.31	Machinery, nuclear reactors, boilers	0.512
Slovenia	Electrical, electronic equipment	1.03	Machinery, nuclear reactors, boilers	0.408
Spain	Electrical, electronic equipment	5.64	Machinery, nuclear reactors, boilers	3.27
Sweden	Electrical, electronic equipment	1.73	Machinery, nuclear reactors, boilers	1.27

(continued)

(continued)

Economy	First category	Value (billion USD)	Second category	Value (billion USD)
Switzerland	Electrical, electronic equipment	0.847	Machinery, nuclear reactors, boilers	0.843
Ukraine	Electrical, electronic equipment	1.27	Machinery, nuclear reactors, boilers	1.16
United Kingdom	Electrical, electronic equipment	14.74	Machinery, nuclear reactors, boilers	11.11

Source United Nations COMTRADE, year 2020

European Economies and China: Two Main Export Categories to China

Germany is the top exporter towards China, with the main exports being "vehicles other than railway, tramway", valued 22.64 billion USD in 2020, and "machinery, nuclear reactors, boilers", valued 22.02 billion USD. Russia and France are the second and the third top exporters towards China. The first exports of Russia are "mineral fuels, oils, distillation products", worth 33.39 billion USD in 2020, and "Wood and articles of wood, wood charcoal", for 3.71 billion USD. The first exports of France are "Essential oils, perfumes, cosmetics, toiletries", worth 4.49 billion USD in 2020, and "Machinery, nuclear reactors, boilers", for 3.63 billion USD.

Economy	First category	Value (billion USD)	Second category	Value (billion USD)
Albania	Ores slag and ash	0.056	Articles of apparel, not knit or crocheted	0.007
Andorra	Optical, photo, technical, medical apparatus	0.0003	Commodities not specified according to kind	0.00006
Austria	Machinery, nuclear reactors, boilers	1.51	Vehicles other than railway, tramway	1.11
Belarus	Fertilizers	0.334	Meat and edible meat offal	0.126
Belgium	Pearls, precious stones, metals, coins	1.43	Pharmaceutical products	1.03
Bosnia and Herzegovina	Wood and articles of wood, wood charcoal	0.023	Articles of apparel, not knit or crocheted	0.014

(continued)

(continued)

Economy	First category	Value (billion USD)	Second category	Value (billion USD)
Bulgaria	Copper	0.739	Electrical, electronic equipment	0.111
Croatia	Electrical, electronic equipment	0.039	Wood and articles of wood, wood charcoal	0.029
Cyprus	Vegetable, fruit, nut food preparations	0.009	Pharmaceutical products	0.009
Czech Republic	Electrical, electronic equipment	1.46	Machinery, nuclear reactors, boilers	1.23
Denmark	Meat and edible meat offal	1.39	Organic chemicals	1.03
Estonia	Electrical, electronic equipment	0.117	Wood and articles of wood, wood charcoal	0.040
Finland	Pulp of wood, fibrous cellulosic material, waste	1.04	Machinery, nuclear reactors, boilers	0.664
France	Essential oils, perfumes, cosmetics, toiletries	4.49	Machinery, nuclear reactors, boilers	3.63
Germany	Vehicles other than railway, tramway	22.64	Machinery, nuclear reactors, boilers	22.02
Greece	Pharmaceutical products	0.243	Salt, sulphur, earth, stone, plaster, lime and cement	0.170
Hungary	Electrical, electronic equipment	1.87	Vehicles other than railway, tramway	0.737
Iceland	Fish, crustaceans, molluscs, aquatics invertebrates	0.075	Aluminum	0.015
Ireland	Electrical, electronic equipment	7.41	Pharmaceutical products	2.59
Italy	Machinery, nuclear reactors, boilers	4.82	Pharmaceutical products	2.23
Latvia	Wood and articles of wood, wood charcoal	0.086	Mineral fuels, oils, distillation products	0.039
Lithuania	Copper	0.098	Cereals	0.092
Luxembourg	Copper	0.071	Wadding, felt, nonwovens, yarns, twine, cordage	0.050

(continued)

(continued)

Economy	First category	Value (billion USD)	Second category	Value (billion USD)
Malta	Electrical, electronic equipment	0.290	Optical, photo, technical, medical apparatus	0.045
Moldova	Electrical, electronic equipment	0.027	Articles of apparel, not knit or crocheted	0.012
Montenegro	Ores slag and ash	0.054	Beverages, spirits and vinegar	0.001
Netherlands	Machinery, nuclear reactors, boilers	3.89	Cereal, flour, starch, milk preparations and products	1.96
North Macedonia	Iron and steel	0.115	Salt, sulphur, earth, stone, plaster, lime and cement	0.029
Norway	Mineral fuels, oils, distillation products	4.27	Organic chemicals	0.713
Poland	Electrical, electronic equipment	0.795	Machinery, nuclear reactors, boilers	0.646
Portugal	Electrical, electronic equipment	1.12	Vehicles other than railway, tramway	0.588
Romania	Electrical, electronic equipment	0.669	Machinery, nuclear reactors, boilers	0.368
Russia	Mineral fuels, oils, distillation products	33.39	Wood and articles of wood, wood charcoal	3.71
San Marino	Miscellaneous edible preparations	0.001	Machinery, nuclear reactors, boilers	0.0005
Serbia	Copper	0.293	Electrical, electronic equipment	0.050
Slovak Republic	Vehicles other than railway, tramway	5.50	Electrical, electronic equipment	0.407
Slovenia	Electrical, electronic equipment	0.186	Machinery, nuclear reactors, boilers	0.069
Spain	Meat and edible meat offal	3.29	Ores slag and ash	0.889
Sweden	Pharmaceutical products	1.87	Machinery, nuclear reactors, boilers	1.52
Switzerland	Pearls, precious stones, metals, coins	5.15	Clocks and watches	3.11
Ukraine	Ores slag and ash	3.01	Cereals	1.87

(continued)

(continued)

Economy	First category	Value (billion USD)	Second category	Value (billion USD)
United Kingdom	Vehicles other than railway, tramway	3.78	Machinery, nuclear reactors, boilers	2.62

Source United Nations COMTRADE, year 2020

European Economies and China: Bilateral Double Tax Agreement

- Northern Europe Region

Definitions of Unctad About Northern Region.

How was the country and area composition of the geographic regions presented in M49 decided?

A: The geographical regional schema was first presented under the 2nd revision of the M49 (1982) based on continental regions; further subdivided into sub-regions and intermediary regions drawn as to obtain greater homogeneity in sizes of population, demographic circumstances and accuracy of demographic statistics. The regional composition of Africa and Americas remain unchanged from that time. The regions of Europe and Asia were extended in 3rd revision (1996) with the new countries resulting from the break-up of the Union of Soviet Socialist Republics (USSR), which was a region in itself in the original schema. The Oceania region was reorganised in the 4th revision (1999) following the cessation of the Pacific Islands (Trust Territory).

The Northern Europe Region is formed by all the economies bordering the North Sea and the Baltic Sea, i.e. the Nordic and Baltic economies, together with the economies of the islands of Great Britain, Ireland, and Iceland. All Northern European economies have signed DTA with China.

Economy	Dividends (%)	Interest (%)	Royalties (%)
Denmark	5–10	0–10	7–10
Estonia	5–10	0–10	10
Finland	5–10	0–10	7–10
Iceland	5–10	0–10	10
Ireland	5–10	0–10	6–10
Latvia	5–10	0–10	7

(continued)

(continued)

Economy	Dividends (%)	Interest (%)	Royalties (%)
Lithuania	5–10	0–10	10
Norway	10	0–10	10
Sweden	5–10	0–10	6–10
United Kingdom	0–5–10	0–10	6–10

Source State Administration of Taxation of China, year 2021
Note Rates of the treaties in force

- Western Europe Region

The Western Europe Region is formed by all the economies in the continent between Poland and Spain (excluded), i.e. Benelux, Switzerland, Austria, Liechtenstein, together with the two largest economies of Europe, France and Germany. Liechtenstein is the only Western European economy which has not signed DTA with China.

Economy	Dividends (%)	Interest (%)	Royalties (%)
Austria	7–10	0–10	6–10
Belgium	5–10	0–10	7
France	5–10	0–10	10
Germany	5–10	0–10	6–10
Liechtenstein	N/A	N/A	N/A
Luxembourg	5–10	0–10	6–10
Netherlands	0–5–10	0–10	6–10
Switzerland	0–5–10	0–10	9

Source State Administration of Taxation of China, year 2021
Note Rates of the treaties in force

- Eastern Europe Region

The Eastern Europe Region is formed by all the economies in the continent east to Germany and Austria, limited by the Balkans and the Baltic economies. These economies used to be part of the Soviet-led Eastern Bloc. All Eastern European economies have signed DTA with China. All 10 economies are also part of the BRI.

Economy	Dividends (%)	Interest (%)	Royalties (%)
Belarus	10	0–10	10
Bulgaria	10	0–10	7–10
Czech Republic	5–10	0–7.5	10
Hungary	10	0–10	10

(continued)

(continued)

Economy	Dividends (%)	Interest (%)	Royalties (%)
Moldova	5–10	0–10	10
Poland	10	0–10	7–10
Romania	0–3	0–3	3
Russia	5–10	0–5–10	6
Slovak Republic	10	10	10
Ukraine	5–10	0–10	10

Source State Administration of Taxation of China, year 2021
Note Rates of the treaties in force

- Southern Europe Region

The economies of the Southern Europe Region span the continent from east to west, including Portugal, Spain from West and the Balkans economies from the east. This region includes also Italy, Malta, and San Marino. Regarding taxation agreements, Andorra, Kosovo, Monaco, and San Marino have not signed DTA with China.

Economy	Dividends (%)	Interest (%)	Royalties (%)
Albania	10	0–10	10
Andorra	N/A	N/A	N/A
Bosnia and Herzegovina	5	0–10	10
Croatia	5	0–10	10
Cyprus	10	10	10
Greece	5–10	0–10	10
Italy	10	0–10	10
Kosovo	N/A	N/A	N/A
Malta	5–10	0–10	7–10
Monaco	N/A	N/A	N/A
Montenegro	5	0–10	10
North Macedonia	5	0–10	10
Portugal	10	0–10	10
San Marino	N/A	N/A	N/A
Serbia	5	0–10	10
Slovenia	5	10	10
Spain	10	10	6–10

Source State Administration of Taxation of China, year 2021
Note Rates of the treaties in force

China—European Double Tax Treaties

For the purpose of this book, the twenty largest economies of Europe have been selected to show a sample of the double tax treaties which the People's Republic of China has signed with nations in Europe. For ease of reference the countries and their respective treaties with China have been listed in alphabetical order.

© The Author(s), under exclusive license to Springer Nature Singapore Pte Ltd. 2022
L. Riccardi and G. Riccardi, *China–Europe Tax Treaties*,
https://doi.org/10.1007/978-981-19-3563-3_8

Austria

Austria, officially the Republic of Austria, is a state in Western Europe. Austria is a landlocked country, bordering Germany to the northwest, the Czech Republic to the north, Slovakia to the northeast, Hungary to the east, Slovenia and Italy to the south, and Switzerland and Liechtenstein to the west. Austria's capital and largest city is Vienna.

Austrians are the majority ethnic group, while minority groups are Slovenes, Croats, Hungarians, Turks, and Bosnian.

The official and predominant spoken language is German. Significant indigenous Slovene-, Hungarian-, and Croatian-speaking minorities are present.

Austria is a federal parliamentary republic. The Österreichische Bundesverfassung is the constitution regulating the political system, in force since 1919. The National Council and Federal Council exert the legislative power forming the parliament. The National Council is elected through direct elections using the open list proportional representation system. The members of the Federal Council are appointed by the parliaments of the federated states.

Executive power is vested in the chancellor and his or her cabinet. The chancellor is appointed by the President of the Republic after being elected by the party or coalition with the parliamentary majority in the National Council.

Austria has a civil law system based on Roman law, however some references to Germanic law are relevant. The Verfassungsgerichtshof acts as Supreme Court, managing constitutional matters, with judicial review powers.

Austria is a federal state, therefore, constituted by nine Bundesländer, constituent states.

From 1995 Austria is part of the European Union.

Category	Value
Population (mln persons)	8.95
Currency	Euro

Source International Monetary Fund, year 2019

© The Author(s), under exclusive license to Springer Nature Singapore Pte Ltd. 2022
L. Riccardi and G. Riccardi, *China–Europe Tax Treaties*,
https://doi.org/10.1007/978-981-19-3563-3_9

Austria is the 12th largest economy of Europe, with a GDP valued 447.7 billion USD in 2019, and has a population of about 8.95 million people. Austria enjoys low inflation (1.5%), while unemployment is over 4.5%. Austria ranked 13 out of 43 in Europe in the 2020 Doing Business ranking, scoring 78.7, and imposes a CIT of 25%. Austria records a trade deficit of 5.9 billion USD, it is the 12th main exporter and the 11th main importer in Europe.

GDP and local economy	
GDP current prices (billion USD)	447.7
GDP per capita (USD)	50,023
GDP growth (%)	1.6
Inflation (%)	1.5
Unemployment (%)	4.5
General government total expenditure (% of GDP)	48.4
General government gross debt (% of GDP)	70.5
Doing business score 2020	78.7

Source International Monetary Fund and UNCTAD, year 2019

Foreign direct investment	
FDI outstock (million USD)	234,578
FDI instock (million USD)	205,634

Source UNCTAD, year 2019

Trade	
Imports (million USD)	184,964
Exports (million USD)	179,021
Trade balance (million USD)	−5943

Source International Monetary Fund and UNCTAD, year 2019

Main import–export	
First import by category	Machinery, nuclear reactors, boilers
Second import by category	Vehicles other than railway, tramway
First export by category	Machinery, nuclear reactors, boilers
Second export by category	Vehicles other than railway, tramway

Source United Nations COMTRADE, year 2020

The legal bases for taxation are established in the constitution. Austria imposes individual income tax, property sales taxes, capital gains, corporate income tax, and value added tax. Progressivity is guaranteed by a system with different bands and various deductions.

Taxes	
Company income tax (%)	25
Top individual income tax (%)	55
Value added tax or sales tax (%)	20
Reduced value added tax or sales tax (%)	10/13

Source RsA Asia report, year 2021

- Economic relation with China

Austria records a trade surplus of 3.23 billion USD in 2020. "Machinery, nuclear reactors, boilers" is the first export category, worth 1.51 billion USD, followed by "Vehicles other than railway, tramway", worth 1.11 billion USD. "Electrical, electronic equipment" is the first import category, valued 0.9 billion USD. Austria is part of the Belt and Road Initiative. In 1991 Austria and China have signed their DTA, which has entered into force in 1992.

Category	Value
Belt road	Yes

Source UNCTAD, year 2020

Import from China	
Import from China (billion USD)	3.41
First import category from China	Electrical, electronic equipment
First import value (billion USD)	0.946
Second import category from China	Machinery, nuclear reactors, boilers
Second import value (billion USD)	0.860

Source United Nations COMTRADE, year 2020

Export to China	
Export to China (billion USD)	6.64
First export category towards China	Machinery, nuclear reactors, boilers
First export value (billion USD)	1.51
Second export category towards China	Vehicles other than railway, tramway
Second export value (billion USD)	1.11

Source United Nations COMTRADE, year 2020

Trade balance	
Trade balance (billion USD)	3.23

Source United Nations COMTRADE, year 2020

Double tax agreement	
DTA effective date	1992.11.1
Dividends (%)	7–10
Interest (%)	0–10
Royalties (%)	6–10

Source State Administration of Taxation of China, year 2021

Title AGREEMENT BETWEEN THE GOVERNMENT OF THE PEOPLE'S REPUBLIC OF CHINA AND THE GOVERNMENT OF THE REPUBLIC OF AUSTRIA FOR THE AVOIDANCE OF DOUBLE TAXATION AND THE PREVENTION OF FISCAL EVASION WITH RESPECT TO TAXES ON INCOME AND CAPITAL

Treaty Text

The Government of the People's Republic of China and the Government of the Republic of Austria;

Desiring to conclude an Agreement for the avoidance of double taxation and the prevention of fiscal evasion with respect to taxes on income and capital;

Have agreed as follows:

Article 1 Personal Scope

This Agreement shall apply to persons who are residents of one or both of the Contracting States.

Article 2 Taxes Covered

This Agreement shall apply to taxes on income and on capital imposed on behalf of a Contracting State or of its political subdivisions of local authorities, irrespective of the manner in which they are levied.

There shall be regarded as taxes on income and on capital all taxes imposed on total income, on total capital, or on elements of income or of capital, including taxes on gains from the alienation of movable or immovable property, as well as taxes on capital appreciation.

The existing taxes to which the Agreement shall apply are in particular:

in the People's Republic of China

the individual income tax;

the income tax concerning joint ventures using Chinese and foreign investment;
the income tax concerning foreign enterprises; and
the local income tax;
(hereinafter referred to as "Chinese tax");

in the Republic of Austria

the income tax;
the corporation tax;
the directors' tax;
the capital tax;
the tax on property eluding death duties;
the tax on commercial and industrial enterprises, including the tax levied on the sum of wages;
the land tax;
the tax on agricultural and forestry enterprises; and
the tax on the value of vacant plots;
(hereinafter referred to as "Austrian tax").

The Agreement shall also apply to any identical or substantially similar taxes which are imposed after the date of signature of this Agreement in addition to, or in place of, the existing taxes referred to in paragraph 3. The competent authorities of the Contracting States shall notify each other of any substantial changes which have been made in their respective taxation laws within a reasonable period of time after such changes.

Article 3 General Definitions

For the purposes of this Agreement, unless the context otherwise requires:

the term "China" means the People's Republic of China and, when used in geographical sense, means all the territory of the People's Republic of China, including its territorial sea, in which the Chinese laws relating to taxation apply, and any area beyond its territorial sea, within which the People's Republic of China has sovereign rights of exploration for and exploitation of resources of the seabed and its sub-soil and superjacent water resources in accordance with international law;
the term "Austria" means the Republic of Austria and, when used in geographical sense, means the territory of the Republic of Austria;
the terms "a Contracting State" and "the other Contracting State" mean China or Austria as the context requires;
the term "tax" means Chinese tax or Austrian tax, as the context requires;
the term "person" includes an individual, a company and any other body of persons;

the term "company" means any body corporate or any entity which is treated as a body corporate for tax purposes;
the terms "enterprise of a Contracting State" and "enterprise of the other Contracting State" mean respectively an enterprise carried on by a resident of a Contracting State and an enterprise carried on by a resident of the other Contracting State;
the term "nationals" means all individuals possessing the nationality of a Contracting State and all juridical persons created or organized under the laws of that Contracting State and all organizations without juridical personality treated for tax purposes as juridical persons created or organized under the laws of that Contracting State;
the term "international traffic" means any transport by a ship or aircraft operated by an enterprise which has its place of head office or of effective management in a Contracting State, except when the ship or aircraft is operated solely between places in the other Contracting State;
the term "competent authority" means, in the case of China, the Ministry of Finance or its authorized representative and, in the case of Austria, the Federal Minister of Finance.

As regards the application of this Agreement by a Contracting State any term not defined therein shall, unless the context otherwise requires, have the meaning which it has under the law of that Contracting State concerning the taxes to which this Agreement applies.

Article 4 Resident

For the purposes of this Agreement, the term "resident of a Contracting State" means any person who, under the laws of that Contracting State, is liable to tax therein by reason of his domicile, residence, place of head office, place of effective management or any other criterion of a similar nature.

Where by reason of the provisions of paragraph 1 an individual is a resident of both Contracting States, then his status shall be determined as follows:

he shall be deemed to be a resident of the Contracting State in which he has a permanent home available to him; if he has a permanent home available to him in both Contracting States, he shall be deemed to be a resident of the Contracting State with which his personal and economic relations are closer (centre of vital interests);
if the Contracting State in which he has his centre of vital interests cannot be determined, or if he has not a permanent home available to him in either Contracting State, he shall be deemed to be a resident of the Contracting State in which he has an habitual abode;
if he has an habitual abode in both Contracting States or in neither of them, he shall be deemed to be a resident of the Contracting State of which he is a national;
if he is a national of both Contracting States or of neither of them, the competent authorities of the Contracting States shall endeavour to settle the question by mutual agreement according to Article 26.

Whereby reason of the provisions of paragraph 1 a person other than an individual is a resident of both Contracting States, then it shall be deemed to be a resident of the Contracting State in which its place of head office or of effective management is situated.

Article 5 Permanent Establishment

For the purposes of this Agreement, the term "permanent establishment" means a fixed place of business through which the business of an enterprise is wholly or partly carried on.

The term "permanent establishment" includes especially:

a place of management;
a branch;
an office;
a factory;
a workshop; and
a mine, an oil or gas well, a quarry or any other place of extraction of natural resources.

The term "permanent establishment" likewise encompasses:

a building site, a construction, assembly or installation project or supervisory activities in connection therewith, but only where such site, project or activities continue for a period of more than six months;
the furnishing of services, including consultancy services, by an enterprise of a Contracting State through employees or other personnel in the other Contracting State, but only where such activities continue (for the same project or a connected project) for a period or periods aggregating more than six months within any twelve-month period.

Notwithstanding the provisions of paragraphs 1 to 3, the term "permanent establishment" shall be deemed not to include:

the use of facilities solely for the purpose of storage, display or delivery of goods or merchandise belonging to the enterprise;
the maintenance of a stock of goods or merchandise belonging to the enterprise solely for the purpose of storage, display or delivery;
the maintenance of a stock of goods or merchandise belonging to the enterprise solely for the purpose of processing by another enterprise;
the maintenance of a fixed place of business solely for the purpose of purchasing goods or merchandise or of collecting information, for the enterprise;
the maintenance of a fixed place of business solely for the purpose of carrying on, for the enterprise, any other activity of a preparatory or auxiliary character;
the maintenance of a fixed place of business solely for any combination of activities mentioned in sub-paragraphs (a) to (e), provided that the overall activity of the fixed place of business resulting from this combination is of a preparatory or auxiliary character.

Notwithstanding the provisions of paragraphs 1 and 2, where a person—other than an agent of an independent status to whom paragraph 6 applies—is acting in a Contracting State on behalf of an enterprise of the other Contracting State and has and habitually exercises an authority to conclude contracts in the name of the enterprise, that enterprise shall be deemed to have a permanent establishment in the first-mentioned Contracting State in respect of any activities which that person undertakes for the enterprise, unless the activities of such person are limited to those mentioned in paragraph 4 which, if exercised through a fixed place of business, would not make this fixed place of business a permanent establishment under the provisions of that paragraph.

An enterprise of a Contracting State shall not be deemed to have a permanent establishment in the other Contracting State merely because it carries on business in that other Contracting State through a broker, general commission agent or any other agent of an independent status, provided that such persons are acting in the ordinary course of their business. However, when the activities of such an agent are devoted wholly or almost wholly on behalf of that enterprise, he will not be considered an agent of an independent status within the meaning of this paragraph.

The fact that a company which is a resident of a Contracting State controls or is controlled by a company which is a resident of the other Contracting State or which carries on business in that other Contracting State (whether through a permanent establishment or otherwise), shall not of itself constitute either company a permanent establishment of the other.

Article 6 Income from Immovable Property

Income derived by a resident of a Contracting State from immovable property situated in the other Contracting State may be taxed in that other Contracting State.

The term “immovable property” shall have the meaning which it has under the law of the Contracting State in which the property in question is situated. The term shall in any case include property accessory to immovable property, livestock and equipment used in agriculture and forestry, rights to which the provisions of general law respecting landed property apply, usufruct of immovable property and rights to variable or fixed payments as consideration for the working of, or the right to work, mineral deposits, sources and other natural resources; ships and aircraft shall not be regarded as immovable property.

The provisions of paragraph 1 shall apply to income derived from the direct use, letting, or use in any other form of immovable property.

The provisions of paragraphs 1 and 3 shall also apply to income from immovable property of an enterprise and to income from immovable property used for the performance of independent personal services.

Article 7 Business Profits

The profits of an enterprise of a Contracting State shall be taxable only in that Contracting State unless the enterprise carries on business in the other Contracting State through a permanent establishment situated therein. If the enterprise carries on business as aforesaid, the profits of the enterprise may be taxed in that other

Contracting State but only so much of them as is attributable to that permanent establishment.

Subject to the provisions of paragraph 3, where an enterprise of a Contracting State carries on business in the other Contracting State through a permanent establishment situated therein, there shall in each Contracting State be attributed to that permanent establishment the profits which it might be expected to make if it were a distinct and separate enterprise engaged in the same or similar activities under the same or similar conditions and dealing wholly independently with the enterprise of which it is a permanent establishment.

In determining the profits of a permanent establishment, there shall be allowed as deductions expenses which are incurred for the purposes of the permanent establishment, including executive and general administrative expenses so incurred, whether in the Contracting State in which the permanent establishment is situated or elsewhere.

Insofar as it has been customary in a Contracting State to determine the profits to be attributed to a permanent establishment on the basis of an apportionment of the total profits of the enterprise to its various parts, nothing in paragraph 2 shall preclude that Contracting State from determining the profits to be taxed by such an apportionment as may be customary; the method of apportionment adopted shall, however, be such that the result shall be in accordance with the principles contained in this Article.

No profits shall be attributed to a permanent establishment by reason of the mere purchase by that permanent establishment of goods or merchandise for the enterprise.

For the purposes of paragraphs 1 to 5, the profits to be attributed to the permanent establishment shall be determined by the same method year by year unless there is good and sufficient reason to the contrary.

Where profits include items of income which are dealt with separately in other Articles of this Agreement, then the provisions of those Articles shall not be affected by the provisions of this Article.

Article 8 Shipping and Air Transport

Profits from the operation of ships or aircraft in international traffic shall be taxable only in the Contracting State in which the place of head office or of effective management of the enterprise is situated.

The provisions of paragraph 1 shall also apply to profits from the participation in a pool, a joint business or an international operating agency.

Article 9 Associated Enterprises

Where an enterprise of a Contracting State participates directly or indirectly in the management, control or capital of an enterprise of the other Contracting State, or the same persons participate directly or indirectly in the management, control or capital of an enterprise of a Contracting State and an enterprise of the other Contracting State, and in either case conditions are made or imposed between the two enterprises in their commercial or financial relations which differ from those which would be made between independent enterprises, then any profits which would, but for those conditions, have accrued to one of the enterprises, but by reason of those conditions, have not so accrued, may be included in the profits of that enterprise and taxed accordingly.

Article 10 Dividends

Dividends paid by a company which is a resident of a Contracting State to a resident of the other Contracting State may be taxed in that other Contracting State.

However, such dividends may also be taxed in the Contracting State of which the company paying the dividends is a resident and according to the laws of that Contracting State, but if the recipient is the beneficial owner of the dividends the tax so charged shall not exceed:

7% of the gross amount of the dividends if the beneficial owner is a company which holds directly at least 25% of the voting shares of the company paying the dividends;

10% of the gross amount of the dividends in all other cases.

the provisions of this paragraph shall not affect the taxation of the company in respect of the profits out of which the dividends are paid.

The term "dividends" as used in this Article means income from shares or other rights, not being debt-claims, participating in profits, as well as income from other corporate rights which is subjected to the same taxation treatment as income from shares by the laws of the Contracting State of which the company making the distribution is a resident.

The provisions of paragraphs 1 and 2 shall not apply if the beneficial owner of the dividends, being a resident of a Contracting State, carries on business in the other Contracting State of which the company paying the dividends is a resident, through a permanent establishment situated therein, or performs in that other Contracting State independent personal services from a fixed base situated therein, and the holding in respect of which the dividends are paid is effectively connected with such permanent establishment of fixed base. In such case the provisions of Article 7 or Article 14, as the case may be, shall apply.

Where a company which is a resident of a Contracting State derives profits or income from the other Contracting State, that other Contracting State may not impose any tax on the dividends paid by the company, except insofar as such dividends are paid to a resident of that other Contracting State or insofar as the holding in respect of which the dividends are paid is effectively connected with a permanent establishment or a fixed base situated in that other Contracting State, nor subject the company's undistributed profits to a tax on the company's undistributed profits, even if the dividends paid or the undistributed profits consist wholly or partly of profits or income arising in that other Contracting State.

Article 11 Interest

Interest arising in a Contracting State and paid to a resident of the other Contracting State may be taxed in that other Contracting State.

However, such interest may also be taxed in the Contracting State in which it arises, and according to the laws of that Contracting State, but if the recipient is the beneficial owner of the interest the tax so charged shall not exceed 10% of the gross amount of the interest.

Notwithstanding the provisions of paragraph 2, interest arising in a Contracting State shall be exempt from tax in that Contracting State, where the interest is paid to:

in the People's Republic of China;
the Government of the People's Republic of China;
the People's Bank of China;
the Bank of China or China International Trust and Investment Corporation by directly or indirectly providing loans;
in the Republic of Austria:
the Government of the Republic of Austria;
the Austrian National Bank;
the Austrian Control Bank Corporation.

The term "interest" as used in this Article means income from debt claims of every kind, whether or not secured by mortgage and whether or not carrying a right to participate in the debtor's profits, and in particular, income from government securities and income from bonds or debentures, including premiums and prizes attaching to such securities, bonds or debentures.

The provisions of paragraphs 1, 2 and 3 shall not apply if the beneficial owner of the interest, being a resident of a Contracting State, carries on business in the other Contracting State in which the interest arises, through a permanent establishment situated therein, or performs in that other Contracting State independent personal services from a fixed base situated therein, and the debt claim in respect of which the interest is paid is effectively connected with such permanent establishment or fixed base. In such case the provisions of Article 7 or Article 14, as the case may be, shall apply.

Interest shall be deemed to arise in a Contracting State when the payer is the Government of that Contracting State, a local authority thereof or a resident of that Contracting State. Where, however, the person paying the interest, whether he is a resident of a Contracting State or not, has in a Contracting State a permanent establishment or a fixed base in connection with which the indebtedness on which the interest is paid was incurred, and such interest is borne by such permanent establishment or fixed base, then such interest shall be deemed to arise in the Contracting State in which the permanent establishment or fixed base is situated.

Where, by reason of a special relationship between the payer and the beneficial owner or between both of them and some other person, the amount of the interest, having regard to the debt claim for which it is paid, exceeds the amount which would have been agreed upon by the payer and the beneficial owner in the absence of such relationship, the provisions of this Article shall apply only to the last-mentioned amount in such case, the excess part of the payments shall remain taxable according to the laws of each Contracting State, due regard being had to the other provisions of this Agreement.

Article 12 Royalties

Royalties arising in a Contracting State and paid to a resident of the other Contracting State may be taxed in that other Contracting State.

However, such royalties may also be taxed in the Contracting State in which they arise, and according to the laws of that Contracting State, but if the recipient is the beneficial owner of the royalties the tax so charged shall not exceed 10 per cent of the gross amount of the royalties.

The term "royalties" as used in this Article means payments of any kind received as a consideration for the use of, or the right to use, any copyright of literary, artistic or scientific work including cinematograph films and films or tapes for radio or television broadcasting, any patent, know-how, trade mark, design or model, plan, secret formula or process, or for the use of, or the right to use, industrial, commercial, or scientific equipment, or for information concerning industrial, commercial or scientific experience.

The provisions of paragraphs 1 and 2 shall not apply if the beneficial owner of the royalties, being a resident of a Contracting State, carries on business in the other Contracting State in which the royalties arise, through a permanent establishment situated therein, or performs in that other Contracting State independent personal services from a fixed base situated therein, and the right or property in respect of which the royalties are paid is effectively connected with such permanent establishment or fixed base. In such case the provisions of Article 7 or Article 14, as the case may be, shall apply.

Royalties shall be deemed to arise in a Contracting State when the payer is the Government of that Contracting State, a local authority thereof or a resident of that Contracting State. Where, however, the person paying the royalties, whether he is a resident of a Contracting State or not, has in a Contracting State a permanent establishment or a fixed base in connection with which the liability to pay the royalties was incurred, and such royalties are borne by such permanent establishment or fixed base, then such royalties shall be deemed to arise in the Contracting State in which the permanent establishment or fixed base is situated.

Where, by reason of a special relationship between the payer and the beneficial owner or between both of them and some other person, the amount of the royalties, having regard to the use, right or information for which they are paid, exceeds the amount which would have been agreed upon by the payer and the beneficial owner in the absence of such relationship, the provisions of this Article shall apply only to the last-mentioned amount. In such case, the excess part of the payments shall remain taxable according to the laws of each Contracting State, due regard being had to the other provisions of this Agreement.

Article 13 Capital Gains

Gains derived by a resident of a Contracting State from the alienation of immovable property referred to in Article 6 and situated in the other Contracting State may be taxed in that other Contracting State.

Gains from the alienation of movable property forming part of the business property of a permanent establishment which an enterprise of a Contracting State has in the other Contracting State or of movable property pertaining to a fixed base available to a resident of a Contracting State in the other Contracting State for the purpose of performing independent personal services including such gains from the alienation of such a permanent establishment (alone or with the whole enterprise) or of such a fixed base, may be taxed in that other Contracting State.

Gains from the alienation of ships or aircraft operated in international traffic or movable property pertaining to the operation of such ships or aircraft shall be taxable only in the Contracting State in which the place of head office or of effective management of the enterprise is situated.

Gains from the alienation of shares of the capital stock of a company the property of which consists directly or indirectly principally of immovable property situated in a Contracting State may be taxed in that Contracting State.

Gains from the alienation of shares other than those mentioned in paragraph 4 representing a participation in a company which is a resident of a Contracting State may be taxed in that Contracting State.

Gains derived by a resident of a Contracting State from the alienation of any property other than that referred to in paragraphs 1 to 5 and arising in the other Contracting State may be taxed in that other Contracting State. Where, however, such gains do not arise in the other Contracting State they shall be taxable only in the Contracting State of which the alienator is a resident.

Article 14 Independent Personal Services

Income derived by a resident of a Contracting State in respect of professional services or other activities of an independent character shall be taxable only in that Contracting State except in one of the following circumstances, when such income may also be taxed in the other Contracting State:

if he has a fixed base regularly available to him in the other Contracting State for the purpose of performing his activities; in that case, only so much of the income as is attributable to that fixed base may be taxed in that other Contracting State;

if his stay in the other Contracting State is for a period or periods exceeding in the aggregate 183 days in the calendar year concerned; in that case, only so much of the income as is derived from his activities performed in that other Contracting State may be taxed in that other Contracting State.

The term "professional services" includes especially independent scientific, literary, artistic, educational or teaching activities as well as the independent activities of physicians, lawyers, engineers, architects, dentists and accountants.

Article 15 Dependent Personal Services

Subject to the provisions of Articles 16, 18, 19, 20 and 21, salaries, wages and other similar remuneration derived by a resident of a Contracting State in respect of an employment shall be taxable only in that Contracting State unless the employment is exercised in the other Contracting State. If the employment is so exercised, such remuneration as is derived therefrom may be taxed in that other Contracting State.

Notwithstanding the provisions of paragraph 1, remuneration derived by a resident of a Contracting State in respect of an employment exercised in the other Contracting State shall be taxable only in the first-mentioned Contracting State if:

the recipient is present in the other Contracting State for a period or periods not exceeding in the aggregate 183 days in the calendar year concerned; and
the remuneration is paid by, or on behalf of, an employer who is not a resident of that other Contracting State; and
the remuneration is not borne by a permanent establishment or a fixed base which the employer has in that other Contracting State.

Notwithstanding the provisions of paragraphs 1 and 2, remuneration derived in respect of an employment exercised aboard a ship or aircraft operated in international traffic may be taxed in the Contracting State in which the place of head office or of effective management of the enterprise is situated.

Article 16 Directors' Fees

Directors' fees and other similar payments derived by a resident of a Contracting State in his capacity as a member of the board of directors of a company which is a resident of the other Contracting State may be taxed in that other Contracting State.

Article 17 Artistes and Athletes

Notwithstanding the provisions of Articles 14 and 15, income derived by a resident of a Contracting State as an entertainer, such as a theatre, motion picture, radio or television artiste, or a musician, or as an athlete, from his personal activities as such exercised in the other Contracting State, may be taxed in that other Contracting State.

Where income in respect of personal activities exercised by an entertainer or an athlete in his capacity as such accrues not to the entertainer or athlete himself but to another person, that income may, notwithstanding the provisions of Articles 7, 14 and 15, be taxed in the Contracting State in which the activities of the entertainer or athlete are exercised.

Notwithstanding the provisions of paragraphs 1 and 2, income derived by entertainers or athletes who are residents of a Contracting State from the activities exercised in the other Contracting State under a plan of cultural exchange between the Governments of both Contracting States, shall be exempted from tax in that other Contracting State.

Article 18 Pensions

Subject to the provisions of paragraph 2 of Article 19, pensions and other similar remuneration paid to a resident of a Contracting State in consideration of past employment shall be taxable only in that Contracting State.

Notwithstanding the provisions of paragraph 1, pensions paid and other similar payments made under a public scheme which is part of the social security system or a special fund of a Contracting State or a local authority thereof shall be taxable only in that Contracting State.

Article 19 Government Service

(a) Remuneration, other than a pension, paid by the Government of a Contracting State or a local authority thereof to an individual in respect of services rendered to the Government of that Contracting State or a local authority thereof, in the discharge of functions of a governmental nature, shall be taxable only in that Contracting State.

However, such remuneration shall be taxable only in the other Contracting State if the services are rendered in that other Contracting State and the individual is a resident of that other Contracting State who:

is a national of that other Contracting State; or

did not become a resident of that other Contracting State solely for the purpose of rendering the services.

(a) Any pension paid by, or out of funds to which contributions are made by, the Government of a Contracting State or a local authority thereof to an individual in respect of services rendered to the Government of that Contracting State or a local authority thereof shall be taxable only in that Contracting State.

(b) However, such pension shall be taxable only in the other Contracting State if the individual is a resident of, and a national of, that other Contracting State.

The provisions of Articles 15, 16, 17 and 18 shall apply to remuneration and pensions in respect of services rendered in connection with a business carried on by the Government of a Contracting State or a local authority thereof.

Article 20 Teachers and Researchers

An individual who is, or was immediately before visiting a Contracting State, a resident of the other Contracting State and is present in the first-mentioned Contracting State for a period not exceeding three years from the date of his first arrival in the first-mentioned Contracting State for the sole purpose of teaching, giving lectures or conducting research at a university, college, school or educational institution or scientific research institution accredited by the Government of that Contracting State in the first-mentioned Contracting State, shall be exempt from tax in the first-mentioned Contracting State in respect of remuneration for such teaching, lectures or research.

Article 21 Students and Trainees

A Student, business apprentice or trainee who is or was immediately before visiting the other Contracting State a resident of a Contracting State, and who is present in the other Contracting State solely for the purpose of his education or training, shall be exempt from tax in the other Contracting State with the following payments:

any payments from abroad of the other Contracting State for the purpose of his maintenance, education or training;

the award, grant and allowance from a State, charitable, scientific, cultural or educational organization for the purpose of his maintenance, education or training; and

income which he derives from an employment which he exercises in the other Contracting State for the purposes of practical training for not longer than a total of six months in any taxable year.

Article 22 Other Income

Items of income of a resident of a Contracting State, wherever arising, not dealt with in the foregoing Articles of this Agreement shall be taxable only in that Contracting State.

The provisions of paragraph 1 shall not apply to income, other than income from immovable property as defined in paragraph 2 of Article 6, if the recipient of such income who is a resident of a Contracting State, carries on business in the other Contracting State through a permanent establishment situated therein, or performs in that other Contracting State independent personal services from a fixed base situated therein, and the right or property in respect of which the income is paid is effectively connected with such permanent establishment or fixed base. In such case the provisions of Article 7 or Article 14, as the case may be, shall apply.

Notwithstanding the provisions of paragraphs 1 and 2 items of income of a resident of a Contracting State not dealt with in the foregoing Articles of this Agreement and arising in the other Contracting State may be taxed in that other Contracting State.

Article 23 Capital

Capital represented by immovable property referred to in Article 6, owned by a resident of a Contracting State and situated, in the other Contracting State, may be taxed in that other Contracting State.

Capital represented by movable property forming part of the business property of a permanent establishment which an enterprise of a Contracting State has in the other Contracting state or by movable property pertaining to a fixed base available to a resident of a Contracting State in the other Contracting State for the purpose of performing independent personal services may be taxed in that other Contracting State.

Capital represented by ships and aircraft operated in international traffic and by movable property pertaining to the operation of such ships and aircraft shall be taxable only in the Contracting State in which the place of head office or of effective management of the enterprise is situated.

All other elements of capital of a resident of a Contracting State shall be taxable only in that Contracting State.

Article 24 Methods for Elimination of Double Taxation

In China, double taxation shall be eliminated as follows:

Where a resident of China derives income from Austria, the amount of Austrian tax payable in respect of that income in accordance with the provisions of this Agreement shall be allowed as a credit against the Chinese tax imposed on that resident. The amount of credit, however, shall not exceed the amount of the Chinese tax computed as appropriate to that income in accordance with the taxation laws and regulations of China.

Where the income derived from Austria is a dividend paid by a company which is a resident of Austria to a company which is a resident of China and which owns not less than 10% of the shares of the company paying the dividends, the credit shall take into account the Austrian tax payable by the company paying the dividends in respect of its income.

In Austria, double taxation shall be eliminated as follows:

Where a resident of Austria derives income or owns capital which, in accordance with the provisions of this Agreement may be taxed in China, Austria shall, subject to the provisions of sub-paragraph (b), exempt such income or capital from tax. Austria may, however, in calculating the amount of tax on the remaining income or capital of such resident, take into account the exempted income or capital.

Where a resident of Austria derives items of income which, in accordance with the provisions of Articles 10, 11, 12, paragraphs 4 to 6 of Article 13 and paragraph 3 of Article 22 may be taxed in China, Austria shall allow as a deduction from the tax on the income of that resident an amount equal to the tax paid in China. Such deduction shall not, however, exceed that part of the tax, as computed before the deduction is given, which is attributable to such items of income derived from China.

For the purposes of subparagraph (b) above the tax paid in China shall be deemed to be

in the case of dividends and interest 10%, and
in the case of royalties 20% of the gross amount of such income.

Where a company resident in Austria owns at least 10% of the capital of a company resident in China, Austria shall, notwithstanding the provisions of sub-paragraphs (b) and (c) and subject to the provisions of the law of Austria regarding the treatment of intercorporate dividends, exempt the dividends from its taxes on income and the value of the shares from its taxes on capital.

Article 25 Non-discrimination

Nationals of a Contracting State shall not be subjected in the other Contracting State to any taxation or any requirement connected therewith, which is other or more burdensome than the taxation and connected requirements to which nationals of that other Contracting State in the same circumstances are or may be subjected. The provisions of this paragraph shall, notwithstanding the provisions of Article 1, also apply to persons who are not residents of one or both of the Contracting States.

The taxation on a permanent establishment which an enterprise of a Contracting State has in the other Contracting State shall not be less favourably levied in that other Contracting State than the taxation levied on enterprises of that other Contracting State carrying on the same activities. The provisions of this paragraph shall not be construed as obliging a Contracting State to grant to residents of the other Contracting

State any personal allowances, reliefs and reductions on account of civil status or family responsibilities which it grants to its own residents.

Except where the provisions of Article 9, paragraph 7 of Article 11, of paragraph 6 of Article 12, apply, interest, royalties and other disbursements paid by an enterprise of a Contracting State to a resident of the other Contracting State shall, for the purpose of determining the taxable profits of such enterprise, be deductible under the same conditions as if they had been paid to a resident of the first-mentioned Contracting State. Similarly, any debts of an enterprise of a Contracting State to a resident of the other Contracting State shall, for the purpose of determining the taxable capital of such enterprise, be deductible under the same conditions as if they had been contracted to a resident of the first-mentioned Contracting State.

Enterprises of a Contracting State, the capital of which is wholly or partly owned or controlled, directly or indirectly, by one or more than one resident of the other Contracting State, shall not be subjected in the first-mentioned Contracting State to any taxation or any requirement connected therewith which is other or more burdensome than the taxation and connected requirements to which other similar enterprises of the first-mentioned Contracting State are or may be subjected.

The provisions of this Article shall, notwithstanding the provisions of Article 2, apply to taxes of every kind and description.

Article 26 Mutual Agreement Procedure

Where a person considers that the measures adopted by one or both of the Contracting States result or will result for him in taxation not in accordance with the provisions of this Agreement, he may, irrespective of the remedies provided by the domestic laws of those Contracting States, present his case to the competent authority of the Contracting State of which he is a resident or, if his case comes under paragraph 1 of Article 25, to that of the Contracting State of which he is a national. The case must be presented within three years from the first notification of the action resulting in taxation not in accordance with the provisions of this Agreement.

The competent authority shall endeavour, if the objection appears to it to be justified and if it is not itself able to arrive at a satisfactory solution, to resolve the case by mutual agreement with the competent authority of the other Contracting State, with a view to the avoidance of taxation which is not in accordance with the provisions of this Agreement. Any agreement reached shall be implemented notwithstanding any time limits in the domestic laws of the Contracting States.

The competent authorities of the Contracting States shall endeavour to resolve by mutual agreement any difficulties or doubts arising as to the interpretation or application of this Agreement. They may also consult together for the elimination of double taxation in cases not provided for in this Agreement.

The competent authorities of the Contracting States may communicate with each other directly for the purpose of reaching an agreement in the sense of paragraphs 2 and 3. When it seems advisable for the purpose of reaching agreement, the representatives of the competent authorities may meet together for an oral exchange of opinions.

Article 27 Exchange of Information

The competent authorities of the Contracting States shall exchange such information as is necessary for carrying out the provisions of this Agreement, in particular for the prevention of evasion of taxes. The exchange of information is not restricted by Article 1. Any information received by a Contracting State shall be treated as secret in the same manner as information obtained under the domestic laws of that Contracting State and shall be disclosed only to persons or authorities (including courts and administrative bodies) involved in the assessment or collection of, the enforcement or prosecution in respect of, or the determination of appeals in relation to, the taxes covered by the Agreement. Such persons or authorities shall use the information only for such purposes. They may disclose the information in public court proceedings or in judicial decisions.

In no case shall the provisions of paragraph 1 be construed so as to impose on a Contracting State the obligation:

to carry out administrative measures at variance with the laws and administrative practice of that or of the other Contracting State;

to supply information which is not obtainable under the laws or in the normal course of the administration of that or of the other Contracting State;

to supply information which would disclose any trade, business, industrial, commercial or professional secret or trade process, or information, the disclosure of which would be contrary to public policy.

Article 28 Diplomatic Agents and Consular Officers

Nothing in this Agreement shall affect the tax privileges of diplomatic agents or consular officers under the general rules of international law or under the provisions of special agreements.

Article 29 Entry Into Force

This Agreement shall enter into force on the first day of the third month next following that in which the Contracting States exchange notes through diplomatic channels notifying each other that the legal procedures necessary in each country for the entry into force of this Agreement have been completed.

This Agreement shall have effect for any taxable year beginning on or after the first day of January in the calendar year next following that in which this exchange of notes takes place.

Article 30 Termination

This Agreement shall continue in effect indefinitely but either of the Contracting State may, on or before the thirtieth day of June in any calendar year beginning after the expiration of a period of five years from the date of its entry into force, give to the other Contracting State, through the diplomatic channel, written notice of termination. In such event this Agreement shall cease to have effect for any taxable year beginning on or after the first day of January in the calendar year next following that in which the notice of termination is given.

IN WITNESS WHEREOF the representatives of the two Contracting State, duly authorized thereto, have signed this Agreement.

DONE at Beijing on the 10th day of April 1991, in duplicate in the Chinese, German and English languages, all three texts being equally authentic. In case of any divergence in the interpretation, the English text shall prevail.

For the Government of the People's Republic of China

For the Government of the Republic of Austria

Belgium

Belgium, officially the Kingdom of Belgium, is a state in Western Europe. Belgium borders the Netherlands to the north, Germany to the east, Luxembourg to the southeast, France to the southwest, and the North Sea to the northwest. Belgium's capital and largest city is Brussels.

Flemish are the majority ethnic group, followed by Walloon and others. The prevalent foreign nationals are Italian, French, Dutch, Moroccan, Portuguese, Spanish, Turkish, and German.

The official and predominant spoken languages are Dutch, French, and German. Both the varieties of Belgian Dutch and Belgian French have minor differences in vocabulary from those spoken in the Netherlands and in France. Many Flemish people speak dialects of Dutch.

Belgium is a federal parliamentary constitutional monarchy. The Belgische Grondwet, also known as Constitution belge or Verfassung Belgiens, is the constitution regulating the political system, in force since 1831. The Chamber of Representatives and the Senate exert the legislative power forming the parliament. The Chamber of Representatives is elected through direct elections using the open list proportional representation system. The members of the Senate are appointed with indirect elections.

Executive power is vested in the Prime Minister and his or her cabinet. The Prime Minister is appointed by the Monarch after being elected by the party or coalition with the parliamentary majority in the Chamber of Representatives.

Belgium has a civil law system based on Roman law. The Court of Cassation is the court of last resort and acts as Supreme Court, managing constitutional matters, with judicial review powers.

Belgium is a federal state, therefore, constituted by three communities and regions.

Belgium is part of the European union, one of the six founding country, together with Germany, France, Italy, Luxemburg, and the Netherlands.

© The Author(s), under exclusive license to Springer Nature Singapore Pte Ltd. 2022
L. Riccardi and G. Riccardi, *China–Europe Tax Treaties*,
https://doi.org/10.1007/978-981-19-3563-3_10

Category	Value
Population (mln persons)	11.458
Currency	Euro

Source International Monetary Fund, year 2019

Belgium is the 11th largest economy of Europe and the fifth of Western Europe, with a GDP of 517.6 billion USD in 2019, and has a population of about 11.5 million people. Belgium enjoys low inflation (1.2%), however, unemployment is over 5% (5.4%). Belgium ranked 25 out of 43 in Europe in the 2020 Doing Business ranking, scoring 75.0, and imposes a CIT of 25%. Belgium records a trade surplus of 18.3 billion USD, it is the sixth main exporter in Europe.

GDP and local economy	
GDP current prices (billion USD)	517.6
GDP per capita (USD)	45,176
GDP growth (%)	1.4
Inflation (%)	1.2
Unemployment (%)	5.4
General government total expenditure (% of GDP)	52.0
General government gross debt (% of GDP)	98.0
Doing business score 2020	75.0

Source International Monetary Fund and UNCTAD, year 2019

Foreign direct investment	
FDI outstock (million USD)	656,429
FDI instock (million USD)	566,116

Source UNCTAD, year 2019

Trade	
Imports (million USD)	426,198
Exports (million USD)	444,563
Trade balance (million USD)	18,365

Source International Monetary Fund and UNCTAD, year 2019

Main import-export	
First import by category	Pharmaceutical products
Second import by category	Vehicles other than railway, tramway
First export by category	Pharmaceutical products

(continued)

(continued)

Main import-export	
Second export by category	Vehicles other than railway, tramway

Source United Nations COMTRADE, year 2020

The legal bases for taxation are established in the constitution. Belgium imposes individual income tax, property sales taxes, capital gains, corporate income tax, and value added tax. Progressivity is guaranteed by a system with different bands and various deductions.

Taxes	
Company income tax (%)	25
Top individual income tax (%)	50
Value added tax or sales tax (%)	21
Reduced value added tax or sales tax (%)	6/12

Source RsA Asia report, year 2021

- Economic relation with China

Belgium records a trade deficit to China of 12.9 billion USD in 2020. "Pearls, precious stones, metals, coins" is the first export category, valued 1.43 billion USD, followed by "Pharmaceutical products", worth 1.03 billion USD. "Machinery, nuclear reactors, boilers" is the first import category, valued 2.9 billion USD. Belgium is not part of the Belt and Road Initiative. The first Belgium-China DTA was signed in 1985, coming into force in 1987. A new agreement has been signed in 2009 and has entered into force at the end of 2013.

Category	Value
Belt road	No

Source UNCTAD, year 2020

Import from China	
Import from China (billion USD)	20.76
First import category from China	Machinery, nuclear reactors, boilers
First import value (billion USD)	2.90
Second import category from China	Electrical, electronic equipment
Second import value (billion USD)	2.76

Source United Nations COMTRADE, year 2020

Export to China	
Export to China (billion USD)	7.84
First export category towards China	Pearls, precious stones, metals, coins
First export value (billion USD)	1.43
Second export category towards China	Pharmaceutical products
Second export value (billion USD)	1.03

Source United Nations COMTRADE, year 2020

Trade balance	
Trade balance (billion USD)	−12.92

Source United Nations COMTRADE, year 2020

Double tax agreement	
DTA effective date	2013.12.29
Dividends (%)	5–10
Interest (%)	0–10
Royalties (%)	7

Source State Administration of Taxation of China, year 2021

Title AGREEMENT BETWEEN THE GOVERNMENT OF THE PEOPLE'S REPUBLIC OF CHINA AND THE GOVERNMENT OF THE KINGDOM OF BELGIUM FOR THE AVOIDANCE OF DOUBLE TAXATION AND THE PREVENTION OF FISCAL EVASION WITH RESPECT TO TAXES ON INCOME

Treaty Text

The Government of the People's Republic of China and the Government of the Kingdom of Belgium,

Desiring to conclude an Agreement for the Avoidance of Double Taxation and the Prevention of Fiscal Evasion with respect to Taxes on Income,

Have agreed to the following:

Article 1 Persons Covered

This Agreement shall apply to persons who are residents of one or both of the Contracting States.

Article 2 Taxes Covered

This Agreement shall apply to taxes on income imposed on behalf of a Contracting State or of its political subdivisions or local authorities, irrespective of the manner in which they are levied.

There shall be regarded as taxes on income all taxes imposed on total income or on elements of income, including taxes on gains from the alienation of movable or immovable property, as well as taxes on capital appreciation.

The existing taxes to which the Agreement shall apply are in particular:

with respect to China:
the individual income tax;
the enterprise income tax;
including any prepayments on these taxes and any surcharges on these taxes and prepayments
(hereinafter referred to as "Chinese tax");
with respect to Belgium:
the individual income tax;
(ii) the corporate income tax;
(iii) the tax on legal entities;
(iv) the tax on non-residents;
(v) the supplementary crisis contribution;

including any prepayments on these taxes and any surcharges on these taxes and prepayments

(hereinafter referred to as "Belgian tax").

The Agreement shall apply also to any identical or substantially similar taxes which are imposed after the date of signature of the Agreement in addition to, or in place of, the existing taxes. The competent authorities of the Contracting States shall notify each other in due time of substantial changes which have been made in their respective taxation laws.

Article 3 General Definitions

For the purposes of this Agreement, unless the context otherwise requires:

the term "Belgium" means the Kingdom of Belgium; when used in a geographical sense, it means the territory of the Kingdom of Belgium including its territorial sea and areas within which, in accordance with international law, the Kingdom of Belgium exercises sovereign rights or its jurisdiction;
the term "China" means the People's Republic of China; when used in a geographical sense, it means all the territory of the People's Republic of China, in which the Chinese laws relating to taxation apply, including its territorial sea, and any area beyond its territorial sea, within which the People's Republic of China has sovereign rights for the purpose of exploring and exploiting the resources of the sea-bed and its subsoil and superjacent water in accordance with international law and its domestic law;
the terms "a Contracting State" and "the other Contracting State" mean Belgium or China, as the context requires;
the term "tax" means Belgian tax or Chinese tax, as the context requires;
the term "person" includes an individual, a company and any other body of persons;

the term “company” means any body corporate or any entity which is treated as a body corporate for tax purposes in the Contracting State of which it is a resident;
the terms “enterprise of a Contracting State” and “enterprise of the other Contracting State” mean respectively an enterprise carried on by a resident of a Contracting State and an enterprise carried on by a resident of the other Contracting State;
the term “national”, in relation to a Contracting State, means:
any individual possessing the nationality or citizenship of that Contracting State; and
any legal person, partnership or association deriving its status as such from the laws in force in that Contracting State;
(i) the term “international traffic” means any transport by a ship or aircraft operated by an enterprise of a Contracting State, except when the ship or aircraft is operated solely between places in the other Contracting State;
the term “competent authority” means:
with respect to China, the State Administration of Taxation or its authorized representative;
with respect to Belgium, the Minister of Finance or his authorized representative.

As regards the application of the Agreement at any time by a Contracting State, any term not defined therein shall, unless the context otherwise requires, have the meaning that it has at that time under the law of that State for the purposes of the taxes to which the Agreement applies, any meaning under the applicable tax laws of that State prevailing over a meaning given to the term under other laws of that State.

Article 4 Resident

For the purposes of this Agreement, the term “resident of a Contracting State” means any person who, under the laws of that State, is liable to tax therein by reason of his domicile, residence, place of incorporation, place of effective management, place of management or any other criterion of a similar nature, and also includes that State and any political subdivision, local authority or statutory body thereof. This term, however, does not include any person who is liable to tax in that State in respect only of income from sources in that State.

Whereby reason of the provisions of paragraph 1 an individual is a resident of both Contracting States, then his status shall be determined as follows:

he shall be deemed to be a resident only of the State in which he has a permanent home available to him; if he has a permanent home available to him in both States, he shall be deemed to be a resident only of the State with which his personal and economic relations are closer (centre of vital interests);
if the State in which he has his centre of vital interests cannot be determined,
or if he has not a permanent home available to him in either State, he shall be deemed to be a resident only of the State in which he has an habitual abode;
if he has an habitual abode in both States or in neither of them, he shall be deemed to be a resident only of the State of which he is a national;

if he is a national of both States or of neither of them, the competent authorities of the Contracting States shall settle the question by mutual agreement.

Where by reason of the provisions of paragraph 1 a person other than an individual is a resident of both Contracting States, then it shall be deemed to be a resident only of the State in which its place of effective management is situated. If its place of effective management cannot be determined, the competent authorities of the Contracting States shall settle the question by mutual agreement.

Article 5 Permanent Establishment

For the purposes of this Agreement, the term "permanent establishment" means a fixed place of business through which the business of an enterprise is wholly or partly carried on.

The term "permanent establishment" includes especially:

a place of management;
a branch;
an office;
a factory;
a workshop, and
a mine, an oil or gas well, a quarry or any other place of extraction of natural resources.

The term "permanent establishment" shall also include:

a building site, a construction, assembly or installation project, or supervisory activities in connection therewith, but only where such site, project or activities continue for a period of more than twelve months;
the furnishing of services, including consultancy services, by an enterprise through employees or other personnel engaged by the enterprise for such purposes, but only where such activities continue (for the same or a connected project) within a Contracting State for a period or periods aggregating more than 183 days within any twelve month period.

Notwithstanding the preceding provisions of this Article, the term "permanent establishment" shall be deemed not to include:

the use of facilities solely for the purpose of storage, display or delivery of goods or merchandise belonging to the enterprise;
the maintenance of a stock of goods or merchandise belonging to the enterprise solely for the purpose of storage, display or delivery;
the maintenance of a stock of goods or merchandise belonging to the enterprise solely for the purpose of processing by another enterprise;
the maintenance of a fixed place of business solely for the purpose of purchasing goods or merchandise or of collecting information, for the enterprise;
the maintenance of a fixed place of business solely for the purpose of carrying on, for the enterprise, any other activity of a preparatory or auxiliary character;

the maintenance of a fixed place of business solely for any combination of activities mentioned in sub-paragraphs a) to e), provided that the overall activity of the fixed place of business resulting from this combination is of a preparatory or auxiliary character.

Notwithstanding the provisions of paragraphs 1 and 2, where a person--other than an agent of an independent status to whom paragraph 6 applies--is acting in a Contracting State on behalf of an enterprise of the other Contracting State and has, and habitually exercises, an authority to conclude contracts in the name of the enterprise, that enterprise shall be deemed to have a permanent establishment in respect of any activities which that person undertakes for the enterprise, unless the activities of such person are limited to those mentioned in paragraph 4 which, if exercised through a fixed place of business, would not make this fixed place of business a permanent establishment under the provisions of that paragraph.

An enterprise of a Contracting State shall not be deemed to have a permanent establishment in the other Contracting State merely because it carries on business in that State through a broker, general commission agent or any other agent of an independent status, provided that such persons are acting in the ordinary course of their business. However, where the activities of such an agent are carried out exclusively or almost exclusively on behalf of that enterprise, that agent is not considered an independent agent for the purposes of this paragraph.

The fact that a company which is a resident of a Contracting State controls or is controlled by a company which is a resident of the other Contracting State, or which carries on business in that other State (whether through a permanent establishment or otherwise), shall not of itself constitute either company a permanent establishment of the other.

Article 6 Income from Immovable Property

Income derived by a resident of a Contracting State from immovable property situated in the other Contracting State may be taxed in that other State.

The term "immovable property" shall have the meaning which it has under the law of the Contracting State in which the property in question is situated. The term shall in any case include property accessory to immovable property, livestock and equipment used in agriculture and forestry, rights to which the provisions of general law respecting landed property apply, usufruct of immovable property and rights to variable or fixed payments as consideration for the working of, or the right to work, mineral deposits, sources and other natural resources; ships and aircraft shall not be regarded as immovable property.

The provisions of paragraph 1 shall apply to income derived from the direct use or right to use, letting, or use in any other form of immovable property.

The provisions of paragraphs 1 and 3 shall also apply to the income from immovable property of an enterprise and to income from immovable property used for the performance of independent personal services.

Article 7 Business Profits

The profits of an enterprise of a Contracting State shall be taxable only in that State unless the enterprise carries on business in the other Contracting State through a permanent establishment situated therein. If the enterprise carries on business as aforesaid, the profits of the enterprise may be taxed in the other State but only so much of them as is attributable to that permanent establishment.

Subject to the provisions of paragraph 3, where an enterprise of a Contracting State carries on business in the other Contracting State through a permanent establishment situated therein, there shall in each Contracting State be attributed to that permanent establishment the profits which it might be expected to make if it were a distinct and separate enterprise engaged in the same or similar activities under the same or similar conditions and dealing wholly independently with the enterprise of which it is a permanent establishment.

In determining the profits of a permanent establishment, there shall be allowed as deductions expenses which are incurred for the purposes of the permanent establishment, including executive and general administrative expenses so incurred, whether in the Contracting State in which the permanent establishment is situated or elsewhere.

Insofar as it has been customary in a Contracting State to determine the profits to be attributed to a permanent establishment on the basis of an apportionment of the total profits of the enterprise to its various parts, nothing in paragraph 2 shall preclude that State from determining the profits to be taxed by such an apportionment as may be customary; the method of apportionment adopted shall, however, be such that the result shall be in accordance with the principles contained in this Article.

No profits shall be attributed to a permanent establishment by reason of the mere purchase by that permanent establishment of goods or merchandise for the enterprise.

For the purposes of the preceding paragraphs, the profits to be attributed to the permanent establishment shall be determined by the same method year by year unless there is good and sufficient reason to the contrary.

Where profits include items of income which are dealt with separately in other Articles of this Agreement, then the provisions of those Articles shall not be affected by the provisions of this Article.

Article 8 Shipping and Air Transport

Profits derived from the operation of ships or aircraft in international traffic by an enterprise of a Contracting State shall be taxable only in that State.

The provisions of paragraph 1 shall also apply to profits from the participation in a pool, a joint business or an international operating agency.

Article 9 Associated Enterprises

Where:

an enterprise of a Contracting State participates directly or indirectly in the management, control or capital of an enterprise of the other Contracting State, or

the same persons participate directly or indirectly in the management, control or capital of an enterprise of a Contracting State and an enterprise of the other Contracting State,
and in either case conditions are made or imposed between the two enterprises in their commercial or financial relations which differ from those which would be made between independent enterprises, then any profits which would, but for those conditions, have accrued to one of the enterprises, but, by reason of those conditions, have not so accrued, may be included in the profits of that enterprise and taxed accordingly.

Where a Contracting State includes in the profits of an enterprise of that State—and taxes accordingly—profits on which an enterprise of the other Contracting State has been charged to tax in that other State and the profits so included are profits which would have accrued to the enterprise of the first-mentioned State if the conditions made between the two enterprises had been those which would have been made between independent enterprises, then that other State shall make an appropriate adjustment to the amount of the tax charged therein on those profits. In determining such adjustment, due regard shall be had to the other provisions of this Agreement and the competent authorities of the Contracting States shall, if necessary, consult each other.

Article 10 Dividends

Dividends paid by a company which is a resident of a Contracting State to a resident of the other Contracting State may be taxed in that other State.

However, such dividends may also be taxed in the Contracting State of which the company paying the dividends is a resident and according to the laws of that State, but if the beneficial owner of the dividends is a resident of the other Contracting State, the tax so charged shall not exceed:

5% of the gross amount of the dividends if the beneficial owner is a company (other than a partnership) which, prior to the moment of the payment of the dividends, has been holding, for an uninterrupted period of at least twelve months, directly at least 25% of the capital of the company paying the dividends;
10% of the gross amount of the dividends in all other cases.
This paragraph shall not affect the taxation of the company in respect of the profits out of which the dividends are paid.
The term "dividends" as used in this Article means income from shares or rights to participate in profits, not being debt-claims, as well as other income which is subjected to the same taxation treatment as income from shares by the laws of the Contracting State of which the company making the payment is a resident.
The provisions of paragraphs 1 and 2 shall not apply if the beneficial owner of the dividends, being a resident of a Contracting State, carries on business in the other Contracting State of which the company paying the dividends is a resident, through a permanent establishment situated therein, or performs in that other State independent personal services from a fixed base situated therein, and the holding in respect of which the dividends are paid is effectively connected with

such permanent establishment or fixed base. In such case the provisions of Article 7 or Article 14, as the case may be, shall apply.

Where a company which is a resident of a Contracting State derives profits or income from the other Contracting State, that other State may not impose any tax on the dividends paid by the company, except insofar as such dividends are paid to a resident of that other State or insofar as the holding in respect of which the dividends are paid is effectively connected with a permanent establishment or a fixed base situated in that other State, nor subject the company's undistributed profits to a tax, even if the dividends paid or the undistributed profits consist wholly or partly of profits or income arising in such other State.

The provisions of this Article shall not apply if it was the main purpose or one of the main purposes of any person concerned with the creation or assignment of the shares or other rights in respect of which the dividends are paid to take advantage of this Article by means of that creation or assignment.

Article 11 Interest

Interest arising in a Contracting State and paid to a resident of the other Contracting State may be taxed in that other State.

However, such interest may also be taxed in the Contracting State in which it arises and according to the laws of that State, but if the beneficial owner of the interest is a resident of the other Contracting State the tax so charged shall not exceed 10% of the gross amount of the interest.

Notwithstanding the provisions of paragraph 2, interest arising in a Contracting State and paid to the Government of the other Contracting State, a political subdivision, a local authority or the Central Bank thereof or any financial institution wholly owned by the Government of the other Contracting State, or paid on loans guaranteed or insured by the Government of a Contracting State, a political subdivision, a local authority or the Central Bank thereof or any financial institution wholly owned by the Government of such Contracting State, shall be exempt from tax in the first-mentioned State.

The term "interest" as used in this Article means income from debt-claims of every kind, whether or not secured by mortgage and whether or not carrying a right to participate in the debtor's profits, and in particular, income from government securities and income from bonds or debentures, including premiums and prizes attaching to such securities, bonds or debentures. However, the term "interest" shall not include for the purpose of this Article penalty charges for late payment nor interest regarded as dividends by the laws of the Contracting State of which the company making the payment is a resident.

The provisions of paragraphs 1 and 2 shall not apply if the beneficial owner of the interest, being a resident of a Contracting State, carries on business in the other Contracting State in which the interest arises, through a permanent establishment situated therein, or performs in that other State independent personal services from a fixed base situated therein, and the debt-claim in respect of which the interest is paid is effectively connected with such permanent establishment or fixed base. In such case the provisions of Article 7 or Article 14, as the case may be, shall apply.

Interest shall be deemed to arise in a Contracting State when the payer is a resident of that Contracting State. Where, however, the person paying the interest, whether he is a resident of a Contracting State or not, has in a Contracting State a permanent establishment or a fixed base in connection with which the indebtedness on which the interest is paid was incurred, and such interest is borne by such permanent establishment or fixed base, then such interest shall be deemed to arise in the Contracting State in which the permanent establishment or fixed base is situated.

Where, by reason of a special relationship between the payer and the beneficial owner or between both of them and some other person, the amount of the interest, having regard to the debt-claim for which it is paid, exceeds the amount which would have been agreed upon by the payer and the beneficial owner in the absence of such relationship, the provisions of this Article shall apply only to the last-mentioned amount. In such case, the excess part of the interest shall remain taxable according to the laws of each Contracting State, due regard being had to the other provisions of this Agreement.

The provisions of this Article shall not apply if it was the main purpose or one of the main purposes of any person concerned with the creation or assignment of the debt-claim in respect of which the interest is paid to take advantage of this Article by means of that creation or assignment.

Article 12 Royalties

Royalties arising in a Contracting State and paid to a resident of the other Contracting State may be taxed in that other State.

However, such royalties may also be taxed in the Contracting State in which they arise and according to the laws of that State, but if the beneficial owner of the royalties is a resident of the other Contracting State, the tax so charged shall not exceed 7% of the gross amount of the royalties.

The term "royalties" as used in this Article means payments of any kind received as a consideration for the use of, or the right to use, any copyright of literary, artistic or scientific work including cinematograph films, or films or tapes for radio or television broadcasting, any patent, know-how, trade mark, design or model, plan, secret formula or process, or for the use of, or the right to use, industrial, commercial, or scientific equipment, or for information concerning industrial, commercial or scientific experience.

The provisions of paragraphs 1 and 2 shall not apply if the beneficial owner of the royalties, being a resident of a Contracting State, carries on business in the other Contracting State in which the royalties arise, through a permanent establishment situated therein, or performs in that other State independent personal services from a fixed base situated therein, and the right or property in respect of which the royalties are paid is effectively connected with such permanent establishment or fixed base. In such case the provisions of Article 7 or Article 14, as the case may be, shall apply.

Royalties shall be deemed to arise in a Contracting State when the payer is a resident of that Contracting State. Where, however, the person paying the royalties, whether he is a resident of a Contracting State or not, has in a Contracting State a permanent establishment or a fixed base in connection with which the obligation to pay the royalties was incurred, and those royalties are borne by that permanent establishment or fixed base, then such royalties shall be deemed to arise in the Contracting State in which the permanent establishment or fixed base is situated.

Where, by reason of a special relationship between the payer and the beneficial owner or between both of them and some other person, the amount of the royalties, having regard to the use, right or information for which they are paid, exceeds the amount which would have been agreed upon by the payer and the beneficial owner in the absence of such relationship, the provisions of this Article shall apply only to the last-mentioned amount. In such case, the excess part of the royalties shall remain taxable according to the laws of each Contracting State, due regard being had to the other provisions of this Agreement.

The provisions of this Article shall not apply if it was the main purpose or one of the main purposes of any person concerned with the creation or assignment of the rights in respect of which the royalties are paid to take advantage of this Article by means of that creation or assignment.

Article 13 Capital Gains

Gains derived by a resident of a Contracting State from the alienation of immovable property referred to in Article 6 and situated in the other Contracting State may be taxed in that other State.

Gains from the alienation of movable property forming part of the business property of a permanent establishment which an enterprise of a Contracting State has in the other Contracting State or of movable property pertaining to a fixed base available to a resident of a Contracting State in the other Contracting State for the purpose of performing independent personal services, including such gains from the alienation of such a permanent establishment (alone or with the whole enterprise) or of such fixed base, may be taxed in that other State.

Gains derived by an enterprise of a Contracting State from the alienation of ships or aircraft operated in international traffic or movable property pertaining to the operation of such ships or aircraft shall be taxable only in that State.

Gains derived by a resident of a Contracting State from the alienation of shares deriving more than 50% of their value directly or indirectly from immovable property situated in the other Contracting State may be taxed in that other State.

Gains derived by a resident of a Contracting State from the alienation of shares, other than shares in which there is substantial and regular trading on a recognized stock exchange provided that the total of the shares alienated by the resident during the fiscal year in which the alienation takes place does not exceed 5% of the quoted shares, of a company which is a resident of the other Contracting State may be taxed in that other Contracting State if the first-mentioned resident, prior to the moment of such alienation, has owned, directly or indirectly, at least 25% of the shares of that company.

Gains from the alienation of any property other than that referred to in paragraphs 1, 2, 3, 4 and 5, shall be taxable only in the Contracting State of which the alienator is a resident.

Article 14 Independent Personal Services

Income derived by a resident of a Contracting State in respect of professional services or other activities of an independent character shall be taxable only in that State. However, such income may also be taxed in the other Contracting State:

if the resident has a fixed base regularly available to him in the other Contracting State for the purpose of performing his activities; in such case only so much of the income as is attributable to that fixed base may be taxed in that other State; or if his stay in the other Contracting State is for a period or periods amounting to or exceeding in the aggregate 183 days in any twelve month period commencing or ending in the fiscal year concerned; in that case only so much of the income as is derived from the activities performed in that other Contracting State may be taxed in that other State.

The term "professional services" includes especially independent scientific, literary, artistic, educational or teaching activities as well as the independent activities of physicians, lawyers, engineers, architects, dentists and accountants.

Article 15 Dependent Personal Services

Subject to the provisions of Articles 16, 18 and 19, salaries, wages and other similar remuneration derived by a resident of a Contracting State in respect of an employment shall be taxable only in that State unless the employment is exercised in the other Contracting State. If the employment is so exercised, such remuneration as is derived therefrom may be taxed in that other State. Notwithstanding the provisions of paragraph 1, remuneration derived by a resident of a Contracting State in respect of an employment exercised in the other Contracting State shall be taxable only in the first-mentioned State if:

the recipient is present in the other State for a period or periods not exceeding in the aggregate 183 days in any twelve month period commencing or ending in the fiscal year concerned; and
the remuneration is paid by, or on behalf of, an employer who is not a resident of the other State; and
the remuneration is not borne by a permanent establishment or a fixed base which the employer has in the other State.

Notwithstanding the preceding provisions of this Article, remuneration derived in respect of an employment exercised aboard a ship or aircraft operated in international traffic by an enterprise of a Contracting State may be taxed in that State.

Article 16 Directors' Fees

Directors' fees and other similar payments derived by a resident of a Contracting State in his capacity as a member of the board of directors or of a similar organ of a company which is a resident of the other Contracting State may be taxed in that other State.

Article 17 Artistes and Sportsmen

Notwithstanding the provisions of Articles 14 and 15, income derived by a resident of a Contracting State as an entertainer, such as a theatre, motion picture, radio or television artiste, or a musician, or as an athlete, from his personal activities as such exercised in the other Contracting State, may be taxed in that other State.

Where income in respect of personal activities exercised by an entertainer or an athlete in his capacity as such accrues not to the entertainer or athlete himself but to another person, that income may, notwithstanding the provisions of Articles 7, 14 and 15, be taxed in the Contracting State in which the activities of the entertainer or athlete are exercised.

Article 18 Pensions

Subject to the provisions of paragraph 2 of Article 19, pensions and other similar remuneration paid to a resident of a Contracting State in consideration of past employment shall be taxable only in that State.

Notwithstanding the provisions of paragraph 1, pensions and other similar remuneration, paid under the social security legislation of a Contracting State may be taxed in that State. This provision shall also apply to pensions and other similar remuneration paid under a public scheme organized by that Contracting State in order to supplement the pension benefits provided for under that legislation.

Article 19 Government Service

Salaries, wages and other similar remuneration paid by a Contracting State or a political subdivision or a local authority thereof to an individual in respect of services rendered to that State or subdivision or authority shall be taxable only in that State.

However, such salaries, wages and other similar remuneration shall be taxable only in the other Contracting State if the services are rendered in that State and the individual is a resident of that State who:

is a national of that State; or

did not become a resident of that State solely for the purpose of rendering the services.

Notwithstanding the provisions of paragraph 1, pensions and other similar remuneration paid by, or out of funds created by, a Contracting State or a political subdivision or a local authority thereof to an individual in respect of services rendered to that State or subdivision or authority shall be taxable only in that State.

However, such pensions and other similar remuneration shall be taxable only in the other Contracting State if the individual is a resident of, and a national of, that State.

The provisions of Articles 15, 16, 17 and 18 shall apply to salaries, wages, pensions and other similar remuneration in respect of services rendered in connection with a business carried on by a Contracting State or a political subdivision or a local authority thereof.

Article 20 Students

Payments which a student who is or was immediately before visiting a Contracting State a resident of the other Contracting State and who is present in the first-mentioned State solely for the purpose of his education receives for the purpose of his maintenance or education shall not be taxed in that State, provided that such payments arise from sources outside that State.

Article 21 Other Income

Items of income not dealt with in the foregoing Articles of this Agreement and arising in a Contracting State may be taxed in that State.

Article 22 Elimination of Double Taxation

In the case of Belgium, double taxation shall be eliminated as follows:

Where a resident of Belgium derives income, not being dividends, interest or royalties, which is taxed in China in accordance with the provisions of this Agreement, Belgium shall exempt such income from tax but may, in calculating the amount of tax on the remaining income of that resident, apply the rate of tax which would have been applicable if such income had not been exempted.

Belgium shall also exempt with progression profits of an enterprise of Belgium attributable to a permanent establishment through which the enterprise carries on business in China which are taxable in China in accordance with the provisions of this Agreement. This exemption shall not apply where the activities exercised through the permanent establishment consist exclusively or mainly:

- in executing collective or finance investments;
- in providing financial services exclusively or mainly for the enterprise or for related enterprises;

or where such permanent establishment holds any portfolio investment or any copyright, patent, trade mark, design, model, plan, secret formula or process which represent in the aggregate more than a third of the assets forming part of the business property of the permanent establishment and such holding is not part of the activities, other than holding such rights or property, exercised through the permanent establishment.

Notwithstanding the provisions of this sub-paragraph and any other provision of this Agreement, Belgium shall, for the determination of the additional taxes established by Belgian municipalities and conurbations, take into account the earned income (revenus professionnels—beroepsinkomsten) that is exempted from tax in Belgium in accordance with this sub-paragraph. These additional taxes shall be calculated on the tax which would be payable in Belgium if the earned income in question had been derived from Belgian sources.

The exemption provided by sub-paragraph (a) shall also be granted with respect to income treated as dividends under Belgian law, which is derived by a resident of Belgium from a participation in an entity that derives its status as such from the laws of China, where that entity has not been taxed as such by China, provided that the resident of Belgium has been taxed by China, proportionally to his participation in such entity, on the income out of which the income treated as dividends under Belgian law is paid. The exempted income is the income received after deduction of the costs incurred in Belgium or elsewhere in relation to the management of the participation in the entity.

Dividends derived by a company which is a resident of Belgium from a company which is a resident of China, shall be exempted from the corporate income tax in Belgium under the conditions and within the limits provided for in Belgian law.

Where a company which is a resident of Belgium derives from a company which is a resident of China dividends which are not exempted according to sub-paragraph c), such dividends shall nevertheless be exempted from the corporate income tax in Belgium if the company which is a resident of China is effectively engaged in the active conduct of a business in China. In such case, such dividends are exempted under the conditions and within the limits provided for in Belgian law except those related to the fiscal regime applicable to the income out of which the dividends are paid.

A company shall not be considered to be effectively engaged in the active conduct of a business in China where such company is an investment company, a financing company (other than a bank) or a treasury company or where such company holds any portfolio investment or any copyright, patent, trade mark, design, model, plan, secret formula or process which represent in the aggregate more than a third of its assets and such holding is not part of the active conduct of a business.

Subject to the provisions of Belgian law regarding the deduction from Belgian tax of taxes paid abroad, where a resident of Belgium derives items of his aggregate income for Belgian tax purposes which are interest or royalties, the Chinese tax levied on that income shall be allowed as a credit against Belgian tax relating to such income.

Where, in accordance with Belgian law, losses incurred by an enterprise carried on by a resident of Belgium in a permanent establishment situated in China, have been effectively deducted from the profits of that enterprise for its taxation in Belgium, the exemption provided for in sub-paragraph a) shall not apply in Belgium to the profits of other taxable periods attributable to that establishment to the extent that those profits have also been exempted from tax in China by reason of compensation for the said losses.

In China, double taxation shall be eliminated as follows:

Where a resident of China derives income from Belgium the amount of tax on that income payable in Belgium in accordance with the provisions of this Agreement, may be credited against the Chinese tax imposed on that resident. The amount of the credit, however, shall not exceed the amount of the Chinese tax on that income computed in accordance with the taxation laws and regulations of China.

Where a dividend is paid by a company which is a resident of Belgium to a company which is a resident of China and which owns not less than 20% of the shares of the company paying the dividend, the credit shall take into account the Belgian tax paid by the company paying the dividend in respect of its income.

Article 23 Miscellaneous Rule

Nothing in this Agreement shall prejudice the right of each Contracting State to apply its domestic laws and measures concerning the prevention of tax evasion and avoidance, whether or not described as such, insofar as they do not give rise to taxation contrary to this Agreement.

Article 24 Non-Discrimination

Nationals of a Contracting State shall not be subjected in the other Contracting State to any taxation or any requirement connected therewith, which is other or more burdensome than the taxation and connected requirements to which nationals of that other State in the same circumstances, in particular with respect to residence, are or may be subjected. This provision shall, notwithstanding the provisions of Article 1, also apply to persons who are not residents of one or both of the Contracting States.

The taxation on a permanent establishment which an enterprise of a Contracting State has in the other Contracting State shall not be less favorably levied in that other State than the taxation levied on enterprises of that other State carrying on the same activities. This provision shall not be construed as obliging a Contracting State to grant to residents of the other Contracting State any personal allowances, reliefs and reductions for taxation purposes on account of civil status or family responsibilities which it grants to its own residents.

Except where the provisions of paragraph 1 of Article 9, paragraph 7 of Article 11, or paragraph 6 of Article 12, apply, interest, royalties and other disbursements paid by an enterprise of a Contracting State to a resident of the other Contracting State shall, for the purpose of determining the taxable profits of such enterprise, be deductible under the same conditions as if they had been paid to a resident of the first-mentioned State.

Enterprises of a Contracting State, the capital of which is wholly or partly owned or controlled, directly or indirectly, by one or more residents of the other Contracting State, shall not be subjected in the first-mentioned State to any taxation or requirement connected therewith which is other or more burdensome than the taxation and connected requirements to which other similar enterprises of the first-mentioned State are or may be subjected.

The provisions of this Article shall, notwithstanding the provisions of Article 2, apply to taxes of every kind and description.

Article 25 Mutual Agreement Procedure

Where a person considers that the actions of one or both of the Contracting States result or will result for him in taxation not in accordance with the provisions of this Agreement, he may, irrespective of the remedies provided by the domestic law of those States, present his case to the competent authority of the Contracting State of which he is a resident or, if his case comes under paragraph 1 of Article 24, to that of the Contracting State of which he is a national. The case must be presented within three years from the first notification of the action resulting in taxation not in accordance with the provisions of the Agreement.

The competent authority shall endeavour, if the objection appears to it to be justified and if it is not itself able to arrive at a satisfactory solution, to resolve the case by mutual agreement with the competent authority of the other Contracting State, with a view to the avoidance of taxation which is not in accordance with the Agreement. Any agreement reached shall be implemented notwithstanding any time limits in the domestic law of the Contracting States.

The competent authorities of the Contracting States shall endeavour to resolve by mutual agreement any difficulties or doubts arising as to the interpretation or application of the Agreement.

The competent authorities of the Contracting States may communicate with each other on the subject of the administrative measures which are necessary for carrying out the provisions of the Agreement and particularly on the subject of the proof to be provided by residents of each State in order to benefit in the other State from the tax exemptions or reductions provided by this Agreement.

The competent authorities of the Contracting States may communicate with each other directly for the application of the Agreement.

Article 26 Exchange of Information

The competent authorities of the Contracting States shall exchange such information as is foreseeably relevant for carrying out the provisions of this Agreement or to the administration or enforcement of the domestic laws concerning taxes of every kind and description imposed on behalf of the Contracting States, in particular for the prevention of fraud or evasion of such taxes, insofar as the taxation thereunder is not contrary to the Agreement. The exchange of information is not restricted by Articles 1 and 2.

Any information received under paragraph 1 by a Contracting State shall be treated as secret in the same manner as information obtained under the domestic laws of that State and shall be disclosed only to persons or authorities (including courts and administrative bodies) concerned with the assessment or collection of, the enforcement or prosecution in respect of, or the determination of appeals in relation to the taxes referred to in paragraph 1, or the oversight of the above. Such persons or authorities shall use the information only for such purposes. They may disclose the information in public court proceedings or in judicial decisions.

In no case shall the provisions of paragraphs 1 and 2 be construed so as to impose on a Contracting State the obligation:

to carry out administrative measures at variance with the laws and administrative practice of that or of the other Contracting State;

to supply information which is not obtainable under the laws or in the normal course of the administration of that or of the other Contracting State;

to supply information which would disclose any trade, business, industrial, commercial or professional secret or trade process, or information the disclosure of which would be contrary to public policy (ordre public).

If information is requested by a Contracting State in accordance with this Article, the other Contracting State shall use its information gathering measures to obtain the requested information, even though that other State may not need such information for its own tax purposes. The obligation contained in the preceding sentence is subject to the limitations of paragraph 3 but in no case shall such limitations be construed to permit a Contracting State to decline to supply information solely because it has no domestic interest in such information.

In no case shall the provisions of paragraph 3 be construed to permit a Contracting State to decline to supply information held by banks or other financial institutions on request by the other Contracting State.

Article 27 Members of Diplomatic Missions and Consular Posts

Nothing in this Agreement shall affect the fiscal privileges of members of diplomatic missions or consular posts under the general rules of international law or under the provisions of special agreements.

Article 28 Entry into Force

Both Contracting States shall notify each other in writing through diplomatic channels that they have completed the internal legal procedures necessary for the entry into force of this Agreement. This Agreement shall enter into force on the 30th day upon the receipt of the latter notification. This Agreement shall apply to income arising as from 1 January of the year following that of its entry into force or to income pertaining to fiscal years beginning as from 1 January of the year following that of its entry into force.

The Agreement between the Government of the People's Republic of China and the Government of the Kingdom of Belgium for the Avoidance of Double Taxation and the Prevention of Fiscal Evasion with respect to Taxes on Income and the Protocol signed at Beijing on April 18, 1985, as amended by the Additional Protocol signed at Beijing on November 27, 1996, shall cease to be effective with respect to income in respect of which the provisions of this Agreement have effect, in accordance with the provisions of paragraph 1.

Article 29 Termination

This Agreement shall continue in effect indefinitely but either of the Contracting States may, on or before the thirtieth day of June in any calendar year beginning after the expiration of a period of five years from the date of its entry into force, give written notice of termination to the other Contracting State through diplomatic channels. In such event, this Agreement shall cease to have effect as respects income derived during the fiscal years beginning on or after the first day of January in the year next following that in which the notice of termination is given.

IN WITNESS WHEREOF, the undersigned, duly authorized thereto by their respective Governments, have signed this Agreement.

DONE at Brussels, in duplicate in the

Chinese, Dutch, French and English languages, the four texts being equally authentic. In case of any divergence of interpretation between the Chinese, Dutch, French and English texts, the English text shall prevail.

For the Government of the People's Republic of China	For the Government of the Kingdom of Belgium

Czech Republic

The Czech Republic, also known by its short-form name Czechia, is a state in Eastern Europe. The Czech Republic borders Austria to the south, Germany to the west, Poland to the northeast, and Slovakia to the east. It is a landlocked country. The Czech Republic's capital and largest city is Prague.

Czechs are the majority ethnic group, while three significant local minorities are Moravians, Slovaks, and Ukrainians. Recognized minorities are Belarusians, Bulgarians, Croatians, Germans, Greeks, Hungarians, Poles, Romani people, Russians, Rusyns, Serbians, Slovaks, Ukrainians and Vietnamese.

The official and predominant spoken language is Czech. Recognized minority languages are Danish, Low German, Low Rhenish, Sorbian, Romany, North Frisian, and Sauerland Frisian. Minority languages used by immigrants and second generations are Turkish, Arabic, Kurdish, Polish, the Balkan languages, and Russian.

The Czech Republic is a unitary parliamentary constitutional republic. The Ústava is the constitution regulating the political system, in force since 1992. The Chamber of Deputies and the Senate exert the legislative power forming the parliament. The Chamber of Deputies is elected through direct elections using the party-list proportional representation system. The members of the Senate are elected in a two-round system.

Executive power is vested in the Prime Minister and his or her cabinet. The Prime Minister is appointed by the President of the Republic after being elected by the party or coalition with the parliamentary majority in the Chamber of Deputies.

The Czech Republic has a civil law system based on Roman law. The Ústavní soud acts as Supreme Court, managing constitutional matters, with judicial review powers.

The Czech Republic is a unitary state, constituted by 13 regions and the capital city.

© The Author(s), under exclusive license to Springer Nature Singapore Pte Ltd. 2022

L. Riccardi and G. Riccardi, *China–Europe Tax Treaties*,
https://doi.org/10.1007/978-981-19-3563-3_11

The Czech Republic has part of the European Union since 2004.

Category	Value
Population (mln persons)	10.638
Currency	Czech koruna

Source International Monetary Fund, year 2019

The Czech Republic is the third largest economy of Eastern Europe, with a GDP valued 247.0 billion USD in 2019, and has a population of about 10.6 million people. The Czech Republic's inflation is 2.9%, while unemployment is 2%, the second lowest in Europe. The Czech Republic ranked 21 out of 43 in the 2020 Doing Business ranking, scoring 76.3, and imposes a CIT of 19%. The Czech Republic records a trade surplus of 20 billion USD, it is the 11th main exporter in Europe.

GDP and local economy	
GDP current prices (billion USD)	247.0
GDP per capita (USD)	23,214
GDP growth (%)	2.6
Inflation (%)	2.9
Unemployment (%)	2.0
General government total expenditure (% of GDP)	41.1
General government gross debt (% of GDP)	30.2
Doing business score 2020	76.3

Source International Monetary Fund and UNCTAD, year 2019

Foreign direct investment	
FDI outstock (million USD)	45,364
FDI instock (million USD)	170,682

Source UNCTAD, year 2019

Trade	
Imports (million USD)	178,248
Exports (million USD)	198,511
Trade balance (million USD)	20,262

Source International Monetary Fund and UNCTAD, year 2019

Main import–export	
First import by category	Electrical, electronic equipment
Second import by category	Machinery, nuclear reactors, boilers
First export by category	Machinery, nuclear reactors, boilers
Second export by category	Electrical, electronic equipment

Source United Nations COMTRADE, year 2020

The legal bases for taxation are established in the constitution. The Czech Republic imposes individual income tax, property sales taxes, capital gains, corporate income tax, and value added tax. Progressivity is guaranteed by a system with different bands and various deductions. Nevertheless, rates are generally low.

Taxes	
Company income tax (%)	19
Top individual income tax (%)	23
Value added tax or sales tax (%)	21
Reduced value added tax or sales tax (%)	10/15

Source RsA Asia report, year 2021

- Economic relation with China

The Czech Republic records a trade deficit to China of 8.61 billion USD in 2020. "Electrical, electronic equipment" is the first export category, worth 1.46 billion USD, followed by "Machinery, nuclear reactors, boilers". "Electrical, electronic equipment" is the first import category, valued 7.22 billion USD. The Czech Republic is part of the Belt and Road Initiative. The Czech Republic and China have signed their DTA in 2009, which has come into force in 2011.

Category	Value
Belt road	YES

Source UNCTAD, year 2021

Import from China	
Import from China (billion USD)	13.74
First import category from China	Electrical, electronic equipment
First import value (billion USD)	7.22
Second import category from China	Machinery, nuclear reactors, boilers
Second import value (billion USD)	3.72

Source United Nations COMTRADE, year 2020

Export to China	
Export to China (billion USD)	5.13
First export category towards China	Electrical, electronic equipment
First export value (billion USD)	1.46
Second export category towards China	Machinery, nuclear reactors, boilers
Second export value (billion USD)	1.23

Source United Nations COMTRADE, year 2020

Trade balance	
Trade balance (billion USD)	−8.61

Source United Nations COMTRADE, year 2020

Double tax agreement	
DTA effective date	2011.5.4
Dividends (%)	5–10
Interest (%)	0–7.5
Royalties (%)	10

Source State Administration of Taxation of China, year 2021

Title AGREEMENT BETWEEN THE GOVERNMENT OF THE PEOPLE'S REPUBLIC OF CHINA AND THE GOVERNMENT OF THE CZECH REPUBLIC FOR THE AVOIDANCE OF DOUBLE TAXATION AND THE PREVENTION OF FISCAL EVASION WITH RESPECT TO TAXES ON INCOME.

Treaty Text

The Government of the People's Republic of China and the Government of the Czech Republic,

Desiring to conclude an Agreement for the Avoidance of Double Taxation and the Prevention of Fiscal Evasion with respect to Taxes on Income,

Have agreed as follows:

Article 1 Persons Covered

This Agreement shall apply to persons who are residents of one or both of the Contracting States.

Article 2 Taxes Covered

This Agreement shall apply to taxes on income imposed on behalf of a Contracting State or of its political subdivisions or local authorities, irrespective of the manner in which they are levied.

There shall be regarded as taxes on income all taxes imposed on total income or on elements of income, including taxes on gains from the alienation of movable or immovable property.

The existing taxes to which the Agreement shall apply are in particular:

in China:
the individual income tax;
the enterprise income tax;
(hereinafter referred to as "the Chinese tax");
in the Czech Republic:
the tax on income of individuals;
the tax on income of legal persons; (hereinafter referred to as "the Czech tax").

The Agreement shall apply also to any identical or substantially similar taxes that are imposed after the date of signature of the Agreement in addition to, or in place of, the existing taxes. The competent authorities of the Contracting States shall notify each other of any significant changes that have been made in their taxation laws.

Article 3 General Definitions

For the purposes of this Agreement, unless the context otherwise requires:

the term "China" means the People's Republic of China; when used in a geographical sense, it means all the territory of the People's Republic of China, in which the Chinese laws relating to taxation apply, including its territorial sea, and any area beyond its territorial sea, within which the People's Republic of China has sovereign rights for the purpose of exploring and exploiting the resources of the sea-bed and its subsoil and suprajacent water in accordance with international law and its domestic law;
the term "the Czech Republic" means the territory of the Czech Republic over which, under Czech legislation and in accordance with international law, the sovereign rights of the Czech Republic are exercised;
the terms "a Contracting State" and "the other Contracting State" mean the Czech Republic or China, as the context requires;
the term "person" includes an individual, a company and any other body of persons;
the term "company" means any body corporate or any entity that is treated as a body corporate for tax purposes;
the term "enterprise" applies to the carrying on of any business;
the terms "enterprise of a Contracting State" and "enterprise of the other Contracting State" mean respectively an enterprise carried on by a resident of a Contracting State and an enterprise carried on by a resident of the other Contracting State;
the term "national" means:
any individual possessing the nationality of a Contracting State; and.
any legal person, partnership or association deriving its status as such from the laws in force in a Contracting State;

the term “business” includes the performance of professional services and of other activities of an independent character;
the term “international traffic” means any transport by a ship or aircraft operated by an enterprise that has its place of effective management in a Contracting State, except when the ship or aircraft is operated solely between places in the other Contracting State;
the term “competent authority” means:
in the case of China, the State Administration of Taxation or its authorised representative;
in the case of the Czech Republic, the Minister of Finance or his authorised representative.

As regards the application of the Agreement at any time by a Contracting State, any term not defined therein shall, unless the context otherwise requires, have the meaning that it has at that time under the law of that State for the purposes of the taxes to which the Agreement applies, any meaning under the applicable tax laws of that State prevailing over a meaning given to the term under other laws of that State.

Article 4 Resident

For the purposes of this Agreement, the term “resident of a Contracting State” means any person who, under the laws of that State, is liable to tax therein by reason of his domicile,

residence, place of incorporation, place of effective management or any other criterion of a similar nature, and also includes that State and any political subdivision or local authority thereof. This term, however, does not include any person who is liable to tax in that State in respect only of income from sources in that State.

Where by reason of the provisions of paragraph 1 an individual is a resident of both Contracting States, then his status shall be determined as follows:

he shall be deemed to be a resident only of the State in which he has a permanent home available to him; if he has a permanent home available to him in both States, he shall be deemed to be a resident only of the State with which his personal and economic relations are closer (centre of vital interests);
if the State in which he has his centre of vital interests cannot be determined, or if he has not a permanent home available to him in either State, he shall be deemed to be a resident only of the State in which he has an habitual abode;
if he has an habitual abode in both States or in neither of them, he shall be deemed to be a resident only of the State of which he is a national;
if he is a national of both States or of neither of them, the competent authorities of the Contracting States shall settle the question by mutual agreement.

Where by reason of the provisions of paragraph 1 a person other than an individual is a resident of both Contracting States, then it shall be deemed to be a resident only of the State in which its place of effective management is situated.

Article 5 Permanent Establishment

For the purposes of this Agreement, the term "permanent establishment" means a fixed place of business through which the business of an enterprise is wholly or partly carried on.

The term "permanent establishment" includes especially:

a place of management;
a branch;
an office;
a factory;
a workshop, and.
a mine, an oil or gas well, a quarry or any other place of extraction of natural resources.

The term "permanent establishment" likewise encompasses:

a building site, or a construction, assembly or installation project or supervisory activities in connection therewith, but only where such site, project or activities continue for a period of more than twelve months;
the furnishing of services, including consultancy services, by an enterprise of a Contracting State or through employees or other personnel engaged by the enterprise for such purpose, but only where activities of that nature continue in the territory of the other Contracting State for a period or periods exceeding in the aggregate nine months in any twelve month period commencing or ending in the fiscal year concerned.

Notwithstanding the preceding provisions of this Article, the term "permanent establishment" shall be deemed not to include:

the use of facilities solely for the purpose of storage, display or delivery of goods or merchandise belonging to the enterprise;
the maintenance of a stock of goods or merchandise belonging to the enterprise solely for the purpose of storage, display or delivery;
the maintenance of a stock of goods or merchandise belonging to the enterprise solely for the purpose of processing by another enterprise;
the maintenance of a fixed place of business solely for the purpose of purchasing goods or merchandise or of collecting information, for the enterprise;
the maintenance of a fixed place of business solely for the purpose of carrying on, for the enterprise, any other activity of a preparatory or auxiliary character;
the maintenance of a fixed place of business solely for any combination of activities mentioned in subparagraphs *a*) to *e*), provided that the overall activity of the fixed place of business resulting from this combination is of a preparatory or auxiliary character.

Notwithstanding the provisions of paragraphs 1 and 2, where a person—other than an agent of an independent status to whom paragraph 6 applies—is acting on behalf of an enterprise and has, and habitually exercises, in a Contracting State an authority to conclude contracts in the name of the enterprise, that enterprise shall be deemed to have a permanent establishment in that State in respect of any activities which that person undertakes for the enterprise, unless the activities of such person are limited to those mentioned in paragraph 4 which, if exercised through a fixed place of business, would not make this fixed place of business a permanent establishment under the provisions of that paragraph.

An enterprise of a Contracting State shall not be deemed to have a permanent establishment in the other Contracting State merely because it carries on business in that other State through a broker, general commission agent or any other agent of an independent status, provided that such persons are acting in the ordinary course of their business.

The fact that a company which is a resident of a Contracting State controls or is controlled by a company which is a resident of the other Contracting State, or which carries on business in that other State (whether through a permanent establishment or otherwise), shall not of itself constitute either company a permanent establishment of the other.

Article 6 Income from Immovable Property

Income derived by a resident of a Contracting State from immovable property (including income from agriculture or forestry) situated in the other Contracting State may be taxed in that other State.

The term "immovable property" shall have the meaning which it has under the law of the Contracting State in which the property in question is situated. The term shall in any case include property accessory to immovable property, livestock and equipment used in agriculture and forestry, rights to which the provisions of general law respecting landed property apply, usufruct of immovable property and rights to variable or fixed payments as consideration for the working of, or the right to work, mineral deposits, sources and other natural resources; ships and aircraft shall not be regarded as immovable property.

The provisions of paragraph 1 shall apply to income derived from the direct use, letting, or use in any other form of immovable property.

The provisions of paragraphs 1 and 3 shall also apply to the income from immovable property of an enterprise.

Article 7 Business Profits

The profits of an enterprise of a Contracting State shall be taxable only in that State unless the enterprise carries on business in the other Contracting State through a permanent establishment situated therein. If the enterprise carries on business as aforesaid, the profits of the enterprise may be taxed in the other State but only so much of them as is attributable to that permanent establishment.

Subject to the provisions of paragraph 3, where an enterprise of a Contracting State carries on business in the other Contracting State through a permanent establishment situated therein, there shall in each Contracting State be attributed to that permanent establishment the profits which it might be expected to make if it were a distinct and separate enterprise engaged in the same or similar activities under the same or similar conditions and dealing wholly independently with the enterprise of which it is a permanent establishment.

In determining the profits of a permanent establishment, there shall be allowed as deductions expenses which are incurred for the purposes of the permanent establishment, including executive and general administrative expenses so incurred, whether in the State in which the permanent establishment is situated or elsewhere.

Insofar as it has been customary in a Contracting State to determine the profits to be attributed to a permanent establishment on the basis of an apportionment of the total profits of the enterprise to its various parts, nothing in paragraph 2 shall preclude that Contracting State from determining the profits to be taxed by such an apportionment as may be customary; the method of apportionment adopted shall, however, be such that the result shall be in accordance with the principles contained in this Article.

No profits shall be attributed to a permanent establishment by reason of the mere purchase by that permanent establishment of goods or merchandise for the enterprise.

For the purposes of the preceding paragraphs, the profits to be attributed to the permanent establishment shall be determined by the same method year by year unless there is good and sufficient reason to the contrary.

Where profits include items of income which are dealt with separately in other Articles of this Agreement, then the provisions of those Articles shall not be affected by the provisions of this Article.

Article 8 Shipping and Air Transport

Profits from the operation of ships or aircraft in international traffic shall be taxable only in the Contracting State in which the place of effective management of the enterprise is situated.

If the place of effective management of a shipping enterprise is aboard a ship, then it shall be deemed to be situated in the Contracting State in which the home harbour of the ship is situated, or, if there is no such home harbour, in the Contracting State of which the operator of the ship is a resident.

The provisions of paragraph 1 shall also apply to profits from the participation in a pool, a joint business or an international operating agency.

Article 9 Associated Enterprises

Where an enterprise of a Contracting State participates directly or indirectly in the management, control or capital of an enterprise of the other Contracting State, or

> the same persons participate directly or indirectly in the management, control or capital of an enterprise of a Contracting State and an enterprise of the other Contracting State,
>
> and in either case conditions are made or imposed between the two enterprises in their commercial or financial relations which differ from those which would be made between independent enterprises, then any profits which would, but for those conditions, have accrued to one of the enterprises, but, by reason of those conditions, have not so accrued, may be included in the profits of that enterprise and taxed accordingly.

Where a Contracting State includes in the profits of an enterprise of that State—and taxes accordingly—profits on which an enterprise of the other Contracting State has been charged to tax in that other State and the profits so included are profits which would have accrued to the enterprise of the first-mentioned State if the conditions made between the two enterprises had been those which would have been made between independent enterprises, then that other State shall make an appropriate adjustment to the amount of the tax charged therein on those profits. In determining such adjustment, due regard shall be had to the other provisions of this Agreement and the competent authorities of the Contracting States shall if necessary consult each other.

The provisions of paragraph 2 shall not apply in the case of fraud, gross negligence or wilful default.

Article 10 Dividends

Dividends paid by a company which is a resident of a Contracting State to a resident of the other Contracting State may be taxed in that other State.

However, such dividends may also be taxed in the Contracting State of which the company paying the dividends is a resident and according to the laws of that State, but if the beneficial owner of the dividends is a resident of the other Contracting State, the tax so charged shall not exceed:

5% of the gross amount of the dividends if the beneficial owner is a company (other than a partnership) which holds directly at least 25% of the capital of the company paying the dividends;
10% of the gross amount of the dividends in all other cases.

The competent authorities of the Contracting States shall by mutual agreement settle the mode of application of these limitations.

This paragraph shall not affect the taxation of the company in respect of the profits out of which the dividends are paid.

The term "dividends" as used in this Article means income from shares or other rights, not being debt-claims, participating in profits, as well as other income which is subjected to the same taxation treatment as income from shares by the laws of the State of which the company making the distribution is a resident.

The provisions of paragraphs 1 and 2 shall not apply if the beneficial owner of the dividends, being a resident of a Contracting State, carries on business in the other Contracting State of which the company paying the dividends is a resident through a permanent establishment situated therein and the holding in respect of which the dividends are paid is effectively connected with such permanent establishment. In such case the provisions of Article 7 shall apply.

Where a company which is a resident of a Contracting State derives profits or income from the other Contracting State, that other State may not impose any tax on the dividends paid by the company, except insofar as such dividends are paid to a resident of that other State or insofar as the holding in respect of which the dividends are paid is effectively connected with a permanent establishment situated in that other State, nor subject the company's undistributed profits to a tax on the company's undistributed profits, even if the dividends paid or the undistributed profits consist wholly or partly of profits or income arising in such other State.

Article 11 Interest

Interest arising in a Contracting State and paid to a resident of the other Contracting State may be taxed in that other State.

However, such interest may also be taxed in the Contracting State in which it arises and according to the laws of that State, but if the beneficial owner of the interest is a resident of the other Contracting State, the tax so charged shall not exceed 7.5% of the gross amount of the interest. The competent authorities of the Contracting States shall by mutual agreement settle the mode of application of this limitation.

Notwithstanding the provisions of paragraph 2, interest arising in a Contracting State and derived by the Government of the other Contracting State, a political subdivision or a local authority thereof, the Central Bank of that other Contracting State or any agency of that Government, or by any other resident of that other Contracting State with respect to debt-claims of that resident which are financed, guaranteed or insured by the Government of that other Contracting State, a political subdivision or a local authority thereof, the Central Bank of that other Contracting State or any agency of that Government, shall be exempt from tax in the first- mentioned Contracting State.

For the purpose of paragraph 3, it is understood that the following institutions are agencies of the Government:

in the case of China:
the China Development Bank;
the Agricultural Development Bank of China;
the Export–Import Bank of China;
the China Export & Credit Insurance Corporation; and.
any other institutions as may be agreed upon between the competent authorities of the Contracting States;
in the case of the Czech Republic:
the Czech Export Bank (CEB);
the Export Guarantee and Insurance Company (EGAP); and.
any other institutions as may be agreed upon between the competent authorities of the Contracting States.

The term "interest" as used in this Article means income from debt-claims of every kind, whether or not secured by mortgage and whether or not carrying a right to participate in the debtor's profits, and in particular, income from government securities and income from bonds or debentures, including premiums and prizes attaching to such securities, bonds or debentures. Penalty charges for late payment shall not be regarded as interest for the purpose of this Article.

The provisions of paragraphs 1, 2 and 3 shall not apply if the beneficial owner of the interest, being a resident of a Contracting State, carries on business in the other

Contracting State in which the interest arises through a permanent establishment situated therein and the debt-claim in respect of which the interest is paid is effectively connected with such permanent establishment. In such case the provisions of Article 7 shall apply.

Interest shall be deemed to arise in a Contracting State when the payer is a resident of that State. Where, however, the person paying the interest, whether he is a resident of a Contracting State or not, has in a Contracting State a permanent establishment in connection with which the indebtedness on which the interest is paid was incurred, and such interest is borne by such permanent establishment, then such interest shall be deemed to arise in the State in which the permanent establishment is situated.

Where, by reason of a special relationship between the payer and the beneficial owner or between both of them and some other person, the amount of the interest, having regard to the debt-claim for which it is paid, exceeds the amount which would have been agreed upon by the payer and the beneficial owner in the absence of such relationship, the provisions of this Article shall apply only to the last-mentioned amount. In such case, the excess part of the payments shall remain taxable according to the laws of each Contracting State, due regard being had to the other provisions of this Agreement.

Article 12 Royalties

Royalties arising in a Contracting State and paid to a resident of the other Contracting State may be taxed in that other State.

However, such royalties may also be taxed in the Contracting State in which they arise and according to the laws of that State, but if the beneficial owner of the royalties is a resident of the other Contracting State, the tax so charged shall not exceed 10% of the gross amount of the royalties. The competent authorities of the Contracting States shall by mutual agreement settle the mode of application of this limitation.

The term "royalties" as used in this Article means payments of any kind received as a consideration for the use of, or the right to use, any copyright of literary, artistic or scientific work including cinematograph films, and films or tapes for television or radio broadcasting, any patent, trade mark, design or model, plan, secret formula or process, or any industrial, commercial or scientific equipment, or for information concerning industrial, commercial or scientific experience.

The provisions of paragraphs 1 and 2 shall not apply if the beneficial owner of the royalties, being a resident of a Contracting State, carries on business in the other Contracting State in which the royalties arise through a permanent establishment situated therein and the right or property in respect of which the royalties are paid is effectively connected with such permanent establishment. In such case the provisions of Article 7 shall apply.

Royalties shall be deemed to arise in a Contracting State when the payer is a resident of that State. Where, however, the person paying the royalties, whether he is a resident of a Contracting State or not, has in a Contracting State a permanent establishment in connection with which the liability to pay the royalties was incurred, and such royalties are borne by such permanent establishment, then such royalties shall be deemed to arise in the State in which the permanent establishment is situated.

Where, by reason of a special relationship between the payer and the beneficial owner or between both of them and some other person, the amount of the royalties, having regard to the use, right or information for which they are paid, exceeds the amount which would have been agreed upon by the payer and the beneficial owner in the absence of such relationship, the provisions of this Article shall apply only to the last-mentioned amount. In such case, the excess part of the payments shall remain taxable according to the laws of each Contracting State, due regard being had to the other provisions of this Agreement.

Article 13 Capital Gains

Gains derived by a resident of a Contracting State from the alienation of immovable property referred to in Article 6 and situated in the other Contracting State may be taxed in that other State.

Gains from the alienation of movable property forming part of the business property of a permanent establishment which an enterprise of a Contracting State has in the other Contracting State, including such gains from the alienation of such a permanent establishment (alone or with the whole enterprise), may be taxed in that other State.

Gains from the alienation of property forming part of the business property of an enterprise and consisting of ships or aircraft operated by that enterprise in international traffic or movable property pertaining to the operation of such ships or aircraft, shall be taxable only in the Contracting State in which the place of effective management of the enterprise is situated.

Gains derived by a resident of a Contracting State from the alienation of shares or other interests in a company which is a resident of the other Contracting State may be taxed in that other State.

Gains from the alienation of any property, other than that referred to in paragraphs 1, 2, 3 and 4, shall be taxable only in the Contracting State of which the alienator is a resident.

Article 14 Income from Employment

Subject to the provisions of Articles 15, 17 and 18, salaries, wages and other similar remuneration derived by a resident of a Contracting State in respect of an employment shall be taxable only in that State unless the employment is exercised in the other Contracting State. If the employment is so exercised, such remuneration as is derived therefrom may be taxed in that other State.

Notwithstanding the provisions of paragraph 1, remuneration derived by a resident of a Contracting State in respect of an employment exercised in the other Contracting State shall be taxable only in the first-mentioned State if:

the recipient is present in the other State for a period or periods not exceeding in the aggregate 183 days in any twelve month period commencing or ending in the fiscal year concerned, and.

the remuneration is paid by, or on behalf of, an employer who is not a resident of the other State, and.

the remuneration is not borne by a permanent establishment which the employer has in the other State.

The term "employer" mentioned in subparagraph *b*) of paragraph 2 means the person having right on the work produced and bearing the responsibility and risk connected with the performance of the work.

Notwithstanding the provisions of paragraphs 1 and 2 of this Article, remuneration derived in respect of an employment exercised aboard a ship or aircraft operated in international traffic may be taxed in the Contracting State in which the place of effective management of the enterprise is situated.

Article 15 Directors' Fees

Directors' fees and other similar payments derived by a resident of a Contracting State in his capacity as a member of the board of directors or any other similar organ of a company which is a resident of the other Contracting State may be taxed in that other State.

Article 16 Artistes and Sportpersons

Notwithstanding the provisions of Articles 7 and 14, income derived by a resident of a Contracting State as an entertainer, such as a theatre, motion picture, radio or television artiste, or a musician, or as a sportsperson, from his or her personal activities as such exercised in the other Contracting State, may be taxed in that other State.

Where income in respect of personal activities exercised by an entertainer or a sportsperson in his or her capacity as such accrues not to the entertainer or sportsperson himself or herself but to another person, that income may, notwithstanding the provisions of Articles 7 and 14, be taxed in the Contracting State in which the activities of the entertainer or sportsperson are exercised.

Article 17 Pensions

Subject to the provisions of paragraph 2 of Article 18, pensions and other similar remuneration paid to a resident of a Contracting State in consideration of past employment shall be taxable only in that State.

Article 18 Government Service

Salaries, wages and other similar remuneration paid by a Contracting State or a political subdivision or a local authority thereof to an individual in respect of services rendered to that State or subdivision or authority shall be taxable only in that State.

However, such salaries, wages and other similar remuneration shall be taxable only in the other Contracting State if the services are rendered in that State and the individual is a resident of that State who:

is a national of that State; or

did not become a resident of that State solely for the purpose of rendering the services.

1. Notwithstanding the provisions of paragraph 1, pensions and other similar remuneration paid by, or out of funds created by, a Contracting State or a political subdivision or a local authority thereof to an individual in respect of services rendered to that State or subdivision or authority shall be taxable only in that State.
2. However, such pensions and other similar remuneration shall be taxable only in the other Contracting State if the individual is a resident of, and a national of, that State.

The provisions of Articles 14, 15, 16 and 17 shall apply to salaries, wages, pensions and other similar remuneration in respect of services rendered in connection with a business carried on by a Contracting State or a political subdivision or a local authority thereof.

Article 19 Students

Payments which a student or business apprentice who is or was immediately before visiting a Contracting State a resident of the other Contracting State and who is present in the first-mentioned State solely for the purpose of his education or training receives for the purpose of his maintenance, education or training shall not be taxed in that State, provided that such payments arise from sources outside that State.

Article 20 Other Income

Items of income of a resident of a Contracting State, wherever arising, not dealt with in the foregoing Articles of this Agreement shall be taxable only in that State.

The provisions of paragraph 1 shall not apply to income, other than income from immovable property as defined in paragraph 2 of Article 6, if the recipient of such income, being a resident of a Contracting State, carries on business in the other Contracting State through a permanent establishment situated therein and the right or property in respect of which the income is paid is effectively connected with such permanent establishment. In such case the provisions of Article 7 shall apply.

Article 21 Preventing Improper Use of the Agreement

Notwithstanding the provisions of any other Articles of this Agreement, benefits provided under this Agreement shall not be granted to companies of either Contracting State if the purpose of such companies is to obtain benefits under this Agreement that would not otherwise be available.

The provisions of this Agreement shall in no case prevent a Contracting State from the application of the provisions of its domestic laws aiming at the prevention of fiscal evasion and avoidance, provided that the taxation in that State on the income concerned is not contrary to the Agreement.

The competent authority of a Contracting State may, after consultation with the competent authority of the other Contracting State, deny the benefits of this Agreement to any person, or with respect to any transaction, if in its opinion the granting of those benefits would constitute an abuse of the Agreement.

Article 22 Elimination of Double Taxation

In China, double taxation shall be eliminated as follows:

Where a resident of China derives income from the Czech Republic the amount of tax on that income payable in the Czech Republic in accordance with the provisions of this Agreement, may be credited against the Chinese tax imposed on that resident. The amount of the credit, however, shall not exceed the amount of the Chinese tax on that income computed in accordance with the taxation laws and regulations of China.

Where the income derived from the Czech Republic is a dividend paid by a company which is a resident of the Czech Republic to a company which is a resident of China and which owns not less than 20% of the shares of the company paying the dividend, the credit shall take into account the tax paid to the Czech Republic by the company paying the dividend in respect of its income.

In the case of a resident of the Czech Republic, double taxation shall be eliminated as follows:

The Czech Republic, when imposing taxes on its residents, may include in the tax base upon which such taxes are imposed the items of income which according to the provisions of this Agreement may also be taxed in China, but shall allow as a deduction from the amount of tax computed on such a base an amount equal to the tax paid in China. Such deduction shall not, however, exceed that part of the Czech tax, as computed before the deduction is given, which is appropriate to the income which, in accordance with the provisions of this Agreement, may be taxed in China.

Where in accordance with any provision of the Agreement income derived by a resident of the Czech Republic is exempt from tax in the Czech Republic, the Czech Republic may nevertheless, in calculating the amount of tax on the remaining income of such resident, take into account the exempted income.

Article 23 Non-discrimination

Nationals of a Contracting State shall not be subjected in the other Contracting State to any taxation or any requirement connected therewith, which is other or more burdensome than the taxation and connected requirements to which nationals of that other State in the same circumstances, in particular with respect to residence, are or may be subjected. This provision shall, notwithstanding the provisions of Article 1, also apply to persons who are not residents of one or both of the Contracting States.

The taxation on a permanent establishment which an enterprise of a Contracting State has in the other Contracting State shall not be less favourably levied in that other State than the taxation levied on enterprises of that other State carrying on the same activities. This provision shall not be construed as obliging a Contracting State to grant to residents of the other Contracting State any personal allowances, reliefs and reductions for taxation purposes on account of civil status or family responsibilities which it grants to its own residents.

Except where the provisions of paragraph 1 of Article 9, paragraph 8 of Article 11, or paragraph 6 of Article 12, apply, interest, royalties and other disbursements paid by an enterprise of a Contracting State to a resident of the other Contracting State shall, for the purpose of determining the taxable profits of such enterprise, be deductible under the same conditions as if they had been paid to a resident of the first-mentioned State.

Enterprises of a Contracting State, the capital of which is wholly or partly owned or controlled, directly or indirectly, by one or more residents of the other Contracting State, shall not be subjected in the first-mentioned State to any taxation or any requirement connected therewith which is other or more burdensome than the taxation and connected requirements to which other similar enterprises of the first-mentioned State are or may be subjected.

The provisions of this Article shall, notwithstanding the provisions of Article 2, apply to taxes of every kind and description.

Article 24 Mutual Agreement Procedure

Where a person considers that the actions of one or both of the Contracting States result or will result for him in taxation not in accordance with the provisions of this Agreement, he may, irrespective of the remedies provided by the domestic law of those States, present his case to the competent authority of the Contracting State of which he is a resident or, if his case comes under paragraph 1 of Article 23, to that of the Contracting State of which he is a national. The case must be presented within three years from the first notification of the action resulting in taxation not in accordance with the provisions of the Agreement.

The competent authority shall endeavour, if the objection appears to it to be justified and if it is not itself able to arrive at a satisfactory solution, to resolve the case by mutual agreement with the competent authority of the other Contracting State, with a view to the avoidance of taxation which is not in accordance with the Agreement. Any agreement reached shall be implemented notwithstanding any time limits in the domestic law of the Contracting States.

The competent authorities of the Contracting States shall endeavour to resolve by mutual agreement any difficulties or doubts arising as to the interpretation or application of the Agreement. They may also consult together for the elimination of double taxation in cases not provided for in the Agreement.

The competent authorities of the Contracting States may communicate with each other directly for the purpose of reaching an agreement in the sense of the preceding paragraphs.

For the purposes of paragraph 3 of Article XXII (Consultation) of the General Agreement on Trade in Services, the Contracting States agree that, notwithstanding that paragraph, any dispute between them as to whether a measure falls within the scope of this Agreement may be brought before the Council for Trade in Services, as provided by that paragraph, only with the consent of both Contracting States. Any doubt as to the interpretation of this paragraph shall be resolved under paragraph 3 of this Article or, failing agreement under that procedure, pursuant to any other procedure agreed to by both Contracting States.

Article 25 Exchange of Information

The competent authorities of the Contracting States shall exchange such information as is foreseeably relevant for carrying out the provisions of this Agreement or to

the administration or enforcement of the domestic laws concerning taxes of every kind and description imposed on behalf of the Contracting States, or of their political subdivisions or local authorities, insofar as the taxation thereunder is not contrary to the Agreement. The exchange of information is not restricted by Articles 1 and 2.

Any information received under paragraph 1 by a Contracting State shall be treated as secret in the same manner as information obtained under the domestic laws of that State and shall be disclosed only to persons or authorities (including courts and administrative bodies) concerned with the assessment or collection of, the enforcement or prosecution in respect of, the determination of appeals in relation to the taxes referred to in paragraph 1, or the oversight of the above. Such persons or authorities shall use the information only for such purposes. They may disclose the information in public court proceedings or in judicial decisions.

In no case shall the provisions of paragraphs 1 and 2 be construed so as to impose on a Contracting State the obligation:

to carry out administrative measures at variance with the laws and administrative practice of that or of the other Contracting State;
to supply information which is not obtainable under the laws or in the normal course of the administration of that or of the other Contracting State;
to supply information which would disclose any trade, business, industrial, commercial or professional secret or trade process, or information the disclosure of which would be contrary to public policy (ordre public).

If information is requested by a Contracting State in accordance with this Article, the other Contracting State shall use its information gathering measures to obtain the requested information, even though that other State may not need such information for its own tax purposes. The obligation contained in the preceding sentence is subject to the limitations of paragraph 3 but in no case shall such limitations be construed to permit a Contracting State to decline to supply information solely because it has no domestic interest in such information.

In no case shall the provisions of paragraph 3 be construed to permit a Contracting State to decline to supply information solely because the information is held by a bank, other financial institution, nominee or person acting in an agency or a fiduciary capacity or because it relates to ownership interests in a person.

Article 26 Members of Diplomatic Missions and Consular Posts

Nothing in this Agreement shall affect the fiscal privileges of members of diplomatic missions or consular posts under the general rules of international law or under the provisions of special agreements.

Article 27 Entry Into Force

Each of the Contracting States shall notify to the other, through the diplomatic channels, the completion of the procedures required by its domestic law for the bringing into force of this Agreement. This Agreement shall enter into force on the date of the later of these notifications and its provisions shall have effect: in respect of taxes withheld at source, to income paid or credited on or after 1st January in the calendar year next following that in which the Agreement enters into force;

in respect of other taxes on income, to income in any taxable year beginning on or after 1st January in the calendar year next following that in which the Agreement enters into force.

The provisions of the Agreement between the Government of the People's Republic of China and the Government of the Czechoslovak Socialist Republic for the Avoidance of Double Taxation and the Prevention of Fiscal Evasion with respect to Taxes on Income, signed at Prague on 11th June 1987, shall cease to be in force and in effect in relations between China and the Czech Republic on the date of the entry into effect of this Agreement.

Article 28 Termination

This Agreement shall remain in force until terminated by a Contracting State. Either Contracting State may terminate the Agreement, through the diplomatic channels, by giving notice of termination at least six months before the end of any calendar year following after the period of five years from the date on which the Agreement enters into force. In such event, the Agreement shall cease to have effect:

in respect of taxes withheld at source, to income paid or credited on or after 1st January in the calendar year next following that in which the notice is given;
in respect of other taxes on income, to income in any taxable year beginning on or after 1st January in the calendar year next following that in which the notice is given.

IN WITNESS WHEREOF the undersigned, duly authorised thereto, have signed this Agreement.

DONE in duplicate at__this__day of______2009 in the Chinese, Czech and English languages, all texts being equally authentic. In case of any divergence of interpretation, the English text shall prevail.

FOR THE GOVERNMENT OF THE PEOPLE'S REPUBLIC OF CHINA.

FOR THE GOVERNMENT OF THE CZECH REPUBLIC.

Denmark

Denmark, officially the Kingdom of Denmark, is a state in Northern Europe. Denmark is located southwest of Sweden and south of Norway, and it is bordered to the south by Germany. The Kingdom of Denmark is constitutionally a unitary state comprising metropolitan Denmark and the two autonomous territories of the Faroe Islands and Greenland. Denmark's capital and largest city is Copenhagen.

There are no official statistics on ethnic groups, nevertheless, Danish descendants are the majority ethnic group, with minorities descending from Turkish, Polish, Syrian, German, Iraqi, and Romanian.

The official and predominant spoken language is Danish. Faroese and Greenlandic are the official languages of the Faroe Islands and Greenland respectively. Minority languages are German and Swedish.

Denmark is a unitary parliamentary constitutional monarchy. The Grundloven is the constitution regulating the political system, in force since 1953. The Folketing exerts the legislative power forming the parliament. The Folketing is elected through direct elections using the open list proportional representation system.

Executive power is vested in the Prime Minister and his or her cabinet. The Prime Minister is appointed by the Monarch after being elected by the party or coalition with the parliamentary majority in the Folketing.

Denmark has a civil law system based on Roman law. The Højesteret acts as Supreme Court, managing constitutional matters, with judicial review powers.

Denmark is a unitary state, divided into five administrative regions, further subdivided into 98 municipalities.

Denmark has been part of the European Union since 1973.

Category	Value
Population (mln persons)	5.806
Currency	Danish krone

Source International Monetary Fund, year 2019

© The Author(s), under exclusive license to Springer Nature Singapore Pte Ltd. 2022

L. Riccardi and G. Riccardi, *China–Europe Tax Treaties*,
https://doi.org/10.1007/978-981-19-3563-3_12

Denmark is the 15th largest economy of Europe and the fifth of Northern Europe, with a GDP valued 347.2 billion USD in 2019, and has a population of about 5.8 million people. Denmark ranks 6th in Europe according to GDP per capita. Denmark enjoys low inflation (0.7%), while unemployment is 5%. Denmark ranked first out of 43 in Europe in the 2020 Doing Business ranking, scoring 85.3, and imposes a CIT of 22%. Denmark records a trade surplus of 13 billion USD.

GDP and local economy	
GDP current prices (billion USD)	347.2
GDP per capita (USD)	59,795
GDP growth (%)	2.4
Inflation (%)	0.7
Unemployment (%)	5.0
General government total expenditure (% of GDP)	49.2
General government gross debt (% of GDP)	33.0
Doing business score 2020	85.3

Source International Monetary Fund and UNCTAD, year 2019

Foreign direct investment	
FDI outstock (million USD)	202,517
FDI instock (million USD)	105,748

Source UNCTAD, year 2019

Trade	
Imports (million USD)	97,533
Exports (million USD)	110,699
Trade balance (million USD)	13,166

Source International Monetary Fund and UNCTAD, year 2019

Main import–export	
First import by category	Machinery, nuclear reactors, boilers
Second import by category	Electrical, electronic equipment
First export by category	Pharmaceutical products
Second export by category	Machinery, nuclear reactors, boilers

Source United Nations COMTRADE, year 2020

The legal bases for taxation are established in the constitution. Denmark imposes individual income tax, property sales taxes, capital gains, corporate income tax, and value added tax. Progressivity is guaranteed by a system with different bands and various deductions.

Taxes	
Company income tax (%)	22
Top individual income tax (%)	15[1]
Value added tax or sales Tax (%)	25
Reduced value added tax or sales tax (%)	0

Source RsA Asia report, year 2021
Note the reported Individual Income Tax is the State tax. Additional local taxes and share taxes, with rates from 8 to 42%, need to be considered

- Economic relation with China.

Denmark records a trade deficit to China of 1.46 billion USD in 2020. "Meat and edible meat" is the first export category, worth 1.39 billion USD, followed by "Organic chemicals". "Electrical, electronic equipment" is the first import category, valued 1.13 billion USD. The first Denmark-China DTA was signed in March 1986, entering into force in October 1986. A new agreement has been signed in June 2012, coming into force on December 27th of the same year. Denmark is not part of the Belt and Road Initiative.

Category	Value
Belt Road	NO

Source UNCTAD, year 2021

Import from China	
Import from China (billion USD)	7.47
First import category from China	Electrical, electronic equipment
First import value (billion USD)	1.13
Second Import category from China	Machinery, nuclear reactors, boilers
Second import value (billion USD)	0.986

Source United Nations COMTRADE, year 2020

Export to China	
Export to China (billion USD)	6.01
First export category towards China	Meat and edible meat offal
First export value (billion USD)	1.39
Second export category towards China	Organic chemicals
Second export value (billion USD)	1.03

Source United Nations COMTRADE, year 2020

Trade balance	
Trade balance (billion USD)	−1.46

Source United Nations COMTRADE, year 2020

Double tax agreement	
DTA effective date	2012.12.27
Dividends (%)	5–10
Interest (%)	0–10
Royalties (%)	7–10

Source State Administration of Taxation of China, year 2021

Title AGREEMENT BETWEEN THE GOVERNMENT OF THE PEOPLE'S REPUBLIC OF CHINA AND THE GOVERNMENT OF THE KINGDOM OF DENMARK FOR THE AVOIDANCE OF DOUBLE TAXATION AND THE PREVENTION OF FISCAL EVASION WITH RESPECT TO TAXES ON INCOME.

Treaty Text

The Government of the People's Republic of China and the Government of the Kingdom of Denmark,

Desiring to conclude an Agreement for the avoidance of double taxation and the prevention of fiscal evasion with respect to taxes on income,

Have agreed as follows:

Article 1 Personal Scope

This Agreement shall apply to persons who are residents of one or both of the Contracting States.

Article 2 Taxes Covered

This Agreement shall apply to taxes on income imposed on behalf of a Contracting State or of its political subdivisions or of its local authorities, irrespective of the manner in which they are levied.

There shall be regarded as taxes on income all taxes imposed on total income, or on elements of income, including taxes on gains from the alienation of movable or immovable property as well as taxes on capital appreciation.

The existing taxes to which the Agreement shall apply are:

In the People's Republic of China:

the individual income tax;
the enterprise income tax; (hereinafter referred to as "Chinese tax");

In the Kingdom of Denmark:

the income tax to the State (indkomstskatten til staten);
the income tax to the municipalities (den kommunale indkomstskat); (hereinafter referred to as "Danish tax").

This Agreement shall apply also to any identical or substantially similar taxes which are imposed after the date of signature of this Agreement in addition to, or in place of, the existing taxes. The competent authorities of the Contracting States shall notify each other of any substantial changes which have been made in their respective taxation laws within a reasonable period of time after such changes.

Article 3 General Definitions

For the purposes of this Agreement, unless the context otherwise requires:

the terms "a Contracting State" and "the other Contracting State" mean the People's Republic of China or the Kingdom of Denmark as the context requires;
the term "China" means the People's Republic of China, when used in a geographical sense, means all the territory of the People's Republic of China, including its territorial sea, in which the laws relating to Chinese tax apply, and any area beyond its territorial sea, within which the People's Republic of China has sovereign rights of exploration for and exploitation of resources of the seabed and its sub-soil and superjacent water resources in accordance with international law;
the term "Denmark" means the Kingdom of Denmark including any area outside the territorial sea of Denmark which in accordance with international law has been or may hereafter be designated under Danish laws as an area within which Denmark may exercise sovereign rights for the purpose of exploring and exploiting the natural resources of the seabed or its subsoil and the superjacent waters and with regard to other activities for the economic exploration and exploitation of the area; the term does not comprise the Faroe Islands and Greenland;
the term "person" includes an individual, a company and any other body of persons;
the term "company" means any body corporate or any entity which is treated as a body corporate for tax purposes;
the terms "enterprise of a Contracting State" and "enterprise of the other Contracting State" mean respectively an enterprise carried on by a resident of a Contracting State and an enterprise carried on by a resident of the other Contracting State;
the term "nationals" means all individuals possessing the nationality of either Contracting State and all juridical persons created or organized under the laws of that Contracting State and any organizations without juridical personality treated for the purposes of tax as juridical persons created or organized under the laws of that Contracting State;
the term "international traffic" means any transport by a ship or aircraft operated by an enterprise which has its place of effective management in a Contracting State, except when the ship or aircraft is operated solely between places in the other Contracting State;
the term "competent authority" means:

in China: The State Administration of Taxation or its authorized representative;
in Denmark:
the Minister for Taxation or his authorised representative.

As regards the application of the Agreement at any time by a Contracting State, any term not defined therein shall, unless the context otherwise requires, have the meaning which it has at that time under the law of that State for the purposes of the taxes to which the Agreement applies, any meaning under the applicable tax laws of that State prevailing over a meaning given to the term under other laws of that State.

Article 4 Resident

For the purposes of this Agreement, the term "resident of a Contracting State" means any person who, under the laws of that State, is liable to tax therein by reason of his domicile, residence, place of incorporation, place of management or any other criterion of a similar nature, and also includes that State and any political subdivision or local authority thereof. This term, however, does not include any person who is liable to tax in that State in respect only of income or capital gains from sources in that State.

Where by reason of the provisions of paragraph 1 an individual is a resident of both Contracting States, then his status shall be determined as follows:

he shall be deemed to be a resident only of the State in which he has a permanent home available to him; if he has a permanent home available to him in both States, he shall be deemed to be a resident only of the State with which his personal and economic relations are closer (centre of vital interests);
if the State in which he has his centre of vital interests cannot be determined, or if he does not have a permanent home available to him in either State, he shall be deemed to be a resident only of the State in which he has an habitual abode;
if he has an habitual abode in both States or in neither of them, he shall be deemed to be a resident only of the State of which he is a national;
if he is a national of both States or of neither of them, the competent authorities of the Contracting States shall settle the question by mutual agreement.

Where by reason of the provisions of paragraph 1 a person other than an individual is a resident of both Contracting States, then it shall be deemed to be a resident only of the State in which its place of effective management is situated.

Article 5 Permanent Establishment

For the purposes of this Agreement, the term "permanent establishment" means a fixed place of business through which the business of an enterprise is wholly or partly carried on.

The term "permanent establishment" includes especially:

a place of management;
a branch;
an office;
a factory;

a workshop, and.
a mine, an oil or gas well, quarry or any other place of extraction of natural resources.

The term “permanent establishment” also includes:

a building site, a construction, assembly or installation project, or supervisory activities in connection therewith, but only where such site, project or activities continue for a period of more than twelve months;
an installation, drilling rig or ship used for the exploration or exploitation of natural resources, but only if so used for a period of more than twelve months; and.
the furnishing of services, including consultancy services, by an enterprise through employees or other personnel engaged by the enterprise for such purpose, but only if activities of that nature continue (for the same or a connected project) within a Contracting State for a period or periods aggregating more than 183 days in any twelve month period commencing or ending in the fiscal year concerned.

Notwithstanding the preceding provisions of this Article, the term “permanent establishment” shall be deemed not to include:

the use of facilities solely for the purpose of storage, display or delivery of goods or merchandise belonging to the enterprise;
the maintenance of a stock of goods or merchandise belonging to the enterprise solely for the purpose of storage, display or delivery;
the maintenance of a stock of goods or merchandise belonging to the enterprise solely for the purpose of processing by another enterprise;
the maintenance of a fixed place of business solely for the purpose of purchasing goods or merchandise or of collecting information, for the enterprise;
the maintenance of a fixed place of business solely for the purpose of carrying on, for the enterprise, any other activity of a preparatory or auxiliary character;
the maintenance of a fixed place of business solely for any combination of activities mentioned in sub-paragraphs (a) to (e) provided that the overall activity of the fixed place of business resulting from this combination is of a preparatory or auxiliary character.

Notwithstanding the provisions of paragraphs 1 and 2, where a person–other than an agent of an independent status to whom paragraph 6 applies–is acting in a Contracting State on behalf of an enterprise of the other Contracting State and has, and habitually exercises an authority to conclude contracts in the name of the enterprise, that enterprise shall be deemed to have a permanent establishment in that Contracting State in respect of any activities which that person undertakes for the enterprise, unless the activities of such person are limited to those mentioned in paragraph 4 which, if exercised through a fixed place of business, would not make this fixed place of business a permanent establishment under the provisions of that paragraph.

An enterprise of a Contracting State shall not be deemed to have a permanent establishment in the other Contracting State merely because it carries on business in that Contracting State through a broker, general commission agent or any other agent of an independent status, provided that such persons are acting in the ordinary course of their business. However, when the activities of such an agent are devoted wholly or almost wholly on behalf of that enterprise, he will not be considered an agent of an independent status within the meaning of this paragraph if it is shown that the transactions between the agent and the enterprise were not made under arm's-length conditions.

The fact that a company which is a resident of a Contracting State controls or is controlled by a company which is a resident of the other Contracting State, or which carries on business in that other Contracting State (whether through a permanent establishment or otherwise), shall not of itself constitute either company a permanent establishment of the other.

Article 6 Income from Immovable Property

Income derived by a resident of a Contracting State from immovable property (including income from agriculture or forestry) situated in the other Contracting State may be taxed in that other Contracting State.

The term "immovable property" shall have the meaning which it has under the law of the Contracting State in which the property in question is situated. The term shall in any case include property accessory to immovable property, livestock and equipment used in agriculture and forestry, rights to which the provisions of general law respecting landed property apply, usufruct of immovable property and rights to variable or fixed payments as consideration for the working of, or the right to work, mineral deposits, sources and other natural resources; ships and aircraft shall not be regarded as immovable property.

The provisions of paragraph 1 shall apply to income derived from the direct use, letting, or use in any other form of immovable property.

The provisions of paragraphs 1 and 3 shall also apply to the income from immovable property of an enterprise and to income from immovable property used for the performance of independent personal services.

Article 7 Business Profits

The profits of an enterprise of a Contracting State shall be taxable only in that Contracting State unless the enterprise carries on business in the other Contracting State through a permanent establishment situated therein. If the enterprise carries on business as aforesaid, the profits of the enterprise may be taxed in the other Contracting State but only so much of them as is attributable to that permanent establishment.

Subject to the provisions of paragraph 3, where an enterprise of a Contracting State carries on business in the other Contracting State through a permanent establishment situated therein, there shall in each Contracting State be attributed to that permanent establishment the profits which it might be expected to make if it were a distinct and separate enterprise engaged in the same or similar activities under the same or similar conditions and dealing wholly independently with the enterprise of which it is a permanent establishment.

In determining the profits of a permanent establishment, there shall be allowed as deductions expenses which are incurred for the purposes of the permanent establishment, including executive and general administrative expenses so incurred, whether in the State in which the permanent establishment is situated or elsewhere.

In so far as it has been customary in a Contracting State to determine the profits to be attributed to a permanent establishment on the basis of an apportionment of the total profits of the enterprise to its various parts, nothing in paragraph 2 shall preclude that Contracting State from determining the profits to be taxed by such an apportionment as may be customary; the method of apportionment adopted shall, however, be such that the result shall be in accordance with the principles contained in this Article.

No profits shall be attributed to a permanent establishment by reason of the mere purchase by that permanent establishment of goods or merchandise for the enterprise.

For the purposes of paragraphs 1 to 5, the profits to be attributed to the permanent establishment shall be determined by the same method year by year unless there is good and sufficient reason to the contrary.

Where profits include items of income which are dealt with separately in other Articles of this Agreement, then the provisions of those Articles shall not be affected by the provisions of this Article.

Article 8 Shipping and Air Transport

Profits from the operation of ships or aircraft in international traffic shall be taxable only in the Contracting State in which the place of effective management of the enterprise is situated.

For the purposes of this Article, profits from the operation of ships or aircraft in international traffic include:

profits from the rental on a bare boat basis of ships or aircraft; and.

profits from the use, maintenance or rental of containers (including trailers and related equipment for the transport of containers) used for the transport of goods or merchandise;

where such rental or such use, maintenance or rental, as the case may be, is incidental to the operation of ships or aircraft in international traffic.

If the place of effective management of a shipping enterprise is aboard a ship, then it shall be deemed to be situated in the Contracting State in which the home harbour of the ship is situated, or, if there is no such home harbour, in the Contracting State of which the operator of the ship is a resident.

The provisions of paragraph 1 shall also apply to profits from the participation in a pool, a joint business or an international operating agency.

Article 9 Associated Enterprises

Where an enterprise of a Contracting State participates directly or indirectly in the management, control or capital of an enterprise of the other Contracting State, or.

the same persons participate directly or indirectly in the management, control or capital of an enterprise of a Contracting State and an enterprise of the other Contracting State,

and in either case conditions are made or imposed between the two enterprises in their commercial or financial relations which differ from those which would be made between independent enterprises, then any profits which would, but for those conditions, have accrued to one of the enterprises, but, by reason of those conditions, have not so accrued, may be included in the profits of that enterprise and taxed accordingly.

Where a Contracting State includes in the profits of an enterprise of that Contracting State—and taxes accordingly—profits on which an enterprise of the other Contracting State has been charged to tax in that other Contracting State and the profits so included are profits which would have accrued to the enterprise of the first-mentioned State if the conditions made between the two enterprises had been those which would have been made between independent enterprises, then that other Contracting State shall make an appropriate adjustment to the amount of the tax charged therein on those profits. In determining such adjustment, due regard shall be had to the other provisions of this Agreement and the competent authorities of the Contracting States shall if necessary consult each other.

Article 10 Dividends

Dividends paid by a company which is a resident of a Contracting State to a resident of the other Contracting State may be taxed in that other Contracting State.

However, such dividends may also be taxed in the Contracting State of which the company paying the dividends is a resident and according to the laws of that State, but if the beneficial owner of the dividends is a resident of the other Contracting State, the tax so charged shall not exceed:

5% of the gross amount of the dividends if the beneficial owner is a company (other than a partnership) which holds directly at least 25% of the capital of the company paying the dividends;

10% of the gross amount of the dividends in all other cases.

This paragraph shall not affect the taxation of the company in respect of the profits out of which the dividends are paid.

The term "dividends" as used in this Article means income from shares or other rights, not being debt-claims, participating in profits, as well as income from other corporate rights which is subjected to the same taxation treatment as income from shares by the laws of the Contracting State of which the company making the distribution is a resident.

The provisions of paragraphs 1 and 2 shall not apply if the beneficial owner of the dividends, being a resident of a Contracting State, carries on business in the other Contracting State of which the company paying the dividends is a resident, through a permanent establishment situated therein, or performs in that other Contracting State independent personal services from a fixed base situated therein, and the holding in respect of which the dividends are paid is effectively connected with such permanent establishment or fixed base. In such case the provisions of Article 7 or Article 14, as the case may be, shall apply.

Where a company which is a resident of a Contracting State derives profits or income from the other Contracting State, that other Contracting State may not impose any tax on the dividends paid by the company, except insofar as such dividends are paid to a resident of that other Contracting State or insofar as the holding in respect of which the dividends are paid is effectively connected with a permanent establishment or a fixed base situated in that other Contracting State, nor subject the company's undistributed profits to a tax on the company's undistributed profits even if the dividends paid or the undistributed profits consist wholly or partly of profits or income arising in that other Contracting State.

The provision of this Article shall not apply if it was the main purpose or one of the main purposes of any person concerned with the creation or assignment of the shares or other rights in respect of which the dividend is paid to take advantage of this Article by means of that creation or assignment.

Article 11 Interest

Interest arising in a Contracting State and paid to a resident of the other Contracting State may be taxed in that other Contracting State.

However, such interest may also be taxed in the Contracting State in which it arises, and according to the laws of that Contracting State, but if the beneficial owner of the interest is a resident of the other Contracting State, the tax so charged shall not exceed 10% of the gross amount of the interest. The competent authorities of the Contracting States shall by mutual agreement settle the mode of application of this limitation.

Notwithstanding the provisions of paragraph 2, interest arising in a Contracting State and derived by the Government of the other Contracting State or a political subdivision or a local authority thereof, the Central Bank of that other Contracting State or any agency of that Government, or by any other resident of that other Contracting State with respect to debt-claims of that resident which are financed, guaranteed or insured by the Government of that other Contracting State or a political subdivision or a local authority thereof, the Central Bank of that other Contracting State or any agency of that Government, shall be exempt from tax in the first-mentioned Contracting State.

The term "interest" as used in this Article means income from debt-claims of every kind, whether or not secured by mortgage, and whether or not carrying a right to participate in the debtor's profits, and in particular income from government securities and income from bonds or debentures, including premiums and prizes attaching to such securities, bonds or debentures.

Penalty charges for late payment shall not be regarded as interest for the purpose of this Article.

The provisions of paragraphs 1 and 2 shall not apply if the beneficial owner of the interest, being a resident of a Contracting State, carries on business in the other Contracting State in which the interest arises, through a permanent establishment situated therein, or performs in that other Contracting State independent personal services from a fixed base situated therein, and the debt-claim in respect of which the interest is paid is effectively connected with such permanent establishment or fixed base. In such case the provisions of Article 7 or Article 14, as the case may be, shall apply.

Interest shall be deemed to arise in a Contracting State when the payer of interest is the Government of that Contracting State, a political subdivision or a local authority or a resident of that Contracting State. Where, however, the person paying the interest, whether he is a resident of a Contracting State or not, has in a Contracting State a permanent establishment or a fixed base in connection with which the indebtedness on which the interest is paid was incurred, and such interest is borne by such permanent establishment or fixed base, then such interest shall be deemed to arise in the Contracting State in which the permanent establishment or fixed base is situated.

Where, by reason of a special relationship between the payer of interest and the beneficial owner or between both of them and some other person, the amount of the interest, having regard to the debt-claim for which it is paid, exceeds the amount which would have been agreed upon by the payer and the beneficial owner in the absence of such relationship, the provisions of this Article shall apply only to the last-mentioned amount. In such case, the excess part of the payments shall remain taxable according to the laws of each Contracting State, due regard being had to the other provisions of this Agreement.

The provision of this Article shall not apply if it was the main purpose or one of the main purposes of any person concerned with the creation or assignment of the debt-claim in respect of which the interest is paid to take advantage of this Article by means of that creation or assignment.

Article 12 Royalties

Royalties arising in a Contracting State and paid to a resident of the other Contracting State may be taxed in that other Contracting State.

However, such royalties may also be taxed in the Contracting State in which they arise and according to the laws of that State, but if the beneficial owner of the royalties is a resident of the other Contracting State, the tax so charged shall not exceed:

in the case of royalties referred to in sub-paragraph a) of paragraph 3, 10% of the gross amount of the royalties; and.

in the case of royalties referred to in sub-paragraph b) of paragraph 3, 10% of the adjusted amount of the royalties. For the purpose of this sub-paragraph "the adjusted amount" means 70% of the gross amount of the royalties.

The competent authorities of the Contracting States shall by mutual agreement settle the mode of application of these limitations.

The term "royalties" as used in this Article means:

payments of any kind received as a consideration for the use of, or the right to use, any copyright of literary, artistic or scientific work including cinematograph films, or films or tapes for radio or television broadcasting, any patent, trade mark, design or model, plan, secret formula or process, or for information (know-how) concerning industrial, commercial or scientific experience; and payments of any kind received as a consideration for the use of, or the right to use, industrial, commercial, or scientific equipment.

The provisions of paragraphs 1 and 2 shall not apply if the beneficial owner of the royalties, being a resident of a Contracting State, carries on business in the other Contracting State in which the royalties arise, through a permanent establishment situated therein, or performs in that other Contracting State independent personal services from a fixed base situated therein, and the right or property in respect of which the royalties are paid is effectively connected with such permanent establishment or fixed base. In such case the provisions of Article 7 or Article 14, as the case may be, shall apply.

Royalties shall be deemed to arise in a Contracting State when the payer of royalties is the Government of that Contracting State or a political subdivision or a local authority thereof or a resident of that Contracting State. Where, however, the person paying the royalties, whether he is a resident of a Contracting State or not, has in a Contracting State a permanent establishment or a fixed base in connection with which the liability to pay the royalties was incurred, and such royalties are borne by such permanent establishment or fixed base, then such royalties shall be deemed to arise in the Contracting State in which the permanent establishment or fixed base is situated.

Where, by reason of a special relationship between the payer of royalties and the beneficial owner or between both of them and some other person, the amount of the royalties, having regard to the use, right or information for which they are paid, exceeds the amount which would have been agreed upon by the payer and the beneficial owner in the absence of such relationship, the provisions of this Article shall apply only to the last-mentioned amount. In such case, the excess part of the payments shall remain taxable according to the laws of each Contracting State, due regard being had to the other provisions of this Agreement.

The provisions of this Article shall not apply if it was the main purpose or one of the main purposes of any person concerned with the creation or assignment of the right in respect of which the royalties are paid to take advantage of this Article by means of that creation or assignment.

Article 13 Capital Gains

Gains derived by a resident of a Contracting State from the alienation of immovable property referred to in Article 6 and situated in the other Contracting State may be taxed in that other State.

Gains from the alienation of movable property forming part of the business property of a permanent establishment which an enterprise of a Contracting State has in the other Contracting State or of movable property pertaining to a fixed base available to a resident of a Contracting State in the other Contracting State for the purpose of performing independent personal services, including such gains from the alienation of such a permanent establishment (alone or with the whole enterprise) or of such a fixed base, may be taxed in that other State.

Gains derived by an enterprise from the alienation of ships or aircraft operated in international traffic by the enterprise, or of containers used in international traffic, or of movable property pertaining to the operation or use of such ships, aircraft or containers, shall be taxable only in the State in which the place of effective management of the enterprise is situated.

Gains derived by a resident of a Contracting State from the alienation of shares deriving more than 50% of their value directly or indirectly from immovable property situated in the other Contracting State may be taxed in that other State.

Gains derived by a resident of a Contracting State from the alienation of shares in a company which is a resident of the other Contracting State may be taxed in that other State if the recipient of the gain, at any time during the 12 month period preceding such alienation, had a participation, directly or indirectly, of at least 25% in the capital of that company.

Gains from the alienation of any property, other than that referred to in paragraphs 1 to 5, shall be taxable only in the Contracting State of which the alienator is a resident.

Article 14 Independent Personal Services

Income derived by a resident of a Contracting State in respect of professional services or other activities of an independent character shall be taxable only in that Contracting State except in one of the following circumstances, when such income may also be taxed in the other Contracting State:

if he has a fixed base regularly available to him in the other Contracting State for the purpose of performing his activities; in that case, only so much of the income as is attributable to that fixed base may be taxed in that other Contracting State;
if his stay in the other Contracting State is for a period or periods amounting to or exceeding in the aggregate 183 days in any twelve month period commencing or ending in the fiscal year concerned; in that case, only so much of the income as is derived from his activities performed in that other State may be taxed in that other State.

The term "professional services" includes, especially, independent scientific, literary, artistic, educational or teaching activities as well as the independent activities of physicians, lawyers, engineers, architects, dentists and accountants.

Article 15 Dependent Personal Services

Subject to the provisions of Articles 16, 18 and 19, salaries, wages and other similar remuneration derived by a resident of a Contracting State in respect of an employment shall be taxable only in that Contracting State unless the employment is exercised in the other Contracting State. If the employment is so exercised, such remuneration as is derived therefrom may be taxed in that other Contracting State.

Notwithstanding the provisions of paragraph 1, remuneration derived by a resident of a Contracting State in respect of an employment exercised in the other Contracting State shall be taxable only in the first-mentioned Contracting State if:

the recipient is present in the other State for a period or periods not exceeding in the aggregate 183 days in any twelve month period commencing or ending in the fiscal year concerned; and.

the remuneration is paid by, or on behalf of, an employer who is not a resident of that other Contracting State, and the remuneration is not borne by a permanent establishment or a fixed base which the employer has in that other Contracting State.

Notwithstanding the preceding provisions of this Article, remuneration derived in respect of an employment exercised aboard a ship or aircraft operated in international traffic may be taxed in the Contracting State in which the place of effective management of the enterprise is situated.

Article 16 Directors' Fees

Directors' fees and other similar payments derived by a resident of a Contracting State in his capacity as a member of the board of directors of a company which is a resident of the other Contracting State may be taxed in that other Contracting State.

Article 17 Artistes and Athletes

Notwithstanding the provisions of Articles 14 and 15, income derived by a resident of a Contracting State as an entertainer, such as a theatre, motion picture, radio or television artiste, or a musician, or as an athlete, from his personal activities as such exercised in the other Contracting State, may be taxed in that other Contracting State.

Where income in respect of personal activities exercised by an entertainer or an athlete in his capacity as such, accrues not to the entertainer or athlete himself but to another person, that income may, notwithstanding the provisions of Articles 7, 14 and 15, be taxed in the Contracting State in which the activities of the entertainer or athlete are exercised.

Notwithstanding the provisions of paragraphs 1 and 2, income derived by entertainers or athletes who are residents of a Contracting State from the activities exercised in the other Contracting State under a plan of cultural exchange between the Governments of both Contracting States, shall be exempted from tax in other Contracting State.

Article 18 Pensions and Social Security Payments

Subject to the provisions of paragraph 2 of Article 19, pensions and other similar remuneration paid to a resident of a Contracting State in consideration of past employment shall be taxable only in that Contracting State.

Notwithstanding the provisions of paragraph 1, pensions paid and other similar payments made under a public welfare scheme of the social security system by the Government of a Contracting State or a political subdivision or a local authority thereof shall be taxable only in that Contracting State.

Notwithstanding the provisions of paragraph 1 of this Article, pensions and other similar remuneration arising in a Contracting State and paid to a resident of the other Contracting State, whether in consideration of past employment or not, may be taxed in the first-mentioned Contracting State where:

contributions paid by the beneficiary to the pension scheme were deducted from the beneficiary's taxable income in the first-mentioned Contracting State under the law of that State; or.

contributions paid by an employer to the pension scheme were not taxable income for the beneficiary in the first-mentioned Contracting State under the law of that State.

The term "beneficiary" as used in this Article is an individual who is entitled to receive payments from the pension scheme.

Article 19 Remuneration and Pensions in Respect of Government Service

Remuneration, other than a pension, paid by the Government of a Contracting State or a political subdivision or a local authority thereof to an individual in respect of services rendered to that Government of that Contracting State or a local authority thereof, in the discharge of functions of a governmental nature shall be taxable only in that Contracting State.

However, such remuneration shall be taxable only in the other Contracting State if the services are rendered in that other Contracting State and the individual is a resident of that other Contracting State who:

is a national of that other Contracting State; or.

did not become a resident of that other Contracting State solely for the purpose of rendering the services.

Any pension paid by, or out of funds created by the Government of a Contracting State or a political subdivision or a local authority thereof to an individual in respect of services rendered to the Government of that Contracting State or a political subdivision or a local authority thereof shall be taxable only in that Contracting State.

However, such pension shall be taxable only in the other Contracting State if the individual is a resident of, and a national of, that other Contracting State.

The provisions of Articles 15, 16, 17 and 18 shall apply to remuneration and pensions in respect of services rendered in connection with a business carried on by the Government of a Contracting State or a political subdivision or a local authority thereof.

Article 20 Students

Payments which a student who is or was immediately before visiting a Contracting State a resident of the other Contracting State and who is present in the first-mentioned State solely for the purpose of his education receives for the purpose of his maintenance or education shall not be taxed in that State, provided that such payments arise from sources outside that State.

Article 21 Other Income

Items of income beneficially owned by a resident of a Contracting State, wherever arising, not dealt with in the foregoing Articles of this Agreement shall be taxable only in that State.

The provisions of paragraph 1 shall not apply to income, other than income from immovable property as defined in paragraph 2 of Article 6, if the beneficial owner of such income, being a resident of a Contracting State, carries on business in the other Contracting State through a permanent establishment situated therein, or performs in that other State independent personal services from a fixed base situated therein, and the right or property in respect of which the income is paid is effectively connected with such permanent establishment or fixed base. In such case the provisions of Article 7 or Article 14, as the case may be, shall apply.

Where, by reason of a special relationship between the resident referred to in paragraph 1 and some other person, or between both of them and some third person, the amount of the income referred to in that paragraph exceeds the amount (if any) which would have been agreed upon between them in the absence of such a relationship, the provisions of this Article shall apply only to the last-mentioned amount. In such a case, the excess part of the income shall remain taxable according to the laws of each Contracting State, due regard being had to the other applicable provisions of this Agreement.

The provisions of this Article shall not apply if it was the main purpose or one of the main purposes of any person concerned with the creation or assignment of the rights in respect of which the income is paid to take advantage of this Article by means of that creation or assignment.

Article 22 Methods for Elimination of Double Taxation

In China, in accordance with the provisions of the law of China, double taxation shall be eliminated as follows.

Where a resident of China derives income from Denmark, the amount of tax on that income payable in Denmark in accordance with the provisions of this Agreement may be credited against the Chinese tax imposed on that resident. The amount of the credit, however, shall not exceed the amount of the Chinese tax on that income computed in accordance with the taxation laws and regulations of China.

Where the income derived from Denmark is dividend paid by a company which is a resident of Denmark to a company which is a resident of China and which owns not less than 20% of the shares of the company paying the dividend, the credit shall take into account the tax paid to Denmark by the company paying the dividend in respect of its income.

In Denmark, double taxation shall be avoided as follows:

Subject to the provisions of sub-paragraph c), where a resident of Denmark derives income which, in accordance with the provisions of this Agreement, may be taxed in China, Denmark shall allow as a deduction from the tax on the income of that resident, an amount equal to the income tax paid in China;

Such deduction shall not, however, exceed that part of the income tax, as computed before the deduction is given, which is attributable to the income which may be taxed in China;

Where a resident of Denmark derives income which, in accordance with the provisions of this Agreement, shall be taxable only in China, Denmark may include this income in the tax base, but shall allow as a deduction from the income tax that part of the income tax which is attributable to the income derived from China.

Article 23 Miscellaneous Rule

Nothing in this Agreement shall prejudice the right of each Contracting State to apply its domestic laws and measures concerning the prevention of tax evasion and avoidance, whether or not described as such, insofar as they do not give rise to taxation contrary to this Agreement.

Article 24 Non-discrimination

Nationals of a Contracting State shall not be subjected in the other Contracting State to any taxation or any requirement connected therewith, which is other or more burdensome than the taxation and connected requirements to which nationals of that other Contracting State in the same circumstances are or may be subjected. This provision shall, notwithstanding the provisions of Article 1, also apply to persons who are not residents of one or both of the Contracting States.

The taxation on a permanent establishment which an enterprise of a Contracting State has in the other Contracting State shall not be less favourably levied in that other Contracting State than the taxation levied on enterprises of that other Contracting State carrying on the same activities. This provision shall not be construed as obliging a Contracting State to grant to residents of the other Contracting State any personal allowances, reliefs and reductions for taxation purposes on account of civil status or family responsibilities which it grants to its own residents.

Except where the provisions of paragraph 1 of Article 9, paragraphs 7 or 8 of Article 11, paragraphs 6 or 7 of Article 12 or paragraphs 3 or 4 of Article 21 apply, interest, royalties and other disbursements paid by an enterprise of a Contracting State to a resident of the other Contracting State shall, for the purpose of determining the taxable profits of such enterprise, be deductible under the same conditions as if they had been paid to a resident of the first-mentioned State.

Enterprises of a Contracting State, the capital of which is wholly or partly owned or controlled, directly or indirectly, by one or more residents of the other Contracting State, shall not be subjected in the first-mentioned Contracting State to any taxation or any requirement connected therewith which is other or more burdensome than the taxation and connected requirements to which other similar enterprises of the first-mentioned Contracting State are or may be subjected.

The provisions of this Article shall, notwithstanding the provisions of Article 2, apply to taxes of every kind.

Article 25 Mutual Agreement Procedure

Where a person considers that the actions of one or both of the Contracting States result or will result for him in taxation not in accordance with the provisions of this Agreement, he may, irrespective of the remedies provided by the domestic law of those Contracting States, present his case to the competent authority of the Contracting State of which he is a resident or, if his case comes under paragraph 1 of Article 24, to the Contracting State of which he is a national. The case must be presented within three years from the first notification of the action resulting in taxation not in accordance with the provisions of the Agreement.

The competent authority shall endeavour, if the objection appears to it to be justified and if it is not itself able to arrive at a satisfactory solution, to resolve the case by mutual agreement with the competent authority of the other Contracting State, with a view to the avoidance of taxation which is not in accordance with this Agreement. Any agreement reached shall be implemented notwithstanding any time limits in the domestic law of the Contracting States.

The competent authorities of the Contracting States shall endeavour to resolve by mutual agreement any difficulties or doubts arising as to the interpretation or application of this Agreement. They may also consult together for the elimination of double taxation in cases not provided for in this Agreement.

The competent authorities of the Contracting States may communicate with each other directly for the purpose of reaching an agreement in the sense of paragraphs 2 and 3. When it seems advisable for the purpose of reaching an agreement the competent authorities of the Contracting States may meet together for an oral exchange of opinions.

Article 26 Exchange of Information

The competent authorities of the Contracting States shall exchange such information as is foreseeably relevant for carrying out the provisions of this Agreement or to the administration or enforcement of the domestic laws concerning taxes of every kind and description imposed on behalf of the Contracting States, or of their political subdivisions or local authorities, insofar as the taxation thereunder is not contrary to the Agreement, in particular, to prevent fraud and to facilitate the administration of statutory provisions against legal avoidance. The exchange of information is not restricted by Articles 1 and 2.

Any information received under paragraph 1 by a Contracting State shall be treated as secret in the same manner as information obtained under the domestic laws of that State and shall be disclosed only to persons or authorities (including courts and administrative bodies) concerned with the assessment or collection of, the enforcement or prosecution in respect of, or the determination of appeals in relation to, the taxes referred to in paragraph 1, or the oversight of the above. Such persons or authorities shall use the information only for such purposes. They may disclose the information in public court proceedings or in judicial decisions.

In no case shall the provisions of paragraph 1 and 2 be construed so as to impose on a Contracting State the obligation:

to carry out administrative measures at variance with the laws and administrative practice of that or of the other Contracting State;

to supply information which is not obtainable under the laws or in the normal course of the administration of that or of the other Contracting State;

to supply information which would disclose any trade, business, industrial, commercial or professional secret or trade process, or information the disclosure of which would be contrary to public policy.

If information is requested by a Contracting State in accordance with this Article, the other Contracting State shall use its information gathering measures to obtain the requested information, even though that other State may not need such information for its own tax purposes. The obligation contained in the preceding sentence is subject to the limitations of paragraph 3 of this Article but in no case shall such limitations be construed to permit a Contracting State to decline to supply information solely because it has no domestic interest in such information.

In no case shall the provisions of paragraph 3 be construed to permit a Contracting State to decline to supply information solely because the information is held by a bank, other financial institution, nominee or person acting in an agency or a fiduciary capacity or because it relates to ownership interests in a person.

Article 27 Diplomatic Agents and Consular Officers
Nothing in this Agreement shall affect the fiscal privileges of diplomatic agents or consular officers under the general rules of international law or under the provisions of special agreements.

Article 28 Entry Into Force
The Governments of the Contracting States shall notify each other through diplomatic channels that they have completed the internal legal procedures necessary for the entry into force of this Agreement.

This Agreement shall enter into force on the thirtieth day upon the receipt of the latter notification referred to in paragraph 1 and its provisions shall have effect in both Contracting States:

in respect of taxes withheld at source, on income derived on or after the first day of January in the calendar year next following the year in which the Agreement enters into force;
in respect of other taxes on income, for taxes chargeable for any tax year beginning on or after the first day of January in the calendar year next following the year in which the Agreement enters into force.

The Agreement between the Government of the People's Republic of China and the Government of the Kingdom of Denmark for the Avoidance of Double Taxation and the Prevention of Fiscal Evasion with Respect to Taxes on Income, signed at Beijing on March 26th 1986, shall cease to have effect with respect to taxes to which this Agreement applies in accordance with paragraph 2 of this Article.

Article 29 Termination
This Agreement shall remain in force until terminated by a Contracting State. Either Contracting State may terminate the Agreement at any time after 5 years from the date on which the Agreement enters into force, by giving a notice of termination through diplomatic channels at least six months in advance.

In such event, the Agreement shall cease to have effect:

in respect of taxes withheld at the source on or after the first day of January next following the date of termination specified in the notice of termination;

in respect of other taxes for any taxable year beginning on or after the first day of January next following the date of termination specified in the notice of termination.

IN WITNESS WHEREOF the undersigned, duly authorized thereto by their respective Governments, have signed this Agreement.

DONE in duplicate at on the day of,, each in the Chinese, Danish and English languages, all texts being equally authentic, except in the case of doubt, when the English text shall prevail.

For the Government of the People's Republic of China.

For the Government of the Kingdom of Denmark.

Protocol

At the moment of signing the Agreement between the Government of the People's Republic of China and the Government of the Kingdom of Denmark for the Avoidance of Double Taxation and the Prevention of Fiscal evasion with Respect to Taxes on Income, the undersigned have agreed that the following provisions shall form an integral part of the Agreement.

When applying the Agreement with respect to the air transport consortium, Scandinavian Airlines System (SAS), the provisions of paragraph 1 of Article 8 and paragraph 3 of Article 13 shall apply only to such part of its profits or capital gains as corresponds to the participation held in that consortium by the Danish partner of Scandinavian Airlines System (SAS).

With respect to Article 11, the term "Central Bank" refers to the People's Bank of China and the National Bank of Denmark, and the term "any agency of that Government" refers to:

in China:
the China Development Bank;
the Agricultural Development Bank of China;
the Export–Import Bank of China;
the National Council for Social Security Fund;
the China Export & Credit Insurance Corporation;
China Investment Corporation, and
any institution wholly owned by the Government of China as may be agreed from time to time between the competent authorities of the Contracting States;
in Denmark:
Industrialisation Fund for Developing Countries (IFU).
Danish Export Credit Fund (EKF).
Danish Fund for Growth (Vaekstfonden).
any institution wholly owned by the Government of Denmark as may be agreed from time to time between the competent authorities of the Contracting States.

IN WITNESS whereof the undersigned, duly authorised thereto, have signed this Protocol.

DONE in duplicate at on the day of,, each in the Chinese, Danish and English languages, all texts being equally authentic, except in the case of doubt, when the English text shall prevail.

For the Government of the People's Republic of China.

For the Government of the Kingdom of Denmark.

Finland

Finland, officially the Republic of Finland, is a state in Northern Europe. Finland borders Sweden to the west, Russia to the east, Norway to the north, and is defined by the Gulf of Bothnia to the west, and the Gulf of Finland of the Baltic Sea across Estonia to the south. Finland's capital and largest city is Helsinki.

Finnish is the majority ethnic group, while other Europeans, Asians, and Africans constitutes 8% of the total population.

The official and predominant spoken languages are Finnish and Swedish. Recognized minority languages are Sámi, Karelian, Finnish Kalo, Finnish Sign Language, and Finland-Swedish Sign Language.

Finland is a unitary parliamentary republic. The Suomen perustuslaki is the constitution regulating the political system, in force since 1917, with its current draft being enacted in 2000. The Eduskunta exerts the legislative power forming the parliament. The Eduskunta is elected through direct elections using the open list proportional representation system.

Executive power is vested in the Prime Minister and his or her cabinet. The Prime Minister is appointed by the President of the Republic after being elected by the party or coalition with the parliamentary majority in the Eduskunta.

Finland has a civil law system based on Roman law. The Korkein Oikeus acts as Supreme Court, managing constitutional matters, with judicial review powers.

Finland is a unitary state, constituted by 19 regions, 70 sub- regions, and 309 municipalities.

Finland has been part of the European Union since 1995.

Category	Value
Population (mln persons)	5.518
Currency	Euro

Source International Monetary Fund, year 2019

Finland follows Denmark as the sixth economy of Northern Europe, with a GDP valued 269.7 billion USD in 2019, and has a population of about 5.5 million people.

© The Author(s), under exclusive license to Springer Nature Singapore Pte Ltd. 2022

L. Riccardi and G. Riccardi, *China–Europe Tax Treaties*,
https://doi.org/10.1007/978-981-19-3563-3_13

It ranks 10th in Europe for GDP per capita. Finland enjoys low inflation (1.1%), while unemployment is over 6% (6.7%). Finland ranked 9 out of 43 in the 2020 Doing Business ranking, scoring more than 80 (80.2). Finland imposes a CIT of 20%. Finland records a trade balance slightly in deficit, 167 million USD.

GDP and local economy	
GDP current prices (billion USD)	269.7
GDP per capita (USD)	48,869
GDP growth (%)	1.0
Inflation (%)	1.1
Unemployment (%)	6.7
General government total expenditure (% of GDP)	53.3
General government gross debt (% of GDP)	59.3
Doing business score 2020	80.2

Source International Monetary Fund and UNCTAD, year 2019

Foreign direct investment	
FDI outstock (million USD)	130,051
FDI instock (million USD)	78,353

Source UNCTAD, year 2019

Trade	
Imports (million USD)	73,500
Exports (million USD)	73,333
Trade balance (million USD)	−167

Source International Monetary Fund and UNCTAD, year 2019

Main import–export	
First import by category	Machinery, nuclear reactors, boilers
Second import by category	Mineral fuels, oils, distillation products
First export by category	Machinery, nuclear reactors, boilers
Second export by category	Paper and paperboard, articles of pulp, paper and board

Source United Nations COMTRADE, year 2020

The legal bases for taxation are established in the constitution. Finland imposes individual income tax, property sales taxes, capital gains, corporate income tax, and value added tax. Progressivity is guaranteed by a system with different bands and various deductions.

Taxes	
Company income tax (%)	20
Top individual income tax (%)	31[1]
Value added tax or sales tax (%)	24
Reduced value added tax or sales tax (%)	10/14

Source RsA Asia report, year 2021
Note Rates of 30–34% apply on income from capital investment. A municipal tax applies with rates of 16.5–23.5%

- Economic relation with China

Finland records a trade surplus to China of 1.24 billion USD in 2020. "Pulp of wood, fibrous cellulosic material, waste" is the first export category, valued 1.04 billion USD, followed by "Machinery, nuclear reactors, boilers". "Electrical, electronic equipment" is the first import category, valued 0.7 billion USD. Finland is not part of the Belt and Road Initiative. Concerning double taxation, in 1986 Finland and China signed their DTA, which had come into force in 1987. In May 2010 the parties have signed a new agreement, which has come into force in November of the same year.

Category	Value
Belt road	NO

Source UNCTAD, year 2021

Import from China	
Import from China (billion USD)	2.95
First import category from China	Electrical, electronic equipment
First Import value (billion USD)	0.698
Second import category from China	Machinery, nuclear reactors, boilers
Second import value (billion USD)	0.562

Source United Nations COMTRADE, year 2020

Export to China	
Export to China (billion USD)	4.19
First export category towards China	Pulp of wood, fibrous cellulosic material, waste
First export value (billion USD)	1.04
Second export category towards China	Machinery, nuclear reactors, boilers
Second export value (billion USD)	0.664

Source United Nations COMTRADE, year 2020

Trade balance	
Trade balance (billion USD)	1.24

Source United Nations COMTRADE, year 2020

Double tax agreement	
DTA effective date	2010.11.25
Dividends (%)	5–10
Interest (%)	0–10
Royalties (%)	7–10

Source State Administration of Taxation of China, year 2021

Title AGREEMENT BETWEEN THE GOVERNMENT OF THE PEOPLE'S REPUBLIC OF CHINA AND THE GOVERNMENT OF THE REPUBLIC OF FINLAND FOR THE AVOIDANCE OF DOUBLE TAXATION AND THE PREVENTION OF FISCAL EVASION WITH RESPECT TO TAXES ON INCOME.

Treaty Text

The Government of the People's Republic of China and the Government of the Republic of Finland,

Desiring to conclude an Agreement for the avoidance of double taxation and the prevention of fiscal evasion with respect to taxes on income,

Have agreed as follows:

Article 1 Persons Covered

This Agreement shall apply to persons who are residents of one or both of the Contracting States.

Article 2 Taxes Covered

This Agreement shall apply to taxes on income imposed on behalf of a Contracting State or its local authorities, irrespective of the manner in which they are levied.

There shall be regarded as taxes on income all taxes imposed on total income, or on elements of income, including taxes on gains from the alienation of movable or immovable property, as well as taxes on capital appreciation.

The existing taxes to which the Agreement shall apply are:

in China:
the individual income tax;
the enterprise income tax; (hereinafter referred to as "Chinese tax");
in Finland:
the state income taxes (valtion tuloverot; de statliga inkomstskatterna);
the corporate income tax (yhteisöjen tulovero; inkomstskatten för samfund);

the communal tax (kunnallisvero; kommunalskatten);
the church tax (kirkollisvero; kyrkoskatten);
the tax withheld at source from interest (korkotulon lähdevero; källskatten på ränteinkomst); and
taxwithheld at source fromnon-residents' income (rajoitetusti verovelvollisen lähdevero; källskatten för begränsat skattskyldig);
(hereinafter referred to as "Finnish tax").

The Agreement shall apply also to any identical or substantially similar taxes that are imposed after the date of signature of the Agreement in addition to, or in place of, the existing taxes. The competent authorities of the Contracting States shall notify each other of any significant changes which have been made in their taxation laws.

Article 3 General Definitions
For the purposes of this Agreement, unless the context otherwise requires:

the term "China" means the People's Republic of China; when used in a geographical sense, it means all the territory of the People's Republic of China, including its territorial sea, in which the Chinese laws relating to taxation apply, and any area beyond its territorial sea, within which the People's Republic of China has sovereign rights of exploration for and exploitation of resources of the sea-bed and its sub-soil and superjacent water resources in accordance with international law and its internal law;
the term "Finland" means the Republic of Finland and, when used in a geographical sense, means the territory of the Republic of Finland, and any area adjacent to the territorial waters of the Republic of Finland within which, under the laws of Finland and in accordance with international law, the rights of Finland with respect to the exploration for and exploitation of the natural resources of the sea bed and its sub soil and of the superjacent waters may be exercised;
the term "person" includes an individual, a company and any other body of persons;
the term "company" means any body corporate or any entity that is treated as a body corporate for tax purposes;
the terms "enterprise of a Contracting State" and "enterprise of the other Contracting State" mean, respectively, an enterprise carried on by a resident of a Contracting State and an enterprise carried on by a resident of the other Contracting State;
the term "international traffic" means any transport by a ship or aircraft operated by an enterprise of a Contracting State, except when the ship or aircraft is operated solely between places in the other Contracting State;
the term "competent authority" means, in the case of China, the State Administration of Taxation or its authorized representative, and in the case of Finland, the Ministry of Finance, its authorised representative or the authority which, by the Ministry of Finance, is designated as competent authority;
the term "national", in relation to a Contracting State, means:

any individual possessing the nationality of a Contracting State; and.
any legal person, partnership or association deriving its status as such from the laws in force in a Contracting State.

As regards the application of the Agreement at any time by a Contracting State, any term not defined therein shall, unless the context otherwise requires, have the meaning which it has at that time under the law of that State for the purposes of the taxes to which the Agreement applies, any meaning under the applicable tax laws of that State prevailing over a meaning given to the term under other laws of that State.

Article 4 Resident

For the purposes of this Agreement, the term "resident of a Contracting State" means any person who, under the laws of that State, is liable to tax therein by reason of his domicile, residence, place of incorporation (registration), place of effective management or any other criterion of a similar nature, and also includes that State and any statutory body or local authority thereof. This term, however, does not include any person who is liable to tax in that State in respect only of income from sources in that State situated therein.

Where by reason of the provisions of paragraph 1 an individual is a resident of both Contracting States, then his status shall be determined as follows:

he shall be deemed to be a resident only of the State in which he has a permanent home available to him; if he has a permanent home available to him in both States, he shall be deemed to be a resident only of the State with which his personal and economic relations are closer (centre of vital interests);
if the State in which he has his centre of vital interests cannot be determined, or if he has not a permanent home available to him in either State, he shall be deemed to be a resident only of the State in which he has an habitual abode;
if he has an habitual abode in both States or in neither of them, he shall be deemed to be a resident only of the State of which he is a national;
if he is a national of both States or of neither of them, the competent authorities of the Contracting States shall settle the question by mutual agreement.

Where by reason of the provisions of paragraph 1 a person other than an individual is a resident of both Contracting States, then it shall be deemed to be a resident only of the State in which its place of effective management is situated.

Article 5 Permanent Establishment

For the purposes of this Agreement, the term "permanent establishment" means a fixed place of business through which the business of an enterprise is wholly or partly carried on.

The term "permanent establishment" includes especially:

a place of management;
a branch;
an office;

a factory;
a workshop; and.
a mine, an oil or gas well, a quarry or any other place of extraction of natural resources.

The term "permanent establishment" likewise encompasses:

A building site, or construction, assembly or installation project or supervisory activities in connection therewith, but only if such site, project or activities last more than 6 months;

The furnishing of services, including consultancy services, by an enterprise through employees or other personnel engaged for such purpose, but only if activities of that nature continue (for the same or a connected project) within a Contracting State for a period or periods aggregating more than 183 days within any twelve-month period.

Notwithstanding the preceding provisions of this Article, the term "permanent establishment" shall be deemed not to include:

the use of facilities solely for the purpose of storage, display or delivery of goods or merchandise belonging to the enterprise;
the maintenance of a stock of goods or merchandise belonging to the enterprise solely for the purpose of storage, display or delivery;
the maintenance of a stock of goods or merchandise belonging to the enterprise solely for the purpose of processing by another enterprise;
the maintenance of a fixed place of business solely for the purpose of purchasing goods or merchandise or of collecting information, for the enterprise;
the maintenance of a fixed place of business solely for the purpose of carrying on, for the enterprise, any other activity of a preparatory or auxiliary character;
the maintenance of a fixed place of business solely for any combination of activities mentioned in sub-paragraphs (a)–(e), provided that the overall activity of the fixed place of business resulting from this combination is of a preparatory or auxiliary character.

Notwithstanding the provisions of paragraphs 1 and 2, where a person—other than an agent of an independent status to whom paragraph 7 applies—is acting in a Contracting State on behalf of an enterprise of the other Contracting State, and has, and habitually exercises, in that Contracting State an authority to conclude contracts in the name of the enterprise, that enterprise shall be deemed to have a permanent establishment in that Contracting State in respect of any activities which that person undertakes for the enterprise, unless the activities of such person are limited to those mentioned in paragraph 4 which, if exercised through a fixed place of business, would not make this fixed place of business a permanent establishment under the provisions of that paragraph.

Notwithstanding the preceding provisions of this Article, an insurance enterprise of a Contracting State shall, except in regard to re-insurance, be deemed to have a permanent establishment in the other Contracting State if it collects premiums in the territory of that other State or insures risks situated therein through a person other than an agent of an independent status to whom paragraph 7 applies.

An enterprise of a Contracting State shall not be deemed to have a permanent establishment in the other Contracting State merely because it carries on business in that other State through a broker, general commission agent or any other agent of an independent status, provided that such persons are acting in the ordinary course of their business. However, when the activities of such an agent are devoted wholly or almost wholly on behalf of that enterprise, he will not be considered an agent of an independent status within the meaning of this paragraph.

The fact that a company which is a resident of a Contracting State controls or is controlled by a company which is a resident of the other Contracting State, or which carries on business in that other State (whether through a permanent establishment or otherwise), shall not of itself constitute either company a permanent establishment of the other.

Article 6 Income from Immovable Property

Income derived by a resident of a Contracting State from immovable property (including income from agriculture or forestry) situated in the other Contracting State may be taxed in that other State.

The term "immovable property" shall have the meaning which it has under the law of the Contracting State in which the property in question is situated. The term shall in any case include property accessory to immovable property, livestock and equipment used in agriculture and forestry, rights to which the provisions of general law respecting landed property apply, usufruct of immovable property and rights to variable or fixed payments as consideration for the working of, or the right to work, mineral deposits, sources and other natural resources; ships and aircraft shall not be regarded as immovable property.

The provisions of paragraph 1 shall apply to income derived from the direct use, letting, or use in any other form of immovable property.

Where the ownership of shares or other corporate rights in a company entitles the owner of such shares or corporate rights to the enjoyment of immovable property held by the company, the income from the direct use, letting, or use in any other form of such right to enjoyment may be taxed in the Contracting State in which the immovable property is situated.

The provisions of paragraphs 1 and 3 shall also apply to the income from immovable property of an enterprise and to income from immovable property used for the performance of independent personal services.

Article 7 Business Profits

The profits of an enterprise of a Contracting State shall be taxable only in that State unless the enterprise carries on business in the other Contracting State through a permanent establishment situated therein. If the enterprise carries on business as aforesaid, the profits of the enterprise may be taxed in the other State, but only so much of them as is attributable to that permanent establishment.

Subject to the provisions of paragraph 3, where an enterprise of a Contracting State carries on business in the other Contracting State through a permanent establishment situated therein, there shall in each Contracting State be attributed to that permanent establishment the profits which it might be expected to make if it were a distinct and separate enterprise engaged in the same or similar activities under the same or similar conditions and dealing wholly independently with the enterprise of which it is a permanent establishment.

In determining the profits of a permanent establishment, there shall be allowed as deductions expenses which are incurred for the purposes of the permanent establishment, including executive and general administrative expenses so incurred, whether in the State in which the permanent establishment is situated or elsewhere.

Insofar as it has been customary in a Contracting State to determine the profits to be attributed to a permanent establishment on the basis of an apportionment of the total profits of the enterprise to its various parts, nothing in paragraph 2 shall preclude that Contracting State from determining the profits to be taxed by such an apportionment as may be customary; the method of apportionment adopted shall, however, be such that the result shall be in accordance with the principles contained in this Article.

No profits shall be attributed to a permanent establishment by reason of the mere purchase by that permanent establishment of goods or merchandise for the enterprise. For the purposes of the preceding paragraphs, the profits to be attributed to the permanent establishment shall be determined by the same method year by year unless there is good and sufficient reason to the contrary.

Where profits include items of income which are dealt with separately in other Articles of this Agreement, then the provisions of those Articles shall not be affected by the provisions of this Article.

Article 8 Shipping and Air Transport

Profits of an enterprise of a Contracting State from the operation of ships or aircraft in international traffic shall be taxable only in that Contracting State.

The provisions of paragraph 1 shall also apply to profits from the participation in a pool, a joint business or an international operating agency.

Article 9 Associated Enterprises

Where

an enterprise of a Contracting State participates directly or indirectly in the management, control or capital of an enterprise of the other Contracting State, or the same persons participate directly or indirectly in the management, control or capital of an enterprise of a Contracting State and an enterprise of the other Contracting State,

and in either case conditions are made or imposed between the two enterprises in their commercial or financial relations which differ from those which would be made between independent enterprises, then any profits which would, but for those conditions, have accrued to one of the enterprises, but, by reason of those conditions, have not so accrued, may be included in the profits of that enterprise and taxed accordingly.

Where a Contracting State includes in the profits of an enterprise of that State—and taxes accordingly—profits on which an enterprise of the other Contracting State has been charged to tax in that other State and the profits so included are profits which would have accrued to the enterprise of the first-mentioned State if the conditions made between the two enterprises had been those which would have been made between independent enterprises, then that other State shall make an appropriate adjustment to the amount of the tax charged therein on those profits, where that other State considers the adjustment justified. In determining such adjustment, due regard shall be had to the other provisions of this Agreement and the competent authorities of the Contracting States shall, if necessary, consult each other.

Article 10 Dividends

Dividends paid by a company which is a resident of a Contracting State to a resident of the other Contracting State may be taxed in that other State.

However, such dividends may also be taxed in the Contracting State of which the company paying the dividends is a resident and according to the laws of that State, but if the beneficial owner of the dividends is a resident of the other Contracting State, the tax so charged shall not exceed:

5% of the gross amount of the dividends if the beneficial owner is a company (other than a partnership) which holds directly at least 25% of the capital of the company paying the dividends;

10% of the gross amount of the dividends in all other cases.

This paragraph shall not affect the taxation of the company in respect of the profits out of which the dividends are paid.

The term "dividends" as used in this Article means income from shares or other rights, not being debt-claims, participating in profits, as well as income from other corporate rights which is subjected to the same taxation treatment as income from shares by the laws of the State of which the company making the distribution is a resident.

The provisions of paragraphs 1 and 2 shall not apply if the beneficial owner of the dividends, being a resident of a Contracting State, carries on business in the other Contracting State of which the company paying the dividends is a resident through a permanent establishment situated therein, or performs in that other State independent personal services from a fixed base situated therein, and the holding in respect of which the dividends are paid is effectively connected with such permanent establishment or fixed base. In such case the provisions of Article 7 or Article 14, as the case may be, shall apply.

Where a company which is a resident of a Contracting State derives profits or income from the other Contracting State, that other State may not impose any tax on the dividends paid by the company, except insofar as such dividends are paid to a resident of that other State or insofar as the holding in respect of which the dividends are paid is effectively connected with a permanent establishment or a fixed base situated in that other State, nor subject the company's undistributed profits to a tax on the company's undistributed profits, even if the dividends paid or the undistributed profits consist wholly or partly of profits or income arising in such other State.

The provision of this Article shall not apply if it was the main purpose or one of the main purposes of any person concerned with the creation or assignment of the shares or other rights in respect of which the dividend is paid to take advantage of this Article by means of that creation or assignment.

Article 11 Interest

Interest arising in a Contracting State and paid to a resident of the other Contracting State may be taxed in that other State.

However, such interest may also be taxed in the Contracting State in which it arises and according to the laws of that State, but if the beneficial owner of the interest is a resident of the other Contracting State, the tax so charged shall not exceed 10% of the gross amount of the interest. The competent authorities of the Contracting States shall by mutual agreement settle the mode of application of this limitation.

Notwithstanding the provisions of paragraph 2, interest arising in a Contracting State and paid to the Government, a local authority, the Central Bank or any institution wholly owned by the Government of the other Contracting State, or paid on loans guaranteed or insured by the Government, a local authority, the Central Bank or any institution wholly owned by the Government of the other Contracting State, shall be exempt from tax in the first-mentioned State.

The term "interest" as used in this Article means income from debt-claims of every kind, whether or not secured by mortgage and whether or not carrying a right to participate in the debtor's profits, and in particular, income from government securities and income from bonds or debentures, including premiums and prizes attaching to such securities, bonds or debentures. Penalty charges for late payment shall not be regarded as interest for the purpose of this Article.

The provisions of paragraphs 1 and 2 shall not apply if the beneficial owner of the interest, being a resident of a Contracting State, carries on business in the other Contracting State in which the interest arises, through a permanent establishment situated therein, or performs in that other State independent personal services from a fixed base situated therein, and the debt-claim in respect of which the interest is paid is effectively connected with such permanent establishment or fixed base. In such case the provisions of Article 7 or Article 14, as the case may be, shall apply.

Interest shall be deemed to arise in a Contracting State when the payer is a resident of that State. Where, however, the person paying the interest, whether he is a resident of a Contracting State or not, has in a Contracting State a permanent establishment or a fixed base in connection with which the indebtedness on which the interest is paid was incurred, and such interest is borne by such permanent establishment or fixed base, then such interest shall be deemed to arise in the State in which the permanent establishment or fixed base is situated.

Where, by reason of a special relationship between the payer and the beneficial owner or between both of them and some other person, the amount of the interest, having regard to the debt-claim for which it is paid, exceeds the amount which would have been agreed upon by the payer and the beneficial owner in the absence of such relationship, the provisions of this Article shall apply only to the last-mentioned amount. In such case, the excess part of the payments shall remain taxable according to the laws of each Contracting State, due regard being had to the other provisions of this Agreement.

The provision of this Article shall not apply if it was the main purpose or one of the main purposes of any person concerned with the creation or assignment of the debt-claim in respect of which the interest is paid to take advantage of this Article by means of that creation or assignment.

Article 12 Royalties

Royalties arising in a Contracting State and beneficially owned by a resident of the other Contracting State may be taxed in that other State.

However, such royalties may also be taxed in the Contracting State in which they arise and according to the laws of that State, but if the beneficial owner of the royalties is a resident of the other Contracting State, the tax so charged shall not exceed 10% of the gross amount of the royalties. The competent authorities of the Contracting States shall by mutual agreement settle the mode of application of this limitation.

The term "royalties" as used in this Article means payments of any kind received as a consideration for the use of, or the right to use, any copyright of literary, artistic or scientific work including cinematograph films, or films or tapes for radio or television broadcasting, any patent, trade mark, design or model, plan, secret formula or process, or for the use of, or the right to use, industrial, commercial, or scientific equipment, or for information concerning industrial, commercial or scientific experience.

The provisions of paragraphs 1 and 2 shall not apply if the beneficial owner of the royalties, being a resident of a Contracting State, carries on business in the other Contracting State in which the royalties arise, through a permanent establishment situated therein, or performs in that other State independent personal services from a fixed base situated therein, and the right or property in respect of which the royalties are paid is effectively connected with such permanent establishment or fixed base. In such case the provisions of Article 7 or Article 14, as the case may be, shall apply.

Royalties shall be deemed to arise in a Contracting State when the payer is a resident of that Contracting State. Where, however, the person paying the royalties, whether he is a resident of a Contracting State or not, has in a Contracting State a permanent establishment or a fixed base in connection with which the liability to pay the royalties was incurred, and such royalties are borne by such permanent establishment or fixed base, then such royalties shall be deemed to arise in the State in which the permanent establishment or fixed base is situated.

Where, by reason of a special relationship between the payer and the beneficial owner or between both of them and some other person, the amount of the royalties, having regard to the use, right or information for which they are paid, exceeds the amount which would have been agreed upon by the payer and the beneficial owner in the absence of such relationship, the provisions of this Article shall apply only to the last-mentioned amount. In such case, the excess part of the payments shall remain taxable according to the laws of each Contracting State, due regard being had to the other provisions of this Agreement.

The provision of this Article shall not apply if it was the main purpose or one of the main purposes of any person concerned with the creation or assignment of the rights in respect of which the royalties are paid to take advantage of this Article by means of that creation or assignment.

Article 13 Capital Gains

Gains derived by a resident of a Contracting State from the alienation of immovable property referred to in Article 6 and situated in the other Contracting State may be taxed in that other State.

Gains from the alienation of movable property forming part of the business property of a permanent establishment which an enterprise of a Contracting State has in the other Contracting State or of movable property pertaining to a fixed base available to a resident of a Contracting State in the other Contracting State for the purpose of performing independent personal services, including such gains from the alienation of such a permanent establishment (alone or with the whole enterprise) or of such a fixed base, may be taxed in that other State.

Gains derived by an enterprise of a Contracting State from the alienation of ships or aircraft operated in international traffic or movable property pertaining to the operation of such ships or aircraft, shall be taxable only in that State.

Gains from the alienation of shares in a company the property of which consists directly or indirectly principally of immovable property situated in a Contracting State may be taxed in that Contracting State.

Gains derived by a resident of a Contracting State from the alienation of shares in a company which is a resident of the other Contracting State may be taxed in that other State if the recipient of the gain, at any time during the 12 month period preceding such alienation, had a participation, directly or indirectly, of at least 25% in the capital of that company.

Gains from the alienation of any property, other than that referred to in paragraphs 1–5, shall be taxable only in the Contracting State of which the alienator is a resident.

Article 14 Independent Personal Services

Income derived by a resident of a Contracting State in respect of professional services or other activities of an independent character shall be taxable only in that State except in the following circumstances, when such income may also be taxed in the other Contracting State:

if he has a fixed base regularly available to him in the other Contracting State for the purpose of performing his activities; in that case, only so much of the income as is attributable to that fixed base may be taxed in that other State; or

if his stay in the other Contracting State is for a period or periods amounting to or exceeding in the aggregate 183 days in any twelve month period commencing or ending in the fiscal year concerned; in that case, only so much of the income as is derived from his activities performed in that other State may be taxed in that other State.

The term “professional services” includes especially independent scientific, literary, artistic, educational or teaching activities as well as the independent activities of physicians, lawyers, engineers, architects, dentists and accountants.

Article 15 Income from Employment

Subject to the provisions of Articles 16, 18, and 19, salaries, wages and other similar remuneration derived by a resident of a Contracting State in respect of an employment shall be taxable only in that State unless the employment is exercised in the other Contracting State. If the employment is so exercised, such remuneration as is derived therefrom may be taxed in that other State.

Notwithstanding the provisions of paragraph 1, remuneration derived by a resident of a Contracting State in respect of an employment exercised in the other Contracting State shall be taxable only in the first-mentioned State if:

the recipient is present in the other State for a period or periods not exceeding in the aggregate 183 days in any twelve-month period commencing or ending in the fiscal year concerned, and

the remuneration is paid by, or on behalf of, an employer who is not a resident of the other State, and

the remuneration is not borne by a permanent establishment or a fixed base which the employer has in the other State.

Notwithstanding the preceding provisions of this Article, remuneration derived in respect of an employment exercised aboard a ship or aircraft operated in international traffic by an enterprise of a Contracting State, may be taxed in that Contracting State.

Article 16 Directors’ Fees

Directors’ fees and other similar payments derived by a resident of a Contracting State in his capacity as a member of the board of directors or any other similar organ of a company which is a resident of the other Contracting State may be taxed in that other State.

Article 17 Artistes and Sportsmen

Notwithstanding the provisions of Articles 7, 14 and 15, income derived by a resident of a Contracting State as an entertainer, such as a theatre, motion picture, radio or television artiste, or a musician, or as a sportsman, from his personal activities as such exercised in the other Contracting State, may be taxed in that other State.

Where income in respect of personal activities exercised by an entertainer or a sportsman in his capacity as such accrues not to the entertainer or sportsman himself but to another person, that income may, notwithstanding the provisions of Articles 7, 14 and 15, be taxed in the Contracting State in which the activities of the entertainer or sportsman are exercised.

Article 18 Pensions

Subject to the provisions of paragraph 2 of Article 19, pensions and other similar remuneration paid to a resident of a Contracting State in consideration of past employment shall be taxable only in that State. Notwithstanding the provisions of paragraph

1, and subject to the provisions of paragraph 2 of Article 19, pensions paid and other similar payments made under the social security legislation or system of a Contracting State or a local authority thereof may be taxed in that State.

Article 19 Government Service

Salaries, wages and other similar remuneration, other than a pension, paid by a Contracting State or a statutory body or a local authority thereof to an individual in respect of services rendered to that State or body or authority, shall be taxable only in that State.

However, such salaries, wages and other similar remuneration shall be taxable only in the other Contracting State if the services are rendered in that State and the individual is a resident of that State who:

is a national of that State; or

did not become a resident of that State solely for the purpose of rendering the services.

Pensions and other similar remuneration paid by, or out of funds created by, a Contracting State or a statutory body or a local authority thereof to an individual in respect of services rendered to that State or body or authority shall be taxable only in that State.

However, such pensions and other similar remuneration shall be taxable only in the other Contracting State if the individual is a resident of, and a national of, that State.

The provisions of Articles 15, 16, 17, and 18 shall apply to salaries, wages, pensions, and other similar remuneration in respect of services rendered in connection with a business carried on by a Contracting State or a statutory body or a local authority thereof.

Article 20 Students

Payments which a student who is or was immediately before visiting a Contracting State a resident of the other Contracting State and who is present in the first-mentioned State solely for the purpose of his education receives for the purpose of his maintenance or education shall not be taxed in that State, provided that such payments arise from sources outside that State.

Article 21 Other Income

Items of income of a resident of a Contracting State, wherever arising, not dealt with in the foregoing Articles of this Agreement shall be taxable only in that State.

The provisions of paragraph 1 shall not apply to income, other than income from immovable property as defined in paragraph 2 of Article 6, if the recipient of such income, being a resident of a Contracting State, carries on business in the other Contracting State through a permanent establishment situated therein, or performs in that other State independent personal services from a fixed base situated therein, and the right or property in respect of which the income is paid is effectively connected with such permanent establishment or fixed base. In such case the provisions of Article 7 or Article 14, as the case may be, shall apply.

Notwithstanding the provisions of paragraphs 1 and 2, items of income of a resident of a Contracting State not dealt with in the foregoing articles of this Agreement and arising in the other Contracting State may also be taxed in the other State.

Article 22 Methods for Elimination Of Double Taxation

In China, in accordance with the provisions of the law of China, double taxation shall be eliminated as follows:

Where a resident of China derives income from Finland, the amount of tax on that income payable in Finland in accordance with the provisions of this Agreement may be credited against the Chinese tax imposed on that resident. The amount of the credit, however, shall not exceed the amount of the Chinese tax on that income computed in accordance with the taxation laws and regulations of China.

Where the income derived from Finland is dividend paid by a company which is a resident of Finland to a company which is a resident of China and which owns not less than 20% of the shares of the company paying the dividend, the credit shall take into account the tax paid to Finland by the company paying the dividend in respect of its income.

In Finland, subject to the provisions of Finnish law regarding the elimination of international double taxation (which shall not affect the general principle hereof), double taxation shall be eliminated as follows:

Where a resident of Finland derives income which, in accordance with the provisions of this Agreement, may be taxed in China, Finland shall, subject to the provisions of sub paragraph b), allow as a deduction from the Finnish tax of that person, an amount equal to the Chinese tax paid under Chinese law and in accordance with the Agreement, as computed by reference to the same income by reference to which the Finnish tax is computed.

Dividends paid by a company being a resident of China to a company which is a resident of Finland and which controls directly at least 10% of the voting power in the company paying the dividends shall be exempt from Finnish tax.

Where in accordance with any provision of the Agreement income derived by a resident of Finland is exempt from tax in Finland, Finland may nevertheless, in calculating the amount of tax on the remaining income of such person, take into account the exempted income.

Article 23 Miscellaneous Rule

Nothing in this Agreement shall prejudice the right of each Contracting State to apply its domestic laws and measures concerning the prevention of tax avoidance, whether or not described as such, insofar as they do not give rise to taxation contrary to this Agreement.

Article 24 Non-discrimination

Nationals of a Contracting State shall not be subjected in the other Contracting State to any taxation or any requirement connected therewith, which is other or more

burdensome than the taxation and connected requirements to which nationals of that other State in the same circumstances, in particular with respect to residence, are or may be subjected. This provision shall, notwithstanding the provisions of Article 1, also apply to persons who are not residents of one or both of the Contracting States.

The taxation on a permanent establishment which an enterprise of a Contracting State has in the other Contracting State shall not be less favourably levied in that other State than the taxation levied on enterprises of that other State carrying on the same activities. This provision shall not be construed as obliging a Contracting State to grant to residents of the other Contracting State any personal allowances, reliefs and reductions for taxation purposes on account of civil status or family responsibilities which it grants to its own residents.

Except where the provisions of paragraph 1 of Article 9, paragraph 7 of Article 11, or paragraph 6 of Article 12, apply, interest, royalties and other disbursements paid by an enterprise of a Contracting State to a resident of the other Contracting State shall, for the purpose of determining the taxable profits of such enterprise, be deductible under the same conditions as if they had been paid to a resident of the first-mentioned State.

Enterprises of a Contracting State, the capital of which is wholly or partly owned or controlled, directly or indirectly, by one or more residents of the other Contracting State, shall not be subjected in the first-mentioned State to any taxation or any requirement connected therewith which is other or more burdensome than the taxation and connected requirements to which other similar enterprises of the first-mentioned State are or may be subjected.

The provisions of this Article shall, notwithstanding the provisions of Article 2, apply to taxes of every kind and description.

Article 25 Mutual Agreement Procedure

Where a person considers that the actions of one or both of the Contracting States result or will result for him in taxation not in accordance with the provisions of this Agreement, he may, irrespective of the remedies provided by the domestic law of those States, present his case to the competent authority of the Contracting State of which he is a resident or, if his case comes under paragraph 1 of Article 24, to that of the Contracting State of which he is a national. The case must be presented within three years from the first notification of the action resulting in taxation not in accordance with the provisions of the Agreement.

The competent authority shall endeavour, if the objection appears to it to be justified and if it is not itself able to arrive at a satisfactory solution, to resolve the case by mutual agreement with the competent authority of the other Contracting State, with a view to the avoidance of taxation which is not in accordance with the Agreement. Any agreement reached shall be implemented notwithstanding any time limits in the domestic law of the Contracting States.

The competent authorities of the Contracting States shall endeavour to resolve by mutual agreement any difficulties or doubts arising as to the interpretation or application of the Agreement. They may also consult together for the elimination of double taxation in cases not provided for in the Agreement.

The competent authorities of the Contracting States may communicate with each other directly for the purpose of reaching an agreement in the sense of paragraphs 2 and 3. When it seems advisable for reaching an agreement, representatives of the competent authorities of the Contracting States may meet together for an oral exchange of opinions.

Article 26 Exchange of Information

The competent authorities of the Contracting States shall exchange such information as is foreseeably relevant for carrying out the provisions of this Agreement or to the administration or enforcement of the domestic laws concerning taxes of every kind and description imposed on behalf of the Contracting States or their local authorities, insofar as the taxation thereunder is not contrary to the Agreement. The exchange of information is not restricted by Articles 1 and 2.

Any information received under paragraph 1 by a Contracting State shall be treated as secret in the same manner as information obtained under the domestic laws of that State and shall be disclosed only to persons or authorities (including courts and administrative bodies) concerned with the assessment or collection of, the enforcement or prosecution in respect of, the determination of appeals in relation to the taxes referred to in paragraph 1, or the oversight of the above. Such persons or authorities shall use the information only for such purposes. They may disclose the information in public court proceedings or in judicial decisions.

In no case shall the provisions of paragraphs 1 and 2 be construed so as to impose on a Contracting State the obligation:

to carry out administrative measures at variance with the laws and administrative practice of that or of the other Contracting State;

to supply information which is not obtainable under the laws or in the normal course of the administration of that or of the other Contracting State;

to supply information which would disclose any trade, business, industrial, commercial or professional secret or trade process, or information, the disclosure of which would be contrary to public policy (ordre public).

If information is requested by a Contracting State in accordance with this Article, the other Contracting State shall use its information gathering measures to obtain the requested information, even though that other State may not need such information for its own tax purposes. The obligation contained in the preceding sentence is subject to the limitations of paragraph 3 but in no case shall such limitations be construed to permit a Contracting State to decline to supply information solely because it has no domestic interest in such information.

In no case shall the provisions of paragraph 3 be construed to permit a Contracting State to decline to supply information solely because the information is held by a bank, other financial institution, nominee or person acting in an agency or a fiduciary capacity or because it relates to ownership interests in a person.

Article 27 Members of Diplomatic Missions and Consular Posts
Nothing in this Agreement shall affect the fiscal privileges of members of diplomatic missions or consular posts under the general rules of international law or under the provisions of special agreements.

Article 28 Entry Into Force
The Governments of the Contracting States shall notify each other through diplomatic channels that they have completed the internal legal procedures necessary for the entry into force of this Agreement.

This Agreement shall enter into force on the thirtieth day upon the receipt of the latter notification referred to in paragraph 1 and its provisions shall have effect in both Contracting States:

in respect of taxes withheld at source, on income derived on or after the first January in the calendar year next following the year in which the Agreement enters into force;
in respect of other taxes on income, for taxes chargeable for any tax year beginning on or after the first January in the calendar year next following the year in which the Agreement enters into force.

The Agreement between the Government of the People's Republic of China and the Government of the Republic of Finland for the Avoidance of Double Taxation and the Prevention of Fiscal Evasion with respect to Taxes on Income and the Protocol thereof, signed at Helsinki on 12th May 1986, as modified by the Protocol signed at Helsinki on 11th September 1995, shall cease to have effect with respect to taxes to which this Agreement applies in accordance with the provisions of paragraph 2.

Article 29 TERMINATION
This Agreement shall remain in force indefinitely but either of the Contracting States may, on or before the thirtieth day of June in any calendar year beginning after the expiration of a period of five years from the date of its entry into force, give written notice of termination to the other Contracting State through diplomatic channels. In such event this Agreement shall cease to have effect in both Contracting States:

in respect of taxes withheld at source, on income derived on or after the first January in the calendar year next following the year in which the notice is given;
in respect of other taxes on income, for taxes chargeable for any tax year beginning on or after the first January in the calendar year next following the year in which the notice is given.

IN WITNESS whereof the undersigned, duly authorized thereto, have signed this Agreement.

Done at___on the___day_________ of, in duplicate in the Chinese, Finnish and English languages, all texts being equally authentic. In case of divergence of interpretation, the English text shall prevail.

For the Government of the People's Republic of China.
For the Government of the Republic of Finland.

France

France, officially the French Republic, is a state in Western Europe. France borders Belgium, Luxembourg, Germany, Switzerland, Monaco, and Italy to the East, while Andorra and Spain to the West. Its coast overlooks the British Channel to the North, and the Mediterranean sea to the South. France's capital and largest city is Paris, being also its financial center. France has the third largest population in Europe (after Russia and Germany).

France is a popular country for immigration due to its economic attractiveness and historical background. White French are the majority ethnic group, while significant groups are Spanish, Italian, Portuguese, and Maghrebi.

The official and predominant spoken language is French. Until the twentieth century, French served as the lingua franca of diplomacy and universities. Regional languages are Occitan, Breton, Catalan, Flemish (Dutch dialect), Alsatian (German dialect), Basque, and Corsican (Italian dialect). Minority languages used by immigrants and second generations are Turkish, Arabic, Italian, Polish, and the Balkan languages.

France is a unitary semi-presidential constitutional republic. The current constitution is the fifth French republican constitution, entered into force on October 4th, 1958. The National Assembly and the Senate exert the legislative power forming the parliament. The National Assembly is elected through direct elections using the two-round voting majority representation system. The members of the Senate are 348, elected in indirect elections by the country's local councilors.

Executive power is vested in the President of the Republic and in the prime minister, who will lead the cabinet. The President of the Republic is elected every 5 years with a two-round voting system. The prime minister is nominated by the President of the Republic after being able to secure a motion of confidence in the National Assembly.

France has a civil law system based on Roman law. The Court of Cassation and the Council of State act as Supreme Court, managing constitutional matters, with judicial review powers.

© The Author(s), under exclusive license to Springer Nature Singapore Pte Ltd. 2022

L. Riccardi and G. Riccardi, *China–Europe Tax Treaties*,
https://doi.org/10.1007/978-981-19-3563-3_14

France is a unitary state, divided into 18 administrative regions, which are divided into 101 departments, subdivided in 335 arrondissements, managed by local governments, elected by the public.

France is part of the European union, one of the six founding country, together with Germany, Italy, Luxemburg, the Netherlands, and Belgium.

Category	Value
Population (mln persons)	64.824
Currency	Euro

Source International Monetary Fund, year 2019

France is the third largest economy of Europe, with a GDP valued 2,707.1 billion USD in 2019, and has a population of 64 million people. France has low inflation, but relatively high unemployment (8.5%). France scored highly in the 2020 Doing Business ranking, but less than Germany and the UK, and imposes a CIT of 25% from January 1st, 2022. It is both a large recipient of FDI and a large investor abroad. France records a trade deficit of 81 billion USD, being the third main importer and exporter in Europe.

GDP and local economy	
GDP current prices (billion USD)	2707.1
GDP per capita (USD)	41,761
GDP growth (%)	1.3
Inflation (%)	1.3
Unemployment (%)	8.5
General government total expenditure (% of GDP)	55.5
General government gross debt (% of GDP)	98.0
Doing business score 2020	76.8

Source International Monetary Fund and UNCTAD, year 2019

Foreign direct investment	
FDI outstock (million USD)	1,532,826
FDI instock (million USD)	868,691

Source UNCTAD, year 2019

Trade	
Imports (million USD)	651,179
Exports (million USD)	569,732
Trade balance (million USD)	– 81,447

Source International Monetary Fund and UNCTAD, year 2019

Main import–export	
First import by category	Machinery, nuclear reactors, boilers
Second import by category	Vehicles other than railway, tramway
First export by category	Machinery, nuclear reactors, boilers
Second export by category	Vehicles other than railway, tramway

Source United Nations COMTRADE, year 2020

The legal bases for taxation are established in the French Constitution, outlining the general principles. France imposes at national and local level different taxes, such as individual income tax, property sales taxes, capital gains, corporate income tax, and value added tax. Progressivity is guaranteed by a system with different bands and various deductions.

Taxes	
Company income tax (%)	25 (from FY 2022)
Top individual income tax (%)	45
Value added tax or sales tax (%)	20
Reduced value added tax or sales tax (%)	2.1 / 5.5 / 10

Source RsA Asia report, year 2021

- Economic relation with China

France records a trade deficit of 7.63 billion USD in 2020. "Essential oils, perfumes, cosmetics, toiletries" is the first export category, while "Electrical, electronic equipment" is the first import category. France is not involved in the Belt and Road Initiative, however, its DTA dates back to 1984, come into force the following year. A new double tax agreement has been signed in 2013 and entered into force in December 2014.

Category	Value
Belt road	No

Source UNCTAD, year 2021

Import from China	
Import from China (billion USD)	37.34
First import category from China	Electrical, electronic equipment
First import value (billion USD)	6.56
Second import category from China	Machinery, nuclear reactors, boilers
Second import value (billion USD)	6.11

Source United Nations COMTRADE, year 2020

Export to China	
Export to China (billion USD)	29.71
First export category towards China	Essential oils, perfumes, cosmetics, toiletries
First export value (billion USD)	4.49
Second Export category towards China	Machinery, nuclear reactors, boilers
Second export value (billion USD)	3.63

Source United Nations COMTRADE, year 2020

Trade balance	
Trade balance (billion USD)	−7.63

Source United Nations COMTRADE, year 2020

Double tax agreement	
DTA effective date	2014.12.28
Dividends (%)	5–10
Interest (%)	0–10
Royalties (%)	10

Source State Administration of Taxation of China, year 2021

Title AGREEMENT BETWEEN THE GOVERNMENT OF THE PEOPLE'S REPUBLIC OF CHINA AND THE GOVERNMENT OF THE FRENCH REPUBLIC FOR THE AVOIDANCE OF DOUBLE TAXATION AND THE PREVENTION OF FISCAL EVASION WITH RESPECT TO TAXES ON INCOME

Treaty Text

The Government of the People's Republic of China and the Government of the French Republic,

Desiring to conclude an Agreement for the avoidance of double taxation and the prevention of fiscal evasion with respect to taxes on income,

Have agreed as follows:

Article 1 Persons Covered

This Agreement shall apply to persons who are residents of one or both of the Contracting States.

Article 2 Taxes Covered

This Agreement shall apply to taxes on income imposed on behalf of a Contracting State or of its local authorities, irrespective of the manner in which they are levied.

There shall be regarded as taxes on income all taxes imposed on total income, or on elements of income, including taxes on gains from the alienation of movable or immovable property, taxes on the total amounts of wages or salaries paid by enterprises, as well as taxes on capital appreciation.

The existing taxes to which the Agreement shall apply are in particular:

in China:
the individual income tax;
the enterprise income tax; (hereinafter referred to as "Chinese tax");
in France:
the income tax ("l'impôt sur le revenu");
the corporation tax ("l'impôt sur les sociétés");
the contributions on corporation tax ("les contributions sur l'impôt sur les sociétés");
including any withholding tax, prepayment (précompte) or advance payment with respect to the aforesaid taxes;
(hereinafter referred to as "French tax").

The Agreement shall apply also to any identical or substantially similar taxes that are imposed after the date of signature of the Agreement in addition to, or in place of, the existing taxes. The competent authorities of the Contracting States shall notify each other of any significant changes which have been made in their taxation laws.

Article 3 General Definitions

For the purposes of this Agreement, unless the context otherwise requires:

the term "China" means the People's Republic of China; when used in geographical sense, means all the territory of the People's Republic of China, in which the Chinese laws relating to taxation apply, including its territorial sea, and any area beyond its territorial sea, within which the People's Republic of China has sovereign rights or jurisdiction in accordance with international law and under its domestic law;
the term "France" means the European and overseas departments of the French Republic, including the territorial sea, and any area outside the territorial sea within which, in accordance with international law, the French Republic has sovereign rights for the purpose of exploring and exploiting the natural resources of the sea bed and its sub-soil and the superjacent waters;
the term "person" includes an individual, a company and any other body of persons;
the term "company" means any body corporate or any entity that is treated as a body corporate for tax purposes;
the terms "enterprise of a Contracting State" and "enterprise of the other Contracting State" mean, respectively, an enterprise carried on by a resident of a Contracting State and an enterprise carried on by a resident of the other Contracting State;

the term “international traffic” means any transport by a ship or aircraft operated by an enterprise that has its place of effective management in a Contracting State, except when the ship or aircraft is operated solely between places in the other Contracting State;
the term “competent authority” means, in the case of China, the State Administration of Taxation or its authorized representative, and in the case of France, the Minister in charge of finance or his authorised representative;
the term “national”, in relation to a Contracting State, means:
any individual possessing the nationality of a Contracting State;
any legal person, partnership or association deriving its status as such from the laws in force in a Contracting State.

As regards the application of the Agreement at any time by a Contracting State, any term not defined therein shall, unless the context otherwise requires, have the meaning which it has at

that time under the law of that State for the purposes of the taxes to which the Agreement applies, any meaning under the applicable tax laws of that State prevailing over a meaning given to the term under other laws of that State.

Article 4 Resident

For the purposes of this Agreement, the term “resident of a Contracting State” means any person who, under the laws of that State, is liable to tax therein by reason of his domicile, residence, place of incorporation, place of effective management or any other criterion of a similar nature, and also includes that State and local authority thereof. This term, however, does not include any person who is liable to tax in that State in respect only of income from sources in that State.

Where by reason of the provisions of paragraph 1 an individual is a resident of both Contracting States, then his status shall be determined as follows:

he shall be deemed to be a resident only of the State in which he has a permanent home available to him; if he has a permanent home available to him in both States, he shall be deemed to be a resident only of the State with which his personal and economic relations are closer (centre of vital interests);
if the State in which he has his centre of vital interests cannot be determined, or if he has not a permanent home available to him in either State, he shall be deemed to be a resident only of the State in which he has an habitual abode;
if he has an habitual abode in both States or in neither of them, he shall be deemed to be a resident only of the State of which he is a national;
if he is a national of both States or of neither of them, the competent authorities of the Contracting States shall settle the question by mutual agreement.

Where by reason of the provisions of paragraph 1 a person other than an individual is a resident of both Contracting States, then it shall be deemed to be a resident only of the State in which its place of effective management is situated.

For the purposes of applying this Agreement:

an item of income, profit or gain:
derived from a Contracting State through a partnership, group of persons or other similar entity that is organised in the other Contracting State; and
treated as the income of beneficiaries, partners, members or participants of that partnership, group of persons or other similar entity under the tax laws of that other Contracting State;
shall be eligible for the benefits of the Agreement that would be granted if it were directly derived by a beneficiary, partner, member or participant of that partnership, group of persons or other similar entity and who is a resident of that other Contracting State, to the extent that such beneficiaries, partners, members or participants are residents of that other Contracting State and satisfy any other conditions specified in the Agreement, without regard to whether the income is treated as the income of such beneficiaries, partners, members or participants under the tax laws of the first-mentioned State;
an item of income, profit or gain:
derived from a Contracting State through a partnership, group of persons or other similar entity that is organised in the other Contracting State; and
treated as the income of that partnership, group of persons or other similar entity under the tax laws of that other Contracting State;
shall be eligible for the benefits of the Agreement that would be granted to a resident of that other Contracting State, without regard to whether the income is treated as the income of that partnership, group of persons or other similar entity under the tax laws of the first-mentioned State, if such partnership, group of persons or other similar entity is a resident of that other Contracting State and satisfies any other conditions specified in the Agreement;
an item of income, profit or gain:
derived from a Contracting State through a partnership, group of persons or any other similar entity that is organised in that Contracting State;
treated as the income of beneficiaries, partners, members or participants of that partnership, group of persons or other similar entity under the tax laws of the other Contracting State; and
treated as the income of that partnership, group of persons or other similar entity under the tax laws of the first-mentioned State;
can be taxed under the tax laws of the first-mentioned State without any restriction;
an item of income, profit or gain:
derived from a Contracting State through a partnership, group of persons or other similar entity that is organised in that Contracting State; and
treated as the income of that partnership, group of persons or other similar entity under the tax laws of the other Contracting State;
shall not be eligible for the benefits of the Agreement;
an item of income, profit or gain:
derived from a Contracting State through a partnership, group of persons or any other similar entity that is organised in a State other than the Contracting States; and

treated as the income of the beneficiaries, partners, members or participants of that partnership, group of persons or other similar entity under the tax laws of the other Contracting State and under the tax laws of the State where the entity is organised;
shall be eligible for the benefits of the Agreement that would be granted if it were directly derived by a beneficiary, partner, member or participant of that partnership, group of persons or other similar entity and who is a resident of that other Contracting State, to the extent that such beneficiaries, partners, members or participants are residents of that other Contracting State and satisfy any other conditions specified in the Agreement, without regard to whether the income is treated as the income of such beneficiaries, partners, members or participants under the tax laws of the first-mentioned State provided that the State where the partnership, group of persons or other similar entity is organised has concluded with the Contracting States an agreement containing a provision for the exchange of information with a view to the prevention of fiscal evasion;
an item of income, profit or gain:
derived from a Contracting State through a partnership, group of persons or any other similar entity that is organised in a State other than the Contracting States; and
treated as the income of that partnership, group of persons or other similar entity under the tax laws of the other Contracting State;
shall not be eligible for the benefits of the Agreement.

Article 5 Permanent Establishment

For the purposes of this Agreement, the term "permanent establishment" means a fixed place of business through which the business of an enterprise is wholly or partly carried on.

The term "permanent establishment" includes especially:

a place of management;
a branch;
an office;
a factory;
a workshop; and
a mine, an oil or gas well, a quarry or any other place of extraction of natural resources.

The term "permanent establishment" likewise encompasses:

a building site, or construction, assembly or installation project or supervisory activities in connection therewith, but only if such site, project or activities last more than twelve months;
the furnishing of services, including consultancy services, by an enterprise through employees or other personnel who are present in a Contracting State for such purpose, but only if activities of that nature continue (for the same or a connected

project) within that Contracting State for a period or periods aggregating more than 183 days within any twelve-month period.

Notwithstanding the preceding provisions of this Article, the term "permanent establishment" shall be deemed not to include:

the use of facilities solely for the purpose of storage, display or delivery of goods or merchandise belonging to the enterprise;
the maintenance of a stock of goods or merchandise belonging to the enterprise solely for the purpose of storage, display or delivery;
the maintenance of a stock of goods or merchandise belonging to the enterprise solely for the purpose of processing by another enterprise;
the maintenance of a fixed place of business solely for the purpose of purchasing goods or merchandise or of collecting information, for the enterprise;
the maintenance of a fixed place of business solely for the purpose of carrying on, for the enterprise, any other activity of a preparatory or auxiliary character;
the maintenance of a fixed place of business solely for any combination of activities mentioned in sub-paragraphs (a) to e), provided that the overall activity of the fixed place of business resulting from this combination is of a preparatory or auxiliary character.

Notwithstanding the provisions of paragraphs 1 and 2, where a person—other than an agent of an independent status to whom paragraph 6 applies—is acting in a Contracting State on behalf of an enterprise of the other Contracting State, and has, and habitually exercises, in that Contracting State an authority to conclude contracts in the name of the enterprise, that enterprise shall be deemed to have a permanent establishment in that Contracting State in respect of any activities which that person undertakes for the enterprise, unless the activities of such person are limited to those mentioned in paragraph 4 which, if exercised through a fixed place of business, would not make this fixed place of business a permanent establishment under the provisions of that paragraph.

An enterprise of a Contracting State shall not be deemed to have a permanent establishment in the other Contracting State merely because it carries on business in that other State through a broker, general commission agent or any other agent of an independent status, provided that such persons are acting in the ordinary course of their business. However, when the activities of such an agent are devoted wholly or almost wholly on behalf of that enterprise, and conditions are made or imposed between that enterprise and the agent in their commercial and financial relations which differ from those which would have been made between independent enterprises, he will not be considered an agent of an independent status within the meaning of this paragraph.

The fact that a company which is a resident of a Contracting State controls or is controlled by a company which is a resident of the other Contracting State, or which carries on business in that other State (whether through a permanent establishment or otherwise), shall not of itself constitute either company a permanent establishment of the other.

Article 6 Income from Immovable Property

Income derived by a resident of a Contracting State from immovable property (including income from agriculture or forestry) situated in the other Contracting State may be taxed in that other State.

The term "immovable property" shall have the meaning which it has under the law of the Contracting State in which the property in question is situated. The term shall in any case include property accessory to immovable property, livestock and equipment used in agriculture and forestry, rights to which the provisions of general law respecting landed property apply, usufruct of immovable property and rights to variable or fixed payments as consideration for the working of, or the right to work, mineral deposits, sources and other natural resources; ships and aircraft shall not be regarded as immovable property.

The provisions of paragraph 1 shall apply to income derived from the direct use, letting, or use in any other form of immovable property.

The provisions of paragraphs 1 and 3 shall also apply to the income from immovable property of an enterprise and to income from immovable property used for the performance of independent personal services, notwithstanding the provisions of Article 7 and Article 14.

Where shares or other rights in a company, trust, entity or any other arrangement give entitlement to the enjoyment of immovable property situated in a Contracting State, income derived from the direct use, letting or use in any other form of that right of enjoyment may be taxed in that State notwithstanding the provisions of Article 7.

Article 7 Business Profits

The profits of an enterprise of a Contracting State shall be taxable only in that State unless the enterprise carries on business in the other Contracting State through a permanent establishment situated therein. If the enterprise carries on business as aforesaid, the profits of the enterprise may be taxed in the other State, but only so much of them as is attributable to that permanent establishment.

Subject to the provisions of paragraph 3, where an enterprise of a Contracting State carries on business in the other Contracting State through a permanent establishment situated therein, there shall in each Contracting State be attributed to that permanent establishment the profits which it might be expected to make if it were a distinct and separate enterprise engaged in the same or similar activities under the same or similar conditions and dealing wholly independently with the enterprise of which it is a permanent establishment.

In determining the profits of a permanent establishment, there shall be allowed as deductions expenses which are incurred for the purposes of the permanent establishment, including executive and general administrative expenses so incurred, whether in the State in which the permanent establishment is situated or elsewhere.

Insofar as it has been customary in a Contracting State to determine the profits to be attributed to a permanent establishment on the basis of an apportionment of the total profits of the enterprise to its various parts, nothing in paragraph 2 shall preclude that Contracting State from determining the profits to be taxed by such an apportionment as may be customary; the method of apportionment adopted shall, however, be such that the result shall be in accordance with the principles contained in this Article.

No profits shall be attributed to a permanent establishment by reason of the mere purchase by that permanent establishment of goods or merchandise for the enterprise.

For the purposes of the preceding paragraphs, the profits to be attributed to the permanent establishment shall be determined by the same method year by year unless there is good and sufficient reason to the contrary.

Where profits include items of income which are dealt with separately in other Articles of this Agreement, then the provisions of those Articles shall not be affected by the provisions of this Article.

Article 8 Shipping and Air Transport

Profits from the operation of ships or aircraft in international traffic shall be taxable only in the Contracting State in which the place of effective management of the enterprise is situated.

If the place of effective management of a shipping enterprise is aboard a ship, then it shall be deemed to be situated in the Contracting State in which the home harbour of the ship is situated, or, if there is no such home harbour, in the Contracting State of which the operator of the ship is a resident.

The provisions of paragraph 1 shall also apply to profits from the participation in a pool, a joint business or an international operating agency.

Article 9 Associated Enterprises

Where

> an enterprise of a Contracting State participates directly or indirectly in the management, control or capital of an enterprise of the other Contracting State, or the same persons participate directly or indirectly in the management, control or capital of an enterprise of a Contracting State and an enterprise of the other Contracting State,
>
> and in either case conditions are made or imposed between the two enterprises in their commercial or financial relations which differ from those which would be made between independent enterprises, then any profits which would, but for those conditions, have accrued to one of the enterprises, but, by reason of those conditions, have not so accrued, may be included in the profits of that enterprise and taxed accordingly.

Where a Contracting State includes in the profits of an enterprise of that State — and taxes accordingly — profits on which an enterprise of the other Contracting State has been charged to tax in that other State and the profits so included are profits which would have accrued to the enterprise of the first-mentioned State if the conditions made between the two enterprises had been those which would have been made between independent enterprises, then that other State shall make an appropriate adjustment to the amount of the tax charged therein on those profits. In determining such adjustment, due regard shall be had to the other provisions of this Agreement and the competent authorities of the Contracting States shall, if necessary, consult each other.

Article 10 Dividends

Dividends paid by a company which is a resident of a Contracting State to a resident of the other Contracting State may be taxed in that other State.

However, such dividends may also be taxed in the Contracting State of which the company paying the dividends is a resident and according to the laws of that State, but if the beneficial owner of the dividends is a resident of the other Contracting State, the tax so charged shall not exceed:

5% of the gross amount of the dividends if the beneficial owner is a company (other than a partnership) which holds directly at least 25% of the capital of the company paying the dividends;

10% of the gross amount of the dividends in all other cases.

The competent authorities of the Contracting States shall by mutual agreement settle the mode of application of these limitations.

This paragraph shall not affect the taxation of the company in respect of the profits out of which the dividends are paid.

The term "dividends" as used in this Article means income from any type of shares or other rights, not being debt-claims, participating in profits as well as income from other corporate rights which is subjected to the same taxation treatment as income from shares by the laws of the State of which the company making the distribution is a resident.

The provisions of paragraphs 1 and 2 shall not apply if the beneficial owner of the dividends, being a resident of a Contracting State, carries on business in the other Contracting State of which the company paying the dividends is a resident through a permanent establishment situated therein, or performs in that other State independent personal services from a fixed base situated therein, and the holding in respect of which the dividends are paid is effectively connected with such permanent establishment or fixed base. In such case the provisions of Article 7 or Article 14, as the case may be, shall apply.

Where a company which is a resident of a Contracting State derives profits or income from the other Contracting State, that other State may not impose any tax on the dividends paid by the company, except insofar as such dividends are paid to a resident of that other State or insofar as the holding in respect of which the dividends are paid is effectively connected with a permanent establishment or a fixed base situated in that other State, nor subject the company's undistributed profits to a tax on the company's undistributed profits, even if the dividends paid or the undistributed profits consist wholly or partly of profits or income arising in such other State.

The provisions of subparagraphs (a) and (b) of paragraph 2 shall not apply to dividends paid out of income or gains derived from immovable property within the meaning of Article 6 by an investment vehicle:

which distributes most of this income annually; and

whose income or gains from such immovable property are exempted from tax; where the beneficial owner of those dividends holds, directly or indirectly, 10% or more of the capital of the vehicle paying the dividends. In such case, the dividends may be taxed at the rate provided for by the domestic law of the Contracting State in which the dividends arise.

The provisions of this Article shall not apply if it was the main purpose or one of the main purposes of any person concerned with the creation or the assignment of the shares or other rights in respect of which the dividends are paid to take advantage of this Article by means of that creation or assignment.

Article 11 Interest

Interest arising in a Contracting State and paid to a resident of the other Contracting State may be taxed in that other State.

However, such interest may also be taxed in the Contracting State in which it arises and according to the laws of that State, but if the beneficial owner of the interest is a resident of the other Contracting State, the tax so charged shall not exceed 10% of the gross amount of the interest. The competent authorities of the Contracting States shall by mutual agreement settle the mode of application of this limitation.

Notwithstanding the provisions of paragraph 2, interest referred to in paragraph 1 shall be taxable only in the Contracting State of which the recipient of the interest is a resident, if it is paid:

in China:
to the Government of China or a local authority thereof;
to the People's Bank of China;
to the China Development Bank Corporation;
to the Agricultural Development Bank of China;
to the Export–Import Bank of China;
to the National Council for Social Security Fund;
on loans directly or indirectly guaranteed or insured by the China Export & Credit Insurance Corporation;
to any financial institution mutually agreed upon by the competent authorities of the Contracting States;
in France:
to the Government of France or a local authority thereof;
to the Bank of France;
to the Public Investment Bank of France (BPIfrance);
to the Deposit and Consignment Office (CDC);
in respect of a loan directly or indirectly financed or subsidized by the French Government within the framework of the public aid to foreign trade or guaranteed or insured by the French Foreign Trade Insurance Company (COFACE);
to any financial institution mutually agreed upon by the competent authorities of the Contracting States.

Regarding entities mentioned in paragraphs (a) (iii), (a) (iv), (a) (v), (a) (vi), (b) (iii) and (b) (iv), it is understood that the exemption only applies as long as those entities are wholly owned—directly or indirectly—by a Contracting State or a local authority thereof.

The term "interest" as used in this Article means income from debt-claims of every kind, whether or not secured by mortgage and whether or not carrying a right to participate in the debtor's profits, and in particular, income from government securities and income from bonds or debentures, including premiums and prizes attaching to such securities, bonds or debentures. Penalty charges for late payment and payments of any kind received as a consideration for the guarantee or insurance of a debt-claim shall not be regarded as interest for the purpose of this Article.

The provisions of paragraphs 1 and 2 shall not apply if the beneficial owner of the interest, being a resident of a Contracting State, carries on business in the other Contracting State in which the interest arises, through a permanent establishment situated therein, or performs in that other State independent personal services from a fixed base situated therein, and the debt-claim in respect of which the interest is paid is effectively connected with such permanent establishment or fixed base. In such case the provisions of Article 7 or Article 14, as the case may be, shall apply.

Interest shall be deemed to arise in a Contracting State when the payer is a resident of that State. Where, however, the person paying the interest, whether he is a resident of a Contracting State or not, has in a Contracting State a permanent establishment or a fixed base in connection with which the indebtedness on which the interest is paid was incurred, and such interest is borne by such permanent establishment or fixed base, then such interest shall be deemed to arise in the State in which the permanent establishment or fixed base is situated.

Where, by reason of a special relationship between the payer and the beneficial owner or between both of them and some other person, the amount of the interest, having regard to the debt-claim for which it is paid, exceeds the amount which would have been agreed upon by the payer and the beneficial owner in the absence of such relationship, the provisions of this Article shall apply only to the last-mentioned amount. In such case, the excess part of the payments shall remain taxable according to the laws of each Contracting State, due regard being had to the other provisions of this Agreement.

The provisions of this Article shall not apply if it was the main purpose or one of the main purposes of any person concerned with the creation or assignment of the debt-claim in respect of which the interest is paid to take advantage of this Article by means of that creation or assignment.

Article 12 Royalties

Royalties arising in a Contracting State and beneficially owned by a resident of the other Contracting State may be taxed in that other State.

However, such royalties may also be taxed in the Contracting State in which they arise and according to the laws of that State, but if the beneficial owner of the royalties is a resident of the other Contracting State, the tax so charged shall not exceed 10%

of the gross amount of the royalties. The competent authorities of the Contracting States shall by mutual agreement settle the mode of application of this limitation.

The term "royalties" as used in this Article means payments of any kind received as a consideration for the use of, or the right to use, any copyright of literary, artistic or scientific work including cinematography films, or films or tapes for radio or television broadcasting, any patent, trade mark, design or model, plan, secret formula or process, or for the use of, or the right to use, industrial, commercial, or scientific equipment, or for information concerning industrial, commercial or scientific experience.

The provisions of paragraphs 1 and 2 shall not apply if the beneficial owner of the royalties, being a resident of a Contracting State, carries on business in the other Contracting State in which the royalties arise, through a permanent establishment situated therein, or performs in that other State independent personal services from a fixed base situated therein, and the right or property in respect of which the royalties are paid is effectively connected with such permanent establishment or fixed base. In such case the provisions of Article 7 or Article 14, as the case may be, shall apply.

Royalties shall be deemed to arise in a Contracting State when the payer is a resident of that Contracting State. Where, however, the person paying the royalties, whether he is a resident of a Contracting State or not, has in a Contracting State a permanent establishment or a fixed base in connection with which the liability to pay the royalties was incurred, and such royalties are borne by such permanent establishment or fixed base, then such royalties shall be deemed to arise in the State in which the permanent establishment or fixed base is situated.

Where, by reason of a special relationship between the payer and the beneficial owner or between both of them and some other person, the amount of the royalties, having regard to the use, right or information for which they are paid, exceeds the amount which would have been agreed upon by the payer and the beneficial owner in the absence of such relationship, the provisions of this Article shall apply only to the last-mentioned amount. In such case, the excess part of the payments shall remain taxable according to the laws of each Contracting State, due regard being had to the other provisions of this Agreement.

The provisions of this Article shall not apply if it was the main purpose or one of the main purposes of any person concerned with the creation or assignment of the rights in respect of which the royalties are paid to take advantage of this Article by means of that creation or assignment.

Article 13 Capital Gains

Gains derived by a resident of a Contracting State from the alienation of immovable property referred to in Article 6 and situated in the other Contracting State may be taxed in that other State.

Gains from the alienation of movable property forming part of the business property of a permanent establishment which an enterprise of a Contracting State has in the other Contracting State or of movable property pertaining to a fixed base available to a resident of a Contracting State in the other Contracting State for the purpose of performing independent personal services, including such gains from the alienation of such a permanent establishment (alone or with the whole enterprise) or of such a fixed base, may be taxed in that other State.

Gains from the alienation of ships or aircraft operated in international traffic, or movable property pertaining to the operation of such ships, or aircraft, shall be taxable only in the Contracting State in which the place of effective management of the enterprise is situated.

Gains from the alienation of shares or other rights in a company, a trust or any other institution or entity the assets or property of which consist, at any time during the preceding 36 months before such alienation, for more than 50% of their value of, or derive more than 50% of their value from, directly or indirectly through the interposition of one or more other companies, trusts, institutions or entities, immovable property referred to in Article 6 and situated in a Contracting State or of rights connected with such immovable property may be taxed in that State.

Gains derived by a resident of a Contracting State from the alienation of shares (other than the ones referred to in paragraph 4) of a company which is a resident of the other Contracting State may be taxed in that other Contracting State if the recipient of the gain, at any time during the twelve-month period preceding such alienation, had a participation, directly or indirectly, of at least 25% in the capital of that company.

Gains from the alienation of any property, other than that referred to in paragraphs 1 to 5, shall be taxable only in the Contracting State of which the alienator is a resident.

Article 14 Independent Personal Services

Income derived by a resident of a Contracting State in respect of professional services or other activities of an independent character shall be taxable only in that State except in the following circumstances, when such income may also be taxed in the other Contracting State:

> if he has a fixed base regularly available to him in the other Contracting State for the purpose of performing his activities; in that case, only so much of the income as is attributable to that fixed base may be taxed in that other State; or
> if his stay in the other Contracting State is for a period or periods amounting to or exceeding in the aggregate 183 days in any twelve-month period commencing or ending in the fiscal year concerned; in that case, only so much of the income as is derived from his activities performed in that other State may be taxed in that other State.

The term "professional services" includes especially independent scientific, literary, artistic, educational or teaching activities as well as the independent activities of physicians, lawyers, engineers, architects, dentists and accountants.

Article 15 Income from Employment

Subject to the provisions of Articles 16, 18 and 19, salaries, wages and other similar remuneration derived by a resident of a Contracting State in respect of an employment shall be taxable only in that State unless the employment is exercised in the other

Contracting State. If the employment is so exercised, such remuneration as is derived therefrom may be taxed in that other State.

Notwithstanding the provisions of paragraph 1, remuneration derived by a resident of a Contracting State in respect of an employment exercised in the other Contracting State shall be taxable only in the first-mentioned State if:

the recipient is present in the other State for a period or periods not exceeding in the aggregate 183 days in any twelve-month period commencing or ending in the fiscal year concerned, and
the remuneration is paid by, or on behalf of, an employer who is not a resident of the other State, and
the remuneration is not borne by a permanent establishment or a fixed base which the employer has in the other State.

Notwithstanding the preceding provisions of this Article, remuneration derived in respect of an employment exercised aboard a ship or aircraft operated in international traffic may be taxed in the Contracting State in which the place of effective management of the enterprise is situated.

Article 16 Directors' Fees

Directors' fees and other similar payments derived by a resident of a Contracting State in his capacity as a member of the board of directors or of a supervisory board of a company which is a resident of the other Contracting State may be taxed in that other State.

Article 17 Artistes and Athletes

Notwithstanding the provisions of Articles 7, 14 and 15, income derived by a resident of a Contracting State as an entertainer, such as a theatre, motion picture, radio or television artiste, or a musician, or as an athlete or a model, from his personal activities as such exercised in the other Contracting State, may be taxed in that other State.

Where income in respect of personal activities exercised by an entertainer, an athlete or a model in his capacity as such accrues not to the entertainer, athlete or model himself but to another person, that income may, notwithstanding the provisions of Articles 7, 14 and 15, be taxed in the Contracting State in which the activities of the entertainer, athlete or model are exercised.

Notwithstanding the provisions of paragraphs 1 and 2, income derived by a resident of a Contracting State as an entertainer or an athlete or a model from his personal activities as such exercised in the other Contracting State, including where such income accrues not to the entertainer, the athlete or the model himself, but to another person whether a resident of a Contracting State or not, shall be taxable only in the first-mentioned State if those activities in the other State are supported mainly by public funds of the first-mentioned State or its local authorities.

Article 18 Pensions

Subject to the provisions of paragraph 2 of Article 19, pensions and other similar remuneration paid to a resident of a Contracting State in consideration of past employment shall be taxable only in that State.

Article 19 Government Service

(a) Salaries, wages and other similar remuneration, other than a pension, paid by the Government of a Contracting State or a local authority thereof to an individual in respect of services rendered to the Government of that State or authority, shall be taxable only in that State.

However, such salaries, wages and other similar remuneration shall be taxable only in the other Contracting State if the services are rendered in that State and the individual is a resident of that State who:

is a national of that State; or
did not become a resident of that State solely for the purpose of rendering the services.

(a) Pensions and other similar remuneration paid by, or out of funds created by, a Contracting State or a local authority thereof to an individual in respect of services rendered to the Government of that State or authority shall be taxable only in that State.
(b) However, such pensions and other similar remuneration shall be taxable only in the other Contracting State if the individual is a resident of, and a national of, that State.

The provisions of paragraph 1 shall also apply to remuneration of personnel of non-profit educational institutions of a Contracting State situated in the other Contracting State, irrespective of the payer of the remuneration, if the resources of such establishments derive solely or mainly from the first-mentioned State.

The provisions of Articles 15, 16, 17 and 18 shall apply to salaries, wages, pensions and other similar remuneration in respect of services rendered in connection with a business carried on by the Government of a Contracting State or a local authority thereof.

Article 20 Teachers and Researchers

Subject to the provisions of Article 19, remuneration which a teacher or a researcher who is or was immediately before visiting a Contracting State a resident of the other Contracting State, and who is present in the first-mentioned State solely for the purpose of teaching or engaging in research, derives in respect of such activities, shall be taxable only in the other State. This provision shall apply for a period not exceeding 36 months from the date of the first arrival of the teacher or researcher in the first-mentioned State for the purpose of teaching or engaging in research. However, when the research is undertaken not in the public interest but primarily for the private benefit of a specific person or persons, the provisions of Article 15 shall apply.

Article 21 Students

Payments which a student, a trainee, an intern or a business apprentice who is or was immediately before visiting a Contracting State a resident of the other Contracting State and who is present in the first-mentioned State solely for the purpose of his education receives for the purpose of his maintenance or education shall not be taxed in that State, provided that such payments arise from sources outside that State.

Article 22 Other Income

Items of income of a resident of a Contracting State, wherever arising, not dealt with in the foregoing Articles of this Agreement shall be taxable only in that State.

The provisions of paragraph 1 shall not apply to income, other than income from immovable property as defined in paragraph 2 of Article 6, if the recipient of such income, being a resident of a Contracting State, carries on business in the other Contracting State through a permanent establishment situated therein, or performs in that other State independent personal services from a fixed base situated therein, and the right or property in respect of which the income is paid is effectively connected with such permanent establishment or fixed base. In such case the provisions of Article 7 or Article 14, as the case may be, shall apply.

Where, by reason of a special relationship between the person referred to in paragraph 1 and some other person, or between both of them and some third person, the amount of the income referred to in paragraph 1 exceeds the amount which would have been agreed upon between them in the absence of such a relationship, the provisions of this Article shall apply only to the last-mentioned amount. In such a case, the excess part of the income shall remain taxable according to the laws of each Contracting State, due regard being had to the other provisions of this Agreement.

The provisions of this Article shall not apply if it was the main purpose or one of the main purposes of any person concerned with the creation or assignment of the rights in respect of which the income is paid to take advantage of this Article by means of that creation or assignment.

Article 23 Methods for Elimination of Double Taxation

In the case of China, double taxation shall be avoided in the following manner:

Where a resident of China derives income from France, the amount of tax on that income payable in France in accordance with the provisions of this Agreement may be credited against the Chinese tax imposed on that resident. The amount of the credit, however, shall not exceed the amount of the Chinese tax on that income computed in accordance with the taxation laws and regulations of China.

Where the income derived from France is dividend paid by a company which is a resident of France to a company which is a resident of China and which owns not less than 20% of the shares of the company paying the dividend, the credit shall take into account the tax paid to France by the company paying the dividend in respect of its income.

In the case of France, double taxation shall be avoided in the following manner:

Notwithstanding any other provision of this Agreement, income which may be taxed or shall be taxable only in China in accordance with the provisions of the Agreement shall be taken into account for the computation of the French tax where such income is not exempted from corporation tax according to French domestic law. In that case, the Chinese tax shall not be deductible from such income, but the resident of France shall, subject to the conditions and limits provided for in sub-paragraphs (i) and (ii), be entitled to a tax credit against French tax. Such tax credit shall be equal:

in the case of income other than that mentioned in sub-paragraph (ii), to the amount of French tax attributable to such income provided that the resident of France is subject to Chinese tax in respect of such income;
in the case of income subject to the corporation tax referred to in Article 7, paragraph 2 of Article 13 and Article 14, and in the case of income referred to in Article 9, Article 10, paragraph 2 of Article 11, paragraph 2 of Article 12, paragraphs 1 and 4 of Article 13, paragraph 3 of Article 15, Article 16 and paragraphs 1 and 2 of Article 17, to the amount of tax paid in China in accordance with the provisions of those Articles; however, such tax credit shall not exceed the amount of French tax attributable to such income.

(a) It is understood that the term "amount of French tax attributable to such income" as used in sub-paragraph (a) means:

- where the tax on such income is computed by applying a proportional rate, the amount of the net income concerned multiplied by the rate which actually applies to that income;
- where the tax on such income is computed by applying a progressive scale, the amount of the net income concerned multiplied by the rate resulting from the ratio of the tax actually payable on the total net income taxable in accordance with French law to the amount of that total net income.

(b) It is understood that the term "amount of tax paid in China" as used in sub-paragraph (a) means the amount of Chinese tax effectively and definitively borne in respect of the items of income concerned, in accordance with the provisions of the Agreement, by a resident of France who is taxed on those items of income according to the French law.

Article 24 Miscellaneous Rule

The benefits of any reduction in or exemption from tax provided for in this Agreement shall not be available where the main purpose for entering into certain transactions or arrangements was to secure a more favourable tax position and obtaining that more favourable treatment in these circumstances would be contrary to the object and purpose of the relevant provisions of this Agreement.

Article 25 Non-discrimination

(a) Nationals of a Contracting State shall not be subjected in the other Contracting State to any taxation or any requirement connected therewith, which is other or more burdensome than the taxation and connected requirements to which nationals of that other State in the same circumstances, in particular with respect to residence, are or may be subjected. This provision shall, notwithstanding the provisions of Article 1, also apply to persons who are not residents of one or both of the Contracting States.

(b) For the purposes of subparagraph (a), it is understood that an individual, a legal person, a partnership or an association who or which is a resident of a Contracting State is not placed in the same circumstances as an individual, a legal person, a partnership or an association who or which is not a resident of that State, whatever the definition of nationality is and even if the legal persons, partnerships or associations are deemed to be nationals of the Contracting State of which they are residents.

The taxation on a permanent establishment which an enterprise of a Contracting State has in the other Contracting State shall not be less favorably levied in that other State than the taxation levied on enterprises of that other State carrying on the same activities. This provision shall not be construed as obliging a Contracting State to grant to residents of the other Contracting State any personal allowances, reliefs and reductions for taxation purposes on account of civil status or family responsibilities which it grants to its own residents.

Except where the provisions of paragraph 1 of Article 9, paragraph 7 of Article 11, or paragraph 6 of Article 12 apply, interest, royalties and other disbursements paid by an enterprise of a Contracting State to a resident of the other Contracting State shall, for the purpose of determining the taxable profits of such enterprise, be deductible under the same conditions as if they had been paid to a resident of the first-mentioned State.

Enterprises of a Contracting State, the capital of which is wholly or partly owned or controlled, directly or indirectly, by one or more residents of the other Contracting State, shall not be subjected in the first-mentioned State to any taxation or any requirement connected therewith which is other or more burdensome than the taxation and connected requirements to which other similar enterprises of the first-mentioned State are or may be subjected.

The provisions of the Article shall, notwithstanding the provisions of Article 2, apply to taxes of every kind and description.

Article 26 Mutual Agreement Procedure

Where a person considers that the actions of one or both of the Contracting States result or will result for him in taxation not in accordance with the provisions of this Agreement, he may, irrespective of the remedies provided by the domestic law of those States, present his case to the competent authority of the Contracting State of which he is a resident or, if his case comes under paragraph 1 of Article 25, to that of the Contracting State of which he is a national. The case must be presented within three years from the first notification of the action resulting in taxation not in accordance with the provisions of the Agreement.

The competent authority shall endeavour, if the objection appears to it to be justified and if it is not itself able to arrive at a satisfactory solution, to resolve the case by mutual agreement with the competent authority of the other Contracting State, with a view to the avoidance of taxation which is not in accordance with the Agreement. Any agreement reached shall be implemented notwithstanding any time limits in the domestic law of the Contracting States.

The competent authorities of the Contracting States shall endeavour to resolve by mutual agreement any difficulties or doubts arising as to the interpretation or application of the Agreement. They may also consult together for the elimination of double taxation in cases not provided for in the Agreement.

The competent authorities of the Contracting States may communicate with each other directly for the purpose of reaching an agreement in the sense of paragraphs 2 and 3. When it seems advisable for reaching an agreement, representatives of the competent authorities of the Contracting States may meet together for an oral exchange of opinions.

Article 27 Exchange of Information

The competent authorities of the Contracting States shall exchange such information as is foreseeably relevant for carrying out the provisions of this Agreement or to the administration or enforcement of the domestic laws concerning taxes of every kind and description imposed on behalf of the Contracting States, or local authorities, insofar as the taxation thereunder is not contrary to the Agreement. The exchange of information is not restricted by Articles 1 and 2.

Any information received under paragraph 1 by a Contracting State shall be treated as secret in the same manner as information obtained under the domestic laws of that State and shall be disclosed only to persons or authorities (including courts and administrative bodies) concerned with the assessment or collection of, the enforcement or prosecution in respect of, the determination of appeals in relation to the taxes referred to in paragraph 1, or the oversight of the above. Such persons or authorities shall use the information only for such purposes. They may disclose the information in public court proceedings or in judicial decisions.

In no case shall the provisions of paragraphs 1 and 2 be construed so as to impose on a Contracting State the obligation:

to carry out administrative measures at variance with the laws and administrative practice of that or of the other Contracting State;

to supply information which is not obtainable under the laws or in the normal course of the administration of that or of the other Contracting State;

to supply information which would disclose any trade, business, industrial, commercial or professional secret or trade process, or information, the disclosure of which would be contrary to public policy (ordre public).

If information is requested by a Contracting State in accordance with this Article, the other Contracting State shall use its information gathering measures to obtain the requested information, even though that other State may not need such information for its own tax purposes. The obligation contained in the preceding sentence is subject to the limitations of paragraph 3 but in no case shall such limitations be construed to permit a Contracting State to decline to supply information solely because it has no domestic interest in such information.

In no case shall the provisions of paragraph 3 be construed to permit a Contracting State to decline to supply information solely because the information is held by a bank, other financial institution, nominee or person acting in an agency or a fiduciary capacity or because it relates to ownership interests in a person.

Article 28 Assistance in the Collection of Taxes

The Contracting States shall endeavour to lend assistance to each other in the collection of revenue claims. The competent authorities of the Contracting States may by mutual agreement settle the mode of application of this Article.

Article 29 Members of Diplomatic Missions and Consular Posts

Nothing in this Agreement shall affect the fiscal privileges of members of diplomatic missions or consular posts under the general rules of international law or under the provisions of special agreements.

Article 30 Entry Into Force

Each of the Contracting States shall notify the other through diplomatic channels the completion of internal procedures required as far as it is concerned for the bringing into force of this Agreement. This Agreement shall enter into force on the thirtieth day following the day when the latter notification is received.

The provisions of this Agreement shall have effect:

in respect of taxes on income withheld at source, for amounts taxable on or after the first day of January of the calendar year next following that in which this Agreement enters into force;

in respect of other taxes, for any tax year or accounting period beginning on or after the first day of January of the calendar year next following that in which the Agreement enters into force.

The Agreement between the Government of the People's Republic of China and the Government of the French Republic for the Avoidance of Double Taxation and the Prevention of Fiscal Evasion with Respect to Taxes on Income signed at Paris on 30 May 1984 shall cease to have effect as from the date on which the provisions of this Agreement become applicable in accordance with the provisions of this Article.

Article 31 Termination

This Agreement shall continue in effect indefinitely but either of the Contracting States may, on or before the thirtieth day of June in any calendar year beginning after the expiration of a period of five years from the date of its entry into force, give written notice of termination to the other Contracting State through diplomatic channels.

In such event this Agreement shall cease to have effect:

in respect of taxes on income withheld at source, for amounts taxable on or after the first day of January of the calendar year next following that in which the notice of termination is given;
in respect of other taxes, for any tax year or accounting period beginning on or after the first day of January of the calendar year next following that in which the notice of termination is given.

IN WITNESS whereof the undersigned, duly authorized thereto, have signed this Agreement.

Done at Beijing on the 26th day of November, 2013, in duplicate in the Chinese and French languages, both texts being equally authentic.

For the Government of the People's Republic of China.

For the Government of the French Republic.

Protocol

At the time of proceeding to the signature of the Agreement between the Government of the People's Republic of China and the Government of the French Republic for the Avoidance of Double Taxation and the Prevention of Fiscal Evasion with Respect to Taxes on Income, both parties have agreed on the following provisions which shall form an integral part of the Agreement.

In respect of Article 7:

where an enterprise of a Contracting State sells goods or merchandise or carries on business in the other Contracting State through a permanent establishment situated therein, the profits of that permanent establishment shall not be determined as the total amount received by the enterprise but only as the remuneration which is attributable to the actual activity of the permanent establishment for such sales or business;
in the case of contracts for the survey, supply, installation or construction of industrial, commercial or scientific equipment or premises, or of public works, where an enterprise of a Contracting State has a permanent establishment in the other Contracting State, the profits of such permanent establishment shall not be determined as the total amount of the contract, but only as that part of the contract which is effectively accomplished by the permanent establishment;
notwithstanding the provisions of subparagraphs (a) and (b), in situations where a permanent establishment fails to report with a reliable account of the income and expenses, the Contracting State where such permanent establishment is situated may assess the profits of such permanent establishment according to its domestic law, insofar as the application of the latter does not give rise to taxation contrary to the other provisions of this Agreement.
In relation to Article 10, it is understood that where a Contracting State applies the exemptions of its domestic regime applicable to investment vehicles as mentioned in paragraph 6 of Article 10 to the permanent establishment of an entity organised in the other Contracting State, no provision of this Agreement restricts the right of the first-mentioned Contracting State to tax, according to its domestic law,

income from immovable property deemed to be distributed by that permanent establishment.

In respect of Articles 10 and 11, an investment vehicle, which is established in a Contracting State where it is not subject to a tax mentioned in sub-paragraphs (a) or (b) of paragraph 3 of Article 2, and which receives dividends or interest arising in the other Contracting State, can ask for the aggregate amount of the tax reductions or exemptions provided by this Agreement in the proportion of such income which corresponds to the rights in the vehicle held by residents of the first-mentioned State and which is taxable in the hands of such residents, provided such residents are beneficial owners of such income.

With respect to paragraph 3 of Article 10, it is understood that the term "dividends" also includes, where the company making the distribution is a resident of France, income treated as a distribution by the tax laws of France.

With respect to Articles 10, 11 and 13, income other than capital gains mentioned in paragraphs 1 and 4 of Article 13 derived from a Contracting State by a sovereign wealth fund created and wholly owned by the other Contracting State for macroeconomic purposes shall be taxable only in that other Contracting State. With respect to capital gains mentioned in paragraphs 1 and 4 of Article 13 derived by a sovereign wealth fund as aforementioned, the exemption or collection shall be decided by the domestic law of the Contracting State in which the immovable property is situated. The sovereign wealth fund as aforementioned refers to:

in China:
the China Investment Corporation;
any institution mutually agreed upon by the competent authorities of the two Contracting States;
in France:
the Retirement Reserve Fund (FRR);
any institution mutually agreed upon by the competent authorities of the two Contracting States.

With respect to paragraph 3 of Article 12 of the Agreement, royalties paid for the use of or the right to use industrial, commercial or scientific equipment shall be subject to tax on 60% of the gross amount of such royalties.

Nothing in this Agreement shall affect the provisions of the Agreement of 23 January 1979 on the reciprocal exemption from taxes and charges on air transport enterprises and of the Agreement on maritime shipping of 10 April 1996 and the Exchange of Letters of 28 September 1975 maintained into force by the Exchange of Letters of 16 September 1996.

In respect of Article 23, notwithstanding the provisions of paragraph 3 of Article 30, the provisions of subparagraph (c) of paragraph 2 of Article 22 of the Agreement between the Government of the People's Republic of China and the Government of the French Republic for the Avoidance of Double Taxation and the Prevention of Fiscal Evasion with Respect to Taxes on Income signed in Paris on 30 May 1984 shall remain applicable to:

any royalties paid during a 24-month period as from the date of entry into force of the Agreement;

payments received in respect to any agreement for the use of, or the right to use, industrial, commercial or scientific equipment, provided the financial terms and conditions of the agreement are set up before 1st March 2012, and provided the equipment is delivered before 1st January 2013, but only for the duration of the agreement that is remaining as at 29th February 2012,

provided that the conduct of operations resulting in a tax credit had not for main purpose to obtain the benefit of such tax credit.

In respect of Article 25, it is understood that the provisions of the last sentence of paragraph 1 (a) apply only to individuals.

IN WITNESS whereof the undersigned, duly authorized thereto, have signed this Protocol.

Done at Beijing on the 26th day of November, 2013, in duplicate in the Chinese and French languages, both texts being equally authentic.

For the Government of the People's Republic of China.

For the Government of the French Republic.

Germany

Germany, officially the Federal Republic of Germany, is a state in Western Europe. Germany borders Denmark to the north, Poland and the Czech Republic to the east, Austria and Switzerland to the south, and France, Luxembourg, Belgium, and the Netherlands to the west. Its coast overlooks the Baltic and North seas. Germany's capital and largest city is Berlin, while Frankfurt is its financial center. Germany has the second largest population in Europe (after Russia, classified by the UN as an Eastern European country, although Russia's territory extends between the European and Asian continents).

Germany is the first most popular immigration destination in Europe and the second in the world after the United States. Germans are the majority ethnic group, while four significant groups are referred to as "national minorities", i.e. the Danish, the Sorbs, the Roma and Sinti, and the Frisians.

The official and predominant spoken language is German. Recognised minority languages are Danish, Low German, Low Rhenish, Sorbian, Romany, North Frisian, and Saterland Frisian. Minority languages used by immigrants and second generations are Turkish, Arabic, Kurdish, Polish, the Balkan languages, and Russian.

Germany is a federal, parliamentary, representative democratic republic. The Grundgesetz (Basic Law) is the constitution regulating the political system, in force since 1949. The Bundestag (Federal Diet) and Bundesrat (Federal Council) exert the legislative power forming the parliament. The Bundestag is elected through direct elections using the mixed-member proportional representation system. The members of the Bundesrat represent, and are appointed by, the governments of the sixteen federated states.

Executive power is vested in the chancellor and his or her cabinet. The chancellor is appointed by the President of the Republic after being elected by the party or coalition with the parliamentary majority in the Bundestag.

Germany has a civil law system based on Roman law, however some references to Germanic law are relevant. The Federal Constitutional Court acts as Supreme Court, managing constitutional matters, with judicial review powers.

© The Author(s), under exclusive license to Springer Nature Singapore Pte Ltd. 2022

L. Riccardi and G. Riccardi, *China–Europe Tax Treaties*,
https://doi.org/10.1007/978-981-19-3563-3_15

Germany is a federal state, therefore, constituted by sixteen constituent states which are collectively referred to as Länder.

Germany is part of the European Union, one of the six founding country, together with France, Italy, Luxemburg, the Netherlands, and Belgium.

Category	Value
Population (mln persons)	82.969
Currency	Euro

Source International Monetary Fund, year 2019

Germany is the largest economy of Europe, with a GDP worth 3,863.3 billion USD in 2019, and has second largest population (after Russia, classified by the UN as an Eastern European country, although Russia's territory extends between the European and Asian continents). Growth has been consistent in the last 10 years, with low inflation and unemployment. Germany scored highly in the 2020 Doing Business, ranking 10th out of 43 in Europe. It is both a large recipient of FDI and a large investor abroad. Germany is an

export-oriented country, marking a trade surplus with the rest of the world, being its first export categories machinery and vehicles.

GDP and local economy	
GDP current prices (billion USD)	3863.3
GDP per capita (USD)	46,564
GDP growth (%)	0.6
Inflation (%)	1.3
Unemployment (%)	3.2
General government total expenditure (% of GDP)	45.1
General government gross debt (% of GDP)	59.6
Doing Business Score 2020	79.7

Source International Monetary Fund and UNCTAD, year 2019

Foreign direct investment	
FDI outstock (million USD)	1,719,389
FDI instock (million USD)	953,306

Source UNCTAD, year 2019

Trade	
Imports (million USD)	1,234,222
Exports (million USD)	1,489,158

(continued)

(continued)

Trade	
Trade balance (million USD)	254,936

Source International Monetary Fund, year 2019

Main import–export	
First import by category	Machinery, nuclear reactors, boilers
Second import by category	Electrical, electronic equipment
First export by category	Machinery, nuclear reactors, boilers
Second export by category	Vehicles other than railway, tramway

Source United Nations COMTRADE, year 2020

The legal bases for taxation are established in the German basic law, outlining the general principles. Germany imposes at federal and local level different taxes, such as individual income tax, property sales taxes, capital gains, corporate income tax, and value added tax. Progressivity is guaranteed by a system with different bands and various deductions.

Taxes	
Company income tax (%)	30
Top individual income tax (%)	45
Value added tax or sales tax (%)	19
Reduced value added tax or sales tax (%)	7

Source RsA Asia report 2021
Note The CIT expressed above is the average estimation in the city of Berlin of the impact of Corporation tax (Körperschaftsteuer) and trade tax (Gewerbesteuer)

- Economic relation with China

Germany is the top importer from China and the top exporter towards China, with a trade surplus of 18 billion USD in 2020. "Vehicles other than railway, tramway" is the first export category, while "Electrical, electronic equipment" is the first import category. Germany is not involved in the Belt and Road Initiative, however, the first DTA dates back to 1985 and had been in force since May 1986. A new agreement has been signed in 2014, becoming effective in April 2016.

Category	Value
belt road	NO

Source UNCTAD, year 2021

Import from China	
Import from China (billion USD)	86.82
First Import category from China	Electrical, electronic equipment
First import value (billion USD)	20.65
Second import category from China	Machinery, nuclear reactors, boilers
Second import value (billion USD)	18.94

Source United Nations COMTRADE, year 2020

Export to China	
Export to China (billion USD)	105.26
First export category towards China	Vehicles other than railway, tramway
First export value (billion USD)	22.64
Second export category towards China	Machinery, nuclear reactors, boilers
Second export value (billion USD)	22.02

Source United Nations COMTRADE, year 2020

Trade balance	
Trade balance (billion USD)	18.44

Source United Nations COMTRADE, year 2020

Double tax agreement	
DTA effective date	2016.4.6
Dividends (%)	5–10
Interest (%)	0–10
Royalties (%)	6–10

Source State Administration of Taxation of China, year 2021

Title **AGREEMENT BETWEEN THE PEOPLE'S REPUBLIC OF CHINA AND THE FEDERAL REPUBLIC OF GERMANY FOR THE AVOIDANCE OF DOUBLE TAXATION AND THE PREVENTION OF FISCAL EVASION WITH RESPECT TO TAXES ON INCOME AND ON CAPITAL**

Treaty Text

The People's Republic of China and the Federal Republic of Germany,

Desiring to conclude an Agreement for the avoidance of double taxation and the prevention of fiscal evasion with respect to taxes on income and on capital,

Have agreed as follows:

Article 1 Persons Covered
This Agreement shall apply to persons who are residents of one or both of the Contracting States.

Article 2 Taxes Covered
This Agreement shall apply to taxes on income and on capital imposed on behalf of a Contracting State or its local authorities, irrespective of the manner in which they are levied.

There shall be regarded as taxes on income and on capital all taxes imposed on total income, on total capital, or on elements of income or of capital, including taxes on gains from the alienation of movable or immovable property, taxes on the total amounts of wages or salaries paid by enterprises, as well as taxes on capital appreciation.

The existing taxes to which the Agreement shall apply are in particular:

in China:
the individual income tax;
the enterprise income tax; (hereinafter referred to as "Chinese tax");
in the Federal Republic of Germany:
the income tax (Einkommensteuer);
the corporation tax (Körperschaftsteuer);
the trade tax (Gewerbesteuer); and
the capital tax (Vermögensteuer); including the supplements levied thereon (hereinafter referred to as "German tax").

The Agreement shall apply also to any identical or substantially similar taxes that are imposed after the date of signature of the Agreement in addition to, or in place of, the existing taxes. The competent authorities of the Contracting States shall notify each other of any significant changes that have been made in their taxation laws.

Article 3 General Definitions
For the purposes of this Agreement, unless the context otherwise requires:

the term "China" means the People's Republic of China, and when used in a geographical sense, means all the territory of the People's Republic of China, including its territorial sea, in so far as the Chinese laws relating to taxation apply, and any area beyond its territorial sea, insofar as the People's Republic of China has sovereign rights of exploration for and exploitation of resources of the sea-bed and its sub-soil and superjacent water resources in accordance with international law and its internal law;
the term "Germany" means the Federal Republic of Germany, and when used in a geographical sense, means the territory of the Federal Republic of Germany as well as the area of the sea-bed, its sub-soil and the superjacent waters adjacent to the territorial sea, in so far as the Federal Republic of Germany may exercise sovereign rights and jurisdiction in conformity with international law and

its national legislation for the purpose of exploring, exploiting, conserving and managing the living and non-living natural resources;
the terms "a Contracting State" and "the other Contracting State" mean China or the Federal Republic of Germany as the context requires;
the term "person" includes an individual, a company and any other body of persons;
the term "company" means any body corporate or any entity that is treated as a body corporate for tax purposes;
the terms "enterprise of a Contracting State" and "enterprise of the other Contracting State" mean respectively an enterprise carried on by a resident of a Contracting State and an enterprise carried on by a resident of the other Contracting State;
the term "international traffic" means any transport by a ship or aircraft operated by an enterprise that has its place of effective management in a Contracting State, except when the ship or aircraft is operated solely between places in the other Contracting State;
the term "national" means:
in respect of the Federal Republic of Germany,
any German within the meaning of the Basic Law for the Federal Republic of Germany and any legal person, partnership and association deriving its status as such from the laws in force in the Federal Republic of Germany;
in respect of China,
any individual possessing the nationality of the People's Republic of China, and any legal person, partnership or association deriving its status as such from the laws in force in the People's Republic of China;
the term "competent authority" means:
in the case of China, the State Administration of Taxation or its authorized representative;
in the case of the Federal Republic of Germany, the Federal Ministry of Finance or the agency to which it has delegated its powers.

As regards the application of the Agreement at any time by a Contracting State, any term not defined therein shall, unless the context otherwise requires, have the meaning which it has at that time under the law of that State for the purposes of the taxes to which the Agreement applies, any meaning under the applicable tax laws of that State prevailing over a meaning given to the term under other laws of that State.

Article 4 Resident

For the purposes of this Agreement, the term "resident of a Contracting State" means any person who, under the laws of that State, is liable to tax therein by reason of his domicile, residence, place of incorporation, place of effective management or any other criterion of a similar nature, and also includes that State or its local authorities. This term, however, does not include any person who is liable to tax in that State in respect only of income from sources in that State or capital situated therein.

Where by reason of the provisions of paragraph 1 an individual is a resident of both Contracting States, then his status shall be determined as follows:

he shall be deemed to be a resident only of the State in which he has a permanent home available to him; if he has a permanent home available to him in both States, he shall be deemed to be a resident only of the State with which his personal and economic relations are closer (centre of vital interests);
if the State in which he has his centre of vital interests cannot be determined, or if he has not a permanent home available to him in either State, he shall be deemed to be a resident only of the State in which he has an habitual abode;
if he has an habitual abode in both States or in neither of them, he shall be deemed to be a resident only of the State of which he is a national;
if he is a national of both States or of neither of them, the competent authorities of the Contracting States shall settle the question by mutual agreement.

Where by reason of the provisions of paragraph 1 a person other than an individual is a resident of both Contracting States, then it shall be deemed to be a resident only of the State in which its place of effective management is situated.

Article 5 Permanent Establishment

For the purposes of this Agreement, the term "permanent establishment" means a fixed place of business through which the business of an enterprise is wholly or partly carried on.

The term "permanent establishment" includes especially:

a place of management;
a branch;
an office;
a factory;
a workshop, and
a mine, an oil or gas well, a quarry or any other place of extraction of natural resources.

The term "permanent establishment" likewise encompasses:

A building site, or construction, assembly or installation project or supervisory activities in connection therewith, but only if such site, project or activities last more than twelve months;

The furnishing of services, including consultancy services, by an enterprise through employees or other personnel engaged for such purpose, but only if activities of that nature continue (for the same or a connected project) within a Contracting State for a period or periods aggregating more than 183 days within any twelve-month period.

Notwithstanding the preceding provisions of this Article, the term "permanent establishment" shall be deemed not to include:

the use of facilities solely for the purpose of storage, display or delivery of goods or merchandise belonging to the enterprise;

the maintenance of a stock of goods or merchandise belonging to the enterprise solely for the purpose of storage, display or delivery;
the maintenance of a stock of goods or merchandise belonging to the enterprise solely for the purpose of processing by another enterprise;
the maintenance of a fixed place of business solely for the purpose of purchasing goods or merchandise or of collecting information, for the enterprise;
the maintenance of a fixed place of business solely for the purpose of carrying on, for the enterprise, any other activity of a preparatory or auxiliary character;
the maintenance of a fixed place of business solely for any combination of activities mentioned in sub-paragraphs (a) to (e), provided that the overall activity of the fixed place of business resulting from this combination is of a preparatory or auxiliary character.

Notwithstanding the provisions of paragraphs 1 and 2, where a person—other than an agent of an independent status to whom paragraph 6 applies—is acting in a Contracting State on behalf of an enterprise of the other Contracting State and has, and habitually exercises, in that Contracting State an authority to conclude contracts in the name of the enterprise, that enterprise shall be deemed to have a permanent establishment in that Contracting State in respect of any activities which that person undertakes for the enterprise, unless the activities of such person are limited to those mentioned in paragraph 4 which, if exercised through a fixed place of business, would not make this fixed place of business a permanent establishment under the provisions of that paragraph.

An enterprise of a Contracting State shall not be deemed to have a permanent establishment in the other Contracting State merely because it carries on business in that other State through a broker, general commission agent or any other agent of an independent status, provided that such persons are acting in the ordinary course of their business. However, when the activities of such an agent are devoted wholly or almost wholly on behalf of that enterprise, and conditions are made or imposed between that enterprise and the agent in their commercial and financial relations which differ from those which would have been made between independent enterprises, he will not be considered an agent of an independent status within the meaning of this paragraph.

The fact that a company which is a resident of a Contracting State controls or is controlled by a company which is a resident of the other Contracting State, or which carries on business in that other State (whether through a permanent establishment or otherwise), shall not of itself constitute either company a permanent establishment of the other.

Article 6 Income from Immovable Property

Income derived by a resident of a Contracting State from immovable property (including income from agriculture or forestry) situated in the other Contracting State may be taxed in that other State.

The term "immovable property" shall have the meaning which it has under the law of the Contracting State in which the property in question is situated. The term shall in any case include property accessory to immovable property, livestock and equipment used in agriculture and forestry, rights to which the provisions of general law respecting landed property apply, usufruct of immovable property and rights to variable or fixed payments as consideration for the working of, or the right to work, mineral deposits, sources and other natural resources; ships and aircraft shall not be regarded as immovable property.

The provisions of paragraph 1 shall apply to income derived from the direct use, letting, or use in any other form of immovable property.

The provisions of paragraphs 1 and 3 shall also apply to the income from immovable property of an enterprise and to income from immovable property used for the performance of independent personal services.

Article 7 Business Profits

The profits of an enterprise of a Contracting State shall be taxable only in that State unless the enterprise carries on business in the other Contracting State through a permanent establishment situated therein. If the enterprise carries on business as aforesaid, the profits of the enterprise may be taxed in the other State, but only so much of them as is attributable to that permanent establishment.

Subject to the provisions of paragraph 3, where an enterprise of a Contracting State carries on business in the other Contracting State through a permanent establishment situated therein, there shall in each Contracting State be attributed to that permanent establishment the profits which it might be expected to make if it were a distinct and separate enterprise engaged in the same or similar activities under the same or similar conditions and dealing wholly independently with the enterprise of which it is a permanent establishment.

In determining the profits of a permanent establishment, there shall be allowed as deductions expenses which are incurred for the purposes of the permanent establishment, including executive and general administrative expenses so incurred, whether in the State in which the permanent establishment is situated or elsewhere.

Insofar as it has been customary in a Contracting State to determine the profits to be attributed to a permanent establishment on the basis of an apportionment of the total profits of the enterprise to its various parts, nothing in paragraph 2 shall preclude that Contracting State from determining the profits to be taxed by such an apportionment as may be customary; the method of apportionment adopted shall, however, be such that the result shall be in accordance with the principles contained in this Article.

No profits shall be attributed to a permanent establishment by reason of the mere purchase by that permanent establishment of goods or merchandise for the enterprise.

For the purposes of the preceding paragraphs, the profits to be attributed to the permanent establishment shall be determined by the same method year by year unless there is good and sufficient reason to the contrary.

Where profits include items of income which are dealt with separately in other Articles of this Agreement, then the provisions of those Articles shall not be affected by the provisions of this Article.

Article 8 Shipping and Air Transport

Profits from the operation of ships or aircraft in international traffic shall be taxable only in the Contracting State in which the place of effective management of the enterprise is situated.

For the purposes of this Article, profits from the operation of ships or aircraft in international traffic shall include:

profits from the rental on a bare-boat basis of ships or aircraft, and
profits from the use, maintenance or rental of containers (including trailers and related equipment used for the transport of the containers) used for the transport of goods or merchandise;
where such use, maintenance or rental, as the case may be, is incidental to the operation of ships or aircraft in international traffic.

If the place of effective management of a shipping enterprise is aboard a ship, then it shall be deemed to be situated in the Contracting State in which the home harbor of the ship is situated, or, if there is no such home harbor, in the Contracting State of which the operator of the ship is a resident.

The provisions of paragraph 1 shall also apply to profits from the participation in a pool, a joint business or an international operating agency.

Article 9 Associated Enterprises

Where

an enterprise of a Contracting State participates directly or indirectly in the management, control or capital of an enterprise of the other Contracting State, or
the same persons participate directly or indirectly in the management, control or capital of an enterprise of a Contracting State and an enterprise of the other Contracting State,
and in either case conditions are made or imposed between the two enterprises in their commercial or financial relations which differ from those which would be made between independent enterprises, then any profits which would, but for those conditions, have accrued to one of the enterprises, but, by reason of those conditions, have not so accrued, may be included in the profits of that enterprise and taxed accordingly.

Where a Contracting State includes in the profits of an enterprise of that State—and taxes accordingly—profits on which an enterprise of the other Contracting State has been charged to tax in that other State and the profits so included are profits which would have accrued to the enterprise of the first-mentioned State if the conditions made between the two enterprises had been those which would have been made between independent enterprises, then that other State shall make an appropriate adjustment to the amount of the tax charged therein on those profits. In determining such adjustment, due regard shall be had to the other provisions of this Agreement and the competent authorities of the Contracting States shall, if necessary, consult each other.

Article 10 Dividends

Dividends paid by a company which is a resident of a Contracting State to a resident of the other Contracting State may be taxed in that other State.

However, such dividends may also be taxed in the Contracting State of which the company paying the dividends is a resident and according to the laws of that State, but if the beneficial owner of the dividends is a resident of the other Contracting State, the tax so charged shall not exceed:

5% of the gross amount of the dividends if the beneficial owner is a company (other than a partnership) which holds directly at least 25% of the capital of the company paying the dividends;
15% of the gross amount of the dividends where those dividends are paid out of income or gains derived directly or indirectly from immovable property within the meaning of Article 6 by an investment vehicle which distributes most of this income or gains annually and whose income or gains from such immovable property is exempted from tax;
10% of the gross amount of the dividends in all other cases.

This paragraph shall not affect the taxation of the company in respect of the profits out of which the dividends are paid.

The term "dividends" as used in this Article means income from shares or other rights, not being debt-claims, participating in profits, or other income which is subjected to the same taxation treatment as income from shares by the laws of the State of which the company making the distribution is a resident.

The provisions of paragraphs 1 and 2 shall not apply if the beneficial owner of the dividends, being a resident of a Contracting State, carries on business in the other Contracting State of which the company paying the dividends is a resident through a permanent establishment situated therein, or performs in that other State independent personal services from a fixed base situated therein, and the holding in respect of which the dividends are paid is effectively connected with such permanent establishment or fixed base. In such case the provisions of Article 7 or Article 14, as the case may be, shall apply.

Where a company which is a resident of a Contracting State derives profits or income from the other Contracting State, that other State may not impose any tax on the dividends paid by the company, except insofar as such dividends are paid to a resident of that other State or insofar as the holding in respect of which the dividends are paid is effectively connected with a permanent establishment or a fixed base situated in that other State, nor subject the company's undistributed profits to a tax on the company's undistributed profits, even if the dividends paid or the undistributed profits consist wholly or partly of profits or income arising in such other State.

Article 11 Interest

Interest arising in a Contracting State and paid to a resident of the other Contracting State may be taxed in that other State.

However, such interest may also be taxed in the Contracting State in which it arises and according to the laws of that State, but if the beneficial owner of the interest is a resident of the other Contracting State, the tax so charged shall not exceed 10% of the gross amount of the interest.

Notwithstanding the provisions of paragraph 2,

interest arising in a Contracting State and paid to the Government of the other Contracting State shall be exempt from tax in the first-mentioned State;
interest arising in a Contracting State and paid in consideration of a loan guaranteed or insured by the other Contracting State or any financial institution wholly owned by it shall be exempt from tax in the first-mentioned State;
interest arising in China and paid to the German Federal Bank (Deutsche Bundesbank), the Development Loan Corporation (Kreditanstalt für Wiederaufbau) or the German Investment and Development Company (DEG—Deutsche Investitions- und Entwicklungsgesellschaft mbH), and any public credit institution of the Federal Republic of Germany, if the competent authorities of both States have agreed thereto, shall be exempt from Chinese tax;
interest arising in the Federal Republic of Germany and paid to:
the People's Bank of China;
the China Development Bank Corporation;
the Agricultural Development Bank of China;
the Export–Import Bank of China;
the National Council for Social Security Fund;
the China Investment Corporation, and
any other public credit institution of the Government of China, if the competent authorities of both States have agreed thereto;
shall be exempt from German tax.

Notwithstanding the provisions of paragraph 2, interest as referred to in paragraph 1 may be taxed only in the Contracting State of which the recipient is a resident if the recipient is the beneficial owner of the interest and the interest is paid in connection with the sale of commercial or scientific equipment on credit.

The term "interest" as used in this Article means income from debt-claims of every kind, whether or not secured by mortgage, and in particular, income from government securities and income from bonds or debentures, including premiums and prizes attaching to such securities, bonds or debentures. Penalty charges for late payment shall not be regarded as interest for the purpose of this Article.

The provisions of paragraphs 1 to 4 shall not apply if the beneficial owner of the interest, being a resident of a Contracting State, carries on business in the other Contracting State in which the interest arises, through a permanent establishment situated therein, or performs in that other State independent personal services from a fixed base situated therein, and the debt-claim in respect of which the interest is paid is effectively connected with such permanent establishment or fixed base. In such case the provisions of Article 7 or Article 14, as the case may be, shall apply.

Interest shall be deemed to arise in a Contracting State when the payer is a resident of that State. Where, however, the person paying the interest, whether he is a resident of a Contracting State or not, has in a Contracting State a permanent establishment or a fixed base in connection with which the indebtedness on which the interest is paid was incurred, and such interest is borne by such permanent establishment or fixed base, then such interest shall be deemed to arise in the State in which the permanent establishment or fixed base is situated.

Where, by reason of a special relationship between the payer and the beneficial owner or between both of them and some other person, the amount of the interest, having regard to the debt-claim for which it is paid, exceeds the amount which would have been agreed upon by the payer and the beneficial owner in the absence of such relationship, the provisions of this Article shall apply only to the last-mentioned amount. In such case, the excess part of the payments shall remain taxable according to the laws of each Contracting State, due regard being had to the other provisions of this Agreement.

Article 12 Royalties

Royalties arising in a Contracting State and beneficially owned by a resident of the other Contracting State may be taxed in that other State.

However, such royalties may also be taxed in the Contracting State in which they arise and according to the laws of that State, but if the beneficial owner of the royalties is a resident of the other Contracting State, the tax so charged shall not exceed:

in the case of royalties referred to in sub-paragraph (a) of paragraph 3, 10% of the gross amount of the royalties, and
in the case of royalties referred to in sub-paragraph (b) of paragraph 3, 10% of the adjusted amount of the royalties. For the purpose of this sub-paragraph "the adjusted amount" means 60% of the gross amount of the royalties.

The term "royalties" as used in this Article means:

payments of any kind received as a consideration for the use of, or the right to use, any copyright of literary, artistic or scientific work, including cinematograph films, and films or tapes for radio or television broadcasting, any patent, trade mark, design or model, plan, secret formula or process, or for information (know-how) concerning industrial, commercial or scientific experience, and

payments of any kind received as a consideration for the use of, or the right to use, any industrial, commercial or scientific equipment.

The provisions of paragraphs 1 and 2 shall not apply if the beneficial owner of the royalties, being a resident of a Contracting State, carries on business in the other Contracting State in which the royalties arise, through a permanent establishment situated therein, or performs in that other State independent personal services from a fixed base situated therein, and the right or property in respect of which the royalties are paid is effectively connected with such permanent establishment or fixed base. In such case the provisions of Article 7 or Article 14, as the case may be, shall apply.

Royalties shall be deemed to arise in a Contracting State when the payer is a resident of that Contracting State. Where, however, the person paying the royalties, whether he is a resident of a Contracting State or not, has in a Contracting State a permanent establishment or a fixed base in connection with which the liability to pay the royalties was incurred, and such royalties are borne by such permanent establishment or fixed base, then such royalties shall be deemed to arise in the State in which the permanent establishment or fixed base is situated.

Where, by reason of a special relationship between the payer and the beneficial owner or between both of them and some other person, the amount of the royalties, having regard to the use, right or information for which they are paid, exceeds the amount which would have been agreed upon by the payer and the beneficial owner in the absence of such relationship, the provisions of this Article shall apply only to the last-mentioned amount. In such case, the excess part of the payments shall remain taxable according to the laws of each Contracting State, due regard being had to the other provisions of this Agreement.

Article 13 Capital Gains

Gains derived by a resident of a Contracting State from the alienation of immovable property referred to in Article 6 and situated in the other Contracting State may be taxed in that other State.

Gains from the alienation of movable property forming part of the business property of a permanent establishment which an enterprise of a Contracting State has in the other Contracting State or of movable property pertaining to a fixed base available to a resident of a Contracting State in the other Contracting State for the purpose of performing independent personal services, including such gains from the alienation of such a permanent establishment (alone or with the whole enterprise) or of such a fixed base, may be taxed in that other State.

Gains from the alienation of ships or aircraft operated in international traffic, or movable property pertaining to the operation of such ships or aircraft, shall be taxable only in the Contracting State in which the place of effective management of the enterprise is situated.

Gains derived by a resident of a Contracting State from the alienation of shares deriving more than 50% of their value directly or indirectly from immovable property situated in the other Contracting State may be taxed in that other State.

Gains derived by a resident of a Contracting State from the alienation of shares, other than shares in which there is substantial and regular trading on a recognized stock exchange provided that the total of the shares alienated by the resident during the fiscal year in which the alienation takes place does not exceed 3% of the quoted shares, of a company which is a resident of the other Contracting State may be taxed in that other Contracting State if the first-mentioned resident, at any time during the 12 month period preceding the alienation has owned, directly or indirectly, at least 25% of the shares of that company.

Gains from the alienation of any property, other than that referred to in paragraphs 1 to 5, shall be taxable only in the Contracting State of which the alienator is a resident.

Article 14 Independent Personal Services

Income derived by a resident of a Contracting State in respect of professional services or other activities of an independent character shall be taxable only in that State except in one of the following circumstances, when such income may also be taxed in the other Contracting State:

if he has a fixed base regularly available to him in the other Contracting State for the purpose of performing his activities; in that case, only so much of the income as is attributable to that fixed base may be taxed in that other State;
if his stay in the other Contracting State is for a period or periods amounting to or exceeding in the aggregate 183 days in any twelve-month period commencing or ending in the fiscal year concerned; in that case, only so much of the income as is derived from his activities performed in that other State may be taxed in that other State.

The term "professional services" includes especially independent scientific, literary, artistic, educational or teaching activities as well as the independent activities of physicians, lawyers, engineers, architects, dentists and accountants.

Article 15 Income from Employment

Subject to the provisions of Articles 16, 18 and 19, salaries, wages and other similar remuneration derived by a resident of a Contracting State in respect of an employment shall be taxable only in that State unless the employment is exercised in the other Contracting State. If the employment is so exercised, such remuneration as is derived therefrom may be taxed in that other State.

Notwithstanding the provisions of paragraph 1, remuneration derived by a resident of a Contracting State in respect of an employment exercised in the other Contracting State shall be taxable only in the first-mentioned State if:
the recipient is present in the other State for a period or periods not exceeding in the aggregate 183 days in any twelve-month period commencing or ending in the fiscal year concerned, and
the remuneration is paid by, or on behalf of, an employer who is not a resident of the other State, and
the remuneration is not borne by a permanent establishment or a fixed base which the employer has in the other State.

Notwithstanding the preceding provisions of this Article, remuneration derived in respect of an employment exercised aboard a ship or aircraft operated in international traffic, may be taxed in the Contracting State in which the place of effective management of the enterprise which operates the ship or aircraft is situated.

Article 16 Directors' Fees

Directors' fees and other similar payments derived by a resident of a Contracting State in his capacity as a member of the board of directors of a company which is a resident of the other Contracting State may be taxed in that other State.

Article 17 Artistes and Sportsmen

Notwithstanding the provisions of Articles 7, 14 and 15, income derived by a resident of a Contracting State as an entertainer, such as a theatre, motion picture, radio or television artiste, or a musician, or as a sportsman, from his personal activities as such exercised in the other Contracting State, may be taxed in that other State.

Where income in respect of personal activities exercised by an entertainer or a sportsman in his capacity as such accrues not to the entertainer or sportsman himself but to another person, that income may, notwithstanding the provisions of Articles 7, 14 and 15, be taxed in the Contracting State in which the activities of the entertainer or sportsman are exercised.

Notwithstanding the provisions of paragraphs 1 and 2, income derived by an entertainer or sportsman who is resident in a Contracting State from activities exercised in the other Contracting State within the framework of a cultural exchange program agreed upon by the Governments of both Contracting States shall not be taxed in that other State.

Article 18 Pensions

Subject to the provisions of paragraph 2 of Article 19, pensions and similar payments or annuities paid to a resident of a Contracting State from the other Contracting State shall only be taxable in the first-mentioned State.

Notwithstanding the provisions of paragraph 1, pensions paid and other payments made under a public scheme which is part of the social security system of a Contracting State or a local authority thereof shall be taxable only in that State.

Article 19 Government Service

(a) Salaries, wages and other similar remuneration, other than a pension, paid by a Contracting State or a local authority thereof to an individual in respect of services rendered to that State or local authority shall be taxable only in that State.

However, such salaries, wages and other similar remuneration shall be taxable only in the other Contracting State if the services are rendered in that State and the individual is a resident of that State who:

is a national of that State; or
did not become a resident of that State solely for the purpose of rendering the services.

(a) Notwithstanding the provisions of paragraph 1, pensions and other similar remuneration paid by, or out of funds created by, a Contracting State or a local authority thereof to an individual in respect of services rendered to that State or local authority shall be taxable only in that State.
(b) However, such pensions and other similar remuneration shall be taxable only in the other Contracting State if the individual is a resident of, and a national of, that State.

The provisions of Articles 15, 16, 17 and 18 shall apply to salaries, wages, pensions and other similar remuneration in respect of services rendered in connection with a business carried on by a Contracting State or a local authority thereof.

Article 20 Visiting Professors, Teachers and Students

An individual who visits a Contracting State at the invitation of that State or of a university, college, school, museum or other cultural institution of that State or under an official programme of cultural exchange for a period not exceeding two years solely for the purpose of teaching, giving lectures or carrying out research at such institution and who is, or was immediately before that visit, a resident of the other Contracting State shall be exempt from tax in the first-mentioned State on his remuneration for such activity, provided that such remuneration is derived by him from outside that State. If the period exceeds two years, the remuneration for such activities may be taxed in the first-mentioned State from the beginning of the visit.

The provisions of paragraph 1 shall not apply to income from research if such research is undertaken not in the public interest but primarily for the private benefit of a specific person or persons.

Payments which a student or business apprentice who is or was immediately before visiting a Contracting State a resident of the other Contracting State and who is present in the first-mentioned State solely for the purpose of his education or training receives for the purpose of his maintenance, education or training shall not be taxed in that State, provided that such payments arise from sources outside that State.

Article 21 Other Income

Items of income of a resident of a Contracting State, wherever arising, not dealt with in the foregoing Articles of this Agreement shall be taxable only in that State.

The provisions of paragraph 1 shall not apply to income, other than income from immovable property as defined in paragraph 2 of Article 6, if the recipient of such income, being a resident of a Contracting State, carries on business in the other Contracting State through a permanent establishment situated therein, or performs in that other State independent personal services from a fixed base situated therein, and the right or property in respect of which the income is paid is effectively connected with such permanent establishment or fixed base. In such case the provisions of Article 7 or Article 14, as the case may be, shall apply.

Article 22 Capital

Capital represented by immovable property referred to in Article 6, owned by a resident of a Contracting State and situated in the other Contracting State, may be taxed in that other State.

Capital represented by movable property forming part of the business property of a permanent establishment which an enterprise of a Contracting State has in the other Contracting State may be taxed in that other State.

Capital represented by ships and aircraft operated in international traffic and by movable property pertaining to the operation of such ships and aircraft shall be taxable only in the Contracting State in which the place of effective management of the enterprise is situated.

All other elements of capital of a resident of a Contracting State shall be taxable only in that State.

Article 23 Methods for Elimination of Double Taxation

In China, in accordance with the provisions of the law of China, double taxation shall be eliminated as follows:

Where a resident of China derives income from the Federal Republic of Germany, the amount of tax on that income payable in the Federal Republic of Germany in accordance with the provisions of this Agreement may be credited against the Chinese tax imposed on that resident. The amount of the credit, however, shall not exceed the amount of the Chinese tax on that income computed in accordance with the taxation laws and regulations of China.

Where the income derived from the Federal Republic of Germany is a dividend paid by a company which is a resident of the Federal Republic of Germany to a company which is a resident of China and which owns not less than 20% of the shares of the company paying the dividend, the credit shall take into account the tax paid to the Federal Republic of Germany by the company paying the dividend in respect of its income.

In the Federal Republic of Germany, in accordance with the provisions of the law of the Federal Republic of Germany, double taxation shall be eliminated as follows:

Unless foreign tax credit is to be allowed under sub-paragraph (b), there shall be exempted from the assessment basis of the German tax any item of income arising in China and any item of capital situated within China which, according to this Agreement, may be taxed in China.

In the case of items of income from dividends, the preceding provision shall apply only to such dividends as are paid to a company (not including partnerships) being a resident of the Federal Republic of Germany by a company being a resident of China at least 25% of the capital of which is owned directly by the German company and which were not deducted when determining the profits of the company distributing these dividends.

There shall be exempted from the assessment basis of the taxes on capital any shareholding the dividends of which if paid, would be exempted, according to the foregoing sentences.

Subject to the provisions of German tax law regarding credit for foreign tax, there shall be allowed as a credit against German tax on income payable in respect of the following items of income the Chinese tax paid under the laws of China and in accordance with this Agreement:

dividends not dealt with in sub-paragraph (a);
interest;
royalties;
items of income that may be taxed in China according to paragraphs 4 and 5 of Article 13;

directors' fees;
items of income that may be taxed according to Article 17.

The provisions of sub-paragraph (b) shall apply instead of the provisions of sub-paragraph (a) to items of income as defined in Articles 7 and 10 and to the assets from which such income is derived if the resident of the Federal Republic of Germany does not prove that the gross income of the permanent establishment in the business year in which the profit has been realised or of the company resident in China in the business year for which the dividends were paid was derived exclusively or almost exclusively from activities within the meaning of nos. 1 to 6 of paragraph 1 of section 8 of the German Law on External Tax Relations (Aussensteuergesetz); the same shall apply to immovable property used by a permanent establishment and to income from this immovable property of the permanent establishment (paragraph 4 of Article 6) and to profits from the alienation of such immovable property (paragraph 1 of Article 13) and of the movable property forming part of the business property of the permanent establishment (paragraph 2 of Article 13).

the Federal Republic of Germany, however, retains the right to take into account in the determination of its rate of tax the items of income and capital, which are under the provisions of this Agreement exempted from German tax.

Notwithstanding the provisions of sub-paragraph (a), double taxation shall be avoided by allowing a tax credit as laid down in sub-paragraph (b)

if in the Contracting States items of income or capital are placed under differing provisions of this Agreement or attributed to different persons (except pursuant to Article 9) and this conflict cannot be settled by a procedure in accordance with paragraph 3 of Article 25 and if as a result of this difference in placement or attribution the relevant income or capital would remain untaxed or be taxed lower than without this conflict or

if after due consultation with the competent authority of China, the German competent authority notifies the Chinese competent authority in writing of other items of income to which it intends to apply the provisions of sub-paragraph (b). Double taxation is then avoided for the notified item of income by allowing a tax credit from the first day of the calendar year next following that in which the notification was made.

Article 24 Non-discrimination

Nationals of a Contracting State shall not be subjected in the other Contracting State to any taxation or any requirement connected therewith, which is other or more burdensome than the taxation and connected requirements to which nationals of that other State in the same circumstances, in particular with respect to residence, are or may be subjected. This provision shall, notwithstanding the provisions of Article 1, also apply to persons who are not residents of one or both of the Contracting States.

The taxation on a permanent establishment which an enterprise of a Contracting State has in the other Contracting State shall not be less favorably levied in that other

State than the taxation levied on enterprises of that other State carrying on the same activities. This provision shall not be construed as obliging a Contracting State to grant to residents of the other Contracting State any personal allowances, reliefs and reductions for taxation purposes on account of civil status or family responsibilities which it grants to its own residents.

Except where the provisions of paragraph 1 of Article 9, paragraph 8 of Article 11, or paragraph 6 of Article 12 apply, interest, royalties and other disbursements paid by an enterprise of a Contracting State to a resident of the other Contracting State shall, for the purpose of determining the taxable profits of such enterprise, be deductible under the same conditions as if they had been paid to a resident of the first-mentioned State. Similarly, any debts of an enterprise of a Contracting State to a resident of the other Contracting State shall, for the purpose of determining the taxable capital of such enterprise, be deductible under the same conditions as if they had been contracted to a resident of the first-mentioned State.

Enterprises of a Contracting State, the capital of which is wholly or partly owned or controlled, directly or indirectly, by one or more residents of the other Contracting State, shall not be subjected in the first-mentioned State to any taxation or any requirement connected therewith which is other or more burdensome than the taxation and connected requirements to which other similar enterprises of the first-mentioned State are or may be subjected.

The provisions of the Article shall, notwithstanding the provisions of Article 2, apply to taxes of every kind and description.

Article 25 Mutual Agreement Procedure

Where a person considers that the actions of one or both of the Contracting States result or will result for him in taxation not in accordance with the provisions of this Agreement, he may, irrespective of the remedies provided by the domestic law of those States, present his case to the competent authority of the Contracting State of which he is a resident or, if his case comes under paragraph 1 of Article 24, to that of the Contracting State of which he is a national. The case must be presented within three years from the first notification of the action resulting in taxation not in accordance with the provisions of the Agreement.

The competent authority shall endeavor, if the objection appears to it to be justified and if it is not itself able to arrive at a satisfactory solution, to resolve the case by mutual agreement with the competent authority of the other Contracting State, with a view to the avoidance of taxation which is not in accordance with the Agreement. Any agreement reached shall be implemented not withstanding any time limits in the domestic law of the Contracting States.

The competent authorities of the Contracting States shall endeavor to resolve by mutual agreement any difficulties or doubts arising as to the interpretation or application of the Agreement. They may also consult together for the elimination of double taxation in cases not provided for in the Agreement.

The competent authorities of the Contracting States may communicate with each other directly for the purpose of reaching an agreement in the sense of the preceding paragraphs. If necessary, representatives of the competent authorities and of the responsible tax administrations may meet for an exchange of opinions.

Article 26 Exchange of Information

The competent authorities of the Contracting States shall exchange such information as is foreseeably relevant for carrying out the provisions of this Agreement or to the administration or enforcement of the domestic laws concerning taxes of every kind and description imposed on behalf of the Contracting States or their local authorities, insofar as the taxation thereunder is not contrary to the Agreement. The exchange of information is not restricted by Articles 1 and 2.

Any information received under paragraph 1 by a Contracting State shall be treated as secret in the same manner as information obtained under the domestic laws of that State and shall be disclosed only to persons or authorities (including courts and administrative bodies) concerned with the assessment or collection of, the enforcement or prosecution in respect of, the determination of appeals in relation to the taxes referred to in paragraph 1, or the oversight of the above with a view to the proper application of this Agreement and the tax laws. Such persons or authorities shall use the information only for such purposes. They may disclose the information in public court proceedings or in judicial decisions.

In no case shall the provisions of paragraphs 1 and 2 be construed so as to impose on a Contracting State the obligation:

to carry out administrative measures at variance with the laws and administrative practice of that or of the other Contracting State;
to supply information which is not obtainable under the laws or in the normal course of the administration of that or of the other Contracting State;
to supply information which would disclose any trade, business, industrial, commercial or professional secret or trade process, or information, the disclosure of which would be contrary to public policy (*ordre public*).

If information is requested by a Contracting State in accordance with this Article, the other Contracting State shall use its information gathering measures to obtain the requested information, even though that other State may not need such information for its own tax purposes. The obligation contained in the preceding sentence is subject to the limitations of paragraph 3 but in no case shall such limitations be construed to permit a Contracting State to decline to supply information solely because it has no domestic interest in such information.

In no case shall the provisions of paragraph 3 be construed to permit a Contracting State to decline to supply information solely because the information is held by a bank, other financial institution, nominee or person acting in an agency or a fiduciary capacity or because it relates to ownership interests in a person.

Article 27 Assistance in the Collection of Taxes

The Contracting States shall endeavour to lend assistance to each other in the collection of revenue claims. The competent authorities of the Contracting States may by mutual agreement settle the mode of application of this Article.

In no case shall the provisions of this Article be construed so as to impose on a Contracting State the obligations:

to carry out administrative measures at variance with the law and administrative practice of that or of the other Contracting State;
to carry out measures which would be contrary to public policy (*ordre public*).

Article 28 Procedural Rules for Taxation at Source

If in one of the Contracting States the taxes on dividends, interest, royalties or other items of income derived by a person who is a resident of the other Contracting State are levied by withholding at source, the right of the first-mentioned State to apply the withholding of tax at the rate provided under its domestic law shall not be affected by the provisions of this Agreement. The tax withheld at source shall be refunded on application by the taxpayer if according to this Agreement, there is no or reduced source tax.

Refund applications must be submitted within the time limits in accordance with the provisions of the laws of the Contracting State in which the items of income arise.

Notwithstanding paragraph 1, each Contracting State shall provide for procedures to the effect,

that payments of income subject under this Agreement to no tax in the state of source may be made without deduction of tax;
that payments of income subject under this Agreement to reduced tax in the state of source may be made with deduction of tax only at the rate provided for in the relevant Article.

The Contracting State in which the items of income arise may ask for a certificate by the competent authority on the residence in the other Contracting State.

The competent authorities may by mutual agreement implement the provisions of this Article and if necessary establish other procedures for the implementation of tax reductions or exemptions provided for under this Agreement.

Article 29 Miscellaneous Rules

The benefits of this Agreement shall not be available where the main purpose for entering into certain transactions or arrangements was to secure these benefits and obtaining those benefits would be contrary to the object and purpose of the relevant provisions of this Agreement.

This Agreement shall not be interpreted to mean that a Contracting State is prevented from applying its domestic legal provisions on the prevention of tax evasion or tax avoidance.

Where a person considers that the application of the preceding paragraphs results for him in taxation not in accordance with the provisions of this Agreement, he may apply for a mutual agreement procedure.

Article 30 Members of Diplomatic Missions and Consular Posts

Nothing in this Agreement shall affect the fiscal privileges of members of diplomatic missions or consular posts under the general rules of international law or under the provisions of special agreements.

Article 31 Protocol

The attached Protocol shall be an integral part of this Agreement.

Article 32 Entry Into Force

This Agreement shall enter into force on the thirtieth day following the day on which the two Contracting States have notified each other that the domestic legal procedures for such entry into force have been fulfilled. The relevant date shall be the day on which the last notification is received.

The provisions of this Agreement shall have effect:

in the case of taxes withheld at source, in respect of amounts paid on or after the first day of January of the calendar year next following that in which the Agreement enters into force;
in the case of other taxes, for any tax year beginning on or after the first day of January of the calendar year next following that in which the Agreement enters into force.

With the entry into force of this Agreement, the Agreement between the People's Republic of China and the Federal Republic of Germany for the Avoidance of Double Taxation with respect to Taxes on Income and Capital signed in Bonn on 10 June 1985 shall expire. The provisions of the Agreement signed in Bonn on 10 June 1985 shall continue to apply to all tax cases having occurred prior to the date upon which this Agreement has entered into force. In any case, the provisions of the Agreement signed in Bonn on 10 June 1985 shall continue to be applicable until this Agreement shall become effective as provided for in paragraph 2 of this Article.

Article 33 Termination

This Agreement shall continue in effect indefinitely but either of the Contracting States may, on or before the thirtieth day of June in any calendar year beginning after the expiration of a period of five years from the date of its entry into force, give to the other Contracting State, through diplomatic channels, written notice of termination and, in such event, this Agreement shall cease to have effect:

in the case of taxes withheld at source, in respect of amounts paid on or after the first day of January of the calendar year next following that in which notice of termination is given;
in the case of other taxes, for any tax year beginning on or after the first day of January of the calendar year next following that in which notice of termination is given.

The date of receipt of such notice by the other Contracting State shall be definitive for the determination of the deadline (the thirtieth day of June in any calendar year).

IN WITNESS whereof the undersigned, duly authorised thereto, have signed this Agreement.

Done at Berlin on the 28th day of March, 2014, in duplicate in the Chinese, German and English languages, all texts being authentic. In case of divergence in interpretation of the Chinese and the German texts, the English text shall prevail.

For the Federal Republic of Germany.

For the People's Republic of China.

Protocol

At the signing of the Agreement between the People's Republic of China and the Federal Republic of Germany for the Avoidance of Double Taxation and the Prevention of Fiscal Evasion with respect to Taxes on Income and on Capital signed on March 28, 2014 (hereinafter referred to as "the Agreement"), both sides have agreed upon the following provisions, which shall form an integral part of the Agreement:

With reference to the term "Contracting State":

In respect of the Federal Republic of Germany, the term "Contracting State" includes "Länder". The term "Länder" means German States in accordance with the Basic Law for the Federal Republic of Germany.

With reference to Article 7:

The Contracting States expressed their willingness to refer to the OECD Model Commentary (2008) in interpreting and applying the provisions of this Article.

With reference to sub-paragraph (b) of paragraph 2 of Article 10:

In the case of the Federal Republic of Germany, an investment vehicle is a company according to paragraph 1 of section 1 of the German Act on German Real Estate Stock Corporations with Listed Shares (REIT Act).

With reference to Articles 10 and 11:

Notwithstanding the provisions of Articles 10 and 11 of this Agreement, dividends and interest may be taxed in the Contracting State in which they arise, and according to the law of that State,

> if they are derived from rights or debt claims carrying a right to participate in profits (including income derived by a silent partner ("stiller Gesellschafter") from his participation as such, or from a loan with an interest rate linked to borrower's profit ("partiarisches Darlehen") or from profit sharing bonds ("Gewinnobligationen") within the meaning of the tax law of the Federal Republic of Germany) and under the condition that they are deductible in the determination of profits of the debtor of such income.

With reference to Article 19:

The provisions of paragraphs 1 and 2 shall also apply in respect of salaries, wages and other similar remuneration and pensions paid to individuals in respect of services rendered to the People's Bank of China and the Deutsche Bundesbank.

The provisions of paragraph 1 shall likewise apply in respect of remuneration paid, under a development assistance programme of a Contracting State or a local authority thereof, out of funds exclusively supplied by that State or local authority, to a specialist or volunteer seconded to the other Contracting State with the consent of that other State.

The provisions of paragraphs 1 and 2 shall also apply in respect of salaries, wages and other similar remuneration and pensions paid:

out of German governmental funds to individuals in respect of services rendered to the Goethe Institute;
out of Chinese governmental funds to individuals in respect of services rendered to the Chinese Cultural Center;
to other comparable institutions mutually agreed by the Contracting States.

With reference to Article 26:

If in accordance with domestic law personal data are exchanged under this Agreement, the following additional provisions shall apply subject to the legal provisions in effect for each Contracting State:

"Personal data" shall mean any information relating to an identified or identifiable natural person; an identifiable person is one who can be identified through the information provided by the requesting agency.

The receiving agency may use such data only for the purposes stated in Article 26 and shall be subject to the conditions prescribed by the supplying agency. Data and information communicated pursuant to this Agreement must not be used in criminal matters without the prior consent of the supplying Contracting State, which is to be given in accordance with national law and in compliance with any applicable bi- or multilateral agreements on mutual assistance in criminal matters.

The receiving agency shall on request inform the supplying agency about the use of the supplied data and the results achieved thereby.

Any subsequent supply to other agencies not mentioned in paragraph 2 of Article 26 may be effected only with the prior approval of the supplying agency.

The supplying agency shall endeavour to their best efforts to ensure that the data to be supplied are accurate and that they are necessary for and proportionate to the purpose for which they are supplied. Any limitations on data supply prescribed under applicable domestic law shall be observed. If it emerges that inaccurate data or data which should not have been supplied have been supplied, the receiving agency shall be informed of this without delay. That agency shall then be obliged to correct or erase such data without delay.

Upon application the person concerned shall be informed of the supplied data relating to him and of the use to which such data are to be put. There shall be no obligation to furnish this information if on balance it turns out that the public interest in withholding it outweighs the interest of the person concerned in receiving it. In all other respects, the right of the person concerned to be informed of the existing data relating to him shall be governed by the domestic law of the Contracting State in whose sovereign territory the application for the information is made.

Where the domestic law of the supplying agency contains special provisions for the deletion of the personal data supplied, that agency shall inform the receiving agency accordingly. Irrespective of such law, supplied personal data shall be erased once they are no longer required for the purpose for which they were supplied.

The supplying and the receiving agencies shall be obliged to keep official records of the supply and receipt of personal data.

The supplying and the receiving agencies shall be obliged to take effective measures to protect the personal data supplied against unauthorised access, unauthorised alteration and unauthorised disclosure.

IN WITNESS whereof the undersigned, duly authorised thereto, have signed this Protocol.

Done at Berlin on the 28th day of March, 2014, in duplicate in the Chinese, German and English languages, all texts being authentic. In case of divergence in interpretation of the Chinese and the German texts, the English text shall prevail.

For the Federal Republic of Germany.

For the People's Republic of China.

Greece

Greece, officially the Hellenic Republic, is a state in Southern Europe. Greece borders with Albania to the northwest, North Macedonia and Bulgaria to the north, and Turkey to the northeast. Greece lies between the Aegean Sea to the east, the Ionian Sea to the west, the Cretan Sea, and the Mediterranean Sea to the south. Greece's capital and largest city is Athens.

Greek is the majority ethnic group, while Turks, Pomaks, and Romani are referred to as "national minorities".

The official and predominant spoken language is Greek.

Greece is a unitary parliamentary republic. The Greek Constitution regulates the political system, in force since 1975. The Hellenic Parliament exerts the legislative power forming the parliament. The Hellenic Parliament is elected through direct elections using the semi-proportional representation system.

Executive power is vested in the Prime Minister and his or her cabinet. The Prime Minister is appointed by the President of the Republic after being elected by the party or coalition with the parliamentary majority in the Hellenic Parliament.

Greece has a civil law system based on Roman law. The Supreme Civil and Criminal Court of Greece acts as Supreme Court, managing constitutional matters, with judicial review powers.

Greece is a unitary state, consisted of 13 regions subdivided into a total of 325.

Greece is part of the European union, entering in 1981.

Category	Value
Population (mln persons)	10.714
Currency	Euro

Source International Monetary Fund, year 2019

Greece is the fourth largest economy of Southern Europe, with a GDP valued 214 billion USD in 2019, and has a population of about 10.7 million people. Greece's inflation is 0.5%, while unemployment is the third highest in Europe (17.3%). Greece

© The Author(s), under exclusive license to Springer Nature Singapore Pte Ltd. 2022
L. Riccardi and G. Riccardi, *China–Europe Tax Treaties*,
https://doi.org/10.1007/978-981-19-3563-3_16

ranked 38 out of 43 in the 2020 Doing Business ranking, scoring 68.4, and imposes a CIT of 22%. Greece records a trade deficit of 24 billion USD.

GDP and local economy	
GDP current prices (billion USD)	214.0
GDP per capita (USD)	19,974
GDP growth (%)	1.9
Inflation (%)	0.5
Unemployment (%)	17.3
General government total expenditure (% of GDP)	47.3
General government gross debt (% of GDP)	184.9
Doing business score 2020	68.4

Source International Monetary Fund and UNCTAD, year 2019

Foreign direct investment	
FDI outstock (million USD)	19,848
FDI instock (million USD)	40,513

Source UNCTAD, year 2019

Trade	
Imports (million USD)	62,218
Exports (million USD)	37,874
Trade balance (million USD)	−24,344

Source International Monetary Fund and UNCTAD, year 2019

Main import–export	
First import by category	Mineral fuels, oils, distillation products
Second import by category	Machinery, nuclear reactors, boilers
First export by category	Mineral fuels, oils, distillation products
Second export by category	Pharmaceutical products

Source United Nations COMTRADE, year 2020

The legal bases for taxation are established in the constitution. Greece imposes individual income tax, property sales taxes, capital gains, corporate income tax, and value added tax. Progressivity is guaranteed by a system with different bands and various deductions.

Taxes	
Company income tax (%)	22
Top individual income tax (%)	44
Value added tax or sales tax (%)	24
Reduced value added tax or sales tax (%)	6 / 13

Source RsA Asia report, year 2021

- Economic relation with China

Greece records a trade deficit towards China of 6.27 billion USD in 2020. "Pharmaceutical products" is the first export category, worth 243 million USD, followed by "Salt, sulphur, earth, stone, plaster, lime and cement". "Machinery, nuclear reactors, boilers" is the first import category, valued 1.29 billion USD, followed by "Electrical, electronic equipment". Greece is part of the Belt and Road Initiative. In 2002 Greece and China have signed their DTA, which has entered into force in 2005.

Category	Value
Belt road	Yes

Source UNCTAD, year 2021

Import from China	
Import from China (billion USD)	7.04
First import category from China	Machinery, nuclear reactors, boilers
First import value (billion USD)	1.29
Second import category from China	Electrical, electronic equipment
Second import value (billion USD)	1.02

Source United Nations COMTRADE, year 2020

Export to China	
Export to China (billion USD)	0.773
First export category towards China	Pharmaceutical products
First export value (billion USD)	0.243
Second export category towards China	Salt, sulphur, earth, stone, plaster, lime and cement
Second export value (billion USD)	0.170

Source United Nations COMTRADE, year 2020

Trade balance	
Trade balance (billion USD)	– 6.27

Source United Nations COMTRADE, year 2020

Double tax agreement	
DTA effective date	2005.11.1
Dividends (%)	5–10
Interest (%)	0–10
Royalties (%)	10

Source State Administration of Taxation of China, year 2021

Title AGREEMENT BETWEEN THE GOVERNMENT OF THE HELLENIC REPUBLIC AND THE GOVERNMENT OF THE PEOPLE'S REPUBLIC OF CHINA FOR THE AVOIDANCE OF DOUBLE TAXATION AND THE PREVENTION OF FISCAL EVASION WITH RESPECT TO TAXES ON INCOME

Treaty Text

The Government of the Hellenic Republic and the Government of the People's Republic of China.

Desiring to conclude an Agreement for the avoidance of double taxation and the prevention of fiscal evasion with respect to taxes on income.

Have agreed as follows:

Article 1 Personal Scope

This Agreement shall apply to persons who are residents of one or both of the Contracting States.

Article 2 Taxes Covered

This Agreement shall apply to taxes on income imposed on behalf of a Contracting State or of its local authorities, irrespective of the manner in which they are levied.

There shall be regarded as taxes on income all taxes imposed on total income, or on elements of income, including taxes on gains from the alienation of movable or immovable property, as well as taxes on capital appreciation.

The existing taxes to which the Agreement shall apply are in particular:

In the Hellenic Republic:

the income tax on individuals;

the income tax on legal entities; (hereinafter referred to as "Hellenic tax").

In China

the individual income tax;

the income tax for enterprises with foreign investment and foreign enterprises; (hereinafter referred to as "Chinese tax").

The Agreement shall apply also to any identical or substantially similar taxes which are imposed after the date of signature of the Agreement in addition to, or in place of, the existing taxes. The competent authorities of the Contracting States shall notify each other of any substantial changes which have been made in their respective taxation laws within a reasonable period of time after such changes.

Article 3 General Definitions

For the purposes of this Agreement, unless the context otherwise requires:

the terms: "a Contracting State" and "the other Contracting State" mean the Hellenic Republic or China as the context requires;
the term "Hellenic Republic" comprises the territory of the Hellenic Republic and the part of the sea, the sea-bed and its subsoil under the Mediterranean Sea, over which the Hellenic Republic, in accordance with international law, has sovereign rights for the purpose of exploration, extraction or exploitation of the natural resources of such areas;
the term "China" means the People's Republic of China; when used in geographical sense, means all the territory of the People's Republic of China, including its territorial sea, in which the Chinese laws relating to taxation apply, and any area beyond its territorial sea, within which the People's Republic of China has sovereign rights of exploration for and exploitation of resources of the sea-bed and its sub-soil and superjacent water resources in accordance with international law;
the term "tax" means Hellenic tax or Chinese tax, as the context requires;
the term "person" includes an individual, a company and any other body of persons;
the term "company" means any body corporate or any entity which is treated as a body corporate for tax purposes;

The terms "enterprise of a Contracting State" and "enterprise of the other Contracting State" mean respectively an enterprise carried on by a resident of a Contracting State and an enterprise carried on by a resident of the other Contracting State;

the term "national" means:
any individual possessing the nationality of a Contracting State;
any legal person, partnership or association deriving its status as such from the laws in force in a Contracting State;
(I) the term "international traffic" means any transport by a ship or aircraft, except when the ship or aircraft is operated solely between places in a Contracting State;
the term "competent authority" means:
in the Hellenic Republic, the Minister of Finance or his authorised representative,
in China, the State Administration of Taxation or its authorized representative;

As regards the application of the Agreement at any time by a Contracting State, any term not defined therein shall, unless the context otherwise requires, have the meaning that it has at that time under the law of that State for the purposes of the taxes to which the Agreement applies, any meaning under the applicable tax laws of that State prevailing over a meaning given to the term under other laws of that State.

Article 4 Resident

For the purposes of this Agreement, the term "resident of a Contracting State" means any person who, under the laws of that State, is liable to tax therein by reason of his domicile, residence, place of management, place of head office or any other criterion of a similar nature, and also includes that State or local authority thereof. This term, however, does not include any person who is liable to tax in that State in respect only of income from sources in that State or capital situated therein.

Where by reason of the provisions of paragraph 1 an individual is a resident of both Contracting States, then his status shall be determined as follows:

he shall be deemed to be a resident only of the State in which he has a permanent home available to him; if he has a permanent home available to him in both States, he shall be deemed to be a resident of the State with which his personal and economic relations are closer (centre of vital interests);

if the State in which he has his centre of vital interests cannot be determined, or if he has not a permanent home available to him in either State, he shall be deemed to be a resident only of the State in which he has an habitual abode;

if he has an habitual abode in both States, or in neither of them, he shall be deemed to be a resident of the State of which he is a national;

if he is a national of both States, or of neither of them, the competent authorities of the Contracting States shall settle the question by mutual agreement.

Where by reason of the provisions of paragraph 1 a person other than an individual is a resident of both Contracting States, then the competent authorities of the Contracting States shall settle the question by mutual agreement.

Article 5 Permanent Establishment

For the purposes of this Agreement, the term "permanent establishment" means a fixed place of business through which the business of an enterprise is wholly or partly carried on.

The term "permanent establishment" includes especially:

a place of management;
a branch;
an office;
a factory;
a workshop, and
a mine, an oil or gas well, a quarry or any other place of extraction of natural resources.

The term "permanent establishment" likewise encompasses:

a building site, a construction, assembly or installation project or supervisory activities in connection therewith, but only where such site, project or activities continue for a period of more than twelve months.

Notwithstanding the preceding provisions of this Article, the term "permanent establishment" shall be deemed not to include:

the use of facilities solely for the purpose of storage, display or delivery of goods or merchandise belonging to the enterprise;

the maintenance of a stock of goods or merchandise belonging to the enterprise solely for the purpose of storage, display or delivery;

the maintenance of a stock of goods or merchandise belonging to the enterprise solely for the purpose of processing by another enterprise;

the maintenance of a fixed place of business solely for the purpose of purchasing goods or merchandise, or of collecting information, for the enterprise;

the maintenance of a fixed place of business solely for the purpose of carrying on, for the enterprise, any other activity of a preparatory or auxiliary character;

the maintenance of a fixed place of business solely for any combination of activities mentioned in subparagraphs (a) to (e), provided that the overall activity of the fixed place of business resulting from the combination is of a preparatory or auxiliary character.

Notwithstanding the provisions of paragraphs 1 and 2, where a person—other than an agent of an independent status to whom paragraph 6 applies—is acting in a Contracting State on behalf of an enterprise of the other Contracting State and has, and habitually exercises, in a Contracting State an authority to conclude contracts in the name of the enterprise, that enterprise shall be deemed to have a permanent establishment in that State in respect of any activities which that person undertakes for the enterprise, unless the activities of such person are limited to those mentioned in paragraph 4 which, if exercised through a fixed place of business, would not make this fixed place of business a permanent establishment under the provisions of that paragraph.

An enterprise of a Contracting State shall not be deemed to have a permanent establishment in the other Contracting State merely because it carries on business in that other State through a broker, general commission agent or any other agent of an independent status, provided that such persons are acting in the ordinary course of their business. However, when the activities of such an agent are devoted wholly or almost wholly on behalf of that enterprise, he will not be considered an agent of an independent status within the meaning of this paragraph.

The fact that a company which is a resident of a Contracting State controls or is controlled by a company which is a resident of the other Contracting State, or which carries on business in that other State (whether through a permanent establishment or otherwise), shall not of itself constitute either company a permanent establishment of the other.

Article 6 Income from Immovable Property

Income derived by a resident of a Contracting State from immovable property (including income from agriculture or forestry) situated in the other Contracting State may be taxed in that other State.

The term "immovable property" shall have the meaning which it has under the law of the Contracting State in which the property in question is situated. The term shall in any case include property accessory to immovable property, livestock and equipment used in agriculture and forestry, rights to which the provisions of general law respecting landed property apply, usufruct of immovable property and rights to variable or fixed payments as consideration for the working of, or the right to work, mineral deposits, sources and other natural resources; ships, and aircraft shall not be regarded as immovable property.

The provisions of paragraph 1 shall apply to income derived from the direct use, letting, or use in any other form of immovable property.

The provisions of paragraphs 1 and 3 shall also apply to the income from immovable property of an enterprise and to income from immovable property used for the performance of independent personal services.

Article 7 Business Profits

The profits of an enterprise of a Contracting State shall be taxable only in that State unless the enterprise carries on business in the other Contracting State through a permanent establishment situated therein. If the enterprise carries on business as aforesaid, the profits of the enterprise may be taxed in the other State but only so much of them as is attributable to that permanent establishment.

Subject to the provisions of paragraph 3, where an enterprise of a Contracting State carries on business in the other Contracting State through a permanent establishment situated therein, there shall in each Contracting State be attributed to that permanent establishment the profits which it might be expected to make if it were a distinct and separate enterprise engaged in the same or similar activities under the same or similar conditions and dealing wholly independently with the enterprise of which it is a permanent establishment.

In determining the profits of a permanent establishment, there shall be allowed as deductions expenses which are incurred for the purposes of the permanent establishment, including executive and general administrative expenses so incurred, whether in the State in which the permanent establishment is situated or elsewhere.

Insofar as it has been customary in a Contracting State to determine the profits to be attributed to a permanent establishment on the basis of an apportionment of the total profits of the enterprise to its various parts, nothing in paragraph 2 shall preclude that Contracting State from determining the profits to be taxed by such an apportionment as may be customary; the method of apportionment adopted shall, however, be such that the result shall be in accordance with the principles contained in this Article.

No profits shall be attributed to a permanent establishment by reason of the mere purchase by that permanent establishment of goods or merchandise for the enterprise.

For the purposes of the preceding paragraphs, the profits to be attributed to the permanent establishment shall be determined by the same method year by year unless there is good and sufficient reason to the contrary.

Where profits include items of income which are dealt with separately in other Articles of this Agreement, then the provisions of those Articles shall not be affected by the provisions of this Article.

Article 8 Shipping and Air Transport

Profits from the operation of ships by an enterprise of a Contracting State in international traffic shall be taxable only in that Contracting State.

Notwithstanding the provisions of paragraph 1, the implementation of the provisions of Article 18 concerning the taxation of income from the operation of ships in international traffic of the Agreement between the Government of the Hellenic Republic and the Government of the People's Republic of China on Maritime Transport signed at Beijing on the 16th of October 1995 shall not be affected.

Profits from the operation of aircraft by an enterprise of a Contracting State in international traffic shall be taxable only in that Contracting State.

The provisions of paragraphs 1, 2 and 3 shall also apply to profits form the participation in a pool, a joint business or an international operating agency.

Article 9 Associated Enterprises

Where

an enterprise of a Contracting State participates directly or indirectly in the management, control or capital of an enterprise of the other Contracting State, or the same persons participate directly of indirectly in the management, control or capital of an enterprise of a Contracting State and an enterprise of the other Contracting State,

and in either case conditions are made or imposed between the two enterprises in their commercial or financial relations which differ from those which would be made between independent enterprises, then any profits which would, but for those conditions, have accrued to one of the enterprises, but, by reason of those conditions, have not so accrued, may be included in the profits of that enterprises and taxed accordingly.

Where a Contracting State includes in the profits of an enterprise of that State—and taxes accordingly—profits on which an enterprise of the other Contracting State has been charged to tax in that other State and the profits so included are profits which would have accrued to the enterprise of the first—mentioned State if the conditions made between the two enterprises had been those which would have been made between independent enterprises, then that other State shall make an appropriate adjustment to the amount of the tax charged therein on those profits. In determining such adjustment, due regard shall be had to the other provisions of this Agreement and the competent authorities of the Contracting States shall if necessary consult each other.

Article 10 Dividends

Dividends paid by a company which is a resident of a Contracting State to a resident of the other Contracting State may be taxed in that other State.

However, such dividends may also be taxed in the Contracting State of which the company paying the dividends is a resident and according to the laws of that State, but if the recipient is the beneficial owner of the dividends the tax so charged shall not exceed:

5% of the gross amount of the dividends if the beneficial owner is a company (other than partnership) which holds directly at least 25% of the capital of the company paying the dividends:

10% of the gross amount of the dividends in all other cases.

The competent authorities of the Contracting States shall by mutual agreement settle the mode of application of these limitations.

This paragraph shall not affect the taxation of the company in respect of the profits out of which the dividends are paid.

The term "dividends", as used in this Article means income from shares, "jouissance" shares or "jouissance" rights, mining shares, founders' shares or other rights, not being debt-claims, participating in profits, as well as income from other corporate rights which is subjected to the same taxation treatment as income from shares by the laws of the State of which the company making the distribution is a resident.

The provisions of paragraphs 1 and 2 shall not apply if the beneficial owner of the dividends, being a resident of a Contracting State, carries on business in the other Contracting State of which the company paying the dividends is a resident, through a permanent establishment situated therin, or performs in that other State independent personal services from a fixed base situated therein, and the holding in respect of which the dividends are paid is effectively connected with such permanent establishment or fixed base. In such case the provisions of Article 7 or Article 14, as the case may be, shall apply.

Where a company which is a resident of a Contracting State derives profits or income from the other Contracting State, that other State may not impose any tax on the dividends paid by the company, except insofar as such dividends are paid to a resident of that other State or insofar as the holding in respect of which the dividends are paid is effectively connected with a permanent establishment or a fixed base situated in that other State, nor subject the company's undistributed profits to a tax on the company's undistributed profits, even if the dividends paid or the undistributed profits consist wholly or partly of profits or income arising in such other State.

Article 11 Interest

Interest arising in a Contracting State and paid to a resident of the other Contracting State may be taxed in that other State.

However, such interest may also be taxed in the Contracting State in which it arises and according to the laws of that State, but if the recipient is the beneficial owner of the interest the tax so charged shall not exceed 10% of the gross amount of the interest. The competent authorities of the Contracting State shall by mutual agreement settle the mode of application of this limitation.

Notwithstanding the provisions of paragraph 2, interest arising in a Contracting State and derived by the Government of the other Contracting State, a local authority and the Central Bank thereof of any financial institutions wholly owned by the Government of that other State, shall be exempt from tax in the first-mentioned State.

The term "interest", as used in this Article, means income from debt-claims of every kind, whether or not secured by mortgage, and whether or not carrying a right to participate in the debtor's profits, and in particular, income from government securities and income from bonds or debentures, including premiums and prizes attaching to such securities, bonds or debentures. Penalty charges for late payment shall not be regarded as interest for the purpose of this Article.

The provisions of paragraphs 1, 2 and 3 shall not apply if the beneficial owner of the interest, being a resident of a Contracting State, carries on business in the other Contracting State in which the interest arises, through a permanent establishment situated therein, or performs in that other State independent personal services from a fixed base situated therein, and the debt-claim in respect of which the interest is paid is effectively connected with such permanent establishment or fixed base. In such case the provisions of Article 7 or Article 14, as the case may be, shall apply.

Interest shall be deemed to arise in a Contracting State when the payer is a resident of that State. Where, however, the person paying the interest, whether he is a resident of a Contracting State or not, has in a Contracting State a permanent establishment or a fixed base in connection with which the indebtedness on which the interest is paid was incurred, and such interest is borne by such permanent establishment or fixed base, then such interest shall be deemed to arise in the State in which the permanent establishment or fixed base is situated.

Where, by reason of a special relationship between the payer and the beneficial owner or between both of them and some other person, the amount of the interest, having regard to the debt-claim for which it is paid, exceeds the amount which would have been agreed upon by the payer and the beneficial owner in the absence of such relationship, the provisions of this Article shall apply only to the last-mentioned amount. In such case, the excess part of the payment shall remain taxable according to the laws of each Contracting State, due regard being had to the other provisions of this Agreement.

Article 12 Royalties

Royalties arising in a Contracting State and paid to a resident of the other Contracting State may be taxed in that other State.

However, such royalties may also be taxed in the Contracting State in which they arise and according to the laws of that State, but if the recipient is the beneficial owner of the royalties the tax so charged shall not exceed 10% of the gross amount of the royalties. The competent authorities of the Contracting States shall by mutual agreement settle the mode of applications of this limitation.

The term "royalties", as used in this Article means payments of any kind received as a consideration for the use of, or the right to use, any copyright of literary, artistic or scientific work including cinematograph films and films or tapes for television or radio broadcasting, any patent, trade mark, design or model, plan, secret formula or process, or for the use of, or the right to use, industrial, commercial or scientific equipment, or for information concerning industrial, commercial or scientific experience.

The provisions of paragraphs 1 and 2 shall not apply if the beneficial owner of the royalties, being a resident of a Contracting State, carries on business in the other Contracting State in which the royalties arise, through a permanent establishment situated therein, or performs in that other State independent personal services from a fixed base situated therein, and the right or property in respect of which the royalties are paid is effectively connected with such permanent establishment or fixed base. In such case the provisions of Article 7 or Article 14, as the case may be, shall apply.

Royalties shall be deemed to arise in a Contracting State where the payer is a resident of that State. Where, however, the person paying the royalties, whether he is a resident of a Contracting State or not, has in a Contracting State a permanent establishment or a fixed base in connection with which the liability to pay the royalties was incurred and such royalties are borne by that permanent establishment or fixed base, then such royalties shall be deemed to arise in the State in which the permanent establishment or fixed base is situated.

Where, by reason of a special relationship between the payer and the beneficial owner or between both of them and some other person, the amount of the royalties, having regard to the use, right or information for which they are paid, exceeds the amount which would have been agreed upon by the payer and the beneficial owner in the absence of such relationship, the provisions of this Article shall apply only to the last-mentioned amount. In such case, the excess part of the payments shall remain taxable according to the laws of each Contracting State, due regard being had to the other provisions of this Agreement.

Article 13 Capital Gains

Gains derived by a resident of a Contracting State from the alienation of immovable property referred to in Article 6 and situated in the other Contracting State may be taxed in that other State.

Gains from the alienation of movable property forming part of the business property of a permanent establishment which an enterprise of a Contracting State has in the other Contracting State or of movable property pertaining to a fixed base available to a resident of a Contracting State in the other Contracting State for the purpose of performing independent personal services, including such gains from the alienation of such a permanent establishment (alone or with the whole enterprise) or of such fixed base, may be taxed in that other State.

Gains from the alienation of ships or aircraft operated in international traffic or movable property pertaining to the operation of such ships or aircraft shall be taxable only in the Contracting State in which the profits of such ships or aircraft are taxable according to the provisions of Article 8.

Gains from the alienation of shares of the capital stock of a company the property of which consists directly or indirectly principally of immovable property situated in a Contracting State may be taxed in that Contracting State.

Gains from the alienation of any property other than that referred to in paragraphs 1 to 4, shall be taxable only in the Contracting State of which the alienator is a resident.

Article 14 Independent Personal Services

Income derived by a resident of a Contracting State in respect of professional services or other activities of an independent character shall be taxable only in that State except in one of the following circumstances, when such income may also be taxed in the other Contracting State if:

he has a fixed base regularly available to him in that other State for the purpose of performing his activities, or

he is present in the other State for a period or periods exceeding in the aggregate 183 days in the calendar year concerned, but only so much thereof as is attributable to that fixed base or to activities performed in that State.

The term "professional services" includes, especially, independent scientific, literary, artistic, educational or teaching activities as well as the independent activities of physicians, lawyers, engineers, architects, dentists and accountants.

Article 15 Dependent Personal Services

Subject to the provisions of Articles 16, 18, 19, 20 and 21 salaries, wages and other similar remuneration derived by a resident of a Contracting State in respect of an employment shall be taxable only in that State unless the employment is exercised, in the other Contracting State. If the employment is so exercised, such remuneration as is derived therefrom may be taxed in that other State.

Notwithstanding the provisions of paragraph 1, remuneration derived by a resident of a Contracting State in respect of an employment exercised in the other Contracting State shall be taxable only in the first-mentioned State if:

the recipient is present in the other State for a period or periods not exceeding in the aggregate 183 days in any twelve month period commencing or ending in the calendar year concerned, and

the remuneration is paid by or on behalf of, an employer who is not a resident of the other State, and

the remuneration is not borne by a permanent establishment or a fixed base which the employer has in the other State.

Notwithstanding the preceding provisions of this Article, remuneration derived in respect of an employment exercised aboard a ship or aircraft operated in international traffic, shall be taxable only in the Contracting State in which the profits from the operation of the ship or aircraft are taxable according to the provisions of Article 8.

Article 16 Directors' Fees

Directors' fees and other similar payments derived by a resident of a Contracting State in his capacity as a member of the board of directors of a company which is a resident of the other Contracting State may be taxed in that other State.

Article 17 Artistes and Sportsmen

Notwithstanding the provisions of Articles 14 and 15, income derived by a resident of a Contracting State as an entertainer, such as a theatre, motion picture, radio or television artiste, or a musician, or as a sportsman, from his personal activities as such exercised in the other Contracting State, may be taxed in that other State.

Where income in respect of personal activities exercised by an entertainer or a sportsman, in his capacity as such accrues not to the entertainer or sportsman, himself but to another person, that income, notwithstanding the provisions of Articles 7, 14 and 15, may be taxed in the Contracting State in which the activities of the entertainer or sportsman are exercised.

Notwithstanding the preceding provisions of this Article, income derived by entertainers or sportsmen who are residents of a Contracting State from the activities exercised in the other Contracting State under a plan of cultural exchange between the Governments of both Contracting States shall be exempt from tax in that other State.

Article 18 Pensions

Subject to the provisions of paragraph 2 of Article 19, pensions and other similar remuneration paid to a resident of a Contracting State in consideration of past employment shall be taxable only in that State.

Notwithstanding the provisions of paragraph 1, pensions paid and other similar payments made by the Government of a Contracting State or a local authority thereof under a public welfare scheme of the social security system of that State may be taxed in that State.

Article 19 Government Services

(a) Salaries, wages and other similar remuneration, other than a pension, paid by a Contracting State or a local authority thereof to an individual in respect of services rendered to that State or authority shall be taxable only in that State.

However, such salaries, wages and other similar remuneration shall be taxable only in the other Contracting State if the services are rendered in that State and the individual is a resident of that State who:

is a national of that State; or

did not become a resident of that State solely for the purpose of rendering the services.

(a) Any pension paid by, or out of funds created by, a Contracting State or a local authority thereof to an individual in respect of services rendered to that State or authority shall be taxable only in that State.

(b) However, such pension shall be taxable only in the other Contracting State if the individual is a resident of, and a national of, that State.

The provisions of Articles 15, 16, 17 and 18 shall apply to remuneration and pensions in respect of services rendered in connection with a business carried on by a Contracting State or a local authority thereof.

Article 20 Teachers and Researchers

Remuneration which an individual who is or was immediately before visiting a Contracting State, a resident of the other Contracting State and who is present in the first-mentioned State for the primary purpose of teaching, giving lectures or conducting research at a university, college, school or educational institution or scientific research institution recognized by the first-mentioned State derives for the purpose of such teaching, lectures or research shall not be taxed in the first-mentioned State, for a period of three years from the date of his first arrival in the first-mentioned State.

The provisions of paragraph 1 shall not apply to income from research if such research is undertaken not in the public interest but primarily for the private benefit of a specific person or persons.

Article 21 Students and Trainees

Payments which a student, business apprentice or trainee who is or was immediately before visiting a Contracting State a resident of the other Contracting State and who is present in the first-mentioned State solely for the purpose of his education or training receives for the purpose of his maintenance, education or training shall not be taxed in that State, provided that such payments arise from sources outside that State.

In respect of grants, scholarships and remuneration from employment not covered by paragraph 1, a student, business apprentice or trainee described in paragraph 1 shall, in addition, be entitled during such education or training to the same exemptions, reliefs or reductions in respect of taxes available to residents of the State which he is visiting.

Article 22 Other Income

Items of income of a resident of a Contracting State, wherever arising, not dealt with, in the foregoing Articles of this Agreement shall be taxable only in that State.

The provisions of paragraph 1 shall not apply to income, other than income from immovable property as defined in paragraph 2 of Article 6, if the recipient of such income being a resident of a Contracting State, carries on business in the other Contracting State through a permanent establishment situated therein, or performs in that other State independent personal services from a fixed base situated therin, and the right or property in respect of which the income is paid is effectively connected with such permanent establishment or fixed base. In such case the provisions of Article 7 or Article 14, as the case may be, shall apply.

Article 23 Methods for Elimination of Double Taxation

In the Hellenic Republic, double taxation shall be eliminated as follows:

Where a resident of the Hellenic Republic derives income which, in accordance with the provisions of this Agreement, may be taxed in China, the Hellenic Republic shall allow as deduction from the tax on the income of that resident, an amount equal to the income tax paid in China.

Such deduction shall not, however, exceed that part of the income tax, as computed before the deduction is given, which is attributable, to the income which may be taxed in China.

Where dividends paid by a company which is a resident of China to a resident of the Hellenic Republic, the credit shall take into account, in addition to any tax creditable under the provisions of subparagraph (a) of this paragraph, the tax payable by the company in respect of the profits out of which such dividends are paid.

In China, double taxation shall be eliminated as follows:

Where a resident of China derives income from the Hellenic Republic the amount of tax on that income payable in the Hellenic Republic in accordance with the provisions of this Agreement, may be credited against the Chinese tax imposed on that resident. The amount of the credit, however, shall not exceed the amount of the Chinese tax on that income computed in accordance with the taxation laws and regulations of China.

Article 24 Non-discrimination

Nationals of a Contracting State shall not be subjected in the other Contracting State to any taxation or any requirement connected therewith, which is other or more burdensome than the taxation and connected requirements to which nationals of that other State in the same circumstances, in particular in the respect to residence, are or may be subjected. This provisions shall, notwithstanding the provisions of Article 1, also apply to persons who are not residents of one or both of the Contracting States.

The taxation on a permanent establishment which an enterprise of a Contracting State has in the other Contracting State shall not be less favourably levied in that other State than the taxation levied on enterprises of that other State carrying on the same activities. This provision shall not be construed as obliging a Contracting State to grant to residents of the other Contracting State any personal allowances, reliefs and reductions for taxation purposes on account of civil status or family responsibilities which it grants to its own residents.

Except where the provisions of paragraph 1 of Article 9, paragraph 7 of Article 11, or paragraph 6 of Article 12, apply, interest, royalties and other disbursements paid by an enterprise of a Contracting State to a resident of the other Contracting State shall, for the purpose of determining the taxable profits of such enterprise, be deductible under the same conditions as if they had been paid to a resident of the first-mentioned State.

Enterprises of a Contracting State, the capital of which is wholly or partly owned or controlled, directly or indirectly, by one or more residents of the other Contracting State, shall not be subjected in the first-mentioned State to any taxation or any requirement connected therewith which is other or more burdensome than the taxation and connected requirements to which other similar enterprises of the first-mentioned State are or may be subjected.

The provisions of this Article shall, notwithstanding the provision of Article 2, apply to taxes of every kind and description.

Article 25 Mutual Agreement Procedure

Where a person considers that the actions of one or both of the Contracting States result or will result for him in taxation not in accordance with this Agreement, he may, irrespective of the remedies provided by the domestic law of those States, present his case to the competent authority of the Contracting State of which he is a resident or, if his case comes under paragraph 1 of Article 24, to that of the Contracting State of which he is a national. The case must be presented within three years from the first notification of the action resulting in taxation not in accordance with the provisions of the Agreement.

The competent authority shall endeavour, if the objection appears to it to be justified and if it is not itself able to arrive at a satisfactory solution, to resolve the case by mutual agreement with the competent authority of the other Contracting State, with a view to the avoidance of taxation which is not in accordance with the Agreement. Any agreement reached shall be implemented notwithstanding any time limits in the domestic law of the Contracting States.

The competent authorities of the Contracting States shall endeavour to resolve by mutual agreement any difficulties or doubts arising as to the interpretation or application of the Agreement. They may also consult together for the elimination of double taxation in cases not provided for in the Agreement.

The competent authorities of the Contracting States may communicate with each other directly for the purpose of reaching an agreement in the sense of paragraphs 2 and 3. When it seems advisable for reaching agreement, representatives of the competent authorities of the Contracting States may meet together for an oral exchange of opinions.

Article 26 Exchange of Information

The competent authorities of the Contracting States shall exchange such information as is necessary for carrying out the provisions of this Agreement or of the domestic laws of the Contracting States concerning taxes covered by the Agreement insofar as the taxation thereunder is not contrary to the Agreement, in particular for the prevention of evasion of such taxes. The exchange of information is not restricted by Article 1. Any information received by a Contracting State shall be treated as secret in the same manner as information obtained under the domestic laws of that State and shall be disclosed only to persons or authorities (including courts and administrative bodies) involved in the assessment or collection of, the enforcement or prosecution in respect of, or the determination of appeals in relation to, the taxes covered by the Agreement. Such persons or authorities shall use the information only for such purposes. They may disclose the information in public court proceedings or in judicial decisions.

In no case shall the provisions of paragraph 1 be construed so as to impose on a Contracting States the obligation:

to carry out administrative measures at variance with the laws and administrative practice of that or of the other Contracting State;
to supply information which is not obtainable under the laws or in the normal course of the administration of that or of the other Contracting State;
to supply information which would disclose any trade, business, industrial, commercial or professional secret or trade process, or information, the disclosure of which would be contrary to public policy (ordre public).

Article 27 Members of Diplomatic Missions and Consular Posts
Nothing in this Agreement shall affect the fiscal privileges of members of diplomatic missions or consular posts under the general rules of international law or under the provisions of special agreements.

Article 28 Entry Into Force
The Contracting States shall notify each other through diplomatic channels that the legal procedures for the entry into force of this Agreement have been completed.

The Agreement shall enter into force on the thirtieth day after the date of the latter of the notifications referred to in paragraph 1 and its provisions shall have effect in respect of income derived during the taxable year beginning on or after the first day of January next following that in which this Agreement enters into force.

Article 29 Termination
This Agreement shall continue in effect indefinitely but either of the Contracting State may, on or before the thirtieth day of June in any calendar year beginning after the expiration of a period of five years from the date of its entry into force, give written notice of termination to the other Contracting State through diplomatic channels. In such event this Agreement shall cease to have effect in respect of income derived during the taxable year beginning on or after the first day of January in the calendar year next following that in which the notice of termination is given.

IN WITNESS WHEREOF the undersigned, duly authorised thereto, have signed this Agreement.

Done at Beijing on the day of 3.6.2002 in duplicate, in the Greek, the Chinese and the English languages, the three texts being equally authentic. In case there is any divergence of interpretation between the Chinese and the Hellenic texts, the English text shall prevail.

For the Government of the Hellenic Republic.

For the Government of the People's Republic of China.

Ireland

Ireland is a state in Northern Europe. Ireland borders Northern-Ireland (part of the United Kingdom) to the north, while its coast overlooks the Atlantic Ocean, with the Celtic Sea to the south, St George's Channel to the south-east, and the Irish Sea to the east. Ireland's capital and largest city is Dublin, also a major financial center.

The Irish are the majority ethnic group, while Asians and Blacks constitute the major minorities.

The predominant spoken and official language is English, while Irish is also an official language but less widely spoken. Minority languages used by immigrants and second generations are Polish and the Baltic languages.

Ireland is a unitary parliamentary republic. The Bunreacht na hÉireann is the constitution regulating the political system, in force since 1937. The Dáil Éireann and Seanad Éireann exert the legislative power forming the parliament. The Dáil is elected through direct elections using the single transferable vote system. The members of the Seanad are also elected with single transferable vote, however 43 members are elected indirectly.

Executive power is vested in the Taoiseach and his or her cabinet. The Taoiseach is appointed by the President of the Republic after being elected by the party or coalition with the parliamentary majority in the Dáil.

Ireland has a common law system based on British law. The Cúirt Uachtarach acts as Supreme Court, managing constitutional matters, with judicial review powers.

Ireland is a unitary state, formed by four provinces and 26 counties.

Ireland is part of the European Union since 1973, when it joined the European Economic Community along with the United Kingdom and Denmark.

Category	Value
Population (mln persons)	4.95
Currency	Euro

Source International Monetary Fund, year 2019

© The Author(s), under exclusive license to Springer Nature Singapore Pte Ltd. 2022
L. Riccardi and G. Riccardi, *China–Europe Tax Treaties*,
https://doi.org/10.1007/978-981-19-3563-3_17

Ireland is the 14th largest economy of Europe, with a GDP valued 384.9 billion USD in 2019, and the economy with the fastest economic growth in Europe (5.5% in 2019). Ireland has a population of about 4.95 million people. Ireland enjoys low inflation (0.9%), while unemployment is 5.0%. Ireland ranked 11 out of 43 in Europe in the 2020 Doing Business ranking, scoring 79.6, and imposes a CIT of 12.5%. Ireland records a trade surplus of 71.2 billion USD, it is the 13th main exporter in Europe.

GDP and local economy	
GDP current prices (billion USD)	384.9
GDP per capita (USD)	77,771
GDP growth (%)	5.5
Inflation (%)	0.9
Unemployment (%)	5.0
General government total expenditure (% of GDP)	24.5
General government gross debt (% of GDP)	57.3
Doing business score 2020	79.6

Source International Monetary Fund and UNCTAD, year 2019

Foreign direct investment	
FDI outstock (million USD)	1,085,167
FDI instock (million USD)	1,120,301

Source UNCTAD, year 2019

Trade	
Imports (million USD)	98,483
Exports (million USD)	169,779
Trade balance (million USD)	71,297

Source International Monetary Fund and UNCTAD, year 2019

Main import–export	
First import by category	Aircraft, spacecraft
Second import by category	Machinery, nuclear reactors, boilers
First export by category	Pharmaceutical products
Second export by category	Organic chemicals

Source United Nations COMTRADE, year 2020

The legal bases for taxation are established in the constitution. Ireland imposes individual income tax, property sales taxes, capital gains, corporate income tax, and value added tax. The Irish corporate tax is one of the lowest in Europe. Progressivity is guaranteed by a system with different bands and various deductions.

Taxes	
Company income tax (%)	12.5
Top individual income tax (%)	40
Value added tax or sales tax (%)	21
Reduced value added tax or sales tax (%)	9/13.5

Source RsA Asia report, year 2021

- Economic relation with China

Ireland records a trade surplus of 10 billion USD in 2020. "Electrical, electronic equipment" is the first export category, worth 7.41 billion USD, followed by "Pharmaceutical products". "Machinery, nuclear reactors, boilers" is the first import category, valued 1.01 billion USD. Ireland is not part of the Belt and Road Initiative. In April 2000, Ireland and China have signed their DTA, which has come into force in December of the same year.

Category	Value
Belt road	No

Source UNCTAD, year 2021

Import from China	
Import from China (billion USD)	4
First import category from China	Machinery, nuclear reactors, boilers
First import value (billion USD)	1.01
Second import category from China	Electrical, electronic equipment
Second import value (billion USD)	0.49

Source United Nations COMTRADE, year 2020

Export to China	
Export to China (billion USD)	14.04
First export category towards China	Electrical, electronic equipment
First export value (billion USD)	7.41
Second export category towards China	Pharmaceutical products
Second export value (billion USD)	2.59

Source United Nations COMTRADE, year 2020

Trade balance	
Trade balance (billion USD)	10.04

Source United Nations COMTRADE, year 2020

Double tax agreement	
DTA effective date	2000.12.29
Dividends (%)	5–10
Interest (%)	0–10
Royalties (%)	6–10

Source State Administration of Taxation of China, year 2021

Title AGREEMENT BETWEEN THE GOVERNMENT OF THE PEOPLE'S REPUBLIC OF CHINA AND THE GOVERNMENT OF IRELAND FOR THE AVOIDANCE OF DOUBLE TAXATION AND THE PREVENTION OF FISCAL EVASION WITH RESPECT TO TAXES ON INCOME

Treaty Text

The Government of the People's Republic of China and the Government of Ireland,

Desiring to conclude an Agreement for the avoidance of double taxation and the prevention of fiscal evasion with respect to taxes on income,

Have agreed as follows:

Article 1 Personal Scope

This Agreement shall apply to persons who are residents of one or both of the Contracting States.

Article 2 Taxes Covered

This Agreement shall apply to taxes on income imposed on behalf of a Contracting State or of its local authorities, irrespective of the manner in which they are levied.

There shall be regarded as taxes on income all taxes imposed on total income, or on elements of income, including taxes on gains from the alienation of movable or immovable property.

The existing taxes to which the Agreement shall apply are in particular:

in China:
the individual income tax;
the income tax for enterprises with foreign investment and foreign enterprises; and
the local income tax; (hereinafter referred to as "Chinese tax").
in the case of Ireland:
the income tax;
the corporation tax; and

the capital gains tax; (hereinafter referred to as "Irish tax").

The Agreement shall also apply to any identical or substantially similar taxes which are imposed after the date of signature of the Agreement in addition to, or in place of, the existing taxes. The competent authorities of the Contracting States shall notify each other of any substantial changes which have been made in their respective taxation laws within a reasonable period of time after such changes.

Article 3 General Definitions

For the purposes of this Agreement, unless the context otherwise requires:

the term "China" means the People's Republic of China; when used in a geographical sense, means all the territory of the People's Republic of China, including its territorial sea, in which the Chinese laws relating to taxation apply, and any area beyond its territorial sea, within which the People's Republic of China has sovereign rights of exploration for and exploitation of resources of the sea-bed and its sub-soil and superjacent water resources in accordance with international law;

the term "Ireland" includes any area outside the territorial waters of Ireland which, in accordance with international law, has been or may hereafter be designated under the laws of Ireland concerning the Continental Shelf, as an area within which the rights of Ireland with respect to the sea-bed and sub-soil and their natural resources may be exercised;

the terms "a Contracting State" and "the other Contracting State" mean China or Ireland, as the context requires;

the term "person" includes an individual, a company, a trust and any other body of persons;

the term "company" means any body corporate or any entity which is treated as a body corporate for tax purposes;

the terms "enterprise of a Contracting State" and "enterprise of the other Contracting State" mean, respectively, an enterprise carried on by a resident of a Contracting State and an enterprise carried on by a resident of the other Contracting State;

the term "national" means:

in the case of China, any individual possessing the nationality of China or any legal person, partnership or association deriving its status as such from the laws in force in China;

in the case of Ireland, any citizen of Ireland and any legal person, association or other entity deriving its status as such from the laws in force in Ireland;

the term "international traffic" means any transport by a ship or aircraft operated by an enterprise of a Contracting State except when the ship or aircraft is operated solely between places in the other Contracting State;

the term "competent authority" means, in the case of China, the State Administration of Taxation or its authorized representative, and in the case of Ireland, the Revenue Commissioners or their authorized representative.

As regards the application of the Agreement by a Contracting State any term not defined therein shall, unless the context otherwise requires, have the meaning which it has under the law of that State concerning the taxes to which the Agreement applies.

Article 4 Resident

For the purposes of this Agreement, the term "resident of a Contracting State" means any person who, under the laws of that State, is liable to tax therein by reason of his domicile, residence, place of effective management, place of head office, or any other criterion of a similar nature. But this term does not include any person who is liable to tax in that State in respect only of income from sources in that State.

Where by reason of the provisions of paragraph 1 an individual is a resident of both Contracting States, then his status shall be determined as follows:

he shall be deemed to be a resident of the State in which he has a permanent home available to him; if he has a permanent home available to him in both States, he shall be deemed to be a resident only of the State with which his personal and economic relations are closer (centre of vital interests);
if the State in which he has his centre of vital interests cannot be determined, or if he has not a permanent home available to him in either State, he shall be deemed to be a resident only of the State in which he has an habitual abode;
if he has an habitual abode in both States or in neither of them, he shall be deemed to be a resident only of the State of which he is a national;
if he is a national of both States or of neither of them, the competent authorities of the Contracting States shall settle the question by mutual agreement.

Where by reason of the provisions of paragraph 1 of this Article a person other than an individual is a resident of both Contracting States, then it shall be deemed to be a resident of the State in which the place of head office (the place of effective management) of its business is situated. However, where such a person has the place of effective management of its business in one of the Contracting States and the place of head office of its business in the other Contracting State, then the competent authorities of the Contracting States shall determine by mutual agreement the State of which the company shall be deemed to be a resident for the purposes of this Agreement.

Article 5 Permanent Establishment

For the purposes of this Agreement, the term "permanent establishment" means a fixed place of business through which the business of an enterprise is wholly or partly carried on.

The term "permanent establishment" includes especially:

a place of management;
a branch;
an office;
a factory;
a workshop;

a mine, an oil or gas well, a quarry or any other place of extraction of natural resources; and

an installation, drilling rig or ship used for the exploration or exploitation of natural resources.

A building site, a construction, assembly or installation project constitutes a permanent establishment only if it lasts more than 6 months.

Notwithstanding the preceding provisions of this Article, the term "permanent establishment" shall be deemed not to include:

the use of facilities solely for the purpose of storage, display or delivery of goods or merchandise belonging to the enterprise;

the maintenance of a stock of goods or merchandise belonging to the enterprise solely for the purpose of storage, display or delivery;

the maintenance of a stock of goods or merchandise belonging to the enterprise solely for the purpose of processing by another enterprise;

the maintenance of a fixed place of business solely for the purpose of purchasing goods or merchandise or of collecting information, for the enterprise;

the maintenance of a fixed place of business solely for the purpose of carrying on, for the enterprise, any other activity of a preparatory or auxiliary character;

the maintenance of a fixed place of business solely for any combination of activities mentioned in sub-paragraphs (a)–(e), provided that the overall activity of the fixed place of business resulting from this combination is of a preparatory or auxiliary character.

Notwithstanding the provisions of paragraphs 1 and 2, where a person—other than an agent of an independent status to whom paragraph 6 applies—is acting in a Contracting State on behalf of an enterprise of the other Contracting State, has and habitually exercises, an authority to conclude contracts in the name of the enterprise, that enterprise shall be deemed to have a permanent establishment in the first-mentioned Contracting State in respect of any activities which that person undertakes for the enterprise, unless the activities of such person are limited to those mentioned in paragraph 4 which, if exercised through a fixed place of business, would not make this fixed place of business a permanent establishment under the provisions of that paragraph.

An enterprise shall not be deemed to have a permanent establishment in a Contracting State merely because it carries on business in that State through a broker, general commission agent or any other agent of an independent status, provided that such persons are acting in the ordinary course of their business. However, when the activities of such an agent are devoted wholly or almost wholly on behalf of that enterprise, he will not be considered an agent of an independent status within the meaning of this paragraph if it is shown that the transactions between the agent and the enterprise were not made under arm's-length conditions.

The fact that a company which is a resident of a Contracting State controls or is controlled by a company which is a resident of the other Contracting State, or which carries on business in that other State (whether through a permanent establishment or otherwise), shall not of itself constitute either company a permanent establishment of the other.

Article 6 Income from Immovable Property

Income derived by a resident of a Contracting State from immovable property (including income from agriculture or forestry) situated in the other Contracting State may be taxed in that other State.

The term "immovable property" shall have the meaning which it has under the law of the Contracting State in which the property in question is situated. The term shall in any case include property accessory to immovable property, livestock and equipment used in agriculture and forestry, rights to which the provisions of general law respecting landed property apply, usufruct of immovable property and rights to variable or fixed payments as consideration for the working of, or the right to work, mineral deposits, sources and other natural resources. Ships and aircraft shall not be regarded as immovable property.

The provisions of paragraph 1 shall apply to income derived from the direct use, letting, or use in any other form of immovable property.

The provisions of paragraphs 1 and 3 shall also apply to the income from immovable property of an enterprise and to income from immovable property used for the performance of independent personal services.

Article 7 Business Profits

The profits of an enterprise of a Contracting State shall be taxable only in that State unless the enterprise carries on business in the other Contracting State through a permanent establishment situated therein. If the enterprise carries on business as aforesaid, the profits of the enterprise may be taxed in the other State, but only so much of them as is attributable to that permanent establishment.

Subject to the provisions of paragraph 3, where an enterprise of a Contracting State carries on business in the other Contracting State through a permanent establishment situated therein, there shall in each Contracting State be attributed to that permanent establishment the profits which it might be expected to make if it were a distinct and separate enterprise engaged in the same or similar activities under the same or similar conditions and dealing wholly independently with the enterprise of which it is a permanent establishment.

In determining the profits of a permanent establishment, there shall be allowed as deductions expenses which are incurred for the purposes of the business of the permanent establishment, including executive and general administrative expenses so incurred, whether in the State in which the permanent establishment is situated or elsewhere.

Insofar as it has been customary in a Contracting State to determine the profits to be attributed to a permanent establishment on the basis of an apportionment of the total profits of the enterprise to its various parts, nothing in paragraph 2 shall preclude that Contracting State from determining the profits to be taxed by such an apportionment as may be customary. The method of apportionment adopted shall, however, be such that the result shall be in accordance with the principles contained in this Article.

No profits shall be attributed to a permanent establishment by reason of the mere purchase by that permanent establishment of goods or merchandise for the enterprise.

For the purposes of the preceding paragraphs, the profits to be attributed to the permanent establishment shall be determined by the same method year by year unless there is good and sufficient reason to the contrary.

Where profits include items of income or gains which are dealt with separately in other Articles of this Agreement, then the provisions of those Articles shall not be affected by the provisions of this Article.

Article 8 Shipping and Air Transport

Profits of an enterprise of a Contracting State from the operation of ships or aircraft in international traffic shall be taxable only in that Contracting State.

If the place of head office (place of effective management) of a shipping enterprise is aboard a ship, then it shall be deemed to be situated in the Contracting State in which the home harbour of the ship is situated, or, if there is no such home harbour, in the Contracting State of which the operator of the ship is a resident.

The provisions of paragraph 1 shall also apply to profits from the participation in a pool, a joint business or an international operating agency.

Article 9 Associated Enterprises

Where

> an enterprise of a Contracting State participates directly or indirectly in the management, control or capital of an enterprise of the other Contracting State, or the same persons participate directly or indirectly in the management, control or capital of an enterprise of a Contracting State and an enterprise of the other Contracting State, and in either case conditions are made or imposed between the two enterprises in their commercial or financial relations which differ from those which would be made between independent enterprises, then any profits which would, but for those conditions, have accrued to one of the enterprises, but, by reason of those conditions, have not so accrued, may be included in the profits of that enterprise and taxed accordingly.

Where a Contracting State includes in the profits of an enterprise of that State—and taxes accordingly—profits on which an enterprise of the other Contracting State has been charged to tax in that other State and the profits so included are profits which would have accrued to the enterprise of the first-mentioned State if the conditions made between the two enterprises had been those which would have been made between independent enterprises, then that other State shall make an appropriate adjustment to the amount of the tax charged therein on those profits. In determining such adjustment, due regard shall be had to the other provisions of this Agreement and the competent authorities of the Contracting States shall, if necessary, consult each other.

Article 10 Dividends

Dividends paid by a company which is a resident of a Contracting State to a resident of the other Contracting State may be taxed in that other State.

However, such dividends may also be taxed in the Contracting State of which the company paying the dividends is a resident and according to the laws of that State, but if the recipient is the beneficial owner of the dividends the tax so charged shall not exceed:

5% of the gross amount of the dividends if the beneficial owner is a company which holds directly at least 25% of the voting power of the company paying the dividends;

10% of the gross amount of the dividends in all other cases.

The competent authorities of the Contracting States shall by mutual agreement settle the mode of application of this limitation.

This paragraph shall not affect the taxation of the company in respect of the profits out of which the dividends are paid.

The term "dividends" as used in this Article means income from shares, or other rights, not being debt-claims, participating in profits, as well as income from other corporate rights which is subjected to the same taxation treatment as income from shares by the laws of the State of which the company making the distribution is a resident.

The provisions of paragraphs 1 and 2 shall not apply if the beneficial owner of the dividends, being a resident of a Contracting State, carries on business in the other Contracting State of which the company paying the dividends is a resident, through a permanent establishment situated therein, or performs in that other State independent personal services from a fixed base situated therein, and the holding in respect of which the dividends are paid is effectively connected with such permanent establishment or fixed base. In such case the provisions of Article 7 or Article 14, as the case may be, shall apply.

Where a company which is a resident of a Contracting State derives profits or income from the other Contracting State, that other State may not impose any tax on the dividends paid by the company, except insofar as such dividends are paid to a resident of that other State or insofar as the holding in respect of which the dividends are paid is effectively connected with a permanent establishment or a fixed base situated in that other State, nor subject the company's undistributed profits to a tax on the company's undistributed profits, even if the dividends paid or the undistributed profits consist wholly or partly of profits or income arising in such other State.

Article 11 Interest

Interest arising in a Contracting State and paid to a resident of the other Contracting State may be taxed in that other State.

However, such interest may also be taxed in the Contracting State in which it arises and according to the laws of that State, but if the recipient is the beneficial owner of the interest the tax so charged shall not exceed 10% of the gross amount of the interest. The competent authorities of the Contracting States shall by mutual agreement settle the mode of application of this limitation.

Notwithstanding the provisions of paragraph 2, interest arising in a Contracting State and derived by the Government of the other Contracting State, a local authority and the Central Bank thereof or any financial institution wholly owned by the Government of that other State, or by any other resident of that other State with respect to debt-claims indirectly financed by the Government of that other State, a local authority and the Central Bank thereof or any financial institution wholly owned by the Government of that other State, shall be exempt from tax in the first-mentioned State.

The term "interest" as used in this Article means income from debt-claims of every kind, whether or not secured by mortgage and whether or not carrying a right to participate in the debtor's profits, and in particular, income from government securities and income from bonds or debentures, including premiums and prizes attaching to such securities, bonds or debentures. Penalty charges for late payment shall not be regarded as interest for the purpose of this Article.

The provisions of paragraphs 1, 2 and 3 shall not apply if the beneficial owner of the interest, being a resident of a Contracting State, carries on business in the other Contracting State in which the interest arises, through a permanent establishment situated therein, or performs in that other State independent personal services from a fixed base situated therein, and the debt-claim in respect of which the interest is paid is effectively connected with such permanent establishment or fixed base. In such case the provisions of Article 7 or Article 14, as the case may be, shall apply.

Interest shall be deemed to arise in a Contracting State when the payer is the Government of that State, a local authority thereof or a resident of that State. Where, however, the person paying the interest, whether he is a resident of a Contracting State or not, has in a Contracting State a permanent establishment or a fixed base in connection with which the indebtedness on which the interest is paid was incurred, and such interest is borne by such permanent establishment or fixed base, then such interest shall be deemed to arise in the State in which the permanent establishment or fixed base is situated.

Where, by reason of a special relationship between the payer and the beneficial owner or between both of them and some other person, the amount of the interest, having regard to the debt-claim for which it is paid, exceeds the amount which would have been agreed upon by the payer and the beneficial owner in the absence of such relationship, the provisions of this Article shall apply only to the last-mentioned amount. In such case, the excess part of the payments shall remain taxable according to the laws of each Contracting State, due regard being had to the other provisions of this Agreement.

Article 12 Royalties

Royalties arising in a Contracting State and paid to a resident of the other Contracting State may be taxed in that other State.

However, such royalties may also be taxed in the Contracting State in which they arise, and according to the laws of that Contracting State, but if the recipient is the beneficial owner of the royalties, the tax so charged shall not exceed:

in the case of royalties referred to in sub-paragraph (a) of paragraph 3 of this Article, 10% of the gross amount of the royalties; and
in the case of royalties referred to in sub-paragraph (b) of paragraph 3 of this Article, 10% of the adjusted amount of the royalties. For the purpose of this sub-paragraph the adjusted amount means 60% of the gross amount of the royalties.

The term "royalties" as used in this Article means:

payments of any kind received as a consideration for the use of, or the right to use, any copyright of literary, artistic or scientific work including cinematograph films and films or tapes for radio or television broadcasting, any patent, trade mark, design or model, plan, secret formula or process, or for information concerning industrial, commercial or scientific experience; and
payments of any kind received as a consideration for the use of, or the right to use, industrial, commercial, or scientific equipment.

The provisions of paragraphs 1 and 2 shall not apply if the beneficial owner of the royalties, being a resident of a Contracting State, carries on business in the other Contracting State in which the royalties arise, through a permanent establishment situated therein, or performs in that other State independent personal services from a fixed base situated therein, and the right or property in respect of which the royalties are paid is effectively connected with such permanent establishment or fixed base. In such case the provisions of Article 7 or Article 14, as the case may be, shall apply.

Royalties shall be deemed to arise in a Contracting State when the payer is the Government of that Contracting State, a local authority thereof or a resident of that Contracting State. Where, however, the person paying the royalties, whether he is a resident of a Contracting State or not, has in a Contracting State a permanent establishment or a fixed base in connection with which the liability to pay the royalties was incurred, and such royalties are borne by such permanent establishment or fixed base, then such royalties shall be deemed to arise in the State in which the permanent establishment or fixed base is situated.

Where, by reason of a special relationship between the payer and the beneficial owner or between both of them and some other person, the amount of the royalties, having regard to the use, right or information for which they are paid, exceeds the amount which would have been agreed upon by the payer and the beneficial owner in the absence of such relationship, the provisions of this Article shall apply only to the last-mentioned amount. In such case, the excess part of the payments shall remain taxable according to the laws of each Contracting State, due regard being had to the other provisions of this Agreement.

Article 13 Capital Gains

Gains derived by a resident of a Contracting State from the alienation of immovable property referred to in Article 6 and situated in the other Contracting State may be taxed in that other State.

Gains from the alienation of movable property forming part of the business property of a permanent establishment which an enterprise of a Contracting State has in the other Contracting State or of movable property pertaining to a fixed base available to a resident of a Contracting State in the other Contracting State for the purpose of performing independent personal services, including such gains from the alienation of such a permanent establishment (alone or with the whole enterprise) or of such a fixed base, may be taxed in that other State.

Gains from the alienation of ships or aircraft operated in international traffic by an enterprise of a Contracting State or movable property pertaining to the operation of such ships or aircraft shall be taxable only in that State.

Gains from the alienation of shares of the capital stock of a company the property of which consists directly or indirectly principally of immovable property situated in a Contracting State may be taxed in that Contracting State.

Gains from the alienation of any property other than that referred to in paragraphs 1–4, shall be taxable only in the Contracting State of which the alienator is a resident.

Article 14 Independent Personal Services

Income derived by a resident of a Contracting State in respect of professional services or other activities of an independent character shall be taxable only in that State except in one of the following circumstances, when such income may also be taxed in the other Contracting State:

if he has a fixed base regularly available to him in the other Contracting State for the purpose of performing his activities; in that case, only so much of the income as is attributable to that fixed base may be taxed in that other State;

if his stay in the other Contracting State is for a period or periods amounting to or exceeding in the aggregate 183 days in the calendar year concerned; in that case, only so much of the income as is derived from his activities performed in that other State may be taxed in that other State.

The term "professional services" includes especially independent scientific, literary, artistic, educational or teaching activities as well as the independent activities of physicians, lawyers, engineers, architects, dentists and accountants.

Article 15 Dependent Personal Services

Subject to the provisions of Articles 16, 18, 19, 20 and 21, salaries, wages and other similar remuneration derived by a resident of a Contracting State in respect of an employment shall be taxable only in that State unless the employment is exercised in the other Contracting State. If the employment is so exercised, such remuneration as is derived therefrom may be taxed in that other State.

Notwithstanding the provisions of paragraph 1, remuneration derived by a resident of a Contracting State in respect of an employment exercised in the other Contracting State shall be taxable only in the first-mentioned State if:

the recipient is present in the other State for a period or periods not exceeding in the aggregate 183 days in the fiscal year concerned; and
the remuneration is paid by, or on behalf of, an employer who is not a resident of the other State; and
the remuneration is not borne by a permanent establishment or a fixed base which the employer has in the other State.

Notwithstanding the preceding provisions of this Article, remuneration derived in respect of an employment exercised aboard a ship or aircraft operated in international traffic by an enterprise of a Contracting State shall be taxable only in that State.

Article 16 Directors' Fees
Directors' fees and other similar payments derived by a resident of a Contracting State in his capacity as a member of the board of directors of a company which is a resident of the other Contracting State may be taxed in that other State.

Article 17 Artistes and Sportsperson
Notwithstanding the provisions of Articles 14 and 15, income derived by a resident of a Contracting State as an entertainer, such as a theatre, motion picture, radio or television artiste, or a musician, or as a sportsman, from his personal activities as such exercised in the other Contracting State, may be taxed in that other State.

Where income in respect of personal activities exercised by an entertainer or a sportsman in his capacity as such accrues not to the entertainer or sportsman himself but to another person, that income may, notwithstanding the provisions of Articles 7, 14 and 15, be taxed in the Contracting State in which the activities of the entertainer or sportsman are exercised.

Notwithstanding the preceding provisions of this Article, income derived by entertainers or sportsmen who are residents of a Contracting State from the activities exercised in the other Contracting State under a plan of cultural exchange between the Governments of both Contracting States shall be exempt from tax in that other State.

Article 18 Pensions
Subject to the provisions of paragraph 2 of Article 19, pensions and other similar remuneration paid to a resident of a Contracting State in consideration of past employment shall be taxable only in that State.

Notwithstanding the provisions of paragraph 1, pensions paid and other similar payments made by the Government of a Contracting State of a local authority thereof under a public welfare scheme of the social security system of that State shall be taxable only in that State.

The provisions of this Article shall also apply to an annuity paid to a resident of a Contracting State. The term "annuity" means a stated sum payable periodically at stae times during life or during a specified or ascertainable period of time under an obligate to make the payments in return for adequate and full consideration in money or more worth.

Article 19 Government Service

Salaries, wages and other similar remuneration, other than a pension, paid by the Government of a Contracting State or a local authority thereof, to an individual in respect of services rendered to the Government of that State or a local authority thereof, in the discharge of functions of a governmental nature, shall be taxable only in that State.

However, such salaries, wages and other similar remuneration shall be taxable only in the other Contracting State if the services are rendered in that other State and the individual is a resident of that State who:

is a national of that State; or

did not become a resident of that State solely for the purpose of rendering the services.

(a) Any pension paid by, or out of funds, to which contributions are made by the Government of a Contracting State or a local authority thereof to an individual in respect of services rendered to the Government of that State or a local authority thereof in the discharge of functions of a governmental nature shall be taxable only in that State.

(b) However, such pension shall be taxable only in the other Contracting State if the individual is a resident of, and a national of, that other State.

The provisions of Articles 15, 16, 17 and 18 shall apply to salaries, wages and other similar remuneration, and to pensions in respect of services rendered in connection with a business carried on by the Government of a Contracting State or a local authority thereof.

Article 20 Teachers and Researchers

An individual who immediately before visiting a Contracting State, was a resident of the other Contracting State and who is present in the first-mentioned State for the purpose of teaching, giving lectures or conducting research at a university, college, school or other recognised educational or scientific research institution in the first-mentioned State shall be exempt from tax in the first-mentioned State for a period of two years from the date of his first arrival in that State in respect of remuneration from such teaching, lectures or research.

This Article shall not apply to income from research if such research is undertaken primarily for the private benefit of a specific person or persons.

Article 21 Students and Trainees

A student, business apprentice or trainee who is or was immediately before visiting a Contracting State, a resident of the other Contracting State and who is present in the first-mentioned Contracting State solely for the purpose of his education, training or obtaining special technical experience shall be exempt from tax in that Contracting State with respect to:

payments received from abroad for the purpose of his maintenance, education, study, research or training;
grants or awards from a government, scientific, educational or other tax exempt organization.

The benefit provided under paragraph 1 shall extend only for such period of tin as is reasonably necessary to complete the education or training.

Article 22 Other Income

Items of income of a resident of a Contracting State, wherever arising, not dealt with in the foregoing Articles of this Agreement shall be taxable only in that State.

The provisions of paragraph 1 shall not apply to income, other than income from immovable property as defined in paragraph 2 of Article 6, if the recipient of such income, being a resident of a Contracting State, carries on business in the other Contracting State through a permanent establishment situated therein, or performs in that other State independent personal services from a fixed base situated therein, and the right or property in respect of which the income is paid is effectively connected with such permanent establishment or fixed base. In such case the provisions of Article 7 or Article 14, as the case may be, shall apply.

Article 23 Methods for Elimination of Double Taxation

In China, double taxation shall be eliminated as follows:

where a resident of China derives income from Ireland the amount of tax on that income payable in Ireland in accordance with the provisions of this Agreement, may be credited against the Chinese tax imposed on that resident. The amount of the credit, however, shall not exceed the amount of the Chinese tax on that income computed in accordance with the taxation laws and regulations of China.
where the income derived from Ireland is a dividend paid by a company which is a resident of Ireland to a company which is a resident of China and which owns more than 10% of the shares of the company paying the dividend, the credit shall take into account the Irish tax payable by the company paying the dividend in respect of its income.

In Ireland, double taxation shall be eliminated as follows:

Subject to the provisions of the laws of Ireland regarding the allowance as a credit against Irish tax of tax payable in a territory outside Ireland (which shall not affect the general principle hereof), Chinese tax payable under the laws of China and in accordance with this Agreement, whether directly or by deduction, on profits, income or gains from sources within China shall be allowed as a credit against any Irish tax computed by reference to the same profits, income or gains by reference to which Chinese tax is computed;
in the case of a dividend paid by a company which is a resident of China to a company which is a resident of Ireland and which controls directly or indirectly 10% or more of the voting power in the company paying the dividend, the credit

shall take into account (in addition to any Chinese tax creditable under the provisions of sub-paragraph (a) of this paragraph) Chinese tax payable by the company in respect of the profits out of which such dividend is paid.

For the purposes of paragraphs 1 and 2 of this Article profits, income or gains owned by a resident of a Contracting State which may be taxed in the other Contracting State in accordance with this Agreement shall be deemed to be derived from sources in that other Contracting State.

Article 24 Non-Discrimination

Nationals of a Contracting State shall not be subjected in the other Contracting State to any taxation or any requirement connected therewith, which is other or more burdensome than the taxation and connected requirements to which nationals of that other State in the same circumstances, in particular with respect to residence, are or may be subjected. This provision shall, notwithstanding the provisions of Article 1, also apply to persons who are not residents of one or both of the Contracting States.

The taxation on a permanent establishment which an enterprise of a Contracting State has in the other Contracting State shall not be less favourably levied in that other State than the taxation levied on enterprises of that other State carrying on the same activities. This provision shall not be construed as obliging a Contracting State to grant to residents of the other Contracting State any personal allowances, reliefs and reductions for taxation purposes on account of civil status or family responsibilities which it grants to its own residents.

Except where the provisions of paragraph 1 of Article 9, paragraph 7 of Article 11, or paragraph 6 of Article 12, apply, interest, royalties and other disbursements paid by an enterprise of a Contracting State to a resident of the other Contracting State shall, for the purpose of determining the taxable profits of such enterprise, be deductible under the same conditions as if they had been paid to a resident of the first-mentioned State.

Enterprises of a Contracting State, the capital of which is wholly or partly owned or controlled, directly or indirectly, by one or more residents of the other Contracting State, shall not be subjected in the first-mentioned State to any taxation or any requirement connected therewith which is other or more burdensome than the taxation and connected requirements to which other similar enterprises of the first-mentioned State are or may be subjected.

Article 25 Mutual Agreement Procedure

Where a person considers that the actions of one or both of the Contracting States result or will result for him in taxation not in accordance with the provisions of this Agreement, he may, irrespective of the remedies provided by the domestic law of those States, present his case to the competent authority of the Contracting State of which he is a resident or, if his case comes under paragraph 1 of Article 24, to that of the Contracting State of which he is a national. The case must be presented within three years from the first notification of the action resulting in taxation not in accordance with the provisions of the Agreement.

The competent authority shall endeavour, if the objection appears to it to be justified and if it is not itself able to arrive at a satisfactory solution, to resolve the case by mutual agreement with the competent authority of the other Contracting State, with a view to the avoidance of taxation which is not in accordance with the Agreement. Any agreement reached shall be implemented notwithstanding any time limits in the domestic law of the Contracting States.

The competent authorities of the Contracting States shall endeavour to resolve by mutual agreement any difficulties or doubts arising as to the interpretation or application of the Agreement. They may also consult together for the elimination of double taxation in cases not provided for in the Agreement.

The competent authorities of the Contracting States may communicate with each other directly for the purpose of reaching an agreement in the sense of paragraphs 2 and 3. When it seems advisable for reaching agreement, representatives of the competent authorities of the Contracting States may meet together for an oral exchange of opinions.

Article 26 Exchange of Information

The competent authorities of the Contracting States shall exchange such information as is necessary for carrying out the provisions of this Agreement or of the domestic laws of the Contracting States concerning taxes covered by the Agreement insofar as the taxation thereunder is not contrary to the Agreement, in particular for the prevention of evasion of such taxes. The exchange of information is not restricted by Article 1. Any information received by a Contracting State shall be treated as secret in the same manner as information obtained under the domestic laws of that State and shall be disclosed only to persons or authorities (including courts and administrative bodies) involved in the assessment or collection of, the enforcement or prosecution in respect of, or the determination of appeals in relation to, the taxes covered by the Agreement. Such persons or authorities shall use the information only for such purposes. They may disclose the information in public court proceedings or in judicial decisions.

In no case shall the provisions of paragraph 1 be construed so as to impose on a Contracting State the obligation:

to carry out administrative measures at variance with the laws and administrative practice of that or of the other Contracting State;

to supply information which is not obtainable under the laws or in the normal course of the administration of that or of the other Contracting State;

to supply information which would disclose any trade, business, industrial, commercial or professional secret or trade process, or information, the disclosure of which would be contrary to public policy (*ordre public*).

Article 27 Members of Diplomatic Missions and Consular Posts

Nothing in this Agreement shall affect the fiscal privileges of members of diplomatic missions or consular posts under the general rules of international law or under the provisions of special agreements.

Article 28 Entry into Force

Each of the Contracting States shall notify to the other the completion of the procedures required by its law for the bringing into force of this Agreement. The Agreement shall enter into force on the thirtieth day following the date of the later of these notifications and shall thereupon have effect:

in China, in respect of profits, income and capital gains arising in any tax year beginning on or after the first day of January in the calendar year next following that in which this Agreement enters into force;
in Ireland:
in respect of income tax and capital gains tax, for any year of assessment beginning on or after 6 April in the calendar year next following that in which this Agreement enters into force;
in respect of corporation tax, for any financial year beginning on or after first day of January in the calendar year next following that in which this Agreement enters into force.

Article 29 Termination

This Agreement shall continue in effect indefinitely but either of the Contracting States may, on or before the thirtieth day of June in any calendar year beginning after the expiration of a period of five years from the date of its entry into force, give to the other Contracting State, through diplomatic channels, written notice of termination. In such event this Agreement shall cease to have effect:

in China, as regards profits, income and capital gains derived during the tax year beginning on or after 1 January in the calendar year next following that in which the notice is given;
in Ireland:
in respect of income tax and capital gains tax, for any year of assessment beginning on or after 6 April in the calendar year next following that in which the notice is given;
in respect of corporation tax, for any financial year beginning on or after 1 January in the calendar year next following that in which the notice is given.

IN WITNESS whereof the undersigned, duly authorized thereto, have signed this Agreement.

Done at Dublin on the 19th day of April 2000, in duplicate in the Chinese and English languages, both texts being equally authentic.

For the Government of Ireland

For the Government of the People's Republic of China

Italy

Italy, officially the Republic of Italy, is a state in Southern Europe. Italy borders with France to the north-west, Switzerland to the north, Austria and Slovenia to the North-East, and the enclaved microstates of Vatican City and San Marino. Its coast overlooks the Mediterranean seas. Italy's capital and largest city is Rome, while Milan is its financial center. Italy has the fifth largest population in Europe.

Italy has recently become an immigration destination, especially from the Balkans and Africa, despite being for most of its history an emigration country. Italians are the majority ethnic group, while other substantial groups are Romanian, Albanian, Moroccan, and Chinese.

The official and predominant spoken language is Italian. Recognized minority languages are Albanian, Catalan, German, Greek, Slovene, Croatian, French, Franco-Provençal, Friulian, Ladin, Occitan and Sardinian. Minority languages used by immigrants and second generations are Arabic, Chinese, Polish, and the Balkan languages.

Italy is a unitary parliamentary constitutional republic. The Costituzione Italiana is the constitution regulating the political system, in force since 1948. The Chamber of Deputies and the Senate are vested with the legislative power, forming the parliament. Both houses are elected through direct elections using the mixed-member proportional representation system, even though until 1992 a purely proportional system was in place.

Executive power is vested in the president of the council (informally called prime minister) and his or her cabinet. The president of the council is appointed by the President of the Republic after a series of consultations ensuring that the president will obtain a majority in a vote of confidence in both houses of parliament.

Italy has a civil law system based on Roman law. The Corte Costituzionale acts as Supreme Court, managing constitutional matters, with judicial review powers.

Italy is a unitary state divided into 20 regions, 107 provinces, and 8000 comuni (town), leaded by local elected governments.

Italy is part of the European Union, one of the six founding country, together with Germany, France, Luxemburg, the Netherlands, and Belgium.

© The Author(s), under exclusive license to Springer Nature Singapore Pte Ltd. 2022

L. Riccardi and G. Riccardi, *China–Europe Tax Treaties*,
https://doi.org/10.1007/978-981-19-3563-3_18

Category	Value
Population (mln persons)	60.360
Currency	Euro

Source International Monetary Fund, year 2019

Italy is the largest economy of Southern Europe, with a GDP valued 1988.6 billion USD in 2019, and has a population of about 60 million people. Italy, similar to France, enjoys low inflation (0.6%), but it has relatively high unemployment (10%), the nineth highest in Europe. Italy scored 34 out of 43 in Europe in the 2020 Doing Business ranking and imposes a CIT of 24%. It is a large investor abroad. Italy records a positive trade balance of 59 billion USD, being the fourth main exporter in Europe.

GDP and local economy	
GDP current prices (billion USD)	1988.6
GDP per capita (USD)	32,947
GDP growth (%)	0.3
Inflation (%)	0.6
Unemployment (%)	10.0
General government total expenditure (% of GDP)	48.6
General government gross debt (% of GDP)	134.5
Doing Business Score 2020	72.9

Source International Monetary Fund and UNCTAD, year 2019

Foreign direct investment	
FDI outstock (million USD)	558,400
FDI instock (million USD)	445,741

Source UNCTAD, year 2019

Trade	
Imports (million USD)	473,512
Exports (million USD)	532,663
Trade balance (million USD)	59,151

Source International Monetary Fund and UNCTAD, year 2019

Main import–export	
First import by category	Machinery, nuclear reactors, boilers
Second import by category	Vehicles other than railway, tramway
First export by category	Machinery, nuclear reactors, boilers
Second export by category	Vehicles other than railway, tramway

Source United Nations COMTRADE, year 2020

The legal bases for taxation are established in the constitution. Italy imposes individual income tax, property sales taxes, capital gains, corporate income tax, and value added tax. Progressivity is guaranteed by a system with different bands and various deductions.

Taxes	
Company income tax (%)	24
Top individual income tax (%)	43
Value added tax or sales tax (%)	22
Reduced value added tax or sales tax (%)	4/5/10

Source RsA Asia report, year 2021

- Economic relation with China

Italy records a trade deficit of 10.69 billion USD in 2020 towards China. "Machinery, nuclear reactors, boilers" is the first export category, worth 4.82 billion USD, while "Electrical, electronic equipment" is the first import category, worth 6.96 billion USD. Italy is the main economy to be part of the Belt and Road Initiative. The Italy-China DTA dates back to 1986, entering into force in 1989. A new agreement has been signed in 2019.

Category	Value
Belt road	Yes

Source UNCTAD, year 2021

Import from China	
Import from China (billion USD)	32.94
First import category from China	Electrical, electronic equipment
First import Value (billion USD)	6.96
Second import category from China	Machinery, nuclear reactors, boilers
Second import Value (billion USD)	5.58

Source United Nations COMTRADE, year 2020

Export to China	
Export to China (billion USD)	22.25
First export category towards China	Machinery, nuclear reactors, boilers
First export value (billion USD)	4.82
Second export category towards China	Pharmaceutical products
Second export value (billion USD)	2.23

Source United Nations COMTRADE, year 2020

Trade balance	
Trade balance (billion USD)	−10.69

Source United Nations COMTRADE, year 2020

Double tax agreement 1986	
DTA effective date	1989.11.14
Dividends (%)	10
Interest (%)	0–10
Royalties (%)	10

Source State Administration of Taxation of China, year 2021
Note Rates of the treaty in force at the time of writing (October 2021)

Double tax agreement 2019	
DTA signature date	2019.3.23
Dividends (%)	5–10
Interest (%)	0–8–10
Royalties (%)	5–10

Source State Administration of Taxation of China, year 2021
Note The DTA is not in force at the time of writing (October 2021)

Title AGREEMENT BETWEEN THE GOVERNMENT OF THE PEOPLE'S REPUBLIC OF CHINA AND THE GOVERNMENT OF THE ITALIAN REPUBLIC FOR THE ELIMINATION OF DOUBLE TAXATION WITH RESPECT TO TAXES ON INCOME AND THE PREVENTION OF TAX EVASION AND AVOIDANCE

Treaty Text

The Government of the People's Republic of China and the Government of the Italian Republic,

Desiring to further develop their economic relationship and to enhance their cooperation in tax matters,

Intending to conclude an Agreement for the elimination of double taxation with respect to taxes on income without creating opportunities for non-taxation or reduced taxation through tax evasion or avoidance (including through treaty-shopping arrangements aimed at obtaining reliefs provided in this Agreement for the indirect benefit of residents of third States),

Have agreed as follows:

Article 1 Persons Covered

This Agreement shall apply to persons who are residents of one or both of the Contracting States.

For the purposes of this Agreement, income derived by or through an entity or arrangement that is treated as wholly or partly fiscally transparent under the tax law of either Contracting State shall be considered to be income of a resident of a Contracting State but only to the extent that the income is treated, for purposes of taxation by that State, as the income of a resident of that State.

This Agreement shall not affect the taxation, by a Contracting State, of its residents except with respect to the benefits granted under paragraph 2 of Article 9, paragraph 2 of Article 18, and Articles 19, 20, 21, 23, 25, 26 and 28.

Article 2 Taxes Covered

This Agreement shall apply to taxes on income imposed on behalf of a Contracting State or of its political subdivisions or local authorities, irrespective of the manner in which they are levied.

There shall be regarded as taxes on income all taxes imposed on total income, or on elements of income, including taxes on gains from the alienation of movable or immovable property, taxes on the total amounts of wages or salaries paid by enterprises, as well as taxes on capital appreciation.

The existing taxes to which the Agreement shall apply are in particular:

in China:
the individual income tax;
the enterprise income tax; (hereinafter referred to as "Chinese tax");
in Italy:
the personal income tax;
the corporate income tax;
the regional tax on productive activities;
whether or not they are collected by withholding at source; (hereinafter referred to as "Italian tax").

The Agreement shall apply also to any identical or substantially similar taxes that are imposed after the date of signature of the Agreement in addition to, or in place of, the existing taxes. The competent authorities of the Contracting States shall notify each other of any significant changes which have been made in their taxation laws.

Article 3 General Definitions

For the purposes of this Agreement, unless the context otherwise requires:

the term "China" means the People's Republic of China; when used in geographical sense, means all the territory of the People's Republic of China, including its land territory, internal waters, territorial sea and the air space above them, in which the Chinese laws relating to taxation apply, and any area beyond its territorial sea within which the People's Republic of China has sovereign rights or exercises jurisdiction in accordance with international law and its internal law;
the term "Italy" means the Italian Republic and includes any area beyond the territorial waters which is designated as an area within which Italy, in compliance with its legislation and in conformity with the International Law, exercises sovereign rights in respect of the exploration and exploitation of the natural resources of the seabed, the subsoil and the superjacent waters;
the terms "a Contracting State" and "the other Contracting State " mean China or Italy, as the context requires;
the term "person" includes an individual, a company and any other body of persons;
the term "company" means any body corporate or any entity that is treated as a body corporate for tax purposes;
the terms "enterprise of a Contracting State" and "enterprise of the other Contracting State" mean, respectively, an enterprise carried on by a resident of a Contracting State and an enterprise carried on by a resident of the other Contracting State;
the term "international traffic" means any transport by a ship or aircraft operated by an enterprise of a Contracting State, except when the ship or aircraft is operated solely between places in the other Contracting State;
the term "competent authority" means, in the case of China, the State Taxation Administration or its authorized representative, and in the case of Italy, the Ministry of Economy and Finance;

the term "national", in relation to a Contracting State, means:

any individual possessing the nationality of a Contracting State; and
any legal person, partnership or association deriving its status as such from the laws in force in a Contracting State.

As regards the application of the Agreement at any time by a Contracting State, any term not defined therein shall, unless the context otherwise requires, have the meaning which it has at that time under the law of that State for the purposes of the taxes to which the Agreement applies, any meaning under the applicable tax laws of that State prevailing over a meaning given to the term under other laws of that State.

Article 4 Resident

For the purposes of this Agreement, the term "resident of a Contracting State" means any person who, under the laws of that State, is liable to tax therein by reason of his domicile, residence, place of incorporation, place of effective management or any other criterion of a similar nature, and also includes that State and any political subdivision or local authority thereof. This term, however, does not include any person who is liable to tax in that State in respect only of income from sources in that State.

Where by reason of the provisions of paragraph 1 an individual is a resident of both Contracting States, then his status shall be determined as follows:

he shall be deemed to be a resident only of the State in which he has a permanent home available to him; if he has a permanent home available to him in both States, he shall be deemed to be a resident only of the State with which his personal and economic relations are closer (centre of vital interests);
if the State in which he has his centre of vital interests cannot be determined, or if he has not a permanent home available to him in either State, he shall be deemed to be a resident only of the State in which he has an habitual abode;
if he has an habitual abode in both States or in neither of them, he shall be deemed to be a resident only of the State of which he is a national;
if he is a national of both States or of neither of them, the competent authorities of the Contracting States shall settle the question by mutual agreement.

Where by reason of the provisions of paragraph 1 a person other than an individual is a resident of both Contracting States, the competent authorities of the Contracting States shall endeavour to determine by mutual agreement the Contracting State of which such person shall be deemed to be a resident for the purposes of the Agreement, having regard to its place of effective management, the place where it is incorporated or otherwise constituted and any other relevant factors. In the absence of such agreement, such person shall not be entitled to any relief or exemption from tax provided by this Agreement except to the extent and in such manner as may be agreed upon by the competent authorities of the Contracting States.

Article 5 Permanent Establishment

For the purposes of this Agreement, the term "permanent establishment" means a fixed place of business through which the business of an enterprise is wholly or partly carried on.

The term "permanent establishment" includes especially:

a place of management;
a branch;
an office;
a factory;
a workshop; and
a mine, an oil or gas well, a quarry or any other place of extraction of natural resources.

The term "permanent establishment" likewise encompasses:

a building site, a construction, assembly or installation project or supervisory activities in connection therewith but only if such site, project or activities last more than 12 months;

the furnishing of services, including consultancy services, by an enterprise through employees or other personnel engaged for such purpose, but only if activities of that nature continue (for the same or a connected project) within a Contracting State for a period or periods aggregating more than 183 days within any twelve-month period.

Notwithstanding the preceding provisions of this Article, the term " permanent establishment" shall be deemed not to include:

the use of facilities solely for the purpose of storage, display or delivery of goods or merchandise belonging to the enterprise;
the maintenance of a stock of goods or merchandise belonging to the enterprise solely for the purpose of storage, display or delivery;
the maintenance of a stock of goods or merchandise belonging to the enterprise solely for the purpose of processing by another enterprise;
the maintenance of a fixed place of business solely for the purpose of purchasing goods or merchandise or of collecting information, for the enterprise;
the maintenance of a fixed place of business solely for the purpose of carrying on, for the enterprise, any activity not listed in subparagraphs (a)–(d), provided that this activity has a preparatory or auxiliary character; or
the maintenance of a fixed place of business solely for any combination of activities mentioned in subparagraphs (a)–(e), provided that the overall activity of the fixed place of business resulting from this combination is of a preparatory or auxiliary character.

Notwithstanding the provisions of paragraphs 1 and 2, where a person—other than an agent of an independent status to whom paragraph 6 applies—is acting in a Contracting State on behalf of an enterprise of the other Contracting State, and has, and habitually exercises, in that Contracting State an authority to conclude contracts in the name of the enterprise, that enterprise shall be deemed to have a permanent establishment in that Contracting State in respect of any activities which that person undertakes for the enterprise, unless the activities of such person are limited to those mentioned in paragraph 4 which, if exercised through a fixed place of business, would not make this fixed place of business a permanent establishment under the provisions of that paragraph.

(a) Paragraph 5 shall not apply where the person acting in a Contracting State on behalf of an enterprise of the other Contracting State carries on business in the first-mentioned State as an independent agent and acts for the enterprise in the ordinary course of that business. Where, however, a person acts exclusively or almost exclusively on behalf of one or more enterprises to which it is closely related, that person shall not be considered to be an independent agent within the meaning of this paragraph with respect to any such enterprise.

(b) For the purposes of this Article, a person is closely related to an enterprise if, based on all the relevant facts and circumstances, one has control of the other or both are under the control of the same persons or enterprises. In any case, a person shall be considered to be closely related to an enterprise if one possesses directly or indirectly more than 50% of the beneficial interest in the other (or, in the case of a company, more than 50% of the aggregate vote and value of the company's shares or of the beneficial equity interest in the company) or if another person possesses directly or indirectly more than 50% of the beneficial interest (or, in the case of a company, more than 50% of the aggregate vote and value of the company's shares or of the beneficial equity interest in the company) in the person and the enterprise.

The fact that a company which is a resident of a Contracting State controls or is controlled by a company which is a resident of the other Contracting State, or which carries on business in that other State (whether through a permanent establishment or otherwise), shall not of itself constitute either company a permanent establishment of the other.

Article 6 Income from Immovable Property

Income derived by a resident of a Contracting State from immovable property (including income from agriculture or forestry) situated in the other Contracting State may be taxed in that other State.

The term "immovable property" shall have the meaning which it has under the law of the Contracting State in which the property in question is situated. The term shall in any case include property accessory to immovable property, livestock and equipment used in agriculture and forestry, rights to which the provisions of general law respecting landed property apply, usufruct of immovable property and rights to variable or fixed payments as consideration for the working of, or the right to work, mineral deposits, sources and other natural resources; ships, boats and aircraft shall not be regarded as immovable property.

The provisions of paragraph 1 shall apply to income derived from the direct use, letting, or use in any other form of immovable property.

The provisions of paragraphs 1 and 3 shall also apply to the income from immovable property of an enterprise and to income from immovable property used for the performance of independent personal services.

Article 7 Business Profits

The profits of an enterprise of a Contracting State shall be taxable only in that State unless the enterprise carries on business in the other Contracting State through a permanent establishment situated therein. If the enterprise carries on business as aforesaid, the profits of the enterprise may be taxed in the other State, but only so much of them as is attributable to that permanent establishment.

Subject to the provisions of paragraph 3, where an enterprise of a Contracting State carries on business in the other Contracting State through a permanent establishment situated therein, there shall in each Contracting State be attributed to that permanent establishment the profits which it might be expected to make if it were a distinct and separate enterprise engaged in the same or similar activities under the same or similar conditions and dealing wholly independently with the enterprise of which it is a permanent establishment.

In determining the profits of a permanent establishment, there shall be allowed as deductions expenses which are incurred for the purposes of the permanent establishment, including executive and general administrative expenses so incurred, whether in the State in which the permanent establishment is situated or elsewhere.

Insofar as it has been customary in a Contracting State to determine the profits to be attributed to a permanent establishment on the basis of an apportionment of the total profits of the enterprise to its various parts, nothing in paragraph 2 shall preclude that Contracting State from determining the profits to be taxed by such an apportionment as may be customary; the method of apportionment adopted shall, however, be such that the result shall be in accordance with the principles contained in this Article.

No profits shall be attributed to a permanent establishment by reason of the mere purchase by that permanent establishment of goods or merchandise for the enterprise.

For the purposes of the preceding paragraphs, the profits to be attributed to the permanent establishment shall be determined by the same method year by year unless there is good and sufficient reason to the contrary.

Where profits include items of income which are dealt with separately in other Articles of this Agreement, then the provisions of those Articles shall not be affected by the provisions of this Article.

Article 8 International Transport

Profits from the operation of ships or aircrafts in international traffic by an enterprise of a Contracting State shall be taxable only in that Contracting State.

The provisions of paragraph 1 shall also apply to profits from the participation in a pool, a joint business or an international operating agency.

Article 9 Associated Enterprises

Where

> an enterprise of a Contracting State participates directly or indirectly in the management, control or capital of an enterprise of the other Contracting State, or the same persons participate directly or indirectly in the management, control or capital of an enterprise of a Contracting State and an enterprise of the other Contracting State,
>
> and in either case conditions are made or imposed between the two enterprises in their commercial or financial relations which differ from those which would be made between independent enterprises, then any profits which would, but for those conditions, have accrued to one of the enterprises, but, by reason of those conditions, have not so accrued, may be included in the profits of that enterprise and taxed accordingly.

Where a Contracting State includes in the profits of an enterprise of that State—and taxes accordingly—profits on which an enterprise of the other Contracting State has been charged to tax in that other State and the profits so included are profits which would have accrued to the enterprise of the first-mentioned State if the conditions made between the two enterprises had been those which would have been made between independent enterprises, then that other State shall make an appropriate adjustment to the amount of the tax charged therein on those profits. Any such adjustment shall be made only in accordance with the mutual agreement procedure provided for by Article 26 of this Agreement.

Article 10 Dividends

Dividends paid by a company which is a resident of a Contracting State to a resident of the other Contracting State may be taxed in that other State.

However, such dividends may also be taxed in the Contracting State of which the company paying the dividends is a resident and according to the laws of that State, but if the beneficial owner of the dividends is a resident of the other Contracting State, the tax so charged shall not exceed:

5% of the gross amount of the dividends if the beneficial owner is a company which holds directly at least 25% of the capital of the company paying the dividends throughout a 365 day period that includes the day of the payment of the dividend (for the purpose of computing that period, no account shall be taken of changes of ownership that would directly result from a corporate reorganisation, such as a merger or divisive reorganisation, of the company that holds the shares or that pays the dividend);

10% of the gross amount of the dividends in all other cases.

This paragraph shall not affect the taxation of the company in respect of the profits out of which the dividends are paid.

The term "dividends" as used in this Article means income from shares, "jouissance" shares or "jouissance" rights, mining shares, founders' shares or other rights, not being debt-claims, participating in profits, as well as income from other corporate rights which is subjected to the same taxation treatment as income from shares by the laws of the State of which the company making the distribution is a resident.

The provisions of paragraphs 1 and 2 shall not apply if the beneficial owner of the dividends, being a resident of a Contracting State, carries on business in the other Contracting State of which the company paying the dividends is a resident through a permanent establishment situated therein, or performs in that other State independent personal services from a fixed base situated therein, and the holding in respect of which the dividends are paid is effectively connected with such permanent establishment or fixed base. In such case the provisions of Article 7 or Article 14, as the case may be, shall apply.

Where a company which is a resident of a Contracting State derives profits or income from the other Contracting State, that other State may not impose any tax on the dividends paid by the company, except insofar as such dividends are paid to a resident of that other State or insofar as the holding in respect of which the dividends are paid is effectively connected with a permanent establishment or a fixed base situated in that other State, nor subject the company's undistributed profits to a tax on the company's undistributed profits, even if the dividends paid or the undistributed profits consist wholly or partly of profits or income arising in such other State.

Article 11 Interest

Interest arising in a Contracting State and paid to a resident of the other Contracting State may be taxed in that other State.

However, such interest may also be taxed in the Contracting State in which it arises and according to the laws of that State, but if the beneficial owner of the interest is a resident of the other Contracting State, the tax so charged shall not exceed:

8% of the gross amount of the interest if the interest is paid to a financial institution on a loan with a term of at least 3 years for the financing of investment projects;
10% of the gross amount of the interest in all other cases.

Notwithstanding the provisions of paragraph 2, interest arising in a Contracting State shall be exempt from tax in that State if:

the payer of the interest is the Government of that Contracting State or a local authority thereof;
the interest is paid to the Government of the other Contracting State or political subdivisions, local authorities thereof, the Central Bank of the other Contracting State, or any public entity or any entity the capital of which is wholly owned by the Government of the other Contracting State, or paid on loans guaranteed or insured by the Government of the other Contracting State, or political subdivisions, local authorities thereof, the Central Bank of the other Contracting State or any public entity or any entity the capital of which is wholly owned by the Government of the other Contracting State.

Notwithstanding the provisions of paragraph 2, interest arising in Italy and paid to any beneficial owner of the interest who is a resident of China, when the issuer is Bank of Italy, Cassa Depositi e Prestiti-CDP, Istituto per i servizi assicurativi del commercio estero-Sace, Societa Italiana per le imprese all'estero-Simest, shall be exempt from Italian tax.

The term "interest" as used in this Article means income from debt-claims of every kind, whether or not secured by mortgage and whether or not carrying a right to participate in the debtor's profits, and in particular, income from government securities and income from bonds or debentures, including premiums and prizes attaching to such securities, bonds or debentures. Penalty charges for late payment shall not be regarded as interest for the purpose of this Article.

The provisions of paragraphs 1 and 2 shall not apply if the beneficial owner of the interest, being a resident of a Contracting State, carries on business in the other Contracting State in which the interest arises through a permanent establishment situated therein, or performs in that other State independent personal services from a fixed base situated therein, and the debt-claim in respect of which the interest is paid is effectively connected with such permanent establishment or fixed base. In such case the provisions of Article 7 or Article 14, as the case may be, shall apply.

Interest shall be deemed to arise in a Contracting State when the payer is a resident of that State. Where, however, the person paying the interest, whether he is a resident of a Contracting State or not, has in a Contracting State a permanent establishment or a fixed base in connection with which the indebtedness on which the interest is paid was incurred, and such interest is borne by such permanent establishment or fixed base, then such interest shall be deemed to arise in the State in which the permanent establishment or fixed base is situated.

Where, by reason of a special relationship between the payer and the beneficial owner or between both of them and some other person, the amount of the interest, having regard to the debt-claim for which it is paid, exceeds the amount which would have been agreed upon by the payer and the beneficial owner in the absence of such relationship, the provisions of this Article shall apply only to the last-mentioned amount. In such case, the excess part of the payments shall remain taxable according to the laws of each Contracting State, due regard being had to the other provisions of this Agreement.

Article 12 Royalties

Royalties arising in a Contracting State and beneficially owned by a resident of the other Contracting State may be taxed in that other State.

However, such royalties may also be taxed in the Contracting State in which they arise and according to the laws of that State, but if the beneficial owner of the royalties is a resident of the other Contracting State, the tax so charged shall not exceed:

in the case of royalties referred to in sub-paragraph (a) of paragraph 3, 10% of the gross amount of the royalties; and
in the case of royalties referred to in sub-paragraph (b) of paragraph 3, 10% of the adjusted amount of the royalties. For the purpose of this sub-paragraph "the adjusted amount" means 50% of the gross amount of the royalties.

The term "royalties" as used in this Article means:

payments of any kind received as a consideration for the use of, or the right to use, any copyright of literary, artistic or scientific work including software, cinematography films, or films or tapes for radio or television broadcasting, any patent, trade mark, design or model, plan, secret formula or process, or for information concerning industrial, commercial or scientific experience;
payments of any kind received as a consideration for the use of, or the right to use, industrial, commercial, or scientific equipment.

The provisions of paragraphs 1 and 2 shall not apply if the beneficial owner of the royalties, being a resident of a Contracting State, carries on business in the other Contracting State in which the royalties arise through a permanent establishment situated therein, or performs in that other State independent personal services from a fixed base situated therein, and the right or property in respect of which the royalties are paid is effectively connected with such permanent establishment or fixed base. In such case the provisions of Article 7 or Article 14, as the case may be, shall apply.

Royalties shall be deemed to arise in a Contracting State when the payer is a resident of that Contracting State. Where, however, the person paying the royalties, whether he is a resident of a Contracting State or not, has in a Contracting State a permanent establishment or a fixed base in connection with which the liability to pay the royalties was incurred, and such royalties are borne by such permanent establishment or fixed base, then such royalties shall be deemed to arise in the State in which the permanent establishment or fixed base is situated.

Where, by reason of a special relationship between the payer and the beneficial owner or between both of them and some other person, the amount of the royalties, having regard to the use, right or information for which they are paid, exceeds the amount which would have been agreed upon by the payer and the beneficial owner in the absence of such relationship, the provisions of this Article shall apply only to the last-mentioned amount. In such case, the excess part of the payments shall remain taxable according to the laws of each Contracting State, due regard being had to the other provisions of this Agreement.

Article 13 Capital Gains

Gains derived by a resident of a Contracting State from the alienation of immovable property referred to in Article 6 and situated in the other Contracting State may be taxed in that other State.

Gains from the alienation of movable property forming part of the business property of a permanent establishment which an enterprise of a Contracting State has in the other Contracting State or of movable property pertaining to a fixed base available to a resident of a Contracting State in the other Contracting State for the purpose of performing independent personal services, including such gains from the alienation of such a permanent establishment (alone or with the whole enterprise) or of such a fixed base, may be taxed in that other State.

Gains from the alienation of ships or aircraft operated in international traffic by an enterprise of a Contracting State, or movable property pertaining to the operation of such ships or aircraft, shall be taxable only in that Contracting State.

Gains derived by a resident of a Contracting State from the alienation of shares deriving more than 50% of their value directly or indirectly from immovable property situated in the other Contracting State may be taxed in that other State.

Gains derived by a resident of a Contracting State from the alienation of shares of a company which is a resident of the other Contracting State may be taxed in that other Contracting State if the alienator at any time during the 12 month period preceding such alienation, had a participation, directly or indirectly, of at least 25% in the capital of that company.

Gains from the alienation of any property, other than that referred to in paragraphs 1 to 5, shall be taxable only in the Contracting State of which the alienator is a resident.

Article 14 Independent Personal Services

Income derived by a resident of a Contracting State in respect of professional services or other activities of an independent character shall be taxable only in that State except in the following circumstances, when such income may also be taxed in the other Contracting State:

if he has a fixed base regularly available to him in the other Contracting State for the purpose of performing his activities; in that case, only so much of the income as is attributable to that fixed base may be taxed in that other State; or if his stay in the other Contracting State is for a period or periods amounting to or exceeding in the aggregate 183 days in any twelve month period commencing or ending in the fiscal year concerned; in that case, only so much of the income as is derived from his activities performed in that other State may be taxed in that other State.

The term "professional services" includes especially independent scientific, literary, artistic, educational or teaching activities as well as the independent activities of physicians, lawyers, engineers, architects, dentists and accountants.

Article 15 Income from Employment

Subject to the provisions of Articles 16, 18, 19 and 21, salaries, wages and other similar remuneration derived by a resident of a Contracting State in respect of an employment shall be taxable only in that State unless the employment is exercised in the other Contracting State. If the employment is so exercised, such remuneration as is derived therefrom may be taxed in that other State.

Notwithstanding the provisions of paragraph 1, remuneration derived by a resident of a Contracting State in respect of an employment exercised in the other Contracting State shall be taxable only in the first-mentioned State if:

the recipient is present in the other State for a period or periods not exceeding in the aggregate 183 days in any twelve month period commencing or ending in the fiscal year concerned, and

the remuneration is paid by, or on behalf of, an employer who is not a resident of the other State, and

the remuneration is not borne by a permanent establishment or a fixed base which the employer has in the other State.

Notwithstanding the preceding provisions of this Article, remuneration derived in respect of an employment exercised aboard a ship or aircraft operated in international traffic by an enterprise of a Contracting State, may be taxed in that Contracting State.

Payments received by a resident of a Contracting State after having ceased to be a resident of the other Contracting State and derived by virtue of his employment in that other Contracting State as severance indemnity or other similar lump sum payments, shall be taxable only in that other Contracting State.

Article 16 Directors' Fees

Directors' fees and other similar payments derived by a resident of a Contracting State in his capacity as a member of the board of directors of a company which is a resident of the other Contracting State may be taxed in that other State.

Article 17 Artistes and Sportsmen

Notwithstanding the provisions of Articles 14 and 15, income derived by a resident of a Contracting State as an entertainer, such as a theatre, motion picture, radio or television artiste, or a musician, or as a sportsman, from his personal activities as such exercised in the other Contracting State, may be taxed in that other State.

Where income in respect of personal activities exercised by an entertainer or a sportsman in his capacity as such accrues not to the entertainer or sportsman himself but to another person, that income may, notwithstanding the provisions of Articles 7, 14 and 15, be taxed in the Contracting State in which the activities of the entertainer or sportsman are exercised.

Notwithstanding the provisions of paragraphs 1 and 2, income derived by a resident of a Contracting State as an entertainer or as a sportsman, whether or not accruing to the entertainer or sportsman himself or to another person, from such activities as are referred to in paragraph 1 performed in the other Contracting State shall be taxed only in the first-mentioned Contracting State if such activities are wholly or mainly supported by public funds of the first-mentioned State, or if such activities are performed in the other State under a plan of cultural exchange between the Governments of both Contracting States.

Article 18 Pensions

Subject to the provisions of paragraph 2 of Article 19, pensions and other similar remuneration paid to a resident of a Contracting State in consideration of past employment shall be taxable only in that State.

Notwithstanding the provisions of paragraph 1, pensions paid and other similar payments made under a public welfare scheme of a Contracting State, a political subdivision or a local authority thereof shall be taxable only in that State.

Article 19 Government Service

(a) Salaries, wages and other similar remuneration, other than a pension, paid by the Government of a Contracting State or a political subdivision or a local authority thereof to an individual in respect of services rendered to the Government of that State or subdivision or authority, shall be taxable only in that State.

However, such salaries, wages and other similar remuneration shall be taxable only in the other Contracting State if the services are rendered in that State and the individual is a resident of that State who:

is a national of that State; or did not become a resident of that State solely for the purpose of rendering the services.

(a) Pensions and other similar remuneration paid by, or out of funds created by, a Contracting State or a political subdivision or a local authority thereof to an individual in respect of services rendered to the Government of that State or subdivision or authority shall be taxable only in that State.

(b) However, such pensions and other similar remuneration shall be taxable only in the other Contracting State if the individual is a resident of, and a national of, that State.

The provisions of Articles 15, 16, 17, and 18 shall apply to salaries, wages, pensions, and other similar remuneration in respect of services rendered in connection with a business carried on by the Government of a Contracting State or a political subdivision or a local authority thereof.

Article 20 Students

Payments which a student or business apprentice who is or was immediately before visiting a Contracting State a resident of the other Contracting State and who is present in the first-mentioned State solely for the purpose of his education receives for the purpose of his maintenance or education shall not be taxed in that State, provided that such payments arise from sources outside that State.

The benefits of this Article shall extend only for a period not exceeding six consecutive years from the date of his first arrival in the first-mentioned State.

Article 21 Teachers and Researchers

Remuneration which an individual who is or was immediately before visiting a Contracting State a resident of the other Contracting State, and who is present in the first-mentioned State solely for the purpose of teaching, giving lectures or engaging in research in a school, institute, university, or any other educational or research institution officially recognized by the Government of that State, receives for such services shall be exempt from tax in that State for a period not exceeding, in total three years, as from the date of his or her arrival in that State.

The provisions of paragraph 1 shall not apply to income from research, if this research is not in the public interest and is primarily for the private benefit of a certain person or persons.

Article 22 Other Income

Items of income of a resident of a Contracting State, wherever arising, not dealt with in the foregoing Articles of this Agreement shall be taxable only in that State.

The provisions of paragraph 1 shall not apply to income, other than income from immovable property as defined in paragraph 2 of Article 6, if the recipient of such income, being a resident of a Contracting State, carries on business in the other Contracting State through a permanent establishment situated therein, or performs in that other State independent personal services from a fixed base situated therein, and the right or property in respect of which the income is paid is effectively connected with such permanent establishment or fixed base. In such case the provisions of Article 7 or Article 14, as the case may be, shall apply.

Article 23 Methods for Elimination of Double Taxation

In China, in accordance with the provisions of the law of China, double taxation shall be eliminated as follows:

> Where a resident of China derives income from Italy, the amount of tax on that income payable in Italy in accordance with the provisions of this Agreement may be credited against the Chinese tax imposed on that resident. The amount of the credit, however, shall not exceed the amount of the Chinese tax on that income computed in accordance with the taxation laws and regulations of China.
>
> Where the income derived from Italy is dividend paid by a company which is a resident of Italy to a company which is a resident of China and which owns not less than 20% of the shares of the company paying the dividend, the credit shall

take into account the tax paid to Italy by the company paying the dividend in respect of its income.

In Italy, double taxation shall be eliminated as follows:

residents of Italy deriving items of income which, in accordance with the provisions of this Agreement, may be taxed in China, may include such items of income in the tax base upon which taxes are imposed in Italy, subject to the applicable provisions of the Italian law.

In such a case, Italy shall allow as a deduction from the taxes so calculated the income tax paid in China but in an amount not exceeding that proportion of the aforesaid Italian tax which such items of income bear to the entire income.

However, no deduction shall be granted if the item of income is subjected in Italy to a substitute tax or to a final withholding tax, or to substitute taxation at the same rate as the final withholding tax, also by request of the recipient, in accordance with Italian law.

Article 24 Entitlement to Benefits

Notwithstanding the other provisions of this Agreement, a benefit under this Agreement shall not be granted in respect of an item of income if it is reasonable to conclude, having regard to all relevant facts and circumstances, that obtaining that benefit was one of the principal purposes of any arrangement or transaction that resulted directly or indirectly in that benefit, unless it is established that granting that benefit in these circumstances would be in accordance with the object and purpose of the relevant provisions of this Agreement.

Article 25 Non-Discrimination

Nationals of a Contracting State shall not be subjected in the other Contracting State to any taxation or any requirement connected therewith, which is other or more burdensome than the taxation and connected requirements to which nationals of that other State in the same circumstances, in particular with respect to residence, are or may be subjected. This provision shall, notwithstanding the provisions of Article 1, also apply to persons who are not residents of one or both of the Contracting States.

The taxation on a permanent establishment which an enterprise of a Contracting State has in the other Contracting State shall not be less favorably levied in that other State than the taxation levied on enterprises of that other State carrying on the same activities. This provision shall not be construed as obliging a Contracting State to grant to residents of the other Contracting State any personal allowances, reliefs and reductions for taxation purposes on account of civil status or family responsibilities which it grants to its own residents.

Except where the provisions of paragraph 1 of Article 9, paragraph 8 of Article 11, or paragraph 6 of Article 12, apply, interest, royalties and other disbursements paid by an enterprise of a Contracting State to a resident of the other Contracting State shall, for the purpose of determining the taxable profits of such enterprise, be deductible under the same conditions as if they had been paid to a resident of the first-mentioned State.

Enterprises of a Contracting State, the capital of which is wholly or partly owned or controlled, directly or indirectly, by one or more residents of the other Contracting State, shall not be subjected in the first-mentioned State to any taxation or any requirement connected therewith which is other or more burdensome than the taxation and connected requirements to which other similar enterprises of the first-mentioned State are or may be subjected.

The provisions of the Article shall, notwithstanding the provisions of Article 2, apply to taxes of every kind and description.

Article 26 Mutual Agreement Procedure

Where a person considers that the actions of one or both of the Contracting States result or will result for him in taxation not in accordance with the provisions of this Agreement, he may, irrespective of the remedies provided by the domestic law of those States, present his case to the competent authority of the Contracting State of which he is a resident or, if his case comes under paragraph 1 of Article 25, to that of the Contracting State of which he is a national. The case must be presented within three years from the first notification of the action resulting in taxation not in accordance with the provisions of the Agreement.

The competent authority shall endeavor, if the objection appears to it to be justified and if it is not itself able to arrive at a satisfactory solution, to resolve the case by mutual agreement with the competent authority of the other Contracting State, with a view to the avoidance of taxation which is not in accordance with the Agreement. Any agreement reached shall be implemented notwithstanding any time limits in the domestic law of the Contracting States.

The competent authorities of the Contracting States shall endeavor to resolve by mutual agreement any difficulties or doubts arising as to the interpretation or application of the Agreement. They may also consult together for the elimination of double taxation in cases not provided for in the Agreement.

The competent authorities of the Contracting States may communicate with each other directly for the purpose of reaching an agreement in the sense of paragraphs 2 and 3. When it seems advisable for reaching an agreement, representatives of the competent authorities of the Contracting States may meet together for an oral exchange of opinions.

Article 27 Exchange of Information

The competent authorities of the Contracting States shall exchange such information as is foreseeably relevant for carrying out the provisions of this Agreement or to the administration or enforcement of the domestic laws concerning taxes of every kind and description imposed on behalf of the Contracting States, or of their political subdivisions or local authorities, insofar as the taxation thereunder is not contrary to the Agreement. The exchange of information is not restricted by Articles 1 and 2.

Any information received under paragraph 1 by a Contracting State shall be treated as secret in the same manner as information obtained under the domestic laws of that State and shall be disclosed only to persons or authorities (including courts and administrative bodies) concerned with the assessment or collection of, the enforcement or prosecution in respect of, the determination of appeals in relation to the taxes referred to in paragraph 1, or the oversight of the above. Such persons or authorities shall use the information only for such purposes. They may disclose the information in public court proceedings or in judicial decisions.

In no case shall the provisions of paragraphs 1 and 2 be construed so as to impose on a Contracting State the obligation:

to carry out administrative measures at variance with the laws and administrative practice of that or of the other Contracting State;
to supply information which is not obtainable under the laws or in the normal course of the administration of that or of the other Contracting State;
to supply information which would disclose any trade, business, industrial, commercial or professional secret or trade process, or information, the disclosure of which would be contrary to public policy (*ordre public*).

If information is requested by a Contracting State in accordance with this Article, the other Contracting State shall use its information gathering measures to obtain the requested information, even though that other State may not need such information for its own tax purposes. The obligation contained in the preceding sentence is subject to the limitations of paragraph 3 but in no case shall such limitations be construed to permit a Contracting State to decline to supply information solely because it has no domestic interest in such information.

In no case shall the provisions of paragraph 3 be construed to permit a Contracting State to decline to supply information solely because the information is held by a bank, other financial institution, nominee or person acting in an agency or a fiduciary capacity or because it relates to ownership interests in a person.

Article 28 Members of Diplomatic Missions and Consular Posts

Nothing in this Agreement shall affect the fiscal privileges of members of diplomatic missions or consular posts under the general rules of international law or under the provisions of special agreements.

Article 29 Entry into Force

Both Contracting States shall notify each other through diplomatic channels that they have completed the internal legal procedures necessary for the entry into force of this Agreement. This Agreement shall enter into force on the thirtieth day upon the receipt of the latter notification and have effect:

in respect of taxes withheld at source, to amounts derived on or after 1st January in the calendar year next following that in which this Agreement enters into force;
in respect of other taxes on income, to taxes chargeable for any taxable period beginning on or after 1st January in the calendar year next following that in which this Agreement enters into force.

The Agreement between the Government of People's Republic of China and the Government of the Republic of Italy for the Avoidance of Double Taxation and the

Prevention of Fiscal Evasion with respect to taxes on Income, signed on 31st October 1986 in Beijing shall cease to have effect as from the date on which the provisions of this Agreement become applicable in accordance with the provisions of this Article.

Article 30 Termination

This Agreement shall continue in effect indefinitely but either of the Contracting States may, on or before the thirtieth day of June in any calendar year beginning after the expiration of a period of five years from the date of its entry into force, give written notice of termination to the other Contracting State through diplomatic channels. In such event this Agreement shall cease to have effect:

in respect of taxes withheld at source, to amounts derived on or after 1st January in the calendar year next following that in which the notice is given;
in respect of other taxes on income, to taxes chargeable for any taxable period beginning on or after 1st January in the calendar year next following that in which the notice is given.

IN WITNESS whereof the undersigned, duly authorized thereto by their respective Governments, have signed this Agreement.

Done at Rome on the 23rd day of March, 2019, in duplicate in the Chinese, Italian and English languages, all texts being equally authentic. In case of divergence in interpretation or application, the English text shall prevail.

For the Government ofthe People's Republic of China

For the Government of the Italian Republic

Protocol

At the signing of the Agreement between the Government of the People's Republic of China and the Government of the Italian Republic for the Elimination of Double Taxation with respect to Taxes on Income and the Prevention of Tax Evasion and Avoidance (hereinafter referred to as "the Agreement"), the undersigned have agreed upon the following provisions which shall form an integral part of the Agreement.

In respect of Article 7:

where an enterprise of a Contracting State sells goods or merchandise or carries on business in the other Contracting State through a permanent establishment situated therein, the profits of that permanent establishment shall not be determined as the total amount received by the enterprise but only as the remuneration which is attributable to the actual activity of the permanent establishment for such sales or business;
in the case of contracts for building sites, a construction, assembly, or installation projects, where an enterprise of a Contracting State has a permanent establishment in the other Contracting State, the profits of such permanent establishment shall not be determined as the total amount of the contract, but only as that part of the contract which is effectively accomplished by the permanent establishment.

The application of this Agreement shall not affect the application of the other agreements between the two Contracting States which provide for more favourable treatment on international traffic.

With reference to paragraph 3 of Article 11,

It is understood that the term "any public entity or any entity the capital of which is wholly owned by the Government of the other Contracting State" means:

in the case of China:
the China Development Bank;
the Agricultural Development Bank of China;
the Export–Import bank of China;
the National Council for Social Security Fund;
the China Export & Credit Insurance Corporation;
the China Investment Corporation;
the China Investment Corporation (CIC) International Co., Ltd.; (viii) the China Investment Corporation (CIC) Capital Corporation;
(ix) the Silk Road Fund Co., Ltd.
in the case of Italy:
Cassa Depositi e Prestiti—CDP;
Istituto per i servizi assicurativi del commercio estero—Sace;
Società italiana per le imprese all'estero—Simest.

With reference to paragraphs 1 and 2 of Article 19, remuneration paid to an individual in respect of services rendered to the Bank of Italy or to the People's Bank of China, and to the Italian Trade Agency (*ICE—Agenzia per la promozione all'estero e l'internazionalizzazione delle imprese italiane*) or to the China Council for the Promotion of International Trade, are covered by the provisions concerning government service. The same treatment may apply to similar entities as it may be agreed upon by the competent authorities through an Exchange of Notes subject to ratification.

Notwithstanding the provisions of Article 27, for data and information communicated pursuant to this Agreement to be used in criminal proceedings, further request shall be put forward in compliance with any other bilateral or multilateral agreement that the two Contracting States signed or participated in.

Both Contracting States allow the direct application of the tax rate limitations provided for in this Agreement. In the case where taxes are withheld at source at the domestic rate, they will be refunded by request of the taxpayer or of the State of which he is a resident, according to the domestic law of each Contracting State.

IN WITNESS whereof the undersigned, duly authorized thereto by their respective Governments, have signed this Protocol.

Done at Rome on the 23rd day of March, 2019, in duplicate in the Chinese, Italian and English languages, all texts being equally authentic. In case of divergence in interpretation or application, the English text shall prevail.

For the Government of the People's Republic of China

For the Government of the Italian Republic

Netherlands

The Netherlands, officially the Kingdom of the Netherlands, is a state in Western Europe. The Netherlands borders Germany to the east, Belgium to the south, and the North Sea to the northwest. The Netherlands' capital and largest city is Amsterdam, also major financial center.

The Netherlands is a most popular immigration destination in Europe. Dutch are the majority ethnic group, while main minorities are constituted by various European groups, Indo, and Turks.

The official and predominant spoken language is Dutch. Recognized minority languages are West Frisian, English, Papiamento, Dutch Low Saxon, and Limburgish. Minority languages used by immigrants and second generations are Arabic, Indonesian, Polish, and Turkish.

The Netherlands is a unitary parliamentary constitutional monarchy. The constitution, regulating the political system, in force since 1848, however, in 1983 a major revision has been carried out. The House of Representatives and the Senate in the States General conduct the legislative power. The House of Representatives is elected through direct elections using the party-list proportional representation system. The members of the Senate are elected by indirect party-list proportional system. The Senate has the right to approve or reject legislative proposals, but it is unable to initiate nor to amend legislation.

Executive power is vested in the Prime Minister and his or her cabinet. The Prime Minister is appointed by the Monarch after consultations are conducted, so that a parliamentary majority will support the new cabinet in a vote of confidence.

The Netherlands has a civil law system based on Roman law, however some references to Germanic law are relevant. The Supreme Court handles constitutional matters, with judicial review powers.

The Netherlands is a unitary state, divided into 12 provinces, divided into 352 municipalities.

The Netherlands is part of the European Union, one of the six founding country, together with Germany, France, Italy, Luxemburg, and Belgium.

© The Author(s), under exclusive license to Springer Nature Singapore Pte Ltd. 2022

L. Riccardi and G. Riccardi, *China–Europe Tax Treaties*,
https://doi.org/10.1007/978-981-19-3563-3_19

Category	Value
Population (mln persons)	17.231
Currency	Euro

Source International Monetary Fund, year 2019

The Netherlands is the third largest economy of Western Europe after Germany and France, with a GDP valued 902.4 billion USD in 2019, and has a population of about 17 million people. The Netherlands inflation is slightly above average in the Eurozone (2.7%), while unemployment is below average at 3.4%. The Netherlands ranked 22 out of 43 in Europe in the 2020 Doing Business ranking, scoring 76.1, and imposes a CIT of 25%. The Netherlands records a trade surplus of 73 billion USD, it is the third main trade surplus in Europe after Germany and Russia. It is the second largest exporter and the fourth larger importer. It should be noted that the figures might be inflated by the Rotterdam effect, however the total trade flow remains unaffected.

GDP and local economy	
GDP current prices (billion USD)	902.4
GDP per capita (USD)	52,368
GDP growth (%)	1.8
Inflation (%)	2.7
Unemployment (%)	3.4
General government total expenditure (% of GDP)	41.2
General government gross debt (% of GDP)	47.5
Doing Business Score 2020	76.1

Source International Monetary Fund and UNCTAD, year 2019

Foreign direct investment	
FDI outstock (million USD)	2,565,287
FDI instock (million USD)	1,749,779

Source UNCTAD, year 2019

Trade	
Imports (million USD)	635,967
Exports (million USD)	709,229
Trade balance (million USD)	73,262

Source International Monetary Fund and UNCTAD, year 2019

Main import–export	
First import by category	Electrical, electronic equipment
Second import by category	Machinery, nuclear reactors, boilers
First export by category	Machinery, nuclear reactors, boilers
Second export by category	Electrical, electronic equipment

Source United Nations COMTRADE, year 2020

The legal bases for taxation are established in the constitution. The Netherlands imposes individual income tax, property sales taxes, capital gains, corporate income tax, and value added tax. Progressivity is guaranteed by a system with different bands and various deductions.

Taxes	
Company income tax (%)	25
Top individual income tax (%)	49.5
Value added tax or sales tax (%)	21
Reduced value added tax or sales tax (%)	9

Source RsA Asia report, year 2021

- Economic relation with China

The Netherlands records a trade deficit towards China of 66 billion USD in 2020. "Machinery, nuclear reactors, boilers" is the first export category, worth 3.89 billion USD. "Electrical, electronic equipment" is the first import category, valued 26.83 billion USD. The Netherlands is not part of the Belt and Road Initiative. The first DTA between the Netherlands and China was signed in 1987 and come into force in 1988. A new agreement has been signed in 2013, entering into force in August 2014.

Category	Value
Belt road	No

Source UNCTAD, year 2021

Import from China	
Import from China (billion USD)	79.01
First import category from China	Electrical, electronic equipment
First import value (billion USD)	26.83
Second import category from China	Machinery, nuclear reactors, boilers
Second import value (billion USD)	20.63

Source United Nations COMTRADE, year 2020

Export to China	
Export to China (billion USD)	12.79
First export category towards China	Machinery, nuclear reactors, boilers
First Export value (billion USD)	3.89
Second export category towards China	Cereal, flour, starch, milk preparations and products
Second export value (billion USD)	1.96

Source United Nations COMTRADE, year 2020

Trade balance	
Trade balance (billion USD)	−66.22

Source United Nations COMTRADE, year 2020

Double tax agreement	
DTA effective date	2014.8.31
Dividends (%)	0–5–10
Interest (%)	0–10
Royalties (%)	6–10

Source State Administration of Taxation of China, year 2021

Title AGREEMENT BETWEEN THE GOVERNMENT OF THE PEOPLE'S REPUBLIC OF CHINA AND THE GOVERNMENT OF THE KINGDOM OF THE NETHERLANDS FOR THE AVOIDANCE OF DOUBLE TAXATION AND THE PREVENTION OF FISCAL EVASION WITH RESPECT TO TAXES ON INCOME

Treaty Text

The Government of the People's Republic of China and the Government of the Kingdom of the Netherlands,

Desiring to conclude an Agreement for the avoidance of double taxation and the prevention of fiscal evasion with respect to taxes on income,

Have agreed as follows:

Article 1 Persons Covered

This Agreement shall apply to persons who are residents of one or both of the Contracting States.

Article 2 Taxes Covered

This Agreement shall apply to taxes on income imposed on behalf of a Contracting State or local authorities, irrespective of the manner in which they are levied.

There shall be regarded as taxes on income all taxes imposed on total income, or on elements of income, including taxes on gains from the alienation of movable or immovable property and taxes on the total amounts of wages or salaries paid by enterprises.

The existing taxes to which the Agreement shall apply are in particular:

in China:
the individual income tax;
the enterprise income tax; (hereinafter referred to as "Chinese tax");
in the Netherlands:
the income tax;
the wages tax;
the company tax, including the Government share in the net profits of the exploitation of natural resources levied pursuant to the Mining Act, the Mining Act BES, the Mining Decree BES or Petroleum Act Saba Bank BES;
the dividend tax;(hereinafter referred to as "Netherlands tax").

The Agreement shall apply also to any identical or substantially similar taxes that are imposed after the date of signature of the Agreement in addition to, or in place of, the existing taxes. The competent authorities of the Contracting States shall notify each other of any significant changes that have been made in their taxation laws.

Article 3 General Definitions

For the purposes of this Agreement, unless the context otherwise requires:

the term "China" means the People's Republic of China; when used in geographical sense, means all the territory of the People's Republic of China, including its territorial sea, in which the Chinese laws relating to taxation apply, and any area beyond its territorial sea, within which the People's Republic of China has jurisdiction or sovereign rights in accordance with international law and its internal law;
the term "the Netherlands" means:
the European part of the Netherlands, including its territorial sea, and any area beyond the territorial sea within which the Kingdom of the Netherlands, in accordance with international law, exercises jurisdiction or sovereign rights; and the Caribbean part of the Netherlands that is situated in the Caribbean Sea and consists of the islands of Bonaire, Saint Eustatius and Saba, including the territorial sea of these islands, and any area beyond the territorial sea of these islands within which the Kingdom of the Netherlands, in accordance with international law, exercises jurisdiction or sovereign rights;
the terms "a Contracting State" and "the other Contracting State" mean China or the Netherlands as the context requires;
the term "person" includes an individual, a company and any other body of persons;
the term "company" means any body corporate or any entity that is treated as a body corporate for tax purposes;

the terms “enterprise of a Contracting State” and “enterprise of the other Contracting State” mean respectively an enterprise carried on by a resident of a Contracting State and an enterprise carried on by a resident of the other Contracting State;
the term “international traffic” means any transport by a ship or aircraft operated by an enterprise that has its place of effective management in a Contracting State, except when the ship or aircraft is operated solely between places in the other Contracting State;
the term “competent authority” means:
in China, the State Administration of Taxation or its authorized representative;
in the Netherlands, the Minister of Finance or his authorized representative;
the term “national”, in relation to a Contracting State, means:
any individual possessing the nationality of a Contracting State;
any legal person, partnership or association deriving its status as such from the laws in force in a Contracting State.

As regards the application of the Agreement at any time by a Contracting State, any term not defined therein shall, unless the context otherwise requires, have the meaning that it has at that time under the law of that State for the purposes of the taxes to which the Agreement applies, any meaning under the applicable tax laws of that State prevailing over a meaning given to the term under other laws of that State.

Article 4 Resident

For the purposes of this Agreement, the term “resident of a Contracting State” means any person who, under the laws of that State, is liable to tax therein by reason of his domicile, residence, place of incorporation, place of effective management or any other criterion of a similar nature, and also includes that State or local authority thereof. This term, however, does not include any person who is liable to tax in that State in respect only of income from sources in that State.

Where by reason of the provisions of paragraph 1 an individual is a resident of both Contracting States, then his status shall be determined as follows:

he shall be deemed to be a resident only of the State in which he has a permanent home available to him; if he has a permanent home available to him in both States, he shall be deemed to be a resident only of the State with which his personal and economic relations are closer (centre of vital interests);
if the State in which he has his centre of vital interests cannot be determined, or if he has not a permanent home available to him in either State, he shall be deemed to be a resident only of the State in which he has an habitual abode;
if he has an habitual abode in both States or in neither of them, he shall be deemed to be a resident only of the State of which he is a national;
if he is a national of both States or of neither of them, the competent authorities of the Contracting States shall settle the question by mutual agreement.

Where by reason of the provisions of paragraph 1 a person other than an individual is a resident of both Contracting States, then it shall be deemed to be a resident only of the State in which its place of effective management is situated.

Article 5 Permanent Establishment

For the purposes of this Agreement, the term "permanent establishment" means a fixed place of business through which the business of an enterprise is wholly or partly carried on.

The term "permanent establishment" includes especially:

a place of management;
a branch;
an office;
a factory;
a workshop; and
a mine, an oil or gas well, a quarry or any other place of extraction of natural resources.

The term "permanent establishment" likewise encompasses:

a building site, or construction, assembly or installation project or supervisory activities in connection therewith, but only if such site, project or activities last more than 12 months;
the furnishing of services, including consultancy services, by an enterprise through employees or other personnel engaged by the enterprise for such purpose, but only if activities of that nature continue (for the same or a connected project) within a Contracting State for a period or periods aggregating more than 183 days within any twelve month period.

Notwithstanding the preceding provisions of this Article, the term "permanent establishment" shall be deemed not to include:

the use of facilities solely for the purpose of storage, display or delivery of goods or merchandise belonging to the enterprise;
the maintenance of a stock of goods or merchandise belonging to the enterprise solely for the purpose of storage, display or delivery;
the maintenance of a stock of goods or merchandise belonging to the enterprise solely for the purpose of processing by another enterprise;
the maintenance of a fixed place of business solely for the purpose of purchasing goods or merchandise or of collecting information, for the enterprise;
the maintenance of a fixed place of business solely for the purpose of carrying on, for the enterprise, any other activity of a preparatory or auxiliary character;
the maintenance of a fixed place of business solely for any combination of activities mentioned in sub-paragraphs (a)–(e), provided that the overall activity of the fixed place of business resulting from this combination is of a preparatory or auxiliary character.

Notwithstanding the provisions of paragraphs 1 and 2, where a person—other than an agent of an independent status to whom paragraph 6 applies—is acting in a Contracting State on behalf of an enterprise of the other Contracting State, and has, and habitually exercises, in that Contracting State an authority to conclude contracts in the name of the enterprise, that enterprise shall be deemed to have a permanent establishment in that Contracting State in respect of any activities which that person undertakes for the enterprise, unless the activities of such person are limited to those mentioned in paragraph 4 which, if exercised through a fixed place of business, would not make this fixed place of business a permanent establishment under the provisions of that paragraph.

An enterprise of a Contracting State shall not be deemed to have a permanent establishment in the other Contracting State merely because it carries on business in that other State through a broker, general commission agent or any other agent of an independent status, provided that such persons are acting in the ordinary course of their business. However, when the activities of such an agent are devoted wholly or almost wholly on behalf of that enterprise, and conditions are made or imposed between that enterprise and the agent in their commercial and financial relations which differ from those which would have been made between independent enterprises, he will not be considered an agent of an independent status within the meaning of this paragraph.

The fact that a company which is a resident of a Contracting State controls or is controlled by a company which is a resident of the other Contracting State, or which carries on business in that other State (whether through a permanent establishment or otherwise), shall not of itself constitute either company a permanent establishment of the other.

Article 6 Income from Immovable Property

Income derived by a resident of a Contracting State from immovable property (including incôme from agriculture or forestry) situated in the other Contracting State may be taxed in that other State.

The term "immovable property" shall have the meaning which it has under the law of the Contracting State in which the property in question is situated. The term shall in any case include property accessory to immovable property, livestock and equipment used in agriculture and forestry, rights to which the provisions of general law respecting landed property apply, usufruct of immovable property and rights to variable or fixed payments as consideration for the working of, or the right to work, mineral deposits, sources and other natural resources; ships and aircraft shall not be regarded as immovable property.

The provisions of paragraph 1 shall apply to income derived from the direct use, letting, or use in any other form of immovable property.

The provisions of paragraphs 1 and 3 shall also apply to the income from immovable property of an enterprise and to income from immovable property used for the performance of independent personal services.

Article 7 Business Profits

The profits of an enterprise of a Contracting State shall be taxable only in that State unless the enterprise carries on business in the other Contracting State through a permanent establishment situated therein. If the enterprise carries on business as aforesaid, the profits of the enterprise may be taxed in the other State but only so much of them as is attributable to that permanent establishment.

Subject to the provisions of paragraph 3, where an enterprise of a Contracting State carries on business in the other Contracting State through a permanent establishment situated therein, there shall in each Contracting State be attributed to that permanent establishment the profits which it might be expected to make if it were a distinct and separate enterprise engaged in the same or similar activities under the same or similar conditions and dealing wholly independently with the enterprise of which it is a permanent establishment.

In determining the profits of a permanent establishment, there shall be allowed as deductions expenses which are incurred for the purposes of the permanent establishment, including executive and general administrative expenses so incurred, whether in the State in which the permanent establishment is situated or elsewhere.

Insofar as it has been customary in a Contracting State to determine the profits to be attributed to a permanent establishment on the basis of an apportionment of the total profits of the enterprise to its various parts, nothing in paragraph 2 shall preclude that Contracting State from determining the profits to be taxed by such an apportionment as may be customary; the method of apportionment adopted shall, however, be such that the result shall be in accordance with the principles contained in this Article.

No profits shall be attributed to a permanent establishment by reason of the mere purchase by that permanent establishment of goods or merchandise for the enterprise.

For the purposes of the preceding paragraphs, the profits to be attributed to the permanent establishment shall be determined by the same method year by year unless there is good and sufficient reason to the contrary.

Where profits include items of income which are dealt with separately in other Articles of this Agreement, then the provisions of those Articles shall not be affected by the provisions of this Article.

Article 8 Shipping and Air Transport

Profits from the operation of ships or aircraft in international traffic shall be taxable only in the Contracting State in which the place of effective management of the enterprise is situated.

If the place of effective management of a shipping enterprise is aboard a ship, then it shall be deemed to be situated in the Contracting State in which the home harbour of the ship is situated, or, if there is no such home harbour, in the Contracting State of which the operator of the ship is a resident.

The provisions of paragraph 1 shall also apply to profits from the participation in a pool, a joint business or an international operating agency.

Article 9 Associated Enterprises

Where

an enterprise of a Contracting State participates directly or indirectly in the management, control or capital of an enterprise of the other Contracting State, or the same persons participate directly or indirectly in the management, control or capital of an enterprise of a Contracting State and an enterprise of the other Contracting State,

and in either case conditions are made or imposed between the two enterprises in their commercial or financial relations which differ from those which would be made between independent enterprises, then any profits which would, but for those conditions, have accrued to one of the enterprises, but, by reason of those conditions, have not so accrued, may be included in the profits of that enterprise and taxed accordingly.

Where a Contracting State includes in the profits of an enterprise of that State—and taxes accordingly—profits on which an enterprise of the other Contracting State has been charged to tax in that other State and the profits so included are profits which would have accrued to the enterprise of the first-mentioned State if the conditions made between the two enterprises had been those which would have been made between independent enterprises, then that other State shall make an appropriate adjustment to the amount of the tax charged therein on those profits. In determining such adjustment, due regard shall be had to the other provisions of this Agreement and the competent authorities of the Contracting States shall, if necessary, consult each other.

Article 10 Dividends

Dividends paid by a company which is a resident of a Contracting State to a resident of the other Contracting State may be taxed in that other State.

However, such dividends may also be taxed in the Contracting State of which the company paying the dividends is a resident and according to the laws of that State, but if the beneficial owner of the dividends is a resident of the other Contracting State, the tax so charged shall not exceed:

5% of the gross amount of the dividends if the beneficial owner is a company (other than a partnership) which holds directly at least 25% of the capital of the company paying the dividends;

10% of the gross amount of the dividends in all other cases.

The competent authorities of the Contracting States shall by mutual agreement settle the mode of application of these limitations.

This paragraph shall not affect the taxation of the company in respect of the profits out of which the dividends are paid.

Notwithstanding the provisions of paragraph 2, dividends paid by a company which is a resident of a Contracting State to a resident of the other Contracting State shall be taxable only in that other Contracting State if the beneficial owner of the dividends is the Government of that other Contracting State, any of its institutions or any other entity the capital of which is wholly owned directly or indirectly by that other Contracting State.

The term "dividends" as used in this Article means income from shares or other rights, not being debt-claims, participating in profits, as well as income from other corporate rights which is subjected to the same taxation treatment as income from shares by the laws of the State of which the company making the distribution is a resident.

The provisions of paragraphs 1 and 2 shall not apply if the beneficial owner of the dividends, being a resident of a Contracting State, carries on business in the other Contracting State of which the company paying the dividends is a resident through a permanent establishment situated therein, or performs in that other State independent personal services from a fixed base situated therein, and the holding in respect of which the dividends are paid is effectively connected with such permanent establishment or fixed base. In such case the provisions of Article 7 or Article 14, as the case may be, shall apply.

Where a company which is a resident of a Contracting State derives profits or income from the other Contracting State, that other State may not impose any tax on the dividends paid by the company, except insofar as such dividends are paid to a resident of that other State or insofar as the holding in respect of which the dividends are paid is effectively connected with a permanent establishment or a fixed base situated in that other State, nor subject the company's undistributed profits to a tax on the company's undistributed profits, even if the dividends paid or the undistributed profits consist wholly or partly of profits or income arising in such other State.

The provisions of this Article shall not apply if it was the main purpose or one of the main purposes of any person concerned with the creation or assignment of the shares or other rights in respect of which the dividends are paid to take advantage of this Article by means of that creation or assignment.

Article 11 Interest

Interest arising in a Contracting State and paid to a resident of the other Contracting State may be taxed in that other State.

However, such interest may also be taxed in the Contracting State in which it arises and according to the laws of that State, but if the beneficial owner of the interest is a resident of the other Contracting State, the tax so charged shall not exceed 10% of the gross amount of the interest. The competent authorities of the Contracting States shall by mutual agreement settle the mode of application of this limitation.

Notwithstanding the provisions of paragraph 2, interest arising in a Contracting State and paid to, or on loans guaranteed or insured by, the Government or a local authority, the Central Bank, or any financial institution wholly owned by the other Contracting State, shall be exempt from tax in the first-mentioned State.

For the purposes of paragraph 3, the term "any financial institution wholly owned by the other Contracting State" means:

in the case of China:

China Development Bank Corporation;

Agricultural Development Bank of China;
Export–Import Bank of China;
National Council for Social Security Fund;
China Export & Credit Insurance Corporation;
China Investment Corporation; and
any other institution as may be agreed from time to time between the competent authorities of the Contracting States;
in the case of the Netherlands:
Netherlands Finance Company for Developing Countries;
Netherlands Investment Bank for Developing Countries; and
any other institution as may be agreed from time to time between the competent authorities of the Contracting States.

The term "interest" as used in this Article means income from debt-claims of every kind, whether or not secured by mortgage and whether or not carrying a right to participate in the debtor's profits, and in particular, income from government securities and income from bonds or debentures, including premiums and prizes attaching to such securities, bonds or debentures. Penalty charges for late payment shall not be regarded as interest for the purpose of this Article.

The provisions of paragraphs 1 and 2 shall not apply if the beneficial owner of the interest, being a resident of a Contracting State, carries on business in the other Contracting State in which the interest arises through a permanent establishment situated therein, or performs in that other State independent personal services from a fixed base situated therein, and the debt-claim in respect of which the interest is paid is effectively connected with such permanent establishment or fixed base. In such case the provisions of Article 7 or Article 14, as the case may be, shall apply.

Interest shall be deemed to arise in a Contracting State when the payer is a resident of that State. Where, however, the person paying the interest, whether he is a resident of a Contracting State or not, has in a Contracting State a permanent establishment or a fixed base in connection with which the indebtedness on which the interest is paid was incurred, and such interest is borne by such permanent establishment or fixed base, then such interest shall be deemed to arise in the State in which the permanent establishment or fixed base is situated.

Where, by reason of a special relationship between the payer and the beneficial owner or between both of them and some other person, the amount of the interest, having regard to the debt-claim for which it is paid, exceeds the amount which would have been agreed upon by the payer and the beneficial owner in the absence of such relationship, the provisions of this Article shall apply only to the last-mentioned amount. In such case, the excess part of the payments shall remain taxable according to the laws of each Contracting State, due regard being had to the other provisions of this Agreement.

The provisions of this Article shall not apply if it was the main purpose or one of the main purposes of any person concerned with the creation or assignment of the debt-claim in respect of which the interest is paid to take advantage of this Article by means of that creation or assignment.

Article 12 Royalties

Royalties arising in a Contracting State and paid to a resident of the other Contracting State may be taxed in that other State.

However, such royalties may also be taxed in the Contracting State in which they arise and according to the laws of that State, but if the beneficial owner of the royalties is a resident of the other Contracting State, the tax so charged shall not exceed:

in the case of royalties referred to in sub-paragraph (a) of paragraph 3, 10% of the gross amount of the royalties; and

in the case of royalties referred to in sub-paragraph (b) of paragraph 3, 10% of the adjusted amount of the royalties. For the purpose of this sub-paragraph "the adjusted amount" means 60% of the gross amount of the royalties.

The competent authorities of the Contracting States shall by mutual agreement settle the mode of application of these limitations.

The term "royalties" as used in this Article means:

payments of any kind received as a consideration for the use of, or the right to use, any copyright of literary, artistic or scientific work including cinematograph films, or films or tapes for radio or television broadcasting, any patent, trade mark, design or model, plan, secret formula or process, or for information (know-how) concerning industrial, commercial or scientific experience; and

payments of any kind received as a consideration for the use of, or the right to use, industrial, commercial, or scientific equipment.

The provisions of paragraphs 1 and 2 shall not apply if the beneficial owner of the royalties, being a resident of a Contracting State, carries on business in the other Contracting State in which the royalties arise, through a permanent establishment situated therein, or performs in that other State independent personal services from a fixed base situated therein, and the right or property in respect of which the royalties are paid is effectively connected with such permanent establishment or fixed base. In such case the provisions of Article 7 or Article 14, as the case may be, shall apply.

Royalties shall be deemed to arise in a Contracting State when the payer is a resident of that Contracting State. Where, however, the person paying the royalties, whether he is a resident of a Contracting State or not, has in a Contracting State a permanent establishment or a fixed base in connection with which the liability to pay the royalties was incurred, and such royalties are borne by such permanent establishment or fixed base, then such royalties shall be deemed to arise in the State in which the permanent establishment or fixed base is situated.

Where, by reason of a special relationship between the payer and the beneficial owner or between both of them and some other person, the amount of the royalties, having regard to the use, right or information for which they are paid, exceeds the amount which would have been agreed upon by the payer and the beneficial owner in the absence of such relationship, the provisions of this Article shall apply only to the last-mentioned amount. In such case, the excess part of the payments shall remain taxable according to the laws of each Contracting State, due regard being had to the other provisions of this Agreement.

The provisions of this Article shall not apply if it was the main purpose or one of the main purposes of any person concerned with the creation or assignment of the rights in respect of which the royalties are paid to take advantage of this Article by means of that creation or assignment.

Article 13 Capital Gains

Gains derived by a resident of a Contracting State from the alienation of immovable property referred to in Article 6 and situated in the other Contracting State may be taxed in that other State.

Gains from the alienation of movable property forming part of the business property of a permanent establishment which an enterprise of a Contracting State has in the other Contracting State or of movable property pertaining to a fixed base available to a resident of a Contracting State in the other Contracting State for the purpose of performing independent personal services, including such gains from the alienation of such a permanent establishment (alone or with the whole enterprise) or of such a fixed base, may be taxed in that other State.

Gains from the alienation of ships or aircraft operated in international traffic, or movable property pertaining to the operation of such ships or aircraft, shall be taxable only in the Contracting State in which the place of effective management of the enterprise is situated.

Gains derived by a resident of a Contracting State from the alienation of shares deriving more than 50% of their value directly or indirectly from immovable property situated in the other Contracting State may be taxed in that other State.

Gains derived by a resident of a Contracting State from the alienation of shares of a company which is a resident of the other Contracting State may be taxed in that other Contracting State if the recipient of the gain, at any time during the twelve month period preceding such alienation, had a participation, directly or indirectly, of at least 25% in the capital of that company.

However, the provisions of paragraphs 4 and 5 shall not apply to gains derived from the alienation of shares: quoted on a recognised stock exchange, provided that the total of the shares alienated by the resident during the fiscal year in which the alienation takes place does not exceed 3% of the quoted shares; or

held by the Government of a Contracting State, any of its institutions or any other entity the capital of which is wholly owned by that Contracting State, provided that such institution or entity is a resident of that Contracting State.

Gains from the alienation of any property, other than that referred to in paragraphs 1–5, shall be taxable only in the Contracting State of which the alienator is a resident.

Article 14 Independent Personal Services

Income derived by a resident of a Contracting State in respect of professional services or other activities of an independent character shall be taxable only in that State except in the following circumstances, when such income may also be taxed in the other Contracting State:

if he has a fixed base regularly available to him in the other Contracting State for the purpose of performing his activities; in that case, only so much of the income as is attributable to that fixed base may be taxed in that other Contracting State; or

if his stay in the other Contracting State is for a period or periods amounting to or exceeding in the aggregate 183 days in any twelve month period commencing or ending in the fiscal year concerned; in that case, only so much of the income as is derived from his activities performed in that other State may be taxed in that other State.

The term "professional services" includes especially independent scientific, literary, artistic, educational or teaching activities as well as the independent activities of physicians, lawyers, engineers, architects, dentists and accountants.

Article 15 Income from Employment

Subject to the provisions of Articles 16, 18 and 19, salaries, wages and other similar remuneration derived by a resident of a Contracting State in respect of an employment shall be taxable only in that State unless the employment is exercised in the other Contracting State. If the employment is so exercised, such remuneration as is derived therefrom may be taxed in that other State.

Notwithstanding the provisions of paragraph 1, remuneration derived by a resident of a Contracting State in respect of an employment exercised in the other Contracting State shall be taxable only in the first-mentioned State if:

the recipient is present in the other State for a period or periods not exceeding in the aggregate 183 days in any twelve month period commencing or ending in the fiscal year concerned, and

the remuneration is paid by, or on behalf of, an employer who is not a resident of the other State, and

the remuneration is not borne by a permanent establishment or a fixed base which the employer has in the other State.

Notwithstanding the preceding provisions of this Article, remuneration derived by a resident of a Contracting State in respect of an employment exercised aboard a ship or aircraft operated in international traffic may be taxed in the Contracting State in which the place of effective management of the enterprise is situated.

Article 16 Directors' Fees

Directors' fees and other remuneration derived by a resident of a Contracting State in his capacity as a member of the board of directors of a company which is a resident of the other Contracting State may be taxed in that other State.

For the purpose of the provisions of paragraph 1, the term "member of the board of directors" includes any person who is charged with the general management of the company and any person who is charged with the supervision thereof.

Article 17 Artistes and Sportsmen

Notwithstanding the provisions of Articles 14 and 15, income derived by a resident of a Contracting State as an entertainer, such as a theatre, motion picture, radio or television artiste, or a musician, or as a sportsman, from his personal activities as such exercised in the other Contracting State, may be taxed in that other State.

Where income in respect of personal activities exercised by an entertainer or a sportsman in his capacity as such accrues not to the entertainer or sportsman himself but to another person, that income may, notwithstanding the provisions of Articles 7, 14 and 15, be taxed in the Contracting State in which the activities of the entertainer or sportsman are exercised.

The provisions of paragraphs 1 and 2 shall not apply to income derived by a resident of a Contracting State from activities exercised in the other Contracting State, if the visit to that other State is wholly or mainly supported by public funds of the first-mentioned State or local authorities thereof, or takes place under a cultural agreement between the Governments of the Contracting States. In such a case, the income shall be taxable only in the Contracting State of which the entertainer or sportsman is a resident.

Article 18 Pensions and Social Security Payments

Subject to the provisions of paragraph 2 of Article 19, pensions and other similar remuneration paid to a resident of a Contracting State shall be taxable only in that State.

However, pensions and other similar remuneration, whether or not periodic in nature, insofar as the contributions or payments associated with the pension or other similar remuneration, or the entitlements received from them, have qualified for tax relief in the other Contracting State, may also be taxed in that State.

Notwithstanding the provisions of paragraph 1, pensions paid and other similar payments made by the Government of a Contracting State or local authority thereof under the social security system of that State, whether or not periodic in nature, shall be taxable only in that State.

Article 19 Government Service

(a) Salaries, wages and other similar remuneration paid by the Government of a Contracting State or a local authority thereof to an individual in respect of services rendered to the Government of that State or authority, shall be taxable only in that State.

However, such salaries, wages and other similar remuneration shall be taxable only in the other Contracting State if the services are rendered in that State and the individual is a resident of that State who:

is a national of that State; or

did not become a resident of that State solely for the purpose of rendering the services.

(a) Notwithstanding the provisions of paragraph 1, pensions and other similar remuneration paid by, or out of funds created by, a Contracting State or a local authority thereof to an individual in respect of services rendered to the Government of that State or authority shall be taxable only in that State.

(b) However, such pensions and other similar remuneration shall be taxable only in the other Contracting State if the individual is a resident of, and a national of, that State.

The provisions of Articles 15, 16, 17 and 18 shall apply to salaries, wages, pensions and other similar remuneration in respect of services rendered in connection with a business carried on by the Government of a Contracting State or a local authority thereof.

Article 20 Students

Payments which a student who is or was immediately before visiting a Contracting State a resident of the other Contracting State and who is present in the first-mentioned State solely for the purpose of his education receives for the purpose of his maintenance or education shall not be taxed in that State, provided that such payments arise from sources outside that State.

Article 21 Other Income

Items of income of a resident of a Contracting State, wherever arising, not dealt with in the foregoing Articles of this Agreement shall be taxable only in that State.

The provisions of paragraph 1 shall not apply to income, other than income from immovable property as defined in paragraph 2 of Article 6, if the recipient of such income, being a resident of a Contracting State, carries on business in the other Contracting State through a permanent establishment situated therein, or performs in that other State independent personal services from a fixed base situated therein, and the right or property in respect of which the income is paid is effectively connected with such permanent establishment or fixed base. In such case the provisions of Article 7 or Article 14, as the case may be, shall apply.

Notwithstanding the provisions of paragraphs 1 and 2, items of income of a resident of a Contracting State not dealt with in the foregoing Articles of this Agreement and arising in the other Contracting State may also be taxed in that other State.

Article 22 Elimination of Double Taxation

In China, in accordance with the provisions of the law of China, double taxation shall be eliminated as follows:

Where a resident of China derives income from the Netherlands, the amount of tax on that income payable in the Netherlands in accordance with the provisions of this Agreement may be credited against the Chinese tax imposed on that resident. The amount of the credit, however, shall not exceed the amount of the Chinese tax on that income computed in accordance with the taxation laws and regulations of China.

Where the income derived from the Netherlands is dividend paid by a company which is a resident of the Netherlands to a company which is a resident of China and which owns not less than 20% of the shares of the company paying the dividend, the credit shall take into account the tax paid in the Netherlands by the company paying the dividend in respect of its income.

In the Netherlands, double taxation shall be eliminated as follows:

The Netherlands, when imposing tax on its residents, may include in the basis upon which such taxes are imposed the items of income which, according to the provisions of this Agreement, may be taxed or shall be taxable only in China.

However, where a resident of the Netherlands derives items of income which according to paragraphs 1, 3 and 4 of Article 6, paragraph 1 of Article 7, paragraphs 1 and 3 of Article 8, paragraph 5 of Article 10, paragraph 6 of Article 11, paragraph 4 of Article 12, paragraphs 1, 2, 3, 4 and 5 of Article 13, paragraph 1 of Article 14, paragraphs 1 and 3 of Article 15, paragraphs 2 and 3 of Article 18, sub-paragraph (a) of paragraph 1 and sub-paragraph (a) of paragraph 2 of Article 19 and paragraph 2 of Article 21 of this Agreement may be taxed or shall be taxable only in China and are included in the basis referred to in sub-paragraph (a) of paragraph 2 of this Article, the Netherlands shall exempt such items of income by allowing a reduction of its tax. This reduction shallbe computed in conformity with the provisions of the Netherlands law for the avoidance of double taxation. For that purpose the said items of income shall be deemed to be included in the amount of the items of income which are exempt from Netherlands tax under those provisions.

Further, the Netherlands shall allow a reduction from the Netherlands tax so computed for the items of income which according to paragraph 2 of Article 10, paragraph 2 of Article 11, paragraph 2 of Article 12, paragraph 1 of Article 16, paragraphs 1 and 2 of Article 17 and paragraph 3 of Article 21 of this Agreement may be taxed or shall be taxable only in China to the extent that these items are included in the basis referred to in sub-paragraph (a) of paragraph 2 of this Article. The amount of this reduction shall be equal to the tax paid in China on these items of income, but shall, in case the provisions of the Netherlands law for the avoidance of double taxation provide so, not exceed the amount of the reduction which would be allowed if the items of income so included were the sole items of income which are exempt from the Netherlands tax under the provisions of the Netherlands law for the avoidance of double taxation.

This paragraph shall not restrict allowance now or hereafter accorded by the provisions of the Netherlands law for the avoidance of double taxation, but only as far as the calculation of the amount of the reduction of the Netherlands tax is concerned with respect to the aggregation of income from more than one country and the carry-forward of the tax paid in China on the said items of income to subsequent years.

Notwithstanding the provisions of sub-paragraph (b) of paragraph 2 of this Article, the Netherlands shall allow a reduction from the Netherlands tax for the tax paid in China on items of income which according to paragraph 1 of Article 7, paragraph 5 of Article 10, paragraph 6 of Article 11, paragraph 4 of Article 12, paragraph 4 of Article 13 and paragraph 2 of Article 21 of this Agreement may be taxed or shall be taxable only in China to the extent that these items are included in the basis referred to in sub-paragraph

(a) of paragraph 2 of this Article, insofar as the Netherlands under the provisions of the Netherlands law for the avoidance of double taxation allows a reduction from the Netherlands tax of the tax levied in another country on such items of income. For the computation of this reduction the provisions of sub-paragraph (c) of paragraph 2 of this Article shall apply accordingly.

Article 23 Miscellaneous Rule

Nothing in this Agreement shall prejudice the right of each Contracting State to apply its domestic laws and measures concerning the prevention of tax evasion and avoidance, whether or not described as such, insofar as they do not give rise to taxation contrary to this Agreement.

Article 24 Non-Discrimination

Nationals of a Contracting State shall not be subjected in the other Contracting State to any taxation or any requirement connected therewith, which is other or more burdensome than the taxation and connected requirements to which nationals of that other State in the same circumstances, in particular with respect to residence, are or may be subjected. This provision shall, notwithstanding the provisions of Article 1, also apply to persons who are not residents of one or both of the Contracting States.

The taxation on a permanent establishment which an enterprise of a Contracting State has in the other Contracting State shall not be less favourably levied in that other State than the taxation levied on enterprises of that other State carrying on the same activities. This provision shall not be construed as obliging a Contracting State to grant to residents of the other Contracting State any personal allowances, reliefs and reductions for taxation purposes on account of civil status or family responsibilities which it grants to its own residents.

Except where the provisions of paragraph 1 of Article 9, paragraph 8 of Article 11, or paragraph 6 of Article 12 apply, interest, royalties and other disbursements paid by an enterprise of a Contracting State to a resident of the other Contracting State shall, for the purpose of determining the taxable profits of such enterprise, be deductible under the same conditions as if they had been paid to a resident of the first-mentioned State.

Enterprises of a Contracting State, the capital of which is wholly or partly owned or controlled, directly or indirectly, by one or more residents of the other Contracting State, shall not be subjected in the first-mentioned State to any taxation or any requirement connected therewith which is other or more burdensome than the taxation and connected requirements to which other similar enterprises of the first-mentioned State are or may be subjected.

The provisions of this Article shall, notwithstanding the provisions of Article 2, apply to taxes of every kind and description.

Article 25 Mutual Agreement Procedure

Where a person considers that the actions of one or both of the Contracting States result or will result for him in taxation not in accordance with the provisions of this Agreement, he may, irrespective of the remedies provided by the domestic law of those States, present his case to the competent authority of the Contracting State of which he is a resident or, if his case comes under paragraph 1 of Article 24, to that of the Contracting State of which he is a national. The case must be presented within three years from the first notification of the action resulting in taxation not in accordance with the provisions of the Agreement.

The competent authority shall endeavour, if the objection appears to it to be justified and if it is not itself able to arrive at a satisfactory solution, to resolve the case by mutual agreement with the competent authority of the other Contracting State, with a view to the avoidance of taxation which is not in accordance with the Agreement. Any agreement reached shall be implemented notwithstanding any time limits in the domestic law of the Contracting States.

The competent authorities of the Contracting States shall endeavor to resolve by mutual agreement any difficulties or doubts arising as to the interpretation or application of the Agreement. They may also consult together for the elimination of double taxation in cases not provided for in the Agreement.

The competent authorities of the Contracting States may communicate with each other directly for the purpose of reaching an agreement in the sense of paragraphs 2 and 3. When it seems advisable for reaching an agreement, representatives of the competent authorities of the Contracting States may meet together for an oral exchange of opinions.

Article 26 Exchange of Information

The competent authorities of the Contracting States shall exchange such information as is foreseeably relevant for carrying out the provisions of this Agreement or to the administration or enforcement of the domestic laws concerning taxes of every kind and description imposed on behalf of the Contracting States or local authorities, insofar as the taxation thereunder is not contrary to the Agreement. The exchange of information is not restricted by Articles 1 and 2.

Any information received under paragraph 1 by a Contracting State shall be treated as secret in the same manner as information obtained under the domestic laws of that State and shall be disclosed only to persons or authorities (including courts and administrative bodies) concerned with the assessment or collection of, the enforcement or prosecution in respect of, the determination of appeals in relation to the taxes referred to in paragraph 1, or the oversight of the above. Such persons or authorities shall use the information only for such purposes. They may disclose the information in public court proceedings or in judicial decisions.

In no case shall the provisions of paragraphs 1 and 2 be construed so as to impose on a Contracting State the obligation:

to carry out administrative measures at variance with the laws and administrative practice of that or of the other Contracting State;

to supply information which is not obtainable under the laws or in the normal course of the administration of that or of the other Contracting State;

to supply information which would disclose any trade, business, industrial, commercial or professional secret or trade process, or information the disclosure of which would be contrary to public policy (*ordre public*).

If information is requested by a Contracting State in accordance with this Article, the other Contracting State shall use its information gathering measures to obtain the requested information, even though that other State may not need such information for its own tax purposes. The obligation contained in the preceding sentence is subject to the limitations of paragraph 3 but in no case shall such limitations be construed to permit a Contracting State to decline to supply information solely because it has no domestic interest in such information.

In no case shall the provisions of paragraph 3 be construed to permit a Contracting State to decline to supply information solely because the information is held by a bank, other financial institution, nominee or person acting in an agency or a fiduciary capacity or because it relates to ownership interests in a person.

Article 27 Assistance in the Collection of Taxes

The Contracting States shall endeavour to lend assistance to each other in the collection of the taxes covered by Article 2. The competent authorities of the Contracting States shall by mutual agreement settle the mode of application of this Article.

In no case shall the provisions of this Article be construed so as to impose on a Contracting State the obligation:

to carry out administrative measures at variance with the laws and administrative practice of that or of the other Contracting State;
to carry out measures which would be contrary to public policy (*ordre public*);
to provide assistance if the other Contracting State has not pursued all reasonable measures of collection or conservancy, as the case may be, available under its laws or administrative practice;
to provide assistance in those cases where the administrative burden for that State is clearly disproportionate to the benefit to be derived by the other Contracting State.

Article 28 Members of Diplomatic Missions and Consular Posts

Nothing in this Agreement shall affect the fiscal privileges of members of diplomatic missions or consular posts under the general rules of international law or under the provisions of special agreements.

Article 29 Entry into Force

Both Contracting States shall notify each other through diplomatic channels that they have completed the internal legal procedures necessary for the entry into force of this Agreement. This Agreement shall enter into force on the last day of the month following the date of the last notification. This Agreement shall have effect as regards income derived during the taxable years and periods beginning on or after the first day of January next following the calendar year in which this Agreement enters into force.

The Agreement between the People's Republic of China and the Kingdom of the Netherlands for the Avoidance of Double Taxation and the Prevention of Fiscal Evasion with Respect to Taxes on Income, with Protocol, signed at Beijing on May 13th, 1987 (the prior Agreement), shall cease to have effect in relation to any tax with effect from the date on which this Agreement has effect in relation to that tax in accordance with paragraph 1 of this Article.

Article 30 Termination

This Agreement shall continue in effect indefinitely but either of the Contracting States may, on or before the thirtieth day of June in any calendar year beginning after the expiration of a period of five years from the date of its entry into force, give written notice of termination to the other Contracting State through diplomatic channels. In such event this Agreement shall cease to have effect as respects income derived during the taxable years and periods beginning on or after the first day of January in the calendar year next following that in which the notice of termination is given.

IN WITNESS whereof the undersigned, duly authorized thereto, have signed this Agreement.

Done at____on the____day of____,____, in duplicate in the Chinese, Netherlands and English languages, all texts being equally authentic. In case of divergence in interpretation, the English text shall prevail.

For the Government of the Kingdom of the Netherlands

For the Government of the People's Republic of China

Protocol

At the moment of signing the Agreement for the avoidance of double taxation and the prevention of fiscal evasion with respect to taxes on income, this day concluded between the Government of the People's Republic of China and the Government of the Kingdom of the Netherlands, the undersigned have agreed that the following provisions shall form an integral part of the Agreement.

Ad Article 1

It is understood that a person who is established in the Netherlands and treated as a tax exempt investment institution under the Netherlands company tax law shall not be entitled to the benefits of this Agreement.

Ad paragraph 2 of Article 3 and Article 25

It is understood that, if the competent authorities of the Contracting States have, by mutual agreement, reached a solution within the context of the Agreement for cases in which

application of paragraph 2 of Article 3 with respect to the interpretation of a term not defined in the Agreement, or

differences in qualification (for example of an element of income or of a person) would result in double taxation or double exemption, this solution, after publication thereof by both competent authorities, shall also be binding for the application of the provisions of the Agreement in other similar cases in the future.

Ad Articles 6, 13 and 22

It is understood that rights to the exploration and exploitation of natural resources shall be regarded as immovable property located in the Contracting State to whose territorial sea, and any area beyond the territorial sea, including the seabed and subsoil thereof—within which that State, in accordance with international law and its internal law, exercises jurisdiction or sovereign rights—these rights apply.

Ad Article 7

It is understood that in the case of profits from survey, supply, installation or construction activities, only so much of these profits shall be attributable to a permanent establishment as results from the functions performed, assets used and risks assumed at or through the permanent establishment.

Ad Article 8

The provisions of Article 8 of this Agreement shall not affect the provisions of Article 8 of the Agreement between the Government of the People's Republic of China and the Government of the Kingdom of the Netherlands relating to maritime shipping, signed at Beijing on 14 August 1975, nor the provisions of paragraph 2 of Article 10 of the Agreement between the Government of the People's Republic of China and the Government of the Kingdom of the Netherlands relating to civil air transport, signed at Beijing on 20 January 1979, nor the provisions of the letters exchanged on 14 December 2004 and 21 December 2004 between the State Administration of Taxation of the People's Republic of China and the Embassy of the Kingdom of the Netherlands relating to the reciprocal exemption from taxation on revenue arising from international transportation by air transport enterprises.

IN WITNESS whereof the undersigned, duly authorized thereto, have signed this Protocol.

Done at Beijing on the 31st day of May, 2013, in duplicate in the Chinese, Netherlands and English languages, all texts being equally authentic. In case of divergence in interpretation, the English text shall prevail.

For the Government of the Kingdom of the Netherlands

For the Government of the People's Republic of China

Norway

Norway, officially the Kingdom of Norway, is a state in Northern Europe. Norway borders Finland and Russia to the north-east and the Skagerrak strait to the south, on the other side of which are Denmark and the United Kingdom. Norway's capital and largest city is Oslo.

In Norway, Norwegians are the majority ethnic group, while important minorities are Pakistani, Somali and Vietnamese.

The official and predominant spoken languages are Norwegian and Sámi. Recognised minority languages are Kven, Romani, Scandoromani, and Norwegian Sign Language.

Norway is a unitary parliamentary constitutional monarchy. The Kongeriget Norges Grundlov is the constitution regulating the political system, in force since 1814. The Stortinget exerts the legislative power forming the parliament. The Stortinget is elected through direct elections using the open list proportional representation system.

Executive power is vested in the Prime Minister and his or her cabinet. The Prime Minister is appointed by the Monarch after being elected by the party or coalition with the parliamentary majority in the Stortinget.

Norway has a civil law system based on Roman law. The Høyesterett acts as Supreme Court, managing constitutional matters, with judicial review powers.

Norway is a unitary state, divided into eleven fylke (first-level administrative counties), whereas the counties are then sub-divided into 356 s-level municipalities (kommuner).

Norway is part of the European Union since 1994.

Category	Value
Population (mln persons)	5.356
Currency	Norwegian krone

Source International Monetary Fund, year 2019

© The Author(s), under exclusive license to Springer Nature Singapore Pte Ltd. 2022

L. Riccardi and G. Riccardi, *China–Europe Tax Treaties*,
https://doi.org/10.1007/978-981-19-3563-3_20

Norway is the 13th largest economy of Europe, with a GDP valued 417.6 billion USD in 2019, and the European economy with the third highest GDP per capita (77,975 USD). It has a population of about 5.4 million people. Norway's inflation is at 2.2%, while unemployment is 3.7%. Norway ranked 3 out of 43 in Europe in the 2020 Doing Business ranking, scoring 82.6, and imposes a CIT of 22%. Norway records a trade surplus of 17.6 billion USD.

GDP and local economy	
GDP current prices (billion USD)	417.6
GDP per capita (USD)	77,975
GDP growth (%)	1.2
Inflation (%)	2.2
Unemployment (%)	3.7
General government total expenditure (% of GDP)	51.5
General government gross debt (% of GDP)	40.8
Doing Business Score 2020	82.6

Source International Monetary Fund and UNCTAD, year 2019

Foreign direct investment	
FDI outstock (million USD)	218,513
FDI instock (million USD)	167,475

Source UNCTAD, year 2019

Trade	
Imports (million USD)	85,013
Exports (million USD)	102,685
Trade balance (million USD)	17,672

Source International Monetary Fund and UNCTAD, year 2019

Main import–export	
First import by category	Machinery, nuclear reactors, boilers
Second import by category	Vehicles other than railway, tramway
First export by category	Mineral fuels, oils, distillation products
Second export by category	Fish, crustaceans, molluscs, aquatics invertebrates

Source United Nations COMTRADE, year 2020

The legal bases for taxation are established in the constitution. Norway imposes individual income tax, property sales taxes, capital gains, corporate income tax, and value added tax. Progressivity is guaranteed by a system with different bands and various deductions.

Taxes	
Company income tax (%)	22
Top individual income tax (%)	22[1]
Value added tax or sales tax (%)	25
Reduced value added tax or sales tax (%)	6/12

Source RsA Asia report, year 2021
Note Individual income is subject to an additional bracket tax which varies from 1.7% to 16.2%

- Economic Relation with China

Norway records a trade surplus of 3.74 billion USD in 2020. "Mineral fuels, oils, distillation products" is the first export category, worth 4.27 billion USD, followed by "Organic chemicals". "Electrical, electronic equipment" is the first import category, valued 0.46 billion USD. Norway is not part of the Belt and Road Initiative. The Norway-China DTA has been signed in February 1986 and has come into force in December of the same year.

Category	Value
Belt road	No

Source UNCTAD, year 2021

Import from China	
Import from China (billion USD)	3.53
First import category from China	Electrical, electronic equipment
First import value (billion USD)	0.461
Second import category from China	Vehicles other than railway, tramway
Second import value (billion USD)	0.455

Source United Nations COMTRADE, year 2020

Export to China	
Export to China (billion USD)	7.27
First export category towards China	Mineral fuels, oils, distillation products
First export value (billion USD)	4.27
Second export category towards China	Organic chemicals
Second export value (billion USD)	0.713

Source United Nations COMTRADE, year 2020

Trade balance	
Trade balance (billion USD)	3.74

Source United Nations COMTRADE, year 2020

Double tax agreement	
DTA effective date	1986.12.21
Dividends (%)	10
Interest (%)	0–10
Royalties (%)	10

Source State Administration of Taxation of China, year 2021

Title AGREEMENT BETWEEN THE GOVERNMENT OF THE PEOPLE'S REPUBLIC OF CHINA AND THE GOVERNMENT OF THE KINGDOM OF NORWAY FOR THE AVOIDANCE OF DOUBLE TAXATION AND THE PREVENTION OF FISCAL EVASION WITH RESPECT TO TAXES ON INCOME AND CAPITAL

Treaty Text

The Government of the People's Republic of China, and the Government of the Kingdom of Norway,

Desiring to conclude an Agreement for the avoidance of double taxation and the prevention of fiscal evasion with respect to taxes on income and on capital,

Have agreed as follows:

Article 1 Personal Scope

This Agreement shall apply to persons who are residents of one or both of the Contracting States.

Article 2 Taxes Covered

This Agreement shall apply to taxes on income and on capital imposed on behalf of a Contracting State or of its political subdivisions or local authorities, irrespective of the manner in which they are levied.

There shall be regarded as taxes on income and on capital all taxes imposed on total income, on total capital, or on elements of income or of capital, including taxes on gains from the alienation of movable or immovable property, as well as taxes on capital appreciation.

The existing taxes to which the Agreement shall apply are:

in China:
the individual income tax;
the income tax concerning joint ventures with Chinese and foreign investment;

the income tax concerning foreign enterprises; and
the local income tax; (hereinafter referred to as "Chinese tax").

in Norway:

the national tax on income (inntektsskatt til staten);
the county municipal tax on income (inntektsskatt til fylkeskommunen);
the municipal tax on income (inntektsskatt til kommunen);
the national contributions to the Tax Equalisation Fund (fellesskatt til Skattefordelingsfondet);
the national tax on capital (formuesskatt til staten);
the municipal tax on capital (formuesskatt til kommunen);
the national tax on income and on capital under the Petroleum Tax Act (skatt til staten vedrΦrende inntekt og formue i henhlΦd til petroleumsskatteloven);
the national dues on remuneration to nonresident artistes (avgift til staten) av honorarer som tilfaller kunstnere bosatt i utlandet);
the seamen's tax (sjΦmannsskatt); (hereinafter referred to as "Norwegian tax").

This Agreement shall also apply to any identical or substantially similar taxes which are imposed after the date of signature of this Agreement in addition to, or in place of, the existing taxes referred to in paragraph 3. The competent authorities of the Contracting States shall notify each other of any substantial changes which have been made in their respective taxation laws within a reasonable period of time after such changes.i

Article 3 General Definitions

For the purposes of this Agreement, unless the context otherwise requires:

the term "China", means the People's Republic of China; when used in a geographical sense, means all the territory of the People's Republic of China, including its territorial sea, in which the Chinese laws relating to Chinese tax apply, and all area beyond its territorial sea, including the seabed and subsoil thereof, over which China has jurisdiction in accordance with international law and in which the laws relating to Chinese tax apply;
the term "Norway" means the Kingdom of Norway, including any area outside the territorial waters of the Kingdom of Norway where the Kingdom of Norway, according to Norwegian legislation and in accordance with international law, may exercise her rights with respect on the seabed and subsoil and their natural resources; the term does not comprise Svalbard, Jan Mayen and the Norwegian dependencies ("bliand");
the terms "a Contracting State" and "the other Contracting State" mean China or Norway as the context requires;
the term "tax" means Chinese tax or Norwegian tax, as the context requires;
the term "person" includes an individual, a company and any other body of persons;

the term “company” means anybody corporate or any entity which is treated as a body corporate for tax purposes;
the terms “enterprise of a Contracting State” and “enterprise of the other Contracting State” mean respectively an enterprise carried on by a resident of a Contracting State and an enterprise carried on by a resident of the other Contracting State;
the term “nationals” means all individuals possessing the nationality of a Contracting State and all legal persons created or organized under the laws of that Contracting State, as well as any organization without legal personality treated for tax purposes as legal persons created and organized under the laws of that Contracting State;
the term “international traffic” means any transport by a ship or aircraft operated by an enterprise which has its place of head office (i.e. effective management) in a Contracting State, except when the ship or aircraft is operated solely between places in the other Contracting State;
the term “competent authority” means in the case of China, the Ministry of Finance or its authorized representative and; in the case of Norway, the Minister of Finance and Customs or his authorized representative.

As regards the application of this Agreement by a Contracting State, any term not defined in this Agreement shall, unless the context otherwise requires, have the meaning which it has under the law of that Contracting State concerning the taxes to which this Agreement applies.

Article 4 Resident

For the purposes of this Agreement, the term “resident of a Contracting State” means any person who, under the laws of that Contracting State, is liable to tax therein by reason of his domicile, residence, place of management or head office or any other criterion of a similar nature.

Where by reason of the provisions of paragraph 1 an individual is a resident of both Contracting States, then his status shall be determined as follows:

He shall be deemed to be a resident of the State in which he has a permanent home available to him; if he has a permanent home available to him in both States, he shall be deemed to be a resident of the State with which his personal and economic relations are closer (center of vital interests);
If the State in which he has his centre of vital interests cannot be determined, or if he has not a permanent home available to him in either State, he shall be deemed to be a resident of the State in which he has an habitual abode;
If he has an habitual abode in both States or in neither of them, he shall be deemed to be a resident of the State of which he is a national;
If he is a national of both States or of neither of them, the competent authorities of the Contracting States shall settle the question by mutual agreement.

Where by reason of the provisions of paragraph 1, a person other than an individual is a resident of both Contracting States, then it shall be deemed to be a resident of the Contracting State in which its place of head office (i.e. effective management) of its business is situated.

Article 5 Permanent Establishment

For the purposes of this Agreement, the term "permanent establishment" means a fixed place of business through which the business of an enterprise is wholly or partly carried on.

The term "permanent establishment" includes especially:

a place of management;
a branch;
an office;
a factory;
a workshop; and
a mine, an oil or gas well, a quarry or any other place of extraction of natural resources.

The term "permanent establishment" likewise encompasses:

a building site, a construction, assembly or installation project or supervisory activities in connection therewith but only where such site, project or activities continue for a period of more than six months;
the furnishing of services, including consultancy services, by an enterprise of a Contracting State through employees or other personnel in the other Contracting State, provided that such activities continue for the same project or a connected project for a period or periods aggregating more than six months within any twelve month period.

Notwithstanding the provisions of paragraphs 1 to 3, the term "permanent establishment" shall be deemed not to include:

the use of facilities solely for the purpose of storage, display or delivery of goods or merchandise belonging to the enterprise;
the maintenance of a stock of goods or merchandise belonging to the enterprise solely for the purpose of storage, display or delivery;
the maintenance of a stock of goods or merchandise belonging to the enterprise solely for the purpose of processing by another enterprise;
the maintenance of a fixed place of business solely for the purpose of purchasing goods or merchandise or of collecting information, for the enterprise;
the maintenance of a fixed place of business solely for the purpose of carrying on, for the enterprise, any other activity of a preparatory or auxiliary character;
the maintenance of a fixed place of business solely for any combination of activities mentioned in sub-paragraphs (a) to (e), provided that the overall activity of the fixed place of business resulting from this combination is of a preparatory or auxiliary character.

Notwithstanding the provisions of paragraphs 1 and 2, where a person—other than an agent of an independent status to whom the provisions of paragraph 6 apply—is acting in a Contracting State on behalf of an enterprise of the other Contracting State and has, and habitually exercises an authority to conclude contracts in the name of the enterprise, that enterprise shall be deemed to have a permanent establishment in the first-mentioned Contracting State in respect of any activities which that person undertakes for the enterprise, unless his activities are limited to those mentioned in paragraph 4 which, if exercised through a fixed place of business, would not make this fixed place of business a permanent establishment under the provisions of that paragraph.

An enterprise of a Contracting State shall not be deemed to have a permanent establishment in the other Contracting State merely because it carries on business in that other Contracting State through a broker, general commission agent or any other agent of an independent status, provided that such persons are acting in the ordinary course of their business.

The fact that a company which is a resident of a Contracting State controls or is controlled by a company which is a resident of the other Contracting State, or which carries on business in that other Contracting State (whether through a permanent establishment or otherwise), shall not of itself constitute either company a permanent establishment of the other.

Article 6 Income from Immovable Property

Income derived by a resident of a Contracting State from immovable property (including income from agriculture or forestry) situated in the other Contracting State may be taxed in that other Contracting State.

The term "immovable property" shall have the meaning which it has under the law of the Contracting State in which the property in question is situated. The term shall in any case include property accessory to immovable property, livestock and equipment used in agriculture and forestry, rights to which the provisions of general law respecting landed property apply, usufruct of immovable property and rights to variable or fixed payments as consideration for the working of, or the right to work, mineral deposits, sources and other natural resources. Ships and aircraft shall not be regarded as immovable property.

The provisions of paragraph 1 shall apply to income derived from the direct use, letting, or use in any other form of immovable property.

The provisions of paragraphs 1 and 3 shall also apply to the income from immovable property of an enterprise and to income from immovable property used for the performance of independent personal services.

Article 7 Business Profits

The profits of an enterprise of a Contracting State shall be taxable only in that Contracting State unless the enterprise carries on business in the other Contracting State through a permanent establishment situated therein. If the enterprise carries on business as aforesaid, the profits of the enterprise may be taxed in the other Contracting State but only so much of them as is attributable to that permanent establishment.

Subject to the provisions of paragraph 3, where an enterprise of a Contracting State carries on business in the other Contracting State through a permanent establishment situated therein, there shall in each Contracting State be attributed to that permanent establishment the profits which it might be expected to make if it were a distinct and separate enterprise engaged in the same or similar activities under the same or similar conditions and dealing wholly independently with the enterprise of which it is a permanent establishment.

In determining the profits of a permanent establishment, there shall be allowed as deductions expenses which are incurred for the purposes of the permanent establishment, including executive and general administrative expenses so incurred, whether in the State in which the permanent establishment is situated or elsewhere. However, no such deduction shall be allowed in respect of amounts, if any, paid (otherwise than towards reimbursement of actual expenses) by the permanent establishment to the head office of the enterprise or any of its other offices, by way of royalities, fees, or other similar payments in return for the use of patents or other rights, or by way of commission, for specific services performed or for management, or, except in the case of a banking enterprise, by way of interest on moneys lent to the permanent establishment. Likewise, no account shall be taken, in the determination of the profits of a permanent establishment, for amounts charged (otherwise than towards reimbursement of actual expenses), by the permanent establishment to the head office of the enterprise or any of its other offices, by way of royalties, fees of other similar payments in return for the use of patents or other rights, or by way of commission for specific services performed or for management, or, except in the case of a banking enterprise by way of interest on moneys lent to the head office of the enterprise or any of its other offices.

Insofar as it has been customary in a Contracting State to determine the profits to be attributed to a permanent establishment on the basis of an apportionment of the total profits of the enterprise to its various parts, nothing in paragraph 2 shall preclude that Contracting State from determining the profits to be taxed by such an apportionment as may be customary. The method of apportionment adopted shall, however, be such that the result shall be in accordance with the principles contained in this Article.

No profits shall be attributed to a permanent establishment by reason of the mere purchase by that permanent establishment of goods or merchandise for the enterprise.

For the purposes of paragraphs 1 to 5, the profits to be attributed to the permanent establishment shall be determined by the same method year by year unless there is good and sufficient reason to the contrary.

Where profits include items of income which are dealt with separately in other Articles of this Agreement, then the provisions of those Articles shall not be affected by the provisions of this Article.

Article 8 Shipping and Air Transport

Profits from the operation of ships or aircraft in international traffic shall be taxable only in the Contracting State in which the place of head office (i.e. effective management) of the enterprise is situated.

If the place of head office of a shipping enterprise is aboard a ship, then it shall be deemed to be situated in the Contracting State in which the home harbour of the ship is situated, or if there is no such home harbour, in the Contracting State of which the operator of the ship is a resident.

The provisions of paragraph 1 shall also apply to profits from the participation in a pool, a joint business or an international operating agency.

Article 9 Associated Enterprises

Where

an enterprise of a Contracting State participates directly or indirectly in the management, control or capital of an enterprise of the other Contracting State, or the same persons participate directly or indirectly in the management, control or capital of an enterprise of a Contracting State and an enterprise of the other Contracting State,

and in either case conditions are made or imposed between the two enterprises in their commercial or financial relations which differ from those which would be made between independent enterprises, then any profits which would, but for those conditions, have accrued to one of the enterprises, but, by reason of those conditions, have not so accrued, may be included in the profits of that enterprise and taxed accordingly.

Article 10 Dividends

Dividends paid by a company which is a resident of a Contracting State to a resident of the other Contracting State may be taxed in that other Contracting State.

However, such dividends may also be taxed in the Contracting State of which the company paying the dividends is a resident and according to the laws of that Contracting State, but if the recipient is the beneficial owner of the dividends the tax so charged shall not exceed 15 per cent of the gross amount of the dividends. The provisions of this paragraph shall not affect the taxation of the company in respect of the profits out of which the dividends are paid.

The term "dividends" as used in this Article means income from shares, or other rights, not being debt-claims, participating in profits, as well as income from other corporate rights which is subject to the same taxation treatment as income from shares by the laws of the State of which the company making the distribution is a resident.

The provisions of paragraphs 1 and 2 shall not apply if the beneficial owner of the dividends, being a resident of a Contracting State, carries on business in the other Contracting State of which the company paying the dividends is a resident, through a permanent establishment situated therein, or performs in that other Contracting State independent personal services from a fixed base situated therein, and the holding in respect of which the dividends are paid is effectively connected with such permanent establishment or fixed base. In such case the provisions of Article 7 or Article 14, as the case may be, shall apply.

Where a company which is a resident of a Contracting State derives profits or income from the other Contracting State, that other Contracting State may not impose any tax on the dividends paid by the company, except insofar as such dividends are paid to a resident of that other Contracting State or insofar as the holding in respect of which the dividends are paid is effectively connected with a permanent establishment or a fixed base situated in that other Contracting State, nor subject the company's undistributed profits to a tax on the company's undistributed profits, even if the dividends paid or the undistributed profits consist wholly or partly of profits or income arising in such other Contracting State.

Article 11 Interest

Interest arising in a Contracting State and paid to a resident of the other Contracting State may be taxed in that other Contracting State.

However, such interest may also be taxed in the Contracting State in which it arises and according to the laws of that Contracting State, but if the recipient is the beneficial owner of the interest the tax so charged shall not exceed 10 per cent of the gross amount of the interest.

Notwithstanding the provisions of paragraph 2, interest arising in a Contracting State and derived by the Government of the other Contracting State, a political subdivision, a local authority or the Central Bank thereof or any financial institution wholly owned by that Government, or by any other resident of that other Contracting State with respect to debt-claims guaranteed by that Government or by any financial institution set up and financed by that Government to give such guarantees, or debt-claims indirectly financed by the Government of that other Contracting State, a political subdivision, a local authority or the Central Bank thereof or any financial institution wholly owned by that Government, shall be exempt from tax in the first-mentioned State.

The term "interest" as used in this Article means income from debt-claims of every kind, whether or not secured by mortgage, and in particular, income from government securities and income from bonds or debentures, including premiums and prizes attaching to such securities, bonds or debentures.

The provisions of paragraphs 1, 2 and 3 shall not apply if the beneficial owner of the interest, being a resident of a Contracting State, carries on business in the other Contracting State in which the interest arises, through a permanent establishment situated therein, or performs in that other Contracting State independent personal services from a fixed base situated therein, and the debt-claim in respect of which the interest is paid is effectively connected with such permanent establishment or fixed base. In such case the provisions of Article 7 or Article 14, as the case may be, shall apply.

Interest shall be deemed to arise in a Contracting State when the payer of the interest is the Government of that Contracting State, a political subdivision or a local authority thereof or a resident of that Contracting State. Where, however, the person paying the interest, whether he is a resident of a Contracting State or not, has in a Contracting State a permanent establishment or a fixed base in connection with which the indebtedness on which the interest is paid was incurred, and such interest is borne by such permanent establishment or fixed base, then such interest shall be deemed to arise in the State in which the permanent establishment or fixed base is situated.

Where, by reason of a special relationship between the payer of the interest and the beneficial owner or between both of them and some other person, the amount of the interest, having regard to the debt-claim for which it is paid, exceeds the amount which would have been agreed upon by the payer and the beneficial owner in the absence of such relationship, the provisions of this Article shall apply only to the last-mentioned amount. In such case, the excess part of the payments shall remain taxable according to the laws of each Contracting State, due regard being had to the other provisions of this Agreement.

Article 12 Royalties

Royalties arising in a Contracting State and paid to a resident of the other Contracting State may be taxed in that other Contracting State.

However, such royalties may also be taxed in the Contracting State in which they arise, and according to the laws of that Contracting State, but if the recipient is the beneficial owner of the royalties, the tax so charged shall not exceed 10 per cent of the gross amount of the royalties.

The term "royalties" as used in this Article means payments of any kind received as a consideration for the use of, or the right to use, any copyright of literary, artistic or scientific work including cinematograph films and films or tapes for radio or television broadcasting, any patent, know-how, trade mark, design or model, plan, secret formula or process, or for the use of, or the right to use, industrial, commercial or scientific equipment, or for information concerning industrial, commercial or scientific experience.

The provisions of paragraphs 1 and 2 shall not apply if the beneficial owner of the royalties, being a resident of a Contracting State, carries on business in the other Contracting State in which the royalties arise, through a permanent establishment situated therein, or performs in that other Contracting State independent personal services from a fixed base situated therein, and the right or property in respect of which the royalties are paid is effectively connected with such permanent establishment or fixed base. In such case, the provisions of Article 7 or Article 14, as the case may be, shall apply.

Royalties shall be deemed to arise in a Contracting State when the payer of the royalty is the Government of that Contracting State, a political subdivision or a local authority thereof or a resident of that Contracting State. Where, however, the person paying the royalties, whether he is a resident of a Contracting State or not, has in a Contracting State a permanent establishment or a fixed base in connection with which the liability to pay the royalties was incurred, and such royalties are borne by such permanent establishment or fixed base, then such royalties shall be deemed to arise in the Contracting State in which the permanent establishment or fixed base is situated.

Where, by reason of a special relationship between the payer of the royalty and the beneficial owner or between both of them and some other person, the amount of the royalties, having regard to the use, right or information for which they are paid, exceeds the amount which would have been agreed upon by the payer and the beneficial owner in the absence of such relationship, the provisions of this Article shall apply only to the last-mentioned amount. In such case, the excess part of the payments shall remain taxable according to the laws of each Contracting State, due regard being had to the other provisions of this Agreement.

Article 13 Capital Gains

Gains derived by a resident of a Contracting State from the alienation of immovable property referred to in Article 6 and situated in the other Contracting State may be taxed in that other Contracting State.

Gains from the alienation of movable property forming part of the business property of a permanent establishment which an enterprise of a Contracting State has in the other Contracting State or of movable property pertaining to a fixed base available to a resident of a Contracting State in the other Contracting State for the purpose of performing independent personal services, including such gains from the alienation of such a permanent establishment (alone or together with the whole enterprise) or of such a fixed base, may be taxed in that other Contracting State.

Gains from the alienation of ships or aircraft operated in international traffic and movable property, pertaining to the operation of such ships or aircraft shall be taxable only in the Contracting State in which the place of head office (i.e. effective management) of the enterprise is situated.

Gains from the alienation of shares in a company the property of which consists directly or indirectly principally of immovable property situated in a Contracting State may be taxed in that Contracting State.

Gains from the alienation of shares other than those mentioned in paragraph 4 representing a participation of 25 per cent in a company which is a resident of Contracting State may be taxed in that Contracting State.

Gains derived by a resident of a Contracting State from the alienation of any property other than that referred to in paragraphs 1 to 5 and arising in the other Contracting State may be taxed in that other Contracting State.

Article 14 Independent Personal Services

Income derived by a resident of a Contracting State in respect of professional services or other activities of an independent character shall be taxable only in that Contracting State except in one of the following circumstances, when such income may also be taxed in the other Contracting State:

if he has a fixed base regularly available to him in the other Contracting State for the purpose of performing his activities; in that case, only so much of the income as is attributable to that fixed base may be taxed in that other Contracting State;
if he is present in the other Contracting State for a period or periods exceeding in the aggregate 183 days in any period of twelve months; in that case, only so much of the income as is derived from his activities performed in that other Contracting State may be taxed in that other Contracting State.

The term “professional services” includes especially independent scientific, literary, artistic, educational or teaching activities as well as the independent activities of physicians, lawyers, engineers, architects, dentists and accountants.

Article 15 Dependent Personal Services

Subject to the provisions of Articles 16, 17, 18, 19, 20 and 21, salaries, wages and other similar remuneration derived by a resident of a Contracting State in respect of an employment shall be taxable only in that Contracting State unless the employment is exercised in the other Contracting State. If the employment is so exercised, such remuneration as is derived therefrom may be taxed in that other Contracting State.

Notwithstanding the provisions of paragraph 1, remuneration derived by a resident of a Contracting State in respect of an employment exercised in the other Contracting State shall be taxable only in the first-mentioned State if:

the recipient is present in the other Contracting State for a period or periods not exceeding in the aggregate 183 days in any period of twelve months; and
the remuneration is paid by, or on behalf of, an employer who is not a resident of the other Contracting State; and
the remuneration is not borne by a permanent establishment or a fixed base which the employer has in the other Contracting State.

Notwithstanding the preceding provisions of this Article, remuneration derived in respect of an employment exercised aboard a ship or aircraft operated in international traffic by an enterprise of a Contracting State, may be taxed in the Contracting State in which the place of head office (i.e. effective management) of the enterprise is situated.

Article 16 Directors’ Fees

Directors’ fees and other similar payments derived by a resident of a Contracting State in his capacity as a member of the board of directors or of a similar organ of a company which is a resident of the other Contracting State may be taxed in that other Contracting State.

Salaries, wages and other similar remuneration derived by a resident of a Contracting State in his capacity as an official in a top-level managerial position of a company which is a resident of the other Contracting State may be taxed in that other Contracting State.

Article 17 Artistes and Athletes

Notwithstanding the provisions of Articles 14 and 15, income derived by a resident of a Contracting State as an entertainer, such as a theatre, motion picture, radio or television artiste, or a musician, or as an athlete, from his personal activities as such exercised in the other Contracting State, may be taxed in that other Contracting State.

Where income in respect of personal activities exercised by an entertainer or an athlete in his capacity as such accrues not to the entertainer or athlete himself but to another person, that income may, notwithstanding the provisions of Articles 7, 14 and 15, be taxed in the Contracting State in which the activities of the entertainer or athlete are exercised.

Notwithstanding the provisions of paragraphs 1 and 2, income derived by entertainers or athletes who are residents of a Contracting State from the activities exercised in the other Contracting State under a plan of cultural exchange between the Governments of the Contracting States shall be exempt from tax in that other Contracting State.

Article 18 Pensions

Subject to the provisions of paragraph 2 of Article 19, pensions and other similar remuneration paid to a resident of a Contracting State shall be taxable only in that Contracting State.

Article 19 Government Service

(a) Remuneration, other than a pension, paid by the Government of a Contracting State or a political subdivision or a local authority thereof to an individual in respect of services rendered to the Government of that Contracting State or political subdivision or local authority thereof, in the discharge of functions of a governmental nature, shall be taxable only in that Contracting State.

However, such remuneration shall be taxable only in the other Contracting State if the services are rendered in that other Contracting State and the individual is a resident of that other Contracting State who:

is a national of that other Contracting State; or
did not become a resident of that other Contracting State solely for the purpose of rendering the services.

(a) Any pension paid by, or out of funds created by the Government of a Contracting State or a political subdivision or a local authority thereof to an individual in respect of services rendered to the Government of that Contracting State or a political subdivision or a local authority thereof shall be taxable only in that Contracting State. However, in the case such pensions are not taxed in that Contracting State, it may be taxed in the other Contracting State.
(b) However, such pension shall be taxable only in the other Contracting State if the individual is a resident of, and a national of, that other Contracting State.

The provisions of Articles 15, 16, 17 and 18 shall apply to remuneration and pensions in respect of services rendered in connection with a business carried on by the Government of a Contracting State or a political subdivision or a local authority thereof.

Article 20 Teachers and Researchers

An individual who is, or immediately before visiting a Contracting State was, a resident of the other Contracting State and is present in the first-mentioned Contracting State for the primary purpose of teaching, giving lectures or conducting research at a university, college, school or educational institution or scientific research institution accredited by the Government of the first-mentioned State shall be exempt from tax in the first-mentioned Contracting State, for a period not exceeding three years from the date of his first arrival in the first-mentioned Contracting State, in respect of remuneration for such teaching, lectures or research, but only in so far as the remuneration is taxed in that other Contracting State.

The provision of paragraph 1 shall not apply to income from research if such research is undertaken not in the public interest but primarily for the private benefit of a specific person or persons.

Article 21 Students, Apprentices and Trainees

A student, business apprentice or trainee who is or was immediately before visiting a Contracting State a resident of the other Contracting State and who is present in the first-mentioned State solely for the purpose of his education or training shall be exempt from tax in that Contracting State on:

payments received from abroad for the purpose of his maintenance, education or training;
scholarships, grants, allowances, and awards from governmental, charitable, scientific, literary or educational organizations for the purposes of his maintenance, education or training.

In respect of remuneration from employment, a student, business apprentice or trainee described in paragraph 1 shall be entitled during such education or training to the same exemptions, reliefs or reductions in respect of taxes available to residents of the State which he is visiting.

Article 22 Other Income

Items of income of a resident of a Contracting State, wherever arising, not dealt with in the foregoing Articles of this Agreement shall be taxable only in that Contracting State.

The provisions of paragraph 1 shall not apply to income, other than income from immovable property as defined in paragraph 2 of Article 6, if the recipient of such income, being a resident of a Contracting State, carries on business in the other Contracting State through a permanent establishment situated therein, or performs in that other Contracting State independent personal services from a fixed base situated therein, and the right or property in respect of which the income is paid is effectively connected with such permanent establishment or fixed base. In such case the provisions of Article 7 or Article 14, as the case may be, shall apply.

Notwithstanding the provisions of paragraphs 1 and 2, items of income of a resident of a Contracting State not dealt with in the foregoing Articles of this Agreement and arising in the other Contracting State may be taxed in that other Contracting State.

Article 23 Offshore Activities

The provisions of this Article shall have effect notwithstanding any other provision of this Agreement.

In this Article the term "offshore activities" means activities which are carried on offshore in connection with the exploration or exploitation of the seabed and subsoil and their natural resources situated in a Contracting State.

A person who is a resident of a Contracting State and carries on offshore activities in the other Contracting State shall, subject to paragraphs 4 and 5 of this Article, be deemed in relation to those activities to be carrying on business in that other Contracting State through a permanent establishment or fixed base situated therein.

The provisions of paragraph 3 shall not apply where the activities are carried on for a period not exceeding 30 days in the aggregate in any twelve months period. However, for the purpose of this paragraph the days referred to shall be calculated in the aggregate as follows:

activities carried on by an enterprise associated with another enterprise shall be regarded as carried on by the enterprise with which it is associated if the activities in question are substantially the same as those carried on by the last-mentioned enterprise;

two enterprises shall be deemed to be associated enterprises if one is controlled directly or indirectly by the other enterprise, or both are controlled directly or indirectly by third persons.

Paragraph 3 of this Article shall not apply where a resident of a Contracting State carries on transportation of supplies or personnel to a location, or between locations, where offshore activities are being carried on in the other Contracting State, or operate tugboats and other vessels auxiliary to such activities.

(a) Subject to sub-paragraph (b) of this paragraph, salaries, wages and similar remuneration, however paid, derived by a resident of a Contracting State in respect of an employment connected with offshore activities in the other Contracting State may, to the extent that the duties are performed offshore in that other Contracting State, be taxed in that other Contracting State provided that the employment offshore is carried on for a period exceeding 30 days in the aggregate in any twelve months period.

(b) Sub-paragraph (a) of this paragraph shall not apply to salaries, wages and similar remuneration derived by a resident of a Contracting State in respect of an employment exercised aboard a ship or aircraft engaged in the transportation of supplies or personnel to a location, or between locations, where offshore activities are being carried on in the other Contracting State, or in respect of an employment exercised aboard tugboats or other vessels operated auxiliary to such activities.

Gains derived by a resident of a Contracting State from the alienation of:

exploration or exploitation rights, or

property situated in the other Contracting State and used in connection with the exploration or exploitation of the seabed and subsoil and their natural resources situated in that other Contracting State, or shares deriving their value or the greater part of their value directly or indirectly from such rights or such property or from such rights and such property taken together may be taxed in that other Contracting State. In this paragraph "exploration or exploitation rights" means rights to assets to be produced by the exploration or exploitation of the seabed and subsoil and their natural resources in the other Contracting State, including rights to interests in or to the benefit of such assets.

Article 24 Capital

Capital represented by immovable property referred to in Article 6, owned by a resident of a Contracting State and situated in the other Contracting State may be taxed in that other Contracting State.

Capital represented by movable property forming part of the business property of a permanent establishment which an enterprise of a Contracting State has in the other Contracting State, or by movable property pertaining to a fixed base available to a resident of a Contracting State in the other Contracting State for the purpose of performing independent personal services, may be taxed in that other Contracting State.

Capital represented by ships and aircraft operated in international traffic and by movable property pertaining to the operation of such ships and aircraft shall be taxable only in the Contracting State in which the place of head office (i.e. effective management) of the enterprise is situated.

All other elements of capital of a resident of a Contracting State shall be taxable only in that Contracting State.

Article 25 Methods for Elimination of Double Taxation

In China, double taxation shall be eliminated as follows:

Where a resident of China derives income from Norway, the amount of tax on that income payable in Norway in accordance with the provisions of this Agreement, may be credited against the Chinese tax imposed on that resident. The amount of credit, however, shall not exceed the amount of the Chinese tax on that income computed in accordance with the taxation laws and regulations of China.

Where the income derived from Norway is a dividend paid by a company which is a resident of Norway to a company which is a resident of China and which owns not less than 10% of the shares of the company paying the dividend, the credit shall take into account the tax paid to Norway by the company paying the dividend in respect of its income.

In Norway, double taxation shall be eliminated as follows:

Where a resident of Norway derives income or owns capital which, in accordance with the provisions of this Agreement, may be taxed in China, Norway shall, subject to the provisions of sub-paragraphs (b), (c) and (d), exempt such income or capital from tax.

Where a resident of Norway derives items of income which, in accordance with the provisions of Articles 10, 11, 12, l6, paragraph 3 of Article 22 and Article 23 may be taxed in China. Norway shall allow as a deduction from the tax on the income of that person an amount equal to the tax paid in China. Such deduction shall not, however, exceed that part of the tax, as computed before the deduction is given, which is attributable to such items of income derived from China.

For the purposes of sub-paragraph (b) and in respect of the items of income referred to in Articles 10, 11 and 12 the amount of Chinese tax levied shall be deemed to be equal to 15% of the gross dividends, 10 per cent of the gross interest and 20% of the gross royalties.

The provisions of this sub-paragraph shall apply only for the first ten years for which this Agreement is effective. This period may be extended by mutual agreement between the competent authorities of the Contracting States,

Where in accordance with any provision of this Agreement income derived or capital owned by a resident of Norway is exempt from tax in Norway, Norway may nevertheless, in calculating the amount of tax on the remaining income or capital of such resident, take into account the exempted income or capital.

Article 26 Non-discrimination

Nationals of a Contracting State shall not be subjected in the other Contracting State to any taxation or any requirement connected therewith, which is other or more burdensome than the taxation and connected requirements to which nationals of that other Contracting State in the same circumstances are or may be subjected. The provisions of this paragraph shall, notwithstanding the provisions of Article 1, also apply to persons who are not residents of one or both of the Contracting States.

The taxation on a permanent establishment which an enterprise of a Contracting State has in the other Contracting State shall not be less favourably levied in that other Contracting State than the taxation levied on enterprises of that other Contracting State carrying on the same activities. The provisions of this paragraph shall not be construed as obliging a Contracting State to grant to residents of the other Contracting State any personal allowances, reliefs and reductions for taxation purposes on account of civil status or family responsibilities which it grants to its own residents.

Except where the provisions of Article 9, paragraph 7 of Article 11, or paragraph 6 of Article 12, apply, interest, royalties and other disbursements paid by an enterprise of a Contracting State to a resident of the other Contracting State shall, for the purpose of determining the taxable profits of such enterprise, be deductible under the same conditions as if they had been paid to a resident of the first-mentioned State. Similarly, and debts of an enterprise of a Contracting State to a resident of the other Contracting State shall, for the purpose of determining the taxable capital of such enterprise, be deductible under the same conditions as if they had been contracted to a resident of the first-mentioned State.

Enterprises of a Contracting State, the capital of which is wholly or partly owned or controlled, directly or indirectly, by one or more residents of the other Contracting

State, shall not be subjected in the first-mentioned State to any taxation or any requirement connected therewith which is other or more burdensome than the taxation and connected requirements to which other similar enterprises of the first-mentioned State are or may be subjected.

The provisions of this Article shall, notwithstanding the provisions of Article 2, apply to taxes of every kind.

Article 27 Mutual Agreement Procedure

Where a person considers that the actions of one or both of the Contracting States result or will result for him in taxation not in accordance with the provisions of this Agreement, he may, irrespective of the remedies provided by the domestic law of those States, present his case to the competent authority of the Contracting State of which he is a resident or, if his case comes under paragraph 1 of Article 26, to that of the Contracting State of which he is a national. The case must be presented within three years from the first notification of the action resulting in taxation not in accordance with the provisions of the Agreement.

The competent authority shall endeavour, if the objection appears to it to be justified and if it is not itself able to arrive at a satisfactory solution, to resolve the case by mutual agreement with the competent authority of the other Contracting State, with a view to the avoidance of taxation which is not in accordance with the provisions of this Agreement. Any agreement reached shall be implemented notwithstanding any time limits in the domestic law of the Contracting States.

The competent authorities of the Contracting States shall endeavour to resolve by mutual agreement any difficulties or doubts arising as to the interpretation or application of the Agreement. They may also consult together for the elimination of double taxation in cases not provided for in this Agreement.

The competent authorities of the Contracting States may communicate with each other directly for the purpose of reaching an agreement in the sense of paragraphs 2 and 3. When it seems advisable for reaching agreement, representatives of the competent authorities of the Contracting States may meet together for an oral exchange of opinions.

Article 28 Exchange of Information

The competent authorities of the Contracting States shall exchange such information as is necessary for carrying out the provisions of this Agreement or of the domestic laws of the Contracting States concerning taxes covered by the Agreement insofar as the taxation thereunder is not contrary to this Agreement, in particular for the prevention of evasion of such taxes. The exchange of information is not restricted by Article 1. Any information received by a Contracting State shall be treated as secret and shall be disclosed only to persons or authorities (including courts and administrative bodies) involved in the assessment or collection of, the enforcement or prosecution in respect of, or the determination of appeals in relation to, the taxes covered by the Agreement. Such persons or authorities shall use the information only for such purposes. They may disclose the information in public court proceedings or in judicial decisions.

In no case shall the provisions of paragraph 1 be construed so as to impose on a Contracting State the obligation:

to carry out administrative measures at variance with the laws and administrative practice of that Contracting State or of the other Contracting State;
to supply information which is not obtainable under the laws or in the normal course of the administration of that Contracting State or of the other Contracting State;
to supply information which would disclose any trade, business, industrial, commercial or professional secret or trade process, or information, the disclosure of which would be contrary to public policy (*order public*).

Article 29 Diplomatic Agents and Consular Officers
Nothing in this Agreement shall affect the fiscal privileges of diplomatic agents or consular officers under the general rules of international law or under the provisions of special agreements.

Article 30 Entry into Force
This Agreement shall enter into force on the thirtieth day after the date on which diplomatic notes indicating the completion of internal legal procedures necessary in each country for the entry into force of this Agreement have been exchanged. This Agreement shall have effect as respects income or capital relating to the taxable years beginning on or after the first day of January next following that in which this Agreement enters into force.

Article 31 Termination
This Agreement shall continue in effect indefinitely but either of the Contracting States may, on or before the thirtieth day of June in any calendar year beginning after the expiration of a period of five years from the date of its entry into force, give written notice of termination to the other Contracting State through the diplomatic channel. In such event this Agreement shall cease to have effect as respects income or capital relating to the taxable years beginning on or after the first day of January in the calendar years next following that in which the notice of termination is given.

DONE at Beijing on the 25th day of February 1986, in duplicate in the Chinese, Norwegian and English languages, the three texts being equally authentic. In case of any divergence of interpretation between the Chinese and Norwegian texts, the English text shall prevail.

For the Government of the People's Republic of China.

For the Government of the Kingdom of Norway.

Poland

Poland, officially the Republic of Poland, is a state in Eastern Europe. Poland borders Lithuania and Russia (Kaliningrad) to the northeast, Belarus and Ukraine to the east, Slovakia and the Czech Republic to the south, and Germany to the west. It fringes the Baltic Sea to the north. Poland's capital and largest city is Warsaw.

Polish are the majority ethnic group, while other major groups are from Ukraine, Belarus, Germany, and Russia.

The only official and predominant spoken language is Polish. Languages having a minority status are Armenian, Belarusian, Czech, German, Yiddish, Hebrew, Lithuanian, Russian, Slovak and Ukrainian.

Poland is a unitary parliamentary constitutional republic. The Konstytucja is the constitution regulating the political system, in force since 1997. The Sejm and the Senate exert the legislative power forming the parliament. The Sejm is elected through direct elections using the open-list proportional representation system. The members of the Senate are elected through First-past-the-post.

Executive power is vested in the Prime Minister. The Prime Minister is appointed by the President of the Republic after being elected by the party or coalition with the parliamentary majority in the Sejm.

Poland has a civil law system based on Roman law. The Sąd Najwyższy acts as Supreme Court, managing constitutional matters, with judicial review powers.

Poland any is a unitary state, divided into voivode ships (provinces) and powiats (counties).

Poland is part of the European Union since 2004.

Category	Value
Population (mln persons)	37.973
Currency	Polish złoty

Source International Monetary Fund, year 2019

Poland is the second largest economy of Eastern Europe, following Russia, with a GDP valued 565.9 billion USD in 2019, and has a population of about 38 million

© The Author(s), under exclusive license to Springer Nature Singapore Pte Ltd. 2022
L. Riccardi and G. Riccardi, *China–Europe Tax Treaties*,
https://doi.org/10.1007/978-981-19-3563-3_21

people. Poland's inflation is slightly above 2% (2.3%), paired with low unemployment figures (3.3%). Polish unemployment is the sixth lowest in Europe. Poland ranked 20 out of 43 in Europe in the 2020 Doing Business ranking, scoring 76.4, and imposes a CIT of 19%. Poland records a trade surplus of 2 billion USD, it is the tenth main exporter in Europe.

GDP and local economy	
GDP current prices (billion USD)	565.9
GDP per capita (USD)	14,902
GDP growth (%)	4.1
Inflation (%)	2.3
Unemployment (%)	3.3
General government total expenditure (% of GDP)	41.7
General government gross debt (% of GDP)	45.6
Doing business score 2020	76.4

Source International Monetary Fund and UNCTAD, year 2019

Foreign direct investment	
FDI outstock (million USD)	24,835
FDI instock (million USD)	236,506

Source UNCTAD, year 2019

Trade	
Imports (million USD)	261,998
Exports (million USD)	264,013
Trade balance (million USD)	2015

Source International Monetary Fund and UNCTAD, year 2019

Main import–export	
First import by category	Electrical, electronic equipment
Second import by category	Machinery, nuclear reactors, boilers
First export by category	Machinery, nuclear reactors, boilers
Second export by category	Electrical, electronic equipment

Source United Nations COMTRADE, year 2020

The legal bases for taxation are established in the constitution. Poland imposes individual income tax, property sales taxes, capital gains, corporate income tax, and value added tax. Progressivity is guaranteed by a system with different bands and various deductions.

Taxes	
Company income tax (%)	19
Top individual income tax (%)	32
Value added tax or sales tax (%)	23
Reduced value added tax or sales tax (%)	5/8

Source RsA Asia report, year 2021

- Economic Relation with China

Poland records a trade deficit of 22 billion USD to China in 2020. "Electrical, electronic equipment" is the first export category, worth 0.8 billion USD, followed by "Machinery, nuclear reactors, boilers". "Electrical, electronic equipment" is also the first import category, valued 7.50 billion USD in 2020. Poland is part of the Belt and Road Initiative. In 1988 Poland and China have signed their DTA, which has been in force since 1989.

Category	Value
Belt road	Yes

Source UNCTAD, year 2020

Import from China	
Import from China (billion USD)	26.74
First import category from China	Electrical, electronic equipment
First import value (billion USD)	7.50
Second import category from China	Machinery, nuclear reactors, boilers
Second import value (billion USD)	4.61

Source United Nations COMTRADE, year 2020

Export to China	
Export to China (billion USD)	4.32
First export category towards China	Electrical, electronic equipment
First export value (billion USD)	0.795
Second export category towards China	Machinery, nuclear reactors, boilers
Second export value (billion USD)	0.646

Source United Nations COMTRADE, year 2020

Trade balance	
Trade balance (billion USD)	−22.42

Source United Nations COMTRADE, year 2020

Double tax agreement	
DTA effective date	1989.1.7
Dividends (%)	10
Interest (%)	0–10
Royalties (%)	7–10

Source State Administration of Taxation of China, year 2021

Title AGREEMENT BETWEEN THE GOVERNMENT OF THE PEOPLE'S REPUBLIC OF CHINA AND THE GOVERNMENT OF THE POLISH PEOPLE'S REPUBLIC FOR THE AVOIDANCE OF DOUBLE TAXATION AND THE PREVENTION OF FISCAL EVASION WITH RESPECT TO TAXES ON INCOME

Treaty Text

The Government of the People's Republic of China and the Government of the Polish People's Republic;

Desiring to conclude an Agreement for the avoidance of double taxation and the prevention of fiscal evasion with respect to taxes on income;

Have agreed as follows:

Article 1 Personal Scope

This Agreement shall apply to persons who are residents of one or both of the Contracting States.

Article 2 Taxes Covered

This Agreement shall apply to taxes on income imposed on behalf of a Contracting State or of its local authorities, irrespective of the manner in which they are levied.

There shall be regarded as taxes on income all taxes imposed on total income, or on elements of income, including taxes on gains from the alienation of movable or immovable property, as well as taxes on capital appreciation.

The existing taxes to which the Agreement shall apply are:

in the People's Republic of China:
the individual income tax;
the income tax concerning joint ventures with Chinese and foreign investment;
the income tax concerning foreign enterprises; and
the local income tax; (hereinafter referred to as "Chinese tax");
in the Polish People's Republic:
the income tax (podatek ochodowy);
the tax on wages and salaries (podatek od wynagrodzen);
the equalisation tax (podatek wyrownawczy);
the tax on immovable property (podatek od nieruchomosci);
the agricultural tax (podatek rolny); (hereinafter referred to as "Polish tax").

This Agreement shall also apply to any identical or substantially similar taxes which are imposed by either Contracting State after the date of signature of this Agreement in addition to, or in place of, the existing taxes referred to in paragraph 3 of this Article. The competent authorities of the Contracting states shall notify each other of any substantial changes which have been made in their respective taxation laws.

Article 3 General Definitions

For the purposes of this Agreement, unless the context otherwise requires:

the term "China" means the People's Republic of China; when used in geographical sense, means all the territory of the People's Republic of China, including its territorial sea, in which the Chinese laws relating to taxation apply, and any area beyond its territorial sea, within which the People's Republic of China has sovereign rights of exploration for and exploitation of resources of the seabed and its sub-soil and superjacent water resources in accordance with international law;
the term "Poland" means the Polish People's Republic; when used in geographical sense, means all the territory of the Polish People's Republic, including its territorial sea, in which the Polish laws relating to taxation apply, and any area beyond its territorial sea, within which the Polish People's Republic has sovereign rights of exploration for and exploitation of resources of the seabed and its sub-soil and superjacent water resources in accordance with international law;
the terms "a Contracting State" and "the other Contracting State" mean China or Poland as the context requires;
the term "tax" means Chinese tax or Polish tax, as the context requires;
the term "person" includes an individual, a company and any other body of persons;
the term "company" means anybody corporate or any entity which is treated as a body corporate for tax purposes;
the terms "enterprise of a Contracting State" and "enterprise of the other Contracting State" mean, respectively, an enterprise carried on by a resident of a Contracting State and an enterprise carried on by a resident of the other Contracting State;
the term "nationals" means all individuals possessing the nationality of a Contracting State and all legal persons, partnerships and associations deriving their status as such from the law in force in a Contracting State.
the term "international traffic" means any transport by a ship or aircraft operated by an enterprise which has its place of effective management of the business in a Contracting State, except when the ship or aircraft is operated solely between places in the other Contracting State;
the term "competent authority" means:
in the case of China, the Ministry of Finance or its authorized representative;
in the case of Poland, the Minister of Finance or his authorized representative.

As regards the application of this Agreement by a Contracting State, any term not defined therein shall, unless the context otherwise requires, have the meaning which it has under the laws of that Contracting State concerning the taxes to which this Agreement applies.

Article 4 Resident

For the purposes of this Agreement, the term "resident of a Contracting State" means any person who, under the law of that State, is liable to tax therein by reason of his domicile, residence, place of head office, place of effective management or any other criterion of a similar nature.

Where by reason of the provisions of paragraph 1 of this Article, an individual is a resident of both Contracting States, then his status shall be determined as follows:

He shall be deemed to be a resident of the Contracting State in which he has a permanent home available to him; if he has a permanent home available to him in both Contracting States, he shall be deemed to be a resident of the Contracting State with which his personal and economic relations are closer (centre of vital interests);

If the State in which he has his centre of vital interests cannot be determined, or if he has not a permanent home available to him in either Contracting State, he shall be deemed to be a resident of the State in which he has an habitual abode;

If he has an habitual abode in both Contracting States or in neither of them, he shall be deemed to be a resident of the Contracting State of which he is a national;

If the status of resident cannot be determined according to sub-paragraphs (a)–(c), the competent authorities of the Contracting States shall settle the question by mutual agreement.

Where by reason of the provisions of paragraph 1 of this Article a person other than an individual is a resident of both Contracting States, then it shall be deemed to be a resident of the State in which the place of effective management of its business is situated. However, where such a person has the place of effective management of its business in one of the Contracting States and the place of head office of its business in the other Contracting State, then the competent authorities of the Contracting States shall determine by mutual agreement the State of which the company shall be deemed to be a resident for the purposes of this Agreement.

Article 5 Permanent Establishment

For the purposes of this Agreement, the term "permanent establishment" means a fixed place of business through which the business of an enterprise is wholly or partly carried on.

The term "permanent establishment" includes especially:

a place of management;
a branch;
an office;
a factory;

a workshop; and
a mine, an oil or gas well, a quarry or any other place of extraction of natural resources.

The term "permanent establishment" likewise encompasses:

a building site, a construction, assembly or installation project or supervisory activities in connection therewith, but only where such site, project or activities continue for a period of more than six months;
the furnishing of services, including consultancy services, by an enterprise of a Contracting State through employees or other engaged personnel in the other Contracting State, provided that such activities continue for the same project or a connected project for a period or periods aggregating more than six months within any twelve-month period.

Notwithstanding the provisions of paragraphs 1 to 3 of this Article, the term "permanent establishment" shall be deemed not to include:

the use of facilities solely for the purpose of storage, display or delivery of goods or merchandise belonging to the enterprise;
the maintenance of a stock of goods or merchandise belonging to the enterprise solely for the purpose of storage, display or delivery;
the maintenance of a stock of goods or merchandise belonging to the enterprise solely for the purpose of processing by another enterprise;
the maintenance of a fixed place of business solely for the purpose of purchasing goods or merchandise or of collecting information, for the enterprise;
the maintenance of a fixed place of business solely for the purpose of carrying on, for the enterprise, any other activity of a preparatory or auxiliary character;
the maintenance of a fixed place of business solely for any combination of activities mentioned in sub-paragraphs (a) to (e) provided that the overall activity of the fixed place of business resulting from this combination is of a preparatory or auxiliary character.

Notwithstanding the provisions of paragraphs 1 and 2 of this Article, where a person other than an agent of an independent status to whom the provisions of paragraph 6 of this Article apply is acting in a Contracting State on behalf of an enterprise of the other Contracting State, has and habitually exercises in a Contracting State an authority to conclude contracts in the name of the enterprise, that enterprise shall be deemed to have a permanent establishment in the first-mentioned Contracting State in respect of any activities which that person undertakes for the enterprise, unless the activities of such person are limited to those mentioned in paragraph 4 of this Article which, if exercised through a fixed place of business, would not make this fixed place of business a permanent establishment under the provisions of that paragraph.

An enterprise of a Contracting State shall not be deemed to have a permanent establishment in the other Contracting State merely because it carries on business in that Contracting State through a broker, general commission agent or any other agent of an independent status, provided that such persons are acting in the ordinary course of their business. However, when the activities of such an agent are devoted wholly or almost wholly on behalf of that enterprise, he will not be considered an agent of an independent status within the meaning of this paragraph.

The fact that a company which is a resident of a Contracting State controls or is controlled by a company which is a resident of the other Contracting State, or which carries on business in that other State (whether through a permanent establishment or otherwise), shall not of itself constitute either company a permanent establishment of the other.

Article 6 Income from Immovable Property

Income derived by a resident of a Contracting State from immovable property situated in the other Contracting State may be taxed in that other Contracting State.

The term "immovable property" shall have the meaning which it has under the law of the Contracting State in which the property in question is situated. The term shall in any case include property accessory to immovable property, livestock and equipment used in agriculture and forestry, rights to which the provisions of general law respecting landed property apply, usufruct of immovable property and rights to variable or fixed payments as consideration for the working of, or the right to work, mineral deposits, sources and other natural resources. Ships, boats and aircraft shall not be regarded as immovable property.

The provisions of paragraph 1 of this Article shall apply to income derived from the direct use, letting, or use in any other form of immovable property.

The provisions of paragraphs 1 and 3 of this Article shall also apply to the income from immovable property of an enterprise and to income from immovable property used for the performance of independent personal services.

Article 7 Business Profits

The profits of an enterprise of a Contracting State shall be taxable only in that State unless the enterprise carries on business in the other Contracting State through a permanent establishment situated therein. If the enterprise carries on business as aforesaid, the profits of the enterprise may be taxed in the other State but only so much of them as is attributable to that permanent establishment.

Subject to the provisions of paragraph 3 of this Article, where an enterprise of a Contracting State carries on business in the other Contracting State through a permanent establishment situated therein, there shall in each Contracting State be attributed to that permanent establishment the profits which it might be expected to make if it were a distinct and separate enterprise engaged in the same or similar activities under the same or similar conditions and dealing wholly independently with the enterprise of which it is a permanent establishment.

In determining the profits of a permanent establishment, there shall be allowed as deductions expenses which are incurred for the purposes of the business of the permanent establishment, including executive and general administrative expenses so incurred, whether in the State in which the permanent establishment is situated or elsewhere. However, no such deduction shall be allowed in respect of amounts, if any, paid (otherwise than towards reimbursement of actual expenses) by the permanent establishment to the head office of the enterprise or any of its other offices, by way of royalties, fees or other similar payments in return for the use of patents or other rights, or by way of commission, for specific services performed or for management, or except in the case of a banking enterprise, by way of interest on moneys lent to the permanent establishment. Likewise, no account shall be taken, in the determination of the profits of a permanent establishment, for amounts charged (otherwise than towards reimbursement of actual expenses) by the permanent establishment to the head office of the enterprise or any of its other offices, by way of royalties, fees or other similar payments in return for the use of patents or other rights, or by way of commission for specific services performed or for management, or, except in the case of a banking enterprise by way of interest on moneys lent to the head office of the enterprise or any of its other offices.

Insofar as it has been customary in a Contracting State to determine the profits to be attributed to a permanent establishment on the basis of an apportionment of the total profits of the enterprise to its various parts, nothing in paragraph 2 of this Article shall preclude that Contracting State from determining the profits to be taxed by such an apportionment as may be customary. The method of apportionment adopted shall, however, be such that the result shall be in accordance with the principles contained in this Article.

No profits shall be attributed to a permanent establishment by reason of the mere purchase by that permanent establishment of goods or merchandise for the enterprise.

For the purposes of paragraphs 1 to 5 of this Article, the profits to be attributed to the permanent establishment shall be determined by the same method year by year unless there is good and sufficient reason to the contrary.

Where profits include items of income which are dealt with separately in other Articles of this Agreement, then the provisions of those Articles shall not be affected by the provisions of this Article.

Article 8 Shipping and Air Transport

Profits from the operation of ships or aircraft in international traffic shall be taxable only in the Contracting State in which the place of effective management of the business of the enterprise is situated.

If the place of effective management of the business of a shipping enterprise is aboard a ship, then it shall be deemed to be situated in the Contracting State in which the home harbour of the ship is situated, or, if there is no such home harbour, in the Contracting State of which the operator of the ship is a resident.

The provisions of paragraph 1 of this Article shall also apply to profits from the participation in a pool, a joint business or an international operating agency.

Article 9 Associated Enterprises

Where

an enterprise of a Contracting State participates directly or indirectly in the management, control or capital of an enterprise of the other Contracting State, or the same persons participate directly or indirectly in the management, control or capital of an enterprise of a Contracting State and an enterprise of the other Contracting State, and in either case conditions are made or imposed between the two enterprises in their commercial or financial relations which differ from those which would be made between independent enterprises, then any profits which would, but for those conditions, have accrued to one of the enterprises, but, by reason of those conditions, have not so accrued, may be included in the profits of that enterprise and taxed accordingly.

Article 10 Dividends

Dividends paid by a company which is a resident of a Contracting State to a resident of the other Contracting State may be taxed in that other Contracting State.

However, such dividends may also be taxed in the Contracting State of which the company paying the dividends is a resident and according to the laws of that Contracting State, but if the recipient is the beneficial owner of the dividends the tax so charged shall not exceed 10% of the gross amount of the dividends.

The provisions of this paragraph shall not affect the taxation of the company in respect of the profits out of which the dividends are paid.

The term "dividends" as used in this Article means income from shares, or other rights, not being debt-claims, participating in profits, as well as income from other corporate rights which is subjected to the same taxation treatment as income from shares by the laws of the State of which the company making the distribution is a resident.

The provisions of paragraphs 1 and 2 of this Article shall not apply if the beneficial owner of the dividends, being a resident of a Contracting State, carries on business in the other Contracting State of which the company paying the dividends is a resident, through a permanent establishment situated therein, or performs in that other State independent personal services from a fixed base situated therein, and the holding in respect of which the dividends are paid is effectively connected with such permanent establishment or fixed base. In such case the provisions of Article 7 or Article 14, as the case may be, shall apply.

Where a company which is a resident of a Contracting State derives profits or income from the other Contracting State, that other State may not impose any tax on the dividends paid by the company, except insofar as such dividends are paid to a resident of that other State or insofar as the holding in respect of which the dividends are paid is effectively connected with a permanent establishment or a fixed base situated in that other State, nor subject the company's undistributed profits to a tax on the company's undistributed profits, even if the dividends paid or the undistributed profits consists wholly or partly of profits or income arising in such other State.

Article 11 Interest

Interest arising in a Contracting State and paid to a resident of the other Contracting State may be taxed in that other Contracting State.

However, such interest may also be taxed in the Contracting State in which it arises and according to the laws of that Contracting State, but if the recipient is the beneficial owner of the interest the tax so charged shall not exceed 10% of the gross amount of the interest.

Notwithstanding the provisions of paragraph 2, interest arising in a Contracting State and derived by the Government of the other Contracting State, a local authority and the Central Bank thereof or any financial institution wholly owned by that Government, or by any other resident of that other Contracting State with respect to debt-claim indirectly financed by the Government of that other Contracting State, a local authority, and the Central Bank thereof or any financial institution wholly owned by that Government, shall be exempt from tax in the first-mentioned State.

The term "interest" as used in this Article means income from debt-claims of every kind, whether or not secured by mortgage and whether or not carrying a right to participate in the debtor's profits, and in particular, income from government securities and income from bonds or debentures, including premiums and prizes attaching to such securities, bonds or debentures. Penalty charges for late payment shall not be regarded as interest for the purpose of this Article.

The provisions of paragraphs 1, 2 and 3 of this Article shall not apply if the beneficial owner of the interest, being a resident of a Contracting State, carries on business in the other Contracting State in which the interest arises, through a permanent establishment situated therein, or performs in that other State independent personal services from a fixed base situated therein, and the debt-claim in respect of which the interest is paid is effectively connected with such permanent establishment or fixed base, In such case the provisions of Article 7 or Article 14, as the case may be, shall apply.

Interest shall be deemed to arise in a Contracting State when the payer is that State itself, a local authority or a resident of that State. Where, however, the person paying the interest, whether he is a resident of a Contracting State or not, has in a Contracting State a permanent establishment or a fixed base in connection with which the indebtedness on which the interest is paid was incurred, and such interest is borne by such permanent establishment or fixed base, then such interest shall be deemed to arise in the State in which the permanent establishment or fixed base is situated.

Where, by reason of a special relationship between the payer and the beneficial owner or between both of them and some other person, the amount of the interest, having regard to the debt-claim for which it is paid, exceeds the amount which would have been agreed upon by the payer and the beneficial owner in the absence of such relationship, the provisions of this Article shall apply only to the last-mentioned amount. In such case, the excess part of the payments shall remain taxable according to the laws of each Contracting State, due regard being had to the other provisions of this Agreement.

Article 12 Royalties

Royalties arising in a Contracting State and paid to a resident of the other Contracting State may be taxed in that other Contracting State.

However, such royalties may also be taxed in the Contracting State in which they arise and according to the law of that State, but if the beneficial owner of the royalties is a resident of the other Contracting State the tax so charged shall not exceed:

in the case of royalties referred to in sub-paragraph (a) of paragraph 3 of this Article, 10% of the gross amount of the royalties; and
in the case of royalties referred to in sub-paragraph (b) of paragraph 3 of this Article, 10% of the adjusted amount of the royalties. For the purpose of this sub-paragraph "the adjusted amount" means 70% of the gross amount of the royalties.

The term "royalties" as used in this Article comprises:

payments of any kind received as a consideration for the use of, or the right to use, any copyright of literary, artistic or scientific work, including cinematograph films, and films or tapes for radio or television broadcasting, or any patent, know-how, trademark, design or model, plan, secret formula or process; and
payments of any kind received as a consideration for the use of, or the right to use, any industrial, commercial or scientific equipment.

The provisions of paragraphs 1 and 2 of this Article shall not apply if the beneficial owner of the royalties, being a resident of a Contracting state, carries on business in the other Contracting State in which the royalties arise, through a permanent establishment situated therein, or performs in that other State independent personal services from a fixed base situated therein, and the right or property in respect of which the royalties are paid is effectively connected with such permanent establishment or fixed base. In such case the provisions of Article 7 or Article 14, as the case may be, shall apply.

Royalties shall be deemed to arise in a Contracting State when the payer is that State itself, a local authority or a resident of that State. Where, however, the person paying the royalties, whether he is a resident of a Contracting State or not, has in a Contracting State a permanent establishment or a fixed base in connection with which the liability to pay the royalties was incurred, and such royalties are borne by such permanent establishment or fixed base, then such royalties shall be deemed to arise in the State in which the permanent establishment of fixed base is situated.

Where, by reason of a special relationship between the payer and the beneficial owner or between both of them and some other person, the amount of the royalties, having regard to the use, right or information for which they are paid, exceeds the amount which would have been agreed upon by the payer and the beneficial owner in the absence of such relationship, the provisions of this Article shall apply only to the last-mentioned amount. In such case, the excess part of the payments shall remain taxable according to the laws of each Contracting State, due regard being had to the other provisions of this Agreement.

Article 13 Capital Gains

Subject to the provisions of paragraph 2 of this Article, capital gains which arise in a Contracting State may be taxed by that State.

Gains from the alienation of ships or aircraft operated in international traffic and any property, other than immovable property, pertaining to the operation of such ships or aircraft shall be taxable only in the Contracting State in which the place of effective management of the business of the enterprise is situated.

Article 14 Independent Personal Services

Income derived by a resident of a Contracting State in respect of professional services or other activities of an independent character shall be taxable only in that Contracting State except in one of the following circumstances, when such income may also be taxed in the other Contracting State:

if he has a fixed base regularly available to him in the other Contracting State for the purpose of performing his activities; in that case, only so much of the income as is attributable to that fixed base may be taxed in that other Contracting State;
if his stay in the other Contracting State is for a period or periods exceeding in the aggregate 183 days in the calendar year concerned, in that case, only so much of the income as is derived from his activities performed in that other Contracting State may be taxed in that other Contracting State.

The term "professional services" includes especially independent scientific, literary, artistic, educational or teaching activities as well as the independent activities of physicians, lawyers, engineers, architects, dentists and accountants.

Article 15 Dependent Personal Services

Subject to the provisions of Articles 16, 18, 19, 20 and 21, salaries, wages and other similar remuneration derived by a resident of a Contracting State in respect of an employment shall be taxable only in that Contracting State unless the employment is exercised in the other Contracting State. If the employment is so exercised, such remuneration as is derived therefrom may be taxed in that other Contracting State.

Notwithstanding the provisions of paragraph 1 of this Article, remuneration derived by a resident of a Contracting State in respect of an employment exercised in the other Contracting State shall be taxable only in the first-mentioned State if:

the recipient is present in the other Contracting State for a period or periods not exceeding in the aggregate 183 days in the calendar year concerned; and
the remuneration is paid by, or on behalf of, an employer who is not a resident of the other Contracting State; and
the remuneration is not borne by a permanent establishment or fixed base which the employer has in the other Contracting State.

Notwithstanding the provisions of paragraphs 1 and 2 of this Article, remuneration derived in respect of an employment exercised aboard a ship or aircraft operated by an enterprise of a Contracting State in international traffic, shall be taxable only in the Contracting State in which the place of effective management of the business of the enterprise is situated.

Article 16 Directors' Fees

Directors' fees and other similar payments derived by a resident of a Contracting State in his capacity as a member of the board of directors of a company which is a resident of the other Contracting State may be taxed in that other Contracting State.

Article 17 Artistes and Athletes

Notwithstanding the provisions of Articles 14 and 15, income derived by a resident of a Contracting State as an entertainer, such as a theatre, motion picture, radio or television artiste, or a musician, or as an athlete, from his personal activities as such exercised in the other Contracting State, may be taxed in that other Contracting State.

Where income in respect of personal activities exercised by an entertainer or an athlete in his capacity as such accrues not to the entertainer or athlete himself but to another person, that income may, notwithstanding the provisions of Articles 7, 14 and 15, be taxed in the Contracting State in which the activities of the entertainer or athlete are exercised.

Notwithstanding the provisions of paragraphs 1 and 2 of this Article, income derived by entertainers or athletes who are residents of a Contracting State from the activities exercised in the other Contracting State under a plan of cultural or sports exchange between the Governments of the both Contracting States shall be exempt from tax in that other Contracting State.

Article 18 Pensions

Subject to the provisions of paragraph 2 of Article 19, pensions and other similar remuneration paid to a resident of a Contracting State in consideration of past employment shall be taxable only in that Contracting State.

Notwithstanding the provisions of paragraph 1 of this Article, pensions paid and other similar payments made by the Government of a Contracting State or a local authority thereof under a public scheme which is part of the social security system of that Contracting State shall be taxable only in that Contracting State.

Article 19 Government Service

(a) Remuneration, other than pension, paid by the Government of a Contracting State or a local authority thereof to an individual in respect of services rendered to the Government of that Contracting State or a local authority thereof shall be taxable only in that Contracting State.

However, such remuneration shall be taxable only in the other Contracting State if the services are rendered in that other Contracting State and the individual is a resident of that other Contracting State who:

is a national of that other Contracting State; or
did not become a resident of that other Contracting State solely for the purpose of rendering the services.

(a) Any pension paid by, or out of funds to which contributions are made by, the Government of a Contracting State or a local authority thereof to an individual in respect of services rendered to the Government of that Contracting State or a local authority thereof shall be taxable only in that Contracting State.

(b) However, such pension shall be taxable only in the other Contracting State if the individual is a resident of, and a national of, that other Contracting State.

The provisions of Articles 15, 16, 17 and 18 shall apply to remuneration and pensions in respect of services rendered in connection with a business carried on by the Government of a Contracting State or a local authority thereof.

Article 20 Teachers and Researchers

An individual who is, or immediately before visiting a Contracting State was, a resident of the other Contracting State and is present in the first-mentioned Contracting State for the primary purpose of teaching, giving lectures or conducting research at a university, college, school or educational institution or scientific research institution recognized by the Government of the first-mentioned State shall be exempt from tax in the first-mentioned Contracting State, for a period of five years from the date of his first arrival in the first-mentioned Contracting State, in respect of remuneration for such teaching, lectures or research.

Article 21 Students, Apprentices and Trainees

A student, business apprentice or trainee who is or was immediately before visiting a Contracting State a resident of the other Contracting State and who is present in the first-mentioned State solely for the purpose of his education or training shall be exempt from tax in that Contracting State on:

payments received from abroad for the purpose of his maintenance, education or training;

scholarships, grants, allowances and awards from governmental, charitable, scientific, literary or educational organizations for the purposes of his maintenance, education or training.

In respect of remuneration from employment, a student, business apprentice or trainee described in paragraph 1 of this Article shall be entitled during such education or training to the same exemptions, reliefs or reductions in respect of taxes available to residents of the State which he is visiting.

Article 22 Other Income

Items of income of a resident of a Contracting State not dealt with in the foregoing Articles of this Agreement and arising in the other Contracting State may be taxed in that other Contracting State.

However, items of income of a resident of a Contracting State, wherever arising, other than those mentioned in paragraph 1 of this Article, which are not dealt with in the foregoing Articles of this Agreement, shall be taxable only in that Contracting State.

The provisions of paragraphs 1 and 2 of this Article shall not apply to income, other than income from immovable property as defined in paragraph 2 of Article 6, if the recipient of such income, being a resident of a Contracting State, carries on business in the other Contracting State through a permanent establishment situated therein, or performs in that other State independent personal services from a fixed base situated therein, and the right or property in respect of which the income is paid is effectively connected with such permanent establishment or fixed base. In such case the provisions of Article 1 or Article 14, as the case may be, shall apply.

Article 23 Methods for the Elimination of Double Taxation
In China, double taxation shall be eliminated as follows:

where a resident of China derives income from Poland, the amount of tax on that income payable in Poland, in accordance with the provisions of this Agreement, may be credited against the Chinese tax imposed on that resident. The amount of credit, however, shall not exceed the amount of the Chinese tax on that income computed in accordance with the taxation laws and regulations of China.
where the income derived from Poland is a dividend paid by a company which is a resident of Poland to a company which is a resident of China and which owns not less than 10% of the shares of the company paying the dividend, the credit shall take into account the tax paid to Poland by the company paying the dividend in respect of its income.

In Poland, double taxation shall be eliminated as follows:

Where a resident of Poland derives income which, in accordance with the provisions of this Agreement may be taxed in China, Poland shall, subject to the provisions of sub-paragraphs (b) to (d) of this paragraph, exempt such income from tax.
Where a resident of Poland derives income which, in accordance with the provisions of Articles 10, 11 and 12 of this Agreement may be taxed in China, Poland shall allow as a deduction from the tax on the income of that resident an amount equal to the tax paid in China. Such deduction shall not, however, exceed that part of the tax, as computed before the deduction is given, which is appropriate to such income derived from China.

For the purpose of sub-paragraph (b) the Chinese tax to be deducted shall be deemed to be 10% of the gross amount of dividend, interest or royalties.
Where in accordance with any provisions of the Agreement income derived by a resident of Poland is exempt from tax in Poland, Poland may in calculating the amount of tax on the remaining income of such resident apply the rate of tax which would have been applicable if the exempted income had not been so exempted.

Article 24 Non-discrimination
National of a Contracting State shall not be subjected in the other Contracting State to any taxation or any requirement connected therewith, which is other or more burdensome than the taxation and connected requirements to which nationals of that other Contracting State in the same circumstances are or may be subjected. The

provisions of this paragraph shall, notwithstanding the provisions of Article 1, also apply to persons who are not residents of one or both of the Contracting States.

The taxation on a permanent establishment which an enterprise of a Contracting State has in the other Contracting State shall not be less favourably levied in that other Contracting State than the taxation levied on enterprises of that other Contracting State carrying on the same activities. The provisions of this paragraph shall not be construed as obliging a Contracting State to grant to residents of the other Contracting State any personal allowances, reliefs and reductions for taxation purposes on account of civil status or family responsibilities which it grants to its own residents.

Except where the provisions of Article 9, paragraph 7 of Article 11, or paragraph 6 of Article 12, apply, interest, royalties and other disbursements paid by an enterprise of a Contracting State to a resident of the other Contracting State shall, for the purpose of determining the taxable profits of such enterprise, be deductible under the same conditions as if they had been paid to a resident of the first-mentioned State.

Enterprises of a Contracting State, the capital of which is wholly or partly owned or controlled, directly or indirectly, by one or more residents of the other Contracting State, shall not be subjected in the first-mentioned State to any taxation or any requirement connected therewith which is other or more burdensome than the taxation and connected requirements to which other similar enterprises of the first-mentioned State are or may be subjected.

The provisions of this Article shall apply to the taxes referred to in Article 2 of this Agreement.

The provisions of this Article shall not be affected by different tax system applicable in the Contracting State to income and profits derived by enterprises of the socialised sector of the economy.

Article 25 Mutual Agreement Procedure

Where a person considers that the actions of one or both of the Contracting States result or will result for him in taxation not in accordance with the provisions of this Agreement, he may, irrespective of the remedies provided by the domestic law of those States, present his case to the competent authority of the Contracting State of which he is a resident or, if his case comes under paragraph 1 of Article 24, to that of the Contracting State of which he is a national. The case must be presented within three years from the first notification of the action resulting in taxation not in accordance with the provisions of the Agreement.

The competent authority shall endeavour, if the objection appears to it to be justified and if it is not itself able to arrive at a satisfactory solution, to resolve the case by mutual agreement with the competent authority of the other Contracting State, with a view to the avoidance of taxation which is not in accordance with the provisions of this Agreement. Any agreement reached shall be implemented notwithstanding any time limits in the domestic law of the Contracting States.

The competent authorities of the Contracting States shall endeavour to resolve by mutual agreement any difficulties or doubts arising as to the interpretation or application of the Agreement. They may also consult together for the elimination of double taxation in cases not provided for in this Agreement.

The competent authorities of the Contracting States may communicate with each other directly for the purpose of reaching an agreement in the sense of paragraphs 2 and 3 of this Article. When it seems advisable for reaching agreement, representatives of the competent authorities of the Contracting State may meet together for an oral exchange of opinions.

Article 26 Exchange of Information

The competent authorities of the Contracting States shall exchange such information as is necessary for carrying out the provisions of this Agreement or of the domestic laws of the Contracting States concerning taxes covered by the Agreement insofar as the taxation thereunder is not contrary to this Agreement, in particular for the prevention of evasion of such taxes. The exchange of information is not restricted by Article 1. Any information received by a Contracting State shall be treated as secret in the same manner as information obtained under the domestic laws of that State and shall be disclosed only to persons or authorities (including courts and administrative bodies) involved in the assessment or collection of, the enforcement or prosecution in respect of, or the determination of appeals in relation to, the taxes covered by the Agreement. Such persons or authorities shall use the information only for such purposes. They may disclose the information in public court proceedings or in judicial decisions.

In no case the provisions of paragraph 1 of this Article shall be construed so as to impose on the competent authority of a Contracting State the obligation:

to carry out administrative measures at variance with the laws and the administrative practice of that or of the other Contracting State;
to supply information which is not obtainable under the laws or in the normal course of the administration of that or of the other Contracting State;
to supply information which would disclose any trade, business, industrial, commercial, professional or official secret or trade process, or information, the disclosure of which would be contrary to public policy (order public).

Article 27 Diplomatic Agents and Consular Officers

Nothing in this Agreement shall affect the fiscal privileges of diplomatic agents or consular officers under the general rules of international law or under the provisions of special agreements.

Article 28 Entry into Force

This Agreement shall enter into force on the thirtieth day after the date on which diplomatic notes indicating the completion of internal legal procedures necessary in each country for the entry into force of this Agreement have been exchanged. This Agreement shall have effect as respects income derived during the taxable years beginning on or after the first day of January next following that in which this Agreement enters into force.

Article 29 Termination

This Agreement shall continue in effect indefinitely but either of the Contracting State may, on or before the thirtieth day of June in any calendar year beginning after the expiration of a period of five years from the date of its entry into force, give written notice of termination to the other Contracting State through the diplomatic channel. In such event this Agreement shall cease to have effect as respects income derived during the taxable years beginning on or after the first day of January in the calendar year next following that in which the notice of termination is given.

DONE at Beijing on the 7th day of June, 1988, in duplicate in the Chinese, Polish, and English languages, the three texts being equally authentic, in case of any divergence of interpretation, the English text shall prevail.

On behalf of the Government of the People's Republic of China.

On behalf of the Government of the Polish People's Republic.

Portugal

Portugal, officially the Federal Republic of Germany, is a state in Southern Europe. Portugal borders with Spain to the east and with the Atlantic Ocean to the west. Portugal's capital and largest city is Lisbon.

Portuguese are the majority ethnic group. Portugal has experienced a steady immigration from Africa, especially from Cape Verde, Angola and Guinea-Bissau, but also São Tomé and Príncipe, Mozambique, and former Portuguese India in Asia.

The official and predominant spoken language is Portuguese. Recognized minority language is Mirandês.

Portugal is a unitary semi-presidential constitutional republic. The Constitution of Portugal regulates the political system, in force since 1933. The Assembly of the Republic exerts the legislative power forming the parliament. The Assembly of the Republic is elected through direct elections using the closed-list representation system.

Executive power is vested in the Prime Minister and his or her cabinet. The Prime Minister is appointed by the President of the Republic after being elected by the party or coalition with the parliamentary majority in the Assembly of the Republic.

Portugal has a civil law system based on Roman law. The Supremo Tribunal de Justiça acts as Supreme Court, managing constitutional matters, with judicial review powers.

Portugal is a unitary state, divided into 308 municipalities.

Portugal has been part of the European Union since 1986.

Category	Value
International Monetary Fund (mln persons)	10.265
Currency	Euro

Source International Monetary Fund, year 2019

Portugal is the third largest economy of Southern Europe, with a GDP valued 236.4 billion USD in 2019, and has a population of about 10.3 million people. Portugal enjoys low inflation (0.3%), while unemployment is over 6% (6.5%). Portugal ranked

© The Author(s), under exclusive license to Springer Nature Singapore Pte Ltd. 2022
L. Riccardi and G. Riccardi, *China–Europe Tax Treaties*,
https://doi.org/10.1007/978-981-19-3563-3_22

18 out of 43 in the 2020 Doing Business ranking, scoring 76.5, and imposes a CIT of 21%. Portugal records a trade deficit of 22.8 billion USD.

GDP and local economy	
GDP current prices (billion USD)	236.4
GDP per capita (USD)	23,031
GDP growth (%)	2.2
Inflation (%)	0.3
Unemployment (%)	6.5
General government total expenditure (% of GDP)	42.5
General government gross debt (% of GDP)	116.8
Doing business score 2020	76.5

Source International Monetary Fund and UNCTAD, year 2019

Foreign direct investment	
FDI outstock (million USD)	58,077
FDI instock (million USD)	161,640

Source UNCTAD, year 2019

Trade	
Imports (million USD)	89,924
Exports (million USD)	67,060
Trade balance (million USD)	−22,864

Source International Monetary Fund and UNCTAD, year 2019

Main import–export	
First import by category	Vehicles other than railway, tramway
Second import by category	Electrical, electronic equipment
First export by category	Vehicles other than railway, tramway
Second export by category	Electrical, electronic equipment

Source United Nations COMTRADE, year 2020

The legal bases for taxation are established in the constitution. Portugal imposes individual income tax, property sales taxes, capital gains, corporate income tax, and value added tax. Progressivity is guaranteed by a system with different bands and various deductions.

Taxes	
Company income tax (%)	21
Top individual income tax (%)	48
Value added tax or sales tax (%)	23
Reduced value added tax or sales tax (%)	6/13

Source RsA Asia report, year 2021

- Economic Relation with China

Portugal records a trade deficit to China of 1.4 billion USD in 2020. "Electrical, electronic equipment" is the first export category, worth 1.12 billion USD, followed by "Vehicles other than railway, tramway". "Electrical, electronic equipment" is the first import category, valued 997 million USD. Portugal is part of the Belt and Road Initiative. In 1998 Portugal and China have signed their DTA, which has come into force in June 2000.

Category	Value
Belt road	Yes

Source UNCTAD, year 2021

Import from China	
Import from China (billion USD)	4.19
First import category from China	Electrical, electronic equipment
First import value (billion USD)	0.997
Second import category from China	Machinery, nuclear reactors, boilers
Second import value (billion USD)	0.673

Source United Nations COMTRADE, year 2020

Export to China	
Export to China (billion USD)	2.77
First export category towards China	Electrical, electronic equipment
First export value (billion USD)	1.12
Second export category towards China	Vehicles other than railway, tramway
Second export value (billion USD)	0.588

Source United Nations COMTRADE, year 2020

Trade balance	
Trade balance (billion USD)	−1.42

Source United Nations COMTRADE, year 2020

Double tax agreement	
DTA effective date	2000.6.7
Dividends (%)	10
Interest (%)	0–10
Royalties (%)	10

Source State Administration of Taxation of China, year 2021

Title AGREEMENT BETWEEN THE GOVERNMENT OF THE PEOPLE'S REPUBLIC OF CHINA AND THE GOVERNMENT OF THE PORTUGUESE REPUBLIC FOR THE AVOIDANCE OF DOUBLE TAXATION AND THE PREVENTION OF FISCAL EVASION WITH RESPECT TO TAXES ON INCOME

Treaty Text

The Government of the People's Republic of China and the Government of the Portuguese Republic,

Desiring to conclude an Agreement for the avoidance of double taxation and the prevention of fiscal evasion with respect to taxes on income,

Have agreed as follows:

Article 1 Personal Scope

This Agreement shall apply to persons who are residents of one or both of the Contracting States.

Article 2 Taxes Covered

This Agreement shall apply to taxes on income imposed on behalf of a Contracting State or of its administrative subdivisions or local authorities, irrespective of the manner in which they are levied.

There shall be regarded as taxes on income all taxes imposed on total income, or on elements of income, including taxes on gains from the alienation of movable or immovable property, as well as taxes on capital appreciation.

The existing taxes to which this Agreement shall apply are:

in the case of China:
the individual income tax;
the income tax for enterprises with foreign investment and foreign enterprises; and.
the local income tax;
(hereinafter referred to as "Chinese tax");

in the case of Portugal:

Personal income tax (Imposto sobre o Rendimento das Pessoas Singulares-IRS);
Corporate income tax (Imposto sobre o Rendimento das Pessoas Colectivas-IRC); and
Local surtax on corporate income tax (Derrama); (hereinafter referred to as "Portuguese tax").

The Agreement shall also apply to any identical or substantially similar taxes which are imposed after the date of signature of the Agreement in addition to, or in place of, the existing taxes referred to in paragraph 3. The competent authorities of the Contracting States shall notify each other of any substantial changes which have been made in their respective taxation laws within a reasonable period of time after such changes.

Article 3 General Definitions
For the purposes of this Agreement, unless the context otherwise requires:

the term "China" means the People's Republic of China; when used in geographical sense, means all the territory of the People's Republic of China, including its territorial sea, in which the Chinese laws relating to taxation apply, and any area beyond its territorial sea, within which the People's Republic of China has sovereign rights of exploration for and exploitation of resources of the sea-bed and its sub-soil and superjacent water resources in accordance with international law;
the term "Portugal" means the Portuguese Republic; when used in a geographical sense, means all the territory of the Portuguese Republic;
situated in the European continent, the archipelagos of Azores and Madeira, the respective territorial sea and any other zone in which, in accordance with the laws of Portugal and international law, the Portuguese Republic has its jurisdiction or sovereign rights with respect to the exploration and exploitation of the natural resources of the sea-bed and sub-soil, and of the superjacent waters;
the terms "a Contracting State" and "the other Contracting State" mean China or Portugal, as the context requires;
the term "tax" means Chinese tax or Portuguese tax, as the context requires;
the term "person" includes an individual, a company and any other body of persons;
the term "company" means anybody corporate or any entity which is treated as a body corporate for tax purposes;

the terms "enterprise of a Contracting State" and "enterprise of the other Contracting State" mean, respectively, an enterprise carried on by a resident of a Contracting State and an enterprise carried on by a resident of the other Contracting State;
the term "national" means:
all individuals possessing the nationality of a Contracting State;
all legal persons, partnerships and associations deriving their status as such from the laws in force in a Contracting State;
(i) the term "international traffic" means any transport by a ship or aircraft operated by an enterprise of a Contracting State, except when the ship or aircraft is operated solely between places in the other Contracting State;
the term "competent authority" means:
in the case of China, the State Administration of Taxation or its authorised representative;
in the case of Portugal, the Minister of Finance, the Director-General of Taxation (Director-Geral dos Impostos) or their authorised representative.

As regards the application of the Agreement by a Contracting State any term not defined therein shall, unless the context otherwise requires, have the meaning which it has under the law of that Contracting State concerning the taxes to which the Agreement applies.

Article 4 Resident

For the purposes of this Agreement, the term "resident of a Contracting State" means any person who, under the laws of that State, is liable to tax therein by reason of his domicile, residence, place of head office, place of effective management or any other criterion of a similar nature.

This term, however, does not include any person who is liable to tax in that State in respect only of income from sources in that State.

Where by reason of the provisions of paragraph 1 an individual is a resident of both Contracting States, then his status shall be determined as follows:

he shall be deemed to be a resident of the Contracting State in which he has a permanent home available to him; if he has a permanent home available to him in both Contracting States, he shall be deemed to be a resident of the Contracting State with which his personal and economic relations are closer (centre of vital interests);
if the State in which he has his centre of vital interests cannot be determined, or if he has not a permanent home available to him in either Contracting State, he shall be deemed to be a resident of the State in which he has an habitual abode;
if he has an habitual abode in both Contracting States or in neither of them, he shall be deemed to be a resident of the Contracting State of which he is a national;
if he is a national of both Contracting States or of neither of them, the competent authorities of the Contracting States shall settle the question by mutual agreement.

Where by reason of the provisions of paragraph 1, a person other than an individual is a resident of both Contracting States, then it shall be deemed to be a resident of the State in which the place of effective management of its business is situated. However, where such a person has the place of effective management of its business in one of the Contracting States and the place of head office of its business in the other Contracting State, then the competent authorities of the Contracting States shall determine by mutual agreement the State of which the person shall be deemed to be resident for the purposes of this Agreement.

Article 5 Permanent Establishment

For the purposes of this Agreement, the term "permanent establishment" means a fixed place of business through which the business of an enterprise is wholly or partly carried on.

The term "permanent establishment" includes especially:

a place of management;
a branch;
an office;
a factory;
a workshop; and
a mine, an oil or gas well, a quarry or any other place of extraction of natural resources.

The term "permanent establishment" likewise encompasses:

a building site, a construction, assembly or installation project or supervisory activities in connection therewith, but only where such site, project or activities continue for a period of more than 6 months;
the furnishing of services, including consultancy services, by an enterprise of a Contracting State through employees or other engaged personnel in the other Contracting State, provided that such activities continue for the same project or a connected project for a period or periods aggregating more than 6 months within any 12-month period.

Notwithstanding the provisions of paragraphs 1 to 3, the term "permanent establishment" shall be deemed not to include:

the use of facilities solely for the purpose of storage, display or delivery of goods or merchandise belonging to the enterprise;
the maintenance of a stock of goods or merchandise belonging to the enterprise solely for the purpose of storage, display or delivery;
the maintenance of a stock of goods or merchandise belonging to the enterprise solely for the purpose of processing by another enterprise;
the maintenance of a fixed place of business solely for the purpose of purchasing goods or merchandise or of collecting information, for the enterprise;
the maintenance of a fixed place of business solely for the purpose of carrying on, for the enterprise, any other activity of a preparatory or auxiliary character;

the maintenance of a fixed place of business solely for any combination of activities mentioned in sub-paragraphs (a) to (e), provided that the overall activity of the fixed place of business resulting from this combination is of a preparatory or auxiliary character.

Notwithstanding the provisions of paragraphs 1 and 2, where a person—other than an agent of an independent status to whom the provisions of paragraph 6 apply—is acting in a Contracting State on behalf of an enterprise of the other Contracting State, has and habitually exercises, an authority to conclude contracts in the name of the enterprise, that enterprise shall be deemed to have a permanent establishment in the first-mentioned Contracting State in respect of any activities which that person undertakes for the enterprise, unless the activities of such person are limited to those mentioned in paragraph 4 which, if exercised through a fixed place of business, would not make this fixed place of business a permanent establishment under the provisions of that paragraph.

An enterprise of a Contracting State shall not be deemed to have a permanent establishment in the other Contracting State merely because it carries on business in that other State through a broker, general commission agent or any other agent of an independent status, provided that such persons are acting in the ordinary course of their business.

The fact that a company which is a resident of a Contracting State controls or is controlled by a company which is a resident of the other Contracting State, or which carries on business in that other Contracting State (whether through a permanent establishment or otherwise), shall not of itself constitute either company a permanent establishment of the other.

Article 6 Income from Immovable Property

Income derived by a resident of a Contracting State from immovable property (including income from agriculture or forestry) situated in the other Contracting State may be taxed in that other Contracting State.

The term "immovable property" shall have the meaning which it has under the law of the Contracting State in which the property in question is situated. The term shall in any case include property accessory to immovable property, livestock and equipment used in agriculture and forestry, rights to which the provisions of general law respecting landed property apply, usufruct of immovable property and rights to variable or fixed payments as consideration for the working of, or the right to work, mineral deposits, sources and other natural resources. Ships and aircraft shall not be regarded as immovable property.

The provisions of paragraph 1 shall apply to income derived from the direct use, letting, or use in any other form of immovable property.

The provisions of paragraphs 1 and 3 shall also apply to the income from immovable property of an enterprise and to income from immovable property used for the performance of independent personal services.

Article 7 Business Profits

The profits of an enterprise of a Contracting State shall be taxable only in that State unless the enterprise carries on business in the other Contracting State through a permanent establishment situated therein. If the enterprise carries on business as aforesaid, the profits of the enterprise may be taxed in the other State, but only so much of them as is attributable to that permanent establishment.

Subject to the provisions of paragraph 3, where an enterprise of a Contracting State carries on business in the other Contracting State through a permanent establishment situated therein, there shall in each Contracting State be attributed to that permanent establishment the profits which it might be expected to make if it were a distinct and separate enterprise engaged in the same or similar activities under the same or similar conditions and dealing wholly independently with the enterprise of which it is a permanent establishment.

In determining the profits of a permanent establishment, there shall be allowed as deductions expenses which are incurred for the purposes of the business of the permanent establishment, including executive and general administrative expenses so incurred, whether in the State in which the permanent establishment is situated or elsewhere.

Insofar as it has been customary in a Contracting State to determine the profits to be attributed to a permanent establishment on the basis of an apportionment of the total profits of the enterprise to its various parts, nothing in paragraph 2 shall preclude that Contracting State from determining the profits to be taxed by such an apportionment as may be customary. The method of apportionment adopted shall, however, be such that the result shall be in accordance with the principles contained in this Article.

No profits shall be attributed to a permanent establishment by reason of the mere purchase by that permanent establishment of goods or merchandise for the enterprise.

For the purposes of paragraphs 1 to 5, the profits to be attributed to the permanent establishment shall be determined by the same method year by year unless there is good and sufficient reason to the contrary.

Where profits include items of income which are dealt with separately in other Articles of this Agreement, then the provisions of those Articles shall not be affected by the provisions of this Article.

Article 8 Shipping and Air Transport

Profits from the operation of ships or aircraft in international traffic by an enterprise of a Contracting State shall be taxable only in that Contracting State.

If the place of head office or the place of effective management of a shipping enterprise is aboard a ship, then it shall be deemed to be situated in the Contracting State in which the home harbour of the ship is situated, or, if there is no such home harbour, in the Contracting State of which the operator of the ship is a resident.

The provisions of paragraph 1 shall also apply to profits from the participation in a pool, a joint business or an international operating agency.

Article 9 Associated Enterprises
Where

an enterprise of a Contracting State participates directly or indirectly in the management, control or capital of an enterprise of the other Contracting State, or the same persons participate directly or indirectly in the management, control or capital of an enterprise of a Contracting State and an enterprise of the other Contracting State,
and in either case conditions are made or imposed between the two enterprises in their commercial or financial relations which differ from those which would be made between independent enterprises, then any profits which would, but for those conditions, have accrued to one of the enterprises, but, by reason of those conditions, have not so accrued, may be included in the profits of that enterprise and taxed accordingly.

Where a Contracting State includes in the profits of an enterprise of that Contracting State—and taxes accordingly—profits on which an enterprise of the other Contracting State has been charged to tax in that other Contracting State and the profits so included are profits which would have accrued to the enterprise of the first-mentioned State if the conditions made between the two enterprises had been those which would have been made between independent enterprises, then that other Contracting State shall make an appropriate adjustment to the amount of the tax charged therein on those profits, where that other Contracting State considers such adjustment justified. In determining such adjustment, due regard shall be had to the other provisions of this Agreement and the competent authorities of the Contracting States shall, if necessary, consult each other.

Article 10 Dividends
Dividends paid by a company which is a resident of a Contracting State to a resident of the other Contracting State may be taxed in that other State.

However, such dividends may also be taxed in the Contracting State of which the company paying the dividends is a resident and according to the laws of that State, but if the recipient is the beneficial owner of the dividends the tax so charged shall not exceed 10% of the gross amount of the dividends The provisions of this paragraph shall not affect the taxation of the company in respect of the profits out of which the dividends are paid.

The term "dividends" as used in this Article means income from shares or other rights, not being debt-claims, participating in profits, as well as income from other corporate rights which is subjected to the same taxation treatment as income from shares by the laws of the State of which the company making the distribution is a resident.

The provisions of paragraphs 1 and 2 shall not apply if the beneficial owner of the dividends, being a resident of a Contracting State, carries on business in the other Contracting State of which the company paying the dividends is a resident, through a permanent establishment situated therein, or performs in that other State independent personal services from a fixed base situated therein, and the holding in respect of which the dividends are paid is effectively connected with such permanent establishment or fixed base. In such case the provisions of Article 7 or Article 14, as the case may be, shall apply.

Where a company which is a resident of a Contracting State derives profits or income from the other Contracting State, that other Contracting State may not impose any tax on the dividends paid by the company, except insofar as such dividends are paid to a resident of that other Contracting State or insofar as the holding in respect of which the dividends are paid is effectively connected with a permanent establishment or a fixed base situated in that other Contracting State, nor subject the company's undistributed profits to a tax on the company's undistributed profits, even if the dividends paid or the undistributed profits consist wholly or partly of profits or income arising in such other Contracting State.

Article 11 Interest

Interest arising in a Contracting State and paid to a resident of the other Contracting State may be taxed in that other Contracting State.

However, such interest may also be taxed in the Contracting State in which it arises and according to the laws of that Contracting State, but if the recipient is the beneficial owner of the interest the tax so charged shall not exceed 10% of the gross amount of the interest.

Notwithstanding the provisions of paragraph 2, interest arising in a Contracting State shall be exempt from tax in that Contracting State, where the interest is paid to:

in China:

the Government of the People's Republic of China, an administrative subdivision or a local authority thereof;
the People's Bank of China;
the State Development Bank;
the Import and Export Bank of China;
the Agriculture Development Bank of China;
any other institution wholly owned by the Government of china or an administrative subdivision or a local authority thereof as may be agreed from time to time between the competent authorities of the Contracting States;

in Portugal:

the Government of the Portuguese Republic, an administrative subdivision or a local authority thereof;
the General Deposits Bank (Caixa Geral de Depositos-CGD);
the National Overseas Bank (Banco Nacional Ultramarino-BNU);
Investment, Trade and Tourism of Portugal (ICEP-Investimentos, Comercio e Turismo de Portugal);

any other institution wholly owned by the Government of Portugal or an administrative subdivision or a local authority thereof as may be agreed from time to time between the competent authorities of the Contracting States.

The term "interest" as used in this Article means income from debt-claims of every kind, whether or not secured by mortgage and whether or not carrying a right to participate in the debtor's profits, and in particular, income from government securities and income from bonds or debentures, including premiums and prizes attaching to such securities, bonds or debentures. Penalty charges for late payment shall not be regarded as interest for the purpose of this Article.

The provisions of paragraphs 1, 2 and 3 shall not apply if the beneficial owner of the interest, being a resident of a Contracting State, carries on business in the other Contracting State in which the interest arises, through a permanent establishment situated therein, or performs in that other Contracting State independent personal services from a fixed base situated therein, and the debt-claim in respect of which the interest is paid is effectively connected with such permanent establishment or fixed base. In such case the provisions of Article 7 or Article 14, as the case may be, shall apply.

Interest shall be deemed to arise in a Contracting State when the payer is that State, an administrative subdivision or a local authority thereof or a resident of that Contracting State. Where, however, the person paying the interest, whether he is a resident of a Contracting State or not, has in a Contracting State a permanent establishment or a fixed base in connection with which the indebtedness on which the interest is paid was incurred, and such interest is borne by such permanent establishment or fixed base, then such interest shall be deemed to arise in the State in which the permanent establishment or fixed base is situated.

Where, by reason of a special relationship between the payer and the beneficial owner or between both of them and some other person, the amount of the interest, having regard to the debt-claim for which it is paid, exceeds the amount which would have been agreed upon by the payer and the beneficial owner in the absence of such relationship, the provisions of this Article shall apply only to the last-mentioned amount. In such case, the excess part of the payments shall remain taxable according to the laws of each Contracting State, due regard being had to the other provisions of this Agreement.

Article 12 Royalties

Royalties arising in a Contracting State and paid to a resident of the other Contracting State may be taxed in that other Contracting State.

However, such royalties may also be taxed in the Contracting State in which they arise, and according to the laws of that State, but if the recipient is the beneficial owner of the royalties the tax so charged shall not exceed 10% of the gross amount of the royalties.

The term "royalties" as used in this Article means payments of any kind received as a consideration for the use of, or the right to use, any copyright of literary, artistic or scientific work including cinematographic films, or films or tapes for radio or television broadcasting, any patent, trade mark, design or model, plan, secret formula or process, or for the use of, or the right to use, industrial, commercial or scientific equipment, or for information concerning industrial, commercial or scientific experience.

The provisions of paragraphs 1 and 2 shall not apply if the beneficial owner of the royalties, being a resident of a Contracting State, carries on business in the other Contracting State in which the royalties arise, through a permanent establishment situated therein, or performs in that other State independent personal services from a fixed base situated therein, and the right or property in respect of which the royalties are paid is effectively connected with such permanent establishment or fixed base. In such case the provisions of Article 7 or Article 14, as the case may be, shall apply.

Royalties shall be deemed to arise in a Contracting State when the payer is that Contracting State, an administrative subdivision or a local authority thereof or a resident of that Contracting State. Where, however, the person paying the royalties, whether he is a resident of a Contracting State or not, has in a Contracting State a permanent establishment or a fixed base in connection with which the liability to pay the royalties was incurred, and such royalties are borne by such permanent establishment or fixed base, then such royalties shall be deemed to arise in the Contracting State in which the permanent establishment or fixed base is situated.

Where, by reason of a special relationship between the payer and the beneficial owner or between both of them and some other person, the amount of the royalties, having regard to the use, right or information for which they are paid, exceeds the amount which would have been agreed upon by the payer and the beneficial owner in the absence of such relationship the provisions of this Article shall apply only to the last-mentioned amount. In such case, the excess part of the payments shall remain taxable according to the laws of each Contracting State, due regard being had to the other provisions of this Agreement.

Article 13 Capital Gains

Gains derived by a resident of a Contracting State from the alienation of immovable property referred to in Article 6 and situated in the other Contracting State may be taxed in that other Contracting State.

Gains from the alienation of movable property forming part of the business property of a permanent establishment which an enterprise of a Contracting State has in the other Contracting State or of movable property pertaining to a fixed base available to a resident of a Contracting State in the other Contracting State for the purpose of performing independent personal services, including such gains from the alienation of such a permanent establishment (alone or with the whole enterprise) or of such fixed base, may be taxed in that other State.

Gains of an enterprise of a Contracting State from the alienation of ships or aircraft operated in international traffic or movable property pertaining to the operation of such ships or aircraft shall be taxable only in that Contracting State.

Gains from the alienation of shares of the capital stock of a company the property of which consists principally of immovable property situated in a Contracting State may be taxed in that Contracting State.

Gains from the alienation of any property other than that referred to in paragraphs 1 to 4, shall be taxable only in the Contracting State of which the alienator is a resident.

Article 14 Independent Personal Services

Income derived by a resident of a Contracting State in respect of professional services or other activities of an independent character shall be taxable only in that State except in one of the following circumstances, when such income may also be taxed in the other Contracting State:

if he has a fixed base regularly available to him in the other Contracting State for the purpose of performing his activities; in that case, only so much of the income as is attributable to that fixed base may be taxed in that other State;

if his stay in the other Contracting State is for a period or periods amounting to or exceeding in the aggregate 183 days in the calendar year concerned; in that case, only so much of the income as is derived from his activities performed in that other State may be taxed in that other State.

The term "professional services" includes especially independent scientific, literary, artistic, educational or teaching activities as well as the independent activities of physicians, lawyers, engineers, architects, dentists and accountants.

Article 15 Dependent Personal Services

Subject to the provisions of Articles 16, 18, 19 and 20, salaries, wages and other similar remuneration derived by a resident of a Contracting State in respect of an employment shall be taxable only in that State unless the employment is exercised in the other Contracting State. If the employment is so exercised, such remuneration as is derived therefrom may be taxed in that other Contracting State.

Notwithstanding the provisions of paragraph 1, remuneration derived by a resident of a Contracting State in respect of an employment exercised in the other Contracting State shall be taxable only in the first-mentioned State if:

the recipient is present in the other Contracting State for a period or periods not exceeding in the aggregate 183 days in the calendar year concerned; and

the remuneration is paid by, or on behalf of, an employer who is not a resident of the other Contracting State; and

the remuneration is not borne by a permanent establishment or a fixed base which the employer has in the other Contracting State.

Notwithstanding the preceding provisions of this Article, remuneration derived in respect of an employment exercised aboard a ship or aircraft operated in international traffic by an enterprise of a Contracting State, may be taxed in that Contracting State.

Article 16 Directors' Fees

Directors' fees and other similar payments derived by a resident of a Contracting State in his capacity as a member of the board of directors of a company which is a resident of the other Contracting State may be taxed in that other Contracting State.

Salaries, wages and other similar remuneration derived by a resident of a Contracting State in his capacity as an official in a top-level managerial position of a company which is a resident of the other Contracting State may be taxed in that other Contracting State.

Article 17 Artistes and Sportsperson

Notwithstanding the provisions of Articles 14 and 15, income derived by a resident of a Contracting State as an entertainer, such as a theatre, motion picture, radio or television artist, or a musician, or as a sportsman, from his personal activities as such exercised in the other Contracting State, may be taxed in that other Contracting State.

Where income in respect of personal activities exercised by an entertainer or a sportsman in his capacity as such accrues not to the entertainer or sportsman himself but to another person, that income may, notwithstanding the provisions of Articles 7, 14 and 15, be taxed in the Contracting State in which the activities of the entertainer or sportsman are exercised.

Notwithstanding the provisions of paragraphs 1 and 2 of this Article, income mentioned in this Article shall be exempt from tax in the Contracting State in which the activity of the entertainer or sportsman is exercised provided that this activity is mainly supported by this Contracting State or by the other Contracting State or the activity is exercised under a cultural agreement or arrangement between the Contracting States.

Article 18 Pensions

Subject to the provisions of paragraph 2 of Article 19, pensions and other similar remuneration paid to a resident of a Contracting State in consideration of past employment shall be taxable only in that Contracting State.

Article 19 Government Service

(a) Salaries, wages and other similar remuneration, other than a pension, paid by the Government of a Contracting State or an administrative subdivision or a local authority thereof to an individual in respect of services rendered to that Contracting State or subdivision or authority thereof shall be taxable only in that Contracting State.

However, such salaries, wages and other similar remuneration shall be taxable only in the other Contracting State if the services are rendered in that other Contracting State and the individual is a resident of that other Contracting State who:

is a national of that Contracting State; or

did not become a resident of that Contracting State solely for the purpose of rendering the services.

(a) Any pension paid by, or out of funds created by the Government of a Contracting State or an administrative subdivision or a local authority thereof to an individual in respect of services rendered to that Contracting State or subdivision or authority thereof shall be taxable only in that Contracting State.
(b) However, such pension shall be taxable only in the other Contracting State if the individual is a resident of, and a national of, that other Contracting State.

The provisions of Articles 15, 16, 17 and 18 shall apply to salaries, wages and other similar remuneration, and to pensions, in respect of services rendered in connection with a business carried on by the Government of a Contracting State or an administrative subdivision or a local authority thereof.

Article 20 Teachers and Researchers
An individual who is, or immediately before visiting a Contracting State, was a resident of the other Contracting State and who is present in the first-mentioned State solely for the purpose of teaching, giving lectures of conducting research at a university, college, school or other similar educational institution or scientific research institution accredited by the Government of the first-mentioned Contracting State and is recognised as non-profitable by that Government of the first-mentioned Contracting State or under an official programme of cultural exchange shall be exempt from tax in the first-mentioned Contracting State, for a period of three years from the date of his first arrival in the first-mentioned Contracting State, in respect of remuneration for such teaching, lectures or research.

The exemption granted under paragraph 1 shall not apply to income from research if such research is undertaken not in the public interest but primarily for the private benefit of a specific person or persons.

Article 21 Students and Trainees
A student, business apprentice or trainee who is or was immediately before visiting a Contracting State a resident of the other Contracting State and who is present in the first-mentioned State solely for the purpose of his education or training shall be exempt from tax in that first-mentioned State on the following payments or income received or derived by him for the purpose of his maintenance, education or training:

payments derived from sources outside that Contracting State for the purpose of his maintenance, education, study, research or training;
grants, scholarships or awards supplied by the Government, or a scientific, educational, cultural or other tax-exempt organisation.

Article 22 Other Income
Items of income of a resident of a Contracting State, wherever arising, not dealt with in the foregoing Articles of this Agreement shall be taxable only in that Contracting State.

The provisions of paragraph 1 shall not apply to income, other than income from immovable property as defined in paragraph 2 of Article 6, if the recipient of such income, being a resident of a Contracting State, carries on business in the other Contracting State through a permanent establishment situated therein, or performs in that other State independent personal services from a fixed base situated therein, and the right or property in respect of which the income is paid is effectively connected with such permanent establishment or fixed base. In such case the provisions of Article 7 or Article 14, as the case may be, shall apply.

Article 23 Methods for Elimination of Double Taxation

In China, double taxation shall be eliminated as follows:

Where a resident of China derives income from Portugal the amount of tax on that income payable in Portugal in accordance with the provisions of this Agreement, may be credited against the Chinese tax imposed on that resident. The amount of the credit, however, shall not exceed the amount of the Chinese tax on that income computed in accordance with the taxation laws and regulations of China.

Where the income derived from Portugal is a dividend paid by a company which is a resident of Portugal to a company which is a resident of China and which owns not less than 10% of the shares of the company paying the dividend, the credit shall take into account the tax paid to Portugal by the company paying the dividend in respect of its income.

In Portugal, double taxation shall be eliminated as follows:

Where a resident of Portugal derives income which, in accordance with the provisions of this Agreement, may be taxed in China, Portugal shall allow as a deduction from the tax on the income of that resident an amount equal to the income tax paid in China; such deduction shall not, however, exceed that part of the income tax as computed before the deduction is given, which is attributable to the income which may be taxed in China; and

Where in accordance with any provision of this Agreement income derived by a resident of Portugal is exempt from tax in this State, Portugal may nevertheless, in calculating the amount of tax on the remaining income of such resident, take into account the exempted income.

The tax paid in a Contracting State mentioned in paragraphs 1 and 2 shall be deemed to include the tax which would have been payable but for the legal provisions concerning tax reduction, exemption or other tax incentives for a limited period of time in accordance with the laws of that State for the promotion of economic development.

The provisions of this paragraph shall apply only to the income foreseen in Articles 7, 10, 11 and 12 and for the period of the first ten years during which this Agreement is effective. This period may be extended by mutual agreement between the competent authorities of the Contracting States.

Article 24 Non-discrimination

Nationals of a Contracting State shall not be subjected in the other Contracting State to any taxation or any requirement connected therewith, which is other or more

burdensome than the taxation and connected requirements to which nationals of that other State in the same circumstances, in particular with respect to residence, are or may be subjected. This provision shall, notwithstanding the provisions of Article 1, also apply to persons who are not residents of one or both of the Contracting States.

The taxation on a permanent establishment which an enterprise of a Contracting State has in the other Contracting State shall not be less favourably levied in that other State than the taxation levied on enterprises of that other State carrying on the same activities. This provision shall not be construed as obliging a Contracting State to grant to residents of the other Contracting State any personal allowances, reliefs and reductions for taxation purposes on account of civil status or family responsibilities which it grants to its own residents.

Except where the provisions of paragraph 1 of Article 9, paragraph 7 of Article 11, or paragraph 6 of Article 12, apply, interest, royalties and other disbursements paid by an enterprise of a Contracting State to a resident of the other Contracting State shall, for the purpose of determining the taxable profits of such enterprise, be deductible under the same conditions as if they had been paid to a resident of the first-mentioned State.

Enterprises of a Contracting State, the capital of which is wholly or partly owned or controlled, directly or indirectly, by one or more residents of the other Contracting State, shall not be subjected in the first-mentioned State to any taxation or any requirement connected therewith which is other or more burdensome than the taxation and connected requirements to which other similar enterprises of the first-mentioned State are or may be subjected.

The provisions of this Article shall, notwithstanding the provisions of Article 2, apply to taxes of every kind and description.

Article 25 Mutual Agreement Procedure

Where a person considers that the actions of one or both of the Contracting States result or will result for him in taxation not in accordance with the provisions of this Agreement, he may, irrespective of the remedies provided by the domestic law of those States, present his case to the competent authority of the Contracting State of which he is a resident or, if his case comes under paragraph 1 of Article 24, to that of the Contracting State of which he is a national. The case must be presented within three years from the first notification of the action resulting in taxation not in accordance with the provisions of the Agreement.

The competent authority shall endeavour, if the objection appears to it to be justified and if it is not itself able to arrive at a satisfactory solution, to resolve the case by mutual agreement with the competent authority of the other Contracting State, with a view to the avoidance of taxation which is not in accordance with the Agreement. Any agreement reached shall be implemented notwithstanding any time limits in the domestic law of the Contracting States.

The competent authorities of the Contracting States shall endeavour to resolve by mutual agreement any difficulties or doubts arising as to the interpretation or application of the Agreement. They may also consult together for the elimination of double taxation in cases not provided for in the Agreement.

The competent authorities of the Contracting States may communicate with each other directly for the purpose of reaching an agreement in the sense of paragraphs 2 and 3. When it seems advisable for reaching agreement, representatives of the competent authorities of the Contracting States may meet together for an oral exchange of opinions.

Article 26 Exchange of Information

The competent authorities of the Contracting States shall exchange such information as is necessary for carrying out the provisions of this Agreement or of the domestic laws of the Contracting States concerning taxes covered by the Agreement, insofar as the taxation thereunder is not contrary to the Agreement, in particular for the prevention of evasion or avoidance of such taxes. The exchange of information is not restricted by Article 1. Any information received by a Contracting State shall be treated as secret in the same manner as information obtained under the domestic laws of that Contracting State and shall be disclosed only to persons or authorities (including courts and administrative bodies) concerned with the assessment or collection of, the enforcement or prosecution in respect of, or the determination of appeals in relation to, the taxes covered by the Agreement. Such persons or authorities shall use the information only for such purposes. They may disclose the information in public court proceedings or in judicial decisions.

In no case shall the provisions of paragraph 1 be construed so as to impose on a Contracting State the obligation:

to carry out administrative measures at variance with the laws and administrative practice of that or of the other Contracting State;

to supply information which is not obtainable under the laws or in the normal course of the administration of that or of the other Contracting State;

to supply information which would disclose any trade, business, industrial, commercial or professional secret or trade process, or information, the disclosure of which would be contrary to public policy (*ordre public*).

Article 27 Members of Diplomatic Missions and Consular Posts

Nothing in this Agreement shall affect the fiscal privileges of members of diplomatic missions or consular posts under the general rules of international law or under the provisions of special agreements.

Article 28 Entry into Force

This Agreement shall enter into force on the thirtieth day after the date on which diplomatic notes indicating the completion of internal legal procedures necessary in each country for the entry into force of this Agreement have been exchanged. This Agreement shall have effect:

in China:

in respect of income derived during the taxable years beginning on or after the first day of January in the calendar year next following that in which this Agreement enters into force;

in Portugal:

in respect of taxes withheld at source, the fact giving rise to them appearing on or after the first day of January in the calendar year next following that in which this Agreement enters into force; and
in respect of other taxes, as to income arising in any fiscal year beginning on or after the first day of January in the calendar year next following that in which this Agreement enters into force.

Article 29 Termination

This Agreement shall continue in effect indefinitely but either of the Contracting States may, on or before the thirtieth day of June in any calendar year beginning after the expiration of a period of five years from the date of its entry into force, give written notice of termination to the other Contracting State through the diplomatic channels. In such event, this Agreement shall cease to have effect:

in China:

in respect of income derived during the taxable years beginning on or after the first day of January in the calendar year next following that in which the notice of termination is given;

in Portugal:

in respect of taxes withheld at source, the fact giving rise to them appearing on or after the first day of January in the calendar year next following that in which the notice of termination is given;
in respect of other taxes, as to income arising in the fiscal year beginning on or after the first day of January in the calendar year next following that in which the notice of termination is given.

IN WITNESS WHEREOF the undersigned, being duly authorised thereto by their respective Governments, have signed this Agreement.

DONE in duplicate at Beijing this 21st day of April of the year 1998, in the Chinese, Portuguese and English languages, all texts being equally authentic. In case of divergency of interpretation, the English text shall prevail.

For the Government of the Portuguese Republic.

For the Government of the People's Republic of China.

Romania

Romania, officially the Republic of Romania, is a state in Eastern Europe. Romania borders Bulgaria to the south, Ukraine to the north, Hungary to the west, Serbia to the southwest, Moldova to the east and the Black Sea to the southeast. Romania's capital and largest city is Bucharest.

Romanians are the majority ethnic group, while Hungarians are the first major minority, followed by Romani.

The official and predominant spoken language is Romanian, while Hungarian, Vlax Romani, and Ukrainian are minority languages.

Romania is a unitary semi-presidential republic. The Constitution of Romania regulates the political system, in force since 1991, and amended in 2003. The Chamber of Deputies and the Senate exert the legislative power forming the parliament. The Chamber of Deputies and the Senate are elected through direct elections using the closed-list system.

Executive power is vested in the Prime Minister and his or her cabinet. The Prime Minister is appointed by the President of the Republic after being elected by the party or coalition with the parliamentary majority in the Chamber of Deputies and the Senate.

Romania has a civil law system based on Roman law. The High Court of Cassation and Justice acts as Supreme Court, managing constitutional matters, with judicial review powers.

Romania is a unitary state, divided into 41 counties and the municipality of Bucharest.

Romania has been part of the European Union since 2007.

Category	Value
Population (mln persons)	19.522
Currency	Romanian leu

Source International Monetary Fund, year 2019

© The Author(s), under exclusive license to Springer Nature Singapore Pte Ltd. 2022
L. Riccardi and G. Riccardi, *China–Europe Tax Treaties*,
https://doi.org/10.1007/978-981-19-3563-3_23

Romania is the fourth largest economy of Eastern Europe, following the Czech Republic, with a GDP valued 243.7 billion USD in 2019, and has a population of about 20 million people. Romania's inflation is 3.8%, while unemployment is almost 4% (3.9%). Romania ranked 32 out of 43 in the 2020 Doing Business ranking, scoring 73.3, and imposes a CIT of 16%. Romania records a trade deficit of almost 20 billion USD, it is the 19th main exporter in Europe.

GDP and local economy	
GDP current prices (billion USD)	243.7
GDP per capita (USD)	12,483
GDP growth (%)	4.1
Inflation (%)	3.8
Unemployment (%)	3.9
General government total expenditure (% of GDP)	33.4
General government gross debt (% of GDP)	36.8
Doing business score 2020	73.3

Source International Monetary Fund and UNCTAD, year 2019

Foreign direct investment	
FDI outstock (million USD)	1349
FDI instock (million USD)	97,095

Source UNCTAD, year 2019

Trade	
Imports (million USD)	96,530
Exports (million USD)	76,873
Trade balance (million USD)	−19,658

Source International Monetary Fund and UNCTAD, year 2019

Main import–export	
First import by category	Electrical, electronic equipment
Second import by category	Machinery, nuclear reactors, boilers
First export by category	Electrical, electronic equipment
Second export by category	Vehicles other than railway, tramway

Source United Nations COMTRADE, year 2020

The legal bases for taxation are established in the constitution. Romania imposes individual income tax, property sales taxes, capital gains, corporate income tax, and value added tax.

Taxes	
Company income tax (%)	16
Top individual income tax (%)	10
Value added tax or sales tax (%)	19
Reduced value added tax or sales tax (%)	5/9

Source RsA Asia report, year 2021

- Economic relation with China

Romania records a trade deficit of 2.49 billion USD in 2020. "Electrical, electronic equipment" is the first export category, worth 669 million USD, followed by "Machinery, nuclear reactors, boilers". "Electrical, electronic equipment" is also the first import category, valued 1.05 billion USD. Romania is part of the Belt and Road Initiative. In 1991 Romania and China signed their first DTA, entered into force in 1992. In 2016 a new agreement has been signed, which has entered into force in 2017.

Category	Value
Belt road	Yes

Source UNCTAD, year 2021

Import from China	
Import from China (billion USD)	5.13
First import category from China	Electrical, electronic equipment
First import Value (billion USD)	1.05
Second import category from China	Machinery, nuclear reactors, boilers
Second import value (billion USD)	1.03

Source United Nations COMTRADE, year 2020

Export to China	
Export to China (billion USD)	2.64
First export category towards China	Electrical, electronic equipment
First export value (billion USD)	0.669
Second export category towards China	Machinery, nuclear reactors, boilers
Second export value (billion USD)	0.368

Source United Nations COMTRADE, year 2020

Trade balance	
Trade balance (billion USD)	−2.49

Source United Nations COMTRADE, year 2020

Double tax agreement	
DTA effective date	2017.6.17
Dividends (%)	0–3
Interest (%)	0–3
Royalties (%)	3

Source State Administration of Taxation of China, year 2021

Title AGREEMENT BETWEEN THE GOVERNMENT OF THE PEOPLE'S REPUBLIC OF CHINA AND THE GOVERNMENT OF ROMANIA FOR THE AVOIDANCE OF DOUBLE TAXATION AND THE PREVENTION OF FISCAL EVASION WITH RESPECT TO TAXES ON INCOME

Treaty Text

The Government of the People's Republic of China and the Government of Romania;

Desiring to promote and strengthen the economic relations between the two countries on the basis of respecting the principles of national sovereignty and independence, equality in rights, mutual benefit and non-interference in domestic matters, have decided to conclude an Agreement for the avoidance of double taxation and the prevention of fiscal evasion with respect to taxes on income;

Have agreed as follows:

Article 1 Personal Scope

This Agreement shall apply to persons who are residents of one or both of the Contracting States.

Article 2 Taxes Covered

This Agreement shall apply to taxes on income imposed on by one of the Contracting States or by its territorial-administrative units, (i.e. local authorities) irrespective of the manner in which they are levied.

There shall be regarded as taxes on income all taxes imposed on total income, or on elements of income including taxes on gains from the alienation of movable or immovable property, as well as taxes on capital appreciation.

The existing taxes to which this Agreement shall apply are:

in the case of Romania:
the tax on income derived by individuals and corporate bodies;
the tax on the profits of foreign representation and companies with participations of foreign capital constituted under Romanian Law;
the tax on income realized from agricultural activities (hereinafter referred to as "Romanian tax").
in the case of the People's Republic of China: (i)
the individual income tax; (ii)
the income tax concerning joint ventures using Chinese and foreign investment; (iii)
the income tax concerning foreign enterprises; and (iv)
the local income tax (hereinafter referred to as "Chinese tax").

The Agreement shall also apply to any identical or substantially similar taxes which are imposed after the date of signature of this Agreement in addition to, or in place of, those referred to in paragraph 3. The competent authorities of the Contracting States shall notify each other of any substantial changes which have been made in their respective taxation laws, within a reasonable period of time after such changes.

Article 3 General Definitions
For the purposes of this Agreement, unless the context otherwise requires:

the terms "a Contracting State" and "the other Contracting State" mean the People's Republic of China or Romania, as the context requires;
the term "China" means the People's Republic of China; when used in geographical sense, means all the territory of the People's Republic of China, including its land territory, internal waters, territorial sea and the air space above them, in which the Chinese laws relating to taxation apply, and any area beyond its territorial sea, within which the People's Republic of China has sovereign rights or jurisdiction in accordance with international law and its internal law;
the term "Romania" means the state territory of Romania, including its territorial sea and air space above them, over which Romania exercises sovereignty, as well as the contiguous zone, the continental shelf and the exclusive economic zone over which Romania exercises sovereign rights and jurisdiction, in accordance with its legislation and with the rules and principles of international law;
the term "person" includes an individual, a company and any other body of persons;
the term "company" means any body corporate or any entity that is treated as a body corporate for tax purposes;
the terms "enterprise of a Contracting State" and "enterprise of the other Contracting State" mean respectively an enterprise carried on by a resident of a Contracting State and an enterprise carried on by a resident of the other Contracting State;

the term "international traffic" means any transport by a ship, aircraft, railway or road vehicle operated by an enterprise of a Contracting State, except when such transport is operated solely between places in the other Contracting State;
the term "competent authority" means:
in China, the State Administration of Taxation or its authorized representative;
in Romania, the Ministry of Public Finance or its authorized representative;
the term "national" means:

in China, any individual possessing the nationality of China and any legal person, partnership or association deriving its status as such from the laws in force in China;
in Romania, any individual possessing the Romanian citizenship in accordance with the laws of Romania and any legal person, body of persons and any other entity set up and deriving its status as such from the laws in force in Romania.

As regards the application of the Agreement at any time by a Contracting State, any term not defined therein shall, unless the context otherwise requires, have the meaning that it has at that time under the law of that State for the purposes of the taxes to which the Agreement applies, any meaning under the applicable tax laws of that State prevailing over a meaning given to the term under other laws of that State.

Article 4 Resident

For the purposes of this Agreement, the term "resident of a Contracting State" means any person who, under the laws of that State, is liable to tax therein by reason of his domicile, residence, place of incorporation, place of effective management, place of registration or any other criterion of a similar nature, and also includes that State and any political subdivision, local authority or administrative—territorial unit thereof. This term, however, does not include any person who is liable to tax in that State in respect only of income from sources in that State.

Where by reason of the provisions of paragraph 1 an individual is a resident of both Contracting States, then his status shall be determined as follows:

he shall be deemed to be a resident only of the State in which he has a permanent home available to him; if he has a permanent home available to him in both States, he shall be deemed to be a resident only of the State with which his personal and economic relations are closer (centre of vital interests);
if the State in which he has his centre of vital interests cannot be determined, or if he has not a permanent home available to him in either State, he shall be deemed to be a resident only of the State in which he has an habitual abode;
if he has an habitual abode in both States or in neither of them, he shall be deemed to be a resident only of the State of which he is a national;
if he is a national of both States or of neither of them, the competent authorities of the Contracting States shall settle the question by mutual agreement.

Where by reason of the provisions of paragraph 1 a person other than an individual is a resident of both Contracting States, then it shall be deemed to be a resident only of the State in which its place of effective management is situated.

Article 5 Permanent Establishment

For the purposes of this Agreement, the term "permanent establishment" means a fixed place of business through which the business of an enterprise is wholly or partly carried on.

The term "permanent establishment" includes especially:

a place of management;
a branch;
an office;
a factory;
a workshop; and
a mine, an oil or gas well, a quarry or any other place of extraction of natural resources.

The term "permanent establishment" also encompasses:

a building site or a construction, assembly or installation project, but only if it lasts more than twelve months;
the furnishing of services, including consultancy services, by an enterprise through employees or other personnel engaged by the enterprise for such purpose, but only if activities of that nature continue (for the same or a connected project) within a Contracting State for a period or periods aggregating more than 183 days within any twelve month period commencing or ending in the fiscal year concerned.

Notwithstanding the preceding provisions of this Article, the term "permanent establishment" shall be deemed not to include:

the use of facilities solely for the purpose of storage, display or delivery of goods or merchandise belonging to the enterprise;
the maintenance of a stock of goods or merchandise belonging to the enterprise solely for the purpose of storage, display or delivery;
the maintenance of a stock of goods or merchandise belonging to the enterprise solely for the purpose of processing by another enterprise;
the maintenance of a stock of goods or merchandise belonging to the enterprise, which is exhibited at a trade fair or exhibition, and which is sold by the enterprise at the end of such fair or exhibition;
the maintenance of a fixed place of business solely for the purpose of purchasing goods or merchandise or of collecting information, for the enterprise;
the maintenance of a fixed place of business solely for the purpose of carrying on, for the enterprise, any other activity of a preparatory or auxiliary character;

the maintenance of a fixed place of business solely for any combination of activities mentioned in sub-paragraphs (a) to (f), provided that the overall activity of the fixed place of business resulting from this combination is of a preparatory or auxiliary character.

Notwithstanding the provisions of paragraphs 1 and 2, where a person—other than an agent of an independent status to whom paragraph 6 applies—is acting on behalf of an enterprise and has, and habitually exercises, in a Contracting State an authority to conclude contracts in the name of the enterprise, that enterprise shall be deemed to have a permanent establishment in that State in respect of any activities which that person undertakes for the enterprise, unless the activities of such person are limited to those mentioned in paragraph 4 which, if exercised through a fixed place of business, would not make this fixed place of business a permanent establishment under the provisions of that paragraph.

An enterprise shall not be deemed to have a permanent establishment in a Contracting State merely because it carries on business in that State through a broker, general commission agent or any other agent of an independent status, provided that such persons are acting in the ordinary course of their business. Where, however, a person acts exclusively or almost exclusively on behalf of one or more enterprises to which it is closely related, that person shall not be considered to be an agent of an independent status within the meaning of this paragraph with respect to any such enterprise.

For the purposes of this Article, a person is closely related to an enterprise if, based on all the relevant facts and circumstances, one has control of the other or both are under the control of the same persons or enterprises. In any case, a person shall be considered to be closely related to an enterprise if one possesses directly or indirectly more than 50% of the beneficial interest in the other (or, in the case of a company, more than 50% t of the aggregate voting rights and value of the company's shares or of the beneficial equity interest in the company) or if another person possesses directly or indirectly more than 50% of the beneficial interest (or, in the case of a company, more than 50% of the aggregate voting rights and value of the company's shares or of the beneficial equity interest in the company) in the person and the enterprise.

The fact that a company which is a resident of a Contracting State controls or is controlled by a company which is a resident of the other Contracting State, or which carries on business in that other State (whether through a permanent establishment or otherwise), shall not of itself constitute either company a permanent establishment of the other.

Article 6 Income from Immovable Property

Income derived by a resident of a Contracting State from immovable property (including income from agriculture or forestry) situated in the other Contracting State may be taxed in that other State.

The term "immovable property" shall have the meaning which it has under the law of the Contracting State in which the property in question is situated. The term shall in any case include property accessory to immovable property, livestock and equipment used in agriculture and forestry, rights to which the provisions of general law respecting landed property apply, usufruct of immovable property and rights to variable or fixed payments as consideration for the working of, or the right to work, mineral deposits, sources and other natural resources; ships, aircraft, railway or road vehicles shall not be regarded as immovable property.

The provisions of paragraph 1 shall apply to income derived from the direct use, letting, or use in any other form of immovable property.

The provisions of paragraphs 1 and 3 shall also apply to the income from immovable property of an enterprise and to income from immovable property used for the performance of independent personal services.

Article 7 Business Profits

The profits of an enterprise of a Contracting State shall be taxable only in that State unless the enterprise carries on business in the other Contracting State through a permanent establishment situated therein. If the enterprise carries on business as aforesaid, the profits of the enterprise may be taxed in the other State, but only so much of them as is attributable to that permanent establishment.

Subject to the provisions of paragraph 3, where an enterprise of a Contracting State carries on business in the other Contracting State through a permanent establishment situated therein, there shall in each Contracting State be attributed to that permanent establishment the profits which it might be expected to make if it were a distinct and separate enterprise engaged in the same or similar activities under the same or similar conditions and dealing wholly independently with the enterprise of which it is a permanent establishment.

In determining the profits of a permanent establishment, there shall be allowed as deductions expenses which are incurred for the purposes of the permanent establishment, including executive and general administrative expenses so incurred, whether in the State in which the permanent establishment is situated or elsewhere.

Insofar as it has been customary in a Contracting State to determine the profits to be attributed to a permanent establishment on the basis of an apportionment of the total profits of the enterprise to its various parts, nothing in paragraph 2 shall preclude that Contracting State from determining the profits to be taxed by such an apportionment as may be customary; the method of apportionment adopted shall, however, be such that the result shall be in accordance with the principles contained in this Article.

No profits shall be attributed to a permanent establishment by reason of the mere purchase by that permanent establishment of goods or merchandise for the enterprise.

For the purposes of the preceding paragraphs, the profits to be attributed to the permanent establishment shall be determined by the same method year by year unless there is good and sufficient reason to the contrary.

Where profits include items of income which are dealt with separately in other Articles of this Agreement, then the provisions of those Articles shall not be affected by the provisions of this Article.

Article 8 International Transport
Profits derived by an enterprise of a Contracting State from the operation of ships, aircraft, railway or road vehicles in international traffic shall be taxable only in that Contracting State.

The provisions of paragraph 1 shall also apply to profits from the participation in a pool, a joint business or an international operating agency.

Article 9 Associated Enterprises
Where

> an enterprise of a Contracting State participates directly or indirectly in the management, control or capital of an enterprise of the other Contracting State, or the same persons participate directly or indirectly in the management, control or capital of an enterprise of a Contracting State and an enterprise of the other Contracting State,
> and in either case conditions are made or imposed between the two enterprises in their commercial or financial relations which differ from those which would be made between independent enterprises, then any profits which would, but for those conditions, have accrued to one of the enterprises, but, by reason of those conditions, have not so accrued, may be included in the profits of that enterprise and taxed accordingly.

Where a Contracting State includes in the profits of an enterprise of that State—and taxes accordingly—profits on which an enterprise of the other Contracting State has been charged to tax in that other State and the profits so included are profits which would have accrued to the enterprise of the first-mentioned State if the conditions made between the two enterprises had been those which would have been made between independent enterprises, then that other State shall make an appropriate adjustment to the amount of the tax charged therein on those profits. In determining such adjustment, due regard shall be had to the other provisions of this Agreement and the competent authorities of the Contracting States shall, if necessary, consult each other.

Article 10 Dividends
Dividends paid by a company which is a resident of a Contracting State to a resident of the other Contracting State may be taxed in that other State.

However, dividends paid by a company which is a resident of a Contracting State may also be taxed in that State according to the laws of that State, but if the beneficial owner of the dividends is a resident of the other Contracting State, the tax so charged shall not exceed 3% of the gross amount of the dividends.

Notwithstanding the provisions of paragraph 2, dividends arising in a Contracting State and paid to the other Contracting State or a political subdivision, local authority or administrative—territorial unit thereof, or any entity wholly or mainly owned by the other Contracting State, shall be exempt from tax in the first-mentioned State.

For the purposes of this paragraph, the term "mainly owned" means the ownership exceeds 50%.

The provisions of paragraphs 2 and 3 shall not affect the taxation of the company in respect of the profits out of which the dividends are paid.

The term "dividends" as used in this Article means income from shares or other rights, not being debt-claims, participating in profits, as well as income from other corporate rights which is subjected to the same taxation treatment as income from shares by the laws of the State of which the company making the distribution is a resident.

The provisions of paragraphs 1 and 2 shall not apply if the beneficial owner of the dividends, being a resident of a Contracting State, carries on business in the other Contracting State of which the company paying the dividends is a resident through a permanent establishment situated therein, or performs in that other State independent personal services from a fixed base situated therein, and the holding in respect of which the dividends are paid is effectively connected with such permanent establishment or fixed base. In such case the provisions of Article 7 or Article 14, as the case may be, shall apply.

Where a company which is a resident of a Contracting State derives profits or income from the other Contracting State, that other State may not impose any tax on the dividends paid by the company, except insofar as such dividends are paid to a resident of that other State or insofar as the holding in respect of which the dividends are paid is effectively connected with a permanent establishment or a fixed base situated in that other State, nor subject the company's undistributed profits to a tax on the company's undistributed profits, even if the dividends paid or the undistributed profits consist wholly or partly of profits or income arising in such other State.

The provisions of this Article shall not apply if it was the main purpose or one of the main purposes of any person concerned with the creation or assignment of the shares or other rights in respect of which the dividend is paid to take advantage of this Article by means of that creation or assignment.

Article 11 Interest

Interest arising in a Contracting State and paid to a resident of the other Contracting State may be taxed in that other State.

However, interest arising in a Contracting State may also be taxed in that State according to the laws of that State, but if the beneficial owner of the interest is a resident of the other Contracting State, the tax so charged shall not exceed 3% of the gross amount of the interest.

Notwithstanding the provisions of paragraph 2, interest arising in a Contracting State and beneficially owned by a resident of the other Contracting State shall be taxable only in that other State to the extent that such interest is paid:

in respect of indebtedness arising as a consequence of the sale on credit of any equipment, merchandise or services; or

on any loan of whatever kind granted by a financial institution of that other State; or

to that other State or a political subdivision, local authority or administrative—territorial unit thereof, or any entity wholly or mainly owned by that other State.

For the purposes of this paragraph, the term "mainly owned" means the ownership exceeds 50%.

The term "interest" as used in this Article means income from debt-claims of every kind, whether or not secured by mortgage and whether or not carrying a right to participate in the debtor's profits, and in particular, income from government securities and income from bonds or debentures, including premiums and prizes attaching to such securities, bonds or debentures. Penalty charges for late payment shall not be regarded as interest for the purpose of this Article.

The provisions of paragraphs 1 and 2 shall not apply if the beneficial owner of the interest, being a resident of a Contracting State, carries on business in the other Contracting State in which the interest arises through a permanent establishment situated therein, or performs in that other State independent personal services from a fixed base situated therein, and the debt-claim in respect of which the interest is paid is effectively connected with such permanent establishment or fixed base. In such case the provisions of Article 7 or Article 14, as the case may be, shall apply.

Interest shall be deemed to arise in a Contracting State when the payer is a resident of that State. Where, however, the person paying the interest, whether he is a resident of a Contracting State or not, has in a Contracting State a permanent establishment or a fixed base in connection with which the indebtedness on which the interest is paid was incurred, and such interest is borne by such permanent establishment or fixed base, then such interest shall be deemed to arise in the Contracting State in which the permanent establishment or fixed base is situated.

Where, by reason of a special relationship between the payer and the beneficial owner or between both of them and some other person, the amount of the interest, having regard to the debt-claim for which it is paid, exceeds the amount which would have been agreed upon by the payer and the beneficial owner in the absence of such relationship, the provisions of this Article shall apply only to the last-mentioned amount. In such case, the excess part of the payments shall remain taxable according to the laws of each Contracting State, due regard being had to the other provisions of this Agreement.

The provisions of this Article shall not apply if it was the main purpose or one of the main purposes of any person concerned with the creation or assignment of the debt-claim in respect of which the interest is paid to take advantage of this Article by means of that creation or assignment.

Article 12 Royalties

Royalties arising in a Contracting State and paid to a resident of the other Contracting State may be taxed in that other State.

However, royalties arising in a Contracting State may also be taxed in that State according to the laws of that State, but if the beneficial owner of the royalties is a resident of the other Contracting State, the tax so charged shall not exceed 3% of the gross amount of the royalties.

The term "royalties" as used in this Article means payments of any kind received as a consideration for the use of, or the right to use, any copyright of literary, artistic or scientific work, including software, cinematograph films, and films or tapes for radio or television broadcasting, transmission of every kind to the public, any patent, trade mark, design or model, plan, secret formula or process, or for the use of, or the right to use, any industrial, commercial or scientific equipment, or for information concerning industrial, commercial or scientific experience.

The provisions of paragraphs 1 and 2 shall not apply if the beneficial owner of the royalties, being a resident of a Contracting State, carries on business in the other Contracting State in which the royalties arise through a permanent establishment situated therein, or performs in that other State independent personal services from a fixed base situated therein, and the right or property in respect of which the royalties are paid is effectively connected with such permanent establishment or fixed base. In such case the provisions of Article 7 or Article 14, as the case may be, shall apply.

Royalties shall be deemed to arise in a Contracting State when the payer is a resident of that State. Where, however, the person paying the royalties, whether he is a resident of a Contracting State or not, has in a Contracting State a permanent establishment or a fixed base in connection with which the liability to pay the royalties was incurred, and such royalties are borne by such permanent establishment or fixed base, then such royalties shall be deemed to arise in the Contracting State in which the permanent establishment or fixed base is situated.

Where, by reason of a special relationship between the payer and the beneficial owner or between both of them and some other person, the amount of the royalties, having regard to the use, right or information for which they are paid, exceeds the amount which would have been agreed upon by the payer and the beneficial owner in the absence of such relationship, the provisions of this Article shall apply only to the last-mentioned amount. In such case, the excess part of the payments shall remain taxable according to the laws of each Contracting State, due regard being had to the other provisions of this Agreement.

The provisions of this Article shall not apply if it was the main purpose or one of the main purposes of any person concerned with the creation or assignment of the rights in respect of which the royalties are paid to take advantage of this Article by means of that creation or assignment.

Article 13 Capital Gains

Gains derived by a resident of a Contracting State from the alienation of immovable property referred to in Article 6 and situated in the other Contracting State may be taxed in that other State.

Gains from the alienation of movable property forming part of the business property of a permanent establishment which an enterprise of a Contracting State has in the other Contracting State or of movable property pertaining to a fixed base available to a resident of a Contracting State in the other Contracting State for the purpose of performing independent personal services, including such gains from the alienation of such a permanent establishment (alone or with the whole enterprise) or of such fixed base, may be taxed in that other State.

Gains derived by an enterprise of a Contracting State from the alienation of ships, aircraft, railway or road vehicles operated in international traffic or movable property pertaining to the operation of such means of transport, shall be taxable only in that State.

Gains derived by a resident of a Contracting State from the alienation of shares, other than shares in which there is substantial and regular trading on a stock exchange, or comparable interests, deriving more than 50% of their value directly or indirectly from immovable property situated in the other Contracting State may be taxed in that other State.

Gains from the alienation of any property, other than that referred to in paragraphs 1, 2, 3 and 4, shall be taxable only in the Contracting State of which the alienator is a resident.

Article 14 Independent Personal Services

Income derived by a resident of a Contracting State in respect of professional services or other activities of an independent character shall be taxable only in that State except in the following circumstances, when such income may also be taxed in the other Contracting State:

if he has a fixed base regularly available to him in the other Contracting State for the purpose of performing his activities; in that case, only so much of the income as is attributable to that fixed base may be taxed in that other State; or

if his stay in the other Contracting State is for a period or periods amounting to or exceeding in the aggregate 183 days in any twelve month period commencing or ending in the fiscal year concerned; in that case, only so much of the income as is derived from his activities performed in that other State may be taxed in that other State.

The term "professional services" includes especially independent scientific, literary, artistic, educational or teaching activities as well as the independent activities of physicians, lawyers, engineers, architects, dentists and accountants.

Article 15 Income from Employment

Subject to the provisions of Articles 16, 18, 19 and 21, salaries, wages and other similar remuneration derived by a resident of a Contracting State in respect of an employment shall be taxable only in that State unless the employment is exercised in the other Contracting State. If the employment is so exercised, such remuneration as is derived therefrom may be taxed in that other State.

Notwithstanding the provisions of paragraph 1, remuneration derived by a resident of a Contracting State in respect of an employment exercised in the other Contracting State shall be taxable only in the first-mentioned State if:

the recipient is present in the other State for a period or periods not exceeding in the aggregate 183 days in any twelve month period commencing or ending in the fiscal year concerned, and

the remuneration is paid by, or on behalf of, an employer who is not a resident of the other State, and

the remuneration is not borne by a permanent establishment or a fixed base which the employer has in the other State.

Notwithstanding the preceding provisions of this Article, remuneration derived in respect of an employment exercised aboard a ship, aircraft, railway or road vehicle operated in international traffic by an enterprise of a Contracting State, may be taxed in that State.

Article 16 Directors' Fees

Directors' fees and other similar payments derived by a resident of a Contracting State in his capacity as a member of the board of directors of a company which is a resident of the other Contracting State may be taxed in that other State.

Article 17 Entertainers and Sportspersons

Notwithstanding the provisions of Articles 14 and 15, income derived by a resident of a Contracting State as an entertainer, such as a theatre, motion picture, radio or television artiste, or a musician, or as a sportsperson, from that resident's personal activities as such exercised in the other Contracting State, may be taxed in that other State.

Where income in respect of personal activities exercised by an entertainer or a sportsperson acting as such accrues not to the entertainer or sportsperson but to another person, that income may, notwithstanding the provisions of Articles 7, 14 and 15, be taxed in the Contracting State in which the activities of the entertainer or sportsperson are exercised.

Notwithstanding the provisions of paragraphs 1 and 2, income derived from the activities referred to in paragraph 1 shall be exempt from tax in the Contracting State in which the activities are exercised if the visit to that State is wholly or mainly supported by public funds of either Contracting State.

For the purposes of this paragraph, the term "mainly supported" means the contribution of public funds exceeds 50%.

Article 18 Pensions

Subject to the provisions of paragraph 2 of Article 19, pensions and other similar remuneration paid to a resident of a Contracting State in consideration of past employment shall be taxable only in that State.

Notwithstanding the provisions of paragraph 1, pensions paid and other similar payments made under a public scheme of the social security system of a Contracting State shall be taxable only in that State.

Article 19 Government Service

(a) Salaries, wages and other similar remuneration, other than a pension, paid by a Contracting State or a political subdivision, local authority or administrative—territorial unit thereof to an individual in respect of services rendered to that State or subdivision, authority or unit shall be taxable only in that State.

However, such salaries, wages and other similar remuneration shall be taxable only in the other Contracting State if the services are rendered in that State and the individual is a resident of that State who:

is a national of that State; or

did not become a resident of that State solely for the purpose of rendering the services.

(a) Pensions and other similar remuneration paid by, or out of funds created by, a Contracting State or a political subdivision, local authority or administrative—territorial unit thereof to an individual in respect of services rendered to that State or subdivision, authority or unit shall be taxable only in that State.

(b) However, such pensions and other similar remuneration shall be taxable only in the other Contracting State if the individual is a resident of, and a national of, that State.

The provisions of Articles 15, 16, 17 and 18 shall apply to salaries, wages, pensions and other similar remuneration in respect of services rendered in connection with a business carried on by a Contracting State or a political subdivision, local authority or administrative—territorial unit thereof.

Article 20 Students

Payments which a student or business apprentice who is or was immediately before visiting a Contracting State a resident of the other Contracting State and who is present in the first-mentioned State solely for the purpose of his education or training receives for the purpose of his maintenance, education or training shall not be taxed in that State, provided that such payments arise from sources outside that State.

Article 21 Teachers and Researchers

Remuneration which an individual who is or was immediately before visiting a Contracting State a resident of the other Contracting State, and who is present in the first-mentioned State solely for the purpose of teaching or carrying out research in a school, institute, university, or any other educational or research institution officially recognized by that State, receives for such activities shall be exempt from tax in that State for a period not exceeding three years from the date of his or her first arrival in that State, provided that such remuneration is derived by him or her from sources outside that State.

Article 22 Other Income

Items of income of a resident of a Contracting State, wherever arising, not dealt with in the foregoing Articles of this Agreement shall be taxable only in that State.

The provisions of paragraph 1 shall not apply to income, other than income from immovable property as defined in paragraph 2 of Article 6, if the recipient of such income, being a resident of a Contracting State, carries on business in the other Contracting State through a permanent establishment situated therein, or performs in that other State independent personal services from a fixed base situated therein, and the right or property in respect of which the income is paid is effectively connected with such permanent establishment or fixed base. In such case the provisions of Article 7 or Article 14, as the case may be, shall apply.

The provisions of this Article shall not apply if it was the main purpose or one of the main purposes of any person concerned with the creation or assignment of the rights in respect of which the income is paid to take advantage of this Article by means of that creation or assignment.

Article 23 Elimination of Double Taxation

In China, in accordance with the provisions of the law of China, double taxation shall be eliminated as follows:

Where a resident of China derives income from Romania, the amount of tax on that income payable in Romania in accordance with the provisions of this Agreement may be credited against the Chinese tax imposed on that resident. The amount of the credit, however, shall not exceed the amount of the Chinese tax on that income computed in accordance with the taxation laws and regulations of China.
Where the income derived from Romania is a dividend paid by a company which is a resident of Romania to a company which is a resident of China and which owns at least 20% of the shares of the company paying the dividend, the credit shall take into account the tax paid in Romania by the company paying the dividend in respect of its income.

In Romania, double taxation shall be eliminated as follows:

Where a resident of Romania derives income which, in accordance with the provisions of this Agreement, may be taxed in China, Romania shall allow as a deduction from the tax on the income of that resident, an amount equal to the income tax paid in China.
Such deduction shall not, however, exceed that part of the income tax, as computed before the deduction is given, which is attributable to the income which may be taxed in China.

Article 24 Miscellaneous Rule

Nothing in this Agreement shall prejudice the right of each Contracting State to apply its domestic laws and measures concerning the prevention of tax avoidance, whether or not described as such, insofar as they do not give rise to taxation contrary to this Agreement.

Article 25 Non-discrimination

Nationals of a Contracting State shall not be subjected in the other Contracting State to any taxation or any requirement connected therewith, which is other or more burdensome than the taxation and connected requirements to which nationals of that other State in the same circumstances, in particular with respect to residence, are or may be subjected. This provision shall, notwithstanding the provisions of Article 1, also apply to persons who are not residents of one or both of the Contracting States.

The taxation on a permanent establishment which an enterprise of a Contracting State has in the other Contracting State shall not be less favorably levied in that other State than the taxation levied on enterprises of that other State carrying on the same activities. This provision shall not be construed as obliging a Contracting State to grant to residents of the other Contracting State any personal allowances, reliefs and reductions for taxation purposes on account of civil status or family responsibilities which it grants to its own residents.

Except where the provisions of paragraph 1 of Article 9, paragraph 7 of Article 11, or paragraph 6 of Article 12, apply, interest, royalties and other disbursements paid by an enterprise of a Contracting State to a resident of the other Contracting State shall, for the purpose of determining the taxable profits of such enterprise, be deductible under the same conditions as if they had been paid to a resident of the first-mentioned State.

Enterprises of a Contracting State, the capital of which is wholly or partly owned or controlled, directly or indirectly, by one or more residents of the other Contracting State, shall not be subjected in the first-mentioned State to any taxation or any requirement connected therewith which is other or more burdensome than the taxation and connected requirements to which other similar enterprises of the first-mentioned State are or may be subjected.

The provisions of this Article shall apply only to taxes which are covered by this Agreement.

Article 26 Mutual Agreement Procedure

Where a person considers that the actions of one or both of the Contracting States result or will result for him in taxation not in accordance with the provisions of this Agreement, he may, irrespective of the remedies provided by the domestic law of those States, present his case to the competent authority of the Contracting State of which he is a resident or, if his case comes under paragraph 1 of Article 25, to that of the Contracting State of which he is a national. The case must be presented within three years from the first notification of the action resulting in taxation not in accordance with the provisions of the Agreement.

The competent authority shall endeavor, if the objection appears to it to be justified and if it is not itself able to arrive at a satisfactory solution, to resolve the case by mutual agreement with the competent authority of the other Contracting State, with a view to the avoidance of taxation which is not in accordance with the Agreement. Any agreement reached shall be implemented notwithstanding any time limits in the domestic law of the Contracting States.

The competent authorities of the Contracting States shall endeavor to resolve by mutual agreement any difficulties or doubts arising as to the interpretation or application of the Agreement. They may also consult together for the elimination of double taxation in cases not provided for in the Agreement.

The competent authorities of the Contracting States may communicate with each other directly for the purpose of reaching an agreement in the sense of paragraphs 2 and 3. When it seems advisable for reaching an agreement, representatives of the competent authorities of the Contracting States may meet together for an oral exchange of opinions.

Article 27 Exchange of Information

The competent authorities of the Contracting States shall exchange such information as is foreseeably relevant for carrying out the provisions of this Agreement or to the administration or enforcement of the domestic laws concerning taxes of every kind and description imposed on behalf of the Contracting States or of their political subdivisions, local authorities or administrative—territorial units, insofar as the taxation thereunder is not contrary to the Agreement. The exchange of information is not restricted by Articles 1 and 2.

Any information received under paragraph 1 by a Contracting State shall be treated as secret in the same manner as information obtained under the domestic laws of that State and shall be disclosed only to persons or authorities (including courts and administrative bodies) concerned with the assessment or collection of, the enforcement or prosecution in respect of, the determination of appeals in relation to the taxes referred to in paragraph 1, or the oversight of the above. Such persons or authorities shall use the information only for such purposes. They may disclose the information in public court proceedings or in judicial decisions. Notwithstanding the foregoing, information received by a Contracting State may be used for other purposes when such information may be used for such other purposes under the laws of both States and the competent authority of the supplying State authorises such use.

In no case shall the provisions of paragraphs 1 and 2 be construed so as to impose on a Contracting State the obligation:

to carry out administrative measures at variance with the laws and administrative practice of that or of the other Contracting State;
to supply information which is not obtainable under the laws or in the normal course of the administration of that or of the other Contracting State;
to supply information which would disclose any trade, business, industrial, commercial or professional secret or trade process, or information, the disclosure of which would be contrary to public policy (*ordre public*).

If information is requested by a Contracting State in accordance with this Article, the other Contracting State shall use its information gathering measures to obtain the requested information, even though that other State may not need such information for its own tax purposes. The obligation contained in the preceding sentence is subject to the limitations of paragraph 3 but in no case shall such limitations be construed to permit a Contracting State to decline to supply information solely because it has no domestic interest in such information.

In no case shall the provisions of paragraph 3 be construed to permit a Contracting State to decline to supply information solely because the information is held by a bank, other financial institution, nominee or person acting in an agency or a fiduciary capacity or because it relates to ownership interests in a person.

Article 28 Members of Diplomatic Missions and Consular Posts

Nothing in this Agreement shall affect the fiscal privileges of members of diplomatic missions or consular posts under the general rules of international law or under the provisions of special agreements.

Article 29 Entry into Force

Both Contracting States shall notify each other through diplomatic channels that they have completed the internal legal procedures necessary for the entry into force of this Agreement. This Agreement shall enter into force on the thirtieth day upon the receipt of the latter notification and shall have effect in respect of income derived during the taxable years beginning on or after the first day of January in the calendar year next following the year in which this Agreement enters into force.

The Agreement between the Government of the People's Republic of China and the Government of Romania for the avoidance of double taxation and the prevention of fiscal evasion with respect to taxes on income, done at Beijing on 16 January 1991, shall be deemed as terminated on the date of entry into force of this Agreement and shall cease to have effect from the date upon which this Agreement has effect.

Article 30 Termination

This Agreement shall remain in force indefinitely but either of the Contracting States may give written notice of termination to the other Contracting State through diplomatic channels, on or before the thirtieth day of June in any calendar year beginning after the expiration of a period of five years from the date of its entry into force. In such event, this Agreement shall be deemed as terminated and cease to have effect in respect of income derived during the taxable years beginning on or after the first day of January in the calendar year next following the year in which the notice of termination is given.

IN WITNESS WHEREOF, the undersigned, duly authorized thereto, have signed this Agreement.

DONE at Bucharest on the 4th day of July, 2016 in duplicate in the Chinese, Romanian and English languages, all texts being equally authentic. In case of divergence in interpretation, the English text shall prevail.

Russia

Russia, officially the Russian Federation, is a state in Eastern Europe. Russia is a transcontinental continent, being the largest country by area, covering over 17 million squared km. Russia has the most borders of any country in the world, as sixteen states border it. Russia borders with Norway, Finland, Estonia, Latvia, Lithuania, Poland, Belarus, Ukraine, Georgia, Azerbaijan, Kazakhstan, China, Mongolia, North Korea, Japan and the United States. Its coast along the Arctic Ocean and the Sea of Japan. Russia's capital and largest city is Moscow, being also its financial center. Russia has the first largest population in Europe.

Russians are the majority ethnic group. Most immigrant in Russia come from Ukraine, Uzbekistan, Tajikistan, Azerbaijan, Moldova, Kazakhstan, Kyrgyzstan, Armenia, Belarus, and China, while temporary migrant workers are about 7 million.

The official and predominant spoken language is Russian, the most spoken native language in Europe. Approximately over 100 minority languages are spoken across Russia, the major ones being Tatar and Ukrainian.

Russia is a Federal semi-presidential constitutional republic. The Konstitútsiya is the constitution regulating the political system, in force since 1993, after the dissolution of the Soviet Union. The State Duma is the lower house while the Federation Council is the upper house, constituting the Federal Assembly, where the legislative power is exerted. The State Duma is elected through direct elections using the parallel voting system. The 170 members of the Federation Council represent the 85 federal subjects of Russia—consisting of 22 republics, 46 oblasts, nine krais, four autonomous okrugs, three federal cities, and one autonomous oblast—sending two senators each.

Executive power is vested in the President and the Prime Minister.

Russia has a civil law system. The Constitutional Court acts as Supreme Court, managing constitutional matters, with judicial review powers.

Russia is a federal state, therefore, constituted by eight federal districts, each administered by an envoy appointed by the President.

Russia is part of the G20, the Shanghai Cooperation Organization (SCO), and BRICS (together with Brazil, India, China, and South Africa).

© The Author(s), under exclusive license to Springer Nature Singapore Pte Ltd. 2022

L. Riccardi and G. Riccardi, *China–Europe Tax Treaties*,
https://doi.org/10.1007/978-981-19-3563-3_24

Category	Value
Population (mln persons)	146.730
Currency	Ruble

Source International Monetary Fund, year 2019

Russia is the largest economy of Eastern Europe, with a GDP valued 1637.9 billion USD in 2019, however, its GDP per capita is 11,163 USD, with a population of about 146.7 million people spanning the European and Asian continent, considerably less than the average recorded for the first four main economies. Inflation marked 4.5%, above the general central bank objective of 2–3%, but it has relatively low unemployment (4.6%). Russia scored 14 out of 43 in Europe in the 2020 Doing Business ranking and imposes a CIT of 20%. Russia records a positive trade balance of 164 billion USD, with an export worth 418 billion USD, pushed by mineral fuels and oil.

GDP and local economy	
GDP current prices (billion USD)	1637.9
GDP per capita (USD)	11,163
GDP growth (%)	1.3
Inflation (%)	4.5
Unemployment (%)	4.6
General government total expenditure (% of GDP)	33.8
General government gross debt (% of GDP)	13.8
Doing business score 2020	78.2

Source International Monetary Fund and UNCTAD, year 2019

Foreign direct investment	
FDI outstock (million USD)	386,622
FDI instock (million USD)	463,860

Source UNCTAD, year 2019

Trade	
Imports (million USD)	254,052
Exports (million USD)	418,796
Trade balance (million USD)	164,744

Source International Monetary Fund and UNCTAD, year 2019

Main import–export	
First import by category	Machinery, nuclear reactors, boilers
Second import by category	Electrical, electronic equipment
First export by category	Mineral fuels, oils, distillation products
Second export by category	Commodities not specified according to kind

Source United Nations COMTRADE, year 2020

The legal bases for taxation are established in the Russian Tax Code, outlining the general principles. France imposes at national and local level different taxes, such as individual income tax, property sales taxes, capital gains, corporate income tax, and value added tax.

Taxes	
Company income tax (%)	20
Top individual income tax (%)	15
Value added tax or sales tax (%)	20
Reduced value added tax or sales tax (%)	10/16.67

Source RsA Asia report, year 2021

- Economic relation with China

Russia records a trade surplus of 6.6 billion USD in 2020. "Mineral fuels, oils, distillation products" is the first export category, worth 33.39 billion USD, followed by "wood and articles of wood, wood charcoal". "Electrical, electronic equipment" is the first import category, worth 10.75 billion USD. Russia is the second main economy to be part of the Belt and Road Initiative. The Russian DTA with China dates back to 1994, coming into force in 1997. A new agreement has been signed in 2014 and has come into force in 2016.

Category	Value
Belt road	Yes

Source UNCTAD, year 2021

Import from China	
Import from China (billion USD)	50.58
First import category from China	Electrical, electronic equipment
First import value (billion USD)	10.75
Second import category from China	Machinery, nuclear reactors, boilers
Second import value (billion USD)	10.19

Source United Nations COMTRADE, year 2020

Export to China	
Export to China (billion USD)	57.18
First export category towards China	Mineral fuels, oils, distillation products
First export value (billion USD)	33.39
Second export category towards China	Wood and articles of wood, wood charcoal
Second export value (billion USD)	3.71

Source United Nations COMTRADE, year 2020

Trade balance	
Trade balance (billion USD)	6.60

Source United Nations COMTRADE, year 2020

Double tax agreement	
DTA effective date	2016.4.9
Dividends (%)	5–10
Interest (%)	0–5–10
Royalties (%)	6

Source State Administration of Taxation of China, year 2021

Title AGREEMENT BETWEEN THE GOVERNMENT OF THE PEOPLE'S REPUBLIC OF CHINA AND THE GOVERNMENT OF THE RUSSIAN FEDERATION FOR THE AVOIDANCE OF DOUBLE TAXATION AND THE PREVENTION OF FISCAL EVASION WITH RESPECT TO TAXES ON INCOME

Treaty Text

The Government of the People's Republic of China and the Government of the Russian Federation,

Desiring to conclude an Agreement for the avoidance of double taxation and the prevention of fiscal evasion with respect to taxes on income,

Have agreed as follows:

Article 1 Persons Covered

This Agreement shall apply to persons who are residents of one or both of the Contracting States.

Article 2 Taxes Covered

This Agreement shall apply to taxes on income imposed on behalf of a Contracting State or of its political subdivisions or local authorities, irrespective of the manner in which they are levied.

There shall be regarded as taxes on income all taxes imposed on total income, or on elements of income, including taxes on gains from the alienation of movable or immovable property and taxes on the total amounts of wages or salaries paid by enterprises.

The existing taxes to which the Agreement shall apply are in particular:

in China:
the individual income tax;
the enterprise income tax.
(hereinafter referred to as "Chinese tax");
in Russia:
the tax on profits of organizations;
the tax on income of individuals (hereinafter referred to as "Russian tax").

The Agreement shall apply also to any identical or substantially similar taxes that are imposed after the date of signature of the Agreement in addition to, or in place of, the existing taxes. The competent authorities of the Contracting States shall notify each other of any significant changes which have been made in their taxation laws.

Article 3 General Definitions

For the purposes of this Agreement, unless the context otherwise requires:

the terms "a Contracting State" and "the other Contracting State" mean the People's Republic of China (China) or the Russian Federation (Russia), as the context requires;
the term "China" means the People's Republic of China; when used in geographical sense, means all the territory of the People's Republic of China, including its territorial sea, in which the Chinese laws relating to taxation apply, and any area beyond its territorial sea, in which the People's Republic of China has in accordance with international law and domestic law sovereign rights of exploration for and exploitation of resources of the sea-bed, its sub-soil and superjacent water resources;
the term "Russia" means the Russian Federation; when used in geographical sense, means all the territory of the Russian Federation, including internal waters and territorial sea, in which the Russian laws relating to taxation apply, and also its exclusive economic zone and continental shelf, in which the Russian Federation has sovereign rights and jurisdiction in accordance with the UN Convention on the Law of the Sea (1982);
the term "person" includes an individual, a company and any other body of persons;
the term "company" means any body corporate or any entity that is treated as a body corporate for tax purposes;
the terms "enterprise of a Contracting State" and "enterprise of the other Contracting State" mean, respectively, an enterprise carried on by a resident of a Contracting State and an enterprise carried on by a resident of the other Contracting State;

the term "international traffic" means any transport by a ship or aircraft operated by an enterprise of a Contracting State, except when the ship or aircraft is operated solely between places in the other Contracting State;
the term "competent authority" means,
in the case of China, the State Administration of Taxation or its authorized representative; and
in the case of Russia, the Ministry of Finance of the Russian Federation or its authorized representative;
the term "national", in relation to a Contracting State, means:
any individual possessing the nationality of a Contracting State; and
any legal person, partnership or association deriving its status as such from the laws in force in a Contracting State.

As regards the application of the Agreement at any time by a Contracting State, any term not defined therein shall, unless the context otherwise requires, have the meaning which it has at that time under the law of that State for the purposes of the taxes to which the Agreement applies, any meaning under the applicable tax laws of that State prevailing over a meaning given to the term under other laws of that State.

Article 4 Resident

For the purposes of this Agreement, the term "resident of a Contracting State" means any person who, under the laws of that State, is liable to tax therein by reason of his domicile, residence, place of incorporation, place of effective management or any other criterion of a similar nature, and also includes that State and any political subdivision or local authority thereof. This term, however, does not include any person who is liable to tax in that State in respect only of income from sources in that State.

Where by reason of the provisions of paragraph 1 an individual is a resident of both Contracting States, then his status shall be determined as follows:

he shall be deemed to be a resident only of the State in which he has a permanent home available to him; if he has a permanent home available to him in both States, he shall be deemed to be a resident only of the State with which his personal and economic relations are closer (centre of vital interests);
if the State in which he has his centre of vital interests cannot be determined, or if he has not a permanent home available to him in either State, he shall be deemed to be a resident only of the State in which he has an habitual abode;
if he has an habitual abode in both States or in neither of them, he shall be deemed to be a resident only of the State of which he is a national;
if he is a national of both States or of neither of them, the competent authorities of the Contracting States shall settle the question by mutual agreement. If the competent authorities are unable to reach such agreement, such person shall not be considered a resident of either Contracting State and not be entitled to any relief from tax provided by this Agreement.

Where by reason of the provisions of paragraph 1 a person other than an individual is a resident of both Contracting States, then it shall be deemed to be a resident only of the State in which its place of effective management is situated.

Article 5 Permanent Establishment

For the purposes of this Agreement, the term "permanent establishment" means a fixed place of business through which the business of an enterprise is wholly or partly carried on.

The term "permanent establishment" includes especially:

a place of management;
a branch;
an office;
a factory;
a workshop; and
a mine, an oil or gas well, a quarry or any other place of extraction of natural resources.

The term "permanent establishment" likewise encompasses:

a building site, or construction, assembly or installation project or supervisory activities in connection therewith, but only if such site, project or activities last more than 18 months;
the furnishing of services, including consultancy services, by an enterprise through employees or other personnel engaged for such purpose, but only if activities of that nature continue (for the same or a connected project) within a Contracting State for a period or periods aggregating 183 days in any twelve month period commencing or ending in the fiscal year concerned.

Notwithstanding the preceding provisions of this Article, the term "permanent establishment" shall be deemed not to include:

the use of facilities solely for the purpose of storage, display or delivery of goods or merchandise belonging to the enterprise;
the maintenance of a stock of goods or merchandise belonging to the enterprise solely for the purpose of storage, display or delivery;
the maintenance of a stock of goods or merchandise belonging to the enterprise solely for the purpose of processing by another enterprise;
the maintenance of a fixed place of business solely for the purpose of purchasing goods or merchandise or of collecting information, for the enterprise;
the maintenance of a fixed place of business solely for the purpose of carrying on, for the enterprise, any other activity of a preparatory or auxiliary character;
the maintenance of a fixed place of business solely for any combination of activities mentioned in sub-paragraphs (a) to (e), provided that the overall activity of the fixed place of business resulting from this combination is of a preparatory or auxiliary character.

Notwithstanding the provisions of paragraphs 1 and 2, where a person—other than an agent of an independent status to whom paragraph 6 applies—is acting in a Contracting State on behalf of an enterprise of the other Contracting State, and has, and habitually exercises, in that Contracting State an authority to conclude contracts in the name of the enterprise, that enterprise shall be deemed to have a permanent establishment in that Contracting State in respect of any activities which that person undertakes for the enterprise, unless the activities of such person are limited to those mentioned in paragraph 4 which, if exercised through a fixed place of business, would not make this fixed place of business a permanent establishment under the provisions of that paragraph.

An enterprise of a Contracting State shall not be deemed to have a permanent establishment in the other Contracting State merely because it carries on business in that other State through a broker, general commission agent or any other agent of an independent status, provided that such persons are acting in the ordinary course of their business.

The fact that a company which is a resident of a Contracting State controls or is controlled by a company which is a resident of the other Contracting State, or which carries on business in that other State (whether through a permanent establishment or otherwise), shall not of itself constitute either company a permanent establishment of the other.

Article 6 Income from Immovable Property

Income derived by a resident of a Contracting State from immovable property (including income from agriculture or forestry) situated in the other Contracting State may be taxed in that other State.

The term "immovable property" shall have the meaning which it has under the law of the Contracting State in which the property in question is situated. The term shall in any case include property accessory to immovable property, livestock and equipment used in agriculture and forestry, rights to which the provisions of general law respecting landed property apply, usufruct of immovable property and rights to variable or fixed payments as consideration for the working of, or the right to work, mineral deposits, sources and other natural resources; ships and aircraft shall not be regarded as immovable property.

The provisions of paragraph 1 shall apply to income derived from the direct use, letting, or use in any other form of immovable property.

The provisions of paragraphs 1 and 3 shall also apply to the income from immovable property of an enterprise and to income from immovable property used for the performance of independent personal services.

Article 7 Business Profits

The profits of an enterprise of a Contracting State shall be taxable only in that State unless the enterprise carries on business in the other Contracting State through a permanent establishment situated therein. If the enterprise carries on business as aforesaid, the profits of the enterprise may be taxed in the other State, but only so much of them as is attributable to that permanent establishment.

Subject to the provisions of paragraph 3, where an enterprise of a Contracting State carries on business in the other Contracting State through a permanent establishment situated therein, there shall in each Contracting State be attributed to that permanent establishment the profits which it might be expected to make if it were a distinct and separate enterprise engaged in the same or similar activities under the same or similar conditions and dealing wholly independently with the enterprise of which it is a permanent establishment.

In determining the profits of a permanent establishment, there shall be allowed as deductions expenses which are incurred for the purposes of the permanent establishment, including executive and general administrative expenses so incurred, whether in the State in which the permanent establishment is situated or elsewhere.

Insofar as it has been customary in a Contracting State to determine the profits to be attributed to a permanent establishment on the basis of an apportionment of the total profits of the enterprise to its various parts, nothing in paragraph 2 shall preclude that Contracting State from determining the profits to be taxed by such an apportionment as may be customary; the method of apportionment adopted shall, however, be such that the result shall be in accordance with the principles contained in this Article.

No profits shall be attributed to a permanent establishment by reason of the mere purchase by that permanent establishment of goods or merchandise for the enterprise.

For the purposes of the preceding paragraphs, the profits to be attributed to the permanent establishment shall be determined by the same method year by year unless there is good and sufficient reason to the contrary.

Where profits include items of income which are dealt with separately in other Articles of this Agreement, then the provisions of those Articles shall not be affected by the provisions of this Article.

Article 8 Shipping and Air Transport

Profits from the operation of ships or aircraft in international traffic by an enterprise of a Contracting State shall be taxable only in that Contracting State.

The provisions of paragraph 1 shall also apply to profits from the participation in a pool, a joint business or an international operating agency.

Article 9 Associated Enterprises

Where an enterprise of a Contracting State participates directly or indirectly in the management, control or capital of an enterprise of the other Contracting State, or

the same persons participate directly or indirectly in the management, control or capital of an enterprise of a Contracting State and an enterprise of the other Contracting State,

and in either case conditions are made or imposed between the two enterprises in their commercial or financial relations which differ from those which would be made between independent enterprises, then any profits which would, but for those conditions, have accrued to one of the enterprises, but, by reason of those conditions, have not so accrued, may be included in the profits of that enterprise and taxed accordingly.

Where a Contracting State includes in the profits of an enterprise of that State—and taxes accordingly—profits on which an enterprise of the other Contracting State has been charged to tax in that other State and the profits so included are profits which would have accrued to the enterprise of the first-mentioned State if the conditions made between the two enterprises had been those which would have been made between independent enterprises, then that other State shall make an appropriate adjustment to the amount of the tax charged therein on those profits. In determining such adjustment, due regard shall be had to the other provisions of this Agreement and the competent authorities of the Contracting States shall, if necessary, consult each other.

Article 10 Dividends

Dividends paid by a company which is a resident of a Contracting State to a resident of the other Contracting State may be taxed in that other State.

However, such dividends may also be taxed in the Contracting State of which the company paying the dividends is a resident and according to the laws of that State, but if the beneficial owner of the dividends is a resident of the other Contracting State, the tax so charged shall not exceed:

5% of the gross amount of the dividends if the beneficial owner is a company (other than a partnership) which holds directly at least 25% of the capital of the company paying the dividends and this holding amounts to at least 80,000 Euros or its equivalent in any other currency;

10% of the gross amount of the dividends in all other cases.

This paragraph shall not affect the taxation of the company in respect of the profits out of which the dividends are paid.

The term "dividends" as used in this Article means income from shares or other rights, not being debt-claims, participating in profits, as well as income from other corporate rights which is subjected to the same taxation treatment as income from shares by the laws of the State of which the company making the distribution is a resident.

The provisions of paragraphs 1 and 2 shall not apply if the beneficial owner of the dividends, being a resident of a Contracting State, carries on business in the other Contracting State of which the company paying the dividends is a resident through a permanent establishment situated therein, or performs in that other State independent personal services from a fixed base situated therein, and the holding in respect of which the dividends are paid is effectively connected with such permanent establishment or fixed base. In such case the provisions of Article 7 or Article 14, as the case may be, shall apply.

Where a company which is a resident of a Contracting State derives profits or income from the other Contracting State, that other State may not impose any tax on the dividends paid by the company, except insofar as such dividends are paid to a resident of that other State or insofar as the holding in respect of which the dividends are paid is effectively connected with a permanent establishment or a fixed base situated in that other State, nor subject the company's undistributed profits to a tax on the company's undistributed profits, even if the dividends paid or the undistributed profits consist wholly or partly of profits or income arising in such other State.

The provisions of this Article shall not apply if it was the main purpose or one of the main purposes of any person concerned with the creation or assignment of the shares or other rights in respect of which the dividend is paid to take advantage of this Article by means of that creation or assignment.

Article 11 Interest

Interest arising in a Contracting State and paid to a resident of the other Contracting State may be taxed in that other State.

However, such interest may also be taxed in the Contracting State in which it arises and according to the laws of that State, but if the beneficial owner of the interest is a resident of the other Contracting State, the tax so charged shall not exceed 5% of the gross amount of the interest.

Notwithstanding the provisions of paragraph 2, interest arising in a Contracting State and paid to the Government of the other Contracting State, a political subdivision or a local authority thereof, its Central Bank or any financial institution wholly owned by the Government of the other Contracting State, or paid on loans guaranteed or insured by the Government of the other Contracting State, a political subdivision or a local authority thereof, its Central Bank or any financial institution wholly owned by the Government of the other Contracting State, shall be exempt from tax in the first-mentioned State. Interest paid on a loan in accordance with an Agreement concluded between the Governments of the Contracting States prior to the signing of the Agreement shall also be exempt from tax in the Contracting State in which the interest arises.

The term "interest" as used in this Article means income from debt-claims of every kind, whether or not secured by mortgage and whether or not carrying a right to participate in the debtor's profits, and in particular, income from government securities and income from bonds or debentures, including premiums and prizes attaching to such securities, bonds or debentures. Penalty charges for late payment shall not be regarded as interest for the purpose of this Article.

The provisions of paragraphs 1 and 2 shall not apply if the beneficial owner of the interest, being a resident of a Contracting State, carries on business in the other Contracting State in which the interest arises, through a permanent establishment situated therein, or performs in that other State independent personal services from a fixed base situated therein, and the debt-claim in respect of which the interest is paid is effectively connected with such permanent establishment or fixed base. In such case the provisions of Article 7 or Article 14, as the case may be, shall apply.

Interest shall be deemed to arise in a Contracting State when the payer is a resident of that State. Where, however, the person paying the interest, whether he is a resident of a Contracting State or not, has in a Contracting State a permanent establishment or a fixed base in connection with which the indebtedness on which the interest is paid was incurred, and such interest is borne by such permanent establishment or fixed base, then such interest shall be deemed to arise in the State in which the permanent establishment or fixed base is situated.

Where, by reason of a special relationship between the payer and the beneficial owner or between both of them and some other person, the amount of the interest, having regard to the debt-claim for which it is paid, exceeds the amount which would have been agreed upon by the payer and the beneficial owner in the absence of such relationship, the provisions of this Article shall apply only to the last-mentioned amount. In such case, the excess part of the payments shall remain taxable according to the laws of each Contracting State, due regard being had to the other provisions of this Agreement.

The provisions of this Article shall not apply if it was the main purpose or one of the main purposes of any person concerned with the creation or assignment of the debt-claim in respect of which the interest is paid to take advantage of this Article by means of that creation or assignment.

Article 12 Royalties

Royalties arising in a Contracting State and beneficially owned by a resident of the other Contracting State may be taxed in that other State.

However, such royalties may also be taxed in the Contracting State in which they arise and according to the laws of that State, but if the beneficial owner of the royalties is a resident of the other Contracting State, the tax so charged shall not exceed 6% of the gross amount of the royalties.

The term "royalties" as used in this Article means payments of any kind received as a consideration for the use of, or the right to use, any copyright of literary, artistic or scientific work including cinematography films, or films or tapes for radio or television broadcasting, any patent, trade mark, design or model, plan, secret formula or process, or for the use of, or the right to use, industrial, commercial, or scientific equipment, or for information concerning industrial, commercial or scientific experience.

The provisions of paragraphs 1 and 2 shall not apply if the beneficial owner of the royalties, being a resident of a Contracting State, carries on business in the other Contracting State in which the royalties arise, through a permanent establishment situated therein, or performs in that other State independent personal services from a fixed base situated therein, and the right or property in respect of which the royalties are paid is effectively connected with such permanent establishment or fixed base. In such case the provisions of Article 7 or Article 14, as the case may be, shall apply.

Royalties shall be deemed to arise in a Contracting State when the payer is a resident of that Contracting State. Where, however, the person paying the royalties, whether he is a resident of a Contracting State or not, has in a Contracting State a permanent establishment or a fixed base in connection with which the liability to pay the royalties was incurred, and such royalties are borne by such permanent establishment or fixed base, then such royalties shall be deemed to arise in the State in which the permanent establishment or fixed base is situated.

Where, by reason of a special relationship between the payer and the beneficial owner or between both of them and some other person, the amount of the royalties, having regard to the use, right or information for which they are paid, exceeds the amount which would have been agreed upon by the payer and the beneficial owner in the absence of such relationship, the provisions of this Article shall apply only to the last-mentioned amount. In such case, the excess part of the payments shall remain taxable according to the laws of each Contracting State, due regard being had to the other provisions of this Agreement.

The provisions of this Article shall not apply if it was the main purpose or one of the main purposes of any person concerned with the creation or assignment of the rights in respect of which the royalties are paid to take advantage of this Article by means of that creation or assignment.

Article 13 Capital Gains

Gains derived by a resident of a Contracting State from the alienation of immovable property referred to in Article 6 and situated in the other Contracting State may be taxed in that other State.

Gains from the alienation of movable property forming part of the business property of a permanent establishment which an enterprise of a Contracting State has in the other Contracting State or of movable property pertaining to a fixed base available to a resident of a Contracting State in the other Contracting State for the purpose of performing independent personal services, including such gains from the alienation of such a permanent establishment (alone or with the whole enterprise) or of such a fixed base, may be taxed in that other State.

Gains from the alienation of ships or aircraft operated in international traffic by an enterprise of a Contracting State, or movable property pertaining to the operation of such ships or aircraft, shall be taxable only in that Contracting State.

Gains derived by a resident of a Contracting State from the alienation of shares deriving more than 50% of their value directly or indirectly from immovable property situated in the other Contracting State may be taxed in that other State.

Gains from the alienation of any property, other than that referred to in paragraphs 1 to 4, shall be taxable only in the Contracting State of which the alienator is a resident.

Article 14 Independent Personal Services

Income derived by a resident of a Contracting State in respect of professional services or other activities of an independent character shall be taxable only in that State except in the following circumstances, when such income may also be taxed in the other Contracting State:

> if he has a fixed base regularly available to him in the other Contracting State for the purpose of performing his activities; in that case, only so much of the income as is attributable to that fixed base may be taxed in that other State; or
> if his stay in the other Contracting State is for a period or periods amounting to or exceeding in the aggregate 183 days in any twelve month period commencing or ending in the fiscal year concerned; in that case, only so much of the income as is derived from his activities performed in that other State may be taxed in that other State.

The term "professional services" includes especially independent scientific, literary, artistic, educational or teaching activities as well as the independent activities of physicians, lawyers, engineers, architects, dentists and accountants.

Article 15 Income from Employment

Subject to the provisions of Articles 16, 18, and 19, salaries, wages and other similar remuneration derived by a resident of a Contracting State in respect of an employment shall be taxable only in that State unless the employment is exercised in the other Contracting State. If the employment is so exercised, such remuneration as is derived therefrom may be taxed in that other State.

Notwithstanding the provisions of paragraph 1, remuneration derived by a resident of a Contracting State in respect of an employment exercised in the other Contracting State shall be taxable only in the first-mentioned State if:

the recipient is present in the other State for a period or periods not exceeding in the aggregate 183 days in any twelve month period commencing or ending in the fiscal year concerned, and

the remuneration is paid by, or on behalf of, an employer who is not a resident of the other State, and

the remuneration is not borne by a permanent establishment or a fixed base which the employer has in the other State.

Notwithstanding the preceding provisions of this Article, remuneration derived in respect of an employment exercised aboard a ship or aircraft operated in international traffic by an enterprise of a Contracting State, may be taxed in that Contracting State.

Article 16 Directors' Fees

Directors' fees and other similar payments derived by a resident of a Contracting State in his capacity as a member of the board of directors of a company which is a resident of the other Contracting State may be taxed in that other State.

Article 17 Artistes and Sportsmen

Notwithstanding the provisions of Articles 7, 14 and 15, income derived by a resident of a Contracting State as an entertainer, such as a theatre, motion picture, radio or television artiste, or a musician, or as a sportsman, from his personal activities as such exercised in the other Contracting State, may be taxed in that other State.

Where income in respect of personal activities exercised by an entertainer or a sportsman in his capacity as such accrues not to the entertainer or sportsman himself but to another person, that income may, notwithstanding the provisions of Articles 7, 14 and 15, be taxed in the Contracting State in which the activities of the entertainer or sportsman are exercised.

Notwithstanding the provisions of paragraphs 1 and 2, income derived from such activities as are referred to in paragraph 1 performed under a cultural agreement or arrangement between the Contracting States shall be exempt from tax in the

Contracting State in which the activities are exercised if the visit to that State is wholly or substantially supported by public or government funds of either Contracting State.

Article 18 Pensions

Subject to the provisions of paragraph 2 of Article 19, pensions and other similar remuneration paid to a resident of a Contracting State in consideration of past employment shall be taxable only in that State.

Notwithstanding the provisions of paragraph 1, pensions paid and other similar payments made by the Government of a Contracting State or a political subdivision or a local authority thereof under a public welfare scheme of the social security system of that State shall be taxable only in that State.

Article 19 Government Service

(a) Salaries, wages and other similar remuneration, other than a pension, paid by the Government of a Contracting State or a political subdivision or a local authority thereof to an individual in respect of services rendered to the Government of that State or subdivision or authority, shall be taxable only in that State.

However, such salaries, wages and other similar remuneration shall be taxable only in the other Contracting State if the services are rendered in that State and the individual is a resident of that State who:

is a national of that State; or

did not become a resident of that State solely for the purpose of rendering the services.

(a) Pensions and other similar remuneration paid by, or out of funds created by, a Contracting State or a political subdivision or a local authority thereof to an individual in respect of services rendered to the Government of that State or subdivision or authority shall be taxable only in that State.

However, such pensions and other similar remuneration shall be taxable only in the other Contracting State if the individual is a resident of, and a national of, that State.

The provisions of Articles 15, 16, 17, and 18 shall apply to salaries, wages, pensions, and other similar remuneration in respect of services rendered in connection with a business carried on by the Government of a Contracting State or a political subdivision or a local authority thereof.

Article 20 Students

Payments which a student who is or was immediately before visiting a Contracting State a resident of the other Contracting State and who is present in the first-mentioned State solely for the purpose of his education receives for the purpose of his maintenance or education shall not be taxed in that State, provided that such payments arise from sources outside that State.

Article 21 Other Income

Items of income of a resident of a Contracting State, wherever arising, not dealt with in the foregoing Articles of this Agreement shall be taxable only in that State.

The provisions of paragraph 1 shall not apply to income, other than income from immovable property as defined in paragraph 2 of Article 6, if the recipient of such income, being a resident of a Contracting State, carries on business in the other Contracting State through a permanent establishment situated therein, or performs in that other State independent personal services from a fixed base situated therein, and the right or property in respect of which the income is paid is effectively connected with such permanent establishment or fixed base. In such case the provisions of Article 7 or Article 14, as the case may be, shall apply.

The provision of this Article shall not apply if it was the main purpose or one of the main purposes of any person concerned with the creation or assignment of the rights in respect of which the income is paid to take advantage of this Article by means of that creation or assignment.

Article 22 Methods for Elimination of Double Taxation

In China, in accordance with the provisions of the law of China, double taxation shall be eliminated as follows:

Where a resident of China derives income from Russia, the amount of tax on that income payable in Russia in accordance with the provisions of this Agreement may be credited against the Chinese tax imposed on that resident. The amount of the credit, however, shall not exceed the amount of the Chinese tax on that income computed in accordance with the taxation laws and regulations of China.
Where the income derived from Russia is dividend paid by a company which is a resident of Russia to a company which is a resident of China and which owns not less than 20% of the shares of the company paying the dividend, the credit shall take into account the tax paid to Russia by the company paying the dividend in respect of its income.

In Russia, double taxation shall be eliminated as follows: Where a resident of Russia derives income from China, the amount of tax on that income payable in China in accordance with the provisions of this Agreement may be credited against the Russian tax imposed on that resident. The amount of credit, however, shall not exceed the amount of the Russian tax on that income computed in accordance with the taxation laws and regulations of Russia.

Article 23 Limitation of Benefits

Except as otherwise provided in this Article, a resident of a Contracting State who derives income from the other Contracting State shall be entitled to all the benefits of this Agreement otherwise accorded to residents of a Contracting State only if such resident is a "qualified person" as defined in paragraph 2 and meets the other conditions of this Agreement for the obtaining of such benefits.

A resident of a Contracting State is a qualified person for a fiscal year only if such resident is either:

an individual;
a qualified governmental entity;

a company, if

the principal class of its shares is listed on a recognized stock exchange specified in subparagraph (a) or (b) of paragraph 6 and is regularly traded on one or more recognized stock exchanges, or

at least 50% of the aggregate vote and value of the shares in the company is owned directly or indirectly by five or fewer companies entitled to benefits under subdivision (i) of this subparagraph, provided that, in the case of indirect ownership, each intermediate owner is a resident of either Contracting State;

a charity or other tax-exempt entity, provided that, in the case of a pension trust or any other organization that is established exclusively to provide pension or other similar benefits, more than 50% of the person's beneficiaries, members or participants are individuals resident in either Contracting State; or

a person other than an individual, if:

on at least half the days of the fiscal year persons that are qualified persons by reason of subparagraph (a), (b) or (d) or subdivision (c) (i) of this paragraph own, directly or indirectly, at least 50% of the aggregate vote and value of the shares or other beneficial interests in the person, and

less than 50% of the person's gross income for the taxable year is paid or accrued, directly or indirectly, to persons who are not residents of either Contracting State in the form of payments that are deductible for purposes of the taxes covered by this Agreement in the person's State of residence (but not including arm's length payments in the ordinary course of business for services or tangible property and payments in respect of financial obligations to a bank, provided that where such a bank is not a resident of a Contracting State such payment is attributable to a permanent establishment of that bank located in one of the Contracting States).

(a) A resident of a Contracting State will be entitled to benefits of the Agreement with respect to an item of income, derived from the other Contracting State, regardless of whether the resident is a qualified person, if the resident is actively carrying on business in the first-mentioned State (other than the business of making or managing investments for the resident's own account, unless these activities are banking, insurance or securities activities carried on by a bank, insurance company or registered securities dealer), and the income derived from the other Contracting State is derived in connection with, or is incidental to, that business and that resident satisfies the other conditions of this Agreement for the obtaining of such benefits.

If the resident of a Contracting State or any of its associated enterprises carries on a business activity in the other Contracting State which gives rise to an item of income, subparagraph (a) shall apply to such item only if the business activity in the first-mentioned State is substantial in relation to business carried on in the other State. Whether a business activity is substantial for purposes of this paragraph will be determined based on all the facts and circumstances.

In determining whether a person is actively carrying on business in a Contracting State under subparagraph (a), activities conducted by a partnership in which that person is a partner and activities conducted by persons connected to such person shall be deemed to be conducted by such person. A person shall be connected to another if one possesses at least 50% of the beneficial interest in the other (or, in the case of a company, at least 50% of the aggregate vote and value of the company's shares) or another person possesses, directly or indirectly, at least 50% of the beneficial interest (or, in the case of a company, at least 50% of the aggregate vote and value of the company's shares) in each person. In any case, a person shall be considered to be connected to another if, based on all the facts and circumstances, one has control of the other or both are under the control of the same person or persons.

Notwithstanding the preceding provisions of this Article, if a company that is a resident of a Contracting State, or a company that controls such a company, has outstanding a class of shares

which is subject to terms or other arrangements which entitle its holders to a portion of the income of the company derived from the other Contracting State that is larger than the portion such holders would receive absent such terms or arrangements ("the disproportionate part of the income"); and

50% or more of the voting power and value of which is owned by persons who are not qualified persons

the benefits of this Agreement shall not apply to the disproportionate part of the income.

A resident of a Contracting State that is neither a qualified person pursuant to the provisions of paragraph 2 or entitled to benefits under paragraph 3 or 4 shall, nevertheless, be granted benefits of the Agreement if the competent authority of the other Contracting State determines that the establishment, acquisition or maintenance of such person and the conduct of its operations did not have as one of its principal purposes the obtaining of benefits under the Agreement.

For the purposes of this Article the term "recognized stock exchange" means:

in China:

Shanghai Stock Exchange; and

Shenzhen Stock Exchange;

in Russia:

Moscow International Currency Exchange (MICEX); and

Russian Trade System (RTS);

any other stock exchange which the competent authorities agree to recognize for the purposes of this Article.

Article 24 Non-discrimination

Nationals of a Contracting State shall not be subjected in the other Contracting State to any taxation or any requirement connected therewith, which is other or more burdensome than the taxation and connected requirements to which nationals of that other State in the same circumstances, in particular with respect to residence, are or may be subjected. This provision shall, notwithstanding the provisions of Article 1, also apply to persons who are not residents of one or both of the Contracting States.

The taxation on a permanent establishment which an enterprise of a Contracting State has in the other Contracting State shall not be less favorably levied in that other State than the taxation levied on enterprises of that other State carrying on the same activities. This provision shall not be construed as obliging a Contracting State to grant to residents of the other Contracting State any personal allowances, reliefs and reductions for taxation purposes on account of civil status or family responsibilities which it grants to its own residents.

Except where the provisions of paragraph 1 of Article 9, paragraph 7 of Article 11, or paragraph 6 of Article 12, apply, interest, royalties and other disbursements paid by an enterprise of a Contracting State to a resident of the other Contracting State shall, for the purpose of determining the taxable profits of such enterprise, be deductible under the same conditions as if they had been paid to a resident of the first-mentioned State.

Enterprises of a Contracting State, the capital of which is wholly or partly owned or controlled, directly or indirectly, by one or more residents of the other Contracting State, shall not be subjected in the first-mentioned State to any taxation or any requirement connected therewith which is other or more burdensome than the taxation and connected requirements to which other similar enterprises of the first-mentioned State are or may be subjected.

The provisions of the Article shall, notwithstanding the provisions of Article 2, apply to taxes of every kind and description.

Article 25 Mutual Agreement Procedure

Where a person considers that the actions of one or both of the Contracting States result or will result for him in taxation not in accordance with the provisions of this Agreement, he may, irrespective of the remedies provided by the domestic law of those States, present his case to the competent authority of the Contracting State of which he is a resident or, if his case comes under paragraph 1 of Article 24, to that of the Contracting State of which he is a national. The case must be presented within three years from the first notification of the action resulting in taxation not in accordance with the provisions of the Agreement.

The competent authority shall endeavor, if the objection appears to it to be justified and if it is not itself able to arrive at a satisfactory solution, to resolve the case by mutual agreement with the competent authority of the other Contracting State, with a view to the avoidance of taxation which is not in accordance with the Agreement. Any agreement reached shall be implemented notwithstanding any time limits in the domestic law of the Contracting States.

The competent authorities of the Contracting States shall endeavor to resolve by mutual agreement any difficulties or doubts arising as to the interpretation or application of the Agreement. They may also consult together for the elimination of double taxation in cases not provided for in the Agreement.

The competent authorities of the Contracting States may communicate with each other directly for the purpose of reaching an agreement in the sense of paragraphs 2 and 3. When it seems advisable for reaching an agreement, representatives of the competent authorities of the Contracting States may meet together for an oral exchange of opinions.

Article 26 Exchange of Information

The competent authorities of the Contracting States shall exchange such information as is foreseeably relevant for carrying out the provisions of this Agreement or to the administration or enforcement of the domestic laws concerning taxes of every kind and description imposed on behalf of the Contracting States, or of their political subdivisions or local authorities, insofar as the taxation thereunder is not contrary to the Agreement. The exchange of information is not restricted by Articles 1 and 2.

Any information received under paragraph 1 by a Contracting State shall be treated as secret in the same manner as information obtained under the domestic laws of that State and shall be disclosed only to persons or authorities (including courts and administrative bodies) concerned with the assessment or collection of, the enforcement or prosecution in respect of, the determination of appeals in relation to the taxes referred to in paragraph 1, or the oversight of the above. Such persons or authorities shall use the information only for such purposes. They may disclose the information in public court proceedings or in judicial decisions.

In no case shall the provisions of paragraphs 1 and 2 be construed so as to impose on a Contracting State the obligation:

to carry out administrative measures at variance with the laws and administrative practice of that or of the other Contracting State;

to supply information which is not obtainable under the laws or in the normal course of the administration of that or of the other Contracting State;

to supply information which would disclose any trade, business, industrial, commercial or professional secret or trade process, or information, the disclosure of which would be contrary to public policy (ordre public).

If information is requested by a Contracting State in accordance with this Article, the other Contracting State shall use its information gathering measures to obtain the requested information, even though that other State may not need such information for its own tax purposes. The obligation contained in the preceding sentence is subject to the limitations of paragraph 3 but in no case shall such limitations be construed to permit a Contracting State to decline to supply information solely because it has no domestic interest in such information.

In no case shall the provisions of paragraph 3 be construed to permit a Contracting State to decline to supply information solely because the information is held by a bank, other financial institution, nominee or person acting in an agency or a fiduciary capacity or because it relates to ownership interests in a person.

Article 27 Members of Diplomatic Missions and Consular Posts

Nothing in this Agreement shall affect the fiscal privileges of members of diplomatic missions or consular posts under the general rules of international law or under the provisions of special agreements.

Article 28 Entry into Force

Both Contracting States shall notify each other through diplomatic channels that they have completed the internal legal procedures necessary for the entry into force of this Agreement. This Agreement shall enter into force on the thirtieth day upon the receipt of the latter notification. This Agreement shall be applicable in respect of income derived during the taxable years beginning on or after the first day of January of the calendar year next following that in which this Agreement enters into force.

The Agreement between the Government of the People's Republic of China and the Government of the Russian Federation for the Avoidance of Double Taxation and the Prevention of Fiscal Evasion with respect to Taxes on Income and the Protocol signed at Beijing on 27 May 1994 shall cease to be effective with respect to income in respect of which the provisions of this Agreement are applicable.

Article 29 Termination

This Agreement shall continue in effect indefinitely but either of the Contracting States may, on or before the thirtieth day of June in any calendar year beginning after the expiration of a period of five years from the date of its entry into force, give written notice of termination to the other Contracting State through diplomatic channels. In such event this Agreement shall cease to have effect as respects income derived during the taxable years beginning on or after the first day of January in the calendar year next following that in which the notice of termination is given.

IN WITNESS whereof the undersigned, duly authorized thereto, have signed this Agreement.

Done at Moscow on the 13th day of October, 2014, in duplicate in the Chinese, Russian and English languages, all texts being equally authentic. In case of divergence in interpretation, the English text shall prevail.

For the Government of the People's Republic of China

For the Government of the Russian Federation

Protocol

At the moment of signing the Agreement between the Government of the People's Republic of China and the Government of the Russian Federation for the Avoidance of Double Taxation and the Prevention of Fiscal Evasion with respect to Taxes on Income (hereinafter referred to as "the Agreement"), the undersigned have agreed upon the following provisions which shall form an integral part of the Agreement.

The term "political subdivisions" in this Agreement means, with respect to the Russian Federation, subjects of the Russian Federation, defined as such according to its legislation.

The term in paragraph 2 of Article 10 of this Agreement "this holding amounts to at least 80,000 Euros" means that the total amount of initial investment or consecutive investments in a company, or the initial acquisition or consecutive acquisitions of shares in a company, reaches 80,000 Euros or more.

The term "fixed base" in this Agreement means a fixed place through which an individual performs his independent personal services.

Any document received under Article 26 of this Agreement or a certificate of residence issued by the competent authority of a Contracting State or its authorised representative shall not require legalisation for the purposes of application in the other Contracting State, including their use in the courts and administrative bodies.

IN WITNESS whereof the undersigned, being duly authorized thereto, have signed this Protocol.

Done at ____ on the ______ day of ______, ________, in duplicate in the Chinese, Russian and English languages, all texts being equally authentic. In case of divergence in interpretation, the English text shall prevail.

For the Government of the People's Republic of China

For the Government of the Russian Federation

Spain

Spain, officially the Kingdom of Spain, is a state in Southern Europe. Spain is bordered to the north by France, Andorra and the Bay of Biscay and to the west by Portugal and the Atlantic Ocean, while it is bordered to the south and east by the Mediterranean Sea. Spain's capital and largest city is Madrid, while Barcelona, Valencia, Seville, Zaragoza, Málaga, Murcia, Palma de Mallorca, Las Palmas de Gran Canaria and Bilbao are major urban areas.

Spain is a popular immigration destination in Europe, with 5.4 million foreign residents in Spain in 2020. The single largest group of immigrants are European, with a majority of Romanians, Britons, Germans, French, with substantial presence of Sub-Saharan people and Asians.

The official and predominant spoken language is Spanish, the only language having official status for the whole country. Specific territories recognize special or co-official status to various other languages.

Spain is a unitary parliamentary constitutional monarchy. The Constitución Española is the constitution regulating the political system, in force since 1978. The Congress of Deputies and the Senate exert the legislative power forming the parliament. The Congress of Deputies is elected through direct elections using the Party-list proportional representation system. 208 of 266 members of the Senate are directly elected by the people, while the legislatures of the autonomous communities elect 57 members.

Executive power is vested in the President of the Council and his or her cabinet. The President of the Council is appointed by the Monarch after being elected by the party or coalition with the parliamentary majority in the Congress of Deputies.

Spain has a civil law system based on Roman law. The Constitutional Court acts as Supreme Court, managing constitutional matters, with judicial review powers.

Spain is a unitary monarchy, divided into 17 autonomous communities and 2 autonomous cities.

Spain is part of the European Union since 1986.

© The Author(s), under exclusive license to Springer Nature Singapore Pte Ltd. 2022

L. Riccardi and G. Riccardi, *China–Europe Tax Treaties*,
https://doi.org/10.1007/978-981-19-3563-3_25

Category	Value
Population (mln persons)	46.656
Currency	Euro

Source International Monetary Fund, year 2019

Spain is the second largest economy of Southern Europe, with a GDP valued 1397.9 billion USD in 2019, and has a population of about 46 million people. Spain, similarly to Italy, enjoys low inflation, but unemployment is over 10% (14%), the sixth highest in Europe. Spain ranked 15 out of 43 in Europe in the 2020 Doing Business ranking, scoring 77.9, and imposes a CIT of 25%. Spain records a trade deficit of 38 billion USD, it is the eighth main exporter in Europe.

GDP and local economy	
GDP current prices (billion USD)	1397.9
GDP per capita (USD)	29,961
GDP growth (%)	2.0
Inflation (%)	0.7
Unemployment (%)	14.1
General government total expenditure (% of GDP)	42.0
General government gross debt (% of GDP)	95.5
Doing business score 2020	77.9

Source International Monetary Fund and UNCTAD, year 2019

Foreign direct investment	
FDI outstock (million USD)	606,549
FDI instock (million USD)	751,510

Source UNCTAD, year 2019

Trade	
Imports (million USD)	371,929
Exports (million USD)	333,622
Trade balance (million USD)	−38,306

Source International Monetary Fund and UNCTAD, year 2019

Main import–export	
First import by category	Vehicles other than railway, tramway
Second import by category	Machinery, nuclear reactors, boilers
First export by category	Vehicles other than railway, tramway

(continued)

(continued)

Main import–export	
Second export by category	Machinery, nuclear reactors, boilers

Source United Nations COMTRADE, year 2020

The legal bases for taxation are established in the constitution. Spain imposes individual income tax, property sales taxes, capital gains, corporate income tax, and value added tax. Progressivity is guaranteed by a system with different bands and various deductions.

Taxes	
Company income tax (%)	25
Top Individual income tax (%)	47
Value added tax or sales tax (%)	21
Reduced value added tax or sales tax (%)	4 / 10

Source RsA Asia report, year 2021

- Economic relation with China

Spain records a trade deficit of 17.2 billion USD in 2020. "Meat and edible meat" is the first export category, worth 3.29 billion USD, followed by "Ores slag and ash". "Electrical, electronic equipment" is the first import category, valued 5.64 billion USD. Spain is not part of the Belt and Road Initiative. In 1990 Spain and China signed their DTA, which had come into force in 1992. In 2018 they have signed a new double tax agreement, coming into force in May 2021.

Category	Value
Belt road	No

Source UNCTAD, year 2021

Import from China	
Import from China (billion USD)	27.54
First import category from China	Electrical, electronic equipment
First import value (billion USD)	5.64
Second import category from China	Machinery, nuclear reactors, boilers
Second import value (billion USD)	3.27

Source United Nations COMTRADE, year 2020

Export to China	
Export to China (billion USD)	10.35
First export category towards China	Meat and edible meat offal
First export Value (billion USD)	3.29
Second export category towards China	Ores slag and ash
Second export value (billion USD)	0.889

Source United Nations COMTRADE, year 2020

Trade balance	
Trade balance (billion USD)	−17.19

Source United Nations COMTRADE, year 2020

Double tax agreement	
DTA effective date	2021.5.2
Dividends (%)	10
Interest (%)	10
Royalties (%)	6–10

Source State Administration of Taxation of China, year 2021

Title AGREEMENT BETWEEN THE PEOPLE'S REPUBLIC OF CHINA AND THE KINGDOM OF SPAIN FOR THE ELIMINATION OF DOUBLE TAXATION WITH RESPECT TO TAXES ON INCOME AND THE PREVENTION OF TAX EVASION AND AVOIDANCE

Treaty Text

The People's Republic of China and the Kingdom of Spain,

Desiring to further develop their economic relationship and to enhance their cooperation in tax matters,

Intending to conclude an Agreement for the elimination of double taxation with respect to taxes on income without creating opportunities for non-taxation or reduced taxation through tax evasion or avoidance (including through treaty-shopping arrangements aimed at obtaining reliefs provided in this Agreement for the indirect benefit of residents of third States),

Have agreed as follows:

Article 1 Persons Covered

This Agreement shall apply to persons who are residents of one or both of the Contracting States.

For purposes of this Agreement, income derived by or through an entity or arrangement that is treated as wholly or partly fiscally transparent under the tax law of either

Contracting State shall be considered to be income of a resident of a Contracting State but only to the extent that the income is treated, for purposes of taxation by that State, as the income of a resident of that State.

This Agreement shall not affect the taxation, by a Contracting State, of its residents except with respect to the benefits granted under paragraph 2 of Article 9, paragraph 2 of Article 18, and Articles 19, 20, 21, 23, 26, 27 and 29.

Article 2 Taxes Covered

This Agreement shall apply to taxes on income imposed on behalf of a Contracting State or of its political subdivisions, irrespective of the manner in which they are levied.

There shall be regarded as taxes on income all taxes imposed on total income, or on elements of income, including taxes on gains from the alienation of movable or immovable property, taxes on the total amounts of wages or salaries paid by enterprises.

The existing taxes to which the Agreement shall apply are in particular:

in China:
the individual income tax;
the enterprise income tax; (hereinafter referred to as "Chinese tax");
in Spain:
the income tax on individuals;
the corporation tax;
the income tax on non residents; (hereinafter referred to as "Spanish Tax").

The Agreement shall apply also to any identical or substantially similar taxes that are imposed after the date of signature of the Agreement in addition to, or in place of, the existing taxes. The competent authorities of the Contracting States shall notify each other of any significant changes which have been made in their taxation laws.

Article 3 General Definitions

For the purposes of this Agreement, unless the context otherwise requires:

the term "China" means the People's Republic of China; when used in geographical sense, means all the territory of the People's Republic of China, including its land territory, internal water, territorial sea and the air space above them, in which the Chinese laws relating to taxation apply, and any area beyond its territorial sea, within which the People's Republic of China has sovereign rights or jurisdiction in accordance with international law and its internal law;
the term "Spain" means the Kingdom of Spain and, when used in a geographical sense, means the territory of the Kingdom of Spain, including inland waters, the air space, the territorial sea and any area outside the territorial sea upon which, in accordance with international law and on application of its domestic legislation, the Kingdom of Spain exercises jurisdiction or sovereign rights with respect to the seabed, its subsoil and superjacent waters, and their natural resources;

the terms “a Contracting State” and “the other Contracting State” mean China and Spain as the context requires;
the term “person” includes an individual, a company and any other body of persons;
the term “company” means any body corporate or any entity that is treated as a body corporate for tax purposes;
the terms “enterprise of a Contracting State” and “enterprise of the other Contracting State” mean, respectively, an enterprise carried on by a resident of a Contracting State and an enterprise carried on by a resident of the other Contracting State;
the term “international traffic” means any transport by a ship or aircraft or railway or a road vehicle operated by an enterprise of a Contracting State, except when the ship, aircraft, railway or road vehicle is operated solely between places in the other Contracting State;
the term “competent authority” means, in the case of China, the State Administration of Taxation or its authorized representative, and in the case of Spain, the Minister of Finance or his authorised representative;
the term “national”, in relation to a Contracting State, means:
any individual possessing the nationality of a Contracting State; and
any legal person, partnership or association deriving its status as such from the laws in force in a Contracting State.

As regards the application of the Agreement at any time by a Contracting State, any term not defined therein shall, unless the context otherwise requires, have the meaning that it has at that time under the law of that State for the purposes of the taxes to which the Agreement applies, any meaning under the applicable tax laws of that State prevailing over a meaning given to the term under other laws of that State.

Article 4 Resident

For the purposes of this Agreement, the term “resident of a Contracting State” means any person who, under the laws of that State, is liable to tax therein by reason of his domicile, residence, place of incorporation, place of effective management or any other criterion of a similar nature, and also includes that State and any political subdivision or local authority thereof. This term, however, does not include any person who is liable to tax in that State in respect only of income from sources in that State.

Where by reason of the provisions of paragraph 1 an individual is a resident of both Contracting States, then his status shall be determined as follows:

he shall be deemed to be a resident only of the State in which he has a permanent home available to him; if he has a permanent home available to him in both States, he shall be deemed to be a resident only of the State with which his personal and economic relations are closer (centre of vital interests);
if the State in which he has his centre of vital interests cannot be determined, or if he has not a permanent home available to him in either State, he shall be deemed to be a resident only of the State in which he has an habitual abode;

if he has an habitual abode in both States or in neither of them, he shall be deemed to be a resident only of the State of which he is a national;
if he is a national of both States or of neither of them, the competent authorities of the Contracting States shall settle the question by mutual agreement. Where by reason of the provisions of paragraph 1 a person other than an individual is a resident of both Contracting States, then it shall be deemed to be a resident only of the State in which its place of effective management is situated.

Article 5 Permanent Establishment

For the purposes of this Agreement, the term "permanent establishment" means a fixed place of business through which the business of an enterprise is wholly or partly carried on.

The term "permanent establishment" includes especially:

a place of management;
a branch;
an office;
a factory;
a workshop; and
a mine, an oil or gas well, a quarry or any other place of extraction of natural resources.

The term "permanent establishment" likewise encompasses:

a building site, or construction, assembly or installation project, but only if such site or project lasts more than twelve months;
the furnishing of services, including consultancy services, by an enterprise of a Contracting State through employees or other personnel engaged for such purpose, but only if activities of that nature continue (for the same or a connected project) within the other Contracting State for a period or periods aggregating more than 183 days within any twelve-month period.

Notwithstanding the preceding provisions of this Article, the term "permanent establishment" shall be deemed not to include:

the use of facilities solely for the purpose of storage, display or delivery of goods or merchandise belonging to the enterprise;
the maintenance of a stock of goods or merchandise belonging to the enterprise solely for the purpose of storage, display or delivery;
the maintenance of a stock of goods or merchandise belonging to the enterprise solely for the purpose of processing by another enterprise;
the maintenance of a fixed place of business solely for the purpose of purchasing goods or merchandise or of collecting information, for the enterprise;
the maintenance of a fixed place of business solely for the purpose of carrying on, for the enterprise, any other activity;
the maintenance of a fixed place of business solely for any combination of activities mentioned in subparagraphs (a) to (e),

provided that such activity or, in the case of subparagraph (f), the overall activity of the fixed place of business, is of a preparatory or auxiliary character.

Paragraph 4 shall not apply to a fixed place of business that is used or maintained by an enterprise if the same enterprise or a closely related enterprise carries on business activities at the same place or at another place in the same Contracting State and

that place or other place constitutes a permanent establishment for the enterprise or the closely related enterprise under the provisions of this Article, or
the overall activity resulting from the combination of the activities carried on by the two enterprises at the same place, or by the same enterprise or closely related enterprises at the two places, is not of a preparatory or auxiliary character,
provided that the business activities carried on by the two enterprises at the same place, or by the same enterprise or closely related enterprises at the two places, constitute complementary functions that are part of a cohesive business operation.

Notwithstanding the provisions of paragraphs 1 and 2 but subject to the provisions of paragraph 6, where a person is acting in a Contracting State on behalf of an enterprise and, in doing so, habitually concludes contracts, or habitually plays the principal role leading to the conclusion of contracts that are routinely concluded without material modification by the enterprise, and these contracts are

in the name of the enterprise, or
for the transfer of the ownership of, or for the granting of the right to use, property owned by that enterprise or that the enterprise has the right to use, or
for the provision of services by that enterprise,
that enterprise shall be deemed to have a permanent establishment in that State in respect of any activities which that person undertakes for the enterprise, unless the activities of such person are limited to those mentioned in paragraph 4 which, if exercised through a fixed place of business, would not make this fixed place of business a permanent establishment under the provisions of that paragraph.

(a) Paragraph 5 shall not apply where the person acting in a Contracting State on behalf of an enterprise of the other Contracting State carries on business in the first-mentioned State as an independent agent and acts for the enterprise in the ordinary course of that business. However, if a person acts exclusively or almost exclusively on behalf of one or more enterprises to which it is closely related, that person shall not be considered to be an independent agent within the meaning of this paragraph with respect to any such enterprise.
(b) For the purposes of this Article, a person or enterprise is closely related to an enterprise if, based on all the relevant facts and circumstances, one has control of the other or both are under the control of the same persons or enterprises. In any case, a person or enterprise shall be considered to be closely related to an enterprise if one possesses directly or indirectly more than 50% of the beneficial interest in the other (or, in the case of a company, more than 50% of the aggregate vote and value of the company's shares or of the beneficial equity interest in the company) or if another

person or enterprise possesses directly or indirectly more than 50% of the beneficial interest (or, in the case of a company, more than 50% of the aggregate vote and value of the company's shares or of the beneficial equity interest in the company) in the person and the enterprise or in the two enterprises.

The fact that a company which is a resident of a Contracting State controls or is controlled by a company which is a resident of the other Contracting State, or which carries on business in that other State (whether through a permanent establishment or otherwise), shall not of itself constitute either company a permanent establishment of the other.

Article 6 Income from Immovable Property

Income derived by a resident of a Contracting State from immovable property (including income from agriculture or forestry) situated in the other Contracting State may be taxed in that other State.

The term "immovable property" shall have the meaning which it has under the law of the Contracting State in which the property in question is situated. The term shall in any case include property accessory to immovable property, livestock and equipment used in agriculture and forestry, rights to which the provisions of general law respecting landed property apply, usufruct of immovable property and rights to variable or fixed payments as consideration for the working of, or the right to work, mineral deposits, sources and other natural resources; ships and aircraft shall not be regarded as immovable property.

The provisions of paragraph 1 shall apply to income derived from the direct use, letting, or use in any other form of immovable property.

The provisions of paragraphs 1 and 3 shall also apply to the income from immovable property of an enterprise and to income from immovable property used for the performance of independent personal services.

Article 7 Business Profits

The profits of an enterprise of a Contracting State shall be taxable only in that State unless the enterprise carries on business in the other Contracting State through a permanent establishment situated therein. If the enterprise carries on business as aforesaid, the profits of the enterprise may be taxed in the other State, but only so much of them as is attributable to that permanent establishment.

Subject to the provisions of paragraph 3, where an enterprise of a Contracting State carries on business in the other Contracting State through a permanent establishment situated therein, there shall in each Contracting State be attributed to that permanent establishment the profits which it might be expected to make if it were a distinct and separate enterprise engaged in the same or similar activities under the same or similar conditions and dealing wholly independently with the enterprise of which it is a permanent establishment.

In determining the profits of a permanent establishment, there shall be allowed as deductions expenses which are incurred for the purposes of the permanent establishment, including executive and general administrative expenses so incurred, whether in the State in which the permanent establishment is situated or elsewhere.

Insofar as it has been customary in a Contracting State to determine the profits to be attributed to a permanent establishment on the basis of an apportionment of the total profits of the enterprise to its various parts, nothing in paragraph 2 shall preclude that Contracting State from determining the profits to be taxed by such an apportionment as may be customary; the method of apportionment adopted shall, however, be such that the result shall be in accordance with the principles contained in this Article.

No profits shall be attributed to a permanent establishment by reason of the mere purchase by that permanent establishment of goods or merchandise for the enterprise.

For the purposes of the preceding paragraphs, the profits to be attributed to the permanent establishment shall be determined by the same method year by year unless there is good and sufficient reason to the contrary.

Where profits include items of income which are dealt with separately in other Articles of this Agreement, then the provisions of those Articles shall not be affected by the provisions of this Article.

Article 8 International Transport

Profits from the operation of ships, aircraft, railway and road vehicles in international traffic by an enterprise of a Contracting State shall be taxable only in that Contracting State.

The provisions of paragraph 1 shall also apply to profits from the participation in a pool, a joint business or an international operating agency.

Article 9 Associated Enterprises

Where an enterprise of a Contracting State participates directly or indirectly in the management, control or capital of an enterprise of the other Contracting State, or

> the same persons participate directly or indirectly in the management, control or capital of an enterprise of a Contracting State and an enterprise of the other Contracting State,
>
> and in either case conditions are made or imposed between the two enterprises in their commercial or financial relations which differ from those which would be made between independent enterprises, then any profits which would, but for those conditions, have accrued to one of the enterprises, but, by reason of those conditions, have not so accrued, may be included in the profits of that enterprise and taxed accordingly.

Where a Contracting State includes in the profits of an enterprise of that State—and taxes accordingly—profits on which an enterprise of the other Contracting State has been charged to tax in that other Contracting State and that other State agrees that the profits so included are profits which would have accrued to the enterprise of the first-mentioned State if the conditions made between the two enterprises had been those which would have been made between independent enterprises, then that other State shall make an appropriate adjustment to the amount of the tax charged therein on those profits. In determining such adjustment, due regard shall be had to the other provisions of this Agreement and the competent authorities of the Contracting States shall, if necessary, consult each other.

Article 10 Dividends

Dividends paid by a company which is a resident of a Contracting State to a resident of the other Contracting State may be taxed in that other State.

However, such dividends may also be taxed in the Contracting State of which the company paying the dividends is a resident and according to the laws of that State, but if the beneficial owner of the dividends is a resident of the other Contracting State, the tax so charged shall not exceed:

5% of the gross amount of the dividends if the beneficial owner is a company (other than a partnership) which holds directly at least 25% of the capital of the company paying the dividends throughout a 365 day period that includes the day of the payment of the dividend;

10% of the gross amount of the dividends in all other cases.

This paragraph shall not affect the taxation of the company in respect of the profits out of which the dividends are paid.

Notwithstanding the provisions of paragraph 2, dividends paid by a company which is a resident of a Contracting State to a resident of the other Contracting State shall be exempt from tax in the first-mentioned State if the beneficial owner of the dividends is the other Contracting State or political subdivisions, local authorities thereof, or the Central Bank of the other Contracting State or any entity the capital of which is wholly owned directly or indirectly by the other Contracting State.

The term "dividends" as used in this Article means income from shares, "jouissance" shares or "jouissance" rights, mining shares, founders' shares or other rights, not being debt- claims, participating in profits, as well as income from other corporate rights which is subjected to the same taxation treatment as income from shares by the laws of the State of which the company making the distribution is a resident.

The provisions of paragraphs 1, 2 and 3 shall not apply if the beneficial owner of the dividends, being a resident of a Contracting State, carries on business in the other Contracting State of which the company paying the dividends is a resident through a permanent establishment situated therein, or performs in that other State independent personal services from a fixed base situated therein and the holding in respect of which the dividends are paid is effectively connected with such permanent establishment or fixed base. In such case the provisions of Article 7 or Article 14, as the case may be, shall apply.

Where a company which is a resident of a Contracting State derives profits or income from the other Contracting State, that other State may not impose any tax on the dividends paid by the company, except insofar as such dividends are paid to a resident of that other State or insofar as the holding in respect of which the dividends are paid is effectively connected with a permanent establishment or a fixed base situated in that other State, nor subject the company's undistributed profits to a tax on the company's undistributed profits, even if the dividends paid or the undistributed profits consist wholly or partly of profits or income arising in such other State.

Article 11 Interest

Interest arising in a Contracting State and paid to a resident of the other Contracting State may be taxed in that other State.

However, such interest may also be taxed in the Contracting State in which it arises and according to the laws of that State, but if the beneficial owner of the interest is a resident of the other Contracting State, the tax so charged shall not exceed 10% of the gross amount of the interest.

Notwithstanding the provisions of paragraph 2, interest arising in a Contracting State and paid to the other Contracting State or political subdivisions, local authorities thereof, the Central Bank of the other Contracting State, or any entity the capital of which is wholly owned directly or indirectly by the other Contracting State, or paid on loans guaranteed or insured by the other Contracting State, or political subdivisions, local authorities thereof, the Central Bank of the other Contracting State or any entity the capital of which is wholly owned directly or indirectly by the other Contracting State, shall be exempt from tax in the first-mentioned State.

Notwithstanding the provisions of paragraph 2, interest arising in a Contracting State beneficially owned by a resident of the other Contracting State shall be exempt from tax in the first-mentioned State if the interest is paid in connection with the sale of commercial or scientific equipment on credit.

The term "interest" as used in this Article means income from debt-claims of every kind, whether or not secured by mortgage and whether or not carrying a right to participate in the debtor's profits, and in particular, income from government securities and income from bonds or debentures, including premiums and prizes attaching to such securities, bonds or debentures, as well as all other income assimilated to income from money lent by the taxation laws of the State in which the income arises. Penalty charges for late payment shall not be regarded as interest for the purpose of this Article.

The provisions of paragraphs 1, 2, 3 and 4 shall not apply if the beneficial owner of the interest, being a resident of a Contracting State, carries on business in the other Contracting State in which the interest arises through a permanent establishment situated therein, or performs in that other State independent personal services from a fixed base situated therein, and the debt-claim in respect of which the interest is paid is effectively connected with such permanent establishment or fixed base. In such case the provisions of Article 7 or Article 14, as the case may be, shall apply.

Interest shall be deemed to arise in a Contracting State when the payer is a resident of that State. Where, however, the person paying the interest, whether he is a resident of a Contracting State or not, has in a Contracting State a permanent establishment or a fixed base in connection with which the indebtedness on which the interest is paid was incurred, and such interest is borne by such permanent establishment or fixed base, then such interest shall be deemed to arise in the State in which the permanent establishment or fixed base is situated.

Where, by reason of a special relationship between the payer and the beneficial owner or between both of them and some other person, the amount of the interest, having regard to the debt-claim for which it is paid, exceeds the amount which would have been agreed upon by the payer and the beneficial owner in the absence of such relationship, the provisions of this Article shall apply only to the last-mentioned amount. In such case, the excess part of the payments shall remain taxable according to the laws of each Contracting State, due regard being had to the other provisions of this Agreement.

Article 12 Royalties

Royalties arising in a Contracting State and paid to a resident of the other Contracting State may be taxed in that other State.

However, such royalties may also be taxed in the Contracting State in which they arise and according to the laws of that State, but if the beneficial owner of the royalties is a resident of the other Contracting State, the tax so charged shall not exceed 10% of the gross amount of the royalties.

The term "royalties" as used in this Article means payments of any kind received as a consideration for the use of, or the right to use, any copyright of literary, artistic, scientific or other work including cinematography films, and films and recordings for radio or television broadcasting, any patent, trade mark, design or model, plan, secret formula or process, or for information concerning industrial, commercial or scientific experience.

The provisions of paragraphs 1 and 2 shall not apply if the beneficial owner of the royalties, being a resident of a Contracting State, carries on business in the other Contracting State in which the royalties arise through a permanent establishment situated therein, or performs in that other State independent personal services from a fixed base situated therein, and the right or property in respect of which the royalties are paid is effectively connected with such permanent establishment or fixed base. In such case the provisions of Article 7 or Article 14, as the case may be, shall apply.

Royalties shall be deemed to arise in a Contracting State when the payer is a resident of that Contracting State. Where, however, the person paying the royalties, whether he is a resident of a Contracting State or not, has in a Contracting State a permanent establishment or a fixed base in connection with which the liability to pay the royalties was incurred, and such royalties are borne by such permanent establishment or fixed base, then such royalties shall be deemed to arise in the State in which the permanent establishment or fixed base is situated.

Where, by reason of a special relationship between the payer and the beneficial owner or between both of them and some other person, the amount of the royalties, having regard to the use, right or information for which they are paid, exceeds the amount which would have been agreed upon by the payer and the beneficial owner in the absence of such relationship, the provisions of this Article shall apply only to the last-mentioned amount. In such case, the excess part of the payments shall remain taxable according to the laws of each Contracting State, due regard being had to the other provisions of this Agreement.

Article 13 Capital Gains

Gains derived by a resident of a Contracting State from the alienation of immovable property referred to in Article 6 and situated in the other Contracting State may be taxed in that other State.

Gains from the alienation of movable property forming part of the business property of a permanent establishment which an enterprise of a Contracting State has in the other Contracting State or of movable property pertaining to a fixed base available to a resident of a Contracting State in the other Contracting State for the purpose of performing independent personal services, including such gains from the alienation of such a permanent establishment (alone or with the whole enterprise) or of such a fixed base, may be taxed in that other State.

Gains from the alienation of ships or aircraft or railway or road vehicles operated in international traffic by an enterprise of a Contracting State, or movable property pertaining to the operation of such ships or aircraft or railway or road vehicles, shall be taxable only in that Contracting State.

Gains derived by a resident of a Contracting State from the alienation of shares or comparable interests deriving more than 50% of their value directly or indirectly from immovable property situated in the other Contracting State may be taxed in that other State. In determining that percentage, immovable property used by a company for exercising its business will not be taken into account.

Gains, other than those to which paragraph 4 applies, derived by a resident of a Contracting State from the alienation of shares, other than shares in which there is substantial and regular trading on a recognized stock exchange provided that the total of the shares alienated by the resident during the fiscal year in which the alienation takes place does not exceed 3% of the quoted shares, of a company which is a resident of the other Contracting State may be taxed in that other Contracting State if the alienator, at any time during the 365 days preceding the alienation, held directly or indirectly, at least 25% of the capital of that company.

Gains from the alienation of any property, other than that referred to in paragraphs 1 to 5, shall be taxable only in the Contracting State of which the alienator is a resident.

Article 14 Independent Personal Services

Income derived by an individual resident of a Contracting State in respect of professional services or other activities of an independent character shall be taxable only in that State except in the following circumstances, when such income may also be taxed in the other Contracting State:

if he has a fixed base regularly available to him in the other Contracting State for the purpose of performing his activities; in that case, only so much of the income as is attributable to that fixed base may be taxed in that other State; or

if his stay in the other Contracting State is for a period or periods amounting to or exceeding in the aggregate 183 days in any twelve-month period commencing or ending in the fiscal year concerned; in that case, only so much of the income as is derived from his activities performed in that other State may be taxed in that other State.

The term "professional services" includes especially independent scientific, literary, artistic, educational or teaching activities as well as the independent activities of physicians, lawyers, engineers, architects, dentists and accountants.

Article 15 Income from Employment

Subject to the provisions of Articles 16, 18, and 19, salaries, wages and other similar remuneration derived by a resident of a Contracting State in respect of an employment shall be taxable only in that State unless the employment is exercised in the other Contracting State. If the employment is so exercised, such remuneration as is derived therefrom may be taxed in that other State.

Notwithstanding the provisions of paragraph 1, remuneration derived by a resident of a Contracting State in respect of an employment exercised in the other Contracting State shall be taxable only in the first-mentioned State if:

the recipient is present in the other State for a period or periods not exceeding in the aggregate 183 days in any twelve-month period commencing or ending in the fiscal year concerned, and
the remuneration is paid by, or on behalf of, an employer who is not a resident of the other State, and the remuneration is not borne by a permanent establishment or a fixed base which the employer has in the other State.

Notwithstanding the preceding provisions of this Article, remuneration derived in respect of an employment exercised aboard a ship, aircraft, railway or road vehicle operated in international traffic by an enterprise of a Contracting State, may be taxed in that Contracting State.

Article 16 Directors' Fees

Directors'' fees and other similar payments derived by a resident of a Contracting State in his capacity as a member of the board of directors of a company which is a resident of the other Contracting State may be taxed in that other State.

Article 17 Entertainers and Sportspersons

Notwithstanding the provisions of Articles 14 and 15, income derived by a resident of a Contracting State as an entertainer, such as a theatre, motion picture, radio or television artiste, or a musician, or as a sportsperson, from that resident's personal activities as such exercised in the other Contracting State, may be taxed in that other State.

Where income in respect of personal activities exercised by an entertainer or a sportsperson acting as such accrues not to the entertainer or sportsperson but to another person, that income may, notwithstanding the provisions of Articles 7, 14 and 15, be taxed in the Contracting State in which the activities of the entertainer or sportsperson are exercised.

Notwithstanding the provisions of paragraphs 1 and 2, income derived from such activities as are referred to in paragraph 1 performed under a cultural agreement or arrangement between the Contracting States or political subdivisions or local authorities thereof shall be exempt from tax in the Contracting State in which the activities are exercised if the visit to that State is wholly or substantially supported by public or government funds of either Contracting State or political subdivisions or local authorities thereof.

Article 18 Pensions

Subject to the provisions of paragraph 2 of Article 19, pensions and other similar remuneration paid to a resident of a Contracting State in consideration of past employment shall be taxable only in that State.

Notwithstanding the provisions of paragraph 1, pensions paid and other similar payments made by the Government of a Contracting State or a local authority thereof under a public welfare scheme of the social security system of that State shall be taxable only in that State.

Article 19 Government Service

(a) Salaries, wages and other similar remuneration, other than a pension, paid by a Contracting State or a political subdivision or a local authority thereof to an individual in respect of services rendered to that State or subdivision or authority, shall be taxable only in that State.

However, such salaries, wages and other similar remuneration shall be taxable only in the other Contracting State if the services are rendered in that State and the individual is a resident of that State who:

is a national of that State; or
did not become a resident of that State solely for the purpose of rendering the services.

(a) Pensions and other similar remuneration paid by, or out of funds created by, a Contracting State or a political subdivision or a local authority thereof to an individual in respect of services rendered to that State or subdivision or authority thereof shall be taxable only in that State.

(b) However, such pensions and other similar remuneration shall be taxable only in the other Contracting State if the individual is a resident of, and a national of, that State.

The provisions of Articles 15, 16, 17, and 18 shall apply to salaries, wages, pensions, and other similar remuneration in respect of services rendered in connection with a business carried on by a Contracting State or a political subdivision or a local authority thereof.

Article 20 Teachers and Researchers

Remuneration which an individual who is or was immediately before visiting a Contracting State a resident of the other Contracting State, and who is present in the first- mentioned State solely for the purpose of teaching, giving lectures or engaging in research in a school, institute, university, or any other educational or research institution officially recognized by the Government of that State, receives for such services shall be exempt from tax in that State for a period not exceeding, in total three years, as from the date of his or her arrival in that State.

The provisions of paragraph 1 shall not apply to income from research, if this research is not in the public interest but primarily for the private benefit of a certain person or persons.

Article 21 Students

Payments which a student or business apprentice who is or was immediately before visiting a Contracting State a resident of the other Contracting State and who is present in the first- mentioned State solely for the purpose of his education or training receives for the purpose of his maintenance, education or training shall not be taxed in that State, provided that such payments arise from sources outside that State.

Article 22 Other Income

Items of income of a resident of a Contracting State, wherever arising, not dealt with in the foregoing Articles of this Agreement shall be taxable only in that State.

The provisions of paragraph 1 shall not apply to income, other than income from immovable property as defined in paragraph 2 of Article 6, if the recipient of such income, being a resident of a Contracting State, carries on business in the other Contracting State through a permanent establishment situated therein, or performs in that other State independent personal services from a fixed base situated therein, and the right or property in respect of which the income is paid is effectively connected with such permanent establishment or fixed base. In such case the provisions of Article 7 or Article 14, as the case may be, shall apply.

Article 23 Methods for Elimination of Double Taxation

In China, in accordance with the provisions of the law of China, double taxation shall be eliminated as follows:

Where a resident of China derives income from Spain, the amount of tax on that income payable in Spain in accordance with the provisions of this Agreement (except to the extent that these provisions allow taxation by Spain solely because the income is also income derived by a resident of Spain) may be credited against the Chinese tax imposed on that resident. The amount of the credit, however, shall not exceed the amount of the Chinese tax on that income computed in accordance with the taxation laws and regulations of China.

Where the income derived from Spain is a dividend paid by a company which is a resident of Spain to a company which is a resident of China and which owns not less than 20% of the shares of the company paying the dividend, the credit shall take into account the tax paid to Spain by the company paying the dividend in respect of its income.

In Spain, double taxation shall be avoided following either the provisions of its internal legislation or the following provisions in accordance with the internal legislation of Spain:

Where a resident of Spain derives income which, in accordance with the provisions of this Agreement (except to the extent that these provisions allow taxation by China solely because the income is also income derived by a resident of China), may be taxed in China, Spain shall allow:

as a deduction from the tax on the income of that resident, an amount equal to the income tax paid in China;
the deduction of the underlying corporation tax shall be given in accordance with the internal legislation of Spain.

Such deduction shall not, however, exceed that part of the income tax, as computed before the deduction is given, which is attributable to the income which may be taxed in China.

Where in accordance with any provision of the Agreement income derived by a resident of Spain is exempt from tax in Spain, Spain may nevertheless, in calculating the amount of tax on the remaining income of such resident, take into account the exempted income.

Article 24 Entitlement to Benefits

Notwithstanding the other provisions of this Agreement, a benefit under this Agreement shall not be granted in respect of an item of income if it is reasonable to conclude, having regard to all relevant facts and circumstances, that obtaining that benefit was one of the principal purposes of any arrangement or transaction that resulted directly or indirectly in that benefit, unless it is established that granting that benefit in these circumstances would be in accordance with the object and purpose of the relevant provisions of this Agreement.

Article 25 Miscellaneous Rule

Nothing in this Agreement shall prejudice the right of each Contracting State to apply its domestic laws and measures concerning the prevention of tax avoidance, whether or not described as such, insofar as they do not give rise to taxation contrary to this Agreement.

Article 26 Non-discrimination

Nationals of a Contracting State shall not be subjected in the other Contracting State to any taxation or any requirement connected therewith, which is other or more burdensome than the taxation and connected requirements to which nationals of that other State in the same circumstances, in particular with respect to residence, are or may be subjected. This provision shall, notwithstanding the provisions of Article 1, also apply to persons who are not residents of one or both of the Contracting States.

The taxation on a permanent establishment which an enterprise of a Contracting State has in the other Contracting State shall not be less favorably levied in that other State than the taxation levied on enterprises of that other State carrying on the same activities. This provision shall not be construed as obliging a Contracting State to grant to residents of the other Contracting State any personal allowances, reliefs and reductions for taxation purposes on account of civil status or family responsibilities which it grants to its own residents.

Except where the provisions of paragraph 1 of Article 9, paragraph 8 of Article 11, or paragraph 6 of Article 12, apply, interest, royalties and other disbursements paid by an enterprise of a Contracting State to a resident of the other Contracting State shall, for the purpose of determining the taxable profits of such enterprise, be deductible under the same conditions as if they had been paid to a resident of the first-mentioned State.

Enterprises of a Contracting State, the capital of which is wholly or partly owned or controlled, directly or indirectly, by one or more residents of the other Contracting State, shall not be subjected in the first-mentioned State to any taxation or any requirement connected therewith which is other or more burdensome than the taxation and connected requirements to which other similar enterprises of the first-mentioned State are or may be subjected.

The provisions of the Article shall, notwithstanding the provisions of Article 2, apply to taxes of every kind and description.

Article 27 Mutual Agreement Procedure

Where a person considers that the actions of one or both of the Contracting States result or will result for him in taxation not in accordance with the provisions of this Agreement, he may, irrespective of the remedies provided by the domestic law of those States, present his case to the competent authority of the Contracting State of which he is a resident or, if his case comes under paragraph 1 of Article 26, to that of the Contracting State of which he is a national. The case must be presented within three years from the first notification of the action resulting in taxation not in accordance with the provisions of the Agreement.

The competent authority shall endeavour, if the objection appears to it to be justified and if it is not itself able to arrive at a satisfactory solution, to resolve the case by mutual agreement with the competent authority of the other Contracting State, with a view to the avoidance of taxation which is not in accordance with the Agreement. Any agreement reached shall be implemented notwithstanding any time limits in the domestic law of the Contracting States.

The competent authorities of the Contracting States shall endeavour to resolve by mutual agreement any difficulties or doubts arising as to the interpretation or application of the Agreement. They may also consult together for the elimination of double taxation in cases not provided for in the Agreement.

The competent authorities of the Contracting States may communicate with each other directly for the purpose of reaching an agreement in the sense of paragraphs 2 and 3. When it seems advisable for reaching an agreement, representatives of the competent authorities of the Contracting States may meet together for an oral exchange of opinions.

Article 28 Exchange of Information

The competent authorities of the Contracting States shall exchange such information as is foreseeably relevant for carrying out the provisions of this Agreement or to

the administration or enforcement of the domestic laws concerning taxes of every kind and description imposed on behalf of the Contracting States, or of their political subdivisions or local authorities, insofar as the taxation thereunder is not contrary to the Agreement. The exchange of information is not restricted by Articles 1 and 2.

Any information received under paragraph 1 by a Contracting State shall be treated as secret in the same manner as information obtained under the domestic laws of that State and shall be disclosed only to persons or authorities (including courts and administrative bodies) concerned with the assessment or collection of, the enforcement or prosecution in respect of, the determination of appeals in relation to the taxes referred to in paragraph 1, or the oversight of the above. Such persons or authorities shall use the information only for such purposes. They may disclose the information in public court proceedings or in judicial decisions. Notwithstanding the foregoing, information received by a Contracting State may be used for other purposes when such information may be used for such other purposes under the laws of both States and the competent authority of the supplying State authorises such use.

In no case shall the provisions of paragraphs 1 and 2 be construed so as to impose on a Contracting State the obligation:

to carry out administrative measures at variance with the laws and administrative practice of that or of the other Contracting State;

to supply information which is not obtainable under the laws or in the normal course of the administration of that or of the other Contracting State;

to supply information which would disclose any trade, business, industrial, commercial or professional secret or trade process, or information, the disclosure of which would be contrary to public policy (*ordre public*).

If information is requested by a Contracting State in accordance with this Article, the other Contracting State shall use its information gathering measures to obtain the requested information, even though that other State may not need such information for its own tax purposes. The obligation contained in the preceding sentence is subject to the limitations of paragraph 3 but in no case shall such limitations be construed to permit a Contracting State to decline to supply information solely because it has no domestic interest in such information.

In no case shall the provisions of paragraph 3 be construed to permit a Contracting State to decline to supply information solely because the information is held by a bank, other financial institution, nominee or person acting in an agency or a fiduciary capacity or because it relates to ownership interests in a person.

Article 29 Members of Diplomatic Missions and Consular Posts

Nothing in this Agreement shall affect the fiscal privileges of members of diplomatic missions or consular posts under the general rules of international law or under the provisions of special agreements.

Article 30 Entry into Force

Both Contracting States shall notify each other through diplomatic channels that they have completed the internal legal procedures necessary for the entry into force of this Agreement.

This Agreement shall enter into force after the period of three months following the date of receipt of the later of the notifications referred to in paragraph 1 and its provisions shall have effect:

in respect of taxes not withheld at source, for taxation years beginning on or after the date on which the Agreement enters into force; and
in all other cases, on or after the date on which the Agreement enters into force.

The Agreement between the Government of Spain and the Government of the People's Republic of China for the Avoidance of Double Taxation and the Prevention of Fiscal Evasion with respect to taxes on Income and on Capital, signed on 22nd November 1990 in Beijing (hereinafter referred to as "the 1990 Agreement") shall cease to have effect as from the date on which the provisions of this Agreement become applicable in accordance with the provisions of this Article. The provisions of Article 23 of the 1990 Agreement shall cease to have effect as from the 31st December following the date of the entry into force of this Agreement.

Article 31 Termination

This Agreement shall remain in force until terminated by a Contracting State. Either Contracting State may terminate the Agreement, through diplomatic channels, by giving written notice of termination at least six months before the end of any calendar year beginning on or after the expiration of a period of five years from the date of its entry into force. In such event, the Agreement shall cease to have effect:

in respect of taxes not withheld at source, for taxation years beginning after the end of that calendar year; and
in all other cases, after the end of that calendar year.

IN WITNESS whereof the undersigned, duly authorized thereto, have signed this Agreement.

Done at Madrid on the 28th day of November, 2018, in duplicate in the Chinese, Spanish and English languages, all texts being equally authentic. In case of divergence of interpretation between the texts, it shall be resolved in accordance with the English text.

For the People's Republic of China
For the Kingdom of Spain

Protocol

At the signing of the Agreement between the People's Republic of China and the Kingdom of Spain for the Elimination of Double Taxation with respect to Taxes on Income and the Prevention of Tax Evasion and Avoidance (hereinafter referred to as "the Agreement"), both sides have agreed upon the following provisions, which shall form an integral part of the Agreement:

With reference to Articles 10, 11 and 12:

It is understood that the tax rates of limitation shall be directly applied rather than through a levy-then-refund procedure, in case such rates are lower than those stipulated in the domestic law of the Contracting State in which such income arises.

With reference to paragraph 3 of Article 10 and paragraph 3 of Article 11:

It is understood that the term "any entity the capital of which is wholly owned directly or indirectly by the other Contracting State" means:

in the case of China:
the China Development Bank;
the Agricultural Development Bank of China;
the Export–Import bank of China;
the National Council for Social Security Fund;
the China Export & Credit Insurance Corporation;
the China Investment Corporation and any entities the capital of which is wholly owned directly or indirectly by it;
the Silk Road Fund Co., Ltd; and
any other wholly-owned entity of China as may be agreed from time to time between the competent authorities of the Contracting States;
in the case of Spain:
the Official Credit Institute (Instituto de Credito Oficial);
the Fund for Orderly Bank Restructuring (Fondo de Restructuracion Ordenada Bancaria); (iii) the Insurance Compensation Consortium (Consorcio de Compensacion de Seguros); (iv) any other wholly-owned entity of Spain as may be agreed from time to time between the competent authorities of the Contracting States.

IN WITNESS whereof the undersigned, duly authorized thereto, have signed this Protocol.

Done at Madrid on the 28th day of November, 2018, in duplicate in the Chinese, Spanish and English languages, all texts being equally authentic. In case of divergence of interpretation between the texts, it shall be resolved in accordance with the English text.

For the People's Republic of China

For the Kingdom of Spain

Sweden

Sweden, officially the Kingdom of Sweden, is a state in Northern Europe. Sweden borders Norway to the west and north, Finland to the east, and is connected to Denmark in the southwest by a bridge-tunnel across the Öresund Strait. Sweden's capital and largest city is Stockholm.

Sweden is a popular immigration destination in Europe. Swedes are the majority ethnic group, while minorities are Sweden Finns, Sami people, Tornedalers, Jewish and Roma.

The official and predominant spoken language is Swedish, very similar to Danish and Norwegian, but differing in pronunciation and orthography. Recognised minority languages are Finnish, Meänkieli, Sami, Romani, and Yiddish.

Sweden is a unitary parliamentary constitutional monarchy. The Basic Laws of Sweden is the constitution regulating the political system. The Riksdag exerts the legislative power. The Riksdag is elected through direct elections using the party-list proportional representation system.

Executive power is vested in the Prime Minister and his or her cabinet. The chancellor is appointed by the Speaker of the Riksdag after being elected by the party or coalition with the parliamentary majority in the Riksdag.

Sweden has a civil law system based on Roman law, however some references to Germanic law are relevant. The Högsta domstolen acts as Supreme Court, managing constitutional matters, with judicial review powers.

Sweden is a unitary state, constituted by 21 county councils (landsting) and 290 municipalities (kommuner).

Sweden has been part of the European Union since 1995.

Category	Value
International Monetary Fund (mln persons)	10.322
Currency	Swedish krona

Source International Monetary Fund, year 2019

© The Author(s), under exclusive license to Springer Nature Singapore Pte Ltd. 2022
L. Riccardi and G. Riccardi, *China–Europe Tax Treaties*,
https://doi.org/10.1007/978-981-19-3563-3_26

Sweden is the second largest economy of Northern Europe, with a GDP valued 528.9 billion USD in 2019, and has a population of about 10.3 million people. Sweden's inflation is below 2% (1.7%), but unemployment is 6.8%. Sweden ranked 4 out of 43 in Europe in the 2020 Doing Business ranking, scoring 82.0, and imposes a CIT of 20.6%. Sweden records a trade surplus of 1.9 billion USD, it is the 14th main exporter in Europe.

GDP and local economy	
GDP current prices (billion USD)	528.9
GDP per capita (USD)	51,242
GDP growth (%)	1.2
Inflation (%)	1.7
Unemployment (%)	6.8
General government total expenditure (% of GDP)	48.2
General government gross debt (% of GDP)	35.1
Doing business score 2020	82.0

Source International Monetary Fund and UNCTAD, year 2019

Foreign direct investment	
FDI outstock (million USD)	396,541
FDI instock (million USD)	339,543

Source UNCTAD, year 2019

Trade	
Imports (million USD)	158,690
Exports (million USD)	160,543
Trade balance (million USD)	1852

Source International Monetary Fund and UNCTAD, year 2019

Main import–export	
First import by category	Electrical, electronic equipment
Second import by category	Machinery, nuclear reactors, boilers
First export by category	Machinery, nuclear reactors, boilers
Second export by category	Vehicles other than railway, tramway

Source United Nations COMTRADE, year 2020

The legal bases for taxation are established in the constitution. Sweden imposes individual income tax, property sales taxes, capital gains, corporate income tax, and value added tax. Progressivity is guaranteed by a system with different bands and various deductions.

Taxes	
Company income tax (%)	20.6
Top individual income tax (%)	52
Value added tax or sales Tax (%)	25
Reduced value added tax or sales tax (%)	6/12

Source RsA Asia report, year 2021

- Economic relation with China

Sweden records a trade surplus with China of 1.1 billion USD in 2020. "Pharmaceutical products" is the first export category, worth 1.87 billion USD, followed by "Machinery, nuclear reactors, boilers". "Electrical, electronic equipment" is the first import category, valued 1.73 billion USD. Sweden is not part of the Belt and Road Initiative. In 1986 Sweden and China have signed their DTA, which has been in force 1987.

Category	Value
Belt road	No

Source UNCTAD, year 2020

Import from China	
Import from China (billion USD)	8.37
First import category from China	Electrical, electronic equipment
First import Value (billion USD)	1.73
Second Import category from China	Machinery, nuclear reactors, boilers
Second Import Value (billion USD)	1.27

Source United Nations COMTRADE, year 2020

Export to China	
Export to China (billion USD)	9.47
First export category towards China	Pharmaceutical products
First export value (billion USD)	1.87
Second export category towards China	Machinery, nuclear reactors, boilers
Second export value (billion USD)	1.52

Source United Nations COMTRADE, year 2020

Trade balance	
Trade balance (billion USD)	1.10

Source United Nations COMTRADE, year 2020

Double tax agreement	
DTA effective date	1987.1.3
Dividends (%)	5–10
Interest (%)	0–10
Royalties (%)	6–10

Source State Administration of Taxation of China, year 2021

Title AGREEMENT BETWEEN THE GOVERNMENT OF THE PEOPLE'S REPUBLIC OF CHINA AND THE GOVERNMENT OF THE KINGDOM OF SWEDEN FOR THE AVOIDANCE OF DOUBLE TAXATION AND THE PREVENTION OF FISCAL EVASION WITH RESPECT TO TAXES ON INCOME.

Treaty Text

The Government of the People's Republic of China and the Government of the Kingdom of Sweden;

Desiring to conclude an Agreement for the avoidance of double taxation and the prevention of fiscal evasion with respect to taxes on income;

Have agreed as follows:

Article 1 Personal Scope

This Agreement shall apply to persons who are residents of one or both of the Contracting States.

Article 2 Taxes Covered

The existing taxes to which this Agreement shall apply are:

in the People's Republic of China:
the individual income tax:
the income tax concerning joint ventures with Chinese and foreign investment;
the income tax concerning foreign enterprises; and
the local income tax (hereinafter referred to as "Chinese tax");
in Sweden:
The state income tax,
The Sailors tax
The coupon tax
the tax on public entertainers

(bevillningsavgiften f·o·r vissa offentliga f·o·rest·a·l ln ingar);
the communal income tax (den kommunala inkomstskatten); and
the profit sharing tax (vinstdelningsskatten) (hereinafter referred to as "Swedish tax").

The Agreement shall also apply to any identical or substantially similar taxes which are imposed after the date of signature of the Agreement in addition to, or in place of, the taxes referred to in paragraph 1. The competent authorities of the Contracting States shall notify each other of any substantial changes which have been made in their respective taxation laws within a reasonable period of time after such changes.

Article 3 General Definitions

For the purposes of this Agreement, unless the context otherwise requires:

the term "China" means the People's Republic of China and, when used in geographical sense, means all the territory of the People's Republic of China, including its territorial sea, in which the Chinese laws relating to taxation apply, and any area beyond its territorial sea, within which the People's Republic of China has sovereign rights of exploration for and exploitation of resources of the seabed and its sub-soil, and superjacent water resources in accordance with international law;
the term "Sweden" means the Kingdom of Sweden and, when used in a geographical sense, includes the national territory, the territorial sea of Sweden as well as other maritime areas over which Sweden in accordance with international law exercises sovereign rights of jurisdiction;
the terms "a Contracting State" and "the other Contracting State" mean China or Sweden as the context requires;
the term "tax" means Chinese tax or Swedish tax, as the context requires;
the term "person" includes an individual, a company and any other body of persons;
the term "company" means any body corporate or any entity which is treated as a body corporate for tax purposes;
the terms "enterprise of a Contracting State" and "enterprise of the other Contracting State" mean, respectively, an enterprise carried on by a resident of a Contracting State and an enterprise carried on by a resident of the other Contracting State;
the term "nationals" means all individuals possessing the nationality of either Contracting State and all juridical persons created or organized under the laws of either Contracting State and all organizations without juridical personality treated for the purposes of tax as juridical persons created or organized under the laws of either Contracting State;
the term "international traffic" means any transport by a ship or aircraft operated by an enterprise which has its head office in a Contracting State, except when the ship or aircraft is operated solely between places in the other Contracting State;

the term “competent authority” means, in the case of China, the Ministry of Finance or its authorized representative and, in the case of Sweden, the Minister of Finance or his authorized representative.

As regards the application of the Agreement by a Contracting State, any term not defined therein shall, unless the context otherwise requires, have the meaning which it has under the laws of that Contracting State concerning the taxes to which the Agreement applies.

Article 4 Resident

For the purposes of this Agreement, the term “resident of a Contracting State” means any person who, under the laws of that Contracting State, is liable to tax therein by reason of his domicile, residence, place of head office or any other criterion of a similar nature.

Where by reason of the provisions of paragraph 1 an individual is a resident of both Contracting States, then his status shall be determined as follows:

he shall be deemed to be a resident of the State in which he has a permanent home available to him; if he has a permanent home available to him in both States, he shall be deemed to be a resident of the State with which his personal and economic relations are closer (centre of vital interests);
if the State in which he has his centre of vital interests cannot be determined, or if he has not a permanent home available to him in either State, he shall be deemed to be a resident of the State in which he has an habitual abode;
if he has an habitual abode in both States or in neither of them, he shall be deemed to be a resident of the State of which he is a national;
if he is a national of both States or of neither of them, the competent authorities of the Contracting States shall settle the question by mutual agreement.

Where by reason of the provisions of paragraph 1 a person other than an individual is a resident of both Contracting States, then it shall be deemed to be a resident of the State in which its head office is situated.

Article 5 Permanent Establishment

For the purposes of this Agreement, the term “permanent establishment” means a fixed place of business through which the business of an enterprise is wholly or partly carried on.

The term “permanent establishment” includes especially:

a place of management;
a branch;
an office;
a factory;
a workshop; and
a mine, an oil or gas well, a quarry or any other place of extraction of natural resources.

The term "permanent establishment" likewise encompasses:

a building site, a construction, assembly or installation project or supervisory activities in connection therewith, but only where such site, project or activities continue for a period of more than six months;
the furnishing of services, including consultancy services, by an enterprise of a Contracting State through employees or other personal in the other Contracting State, but only where such activities continue (for the same project or a connected project) within the country for a period or periods aggregating more than six months within any twelve-month period.

Notwithstanding the provisions of paragraphs 1–3, the term "permanent establishment" shall be deemed not to include:

the use of facilities solely for the purpose of storage, display or delivery of goods or merchandise belonging to the enterprise;
the maintenance of a stock of goods or merchandise belonging to the enterprise solely for the purpose of storage, display or delivery;
the maintenance of a stock of goods or merchandise belonging to the enterprise solely for the purpose of processing by another enterprise;
the maintenance of a fixed place of business solely for the purpose of purchasing goods or merchandise, or of collecting information, for the enterprise;
the maintenance of a fixed place of business solely for the purpose of carrying on, for the enterprise, any other activity of a preparatory or auxiliary character.
the maintenance of a fixed place of business solely for any combination of activities mentioned in sub-paragraphs (a)–(e), provided that the overall activity of the fixed place of business resulting from this combination is of a preparatory or auxiliary character.

Notwithstanding the provisions of paragraphs 1 and 2, where a parson—other than an agent of an independent status to whom the provisions of paragraph 6 apply—is acting on behalf of an enterprise and has and habitually exercises in a Contracting State an authority to conclude contracts in the name of the enterprise, that enterprise shall be deemed to have a permanent establishment in that Contracting State in respect of any activities which that person undertakes for the enterprise, unless his activities are limited to those mentioned in paragraph 4 which, if exercised through a fixed place of business, would not make this fixed place of business a permanent establishment under the provisions of that paragraph.

An enterprise of a Contracting State shall not be deemed to have a permanent establishment in the other Contracting State merely because it carries on business in that other Contracting State through a broker, general commission agent or any other agent of an independent status, provided that such persons are acting in the ordinary course of their business. However, when the activities of such an agent are devoted wholly or almost wholly on behalf of that enterprise, he will not be considered an agent of an independent status within the meaning of this paragraph.

The fact that a company which is a resident of a Contracting State controls or is controlled by a company which is a resident of the other Contracting State, or which carries on business in that other Contracting State (whether through a permanent establishment or otherwise), shall not of itself constitute either company a permanent establishment of the other.

Article 6 Income From Immovable Property

Income derived by a resident of a Contracting State from immovable property situated in the other Contracting State may be taxed in that other Contracting State.

The term "immovable property" shall have the meaning which it has under the laws of the Contracting State in which the property in question is situated. The term shall in any case include property accessory to immovable property, livestock and equipment used in agriculture and forestry, rights to which the provisions of general law respecting landed property apply, usufruct of immovable property and rights to variable or fixed payments as consideration for the working of, or the right to work, mineral deposits, sources and other natural resources; ships and aircraft shall not be regarded as immovable property.

The provisions of paragraph 1 shall apply to income derived from the direct use, letting, or use in any other form of immovable property.

The provisions of paragraphs 1 and 3 shall also apply to the income from immovable property of an enterprise and to income from immovable property used for the performance of independent personal services.

Article 7 Business Profits

The profits of an enterprise of a Contracting State shall be taxable only in that Contracting State unless the enterprise carries on business in the other Contracting State through a permanent establishment situated therein. If the enterprise carries on business as aforesaid, the profits of the enterprise may be taxed in that other Contracting State but only so much of them as is attributable to that permanent establishment.

Subject to the provisions of paragraph 3, where an enterprise of a Contracting State carries on business in the other Contracting State through a permanent establishment situated therein, there shall in each Contracting State be attributed to that permanent establishment the profits which it might be expected to make if it were a distinct and separate enterprise engaged in the same or similar activities under the same or similar conditions and dealing wholly independently with the enterprise of which it is a permanent establishment.

In determining the profits of a permanent establishment, there shall be allowed as deductions expenses which are incurred for the purposes of the permanent establishment, including executive and general administrative expenses so incurred, whether in the State in which the permanent establishment is situated or elsewhere. However, no such deduction shall be allowed in respect of amounts, if any, paid (otherwise than towards reimbursement of actual expenses) by the permanent establishment to the head office of the enterprise or any of its other offices, by way of royalties, fees or other similar payments in return for the use of patents or other rights, or by way of commission, for specific services performed or for management, or, except in the case of a banking enterprise, by way of interest on moneys lent to the permanent establishment. Likewise, no account shall be taken, in the determination of the profits of a permanent establishment, for amounts charged (otherwise than towards reimbursement of actual expenses), by the permanent establishment to the head office of the enterprise or any of its other offices, by way of royalties, fees or other similar payments in return for the use of patents or other rights, or by way of commission for specific services performed or for management, or, except in the case of a banking enterprise, by way of interest on moneys lent to the head office of the enterprise or any of its other offices.

Insofar as it has been customary in a Contracting State to determine the profits to be attributed to a permanent establishment on the basis of an apportionment of the total profits of the enterprise to its various parts, nothing in paragraph 2 shall preclude that Contracting State from determining the profits to be taxed by such an apportionment as may be customary; the method of apportionment adopted shall, however, be such that the result shall be in accordance with the principles contained in this Article.

No profits shall be attributed to a permanent establishment by reason of the mere purchase by that permanent establishment of goods or merchandise for the enterprise.

For the purposes of paragraphs 1–5, the profits to be attributed to the permanent establishment shall be determined by the same method year by year unless there is good and sufficient reason to the contrary.

Where profits include items of income which are dealt with separately in other Articles of this Agreement, then the provisions of those Articles shall not be affected by the provisions of this Article.

Article 8 Shipping and Air Transport

Profits from the operation of ships or aircraft in international traffic shall be taxable only in the Contracting State where the head office of the enterprise is situated.

The provisions of paragraph 1 shall also apply to profits from the participation in a pool, a joint business or an international operating agency.

Article 9 Associated Enterprises

Where

> an enterprise of a Contracting State participates directly or indirectly in the management, control or capital of an enterprise of the other Contracting State, or the same persons participate directly or indirectly in the management, control or capital of an enterprise of a Contracting State and an enterprise of the other Contracting State, and in either case conditions are made or imposed between the two enterprises in their commercial or financial relations which differ from those which would be made between independent enterprises, then any profits which would, but for those conditions, have accrued to one of the enterprises, but, by reason of those conditions, included in the profits of that enterprise and taxed accordingly.

Where a Contracting State includes in the profits of an enterprise of that Contracting State and taxes accordingly profits on which an enterprise of the other Contracting State has been charged to tax in that other Contracting State, and the profits so included are profits which would have accrued to the enterprise of the first-mentioned Contracting State if the conditions made between the two enterprises had been those which would have been made between independent enterprises, then that other Contracting State shall make an appropriate adjustment to the amount of the tax charged therein on those profits. In determining such adjustment, due regard shall be had to the other provisions of this Agreement and the competent authorities of the Contracting States shall if necessary consult each other.

Article 10 Dividends

Dividends paid by a company which is a resident of a Contracting State to a resident of the other Contracting State may be taxed in that other Contracting State.

However, such dividends may also be taxed in the Contracting State of which the company paying the dividends is a resident, and according to the laws of that Contracting State, but if the recipient is the beneficial owner of the dividends the tax so charged shall not exceed.

10% of the gross amount of the dividends.

The provisions of this paragraph shall not affect the taxation of the company in respect of the profits out of which the dividends are paid.

The term "dividends" as used in this Article means income from shares or other rights, not being debt-claims, participating in profits, as well as income from other corporate rights which is subjected to the same taxation treatment as income from shares by the laws of the Contracting State of which the company making the distribution is a resident.

The provisions of paragraphs 1 and 2 shall not apply if the beneficial owner of the dividends, being a resident of a Contracting State, carries on business in the other Contracting State of which the company paying the dividends is a resident, through a permanent establishment situated therein, or performs in that other Contracting State independent personal services from a fixed base situated therein, and the holding in respect of which the dividends are paid is effectively connected with such permanent establishment or fixed base. In such case the provisions of Article 7 or Article 14, as the case may be, shall apply.

Where a company which is a resident of a Contracting State derives profits or income from the other Contracting State, that other Contracting State may not impose any tax on the dividends paid by the company, except insofar as such dividends are paid to a resident of that other Contracting State or insofar as the holding in respect of which the dividends are paid is effectively connected with a permanent establishment or a fixed base situated in that other Contracting State, nor subject the company's undistributed profits to a tax on the company's undistributed profits, even if the dividends paid or the undistributed profits consist wholly or partly of profits or income arising in that other Contracting State.

Article 11 Interest

Interest arising in a Contracting State and paid to a resident of the other Contracting State may be taxed in that other Contracting State.

However, such interest may also be taxed in the Contracting State in which it arises, and according to the laws of that Contracting State, but if the recipient is the beneficial owner of the interest the tax so charged shall not exceed 10% of the gross amount of the interest.

Notwithstanding the provisions of paragraph 2, interest derived from a Contracting State is exempt from tax in that State, if it is paid:

in the case of China:
to the Government of the People's Republic of China;
to the People's Bank of China;
on a loan directly or indirectly financed or guaranteed by the Bank of China or the China International Trust and Investment Company (CITIC);
to a financial institution appointed by the Government of the People's Republic of China and mutually agreed upon by the competent authorities of the two Contracting States;
in the case of Sweden:
to the Government of Sweden;
to the Bank of Sweden;
on a loan, directly or indirectly financed or guaranteed by the Swedish Export Credit Guarantee Board, the National Debt Office or the Swedish Fund for Industrial Cooperation with Developing Countries ("Swedfund");
to a financial institution appointed by the Government of Sweden and mutually agreed upon by the competent authorities of the two Contracting States.

The term "interest" as used in this Article means income from debt-claims of every kind, whether or not secured by mortgage and whether or not carrying a right to participate in the debtor's profits, and in particular, income from Government securities and income from bonds or debentures, including premiums and prizes attaching to such securities, bonds or debentures. Penalty charges for late payment shall not be regarded as interest for the purpose of this Article.

The provisions of paragraphs 1 and 2 shall not apply if the beneficial owner of the interest, being a resident of a Contracting State, carries on business in the other Contracting State in which the interest arises, through a permanent establishment situated therein, or performs in that other Contracting State independent personal services from a fixed base situated therein, and the debt-claim in respect of which the interest is paid is effectively connected with such permanent establishment or fixed base. In such case the provisions of Article 7 or Article 14, as the case may be, shall apply.

Interest shall be deemed to arise in a Contracting State when the payer is the Government of that Contracting State, a local authority thereof or a resident of that Contracting State. Where, however, the person paying the interest, whether he is a resident of a Contracting State or not, has in a Contracting State a permanent establishment or a fixed base in connection with which the indebtedness on which the interest is paid was incurred, and such interest is borne by such permanent establishment or fixed base, then such interest shall be deemed to arise in the Contracting State in which the permanent establishment or fixed base is situated.

Where, by reason of a special relationship between the payer and the beneficial owner or between both of them and some other person, the amount of the interest, having regard to the debt-claim for which it is paid, exceeds the amount which would have been agreed upon by the payer and the beneficial owner in the absence of such relationship, the provisions of this Article shall apply only to the last-mentioned amount. In such case, the excess part of the payments shall remain taxable according to the laws of each Contracting State, due regard being had to the other provisions of this Agreement.

Article 12 Royalties

Royalties arising in a Contracting State and paid to a resident of the other Contracting State may be taxed in that other Contracting State.

However, such royalties may also be taxed in the Contracting State in which they arise, and according to the laws of that Contracting State, but if the recipient is the beneficial owner of the royalties the tax so charged shall not exceed 10% of the gross amount of the royalties.

The term "royalties" as used in this Article means payments of any kind received as a consideration for the use of, or the right to use, any copyright of literary, artistic or scientific work including cinematograph films and films or tapes for radio or television broadcasting, any patent, know-how, trade mark, design or model, plan, secret formula or process, or for the use of, or the right to use, industrial, commercial or scientific equipment, or for information concerning industrial, commercial or scientific experience.

The provisions of paragraphs 1 and 2 shall not apply if the beneficial owner of the royalties, being a resident of a Contracting State, carries on business in the other Contracting State in which the royalties arise, through a permanent establishment situated therein, or performs in that other Contracting State independent personal services from a fixed base situated therein, and the right or property in respect of which the royalties are paid is effectively connected with such permanent establishment or fixed base. In such case the provisions of Article 7 or Article 14, as the case may be, shall apply.

Royalties shall be deemed to arise in a Contracting State when the payer is the Government of that Contracting State, a local authority thereof or a resident of that Contracting State. Where, however, the person paying the royalties, whether he is a resident of a Contracting State or not, has in a Contracting State a permanent establishment or a fixed base in connection with which the liability to pay the royalties was incurred, and such royalties are borne by such permanent establishment or fixed base, then such royalties shall be deemed to arise in the Contracting State in which the permanent establishment or fixed base is situated.

Where, by reason of a special relationship between the payer and the beneficial owner or between both of them and some other person, the amount of the royalties, having regard to the use, right or information for which they are paid, exceeds the amount which would have been agreed upon by the payer and the beneficial owner in the absence of such relationship, the provisions of this Article shall apply only to the last-mentioned amount. In such case, the excess part of the payments shall remain taxable according to the laws of each Contracting State, due regard being had to the other provisions of this Agreement.

Article 13 Capital Gains

Gains derived by a resident of a Contracting State from the alienation of immovable property referred to in Article 6 and situated in the other Contracting State may be taxed in that other Contracting State.

Gains from the alienation of movable property forming part of the business property of a permanent establishment which an enterprise of a Contracting State has in the other Contracting State or of movable property pertaining to a fixed base available to a resident of a Contracting State in the other Contracting State for the purpose of performing independent personal services, including such gains from the alienation of such a permanent establishment (alone or together with the whole enterprise) or of such a fixed base, may be taxed in that other Contracting State.

Gains from the alienation of ships or aircraft operated in international traffic and movable property, pertaining to the operation of such ships or aircraft shall be taxable only in the Contracting State in which the head office of the enterprise is situated.

Gains from the alienation of shares of the capital stock of a company the property of which consists directly or indirectly principally of immovable property situated in a Contracting State may be taxed in that Contracting State.

Gains from the alienation of shares other than those mentioned in paragraph 4 representing a participation of at least 25% in a company which is a resident of a Contracting State may be taxed in that Contracting State.

Gains derived by a resident of a Contracting State from the alienation of any property other than that referred to in paragraphs 1–5 and arising in the other Contracting State may be taxed in that other Contracting State.

Article 14 Independent Personal Services

Income derived by a resident of a Contracting State in respect of professional services or other activities of an independent character shall be taxable only in that Contracting State except in one of the following circumstances, when such income may also be taxed in the other Contracting State:

if he has a fixed base regularly available to him in the other Contracting State for the purpose of performing his activities; in that case, only so much of the income as is attributable to that fixed base may be taxed in that other Contracting State;

if his stay in the other Contracting State is for a period or periods exceeding in the aggregate 183 days in the calendar year concerned; in that case, only so much of the income as is derived from his activities performed in that other Contracting State may be taxed in that other Contracting State.

The term "professional services" includes, especially, independent scientific, literary, artistic, educational or teaching activities as well as the independent activities of physicians, lawyers, engineers, architects, dentists and accountants.

Article 15 Dependent Personal Services

Subject to the provisions of Articles 16, 18, 19, 20 and 21, salaries, wages and other similar remuneration derived by a resident of a Contracting State in respect of an employment shall be taxable only in that Contracting State unless the employment is exercised in the other Contracting State. If the employment is so exercised, such remuneration as is derived therefrom may be taxed in that other Contracting State.

Notwithstanding the provisions of paragraph 1, remuneration derived by a resident of a Contracting State in respect of an employment exercised in the other Contracting State shall be taxable only in the first mentioned Contracting State, if:

the recipient is present in that other Contracting State for a period or periods not exceeding in the aggregate 183 days in the calendar year concerned; and the remuneration is paid by, or on behalf of, an employer who is not a resident of that other Contracting State; and
the remuneration is not borne by a permanent establishment or a fixed base which the employer has in that other Contracting State.

Notwithstanding the provisions of paragraphs 1 and 2, remuneration derived in respect of an employment exercised aboard a ship or aircraft operated in international traffic by an enterprise of a Contracting State may be taxed in that Contracting State.

Article 16 Directors' Fees and Remuneration of Top-Level Managerial Officials

Directors' fees and other similar payments derived by a resident of a Contracting State in his capacity as a member of the board of directors of a company which is a resident of the other Contracting State may be taxed in that other Contracting State.

Salaries, wages and other similar remuneration derived by a resident of a Contracting State in his capacity as an official in a top-level managerial position of a company which is a resident of the other Contracting State may be taxed in that other Contracting State.

Article 17 Artistes and Athletes

Notwithstanding the provisions of Articles 14 and 15, income derived by a resident of a Contracting State as an entertainer, such as a theatre, motion picture, radio or television artiste, or a musician, or as an athlete, from his personal activities as such exercised in the other Contracting State, may be taxed in that other Contracting State.

Where income in respect of personal activities exercised by an entertainer or an athlete in his capacity as such accrues not to the entertainer or athlete himself but to another person, that income may, notwithstanding the provisions of Articles 7, 14 and 15, be taxed in the Contracting State in which the activities of the entertainer or athlete are exercised.

Notwithstanding the provisions of paragraphs 1 and 2, income derived by entertainers or athletes who are residents of a Contracting State from activities referred to in paragraphs 1 and 2 exercised in the other Contracting State under a plan of cultural exchange between the Governments of the Contracting States, shall be exempt from tax in that other Contracting State.

Article 18 Pensions

Subject to the provisions of paragraph 2 of Article 19, pensions and other similar remuneration paid to a resident of a Contracting State in consideration of past employment shall be taxable only in that Contracting State.

Notwithstanding the provisions of paragraph 1, pensions paid and other similar payments made under the social security system or from a special fund of a Contracting State or local authority thereof shall be taxable only in that Contracting State.

Article 19 Government Service

Remuneration, other than a pension, paid by the Government of a Contracting State or a local authority thereof to an individual in respect of services rendered to the Government of that Contracting State or a local authority thereof, in the discharge of functions of a governmental nature, shall be taxable only in that Contracting State.

However, such remuneration shall be taxable only in the other Contracting State if the services are rendered in that other Contracting State and the individual is a resident of that other Contracting State who:

is a national of that other Contracting State; or
did not become a resident of that other Contracting State solely for the purpose of rendering the services.

(a) Any pension paid by, or out of funds created by, the Government of a Contracting State or a local authority thereof to an individual in respect of services rendered to the Government of that Contracting State or a local authority thereof, in the discharge of functions of a governmental nature, shall be taxable only in that Contracting State.

(b) However, such pension shall be taxable only in the other Contracting State if the individual is a resident of, and a national of, that other Contracting State.

The provisions of Articles 15, 16, 17 and 18 shall apply to remuneration and pensions in respect of services rendered in connection with a business carried on by the Government of a Contracting State or a local authority thereof.

Article 20 Students and Trainees

A student, business apprentice or trainee who is or was immediately before visiting a Contracting State, a resident of the other Contracting State and who is present in the first-mentioned Contracting State solely for the purpose of his education, training or obtaining special technical experience shall be exempt from tax in that first-mentioned Contracting State with respect to:

payments received from sources outside that Contracting State for the purpose of his maintenance, education, study, research or training;

grants, scholarships or awards from a government or a scientific, educational or other tax-exempt organization; and

income from personal services performed in that Contracting State provided that the income does not exceed 18,000 Swedish kronor or its equivalent in Chinese yuan for any taxable year.

The benefits provided under sub-paragraph (c) shall extend only for such period of time as is reasonably necessary to complete the education or training, but shall in no event exceed a period of seven consecutive years.

Article 21 Teachers and Researchers

An individual who is a resident of a Contracting State at the beginning of his visit to the other Contracting State and who, at the invitation of the Government of that other Contracting State or of a university or other educational or scientific research institution situated in that other Contracting State and approved by an educational authority of that other Contracting State, is present in that other Contracting State for the primary purpose of teaching, giving lectures or engaging in research at such university or other educational or scientific research institution shall be exempt from tax by that other Contracting State on his income from personal services for teaching, giving lectures or engaging in research at such university or other educational or scientific research institution for a period not exceeding three years from the date of his arrival in that other Contracting State.

The exemption granted under paragraph 1 shall not apply to income from research if such research is undertaken not in the public interest but primarily for the private benefit of a specific person or specific persons.

Article 22 Other Income

Items of income of a resident of a Contracting State not dealt with in the foregoing Articles of this Agreement and arising in the other Contracting State may be taxed in that other Contracting State.

However, items of income of a resident of a Contracting State, wherever arising, not dealt with in the foregoing Articles of this Agreement, and other than those referred to in paragraph 1, shall be taxable only in that Contracting State.

The provisions of paragraphs 1 and 2 shall not apply to income, other than income from immovable property as defined in paragraph 2 of Article 6, if the recipient of such income who is a resident of a Contracting State, carries on business in the other Contracting State through a permanent establishment situated therein, or performs in that other Contracting State independent personal services from a fixed base situated therein, and the right or property in respect of which the income is paid is effectively connected with such permanent establishment or fixed base. In such case the provisions of Article 7 or Article 14, as the case may be, shall apply.

Article 23 Methods for Elimination of Double Taxation

In the case of China, double taxation shall be avoided as follows:

Where a resident of China derives income from Sweden the amount of Swedish tax payable in respect of that income in accordance with the provisions of this Agreement may be allowed as a credit against the Chinese tax imposed on that resident. The amount of credit, however, shall not exceed the amount of the Chinese tax computed as appropriate to that income in accordance with the taxation laws and regulations of China.

Where the income derived from Sweden is a dividend paid by a company which is a resident of Sweden to a company which is a resident of China and which owns not less than 10% of the share capital of the company paying the dividend, the credit shall take into account the Swedish tax payable by the company paying the dividend in respect of its income.

In the case of Sweden, double taxation shall be avoided as follows:

Where a resident of Sweden derives income which under the laws of China and in accordance with the provisions of this Agreement may be taxed in China, Sweden shall allow—subject to the provisions of the law of Sweden concerning credit for foreign tax (as it may be amended from time to time without changing the general principle hereof)—as a deduction from the tax on such income, an amount equal to the Chinese tax paid in respect of such income.

Notwithstanding the provisions of sub-paragraph (a) where a resident of Sweden derives income which in accordance with the provisions of Article 7 or Article 14, or gains which in accordance with the provisions of paragraph 2 of Article 13, may be taxed in China, Sweden shall exempt such income or gains from tax provided that the principal part of the income or gains arises from business activities or independent personal services carried on within China.

Notwithstanding the provisions of sub-paragraph (a), dividends paid by a company being a resident of China to a company which is a resident of Sweden shall be exempt from Swedish tax to the extent that the dividends would have been exempt under Swedish law if both companies had been Swedish companies.

Where a resident of Sweden derives income which, in accordance with the provisions of Article 8, paragraph 3 of Article 13, paragraph 2 of Article 18 and paragraphs 1 and 2 of Article 19, shall be taxable only in China, or derives income or gains which in accordance with sub-paragraph (b) of this paragraph shall be exempt from Swedish tax, Sweden may take such income or gains into account when determining the graduated rate of Swedish tax.

For the purpose of sub-paragraph (a) of paragraph 2, in respect of the items of income referred to in Articles 10, 11 and 12 the amount of "Chinese tax paid" shall be deemed to be equal to 10% of the gross dividends, 10% of the gross interest and 20% of the gross royalties.

The provisions of this paragraph shall apply only for the first ten years for which this Agreement is effective. This period may be extended by mutual agreement between the competent authorities of the Contracting States.

Article 24 Non-discrimination

Nationals of a Contracting State shall not be subjected in the other Contracting State to any taxation or any requirement connected therewith, which is other or more

burdensome than the taxation and connected requirements to which nationals of that other Contracting State in the same circumstances are or may be subjected. The provisions of this paragraph shall, notwithstanding the provisions of Article 1, also apply to persons who are not residents of one or both of the Contracting States.

The taxation on a permanent establishment which an enterprise of a Contracting State has in the other Contracting State shall not be less favourably levied in that other Contracting State than the taxation levied on enterprises of that other Contracting State carrying on the same activities. The provisions of this paragraph shall not be construed as obliging a Contracting State to grant to residents of the other Contracting State any personal allowances, reliefs and reductions based on its policy or on account of civil status or family responsibilities which it grants to its own residents.

Except where the provisions of paragraph 1 of Article 9, paragraph 7 of Article 11, or paragraph 6 of Article 12, apply, interest, royalties and other disbursements paid by an enterprise of a Contracting State to a resident of the other Contracting State shall, for the purpose of determining the taxable profits of such enterprise, be deductible under the same conditions as if they had been paid to a resident of the first-mentioned Contracting State.

Enterprises of a Contracting State, the capital of which is wholly or partly owned or controlled, directly or indirectly, by one or more residents of the other Contracting State, shall not be subjected in the first-mentioned Contracting State to any taxation or any requirement connected therewith which is other or more burdensome than the taxation and connected requirements to which other similar enterprises of the first-mentioned Contracting State are or may be subjected.

The provisions of this Article shall, notwithstanding the provisions of Article 2, apply to taxes of every kind and description.

Article 25 Mutual Agreement Procedure

Where a person considers that the actions of one or both of the Contracting States result or will result for him in taxation not in accordance with the provisions of this Agreement, he may, irrespective of the remedies provided by the domestic laws of those Contracting States, present his case to the competent authority of the Contracting State of which he is a resident or, if his case comes under paragraph 1 of Article 24, to that of the Contracting State of which he is a national. The case must be presented within three years from the first notification of the action resulting in taxation not in accordance with the provisions of the Agreement.

The competent authority shall endeavour, if the objection appears to it to be justified and if it is not itself able to arrive at a satisfactory solution, to resolve the case by mutual agreement with the competent authority of the other Contracting State, with a view to the avoidance of taxation which is not in accordance with the provisions of the Agreement. Any agreement reached shall be implemented notwithstanding any time limits in the domestic laws of the Contracting States.

The competent authorities of the Contracting States shall endeavour to resolve by mutual agreement any difficulties or doubts arising as to the interpretation or application of the Agreement. They may also consult together for the elimination of double taxation in cases not provided for in the Agreement.

The competent authorities of the Contracting States may communicate with each other directly for the purpose of reaching an agreement in the sense of paragraphs 2 and 3. When it seems advisable for the purpose of reaching agreement, the competent authorities may meet together for an oral exchange of opinions.

Article 26 Exchange of Information

The competent authorities of the Contracting States shall exchange such information as is necessary for carrying out the provisions of this Agreement or of the domestic laws of the Contracting States concerning taxes covered by the Agreement, insofar as the taxation there under these laws is not contrary to the Agreement, in particular for the prevention of fraud or evasion of such taxes. The exchange of information is not restricted by Article 1. Any information received by a Contracting State shall be treated as secret in the same manner as information obtained under the domestic laws of that State and shall be disclosed only to persons or authorities, including courts and administrative bodies, involved in the assessment or collection of, the enforcement or prosecution in respect of the taxes covered by this Agreement or the determination of appeals in relation thereto. Such persons or authorities shall use the information only for such purposes. Such information may be disclosed in public court proceedings or in judicial decisions.

In no case shall the provisions of paragraph 1 be construed so as to impose on a Contracting State the obligation:

to carry out administrative measures at variance with the laws and administrative practice of that or of the other Contracting State;

to supply information which is not obtainable under the laws or in the normal course of the administration of that or of the other Contracting State; or

to supply information which would disclose any trade, business, industrial, commercial or professional secret or trade process, or information, the disclosure of which would be contrary to public policy.

Article 27 Diplomatic Agents and Consular Officers

Nothing in this Agreement shall affect the fiscal privileges of diplomatic agents or consular officers under the general rules of international law or under the provisions of special agreements.

Article 28 Entry Into Force

This Agreement shall enter into force on the thirtieth day after the date on which diplomatic notes indicating the completion of internal legal procedures necessary in each Contracting State for the entry into force of the Agreement have been exchanged. The Agreement shall have effect as respects income derived during any taxable year beginning on or after the first day of January in the year in which the Agreement enters into force.

Article 29 Termination

This Agreement shall continue in effect indefinitely but either of the Contracting States may, on or before the thirtieth day of June in any calendar year beginning after the expiration of a period of five years from the date of its entry into force, give to the other Contracting State, through the diplomatic channel, written notice of termination. In such event the Agreement shall cease to have effect as respects income derived during the taxable years beginning on or after the first day of January in the calendar year next following that in which the notice of termination is given.

IN WITNESS WHEREOF the undersigned being duly authorized thereto have signed the present Agreement.

DONE at Stockholm, this 16th day of May, 1986, in duplicate in the Chinese, Swedish and English languages, all texts being equally authentic. In the case of doubt, however, the English text shall prevail.

On behalf of the Government of the People's Republic of China.

On behalf of the Government of the Kingdom of Sweden.

Switzerland

Switzerland, officially the Swiss Confederation, is a state in Western Europe. Switzerland borders Italy to the south, France to the west, Germany to the north and Austria and Liechtenstein to the east. It is a landlocked country. Switzerland has *de iure* no capital, even though de facto Bern functions as the capital, while the largest city is Zürich.

Switzerland is a popular immigration destination in Europe. Swiss are the majority ethnic group, while around a quarter of the population is made by foreigners, mostly Europeans, i.e. Italians, Germans, and French.

The three official and languages are German, French, Italian, and Romansh.

Switzerland is a Federal semi-direct democracy under an assembly-independent directorial republic. The Federal Constitution of 1848 regulates the political system. The National Council and the Council of States exert the legislative power forming the parliament. The National Council is elected through direct elections using the party-list proportional representation system. The Council of States members are elected by the cantons with different methods. Another way legislative power is exerted is by referenda on various subjects across the year. Citizens are called to vote on average on 10 referendum questions every year.

Executive power is vested in the Federal Council, with a president nominated for a non-renewable 1-year term.

Switzerland has a civil law system based on Roman law, however some references to Germanic law are relevant. The Federal Supreme Court acts as Supreme Court, managing constitutional matters, with judicial review powers, to hear appeals against rulings of cantonal or federal courts.

Switzerland is a federal state, therefore, constituted by 26 cantons.

Switzerland is not part of the European Union, but it is part of the European Economic Area and participates in the Schengen Area.

© The Author(s), under exclusive license to Springer Nature Singapore Pte Ltd. 2022

L. Riccardi and G. Riccardi, *China–Europe Tax Treaties*,
https://doi.org/10.1007/978-981-19-3563-3_27

Category	Value
Population (mln persons)	8.545
Currency	Swiss Franc

Source International Monetary Fund, year 2019

Switzerland is the eight largest economy of Europe, with a GDP valued 715.4 billion USD in 2019. It hosts a population of about 8.5 million people and is the second country in Europe for GDP per capita (83,717 USD). Switzerland enjoys both low inflation (0.4%) and low unemployment (2.3%). Swiss unemployment is the third lowest in Europe. Switzerland ranked 17 out of 43 in Europe in the 2020 Doing Business ranking, scoring 76.6, and imposes a CIT between 11.9% and 21.6%, compounding federal, cantonal, and communal CITs. Switzerland marked a trade surplus of 36.8 billion USD in 2019, it is the nineth main exporter in Europe.

GDP and local economy	
GDP current prices (billion USD)	715.4
GDP per capita (USD)	83,717
GDP growth (%)	0.9
Inflation (%)	0.4
Unemployment (%)	2.3
General government total expenditure (% of GDP)	31.5
General government gross debt (% of GDP)	39.7
Doing business score 2020	76.6

Source International Monetary Fund and UNCTAD, year 2019

Foreign direct investment	
FDI outstock (million USD)	1,526,228
FDI instock (million USD)	1,350,682

Source UNCTAD, year 2019

Trade	
Imports (million USD)	277,001
Exports (million USD)	313,866
Trade balance (million USD)	36,865

Source International Monetary Fund and UNCTAD, year 2019

Main import–export	
First import by category	Pearls, precious stones, metals, coins
Second import by category	Pharmaceutical products
First export by category	Pharmaceutical products
Second export by category	Pearls, precious stones, metals, coins

Source United Nations COMTRADE, year 2020

The legal bases for taxation are established in the constitution. Switzerland imposes at federal, cantonal, and communal level individual income tax, property sales taxes, capital gains, corporate income tax, and value added tax. Progressivity is guaranteed by a system with different bands and various deductions.

Taxes	
Company income tax (%)	11.9 – 21.6
Top individual income tax (%)	19
Value added tax or sales tax (%)	7.7
Reduced value added tax or sales tax (%)	2.5 / 3.7

Source RsA Asia report, year 2021
Note The effective Company Income Tax rates are expressed in a range between 11.9% and 21.6% due to the different compounding of federal, cantonal, and communal CITs in different locations

- Economic relation with China

Switzerland records a trade surplus of 12.4 billion USD in 2020. "Pearls, precious stones, metals, coins" is the first export category, worth 5.15 billion USD, followed by "Clocks and watches", valued 3.11 billion USD. "Electrical, electronic equipment" is the first import category, valued 0.8 billion USD. Switzerland is not part of the Belt and Road Initiative. In 1990 Switzerland and China signed their first DTA, which entered into force in 1991. A new agreement has been signed in 2013 and has come into force since 2014.

Category	Value
Belt road	No

Source UNCTAD, year 2021

Import from China	
Import from China (billion USD)	5.09
First import category from China	Electrical, electronic equipment
First import value (billion USD)	0.847
Second import category from China	Machinery, nuclear reactors, boilers
Second import value (billion USD)	0.843

Source United Nations COMTRADE, year 2020

Export to China	
Export to China (billion USD)	17.49
First export category towards China	Pearls, precious stones, metals, coins
First export value (billion USD)	5.15
Second export category towards China	Clocks and watches
Second export value (billion USD)	3.11

Source United Nations COMTRADE, year 2020

Trade balance	
Trade balance (billion USD)	12.40

Source United Nations COMTRADE, year 2020

Double tax agreement	
DTA effective date	2014.11.15
Dividends (%)	0–5–10
Interest (%)	0–10
Royalties (%)	9

Source State Administration of Taxation of China, year 2021

Title AGREEMENT BETWEEN THE GOVERNMENT OF THE PEOPLE'S REPUBLIC OF CHINA AND THE SWISS FEDERAL COUNCIL FOR THE AVOIDANCE OF DOUBLE TAXATION WITH RESPECT TO TAXES ON INCOME AND ON CAPITAL.

Treaty Text

The Government of the People's Republic of China and the Swiss Federal Council,

Desiring to conclude an Agreement for the avoidance of double taxation with respect to taxes on income and on capital,

Have agreed as follows:

Article 1 Persons Covered

This Agreement shall apply to persons who are residents of one or both of the Contracting States.

Article 2 Taxes Covered

This Agreement shall apply to taxes on income and on capital imposed on behalf of a Contracting State or of its political subdivisions or local authorities, irrespective of the manner in which they are levied.

There shall be regarded as taxes on income and on capital all taxes imposed on total income, on total capital, or on elements of income or of capital, including taxes on gains from the alienation of movable or immovable property, taxes on the total amounts of wages or salaries paid by enterprises, as well as taxes on capital appreciation.

The existing taxes to which the Agreement shall apply are in particular:

in China:
the individual income tax;
the enterprise income tax; (hereinafter referred to as "Chinese tax");
in Switzerland:
the federal, cantonal and communal taxes
on income (total income, earned income, income from capital, industrial and commercial profits, capital gains, and other items of income); and
on capital (total property, movable and immovable property, business assets, paid-up capital and reserves, and other items of capital);
(hereinafter referred to as "Swiss tax").

The Agreement shall apply also to any identical or substantially similar taxes that are imposed after the date of signature of the Agreement in addition to, or in place of, the existing taxes. The competent authorities of the Contracting States shall notify each other of any significant changes which have been made in their taxation laws.

Article 3 General Definitions

For the purposes of this Agreement, unless the context otherwise requires:

the term "China" means the People's Republic of China; when used in geographical sense, means all the territory of the People's Republic of China, including its territorial sea, in which the Chinese laws relating to taxation apply, and any area beyond its territorial sea, within which the People's Republic of China has sovereign rights or jurisdiction in accordance with international law and its domestic law;
the term "Switzerland" means the territory of the Swiss Confederation as defined by its laws in accordance with international law;
the term "person" includes an individual, a company and any other body of persons;
the term "company" means any body corporate or any entity that is treated as a body corporate for tax purposes;
the terms "enterprise of a Contracting State" and "enterprise of the other Contracting State" mean, respectively, an enterprise carried on by a resident of a Contracting State and an enterprise carried on by a resident of the other Contracting State;
the term "international traffic" means any transport by a ship or aircraft operated by an enterprise that has its place of effective management in a Contracting State, except when the ship or aircraft is operated solely between places in the other Contracting State;

the term “competent authority” means:
in the case of China, the State Administration of Taxation or its authorised representative;
in the case of Switzerland, the Head of the Federal Department of Finance or his authorised representative;
the term “national”, in relation to a Contracting State, means:
any individual possessing the nationality of a Contracting State; and
any legal person, partnership or association deriving its status as such from the laws in force in a Contracting State.

As regards the application of the Agreement at any time by a Contracting State, any term not defined therein shall, unless the context otherwise requires, have the meaning which it has at that time under the law of that State for the purposes of the taxes to which the Agreement applies, any meaning under the applicable tax laws of that State prevailing over a meaning given to the term under other laws of that State.

Article 4 Resident

For the purposes of this Agreement, the term “resident of a Contracting State” means any person who, under the laws of that Contracting State, is liable to tax therein by reason of his domicile, residence, place of incorporation, place of effective management or any other criterion of a similar nature, and also includes that State and any political subdivision or local authority thereof. This term, however, does not include any person who is liable to tax in that State in respect only of income from sources in that State or capital situated therein.

Where by reason of the provisions of paragraph 1 an individual is a resident of both Contracting States, then his status shall be determined as follows:

he shall be deemed to be a resident only of the State in which he has a permanent home available to him; if he has a permanent home available to him in both States, he shall be deemed to be a resident only of the State with which his personal and economic relations are closer (centre of vital interests);
if the State in which he has his centre of vital interests cannot be determined, or if he has not a permanent home available to him in either State, he shall be deemed to be a resident only of the State in which he has an habitual abode;
if he has an habitual abode in both States or in neither of them, he shall be deemed to be a resident only of the State of which he is a national;
if he is a national of both States or of neither of them, the competent authorities of the Contracting States shall settle the question by mutual agreement.

Where by reason of the provisions of paragraph 1 a person other than an individual is a resident of both Contracting States, then it shall be deemed to be a resident only of the State in which its place of effective management is situated.

Article 5 Permanent Establishment

For the purposes of this Agreement, the term “permanent establishment” means a fixed place of business through which the business of an enterprise is wholly or partly carried on.

The term "permanent establishment" includes especially:

a place of management;
a branch;
an office;
a factory;
a workshop; and
a mine, an oil or gas well, a quarry or any other place of extraction of natural resources.

A building site, or construction, assembly, or installation project or supervisory activities in connection therewith, constitutes a permanent establishment only if it lasts more than twelve months.

Notwithstanding the provisions of paragraphs 1, 2 and 3, the term "permanent establishment" also encompasses the furnishing of services, including consultancy services, by an enterprise through employees or other personnel engaged for such purpose, but only if activities of that nature continue (for the same or a connected project) within a Contracting State for a period or periods aggregating more than 183 days within any twelve-month period.

Notwithstanding the preceding provisions of this Article, the term "permanent establishment" shall be deemed not to include:

the use of facilities solely for the purpose of storage, display or delivery of goods or merchandise belonging to the enterprise;
the maintenance of a stock of goods or merchandise belonging to the enterprise solely for the purpose of storage, display or delivery;
the maintenance of a stock of goods or merchandise belonging to the enterprise solely for the purpose of processing by another enterprise;
the maintenance of a fixed place of business solely for the purpose of purchasing goods or merchandise or of collecting information, for the enterprise;
the maintenance of a fixed place of business solely for the purpose of carrying on, for the enterprise, any other activity of a preparatory or auxiliary character;
the maintenance of a fixed place of business solely for any combination of activities mentioned in subparagraphs (a)–(e), provided that the overall activity of the fixed place of business resulting from this combination is of a preparatory or auxiliary character.

Notwithstanding the provisions of paragraphs 1 and 2, where a person—other than an agent of an independent status to whom paragraph 7 applies—is acting in a Contracting State on behalf of an enterprise of the other Contracting State, and has, and habitually exercises, in that Contracting State an authority to conclude contracts in the name of the enterprise, that enterprise shall be deemed to have a permanent establishment in that Contracting State in respect of any activities which that person undertakes for the enterprise, unless the activities of such person are limited to those mentioned in paragraph 5 which, if exercised through a fixed place of business, would not make this fixed place of business a permanent establishment under the provisions of that paragraph.

An enterprise of a Contracting State shall not be deemed to have a permanent establishment in the other Contracting State merely because it carries on business in that other State through a broker, general commission agent or any other agent of an independent status, provided that such persons are acting in the ordinary course of their business. However, when the activities of such an agent are devoted wholly or almost wholly on behalf of that enterprise, he will not be considered an agent of an independent status within the meaning of this paragraph.

The fact that a company which is a resident of a Contracting State controls or is controlled by a company which is a resident of the other Contracting State, or which carries on business in that other State (whether through a permanent establishment or otherwise), shall not of itself constitute either company a permanent establishment of the other.

Article 6 Income From Immovable Property

Income derived by a resident of a Contracting State from immovable property (including income from agriculture or forestry) situated in the other Contracting State may be taxed in that other State.

The term "immovable property" shall have the meaning which it has under the law of the Contracting State in which the property in question is situated. The term shall in any case include property accessory to immovable property, livestock and equipment used in agriculture and forestry, rights to which the provisions of general law respecting landed property apply, usufruct of immovable property and rights to variable or fixed payments as consideration for the working of, or the right to work, mineral deposits, sources and other natural resources; ships and aircraft shall not be regarded as immovable property.

The provisions of paragraph 1 shall apply to income derived from the direct use, letting, or use in any other form of immovable property.

The provisions of paragraphs 1 and 3 shall also apply to the income from immovable property of an enterprise and to income from immovable property used for the performance of independent personal services.

Article 7 Business Profits

The profits of an enterprise of a Contracting State shall be taxable only in that State unless the enterprise carries on business in the other Contracting State through a permanent establishment situated therein. If the enterprise carries on business as aforesaid, the profits of the enterprise may be taxed in the other State, but only so much of them as is attributable to that permanent establishment.

Subject to the provisions of paragraph 3, where an enterprise of a Contracting State carries on business in the other Contracting State through a permanent establishment situated therein, there shall in each Contracting State be attributed to that permanent establishment the profits which it might be expected to make if it were a distinct and separate enterprise engaged in the same or similar activities under the same or similar conditions and dealing wholly independently with the enterprise of which it is a permanent establishment.

In determining the profits of a permanent establishment, there shall be allowed as deductions expenses which are incurred for the purposes of the permanent establishment, including executive and general administrative expenses so incurred, whether in the State in which the permanent establishment is situated or elsewhere.

Insofar as it has been customary in a Contracting State to determine the profits to be attributed to a permanent establishment on the basis of an apportionment of the total profits of the enterprise to its various parts, nothing in paragraph 2 shall preclude that Contracting State from determining the profits to be taxed by such an apportionment as may be customary; the method of apportionment adopted shall, however, be such that the result shall be in accordance with the principles contained in this Article.

No profits shall be attributed to a permanent establishment by reason of the mere purchase by that permanent establishment of goods or merchandise for the enterprise.

For the purposes of the preceding paragraphs, the profits to be attributed to the permanent establishment shall be determined by the same method year by year unless there is good and sufficient reason to the contrary.

Where profits include items of income which are dealt with separately in other Articles of this Agreement, then the provisions of those Articles shall not be affected by the provisions of this Article.

Article 8 Shipping and Air Transport

Profits from the operation of ships or aircraft in international traffic shall be taxable only in the Contracting State in which the place of effective management of the enterprise is situated.

If the place of effective management of a shipping enterprise is aboard a ship, then it shall be deemed to be situated in the Contracting State in which the home harbor of the ship is situated, or, if there is no such home harbor, in the Contracting State of which the operator of the ship is a resident.

The provisions of paragraph 1 shall also apply to profits from the participation in a pool, a joint business or an international operating agency.

Article 9 Associated Enterprises

Where an enterprise of a Contracting State participates directly or indirectly in the management, control or capital of an enterprise of the other Contracting State, or

the same persons participate directly or indirectly in the management, control or capital of an enterprise of a Contracting State and an enterprise of the other Contracting State,

and in either case conditions are made or imposed between the two enterprises in their commercial or financial relations which differ from those which would be made between independent enterprises, then any profits which would, but for those conditions, have accrued to one of the enterprises, but, by reason of those conditions, have not so accrued, may be included in the profits of that enterprise and taxed accordingly.

Where a Contracting State includes in the profits of an enterprise of that State—and taxes accordingly—profits on which an enterprise of the other Contracting State has been charged to tax in that other State and the profits so included are profits which would have accrued to the enterprise of the first-mentioned State if the conditions made between the two enterprises had been those which would have been made between independent enterprises, then that other State shall make an appropriate adjustment to the amount of the tax charged therein on those profits. In determining such adjustment, due regard shall be had to the other provisions of this Agreement and the competent authorities of the Contracting States shall, if necessary, consult each other.

Article 10 Dividends

Dividends paid by a company which is a resident of a Contracting State to a resident of the other Contracting State may be taxed in that other State.

However, such dividends may also be taxed in the Contracting State of which the company paying the dividends is a resident and according to the laws of that State, but if the beneficial owner of the dividends is a resident of the other Contracting State, the tax so charged shall not exceed:

5% of the gross amount of the dividends if the beneficial owner is a company (other than a partnership) which holds directly at least 25% of the capital of the company paying the dividends;
10% of the gross amount of the dividends in all other cases.

The competent authorities of the Contracting States shall by mutual agreement settle the mode of application of these limitations.

This paragraph shall not affect the taxation of the company in respect of the profits out of which the dividends are paid.

Notwithstanding the provisions of paragraph 2, the Contracting State of which the company is a resident shall exempt from tax dividends paid by that company, if the beneficial owner of the dividends is the other Contracting State itself, a political subdivision or a local authority thereof, or an institution or fund wholly owned by that other State as shall be agreed by mutual agreement of the competent authorities of the Contracting States, or the central bank.

The term "dividends" as used in this Article means income from shares, "jouissance" shares or "jouissance" rights, mining shares, founders' shares or other rights, not being debt-claims, participating in profits, as well as income from other corporate rights which is subjected to the same taxation treatment as income from shares by the laws of the State of which the company making the distribution is a resident.

The provisions of paragraphs 1 and 2 shall not apply if the beneficial owner of the dividends, being a resident of a Contracting State, carries on business in the other Contracting State of which the company paying the dividends is a resident through a permanent establishment situated therein, or performs in that other State independent personal services from a fixed base situated therein, and the holding in respect of which the dividends are paid is effectively connected with such permanent establishment or fixed base. In such case the provisions of Article 7 or Article 14, as the case may be, shall apply.

Where a company which is a resident of a Contracting State derives profits or income from the other Contracting State, that other State may not impose any tax on the dividends paid by the company, except insofar as such dividends are paid to a resident of that other State or insofar as the holding in respect of which the dividends are paid is effectively connected with a permanent establishment or a fixed base situated in that other State, nor subject the company's undistributed profits to a tax on the company's undistributed profits, even if the dividends paid or the undistributed profits consist wholly or partly of profits or income arising in such other State.

The provisions of this Article shall not apply if it was the main purpose of any person concerned with the creation or assignment of the shares or other rights in respect of which the dividends are paid to take advantage of this Article by means of that creation or assignment.

Article 11 Interest

Interest arising in a Contracting State and paid to a resident of the other Contracting State may be taxed in that other State.

However, such interest may also be taxed in the Contracting State in which it arises and according to the laws of that State, but if the beneficial owner of the interest is a resident of the other Contracting State, the tax so charged shall not exceed 10% of the gross amount of the interest. The competent authorities of the Contracting States shall by mutual agreement settle the mode of application of this limitation.

Notwithstanding the provisions of paragraph 2, interest arising in a Contracting State and derived by the Government of the other Contracting State, a political subdivision or local authority thereof, the central bank or any agency of, or any entity wholly owned by, that other Contracting State, or by any other resident of that other Contracting State with respect to debt-claims of that resident which are financed, guaranteed or insured by the Government of the other Contracting State, a political subdivision or local authority thereof, the central bank or any agency of, or any entity wholly owned by, that other Contracting State, shall be exempt from tax in the first-mentioned Contracting State.

The term "interest" as used in this Article means income from debt-claims of every kind, whether or not secured by mortgage and whether or not carrying a right to participate in the debtor's profits, and in particular, income from government securities and income from bonds or debentures, including premiums and prizes attaching to such securities, bonds or debentures. Penalty charges for late payment shall not be regarded as interest for the purpose of this Article.

The provisions of paragraphs 1 and 2 shall not apply if the beneficial owner of the interest, being a resident of a Contracting State, carries on business in the other Contracting State in which the interest arises, through a permanent establishment situated therein, or performs in that other State independent personal services from a fixed base situated therein, and the debt-claim in respect of which the interest is paid is effectively connected with such permanent establishment or fixed base. In such case the provisions of Article 7 or Article 14, as the case may be, shall apply.

Interest shall be deemed to arise in a Contracting State when the payer is a resident of that State. Where, however, the person paying the interest, whether he is a resident of a Contracting State or not, has in a Contracting State a permanent establishment or a fixed base in connection with which the indebtedness on which the interest is paid was incurred, and such interest is borne by such permanent establishment or fixed base, then such interest shall be deemed to arise in the State in which the permanent establishment or fixed base is situated.

Where, by reason of a special relationship between the payer and the beneficial owner or between both of them and some other person, the amount of the interest, having regard to the debt-claim for which it is paid, exceeds the amount which would have been agreed upon by the payer and the beneficial owner in the absence of such relationship, the provisions of this Article shall apply only to the last-mentioned amount. In such case, the excess part of the payments shall remain taxable according to the laws of each Contracting State, due regard being had to the other provisions of this Agreement.

The provisions of this Article shall not apply if it was the main purpose of any person concerned with the creation or assignment of the debt-claim in respect of which the interest is paid to take advantage of this Article by means of that creation or assignment.

Article 12 Royalties

Royalties arising in a Contracting State and beneficially owned by a resident of the other Contracting State may be taxed in that other State.

However, such royalties may also be taxed in the Contracting State in which they arise and according to the laws of that State, but if the beneficial owner of the royalties is a resident of the other Contracting State, the tax so charged shall not exceed 9% of the gross amount of the royalties. The competent authorities of the Contracting States shall by mutual agreement settle the mode of application of this limitation.

The term "royalties" as used in this Article means payments of any kind received as a consideration for the use of, or the right to use, any copyright of literary, artistic or scientific work including cinematography films, or films or tapes for radio or television broadcasting, any patent, trade mark, design or model, plan, secret formula or process, or for the use of, or the right to use, industrial, commercial, or scientific equipment, or for information concerning industrial, commercial or scientific experience.

The provisions of paragraphs 1 and 2 shall not apply if the beneficial owner of the royalties, being a resident of a Contracting State, carries on business in the other Contracting State in which the royalties arise, through a permanent establishment situated therein, or performs in that other State independent personal services from a fixed base situated therein, and the right or property in respect of which the royalties are paid is effectively connected with such permanent establishment or fixed base. In such case the provisions of Article 7 or Article 14, as the case may be, shall apply.

Royalties shall be deemed to arise in a Contracting State when the payer is a resident of that Contracting State. Where, however, the person paying the royalties, whether he is a resident of a Contracting State or not, has in a Contracting State a permanent establishment or a fixed base in connection with which the liability to pay the royalties was incurred, and such royalties are borne by such permanent establishment or fixed base, then such royalties shall be deemed to arise in the State in which the permanent establishment or fixed base is situated.

Where, by reason of a special relationship between the payer and the beneficial owner or between both of them and some other person, the amount of the royalties, having regard to the use, right or information for which they are paid, exceeds the amount which would have been agreed upon by the payer and the beneficial owner in the absence of such relationship, the provisions of this Article shall apply only to the last-mentioned amount. In such case, the excess part of the payments shall remain taxable according to the laws of each Contracting State, due regard being had to the other provisions of this Agreement.

The provisions of this Article shall not apply if it was the main purpose of any person concerned with the creation or assignment of the rights in respect of which the royalties are paid to take advantage of this Article by means of that creation or assignment.

Article 13 Capital Gains

Gains derived by a resident of a Contracting State from the alienation of immovable property referred to in Article 6 and situated in the other Contracting State may be taxed in that other State.

Gains from the alienation of movable property forming part of the business property of a permanent establishment which an enterprise of a Contracting State has in the other Contracting State or of movable property pertaining to a fixed base available to a resident of a Contracting State in the other Contracting State for the purpose of performing independent personal services, including such gains from the alienation of such a permanent establishment (alone or with the whole enterprise) or of such a fixed base, may be taxed in that other State.

Gains from the alienation of ships or aircraft operated in international traffic, or movable property pertaining to the operation of such ships or aircraft, shall be taxable only in the Contracting State in which the place of effective management of the enterprise is situated.

Gains derived by a resident of a Contracting State from the alienation of shares deriving more than 50% of their value directly or indirectly from immovable property situated in the other Contracting State may be taxed in that other State.

Gains derived by a resident of a Contracting State from the alienation of shares of a company which is a resident of the other Contracting State may be taxed in that other Contracting State if the recipient of the gain s, at any time during the twelve-month period preceding such alienation, had a participation, directly or indirectly, of at least 25% in the capital of that company.

Gains from the alienation of any property, other than that referred to in the preceding paragraphs, shall be taxable only in the Contracting State of which the alienator is a resident.

Article 14 Independent Personal Services

Income derived by a resident of a Contracting State in respect of professional services or other activities of an independent character shall be taxable only in that State except in the following circumstances, when such income may also be taxed in the other Contracting State:

if he has a fixed base regularly available to him in the other Contracting State for the purpose of performing his activities; in that case, only so much of the income as is attributable to that fixed base may be taxed in that other State; or
if his stay in the other Contracting State is for a period or periods exceeding in the aggregate 183 days in the fiscal year concerned; in that case, only so much of the income as is derived from his activities performed in that other State may be taxed in that other State.

The term "professional services" includes especially independent scientific, literary, artistic, educational or teaching activities as well as the independent activities of physicians, lawyers, engineers, architects, dentists and accountants.

Article 15 Income From Employment

Subject to the provisions of Articles 16, 18 and 19, salaries, wages and other similar remuneration derived by a resident of a Contracting State in respect of an employment shall be taxable only in that State unless the employment is exercised in the other Contracting State. If the employment is so exercised, such remuneration as is derived therefrom may be taxed in that other State.

Notwithstanding the provisions of paragraph 1, remuneration derived by a resident of a Contracting State in respect of an employment exercised in the other Contracting State shall be taxable only in the first-mentioned State if:

the recipient is present in the other State for a period or periods not exceeding in the aggregate 183 days in the fiscal year concerned, and
the remuneration is paid by, or on behalf of, an employer who is not a resident of the other State, and
the remuneration is not borne by a permanent establishment or a fixed base which the employer has in the other State.

Notwithstanding the preceding provisions of this Article, remuneration derived in respect of an employment exercised aboard a ship or aircraft operated in international traffic, may be taxed in the Contracting State in which the place of effective management of the enterprise is situated.

Article 16 Directors' Fees

Directors' fees and other similar payments derived by a resident of a Contracting State in his capacity as a member of the board of directors of a company which is a resident of the other Contracting State may be taxed in that other State.

Article 17 Artistes and Sportsmen

Notwithstanding the provisions of Articles 14 and 15, income derived by a resident of a Contracting State as an entertainer, such as a theatre, motion picture, radio or television artiste, or a musician, or as a sportsman, from his personal activities as such exercised in the other Contracting State, may be taxed in that other State.

Where income in respect of personal activities exercised by an entertainer or a sportsman in his capacity as such accrues not to the entertainer or sportsman himself but to another person, that income may, notwithstanding the provisions of Articles 7, 14 and 15, be taxed in the Contracting State in which the activities of the entertainer or sportsman are exercised.

The provisions of paragraphs 1 and 2 shall not apply to remuneration or profits, salaries, wages and similar income derived from activities performed in a Contracting State by entertainers or athletes if their visit to that Contracting State is substantially supported from public or governmental funds of the other Contracting State, a political subdivision or a local authority thereof. In such case the provisions of Articles 7, 14 or 15, as the case may be, shall apply.

Article 18 Pensions

Subject to the provisions of paragraph 2 of Article 19, pensions and other similar remuneration paid to a resident of a Contracting State in consideration of past employment shall be taxable only in that State.

Article 19 Government Service

(a) Salaries, wages and other similar remuneration paid by the Government of a Contracting State or a political subdivision or a local authority thereof to an individual in respect of services rendered to the Government of that State or subdivision or authority, shall be taxable only in that State.

However, such salaries, wages and other similar remuneration shall be taxable only in the other Contracting State if the services are rendered in that State and the individual is a resident of that State who:

is a national of that State; or
did not become a resident of that State solely for the purpose of rendering the services.

(a) Pensions and other similar remuneration paid by, or out of funds created by, a Contracting State or a political subdivision or a local authority thereof to an individual in respect of services rendered to the Government of that State or subdivision or authority shall be taxable only in that State.

(b) However, such pensions and other similar remuneration shall be taxable only in the other Contracting State if the individual is a resident of, and a national of, that State.

The provisions of Articles 15, 16, 17 and 18 shall apply to salaries, wages, pensions and other similar remuneration in respect of services rendered in connection with a business carried on by the Government of a Contracting State or a political subdivision or a local authority thereof.

Article 20 Students

Payments which a student or business apprentice who is or was immediately before visiting a Contracting State a resident of the other Contracting State and who is present in the first-mentioned Contracting State solely for the purpose of his education or training receives for the purpose of his maintenance, education or training shall not be taxed in that Contracting State, provided that such payments arise from sources outside that State.

Article 21 Other Income

Items of income of a resident of a Contracting State, wherever arising, not dealt with in the foregoing Articles of this Agreement shall be taxable only in that State.

The provisions of paragraph 1 shall not apply to income, other than income from immovable property as defined in paragraph 2 of Article 6, if the recipient of such income, being a resident of a Contracting State, carries on business in the other Contracting State through a permanent establishment situated therein, or performs in that other State independent personal services from a fixed base situated therein, and the right or property in respect of which the income is paid is effectively connected with such permanent establishment or fixed base. In such case the provisions of Article 7 or Article 14, as the case may be, shall apply.

Where, by reason of a special relationship between the resident referred to in paragraph 1 and some other person, or between both of them and some third person, the amount of the income referred to in paragraph 1 exceeds the amount which would have been agreed upon between them in the absence of such a relationship, the provisions of this Article shall apply only to the last-mentioned amount. In such a case, the excess part of the income shall remain taxable according to the laws of each Contracting State, due regard being had to the other applicable provisions of this Agreement.

The provisions of this Article shall not apply if it was the main purpose of any person concerned with the creation or assignment of the rights in respect of which the income is paid to take advantage of this Article by means of that creation or assignment.

Article 22 Capital

Capital represented by immovable property referred to in Article 6, owned by a resident of a Contracting State and situated in the other Contracting State, may be taxed in that other Contracting State.

Capital represented by movable property forming part of the business property of a permanent establishment which an enterprise of a Contracting State has in the other.

Contracting State or by movable property pertaining to a fixed base available to a resident of a Contracting State in the other Contracting State for the purpose of performing independent personal services, may be taxed in that other Contracting State.

Capital represented by ships and aircraft operated in international traffic, and by movable property pertaining to the operation of such ship and aircraft, shall be taxable only in the Contracting State in which the place of effective management of the enterprise is situated.

All other elements of capital of a resident of a Contracting State shall be taxable only in that Contracting State.

Article 23 Miscellaneous Rule

Nothing in this Agreement shall prejudice the right of each Contracting State to apply its domestic laws and measures concerning special adjustments of taxation, whether or not described as such, insofar as they do not give rise to taxation contrary to this Agreement.

Article 24 Methods for Elimination of Double Taxation

In China, double taxation shall be eliminated as follows:

Where a resident of China derives income from Switzerland, the amount of tax on that income payable in Switzerland, in accordance with the provisions of this Agreement, may be credited against the Chinese tax imposed on that resident. The amount of credit, however, shall not exceed the amount of the Chinese tax on that income computed in accordance with the taxation laws and regulations of China.

Where the income derived from Switzerland is a dividend paid by a company which is a resident of Switzerland to a company which is a resident of China and which owns not less than 20% of the shares of the company paying the dividend, the credit shall take into account the tax payable in Switzerland by the company paying the dividend in respect of its income.

In Switzerland, double taxation shall be eliminated as follows:

Where a resident of Switzerland derives income or owns capital which, in accordance with the provisions of this Agreement, may be taxed in China, Switzerland shall, subject to the provisions of subparagraph (b), exempt such income or capital from tax but may, in calculating tax on the remaining income or capital of that resident, apply the rate of tax which would have been applicable if the exempted income or capital had not been so exempted. However, such exemption shall apply to gains referred to in paragraph 4 of Article 13 only if actual taxation of such gains in China is demonstrated.

Where a resident of Switzerland derives dividends, interest or royalties which, in accordance with the provisions of Articles 10, 11 and 12, may be taxed in China, Switzerland shall allow, upon request, a relief to such resident. The relief may consist of:

a deduction from the tax on the income of that resident of an amount equal to the tax levied in China in accordance with the provisions of Articles 10, 11 and 12; such deduction shall not, however, exceed that part of the Swiss tax, as computed before the deduction is given, which is appropriate to the income which may be taxed in China; or

a lump sum deduction of the Swiss tax determined by standardised formula which have regard to the general principles of the relief referred to in subparagraph (i) above; or

a deduction from such dividends, interest or royalties consisting at least of the tax levied in China on the gross amount of the dividends, interest or royalties.

Switzerland shall determine the applicable relief and regulate the procedure in accordance with the Swiss provisions relating to the carrying out of international agreements of the Swiss Confederation for the avoidance of double taxation.

A company which is a resident of Switzerland and which derives dividends from a company which is a resident of China shall be entitled for the purposes of Swiss tax with respect to such dividends, to the same relief which would be granted to the company if the company paying the dividends were a resident of Switzerland.

Article 25 Non-discrimination

Nationals of a Contracting State shall not be subjected in the other Contracting State to any taxation or any requirement connected therewith, which is other or more burdensome than the taxation and connected requirements to which nationals of that other State in the same circumstances, in particular with respect to residence, are or may be subjected. This provision shall, notwithstanding the provisions of Article 1, also apply to persons who are not residents of one or both of the Contracting States.

The taxation on a permanent establishment which an enterprise of a Contracting State has in the other Contracting State shall not be less favorably levied in that other State than the taxation levied on enterprises of that other State carrying on the same activities. This provision shall not be construed as obliging a Contracting State to grant to residents of the other Contracting State any personal allowances, reliefs and reductions for taxation purposes on account of civil status or family responsibilities which it grants to its own residents.

Except where the provisions of paragraph 1 of Article 9, paragraph 7 of Article 11, paragraph 6 of Article 12, or paragraph 3 of Article 21 apply, interest, royalties and other disbursements paid by an enterprise of a Contracting State to a resident of the other Contracting State shall, for the purpose of determining the taxable profits of such enterprise, be deductible under the same conditions as if they had been paid to a resident of the first-mentioned State. Similarly, any debts of an enterprise of a Contracting State to a resident of the other Contracting State shall, for the purpose of determining the taxable capital of such enterprise, be deductible under the same conditions as if they had been contracted to a resident of the first-mentioned State.

Enterprises of a Contracting State, the capital of which is wholly or partly owned or controlled, directly or indirectly, by one or more residents of the other Contracting

State, shall not be subjected in the first-mentioned State to any taxation or any requirement connected therewith which is other or more burdensome than the taxation and connected requirements to which other similar enterprises of the first-mentioned State are or may be subjected.

The provisions of the Article shall, notwithstanding the provisions of Article 2, apply to taxes of every kind and description.

Article 26 Mutual Agreement Procedure

Where a person considers that the actions of one or both of the Contracting States result or will result for him in taxation not in accordance with the provisions of this Agreement, he may, irrespective of the remedies provided by the domestic law of those States, present his case to the competent authority of the Contracting State of which he is a resident or, if his case comes under paragraph 1 of Article 25, to that of the Contracting State of which he is a national. The case must be presented within three years from the first notification of the action resulting in taxation not in accordance with the provisions of the Agreement.

The competent authority shall endeavor, if the objection appears to it to be justified and if it is not itself able to arrive at a satisfactory solution, to resolve the case by mutual agreement with the competent authority of the other Contracting State, with a view to the avoidance of taxation which is not in accordance with the Agreement.

The competent authorities of the Contracting States shall endeavor to resolve by mutual agreement any difficulties or doubts arising as to the interpretation or application of the Agreement. They may also consult together for the elimination of double taxation in cases not provided for in the Agreement.

The competent authorities of the Contracting States may communicate with each other directly for the purpose of reaching an agreement in the sense of paragraphs 2 and 3. When it seems advisable for reaching an agreement, representatives of the competent authorities of the Contracting States may meet together for an oral exchange of opinions.

Article 27 Exchange of Information

The competent authorities of the Contracting States shall exchange such information as is foreseeably relevant for carrying out the provisions of this Agreement or to the administration or enforcement of the domestic laws concerning taxes of every kind and description imposed on behalf of the Contracting States, or of their political subdivisions or local authorities, insofar as the taxation thereunder is not contrary to the Agreement. The exchange of information is not restricted by Articles 1 and 2.

Any information received under paragraph 1 by a Contracting State shall be treated as secret in the same manner as information obtained under the domestic laws of that State and shall be disclosed only to persons or authorities (including courts and administrative bodies) concerned with the assessment or collection of, the enforcement or prosecution in respect of, or the determination of appeals in relation to the taxes referred to in paragraph 1, or the oversight of the above. Such persons or authorities shall use the information only for such purposes. They may disclose the information in public court proceedings or in judicial decisions. Notwithstanding the foregoing, information received by a Contracting State may be used for other purposes when such information may be used for such other purposes under the laws of both States and the competent authority of the supplying State authorises such use.

In no case shall the provisions of paragraphs 1 and 2 be construed so as to impose on a Contracting State the obligation:

to carry out administrative measures at variance with the laws and administrative practice of that or of the other Contracting State;
to supply information which is not obtainable under the laws or in the normal course of the administration of that or of the other Contracting State;
to supply information which would disclose any trade, business, industrial, commercial or professional secret or trade process, or information the disclosure of which would be contrary to public policy (*ordre public*).

If information is requested by a Contracting State in accordance with this Article, the other Contracting State shall use its information gathering measures to obtain the requested information, even though that other State may not need such information for its own tax purposes. The obligation contained in the preceding sentence is subject to the limitations of paragraph 3 but in no case shall such limitations be construed to permit a Contracting State to decline to supply information solely because it has no domestic interest in such information.

In no case shall the provisions of paragraph 3 be construed to permit a Contracting State to decline to supply information solely because the information is held by a bank, other financial institution, nominee or person acting in an agency or a fiduciary capacity or because it relates to ownership interests in a person. In order to obtain such information, the tax authorities of the requested Contracting State, if necessary to comply with its obligations under this paragraph, shall have the power to enforce the disclosure of information covered by this paragraph, notwithstanding paragraph 3 or any contrary provisions in its domestic laws.

Article 28 Members of Diplomatic Missions and Consular Posts

Nothing in this Agreement shall affect the fiscal privileges of members of diplomatic missions or consular posts under the general rules of international law or under the provisions of special agreements.

This Agreement shall not apply to international organisations, to organs or officials thereof and to persons who are members of a diplomatic mission, consular post or permanent mission of a third State, being present in a Contracting State and not treated in either Contracting State as residents in respect of taxes on income or on capital.

Article 29 Entry Into Force

Both Contracting States shall notify each other through diplomatic channels that they have completed the internal legal procedures necessary for the entry into force of this Agreement. This Agreement shall enter into force on the thirtieth day upon the receipt of the latter notification. This Agreement shall be applicable in respect of all taxes for fiscal years beginning on or after the first day of January next following that in which this Agreement enters into force.

The Agreement between the Government of the People's Republic of China and the Swiss Federal Council for the Avoidance of Double Taxation with Respect to Taxes on Income and Capital and the Protocol, signed at Beijing on July 6th, 1990, shall cease to have effect in relation to any tax with effect from the date on which this Agreement has effect in relation to that tax in accordance with paragraph 1 of this Article.

Article 30 Termination

This Agreement shall continue in effect indefinitely but either of the Contracting States may, on or before the thirtieth day of June in any calendar year beginning from the date of its entry into force, give written notice of termination to the other Contracting State through diplomatic channels. In such event this Agreement shall cease to have effect as respects income derived or capital owned during the fiscal years beginning on or after the first day of January in the calendar year next following that in which the notice of termination is given.

IN WITNESS whereof the undersigned, duly authorized thereto, have signed this Agreement.

Done at Beijing on the 25th day of September, 2013, in duplicate in the Chinese, German and English languages, all texts being equally authentic. In case of divergence in interpretation, the English text shall prevail.

For the Government of The People's Republic of China.

For the Swiss Federal Council.

Protocol

The Government of the People's Republic of China and the Swiss Federal Council have agreed at the signing of this Agreement between the two States for the avoidance of double taxation with respect to taxes on income and on capital upon the following provisions which shall form an integral part of the said Agreement:

It is understood that in case there is any double taxation due to a capital tax that may be introduced by either Contracting State in the future, that tax shall be covered by Article 2 of this Agreement.

With reference to Article 2, it is understood that the Agreement, except for Article 25, shall not apply to taxes withheld at source on prizes in a lottery.

With respect to paragraphs 1 and 2 of Article 7, where an enterprise of a Contracting State, having a permanent establishment in the other Contracting State, sells goods or merchandise or carries on any other business activity in the other Contracting State, the profits of that permanent establishment shall be determined only on the basis of that part of the receipts which is attributable to the actual activity of the permanent establishment for such sales or business activity.

With reference to Article 8, it is understood that:

for residents of Switzerland carrying on the operation of ships or aircraft in international traffic, supplies of international transportation shall be exempt from Business Tax or any other similar tax imposed on the gross receipts in China, or shall be zero-rated under Value Added Tax in China and the input tax attributable to such supplies shall be creditable to the same extent as it is to business enterprises resident in China; and

for residents of China carrying on the operation of ships or aircraft in international traffic, supplies of international transportation shall be zero-rated under Value Added Tax in Switzerland and the input tax attributable to such supplies shall be creditable to the same extent as it is to business enterprises resident in Switzerland.

With reference to paragraph 3 of Article 10, "institution or fund wholly owned by that other State" includes, in the case of China, the China Investment Corporation (CIC) and the National Council for Social Security Fund.

With reference to Articles 18 and 19, the term "pensions" may cover both periodic payments and lump sum payments.

When, according to Article 18, pensions shall be relieved from tax in a Contracting State, and these pensions, according to the law in force in the other Contracting State, are not effectively taxed in that other Contracting State, the first-mentioned Contracting State may tax such pensions pursuant to its domestic law.

With reference to Articles 18 and 21, pensions paid and other similar payments made by the Government of a Contracting State or a political subdivision or local authority thereof under a public welfare scheme of the social security system of that State shall be taxable only in that State.

With reference to Article 27:

It is understood that an exchange of information will only be requested once the requesting Contracting State has pursued all reasonable means available under its internal taxation procedure to obtain the information.

It is understood that the tax authorities of the requesting State shall provide the following information to the tax authorities of the requested State when making a request for information under this Article:

the identity of the person under examination or investigation;

the period of time for which the information is requested;

a statement of the information sought including its nature and the form in which the requesting State wishes to receive the information from the requested State;

the tax purpose for which the information is sought;

to the extent known, the name and address of any person believed to be in possession of the requested information.

The purpose of referring to information that may be foreseeably relevant is intended to provide for exchange of information in tax matters to the widest possible extent without allowing the Contracting States to engage in "fishing expeditions" or to request information that is unlikely to be relevant to the tax affairs of a given taxpayer. While this subparagraph contains important procedural requirements that are intended to ensure that fishing expeditions do not occur, clauses (i) through (v) nevertheless need to be interpreted with a view not to frustrate effective exchange of information.

Although this Article does not restrict the possible methods for exchanging information, it is understood that the Article does not require the Contracting States to exchange information on an automatic or a spontaneous basis.

It is understood that in case of an exchange of information, the administrative procedural rules regarding taxpayers' rights provided for in the requested Contracting State remain applicable before the information is transmitted to the requesting Contracting State. It is further understood that these provisions aim at guaranteeing the taxpayer a fair procedure and not at preventing or unduly delaying the exchange of information process.

With reference to Articles 27 and 29, this Agreement shall be applicable to information that relates to taxable years beginning on or after the first day of January next following that in which this Agreement enters into force.

IN WITNESS whereof the undersigned, duly authorized thereto, have signed this Protocol.

Done at Beijing on the 25th day of September, 2013, in duplicate in the Chinese, German and English languages, all texts being equally authentic. In case of divergence in interpretation, the English text shall prevail.

For the Government of The People's Republic of China.

For the Swiss Federal Council.

United Kingdom

The United Kingdom, officially the United Kingdom of Great Britain and Northern Ireland, is a state in Northern Europe. The United Kingdom includes the island of Great Britain and the northeastern part of the island of Ireland. Northern Ireland shares a border with the Republic of Ireland. The United Kingdom is surrounded by the Atlantic Ocean, with the North Sea to the east, the English Channel to the south. The island of Great Britain and the island of Ireland are separated by the Irish Sea. The UK's capital, financial center, and largest city is London. In terms of population, the UK is the third country in Europe after Russia and Germany.

Due to its historical background, the UK is a popular destination for immigrant. White British are the majority ethnic group, while around 8 million people in the UK are from an ethnic minority background. Significant groups are Indian, Polish, Pakistani, and Romanian.

The official and predominant spoken language is English. Recognized indigenous languages are the three Celtic languages of Welsh, Irish, and Scottish Gaelic. Minority languages used by immigrants and second generations include Punjabi, Urdu, Bengali, Sylheti, and Hindi.

The UK is a democratic constitutional monarchy, made by four home nations: England, Wales, Scotland, and Northern Ireland. The UK does not a written constitution, however, such matters are regulated by conventions and precedents. The House of Commons and the House of Lords form the parliament, which exert the legislative power. The 650 members of the House of Commons are elected through direct elections using the first-past-the-post representation system. The members of the House of Lords, whose number is not set nor limited, are nominated by the King or the Queen, on the advice of the Prime Minister, and serve for life, while a limited number of seats are inherited.

Executive power is vested in the prime minister and his or her cabinet. The prime minister is appointed by the King or the Queen after being elected by the party with the parliamentary majority in the House of Commons.

The UK has a common law system, regulated by precedents and by the laws passed by the Houses of parliament and on which a royal assent is given. The Supreme Court

© The Author(s), under exclusive license to Springer Nature Singapore Pte Ltd. 2022

L. Riccardi and G. Riccardi, *China–Europe Tax Treaties*,
https://doi.org/10.1007/978-981-19-3563-3_28

of the United Kingdom acts as Supreme Court, managing constitutional matters, with judicial review powers.

The UK is formed by four home nations, with three devolved governments for Wales, Scotland, and Northern Ireland. These have their own assemblies and cabinets.

The UK has been part of the European Union from 1973 to 2020, being the first country to leave the Union after the result of the 2016 referendum.

Category	Value
Population (mln persons)	66.867
Currency	Pound sterling

Source International Monetary Fund, year 2019

The United Kingdom is the second largest economy of Europe, with a GDP worth 2743.6 billion USD in 2019, with a population of 66.8 million people. Growth has been consistent in the last 10 years, with low inflation and unemployment, below 2% and 4% respectively. The UK scored highly in the 2020 Doing Business ranking, second in Europe out of 43, with a score of 83.5, and it imposes a CIT of 19%. It is both a large recipient of FDI and a large investor abroad. The UK is one of the top importers in Europe with a trade deficit of 222,983 million USD in 2019.

GDP and local economy	
GDP current prices (billion USD)	2743.6
GDP per capita (USD)	41,030
GDP growth (%)	1.4
Inflation (%)	1.8
Unemployment (%)	3.8
General government total expenditure (% of GDP)	38.8
General government gross debt (% of GDP)	85.2
Doing business score 2020	83.5

Source International Monetary Fund and UNCTAD, year 2019

Foreign direct investment	
FDI outstock (million USD)	1,949,442
FDI instock (million USD)	2,075,271

Source UNCTAD, year 2019

Trade	
Imports (million USD)	691,801

(continued)

(continued)

Trade	
Exports (million USD)	468,817
Trade balance (million USD)	−222,983

Source International Monetary Fund and UNCTAD, year 2019

Main import–export	
First import by category	Pearls, precious stones, metals, coins
Second import by category	Machinery, nuclear reactors, boilers
First export by category	Machinery, nuclear reactors, boilers
Second export by category	Pearls, precious stones, metals, coins

Source United Nations COMTRADE, year 2020

The legal bases for taxation are established by precedent and conventions. The UK imposes individual income tax, property sales taxes, capital gains, corporate income tax, and value added tax. Progressivity is guaranteed by a system with different bands and various deductions.

Taxes	
Company income tax (%)	19
Top individual income tax (%)	45
Value added tax or sales tax (%)	20
Reduced value added tax or sales tax (%)	5

Source RsA Asia report, year 2021

- Economic relation with China

The United Kingdom is the third top importer from China, with a trade deficit of 52.85 billion USD in 2020. "Electrical, electronic equipment" is the first import category to the UK, while "vehicles other than railway, tramway" is the first export category towards China. The UK is not involved in the Belt and Road Initiative. The first DTA between the UK and China was signed in July 1984, effective from December 1984, while the second agreement has been signed in 2011 and has come into force in 2013.

Category	Value
Belt road	No

Source UNCTAD, year 2021

Import from China	
Import from China (billion USD)	72.61
First import category from China	Electrical, electronic equipment
First import value (billion USD)	14.74
Second import category from China	Machinery, nuclear reactors, boilers
Second import value (billion USD)	11.11

Source United Nations COMTRADE, year 2020

Export to China	
Export to China (billion USD)	19.76
First export category towards China	Vehicles other than railway, tramway
First export value (billion USD)	3.78
Second export category towards China	Machinery, nuclear reactors, boilers
Second export value (billion USD)	2.62

Source United Nations COMTRADE, year 2020

Trade balance	
Trade balance (billion USD)	−52.85

Source United Nations COMTRADE, year 2020

Double tax agreement	
DTA effective date	2013.12.13
Dividends (%)	0–5–10
Interest (%)	0–10
Royalties (%)	6–10

Source State Administration of Taxation of China, year 2021

Title AGREEMENT BETWEEN THE GOVERNMENT OF THE PEOPLE'S REPUBLIC OF CHINA AND THE GOVERNMENT OF THE UNITED KINGDOM OF GREAT BRITAIN AND NORTHERN IRELAND FOR THE AVOIDANCE OF DOUBLE TAXATION AND THE PREVENTION OF FISCAL EVASION WITH RESPECT TO TAXES ON INCOME AND ON CAPITAL GAINS.

Treaty Text The Government of the People's Republic of China and the Government of the United Kingdom of Great Britain and Northern Ireland,

Desiring to conclude an Agreement for the avoidance of double taxation and the prevention of fiscal evasion with respect to taxes on income and on capital gains,

Have agreed as follows:

Article 1 Persons Covered
This Agreement shall apply to persons who are residents of one or both of the Contracting States.

Article 2 Taxes Covered
This Agreement shall apply to taxes on income and on capital gains imposed on behalf of a Contracting State or of its political subdivisions or of its local authorities, irrespective of the manner in which they are levied.

There shall be regarded as taxes on income and on capital gains all taxes imposed on total income, or on elements of income, including taxes on gains from the alienation of movable or immovable property.

The existing taxes to which the Agreement shall apply are in particular:

in China:
the individual income tax;
the enterprise income tax; (hereinafter referred to as "Chinese tax");
in the United Kingdom:
the income tax;
the corporation tax;
the capital gains tax;
(hereinafter referred to as "United Kingdom tax").

The Agreement shall also apply to any identical or substantially similar taxes which are imposed after the date of signature of the Agreement in addition to, or in place of, the existing taxes. The competent authorities of the Contracting States shall notify each other of any significant changes which have been made in their taxation laws within a reasonable period of time after such changes.

Article 3 General Definitions

For the purposes of this Agreement, unless the context otherwise requires:

the term "China" means the People's Republic of China and, when used in a geographical sense, means all the territory of the People's Republic of China, including its territorial sea, in which the Chinese laws relating to taxation apply, and any area beyond its territorial sea, within which the People's Republic of China has sovereign rights of exploration for and exploitation of resources of the sea bed and its sub-soil and superjacent water resources in accordance with international law;
the term "United Kingdom" means Great Britain and Northern Ireland, including any area outside the territorial sea of the United Kingdom designated under its laws concerning the Continental Shelf and in accordance with international law as an area within which the rights of the United Kingdom with respect to the sea bed and sub-soil and their natural resources may be exercised;
the terms "a Contracting State" and "the other Contracting State" mean China or the United Kingdom as the context requires;

the term "person" includes an individual, a company and any other body of persons;
the term "company" means anybody corporate or any entity which is treated as a body corporate for tax purposes;
the terms "enterprise of a Contracting State" and "enterprise of the other Contracting State" mean, respectively, an enterprise carried on by a resident of a Contracting State and an enterprise carried on by a resident of the other Contracting State;
the term "international traffic" means any transport by a ship or aircraft operated by an enterprise of a Contracting State, except when the ship or aircraft is operated solely between places in the other Contracting State;
the term "competent authority" means, in the case of China, the State Administration of Taxation or its authorised representative, and in the case of the United Kingdom, the Commissioners for Her Majesty's Revenue and Customs or their authorised representative;
the term "national" means:
in relation to China, any individual who under the law in China possesses Chinese nationality; and any legal person, partnership or other body of persons deriving its status as such from the law in force in China;
in relation to the United Kingdom, any British citizen, or any British subject not possessing the citizenship of any other Commonwealth country or territory, provided he has the right of abode in the United Kingdom; and any legal person, partnership, association or other entity deriving its status as such from the laws in force in the United Kingdom.

As regards the application of the Agreement at any time by a Contracting State, any term not defined therein shall, unless the context otherwise requires, have the meaning that it has at that time under the law of that State for the purposes of the taxes to which this Agreement applies, any meaning under the applicable tax laws of that State prevailing over a meaning given to the term under other laws of that State.

Article 4 Resident

For the purposes of this Agreement, the term "resident of a Contracting State" means any person who, under the laws of that State, is liable to tax therein by reason of his domicile, residence, place of incorporation, place of management or any other criterion of a similar nature, and also includes that State and any political subdivision or local authority thereof. This term, however, does not include any person who is liable to tax in that State in respect only of income or capital gains from sources in that State.

Where by reason of the provisions of paragraph 1 an individual is a resident of both Contracting States, then his status shall be determined as follows:

he shall be deemed to be a resident only of the State in which he has a permanent home available to him; if he has a permanent home available to him in both States, he shall be deemed to be a resident only of the State with which his personal and economic relations are closer (centre of vital interests);

if the State in which he has his centre of vital interests cannot be determined, or if he does not have a permanent home available to him in either State, he shall be deemed to be a resident only of the State in which he has an habitual abode;
if he has an habitual abode in both States or in neither of them, he shall be deemed to be a resident only of the State of which he is a national;
if he is a national of both States or of neither of them, the competent authorities of the Contracting States shall settle the question by mutual agreement.

Where by reason of the provisions of paragraph 1 a person other than an individual is a resident of both Contracting States, then it shall be deemed to be a resident only of the State in which its place of effective management is situated.

Article 5 Permanent Establishment
For the purposes of this Agreement, the term "permanent establishment" means a fixed place of business through which the business of an enterprise is wholly or partly carried on.

The term "permanent establishment" includes especially:

a place of management;
a branch;
an office;
a factory;
a workshop;
a mine, an oil or gas well, a quarry or any other place of extraction of natural resources; and.
an installation or structure used for the exploration or exploitation of natural resources.
The term "permanent establishment" likewise encompasses:
a building site, a construction, assembly or installation project or supervisory activities in connection therewith, but only where such site, project or activities continue for a period of more than 12 months;
the furnishing of services, including consultancy services, by an enterprise through employees or other personnel engaged by the enterprise for such purpose, but only if activities of that nature continue (for the same or a connected project) within a Contracting State for a period or periods aggregating more than 183 days in any twelve-month period commencing or ending in the fiscal year concerned.

Notwithstanding the preceding provisions of this Article, the term "permanent establishment" shall be deemed not to include:

the use of facilities solely for the purpose of storage, display or delivery of goods or merchandise belonging to the enterprise;
the maintenance of a stock of goods or merchandise belonging to the enterprise solely for the purpose of storage, display or delivery;
the maintenance of a stock of goods or merchandise belonging to the enterprise solely for the purpose of processing by another enterprise;

the maintenance of a fixed place of business solely for the purpose of purchasing goods or merchandise or of collecting information, for the enterprise;
the maintenance of a fixed place of business solely for the purpose of carrying on, for the enterprise, any other activity of a preparatory or auxiliary character;
the maintenance of a fixed place of business solely for any combination of activities mentioned in sub-paragraphs a) to e), provided that the overall activity of the fixed place of business resulting from this combination is of a preparatory or auxiliary character.

Notwithstanding the provisions of paragraphs 1 and 2, where a person—other than an agent of an independent status to whom paragraph 6 applies—is acting on behalf of an enterprise and has, and habitually exercises, in a Contracting State an authority to conclude contracts on behalf of the enterprise, that enterprise shall be deemed to have a permanent establishment in that State in respect of any activities which that person undertakes for the enterprise, unless the activities of such person are limited to those mentioned in paragraph 4 which, if exercised through a fixed place of business, would not make this fixed place of business a permanent establishment under the provisions of that paragraph.

An enterprise of a Contracting State shall not be deemed to have a permanent establishment in the other Contracting State merely because it carries on business in that other State through a broker, general commission agent or any other agent of an independent status, provided that such persons are acting in the ordinary course of their business. However, when the activities of such an agent are devoted wholly or almost wholly on behalf of that enterprise, and conditions are made or imposed between that enterprise and the agent in their commercial and financial relations which differ from those which would have been made between independent enterprises, he will not be considered an agent of an independent status within the meaning of this paragraph.

The fact that a company which is a resident of a Contracting State controls or is controlled by a company which is a resident of the other Contracting State, or which carries on business in that other State (whether through a permanent establishment or otherwise), shall not of itself constitute either company a permanent establishment of the other.

Article 6 Income from Immovable Property

Income derived by a resident of a Contracting State from immovable property (including income from agriculture or forestry) situated in the other Contracting State may be taxed in that other State.

The term "immovable property" shall have the meaning which it has under the law of the Contracting State in which the property in question is situated. The term shall in any case include property accessory to immovable property, livestock and equipment used in agriculture and forestry, rights to which the provisions of general law respecting landed property apply, usufruct of immovable property and rights to variable or fixed payments as consideration for the working of, or the right to work, mineral deposits, sources and other natural resources. Ships and aircraft shall not be regarded as immovable property.

The provisions of paragraph 1 shall apply to income derived from the direct use, letting, or use in any other form of immovable property.

The provisions of paragraphs 1 and 3 shall also apply to the income from immovable property of an enterprise and to income from immovable property used for the performance of independent personal services.

Article 7 Business Profits

The profits of an enterprise of a Contracting State shall be taxable only in that State unless the enterprise carries on business in the other Contracting State through a permanent establishment situated therein. If the enterprise carries on business as aforesaid, the profits of the enterprise may be taxed in the other State, but only so much of them as is attributable to that permanent establishment.

Subject to the provisions of paragraph 3, where an enterprise of a Contracting State carries on business in the other Contracting State through a permanent establishment situated therein, there shall in each Contracting State be attributed to that permanent establishment the profits which it might be expected to make if it were a distinct and separate enterprise engaged in the same or similar activities under the same or similar conditions and dealing wholly independently with the enterprise of which it is a permanent establishment.

In determining the profits of a permanent establishment, there shall be allowed as deductions expenses which are incurred for the purposes of the business of the permanent establishment, including executive and general administrative expenses so incurred, whether in the State in which the permanent establishment is situated or elsewhere.

Insofar as it has been customary in a Contracting State to determine the profits to be attributed to a permanent establishment on the basis of an apportionment of the total profits of the enterprise to its various parts, nothing in paragraph 2 shall preclude that Contracting State from determining the profits to be taxed by such an apportionment as may be customary. The method of apportionment adopted shall, however, be such that the result shall be in accordance with the principles contained in this Article.

No profits shall be attributed to a permanent establishment by reason of the mere purchase by that permanent establishment of goods or merchandise for the enterprise.

For the purposes of the preceding paragraphs, the profits to be attributed to the permanent establishment shall be determined by the same method year by year unless there is good and sufficient reason to the contrary.

Where profits include items of income or capital gains which are dealt with separately in other Articles of this Agreement, then the provisions of those Articles shall not be affected by the provisions of this Article.

Article 8 Shipping and Air Transport

Profits of an enterprise of a Contracting State from the operation of ships or aircraft in international traffic shall be taxable only in that State.

For the purposes of this Article, profits from the operation of ships or aircraft in international traffic include:

profits from the rental on a bare boat basis of ships or aircraft; and
profits from the use, maintenance or rental of containers (including trailers and related equipment for the transport of containers) used for the transport of goods or merchandise;
where such rental or such use, maintenance or rental, as the case may be, is incidental to the operation of ships or aircraft in international traffic.

The provisions of paragraph 1 shall also apply to profits from the participation in a pool, a joint business or an international operating agency, but only to so much of the profits so derived as is attributable to the participant in proportion to its share in the joint operation.

Nothing in this Agreement shall affect the provisions of the Agreement between the Government of the People's Republic of China and the Government of the United Kingdom of Great Britain and Northern Ireland for the Reciprocal Avoidance of Double Taxation on Revenues arising from the Business of Air Transport, signed at Beijing on 10 March 1981, to the extent that they have effect as regards taxes to which this Agreement applies. However, where any greater relief for such taxes is afforded by any provision of this Agreement, that provision shall apply.

Article 9 Associated Enterprises
Where

an enterprise of a Contracting State participates directly or indirectly in the management, control or capital of an enterprise of the other Contracting State, or.
the same persons participate directly or indirectly in the management, control or capital of an enterprise of a Contracting State and an enterprise of the other Contracting State,
and in either case conditions are made or imposed between the two enterprises in their commercial or financial relations which differ from those which would be made between independent enterprises, then any profits which would, but for those conditions, have accrued to one of the enterprises, but, by reason of those conditions, have not so accrued, may be included in the profits of that enterprise and taxed accordingly.

Where a Contracting State includes in the profits of an enterprise of that State and taxes accordingly profits on which an enterprise of the other Contracting State has been charged to tax in that other State and the profits so included are profits which would have accrued to the enterprise of the first-mentioned State if the conditions made between the two enterprises had been those which would have been made between independent enterprises, then that other State shall make an appropriate adjustment to the amount of the tax charged therein on those profits. In determining such adjustment, due regard shall be had to the other provisions of this Agreement and the competent authorities of the Contracting States shall, if necessary, consult each other.

Article 10 Dividends

Dividends paid by a company which is a resident of a Contracting State to a resident of the other Contracting State may be taxed in that other State.

However, such dividends may also be taxed in the Contracting State of which the company paying the dividends is a resident and according to the laws of that State, but if the beneficial owner of the dividends is a resident of the other Contracting State, the tax charged shall not exceed:

5% of the gross amount of the dividends if the beneficial owner is a company which holds directly or indirectly at least 25% of the capital of the company paying the dividends;
15% of the gross amount of the dividends where those dividends are paid out of income or gains derived directly or indirectly from immovable property within the meaning of Article 6 by an investment vehicle which distributes most of this income or gains annually and whose income or gains from such immovable property is exempted from tax;
10% of the gross amount of the dividends in all other cases.

The competent authorities of the Contracting States shall by mutual agreement settle the mode of application of these limitations.

This paragraph shall not affect the taxation of the company in respect of the profits out of which the dividends are paid.

Notwithstanding the provisions of paragraphs 1 and 2, dividends paid by a company which is a resident of a Contracting State to a resident of the other Contracting State shall be taxable only in that other Contracting State if the beneficial owner of the dividend is the Government of that other Contracting State or any of its institutions; or other entity the capital of which is wholly-owned directly or indirectly by the Government of that other Contracting State.

The term "dividends" as used in this Article means income from shares, or other rights, not being debt-claims, participating in profits, as well as income from other corporate rights and any other item which, under the laws of the Contracting State of which the company paying the dividend is a resident, is treated as a dividend or distribution of a company.

The provisions of paragraphs 1 and 2 shall not apply if the beneficial owner of the dividends, being a resident of a Contracting State, carries on business in the other Contracting State of which the company paying the dividends is a resident through a permanent establishment situated therein, or performs in that other State independent personal services from a fixed base situated therein, and the holding in respect of which the dividends are paid is effectively connected with such permanent establishment or fixed base. In such case the provisions of Article 7 or Article 14, as the case may be, shall apply.

6. Where a company which is a resident of a Contracting State derives profits or income from the other Contracting State, that other State may not impose any tax

on the dividends paid by the company, except insofar as such dividends are paid to a resident of that other State or insofar as the holding in respect of which the dividends are paid is effectively connected with a permanent establishment or a fixed base situated in that other State, nor subject the company's undistributed profits to a tax on the company's undistributed profits, even if the dividends paid or the undistributed profits consist wholly or partly of profits or income arising in that other State.

7. The provisions of this Article shall not apply if it was the main purpose or one of the main purposes of any person concerned with the creation or assignment of the shares or other rights in respect of which the dividend is paid to take advantage of this Article by means of that creation or assignment.

Article 11 Interest

Interest arising in a Contracting State and paid to a resident of the other Contracting State may be taxed in that other State.

However, such interest may also be taxed in the Contracting State in which it arises and according to the laws of that State, but if the beneficial owner of the interest is a resident of the other Contracting State, the tax so charged shall not exceed 10% of the gross amount of the interest. The competent authorities of the Contracting States shall by mutual agreement settle the mode of application of this limitation.

Notwithstanding the provisions of paragraph 2, interest arising in a Contracting State and derived by the Government of the other Contracting State, a political subdivision or local authority thereof, the Central Bank of that other Contracting State or any agency of, or entity wholly owned by, that Government, or by any other resident of that other Contracting State with respect to debt-claims of that resident which are financed, guaranteed or insured by the Government of that other Contracting State, a political sub-division or local authority thereof, the Central Bank of that other Contracting State or any agency of, or entity wholly owned by, that Government, shall be exempt from tax in the first-mentioned Contracting State.

The term "interest" as used in this Article means income from debt-claims of every kind, whether or not secured by mortgage and whether or not carrying a right to participate in the debtor's profits, and in particular, income from government securities and income from bonds or debentures, including premiums and prizes attaching to such securities, bonds or debentures. Penalty charges for late payment shall not be regarded as interest for the purpose of this Article. The term shall not include any item which is treated as a dividend under the provisions of Article 10 of this Agreement.

The provisions of paragraphs 1, 2 and 3 shall not apply if the beneficial owner of the interest, being a resident of a Contracting State, carries on business in the other Contracting State in which the interest arises through a permanent establishment situated therein, or performs in that other State independent personal services from a fixed base situated therein, and the debt-claim in respect of which the interest is paid is effectively connected with such permanent establishment or fixed base. In such case the provisions of Article 7 or Article 14, as the case may be, shall apply.

Interest shall be deemed to arise in a Contracting State when the payer is a resident of that State. Where, however, the person paying the interest, whether he is a resident of a Contracting State or not, has in a Contracting State a permanent establishment or a fixed base in connection with which the indebtedness on which the interest is paid was incurred, and such interest is borne by such permanent establishment or fixed base, then such interest shall be deemed to arise in the State in which the permanent establishment or fixed base is situated.

Where, by reason of a special relationship between the payer and the beneficial owner or between both of them and some other person, the amount of the interest paid exceeds, for whatever reason, the amount which would have been agreed upon by the payer and the beneficial owner in the absence of such relationship, the provisions of this Article shall apply only to the last-mentioned amount. In such case, the excess part of the payments shall remain taxable according to the laws of each Contracting State, due regard being had to the other provisions of this Agreement.

The provisions of this Article shall not apply if it was the main purpose or one of the main purposes of any person concerned with the creation or assignment of the debt-claim in respect of which the interest is paid to take advantage of this Article by means of that creation or assignment.

Article 12 Royalties

Royalties arising in a Contracting State and paid to a resident of the other Contracting State may be taxed in that other State.

However, such royalties may also be taxed in the Contracting State in which they arise and according to the laws of that State, but if the beneficial owner of the royalties is a resident of the other Contracting State, the tax so charged shall not exceed:

in the case of royalties referred to in sub-paragraph (a) of paragraph 3, 10% of the gross amount of the royalties; and
in the case of royalties referred to in sub-paragraph (b) of paragraph 3, 10% of the adjusted amount of the royalties. For the purpose of this sub-paragraph "the adjusted amount" means 60% of the gross amount of the royalties.

The competent authorities of the Contracting States shall by mutual agreement settle the mode of application of these limitations.

The term "royalties" as used in this Article means:

payments of any kind received as a consideration for the use of, or the right to use, any copyright of literary, artistic or scientific work including cinematograph films, or films or tapes for radio or television broadcasting, any patent, trade mark, design or model, plan, secret formula or process, or for information (know-how) concerning industrial, commercial or scientific experience; and
payments of any kind received as a consideration for the use of, or the right to use, industrial, commercial, or scientific equipment.

The provisions of paragraphs 1 and 2 shall not apply if the beneficial owner of the royalties, being a resident of a Contracting State, carries on business in the other Contracting State in which the royalties arise through a permanent establishment situated therein, or performs in that other State independent personal services from a fixed base situated therein, and the right or property in respect of which the royalties are paid is effectively connected with such permanent establishment or fixed base. In such case the provisions of Article 7 or Article 14, as the case may be, shall apply.

Royalties shall be deemed to arise in a Contracting State when the payer is a resident of that Contracting State. Where, however, the person paying the royalties, whether he is a resident of a Contracting State or not, has in a Contracting State a permanent establishment or a fixed base in connection with which the liability to pay the royalties was incurred, and such royalties are borne by such permanent establishment or fixed base, then such royalties shall be deemed to arise in the State in which the permanent establishment or fixed base is situated.

Where, by reason of a special relationship between the payer and the beneficial owner or between both of them and some other person, the amount of the royalties paid exceeds, for whatever reason, the amount which would have been agreed upon by the payer and the beneficial owner in the absence of such relationship, the provisions of this Article shall apply only to the last-mentioned amount. In such case, the excess part of the payments shall remain taxable according to the laws of each Contracting State, due regard being had to the other provisions of this Agreement.

The provisions of this Article shall not apply if it was the main purpose or one of the main purposes of any person concerned with the creation or assignment of the right in respect of which the royalties are paid to take advantage of this Article by means of that creation or assignment.

Article 13 Capital Gains

Gains derived by a resident of a Contracting State from the alienation of immovable property referred to in Article 6 and situated in the other Contracting State may be taxed in that other State.

Gains from the alienation of movable property forming part of the business property of a permanent establishment which an enterprise of a Contracting State has in the other Contracting State or of movable property pertaining to a fixed base available to a resident of a Contracting State in the other Contracting State for the purpose of performing independent personal services, including such gains from the alienation of such a permanent establishment (alone or with the whole enterprise) or of such fixed base, may be taxed in that other State.

Gains derived by an enterprise of a Contracting State from the alienation of ships or aircraft operated in international traffic by the enterprise, or of containers used in international traffic, or of movable property pertaining to the operation or use of such ships, aircraft or containers, shall be taxable only in that State.

Gains derived by a resident of a Contracting State from the alienation of shares deriving more than 50% of their value directly or indirectly from immovable property situated in the other Contracting State may be taxed in that other State.

Gains derived by a resident of a Contracting State from the alienation of shares in a company which is a resident of the other Contracting State may be taxed in that other Contracting State if the first-mentioned resident, at any time during the twelve-month period preceding such alienation, owned directly or indirectly, at least 25% of the shares of that company.

Gains from the alienation of any property, other than that referred to in paragraphs 1–5, shall be taxable only in the Contracting State of which the alienator is a resident.

Article 14 Independent Personal Services

Income derived by an individual who is a resident of a Contracting State in respect of professional services or other activities of an independent character shall be taxable only in that State except in the following circumstances, when such income may also be taxed in the other Contracting State:

if he has a fixed base regularly available to him in the other Contracting State for the purpose of performing his activities; in that case, only so much of the income as is attributable to that fixed base may be taxed in that other State; or
if his stay in the other Contracting State is for a period or periods amounting to or exceeding in the aggregate 183 days in any twelve month period commencing or ending in the fiscal year concerned; in that case, only so much of the income as is derived from his activities performed in that other State may be taxed in that other State.

The term "professional services" includes especially independent scientific, literary, artistic, educational or teaching activities as well as the independent activities of physicians, lawyers, engineers, architects, dentists and accountants.

Article 15 Income from Employment

Subject to the provisions of Articles 16, 18 and 19, salaries, wages and other similar remuneration derived by a resident of a Contracting State in respect of an employment shall be taxable only in that State unless the employment is exercised in the other Contracting State. If the employment is so exercised, such remuneration as is derived therefrom may be taxed in that other State.

Notwithstanding the provisions of paragraph 1, remuneration derived by a resident of a Contracting State in respect of an employment exercised in the other Contracting State shall be taxable only in the first-mentioned State if:

the recipient is present in the other State for a period or periods not exceeding in the aggregate 183 days in any twelve month period commencing or ending in the fiscal year concerned; and
the remuneration is paid by, or on behalf of, an employer who is not a resident of the other State; and
the remuneration is not borne by a permanent establishment or a fixed base which the employer has in the other State.

Notwithstanding the preceding provisions of this Article, remuneration derived in respect of an employment exercised aboard a ship or aircraft operated in international traffic by an enterprise of a Contracting State may be taxed in that State.

Article 16 Directors' Fees

Directors' fees and other similar payments derived by a resident of a Contracting State in his capacity as a member of the board of directors of a company which is a resident of the other Contracting State may be taxed in that other State.

Article 17 Artistes and Sportsmen

Notwithstanding the provisions of Articles 14 and 15, income derived by a resident of a Contracting State as an entertainer, such as a theatre, motion picture, radio or television artiste, or a musician, or as a sportsman, from his personal activities as such exercised in the other Contracting State, may be taxed in that other State.

Where income in respect of personal activities exercised by an entertainer or a sportsman in his capacity as such accrues not to the entertainer or sportsman himself but to another person, that income may, notwithstanding the provisions of Articles 7, 14 and 15, be taxed in the Contracting State in which the activities of the entertainer or sportsman are exercised.

Article 18 Pensions

Subject to the provisions of paragraph 2 of Article 19, pensions and other similar remuneration paid (including annuities paid as part of a pension arrangement) to an individual who is a resident of a Contracting State shall be taxable only in that State.

Article 19 Government Service

(a) Salaries, wages and other similar remuneration, other than a pension, paid by a Contracting State or a political subdivision or a local authority thereof to an individual in respect of services rendered to that State or subdivision or authority shall be taxable only in that State.

However, such salaries, wages and other similar remuneration shall be taxable only in the other Contracting State if the services are rendered in that State and the individual is a resident of that State who:

is a national of that State; or.
did not become a resident of that State solely for the purpose of rendering the services.

(a) Any pension paid by, or out of funds created by, a Contracting State or a political subdivision or a local authority thereof to an individual in respect of services rendered to that State or subdivision or authority shall be taxable only in that State.

(b) However, such pension shall be taxable only in the other Contracting State if the individual is a resident of, and a national of, that State.

The provisions of Articles 15, 16, 17 and 18 shall apply to salaries, wages and other similar remuneration, and to pensions in respect of services rendered in connection with a business carried on by a Contracting State or a political subdivision or a local authority thereof.

Article 20 Students

Payments which a student who is or was immediately before visiting a Contracting State a resident of the other Contracting State and who is present in the first-mentioned State solely for the purpose of his education receives for the purpose of his maintenance or education shall not be taxed in that State, provided that such payments arise from sources outside that State.

Article 21 Other Income

Items of income beneficially owned by a resident of a Contracting State, wherever arising, not dealt with in the foregoing Articles of this Agreement (other than income paid out of trusts or the estates of deceased persons in the course of administration) shall be taxable only in that State.

The provisions of paragraph 1 shall not apply to income, other than income from immovable property as defined in paragraph 2 of Article 6, if the beneficial owner of such income, being a resident of a Contracting State, carries on business in the other Contracting State through a permanent establishment situated therein, or performs in that other State independent personal services from a fixed base situated therein, and the right or property in respect of which the income is paid is effectively connected with such permanent establishment or fixed base. In such case the provisions of Article 7 or Article 14, as the case may be, shall apply.

Where, by reason of a special relationship between the resident referred to in paragraph 1 and some other person, or between both of them and some third person, the amount of the income referred to in that paragraph exceeds the amount (if any) which would have been agreed upon between them in the absence of such a relationship, the provisions of this Article shall apply only to the last-mentioned amount. In such a case, the excess part of the income shall remain taxable according to the laws of each Contracting State, due regard being had to the other applicable provisions of this Agreement.

The provisions of this Article shall not apply if it was the main purpose or one of the main purposes of any person concerned with the creation or assignment of the rights in respect of which the income is paid to take advantage of this Article by means of that creation or assignment.

Article 22 Elimination of Double Taxation

In China, double taxation shall be eliminated as follows:

Where a resident of China derives profit, income or capital gains from the United Kingdom, the amount of the United Kingdom tax payable in respect of such profit, income or capital gain in accordance with the provisions of this Agreement shall be allowed as a credit against the Chinese tax imposed on that resident. The amount of credit, however, shall not exceed the amount of the Chinese tax computed with respect to such profit, income or capital gains in accordance with the tax laws and regulations of China;

Where the income derived from the United Kingdom is a dividend paid by a company which is a resident of the United Kingdom to a company which is a resident of China and which owns more than 20% of the shares of the company paying the dividend, the credit shall take into account the United Kingdom tax payable by the company paying the dividend in respect of its income.

Subject to the provisions of the law of the United Kingdom regarding the allowance as a credit against United Kingdom tax of tax payable in a territory outside the United Kingdom or, as the case may be, regarding the exemption from United Kingdom tax of a dividend arising in a territory outside the United Kingdom (which shall not affect the general principle hereof):

Chinese tax payable under the laws of China and in accordance with this Agreement, whether directly or by deduction, on profits, income or chargeable gains from sources within China (excluding in the case of a dividend tax payable in respect of the profits out of which the dividend is paid) shall be allowed as a credit against any United Kingdom tax computed by reference to the same profits, income or chargeable gains by reference to which the Chinese tax is computed;

a dividend which is paid by a company which is a resident of China to a company which is a resident of the United Kingdom shall be exempted from United Kingdom tax, when the conditions for exemption under the law of the United Kingdom are met;

in the case of a dividend not exempted from tax under sub-paragraph b) above (because the conditions for exemption under the law of the United Kingdom are not met) which is paid by a company which is a resident of China to a company which is a resident of the United Kingdom and which controls directly or indirectly at least 10% of the voting power in the company paying the dividend, the credit mentioned in sub-paragraph (a) above shall also take into account the Chinese tax payable by the company in respect of its profits out of which such dividend is paid;

for the purposes of this paragraph, profits, income and capital gains owned by a resident of the United Kingdom which may be taxed in China in accordance with this Agreement shall be deemed to arise from sources in China.

ARTICLE 23 Miscellaneous Rule

Nothing in this Agreement shall prejudice the right of each Contracting State to apply its domestic laws and measures concerning the prevention of tax evasion and avoidance, whether or not described as such, insofar as they do not give rise to taxation contrary to this Agreement.

Article 24 Non-discrimination

Nationals of a Contracting State shall not be subjected in the other Contracting State to any taxation or any requirement connected therewith, which is other or more burdensome than the taxation and connected requirements to which nationals of that other State in the same circumstances, in particular with respect to residence, are or may be subjected.

The taxation on a permanent establishment which an enterprise of a Contracting State has in the other Contracting State shall not be less favourably levied in that other State than the taxation levied on enterprises of that other State carrying on the same activities.

Except where the provisions of paragraph 1 of Article 9, paragraphs 7 or 8 of Article 11, paragraphs 6 or 7 of Article 12 or paragraphs 3 or 4 of Article 21 apply, interest, royalties and other disbursements paid by an enterprise of a Contracting State to a resident of the other Contracting State shall, for the purpose of determining the taxable profits of such enterprise, be deductible under the same conditions as if they had been paid to a resident of the first-mentioned State.

Enterprises of a Contracting State, the capital of which is wholly or partly owned or controlled, directly or indirectly, by one or more residents of the other Contracting State, shall not be subjected in the first-mentioned State to any taxation or any requirement connected therewith which is other or more burdensome than the taxation and connected requirements to which other similar enterprises of the first-mentioned State are or may be subjected.

Nothing contained in this Article shall be construed as obliging either Contracting State to grant to individuals not resident in that State any of the personal allowances, reliefs and reductions for tax purposes which are granted to individuals so resident or to its nationals.

The provisions of this Article shall apply to the taxes which are covered by Article 2 of this Agreement.

Article 25 Mutual Agreement Procedure

Where a resident of a Contracting State considers that the actions of one or both of the Contracting States result or will result for him in taxation not in accordance with the provisions of this Agreement, he may, irrespective of the remedies provided by the domestic law of those States, present his case to the competent authority of the Contracting State of which he is a resident or, if his case comes under paragraph 1 of Article 24, to that of the Contracting State of which he is a national.

The competent authority shall endeavour, if the objection appears to it to be justified and if it is not itself able to arrive at a satisfactory solution, to resolve the case by mutual agreement with the competent authority of the other Contracting State, with a view to the avoidance of taxation which is not in accordance with the Agreement. Any agreement reached shall be implemented notwithstanding any time limits or other procedural limitations in the domestic law of the Contracting States.

The competent authorities of the Contracting States shall endeavour to resolve by mutual agreement any difficulties or doubts arising as to the interpretation or application of this Agreement. They may also consult together for the elimination of double taxation in cases not provided for in the Agreement.

The competent authorities of the Contracting States may communicate with each other directly for the purpose of reaching an agreement in the sense of the preceding paragraphs.

Article 26 Exchange of Information

The competent authorities of the Contracting States shall exchange such information as is foreseeably relevant for carrying out the provisions of this Agreement or to

the administration or enforcement of the domestic laws concerning taxes of every kind and description imposed on behalf of the Contracting States, or of their political subdivisions or local authorities, insofar as the taxation thereunder is not contrary to the Agreement, in particular, to prevent fraud and to facilitate the administration of statutory provisions against legal avoidance. The exchange of information is not restricted by Articles 1 and 2.

Any information received under paragraph 1 by a Contracting State shall be treated as secret in the same manner as information obtained under the domestic laws of that State and shall be disclosed only to persons or authorities (including courts and administrative bodies) concerned with the assessment or collection of, the enforcement or prosecution in respect of, or the determination of appeals in relation to, the taxes referred to in paragraph 1, or the oversight of the above. Such persons or authorities shall use the information only for such purposes. They may disclose the information in public court proceedings or in judicial decisions.

In no case shall the provisions of paragraph 1 and 2 be construed so as to impose on a Contracting State the obligation:

to carry out administrative measures at variance with the laws and administrative practice of that or of the other Contracting State;
to supply information which is not obtainable under the laws or in the normal course of the administration of that or of the other Contracting State;
to supply information which would disclose any trade, business, industrial, commercial or professional secret or trade process, or information the disclosure of which would be contrary to public policy.

If information is requested by a Contracting State in accordance with this Article, the other Contracting State shall use its information gathering measures to obtain the requested information, even though that other State may not need such information for its own tax purposes. The obligation contained in the preceding sentence is subject to the limitations of paragraph 3 of this Article but in no case shall such limitations be construed to permit a Contracting State to decline to supply information solely because it has no domestic interest in such information.

In no case shall the provisions of paragraph 3 be construed to permit a Contracting State to decline to supply information solely because the information is held by a bank, other financial institution, nominee or person acting in an agency or a fiduciary capacity or because it relates to ownership interests in a person.

Article 27 Members of Diplomatic Missions and Consular Posts
Nothing in this Agreement shall affect the fiscal privileges of members of diplomatic missions or consular posts under the general rules of international law or under the provisions of special agreements.

Article 28 Entry into Force
Each of the Contracting States shall notify the other, through diplomatic channels in writing, of the completion of the procedures required by its law for the bringing

into force of this Agreement. This Agreement shall enter into force on the date of the later of these notifications and shall thereupon have effect:

in China, in respect of profit, income and capital gains arising in any tax year beginning on or after 1st January in the calendar year next following that in which this Agreement enters into force;
in the United Kingdom,
in respect of income tax and capital gains tax, for any year of assessment beginning on or after 6th April next following the date on which this Agreement enters into force;
in respect of corporation tax, for any financial year beginning on or after 1st April next following the date on which this Agreement enters into force;

The Agreement between the Government of the People's Republic of China and the Government of the United Kingdom of Great Britain and Northern Ireland for the Reciprocal Avoidance of Double Taxation and the Prevention of Fiscal Evasion with Respect to Taxes on Income and Capital Gains, signed at Beijing on July 26th, 1984, as amended by the protocol signed at Beijing on September 2nd 1996 (the prior Agreement) shall cease to have effect in relation to any tax with effect from the date on which this Agreement has effect in relation to that tax in accordance with paragraph 1 of this Article.

Notwithstanding the entry into force of this Agreement, an individual who is entitled to the benefits of Article 21 (Teachers and Researchers) and Article 22 (Students, Apprentices and Trainees) of the prior Agreement at the time of the entry into force of this Agreement shall continue to be entitled to such benefits until such time as the individual would have ceased to be entitled to such benefits if the prior Agreement had remained in force.

Article 29 Termination

This Agreement shall continue in effect indefinitely but either of the Contracting States may terminate this Agreement through diplomatic channels in writing, by giving notice of termination at least six months before the end of any calendar year beginning after the expiry of five years from the date of entry into force of this Agreement. In such event this Agreement shall cease to have effect:

in China, as regards profits, income and capital gains derived during the tax year beginning on or after 1st January in the calendar year next following that in which the notice is given;
in the United Kingdom,
in respect of income tax and capital gains tax, for any year of assessment beginning on or after 6th April next following the date on which the notice is given;
in respect of corporation tax, for any financial year beginning on or after 1st April next following the date on which the notice is given.

IN WITNESS whereof the undersigned, duly authorised thereto, have signed this Agreement.

DONE at____on the____day of____, ____, in duplicate in the Chinese and English languages, both texts being equally authoritative.

For the Government of the People's Republic of China.

For the Government of the United Kingdom of Great Britain and Northern Ireland.